History *of the* Territory *of* Wisconsin *from* 1836–1848

Preceded by an Account of Some Events During the Period in Which It Was Under the Dominion of Kings, States or Other Territories, Previous to the Year 1836

Compiled by
Moses M. Strong, A. M.

HERITAGE BOOKS
2009

HERITAGE BOOKS
AN IMPRINT OF HERITAGE BOOKS, INC.

Books, CDs, and more—Worldwide

For our listing of thousands of titles see our website
at
www.HeritageBooks.com

A Facsimile Reprint
Published 2009 by
HERITAGE BOOKS, INC.
Publishing Division
100 Railroad Ave. #104
Westminster, Maryland 21157

Copyright © 1885 Moses M. Strong

Index Copyright © 2002 Heritage Books, Inc.

Originally published by authority of the state
Madison, Wis.:
Democrat Printing Co., State Printers
1885

— Publisher's Notice —
In reprints such as this, it is often not possible to remove blemishes from the original. We feel the contents of this book warrant its reissue despite these blemishes and hope you will agree and read it with pleasure.

International Standard Book Numbers
Paperbound: 978-0-7884-2231-7
Clothbound: 978-0-7884-8127-7

NOTICE.

At the last session of the legislature an act was passed (chapter 285, laws of 1885) to provide for the purchase of certain copies of this history.

The act appointed a commission consisting of ROBERT GRAHAM, state superintendent; JAMES D. BUTLER, late professor of the University of Wisconsin; and J. W. STEARNS, professor in the University, who were authorized and requested to examine and read the manuscript of the book; and if they should be satisfied that it would when published be a work of merit and a valuable compilation of the history of the territory of Wisconsin, and of the preceding period to which it relates, they were to give notice thereof to the commissioners of public printing, who were authorized on behalf of the state to cause to be printed and suitably bound in cloth by the state printer under the existing contract for state printing, and cause to be delivered to the superintendent of public property, for the use of the state, on or before the first day of September, 1885, such number of copies of said book, not exceeding two thousand, as would enable him as far as practicable to make the distribution provided for by the act.

The commission appointed to examine and read the manuscript, made and unanimously signed on the 7th of May, 1885, the certificate contemplated by the said act.

Upon notice of said certificate given to the commissioners of public printing, they directed the book to be printed and bound by the state printer as required by said act.

The distribution of the two thousand copies, printed by the state, provided for by said act, was required to be made among the educational institutions of the state, school-districts having libraries, other libraries, the public institutions and societies of the state, public officers and to members and employés of the legislature.

The compiler has procured the state printer to stereotype the work and to print an edition for sale by subscription.

PREFACE.

In the winter of 1870, the compiler of this book was invited to deliver the annual address before the State Historical Society, and the members of the legislature. Having accepted the invitation, he took as his theme "Territorial Legislation of Wisconsin."

The address was a brief condensation of what had occurred in the legislative halls during the territorial period of twelve years.

This mere epitome of the history of Territorial Legislation, short and fragmentary as it was from the necessities of the occasion, was received with unexpected favor. The author was urged by many who heard it, among whom were those for whose judgment he felt the utmost deference, to enlarge the work of which the address was an abridgment, and to publish a more complete history of the subject to which it related.

These flattering solicitations induced the author to make the experiment, although with great hesitation and very serious doubts as to his ability to compile a work which would not disappoint the too generous confidence of his friends. The result is the book now presented to the public.

It seemed to the compiler that some account of the pre-territorial period, while the country within the present restricted boundaries of Wisconsin was under the dominion of the successive kings, states and territories, which at different epochs had jurisdiction over it, was a suitable introduction to the history of the territory proper, which

Hence the first chapter, of about twelve pages, contains the briefest possible account of the early explorations of "Florida" and "Louisiana," under which names the whole country from the Gulf of Mexico to Newfoundland was claimed successively by Spain, France and Great Britain, during a period of more than two hundred and fifty years in the sixteenth, seventeenth and eighteenth centuries.

was the principal object of the work.

This naturally led to a notice of the wars in the eighteenth century with the Fox Indians on the Fox and Wisconsin rivers; and in immediate connection with them a sketch of the Langlade family — the first permanent settlers in Wisconsin, whose descendants have remained upon its soil.

The explorations of JONATHAN CARVER in 1766–7, are, it is thought, appropriately referred to; as well as the progress of settlements in the northwest, and the development of their social relations.

To have omitted a notice of the ancient settlements at Green Bay and Prairie du Chien, and the less numerous and less important ones at Chequamegon, Portage and Milwaukee, would, it is believed, have been inexcusable.

The migration of semi-civilized Indians to Wisconsin in the third and fourth decades of this century seemed to demand notice.

The history of the settlement of the lead mines nearly fifteen years before the organization of Wisconsin Territory, and the consequent Winnebago war, followed five years later by the Black Hawk war, occupy nearly forty pages of the preliminary history. These are succeeded by nearly one hundred pages, devoted to an account of civil government, social development, legislation and cognate matters, which complete the pre-territorial history and bring the compilation down to the period when the history of Wisconsin Territory properly commences.

Although the principal design of the work is to present a history of Territorial Legislation, in the execution of which design a chapter is devoted to the events of each year in chronological order, the design has been departed from so far as to incorporate into each chapter the most important of the contemporaneous events of the period to which it relates, although they may have no direct connection with legislation.

History and story are the same word differently written. And the compiler of this book desires to say that his compilation consists almost entirely of the story of the events to which it relates, that had been told or written by others. He disclaims all pretentions to originality, which implies rather the creation than the repetition of a story. He claims credit — if it be any credit — only for the order of the compilation, and of putting the words, deeds and writings of others relating to territorial and ante-territorial times into such convenient form that they may be read without resort to the numerous sources of information from which they have been derived. If the attractions of rhetoric, or the interest of sensational description are expected to be found, the reader will be disappointed, and even the opinions of the compiler, in respect to the events which are recorded, will be looked for in vain, and are not permitted to affect in any manner the statement of facts presented.

The compilation being made so largely from the writings of others, it would be next to impossible, either in the text or by notes, to give the credit which is justly due, and it is hoped that any imputation of plagiarism will be found undeserved in view of this acknowledgment.

Very liberal extracts have been made from the history of GENERAL SMITH and entire paragraphs used without alteration or change of a sentence or word. The collections of the State Historical Society have been drawn upon whenever they would aid in promoting the desired object. The graphic description of the surrender of RED BIRD, in the eleventh chapter, is copied bodily from an article on the Winnebago war by COL. THOMAS L. McKENNEY. Other extracts have been made from other writings, which it is not possible to specify in detail.

The compiler wishes to say, in justice to himself, that the compilation now presented is his first attempt at anything of this kind. He is but little practiced in literary composition, and is but too conscious of his inability to give such form to the materials he has been able to obtain, as to make them worthy of publication. The work, however, is now laid before the public, whose favorable consideration of it is invoked, while no complaint will be made of fair criticism founded upon a knowledge of its contents. It has been undertaken for the reasons already stated, and because the author felt a considerable degree of obligation resting upon him to contribute whatever might be in his power, to the preservation of the history of those events with which he was contemporary, and which in a few years will have passed into oblivion.

MOSES M. STRONG.

TABLE OF CONTENTS.

CHAPTER I.

EARLY EXPLORATIONS OF "FLORIDA AND "LOUISIANA."—1512 TO 1719.

Gen. W. R. Smith's history — Juan Ponce de Leon — Diego Miruelo — Narvaez — De Soto — Champlain — Le Caron — Charter of New France — First Jesuit missions — Brebeuf, Daniel & Zallemand — Nicollet, the first to visit Wisconsin — Raymbault and Jogues — Dequerre — Fur-traders in 1654 — Drocoux — Mèsnard — Allouez and his grand intertribal Council at Chegoiemegon — Dablon and Marquette — Perot, his visit to Green Bay and Chicago — Mission of St. Francis Xavier established at Green Bay — French take formal possession at St. Mary's — The cross borne by Allouez and Dablon to the Milwaukee and Waukesha rivers — Marquette and Joliet explore the Fox, Wisconsin and Mississippi rivers and return to Green Bay via Chicago — Marquette, his sickness and death — La Salle erects fort at Frontenac, builds the Griffin, anchors at Green Bay, goes to the Illinois, begins to build Fort Crèvecœur, returns to Frontenac, and back to the Illinois — Hennepin, with Accau and Du Gay explores the Upper Mississippi, made prisoners, liberated, visited St. Anthony, meet Du Lhut and his party, all reach Green Bay, Hennepin returns to Europe and dies — La Salle goes to Mackinaw and returns to Crèvecœur, descends the Mississippi to its mouth, and takes possession of all the country for France, returns to France, attempts to colonize Louisiana — War between England and France — Peace of Ryswick — Iberville and Chateaumorand — Iberville ascends the Mississippi — Le Sueur — he explores the St. Peter's river for minerals and winters there — Cadillac takes possession of Detroit — Kaskaskia — Peace of Utrecht — Boisbraint — Fort Chartres, Cahokia and Prairie de Rocher — Artaguette — New Orleans — Renault.

CHAPTER II.

WARS WITH FOX INDIANS—1712 TO 1746.

The Foxes concentrate their bands on Fox River — De Louvigny's expedition against the Foxes — His report to the council — Little Butte des Mortes — De Louvigny's death by shipwreck — Gov. Vaudreuil's letter of approbation — Bad faith of the Foxes — Peaceable efforts of the French — Indian council — De Lignery sent to destroy the Foxes — Troops commence march — Foxes escape — Expedition continues up Fox River — Burn villages and return — Lignery criticised — Taken prisoner — Friendly Indians attack the Foxes — Marin — His traffic on Fox and Wisconsin Rivers — Piratical exactions of the Foxes — Marin determines to drive them out — His stratagem — Foxes awaiting the boats — The attack — Village burned — The battle — Result — Letter of De Beauharnois — Du Buisson attacks the Foxes — De Villers defeats and routes the Foxes — Surviving Foxes retire to the Wisconsin River — Marin again attacks them — They are driven across the Mississippi — Marin commands at Green Bay — Taken prisoner — Final expulsion of Foxes — Sacs and Foxes confederated — Sacs at Green Bay — Expulsion of the Sacs — Sacs at Sauk Prairie — Sacs remove to the Mississippi River — Sacs and Foxes at Mouth of Rock River.

CHAPTER III.

THE LANGLADE FAMILY—1745 TO 1800.

Biography no part of history — De Langlade's family — birth of Augustin — and Indian trader — married — children — Charles has a son — Augustin and family remove to Green Bay — his death — marriage of Charles — French War — Vaudreuil selects him to raise the Indian tribes, and lead them in the war — He raises 1500 — they march to

Fort Du Quesne — Braddock's defeat — The fight owing to the importunities of Charles De Langlade — De Beaujeu consents to order an attack — Casualties — De Langlade ordered to strike Fort Cumberland — At capture of Fort William Henry — Second in command at Mackinaw — At Ticonderoga — Again at Fort Du Quesne — French burn the fort and retire before Washington — At Fort Niagara — Battle of Quebec — Surrender of Canada and discharge of De Langlade's troops and Indians — His hardships — His children — Takes active part for the British in the Revolutionary War — Attends Indian Council — Goes to St. Josephs — Superintendent of Indian affairs at Green Bay — His death — Pierre Grignon, Sen. — Augustin Grignon's Recollections.

CHAPTER IV.

JONATHAN CARVER'S EXPLORATIONS — 1766 AND 1767.

Treaty of Paris; cession of Louisiana — Captain Jonathan Carver — His birth — His military record — Sets out from Boston — At Mackinaw — Leaves Green Bay — Leaves Doty's island — At Portage — At Prairie du Sac — The deserted Fox village — La Prairie des Chiens — Traders stop at Yellow river — At Lake Pepin — Nicholas Perrot — Prehistoric tumuli — Makes a treaty between Dakotas and Chippewas — " Carver's Cave " — Leaves canoe and walks to Falls of St. Anthony — St. Francis River — Ascends the Minnesota River — Returns to the Mississippi — Grand Council — " Carver's Grant " — Doubts as to the validity of the deed — In violation of the King's proclamation — Petition presented to Congress — Adverse report — Another adverse report — " Murray Claim " — Private Land claims — Returns to Prairie du Chien — Leaves Prairie du Chien and ascends the Chippewa River — On the St. Croix — Copper — Descends to Lake Superior — Reaches Grand Portage — Returns to Mackinaw and Boston.

CHAPTER V.

PROGRESS OF SETTLEMENTS IN THE NORTHWEST, AND TRANSFER TO BRITISH JURISDICTION — 1765 TO 1775.

Digression — Progress of settlement in the Wabash country — Population of Illinois county — Gist's settlement in the Youghiogeny — Washington sent to the Ohio River — Beginning of the French war — English forces withdrawn from the valley of the Ohio — Braddock's defeat — French power overthrown — Indian affection for the French — First settlements of French east of the Mississippi — Settlement of Upper Louisiana — 1721, Jesuit college — "American Bottom " — French Forts — Fort Massac — Fort Charters — 1765 Great Britain succeeds to France — De Villiers — St. Ange de Bellerive — Retires to St. Louis — Exodus of the French — Population of Illinois settlements — Capt. Sterling — British proclamation — Right of emigration — Equal rights guaranteed — M. St. Ange returns — Maj. Frazer — Col. Reid — Col. Wilkins — First Common Law Court — 1774 Civil Law restored — " Quebec Bill " — Grants of land by Col. Wilkins — Settlements on the Monongahela — Pittsburgh — Gov. Dunmore encourages emigration — French settlers support the American cause — Detroit in 1763 — The Pontiac war — Grand council of Indian tribes — Capture and slaughter of English garrisons — Mackinaw surprised and captured by a game of ball — Green Bay abandoned — Detroit alone remains — Pontiac invests Detroit — Siege — Great distress of the English — Peace concluded with the Indian tribes — Pontiac killed — Peace did not bring settlements — Green Bay — Capt. Stirling takes command of the " Illinois Country " — Indian tribes of the Northwest unfriendly to the Americans and allied to the British — Col. Geo. Rogers Clark sent from Virginia by Gov. Patrick Henry to reduce the British posts in the Northwest — Col. Clark takes Kaskaskia and captures the fort — French inhabitants declare for America, and secure submission at Cahokia — Vincennes declares allegiance to Virginia — Jurisdiction of Virginia established in the Northwest — British capture Post Vincennes — Col. Clark recaptures it and sends the British to Virginia as prisoners — Capt. Helm captures a convoy of supplies — Virginia in the possession of the entire Northwest — Slow progress of settlement.

TABLE OF CONTENTS. 11

CHAPTER VI.

UNDER AMERICAN JURISDICTION — 1787 TO 1820.

Ordinance of 1787 — Slavery at Green Bay — British posts in Northwest not immediately surrendered — Indian wars — Harmar's defeat on the Maumee — Successful and decisive campaign of Gen. Anthony Wayne — Preliminary articles of peace — Treaty of Greenville, "great and abiding peace document." — Disputes about the right to the free navigation of the Lower Mississippi — Free navigation secured by the treaty of Madrid — Spain cedes Louisiana to France — France cedes Louisiana to the United States — Indian Territory established — Genl. W. H. Harrison appointed Governor — Treaty with the Sacs and Foxes — Boundaries of the ceded land — Two treaties with Sacs and Foxes — Treaty with Sacs of Rock River — Black Hawk signs treaty — Fort Madison — Pike's expedition — Cession of site of Fort Snelling — Battle of Tippecanoe — Indians seek the aid of British allies — British incite Indian traders — Robert Dickson and his Indian forces — Capture of Mackinaw — Fort Meigs — Col. Dickson and his Indians join the British at Detroit — Hull's surrender of Detroit — Evacuation of Fort Dearborn and massacre of Capt. Heald and party — Fort at Prairie du Chien — Unsuccessful expedition of Maj. Campbell — Col. McKay places guns at Rock Island — Fort Armstrong commenced at Rock Island — John Shaw, trades between St. Louis and Prairie du Chien — Lead smelting at Galena by Indians — Steam Boat Navigation on the Mississippi — The first saw-mills in Wisconsin.

CHAPTER VII.

GREEN BAY — 1634 TO 1836.

Earliest abodes of civilization — Nicollet — Fur traders — Mesnard — Allouez — Mission of St. Francis Xavier — Fort — Tonti in command — Du Luth — Marquette and Joliet — Hennepin and Du Luth — Thirty barren years — De Louvigney — De Lignery — Capt. De Velie — Garrison withdrawn — Settlement of Augustin De Langlade — Arrival of Capt. Belfour and twenty men — Fort called "Edward Augustus" in charge of Lieut. Gorrell — Lieut. Gorrell abandons the post — Slow progress of the settlement — Jaques Porlier — Charles Reaume — John Lawe — Population 250 in 1812 — Ogilvie, Gillaspie & Co.—Honesty of the Indian trade — Jacob Franks builds a mill — Indian agent and factor — Government saw-mill — Fort Howard located by Gen. Chas. Gratiot — In command of Col. Chambers — Col. Smith removes troops to Camp Smith — Col. Pinkney moves back to Fort Howard — Col. McNeill — Gen. Brady — Shantytown — Robert Irwin, Jr. — Daniel Whitney — Wm. Dickinson — H. S. Baird — J. D. Doty — Court House and Jail — Mission School and Rev. R. F. Cadel — Episcopal Church incorporated — First Newspaper — Indian agency under Maj. Brevort — Catholic Church and school — Father Richard — Shantytown absorbed by Navarino, Astor and Depere — Only eight American families — Character of population — Ebenezer Childs — John P. Arndt — Albert G. Ellis — J. D. Doty — Removes to Green Bay — Madison and Doty's island — His official positions — Is appointed Governor of Utah, where he dies — Morgan L. Martin.

CHAPTER VIII.

PRAIRIE DU CHIEN — 1630 TO 1830.

Uncertainty of time of first settlement — Hennepin — Marquet and Joliet — First military post — Cardinelle — Ganier — French trading post — French military post — Carver — Gov. Sinclair's purchase — Michael Brisbois — His statement of the settlement — His bakery — He issued currency — Campbell appointed Indian agent — Marriage customs — Joseph Rolette — Settlement before the war of 1812 — British meditate building a fort — U. S. Government build Fort Shelby — McKay's expedition for recapture of the fort — Force consisted of 150 whites and 450 Indians — Col. McKay reaches the town — Attack upon the boats — Investment of the garrison — Surrender demanded and refused — Hot shot — Capitulation — American troops retire down the river — Fruitless Indian pursuit — Capt. Pohlman in command — British evacuation — Fort Crawford erected — Col. Chambers in command — Tyranny of the officers — Charles Menard court-martialled — Joseph Rolette banished — New fort erected — John Shaw trades and builds a grist mill — James H. Lockwood — Officers and traders — Origin of name of town — Farming — Habits of settlers — It was neutral ground — Indian trade — Catholic priest — Maj. Forsyth's visit — Col. Leavenworth and troops leave for St. Peters — Fort Snelling located — Troops occupy Fort Crawford — Private land claims — H. L. Dousman — Joseph M. Street — Thomas P. Burnett — Mackinaw county laid out — Brown and Crawford counties laid out — First officers of Brown county — First officers of Crawford county — First court in Brown county — Changes in office in Crawford county — 1823, first court — 1824 — 1826 and 1830 — 1831.

CHAPTER IX.

CHEQUAMEGON — PORTAGE — MILWAUKEE.

Chequamegon, the field of first missionary work — Portage — Its early settlement — Laurent Barth, first settler — Jean L'Ecuyer — Barth sells to Campbell — Laurent Fily — Francis Roy — Pierre Pauquette employed by Joseph Rolette — Indian trade — Settlement did not increase — Erection of Fort Winnebago — Major Twiggs and his officers — Site of fort — Fort completed — Houses at Portage — Change of troops — Military road from Fort Howard to Fort Crawford — Manner of transporting goods up Fox River — Henry Merrill — Milwaukee — First mention in Gorrell's journal — English trader probably Goddard — Là Frambois — Stanislaus Chappue — John B. Beaubien — Laurent Fily — Jaques Vieau — Solomon Juneau — James Kinzie — Hypolite Grignon — Newspaper notices — Juneau purchases land — Byron Kilbourn purchases west side of river — George H. Walker makes claim on south side of river and finally gets patent — Names of some early settlers — First public meeting — Digression — Copper Mines of Lake Superior — Pre-historic implements.

CHAPTER X.

NEW YORK INDIANS — 1820 TO 1839.

N. Y. Indians — Ogden Land Co. — Stockbridge and Brothertown Indians — Jedediah Morse — Eleazer Williams — He proposes emigration scheme — "South" jealous of free States — Calhoun sanctions a plan to set apart Wisconsin for Indians — War Department favors the emigration scheme — Dr. Morse at Green Bay — N. Y. Indians aided by Government in going to Green Bay — Williams arrives at Detroit — He learns the Menomonees had sold their land to U. S. — He returns to New York — Treaty rejected — Renewed aid from War Department — Arrival at Green Bay — Treaty made — Validity of treaty denied — N. Y. Indians opposed to the treaty — War Department favors another visit to Green Bay — Reach Green Bay — New treaty made — Treaty approved — N. Y. Indians emigrate — Opposition to treaty — Cass and McKinney treaty — Senate amendment — Abortive attempt at reconciliation — Samuel C. Stambaugh — He visits Washington with Menomonees — Treaty made — Supplementary article — Continued till next session — Treaty ratified with amendment — Two townships to Stockbridges — One township to Brothertowns — Alteration of boundary — Senate amendment agreed to with modification — Conflict terminated — Williams abandons his schemes — Scheme of Ogden Land Co. abandoned — Area of freedom unabridged — N. Y. Indians emigrate to Wisconsin — Condition of six nations in Wisconsin — Brothertowns become citizens.

CHAPTER XI.

THE LEAD MINES AND WINNEBAGO WAR — 1822 TO 1828.

Gen. Smith's history of Indian disturbances — Indian wars concomitants of settlements — Indians friendly to French settlers — Hostility to agricultural settlements — Winnebagos opposed to the occupancy of the Lead Mines — Mr. Shaw's visit to Fever river — Description of Indian smelting furnaces — First occupation of the Lead Mines — Increase of population — Hazel Green and New Diggings — Government agents — Early settlement of the Lead Mines — "Suckers" and "sucker-holes" — Galena was the objective point — Other points — Product of first three years — Apprehensions of danger from

TABLE OF CONTENTS. 13

Winnebagos — Treaty at Prairie du Chien — Troops removed from Fort Crawford to Fort Snelling — Fears at Prairie du Chien of Indian outrages — Murder of Methode — Wa-man-doos-ga-ra-ka confesses the murder — False rumors — Red Bird — Winnebagos resolved on retaliation — Attempt to kill Mrs. J. H. Lockwood — Murder of Gagnier and Lightcap — Capt. Lindsay and his two keel-boats — The two boats part company — Winnebagos concealed on an island — Description of the boats — Attack upon the boat — "O. H. Perry" — The second attack — The boat is grounded, hand-to-hand conflict — The boat afloat, and survivors escape — Casualties — Harmless attack upon the other boat — Slander contradicted — Alarm at Prairie du Chien — Military company organized — Preparations for defence — Col. Snelling notified, and comes down the river — Consternation at Galena and vicinity — Gov. Cass arrives at Prairie du Chien — He proceeds to Galena — Lieut. Martin Thomas — Col. Snelling assumes command — Gov. Cass proceeds to St. Louis — Col. Henry Dodge chosen Commander of Volunteers — Col. Dodge scours both sides of the Wisconsin river — Maj. Whistler arrives at the Portage — Winnebagos in a desperate plight — Red Bird surrendered by the Winnebagos — Red Bird's appearance — His dress — His calmness — Talk between the Winnebagos and Maj. Whistler — Red Bird ready to die — Prisoners sent to Fort Crawford — Volunteers discharged — Results — Winnebagos contemplated a general rising — Death of Red Bird — Other prisoners convicted and pardoned.

CHAPTER XII.

THE BLACK HAWK WAR — 1831 AND 1832.

Progress in the "Lead Mines" — Black Hawk's village — He crosses the Mississippi — Threatened disturbances in 1831 — Indians agree to remain west of the Mississippi — Black Hawk war ensued a year later — Alarm in the Lead mine Region — Col. Dodge meets the Winnebagos in council — His "talk" — Treacherous promises of the Winnebagos — Beginning of the war in 1832 — Gen. Whiteside's command — Gen. Atkinson and the regulars — Black Hawk moves up Rock river — Troops at Dixon — Stillman's defeat — First blood shed in the war — Col. Dodge writes to Gen. Reynolds — Col. Dodge and his neighbors go on an expedition after the Indians — Inhabitants of the Lead Mines thoroughly alarmed — Forts erected — Indian mode of warfare — Indian Creek massacre — Surrender of female captives — Suspicious conduct of the Winnebagos — Brave and decisive conduct of Col. Dodge — Captive Winnebago chiefs sent to Gratiot's Grove and held as hostages — Dodge's volunteers meet Galena volunteers at Gratiot's Grove — Five murders near Buffalo Grove — Henry Dodge; brief sketch of — March to Kirker's farm — Col. Dodge's address to the volunteers — He, with his forces, joins the regulars at Dixon — He escorts Gen. Brady to Ottawa — He returns to his headquarters — Gen. Atkinson engages the Sioux and Menomonees as allies — Col. W. S. Hamilton commands the Sioux — Col. Stambaugh commands the Menomonees — Menomonees kill two fugitive Sacs — James Aubrey killed — Murders near Spafford's ford — "Apple" killed in his saddle — Col. Dodge pursues the savages and overtakes them at the Peckatonica — Battle of the Peckatonica — Official account — Names of those engaged — Arrival of Sioux — Three of Capt. Stephenson's men killed — Attack on Apple river fort — Black Hawk's account of it — Contest with Maj. Dement's Spy battalion — Black Hawk's account of the engagement — Murder at Helena — Battle of the Blue mound — Number of settlers killed — Indians concentrated near Lake Koshkonong — Gen. Posey and Col. Dodge meet at Fort Hamilton and form left wing — Division of the army — The left wing marches to the First lake — Change of position — March to Fort Atkinson — Judge Charles Dunn shot by a sentinel — Ambush — Indians anxious to escape — Troops sent to Fort Winnebago for provisions, the return route via rapids of Rock River — Effective force — Fresh trail of Indians found — Hot pursuit to the Four Lakes — Pursuit continued to the Wisconsin River — Battle of Wisconsin Heights — Casualties — Indians disappear — Army re-united at Helena — Pursuit — Battle of the Bad Axe — Casualties — Flight of Black Hawk and Prophet to the Lemonweir — Capture and surrender of the fugitives — Gen. Scott and his forces — Victims of the cholera — Losses by the war — Roster of Col. Dodge's command — Black Hawk a prisoner — At Washington — At Fortress Monroe — Sent home — His death.

CHAPTER XIII.

CIVIL GOVERNMENT — 1512 TO 1834.

Claims of Dominion — Military authority — Ponce de Leon first Governor — 1537, De Soto Governor — 1565, Melendez de Aviles, hereditary Governor — French claims of dominion — 1627, Charter of 100 associates — 1663, company of the West Indies — 1671, French claims of Sault St. Mary — 1682, Lá Salle claimed Louisiana for France — 1689 to 1697, Frontenac Governor — 1700, De Calliers Governor-General — 1711, Louisiana an independent government — DeMuys — Artaquette — 1712, Cadillac — 1714, Vaudreuil — 1728, Beauharnois — 1753, Gov. Dinwiddie claims dominion in the valley of the Mississippi — War between France and England — 1762–3, treaty of peace — Division of territory — Inhabitants of "Illinois county" acknowledge jurisdiction of U. S. and Virginia — County of Illinois established — The Revolution a barren period — Ordinance of 1787 — Boundaries — Population — Characteristics of ordinance — Articles of compact — First officers — Creation of legislature — W. H. Harrison, delegate — His successors — 1789, Powers of Congress transferred to President — 1792, Amendment of ordinance — 1810, Franking Privilege extended to delegates — Indiana Territory — Boundaries — Territorial government established — Vincennes the seat of government — 1802, act enabling Ohio to form state government — 1803, admitted into the Union — Population — 1805, Michigan Territory established — Ordinance of 1787 extended over it — Detroit the seat of government — 1809, Illinois Territory established — Boundaries — Powers — Kaskaskia the seat of government — Judicial circuits established — Act enabling Illinois to form state government — North boundary — 5th article of compact disregarded — Proviso requiring ratification of boundaries — People of Wisconsin not consulted — Convention to form constitution provided for — 1818, Illinois admitted into the Union — Wisconsin attached to Michigan Territory — Michigan Territory authorized to elect delegate to Congress — Elective franchise — 1823, additional judge appointed west of Lake Michigan — Appeals and writs of error — Terms of court — Clerks — Residence and salary of judge — James D. Doty, first judge — David Irvin, second judge — Legislative council in Michigan — Territory established — Legislative assembly provided for — Tenure of office for judges — Legislative council increased from 9 to 13 — Township and county officers — Council to be elective — Congress reserves right of repeal — 1830, term of court changed from Prairie du Chien to Mineral Point — Michigan territory extended to Missouri River.

CHAPTER XIV.

LEGISLATION PREVIOUS TO 1835.

Coutume de Paris — Notary Public — Commander of Post administered justice — Limited administration of law in Wisconsin — 1763, British king establishes government of Quebec — 1774, Northwestern territory annexed to Quebec — Rights of Canadian subjects defined — Act denounced by Congress in 1774 — One of the grievances in Declaration of Independence — Court of Trustees — Hesse — Quebec divided into Upper and Lower Canada — 1792, Law of Canada repealed — Places of holding courts established — Slavery limited — 1794, Practice of courts — Inferior courts — Licensing attorneys — 1795, recording conveyances — 1796, British jurisdiction surrendered to United States — Wayne county organized — Common law of England adopted — Woodward code — 1816, "Cass" code — 1818, Illinois admitted, and Wisconsin remanded to jurisdiction of Michigan — 1810, laws of England repealed — *Coutume de Paris* and laws of Louisiana and Canada annulled — Laws of Northwest territory and Indiana territory annulled — Laws passed between 1807 and 1810 repealed — Code of 1820 — 1818, new counties established — Mackinaw, Brown and Crawford — Courts in these counties — 1824, County seats of Brown and Crawford counties — Style of acts changed — 1826, Chippewa county — Sault de St. Mary — 1827, townships of St. Anthony and Green Bay — Census — Apportionment — Counties west of Lake Michigan represented — 1828, special term in Crawford county to try Red Bird — Jurisdiction of county courts transferred to circuit courts — New apportionment — Iowa county organized — Boundaries — County seat — County courts — P. E. Church incorporated at Green Bay — 1830, act in relation to Iowa county — 1831, another apportionment — 1832, first vote on state

TABLE OF CONTENTS. 15

government — Special sessions of circuit court in Brown and Iowa counties — Places of election in Iowa county — County seat of Iowa county — 1834, Milwaukee county established and attached to Brown — 1835, fully organized — Dubuque and Des Moines counties established — Census in 1834 — Bank of Wisconsin — Des Peres — Act to provide for state government — Aug., 1835, special session on account of boundary trouble with Ohio — Laws of Michigan in force in Wisconsin — Judicial system — Supreme court — Circuit courts — County courts — Probate court — Justices of the peace — Poor-debtors — Proscription of negroes — Sabbath — Interest — Militia — Paupers — Autioneers — Highways.

CHAPTER XV.

WISCONSIN IN A TRANSITION STATE — 1835-6.

1825-1832, early settlements of the lead mines — 1825, Col. Wm. S. Hamilton drives 700 head of cattle from Illinois to Green Bay — Efforts to divide Michigan and organize Wisconsin territory — 1832, inhabitants of Michigan vote in favor of state government — Territory west of the Mississippi attached to Michigan territory — 1836, June 16, provisional act for the admission of Michigan — 1837, Jan. 26, admission consumated — 1834, June 28, "Wisconsin" and "Green Bay" land districts established — 1835, 1836, June 15, "Milwaukee" land district established — Provision for election of delegate and legislature — Governor to make apportionment west of Lake Michigan — Mode of canvassing votes changed — Members of legislature apportioned to counties west of Lake Michigan — Proclamation for session of Legislature at Green Bay, Jan. 1, 1836 — Michigan a State out of the Union — S. T. Mason, Governor of State of Michigan — John S. Horner, Secretary of Territory of Michigan — Election of delegate in 1835 — Candidates, Doty, Martin, Jones, Woodbridge — Jones elected — Members elect of Council — Proclamation of Horner creates confusion — Disregarded — Council meets at Green Bay, Jan. 1 — 9 present, 4 absent — Organization — Committee to wait on Governor — Could not find him — His reason for not attending — Committee appointed to inquire into obstructions to legislation — Report — Council can do nothing but pass resolutions and memorials — Resolutions — President requested to remove Secretary — Not removed — Geo. H. Walker's letter explaining Horner's absence — Memorial to Congress for Territorial government — Cassville proposed for capital — Debate—Col. Hamilton — Col. Slaughter — Burnett — Eastern and western portions of territory — Comparative population — Cassville successful — Mr. Knapp — Report of committee on new territory — Amendments — Proposition that Governor be elected — Opposed by Hamilton — Supported by Burnett — Adoption of memorial — Report on internal improvements — Doty as fiscal agent — Propositions to adjourn laid on table — Final adjournment.

CHAPTER XVI.

ORGANIZATION OF WISCONSIN TERRITORY.

Earliest land sales — Floats — Protection of settlers' rights — Territory of Wisconsin organized — Took effect July 4, 1836 — Boundaries — Executive power; Governor; Secretary — Legislative power; Council and House of Representatives — Census — Apportionment — Right of suffrage — Extent of Legislative power — Appointment of county and town officers — Judicial power; Supreme Court; District Courts; Jurisdiction; Writs of Error and Appeals — Attorney and Marshal — Territorial officers appointed by the President — Territorial expenses — Laws of Michigan in force — First session of Legislative Assembly — Public Buildings — Delegate to House of Representatives — Transfer of Judicial proceedings — Library — Summary — Spain, France, Great Britain — Virginia — Northwestern Territory — Indiana Territory — Michigan Territory — Illinois Territory — Michigan Territory.

CHAPTER XVII.

TERRITORY OF WISCONSIN — 1836.

Land speculation in 1836, and its effects — Specie circular — Eastern counties settled most rapidly — Territorial officers took oath of office at Mineral Point, July 4, 1836 — Census apportionment — Election of delegate and members of Legislature on second Monday

16   TABLE OF CONTENTS.

of October — Candidates in each county — Legislature met October 25th — Governor's Message — Statement of the various acts — Judicial districts — Creation of counties — Three banks incorporated — Seat of government established at Madison — Great Seal adopted — Memorials for improvements —'Laws were passed in relation to sheriff's bonds; duties of coroner; incorporation of towns and villages; licensing sale of liquors; bridge across Milwaukee river; Territorial road; railroads; joint resolution to purchase State library — An effort to codify the laws failed and Legislature adjourned Dec. 9, after a session of 46 days — Numerous appointments to office were made by Governor and council — Supreme court held its first session Dec. 8 — All the judges present — Clerk and Reporter appointed — First newspaper in Milwaukee — First in Belmont

CHAPTER XVIII.

TERRITORY OF WISCONSIN — 1837.

Interest of people in proceedings of Congress — Sketch of George W. Jones, delegate — Measures proposed for Wisconsin — Ratification of treaty with Menomonees — Appropriations for arrearages of Legislative expenses and for ordinary expenses — One section of land granted to Mineral Point and to other towns — The acts incorporating banks were approved — Appropriations for light houses at Milwaukee, Manitowoc, Sheboygan, Green Bay and Racine were made — Proceedings to protect "claims" — Newspapers — Local jealousies in Milwaukee — Copper ore developments — County seats in Brown, Grant and Green counties — Mail routes and post offices — Judge Frazer's first court at Milwaukee — Commencement of the capitol at Madison — Purchase of library — Suspension of specie payments and its effects — Legislative session at Burlington Nov. 6 — 1837, changes of membership — Governor's message — Legislature adjourned on the 20th January, 1838, having been in session 75 days, having resolved to meet again at same place on second Monday of June.

CHAPTER XIX.

TERRITORY OF WISCONSIN — 1838.

George W. Jones — Delegate in Congress and his connection as second of Mr. Cilley in a duel between him and Wm. J. Graves — Progress of work on the capitol at Madison — Appropriation by Congress — Indian treaties — Surveyor General's office established for Wisconsin and Iowa — University of Wisconsin — Post offices and post routes — Appropriations by Congress for internal improvements — A preëmption law which furnished partial relief was passed — Wisconsin Territory divided and Iowa Territory organized June 12, 1838 — Land sale at Green Bay, Oct. 22 — Sale at Milwaukee for Nov. 19 postponed until next year — In June a short session of Legislature was held, a census of the population in May, 1838, showed 18,149 — A new apportionment was made — An election held. The candidates for delegate were Jones, Doty and Burnett; Doty was elected — Distribution of money among traders and half-breeds of Winnebago Indians — First session of new Legislature met 26th Nov., and on the 22d Dec. adjourned to 21st of Jan. — County of Walworth was organized and county seat fixed at Elk Horn — Most of the acts related to roads, bridges and ferries and other private and local objects.

CHAPTER XX.

TERRITORY OF WISCONSIN — 1839.

Contest for seat in Congress between Jones and Doty — Doty got the seat and Jones per diem and mileage — Appropriations — Veto power modified — Brothertown Indians — Defining boundary line between Wisconsin and Iowa — Bills which failed — Legislature met Jan. 21 — Governor's message — Winnebago Indians — Acts of fiscal agent ratified — Report of United States attorney as to title to the public park at Madison — Commissioners of public buildings investigated — Old law repealed and new commissioners appointed — New commissioners could make no settlement with the old — Bank investigations — Attorney General ordered to wind up Bank of Wisconsin — State Bank

TABLE OF CONTENTS. 17

incorporated — Several acts creating corporations were passed — Territorial roads were provided for — Building two dams across Rock River authorized — Rock, Dane, Jefferson and Fond du Lac counties were organized — Many towns established — University land located — Judicial districts established and judges assigned — Time of annual session changed to first Monday of December — Revision of laws — Time of service of delegate fixed and an election provided for first Monday in August — Futile attempts to draw party lines — Doty, Kilbourn and Burnett were candidates — Doty was elected — Gov. Dodge's term expired 4th of July — He was reappointed for three years — The land sales at Milwaukee, which had been postponed, took place on 18th of February and 4th of March — The action of commissioners to distribute money under Winnebago treaty was annulled and a new commission appointed.

CHAPTER XXI.

TERRITORY OF WISCONSIN — 1840.

Seven important measures introduced by the delegate, none of which were adopted — No appropriations were made, except for ordinary territorial expenses — The preëmption act extended for two years — In the Legislature of 1839–40, which met December 2, there were seven changes of membership — Names of members, nativity and occupation are given — Governor's message and its recommendations — More about Madison titles — The public buildings unfinished — Suits commenced — Report of committee on the subject — Doty's position that acts of Legislative Assembly did not take effect until submitted to Congress, and letters on that subject from H. N. Wells, E. V. Whiton, Hans Crocker, Morgan L. Martin, and others — Southern boundary and State government — Banks — Capt. Cram's estimates of appropriations for roads' $130,000 — Land sale at Green Bay and at Milwaukee in April — Legislature adjourned on 13th January to 3d of August — Census, 30,747 — New apportionment of House of Representatives — Several new towns were created — Winnebago county was laid off in January, 1840, as also St. Croix and Sauk — Dodge and Washington counties organized — Milwaukee "Bridge War" — Several acts of incorporation passed — Time of general election changed from first Monday of August to fourth Monday of September — Election of President in 1840 — Doty's address, entitled, "Voice of an Injured Territory" — its effect.

CHAPTER XXII.

TERRITORY OF WISCONSIN — 1841.

Appropriation for Legislative expenses reduced from $34,000 to $20,000 — No appropriation for harbors or internal improvements — Legislature of 1840-1 met Dec. 7 — House of Representatives under new apportionment was almost entirely changed — Message and its recommendation — Contested election case of Bruce and Ellis — Brothertown Indians — Also La'Chappelle against Brunson — Condition of the capitol — Territorial suits — Reports of committees on subject — Territorial bonds for $7,000 authorized to be issued for completing capitol and contract let to Daniel Baxter — State government and southern boundary — Nothing done — Banks and safety fund — Examination of bank of Mineral Point — Favorable report — The bank failed in about four months — Memorials were passed asking Congress for appropriations for harbors and other improvements — Territorial Geologist — Schools — Act for township government, optional with counties — Numerous towns established and territorial roads provided for — Portage county extended to north line of the Territory, and organized for county purposes — University lands — Certificates bearing 10 per cent. interest were issued for Territorial indebtedness — President Harrison died April 4, 1841, and Tyler became President — He removed Dodge and appointed Doty, also removed the Secretary, Attorney, Marshal, Surveyor General and most of the Land officers, and many other U. S. officers — Gov. Doty also made numerous removals of Territorial officers — Whig party organized in 1841, and nominated Jonathan E. Arnold, candidate for delegate. The Democratic party organized and nominated Henry Dodge, who was elected.

2

CHAPTER XXIII.

TERRITORY OF WISCONSIN — 1842.

Congressional action — Appropriation for Legislative expenses — Settlement of arrearages — Appropriations must precede sessions of Legislature — Doubts whether appropriation should be made to Mr. Dunn the old or Mr. Field the new secretary — Equivalents for preëmption rights — Post routes — Gov. Doty's minor son appointed pension agent — Appointment withdrawn and Paraclete Potter appointed — Changes in membership of Legislature — Contest of Parmelee and Sill — La'Chappel *vs.* Brunson — Party affiliations exhibited — Contest for president of the council — Democratic speaker — Secret executive sessions abolished — Governor's message; a long paper — Referred to committees in each branch and numerous reports made — The Governor's message strongly recommended State government — Legislature thought it too soon — Gov. Doty issues proclamation for vote on State government; but little attention paid to it — Boundary line between Michigan and Wisconsin — New apportionment of members — New counties — What counties adopted town system — New towns — Acts to amend village incorporations vetoed — Passed notwithstanding veto — Other bills passed over vetoes — Fond du Lac association incorporated — Banks — Imprisonment for debt abolished — Numerous private acts passed — Territorial roads — Contest over the office of State Treasurer — Public buildings and Territorial suits — Lead mines — Leasing system revived — Public feeling — The killing of C. C. P. Arndt by James R. Vineyard.

CHAPTER XXIV.

TERRITORY OF WISCONSIN — 1843.

Harbor and Light house appropriations — Appropriations for Territorial expenses — Certain officers made elective — Term of office of members of the Legislature reduced — Stockbridge Indians — Legislative Assembly meet Dec. 5, 1842 — Mostly new members — Organization — Governor Doty refuses to meet the Legislature — Action of the Legislature on the matter — The Governor's reasons — Memorial to the President asking the removal of the Governor — Both houses adjourn until the fourth Monday of January — Governor appoints special session for 6th March — Adjourned session — Governor still refuses to meet the Legislature — Adjournment to 6th March — Both houses meet on 6th March — Committee wait on Governor, who said he would send a written message at 2 o'clock that day — Message — A question of grammar — Recommendations of message — State government — Territorial debt — Proceeds of public lands — Internal improvements — Short session — Message referred — Conflict between Governor and Legislature renewed — "Special" session or "Adjourned" session — Resolutions adopted that the session is "special" — President of council resigns — Governor willing to coöperate — Session terminates on 25th March — New session on 27th March — Organization continued — Peace restored — Various acts passed — To extend term of court in Walworth county — Appoint superintendent of Territorial property, passed over Governor's veto — Repairs of capitol — Baxter's claim — Territorial suits — Controversy with the librarian, B. Shakelford — Controversy with the auditor, J. T. Clark — Reporter expelled from seat in the House of Representatives — Legislature make no provision for vote on State government — Proclamation of Governor for vote — But little attention paid to it — Governor's vetoes — Bills passed by ⅔ — Errors in Governor's estimates of Legislative expenses — Report of Treasurer — Territorial tax — Ashburton treaty, fixing northwestern boundary — Division of Grant county defeated — Dodge county — St. Croix county — Creation and division of towns — Territorial roads — Dams — Racine to levy tax for harbor — Election of sheriff, etc. — Feeling about abolition — Banks — Small-pox — Death of Gov. Stevens T. Mason — Election of delegate — A party question, H. Dodge and Geo. W. Hickox, candidates.

TABLE OF CONTENTS. 19

CHAPTER XXV.

TERRITORY OF WISCONSIN — 1844

Appropriations by Congress for harbors and legislative expenses — A section of land granted to improve Grant Slough and Potosi — Legislature met Dec. 4, 1843 — Slight changes in membership — Organization — Death of Dr. Lewis F. Linn — Message of Gov. Doty — State government — Short session — Debt — Taxation — "Fifth state" and its boundaries — Shall foreigners vote for state government ? — Question of forming state government submitted to the people — Large majority against it — Negro suffrage — Infringement of boundaries — Report of committee — It shows the infringement, suggests a mode of restitution, and the effect on state government — Receipt and disbursement of share of proceeds of the public lands — Bill to pay Territorial debt — Report of Auditor and Treasurer of the Territory, was misleading — Their nominations were rejected — Territorial suits — Completion of the capitol — J. Y. Smith reëlected superintendent — Baxter claim — University lands — Railroads — Wisconsin Marine and Fire Ins. Co. — Betterments — Terms of courts — Trespass on University and Canal lands — Redemption from tax sales and limitation of suits — Organization of Portage county — Fond du Lac — Dodge — Sauk — Copies of record of deeds to be obtained in Grant, Green, Portage and Winnebago counties — Towns organized — Villages incorporated — Dams authorized — Free bridges in Milwaukee and Racine — Territorial roads — Academies — Special tax for harbors in Milwaukee, Racine and Southport — Vetoes by Governor — Wit and mirth — Adjutant General — Memorials to Congress — Length of session and small appropriation — Adjournment *sine die* — Future sessions to commence first Monday of January — Murder of Robert D. Lester — Politics — Whig convention — Removal of Rufus Parks — Nathaniel P. Tallmadge appointed to succeed Governor Doty.

CHAPTER XXVI.

TERRITORY OF WISCONSIN — 1845.

Congress — Appropriation for Legislature only $13,700 — None for harbors except at Southport — $10,000 for roads — Meeting of Legislature — Change of membership — Organization — Rock and Walworth counties — Harmony between the Governor and Legislature — Contrast between Tallmadge and Doty — Message — Approves the act of last session as to suffrage of foreign-born citizens — Militia — Internal improvements and harbors — Debt — Education — Agriculture — Benediction — No recommendation of State government — Action of Legislature on the subject — Futile efforts to repeal suffrage act — Modified by its friends — Auditor and Treasurer — Their reports — Secretary of the Territory — His reports — Complimented by resolution — Judge Irvin — Dissatisfaction at his absence — Office of Supreme Court Commissioner abolished — Territorial suits, more delay — Baxter claim — Territory cannot be sued — Territorial tax to pay debt — New counties, Chippewa, La Pointe — Washington county organized — Dodge county seat located — Winnebago county — Milwaukee county — Town government in Marquette county and Brown — Futile efforts to divide Jefferson, Dodge and Portage counties — Sauk county seat — Amendments of town government law — Act of Congress granting lands for town sites — Portage City — Fairplay — Boundaries of Milwaukee extended — Beloit incorporated — New towns — Banks — Unauthorized banking — Orthography of Wisconsin — Territorial printer — Liquor license — University lands — Relative to County Treasurers, Clerks and Judges of Probate — Territorial roads — Special tax for roads in Milwaukee and Brown counties — Quietus of bridge controversy in Milwaukee — Improvement of Grant river at Potosi — Penitentiary — Dams — Divorce — Change of name — Wisconsin Phalanx — Janesville Academy — Congregational society in Milwaukee — Memorials to Congress — Fees of Clerk of Supreme Court and Secretary of State — Sheep and dogs — When laws take effect — Adjournment *sine die* — Claim of preëmption to lands reserved as mineral lands — Not sustained by Supreme Court of U. S. — Efforts of agents to lease lands — President's message recommends sale of mineral lands — Henry Dodge appointed Governor in place of Tallmadge, removed —

TABLE OF CONTENTS.

Welcomed at Mineral Point by dinner and ball — Other appointments — Surveyor General, Marshal, Attorney, Land Officers — Morgan L. Martin nominated as delegate by the Democratic convention, James Collins by the Whig convention, and Edward D. Holton by the Liberty party — Martin elected — Stage lines — Disastrous conflagration in Milwaukee.

CHAPTER XXVII.

TERRITORY OF WISCONSIN — 1846.

Certainty of early State government — Enabling act passes Congress — No contest about boundaries — Propositions of Congress — Harbor appropriation defeated by veto — Appropriation of $25,000 for roads reported did not pass — Appropriation of land for Fox and Wisconsin rivers — Appropriations for Territorial government — Surveyor General's salary increased — Stockbridge Indians — Sale of mineral lands authorized — Legislature meets 5th January — Change of membership — Organization — Nativity, age, residence and occupation of members — Governor's message — Referred to State government, school, debt, penitentiary, sale of mineral lands, rivers and harbors, militia and Indians — Message referred — Bill for State government reported and passed both houses — Election for or against to be on first Tuesday of April — Census first June — Apportionment for convention — When delegates elected — When convention to meet — Apportionment of Legislature — Wis. M. & F. Ins. Co. — Bank of Mineral Point — Debt — Auditor's report — Baxter claim — Territorial suits — Escheat of lands to the Territory — New counties: Waukesha, La Fayette and Columbia — New county out of Jefferson and Dodge defeated by vote of people — New towns — Sheboygan county organized — County seats; Sauk, St. Croix — Line between Crawford and Chippewa established — Milwaukee incorporated as a city — Villages incorporated; Madison, Prairieville, Sheboygan and Potosi — University lands — Beloit college incorporated — Carroll college — Madison academy — Common schools — Terms of courts in 2d district — Court practice — Railroad charters — Plank roads — Territorial roads. — Bridges in Milwaukee — Toll bridge in Darlington — Improvement of Grant river — Ferry at Potosi — Dams — Rochester cemetery — Religious societies to sell property — Manufacturing Co. — Filing of ministers' credentials — Divorce — Change of name — Liquor license — Militia — War with Mexico — Wisconsin Volunteers — Indian scare near Muscoda — John Catlin Secretary of Territory vice Floyd — Confirmation of Governor's nominations — Territorial printer and superintendent of property elected — Memorials to Congress — Proceeds of canal lands turned over to Territorial treasury — Burning of wife and children of Marshall M. Strong, and his house — Adjournment sine die — Sale of mineral lands — Political parties — Newspapers — Vote on State government — Census — Governor issues two proclamations; one apportions members of Legislature, the other delegates to convention — Effect of party in election of delegates — Meeting of Constitutional convention — Delegates elect — Absentees — Not sworn — Election of president; influences affecting it — Other officers — Rules — — Standing committees — Judiciary committee increased — Mr. Ryan is indignant and refuses to serve on the committee — Disposition of the printing — Article on banks and banking — On suffrage and the elective franchise — Death of Thomas P. Burnett and his wife and mother — Article on judiciary — Rights of married women and homestead exemption — Resignation of Marshall M. Strong of his seat — To be submitted to vote on first Tuesday of April — Adjournment sine die.

CHAPTER XXVIII.

TERRITORY OF WISCONSIN — 1847.

Division of the Democratic party upon adoption of constitution — Congress passes act for admission of the State — Assents to the change of boundary proposed in the constitution — Proviso of ratification by vote of people — Same appropriations for Territorial expenses — None for harbors — Two for light-houses — Chippewa Land District created — Land for Beetown — Preëmption to Champion and Deering at New Diggins — Legislature meets January 4th — List of members — Organization — Message — It refers to admission of State into the Union; Territorial debt; Harbors; Militia; Capt. Knowlton's volunteer company in U. S. service; Indians and purchase of lands — Incident as to W. A. Barstow — Opposition to constitution developed — Committee report a bill for

TABLE OF CONTENTS. 21

a new convention in June, if the constitution shall be rejected — Passes the council; indefinitely postponed in House — Railroads — Report of Grant river improvement — Improvement of Grand Rapids, of Wisconsin river — Memorial to Congress for improvement of rapids in Mississippi river — Dams — Bridge at Oshkosh — Special harbor tax at Racine — Navigation Co. at Green Bay — Removal of suits from Milwaukee to Waukesha — County seats: Washington county; Iowa county; Columbia county — Organization of La Fayette county — Winnebago county — New towns organized — Villages of Southport and Fond du Lac incorporated; Prairieville changed to Waukesha; Beloit repealed, and Milwaukee city charter amended, and authorized to borrow money for school-house sites — Territorial roads laid out — Memorial asking for U. S. road from Prairie du Chien to La Pointe — Insurance Co. incorporated — Churches authorized to become corporations — "Nashotah House" incorporated; Lawrence Institute incorporated; Memorial for grant of land to it; passed council, but not the House — Academies or seminaries were incorporated at Monroe, Watertown, Sheboygan, Beaver Dam and Prairie du Sac, and a library association at Beloit — Sumptuary laws — University lands — Divorces and change of names — Dower — Election of Printer and Superintendent — Baxter claim — Penitentiary — Facetious report on quackery — Sale of the mineral lands — The voting for the ratification or rejection of the constitution — Official result — Democratic convention to nominate a candidate for delegate — The result — Whig convention nominate John H. Tweedy — Charles Durkee, Abolition candidate — Official statement of result; Mr. Tweedy elected — Proclamation of Governor for special session — Convened on 18th October — Two changes in council — House all new; list of members — Organization — Message; limited to question of State government — Action of Legislature confined to the passage of a law for another convention of sixty-nine delegates to be elected on the 29th of November — Apportionment of delegates — Convention to meet December 15th — Census — Another convention, if constitution should not be adopted — Session of Legislature postponed — Political division of the convention — Population.

CHAPTER XXIX.

TERRITORY OF WISCONSIN — 1848.

Second convention meets — List of members — Organization — William S. Hamilton contests the seat of John O'Connor — Commission to take testimony — Contest unsuccessful — Rules — Prayers — Standing committees — Printing — Article on "Executive," Veto; Lieutenant Governor — "Organization and functions of the Judiciary" — "Boundaries" — "Legislative" — "Suffrage" — "Exemptions from forced sale" — "Banks and Banking" — Other articles adopted without contest — Submitted to popular vote second Monday of March — Elections of State officers, etc., second Monday in May — Legislature meet first Monday in June — Convention adjourned sine die February 1st — Constitution adopted by the people on the 13th March — Admitted into the Union May 19th — Last session of Legislature met February 7th — Members the same — Organization — Message — It refers to harbors; Grant river improvement, Death of Silas Wright, and does not deem it proper to submit "subjects of general legislation" — appropriation only sufficient for session of 24 days — Laws were passed in relation to making land office certificates evidence; publication of notices; conveyances; commitments; cemeteries and telegraph — Resolutions in relation to the death of Silas Wright, John Quincy Adams and Captain Augustus Quarles — Settlement of the Territorial suits — Baxter claim — Memorials to Congress — Repudiating resolutions of 1842 rescinded — Divorces; 42 asked and 24 granted — Change of names — Appropriation to heirs of T. P. Burnett — County seat of La Fayette county — Vote on division of Grant county — Boundaries of Fond du Lac, Winnebago and Calumet counties in Lake Winnebago — Adams county organized; and Manitowoc — County seats; Sauk, Columbia and Washington — Records transferred from Milwaukee to Waukesha county — Mr. Mooers of Washington county resigns his seat — New towns organized — Village charters amended and repealed — Beetown — Incorporation of "Du Lac Academy;" "Sinsinawa Mound College;" "Wisconsin Medical College," at Milwaukee — Milwaukee & Waukesha R. R. Co.; supplementary act — Sixteen plank or turnpike roads incorporated — Numerous Territorial roads — Five ferry charters — Eleven acts were passed authorizing the erection of dams on navigable rivers — "Wisconsin Iron Co.," incorporated — Lumber inspector for St. Croix county — Territorial Printer and Superintendent — Legislature adjourns sine die — TERRITORY OF WISCONSIN becomes only a memory.

TABLE OF CONTENTS.

CHAPTER XXX.
MILWAUKEE AND ROCK RIVER CANAL.

Early navigation of Rock River — Public attention directed to canal in 1836 — Petition for canal charter in 1836; no action — Survey in 1837 — Charter of Canal Co., January 5, 1838 — Provisions of the act — Co. authorized to apply to Congress for aid — Co. organized February 3, 1838 — Co. memorialize Congress for grant of land — Engineer submits estimate of cost — Byron Kilbourn appointed agent to go to Washington, and goes — Memorial presented in Senate — Favorable report and bill — Bill passed Senate June 1, excluding preëmptions — Referred in House — Passed House with amendments which were concurred in by Senate — Bill became a law June 18th — Kilbourn presents bill to Legislature at session of 1838, which Canal Co. wished passed — It authorized the Territory to borrow $500,000 — Provided for Territorial offices, for the appraisal and sale of the granted lands — Bill introduced in Council on 15th of December — Adjournment to 21st of January — Popular hostility to canal — Another bill introduced in Council on 25th of January, which became a law on the 26th of February, 1839 — It authorized loan of only $50,000 — Change in Territorial officers and their duties — Other provisions unsatisfactory to Canal Co. — Officers appointed by governor — Final location of canal 6th May — Plats of location sent to Commissioner General Land Office, and lands designated; 139,191 acres — Session of Legislature 1839 — Report of canal commissioners — Land sales — Settlers protected — Bonds for $50,000 had been executed, agent appointed to sell them, who reported that he could not — Even numbered sections and preëmption — Canal Co. present memorial, which complains of act of last session — Salaries too high — Resolutions of inquiry adopted — Kilbourn's reply — Resolution of inquiry by the House and response — Resolution of Council that president of company present plans and estimates of cost of canal — They are submitted — Proceedings in House — Report of committee — Bill to abandon construction of canal — Amendments adopted providing an opposite policy — Concurred in and became a law — Compensation of officers reduced — To be elected by Legislature — Canal fund to be used for constructing canal, if no loan is made by September — Kilbourn appointed loan agent — Mr. Higginbotham's proposition — Declined by the Governor — Special session of Legislature in August, 1840 — Nothing done about canal — No loan in 1840 — Legislature meet December 7, 1840 — Report of canal company and of canal commissioners — Referred to a committee — Bill reported — Becomes a law February 12th — Substitutes wooden locks for stone; authorized bonds for $100,000, and 7 per cent. interest; proceeds to be deposited in any sound specie paying banks, selected by commissioners and Governor, subject to draft of receiver — Old bonds to be recalled — Kilbourn reappointed loan agent May, 1841 — James D. Doty appointed Governor vice Dodge, removed — Doty revokes Kilbourn's authority September 1, 1841 — On 22d of June Kilbourn negotiated loan for $31,000 at Cincinnati — On the 4th of August he negotiated a loan for $5,000 in New York — On 14th August he negotiated another loan for $15,000 at Oneida, N. Y. — On 26th August he negotiated another loan for $5,000 at Albany, N. Y. — The loans, except $1,000, were not sanctioned by the Receiver for the reasons assigned that they were not authorized by the law or the authority of the loan agent — Legislature met December, 1841 — Gov. Doty in his message says canal is impracticable and work ought not to be continued — Message and report of loan agent referred to committee in council — Committee report resolutions which passed both Houses; approved by Governor February 18, 1842 — They declare 55 of the bonds negotiated to be null and void — And that the other 44 are null and void — Vote upon the resolutions — One bond was paid and all the others but ten afterwards returned and canceled — Work on the canal stopped — February 15, 1843, Gov. Dodge recommends rescinding the repudiating resolutions — Resolutions were rescinded — At session of 1842 resolutions passed that the Territory ought not further to execute the canal trust — Authority to make loans repealed — Efforts to change the grant from canal to railroad — Payment for canal lands indefinitely postponed in 1844 — In 1845 all unsold canal lands to be offered for sale at $1.25 per acre, and lands previously sold to be paid for at same rate — Report of Register and Receiver in 1846 — Canal fund diverted to Territorial treasury — Report of Register and Receiver in 1847 — Appropriation to John Anderson in 1847 — Report of Register and Receiver in 1848 — Payment of interest on repudiated bonds — Refunding excess to purchasers of canal lands — Duties of Register and Receiver transferred to Secretary of State and State Treasurer — Unsold canal lands made part of the 500,000 acre grant — Unsettled canal matters left a legacy to the STATE OF WISCONSIN.

HISTORY

OF THE

TERRITORY OF WISCONSIN.

CHAPTER I.

EARLY EXPLORATIONS OF "FLORIDA" AND "LOUISIANA."

The historical compilation made by General WILLIAM R. SMITH, and published in 1854 by authority of the Legislature, and now out of print, presents an elaborate review of the early history of Wisconsin, previously to 1836, and as intimately connected with it, a retrospective view of the explorations of the whole valley of the Mississippi river.

An epitome of this historical retrospect of these early explorations will be given, consisting chiefly of extracts from that valuable work, sustaining as they do, a relation to the more modern history of the Territory, no less intimate than interesting.

The southern coast of the North American continent, near St. Augustine, Florida, was discovered on Easter Sunday, 1512, by JUAN PONCE DE LEON, a companion of Columbus. He named the new found country Pascua Florida. The Spaniards of early times designated all of North America, from the Gulf of Mexico to the great lakes, by the name of Florida, and under that name claimed the whole sea-coast as far as Newfoundland. PONCE DE LEON was appointed Governor of the country, and in 1521 was killed by the natives.

In 1516 DIEGO MIRUELO sailed for Havana and landed at some point in Florida, which he has not distinctly described.

Ten years later PAMPHILO DE NARVAEZ obtained permission from Spain to prosecute discoveries and make further conquest of Florida. In 1528, he, with three hundred men (of whom eighty were mounted), landed near Appalachee

Bay. In a fruitless search for gold they wandered over the lands lying north of the Gulf for six months, when they again sought the gulf coast, where they desperately embarked in rude boats which they had manufactured, and finally perished in a storm.

The chivalric and romantic adventures of FERDINAND DE SOTO are so familiar to every American, that only the briefest possible reference to them is demanded:

In May, 1539, DE SOTO, having participated with PIZARRO in the conquest of Peru, and having obtained leave from the Spanish king to conquer Florida, accompanied by a well armed and brilliant band of six hundred men, with between two and three hundred horses, landed in the bay of Spiritu Santo, or Tampa Bay, eager to prosecute his contemplated enterprise, and filled with hope and spirit of adventure.

Nearly two years were spent by DE SOTO and his band of adventurous followers, during which they climbed the mountains of Georgia, captured the town of Mavila or Mobile, passed the winter (1540–1) near the Yazoo, and finally on the first of April, 1541, reached the Mississippi River not far from the 35th parallel of latitude. After spending months in explorations west of the Great River, and spending the third winter of their wanderings on the Washita, they descended this river to its junction with the Mississippi, where, in May, 1542, DE SOTO died of a malignant fever. His body was wrapped in a mantle, and sunk in the middle of the stream. The discoverer of the Father of Waters, the most remarkable of all his discoveries; he slept beneath its turbid current, and one-half of his six hundred followers had left their bones among the mountains and in the morasses of the south, from Georgia to Arkansas.

A desire of conquest and a greed for gold were the incentives of all these adventurers. More than a century later, the missionary spirit of religion led to numerous explorations of the Mississippi valley by the route of the great lakes. CHAMPLAIN had discovered the lake which bears his name more than ten years before the landing of the pilgrims at Plymouth.

In 1616, LE CARON, a Franciscan friar, reached the rivers of Lake Huron.

In 1627, a charter grant of New France was obtained from Louis XIII. by a number of French merchants, organized by a French nobleman — the Duke de RICHLIEU — which included the whole basin of the St. Lawrence, and of such other rivers as flowed directly into the sea, and also Florida. After the restoration of Quebec in 1632, by the English, they entered on the government of their province.

The Jesuits BREBEUF and DANIEL, followed soon by LALLEMAND, in 1634 penetrated to the heart of the Huron wilderness, where soon after two villages, St. Louis and St. Ignatius, sprung up, and where was raised the first house of the Society of Jesus.

As early as 1618, M. NICOLLET lived with the Indians on the Ottawa river, and two years later, with tribes bordering on Lake Huron.

It is well authenticated that before 1640, NICOLLET penetrated Wisconsin as far as the Wisconsin river. In the Jesuit relation for 1640 is found this passage written from Quebec to France, by Pere LE JEUNI:

"M. NICOLLET, who has penetrated farthest into these most distant regions, has assured me that if he had pushed on three days longer, on a great river which issues from the second lake of the Hurons (Lake Michigan), he would have found the sea. Now I strongly suspect this sea is on the north of Mexico, and that thereby we could have an entrance in Japan and China."

PARKMAN in his "Jesuits in North America" writes as follows:

"As early as 1639, NICOLLET ascended the Green Bay of Michigan, and crossed the waters of the Mississippi."

It is not probable that NICOLLET saw the river that is now known as the "Mississippi," while it is certain that his visit to the Wisconsin river was in 1634, and not in 1639. A record in the Canadian Archives shows that NICOLLET started from Three Rivers on a western voyage in July, 1634.

It is not improbable that NICOLLET may have trod the soil of Wisconsin earlier than 1634, but no reasonable doubt exists of his visiting the Wisconsin tribes in council during that year, where, it is recorded, there were assembled

"Four thousand warriors, who feasted on six score of beavers. He appeared before them in a robe of state, adorned with figures of flowers and birds. Approaching with a pistol in each hand, he fired both at once. The astonished natives hence styled him 'Thunder Beaver.'"

In 1641, the fathers RAYMBAULT and JOGUES, the first envoys from Christendom, met at the Falls of St. Mary two thousand Indians who had assembled to receive them.

As early as 1652, Eather JEAN DEQUERRE, Jesuit, went from Sault St. Marie to the Illinois and established a flourishing mission, probably that of "St. Louis," where Peoria is now situated. He visited various Indian tribes and was killed in 1661, in the midst of his apostolic labors.

In 1654, two fur traders joined a band of Ottowas and made a western voyage of five hundred leagues. In two years they returned, accompanied with fifty canoes and two hundred and fifty men.

The traders visited Green Bay, and two of them passed the winter of 1659 on the banks of Lake Superior.

In 1657, Father JEAN CHARLES DROCOUX, Jesuit, went to Illinois, and returned to Quebec the same year.

In the autumn of 1660, PERE RENE MESNARD, having been chosen by the bishops of Quebec to visit Lake Superior and Green Bay, reached Keweena, and the next year having wandered in the forest, was never more seen.

In 1665, PERE CLAUDE ALLOUEZ embarked on a mission to the far west. He reached the falls of St. Mary in September, and from thence went to the great village of the Chippewas at Chegoiemegon. Here a grand inter-tribal council was held. There were present the Potowatamies from Lake Michigan; the Sacs and Foxes from the west; the Hurons from north of Lake Superior; the Sioux from the headwaters of the Mississippi, as well also as the Illinois, whose enticing description of the noble river flowing to the south, on which they dwelt, and their vast prairies replete with buffalo and deer, created a desire to explore their country, which was not long to remain ungratified.

In 1667, ALLOUEZ returned to Quebec, and in 1668, CLAUDE DABLON and JAMES MARQUETTE returned to the Sault, where they established the mission of St. Mary's, the oldest European settlement within the bounds of the state of Michigan.

In 1669, NICHOLAS PERROT was despatched to the west as the agent of the Intendant Talon, to prepare a congress of the Indian nations at St. Mary's. PERROT visited Green Bay, and from there was escorted by the Potowatamies, to the Miamis at Chicago, being the pioneer of European explorers to the southern part of Lake Michigan.

There is reason to suppose that about the same time, ROBERT CAVELIER DE LA SALLE reached the Ohio river by way of Lake Erie, and descended it as far as the rapids at Louisville.

In 1669, ALLOUEZ made an excursion to Green Bay, and up the Fox river as far as the town of the Mascoutins, and in the autumn of 1670, having been joined by DABLON, the

EARLY EXPLORATIONS. 27

two fathers again visited Green Bay, and established there the mission of St. Francois Xavier.

The great congress of the Indian nations was held at St. Mary's, in May, 1671. The cross was raised and by its side a column was planted and marked with the lilies of the Bourbons and it was formally announced to the natives that they were placed under the protection of the French king.

The cross was born by ALLOUEZ and DABLON through eastern Wisconsin and the north of Illinois, among the Mascoutins and the Kickapoos on the Milwaukee, and the Miamis at the head of Lake Michigan, as well as the Foxes on the river which bears their name, and which, in their language, was the Wau-ke-sha.

In 1673, MARQUETTE, with the SIEUR JOLIET, explored the Fox and Wisconsin rivers, and descended the Mississippi below the entrance of the Arkansas, and then returning, ascended the Illinois and making a portage to the Chicago river, descended it to Lake Michigan, and returned by that Lake to Green Bay. They left Sault St. Mary, May, 13. They arrived safely at Green Bay and thence went up Fox river to the town of the Mascoutins, which was three leagues from the "portage" and was probably near the head of Buffalo lake. On June 10, they left this Indian town and embarked upon the Wisconsin, then called Mascousin. In seven days, they reached the Mississippi by the route of the great highway of nature, which the Fox and Wisconsin rivers furnished, and which NICOLLET had partially explored thirty-nine years before. The voyagers, having descended the Mississippi river to the Indian village of Akansea, near the latitude of 33 degrees, on the 17th of July, commenced their return voyage. In passing up the Illinois, MARQUETTE was entreated by the tribe of that name to come and reside among them. One of their chiefs, with their young men, conducted the voyagers to the Chicago river and Lake Michigan, and before the end of September they were safe in Green Bay.

JOLIET returned to Quebec, and MARQUETTE remained. He spent the winter and the following summer at the mission of Green Bay, suffering from sickness. In October, 1674, he left Green Bay, intent upon establishing a mission on the Illinois river. In November he reached the Chicago river. His malady had returned upon him and he was compelled to spend the winter on its banks, about two leagues from its mouth, where his companions built a log hut.

On the 30th of March, 1675, MARQUETTE was able to resume his journey, and making the portage to the Des Plaines, he descended the Illinois river until he came to an Indian town, which he called Kaskaskia, which is on the right bank of the Illinois about midway between the present towns of Ottawa and La Salle. Here he met several thousand Indians and harrangued them on the mysteries of the Faith. They begged him to stay among them, but his life was fast ebbing away, and it behooved him to depart. He returned to Chicago, and while sailing thence along the eastern shore of Lake Michigan, on the 19th of May, they entered a small stream, which bears the name of Marquette, and he breathed his last upon its banks, and was buried in the sand. The next year his relics were borne to the Chapel of St. Ignace, of Michilimacina, and buried beneath its floor.

The SIEUR LA SALLE was born at Rouen, 1643, of good family. In 1666, he sailed for Canada. The Jesuits of St. Sulpice had a settlement at Montreal and control of all the land in that vicinity. From them he obtained a grant at La Chène, nine miles above Montreal, and engaged in the fur trade. In 1675, LA SALLE obtained from the king the rank of nobility and the concession of a large domain at the outlet of Lake Ontario, and the exclusive traffic with the Five Nations. Here he erected a fort, which he named Frontenac, where is now the city of Kingston.

In 1679, with TONTI as his lieutenant, the FRANCISCAN HENNEPIN and a party of mechanics and traders, he constructed a vessel of sixty tons on the upper Niagara river, which he called the Griffin. On the 7th of August the sails of the Griffin were spread to the breezes of Lake Erie; and planting a trading post at Mackinaw, he cast anchor in Green Bay early in September.

Having dispatched the Griffin to Niagara river richly laden with furs, he, with his company, made their way in bark canoes to the head of Lake Michigan, and at the mouth of the St. Joseph river constructed the trading house with palisades, known as the Fort of the Miamis.

In December, LA SALLE with TONTI, HENNEPIN, and two other Franciscans and about thirty other followers, ascended the St. Joseph, as far as the present town of South

Bend, and by a short portage, entered the Kankakee and descended to the site of the Indian village below Ottowa, which MARQUETTE had left nearly five years before. The tribe was absent, passing the winter in the chase. He continued on to the site of the present city of Peoria, where he found many Indians, with whom he remained a few days. About the middle of January (1680) he moved with his party a short distance down the river, where he planned and began to build a fort on the left bank, which he called Crèvecœur—broken heart.

In the month of March, he set off on foot with three companions for Fort Frontenac, where he arrived May 6th. He embarked again from Fort Frontenac August 10, with large supplies of men and stores for rigging a brigantine. His route was by Lake Simcoe and the Georgian Bay. On the 4th of November he reached the ruined fort at the mouth of the St. Joseph, and in a few days, by the route he had taken about a year before, he again reached the post in Illinois, which was now deserted. Hence came the delay of another year, which after exploring the Illinois river to its mouth, was occupied in visiting Green Bay, and conducting traffic there; in finding TONTI, who had been driven from Crèvecœur — and his men, and perfecting a capacious barge with which to explore the Mississippi.

On the 28th of February 1680, HENNEPIN with his two companions, ACCAU and DUGAY, set out by direction of LA-SALLE to explore the upper Mississippi. HENNEPIN left the mouth of the Illinois on the 12th of March. He ascended the Mississippi, and after passing the mouth of the Wisconsin, and below Lake Pepin, the voyagers, on the 12th of April, were made prisoners by the Siouxs. They were taken in their canoes as far as the present site of St. Paul, where their captors took them across the country to their villages near Lake Buade, now called Mille Lacs. After remaining prisoners at the Indian village about two months, the Indians set out in a body on a buffalo hunt, taking their captives with them. They descended Rum river which forms the outlet of Mille Lac. At the mouth of Rum river, HENNEPIN and DU GAY were liberated, and furnished a small canoe, an earthen pot, a gun, a knife and a robe of beaver skin. Thus equipped, they began their journey, and soon beheld for the first time the Falls of St. Anthony. They descended the great river as far as the mouth of the Chippewa, and being in danger of starvation, they ascended that stream and joined a large body of Sioux hunters. They soon after met DANIEL GREYSOLON DU LHUT, a cousin of TONTI, with four well-armed Frenchmen. When HENNEPIN met DULHUT, the latter had been about two years in the wilderness. He had left Quebec in September, 1678. In 1679, he visited several of the Sioux villages. In June, 1680, he, with the four Frenchmen and an Indian, set out from the head of Lake Superior and reached the Mississippi river by the route of the Brule and the St. Croix. HENNEPIN and DU GAY returned with DU LHUT and his companions to Mille Lac. The Indians had become more friendly, and when in the autumn the travelers proposed to go home, the Sioux did not oppose their departure, and they set out together — eight white men in all, well equipped for supplying themselves with game.

After various adventures, the party reached the Jesuit mission at Green Bay, by the route of the Wisconsin and Fox Rivers, and soon after reached Mackinaw, where they spent the winter. The following spring HENNEPIN descended the lakes and their connecting rivers to Fort Frontenac and thence to Montreal, and soon after went to Europe, and died in obscurity.

In May, 1681, LA SALLE set out in canoes from Fort Miami and soon reached Mackinaw, where he found TONTI. The two embarked for Frontenac, and returned late in the autumn to Fort Miami. In December, they went in canoes to the Chicago river, and placing their canoes on sledges, dragged them to the open water of the Illinois river below Lake Peoria, upon which the party soon embarked and on the 6th of February (1682), they issued forth on the majestic bosom of the Mississippi. They reached the mouth of the river in about two months, and LA SALLE erected a column and a cross bearing the arms of France, and inscribed upon it the words, "Louis the Great, king of France and Navarre, reigning April 9, 1682;" and formally taking possession for France of all the country watered by the Mississippi, he named it Louisiana. He ascended the river and the Illinois, and in May, 1683, returned to Quebec to embark for France.

The disastrous attempt of LA SALLE during the next three or four years to colonize "Louisiana," in which he sailed from France with four vessels, bearing two hundred and eighty persons, and missing the mouth of the Mississippi,

EARLY EXPLORATIONS. 31

landed at Matagorda Bay, and in which this daring adventurer was assassinated by three of his own men on the 20th of March, 1687, in a branch of the Trinity river, need not be detailed. It is, however, to him that must mainly be ascribed the discovery of the vast regions of the Mississippi valley and the subsequent occupation and settlement of them by the French.

In June, 1689, France declared war against England, in which the American colonies of two kingdoms were so involved that no further settlements in Louisiana were attempted until after the peace of Ryswick in September, 1697.

In 1689, Green Bay contained a fort, chapel and missionary house, which were situated among the villages of the Sacs, Potawatamies and Menomonies.

In October, 1689, two vessels under the command respectively of M. D'IBERVILLE and the Marquis CHATEAUMORAND, sailed from France for the mouth of the Great River. They touched at Pensacola in January, 1699, and passing Mobile Bay, landed on Dauphin Island. IBERVILLE with more than fifty men, departed in barges, entered the Mississippi on the 2d of March, which he ascended for some distance, when he returned to the Bay of Biloxi. Here they built a fort, three leagues west of the Pensacola river, and leaving his brothers De Bienville and Sanvole in command, the explorers returned to France.

In December, 1699, IBERVILLE returned from Europe with two armed vessels and several officers for garrisons, accompanied by M. LE SUEUR and thirty workmen. In April, 1700, LE SUEUR led a company to explore the river for minerals. They ascended to the St. Peters, and up that river to the mouth of the Blue Earth, where they spent the winter and returned in the spring to Biloxi.

In the month of June, 1701, DE LA MOTTE CADILLAC, with a Jesuit missionary and one hundred Frenchmen was sent to take possession of Detroit. In 1712, the Outagamies or Foxes attempted the destruction of the fort. They were repulsed and compelled to surrender at discretion.

The oldest permanent European settlement in the valley of the Mississippi is Kaskaskia, the seat of a Jesuit mission. FATHER GRAVIER was its founder, but the exact date of its origin is uncertain. Land titles were issued for purposes of settlement and cultivation. The date of the earliest one on record being May 10, 1722, signed "Boisbriant."

England, by the peace of UTRECHT in April, 1713, obtained from France large but not well defined concessions of territory in America.

As early as 1720, a lucrative trade had sprung up between the Illinois country and the province of Lower Louisiana. In that year, MONSEUR BOISBRIANT, the commandant on the Illinois, removed his headquarters to the bank of the Mississippi, twenty-five miles below the village of Kaskaskia, where Fort Charters was built. Its walls were of strong masonry, but within a hundred years were overgrown with almost impenetrable vines and forest trees.

Soon after the construction of Fort Charters, the villages of Cahokia, Prairie de Rocher and some others sprung into note in its vicinity. All the settlements continued to extend and multiply. In 1721, the Jesuits had established a monastery and college in Kaskaskia, and four years later, the village became a chartered town. During the first twelve years of the eighteenth century, not less than twenty-five hundred settlers had been introduced in "Louisiana," and in 1717, the number of inhabitants was not more than seven hundred, including persons of every age, sex and color.

In 1711, the government of Louisiana, comprising all the "Illinois country," was placed in the hands of a governor-general — DIRAU D'ARTAGUETTE — with headquarters at the site of the present city of Mobile, where a new fort was erected. "Louisiana" was at this time held by France to embrace the whole valley of the Mississippi and all its tributaries, and to extend north to the great lakes, and the waters of Hudson's Bay, and, of course, included all of the present state of Wisconsin.

In August, 1718, eight hundred emigrants for Louisiana, attracted by visions of wealth to result from the "Mississippi Scheme" of JOHN LAW, landed at Dauphine Island, and made their way to lands that had been ceded them, and which had been selected by BIENVILLE, where is now the city of New Orleans.

In 1719, PHILIPPE FRANCIS RENAULT, "Director General of the mines of Louisiana," arrived in the Illinois country with two hundred miners and artificers. They made fruitless explorations for mines as far as the sources of the St. Peters, the Arkansas, the tributaries of the Missouri and even to the Rocky Mountains.

CHAPTER II.

WARS WITH FOX INDIANS.

The ability of the Outagamies to annoy the French and to war with their savage enemies, was materially affected by their futile attempt to destroy Detroit in 1712, and by the desperate fight which ensued near Lake St. Clair; yet their failure only added fresh and implacable inspiration to the savage spirit of hate and revenge which prompted them to resort to another locality for its gratification.

They collected their dispersed bands on the Fox river, where they robbed and butchered all travelers on this great highway of nature from the lakes to the Mississippi. The Sauks were their old and natural allies, and the Sioux were induced to openly join them, while many of the Iroquois were allied to them clandestinely. Indeed, the danger of a general alliance among the savages against the whites appeared threatening.

This threatened danger induced the French governor of Canada to propose a union of the friendly tribes with the French, in a war of extermination against the common enemy, to which these tribes readily consented. A party of French was raised, and the command of the expedition was wisely confided to the brave, energetic and discreet DE LOUVIGNY, the king's lieutenant at Quebec.

DE LOUVIGNY and his command left Quebec on the 14th of March, 1716, and was joined on his route by a number of savages, so that his force amounted to eight hundred men, resolved upon the total destruction of the Fox nation. He returned to Quebec on the 12th of October, and the next day gave to the council the following account of his expedition:

"After three days of open trenches, sustained by a continuous fire of fusileers with two pieces of cannon and a grenade mortar, they were reduced to ask for peace, notwithstanding they had five hundred warriors in the fort who fired briskly, and more than three thousand women; they also expected shortly a reinforcement of three hundred men. But the promptitude with which the officers, who were in this action, pushed forward the trenches that I had opened at only seventy yards from their fort, made the enemy fear the third night that they would be taken. As I was only twenty-four yards from their fort, my design was to reach the triple oak stakes by a ditch of a foot and a half in the rear. Perceiving very well that my balls had not the effect I anticipated, I decided to take the place at the first onset, and to explode two mines under their curtains. The boxes being properly placed for the purpose, I did not listen to the enemie's first proposition; but they having made a second one, I submitted it to my allies who consented to it on the following conditions: That the Foxes and their allies would make peace with all the Indians who are submissive to the king, and with whom the French are engaged in trade and commerce, and that they would return to me all the French prisoners that they have, and those captured during the war from our allies. This was complied with immediately. That they would take slaves from distant natives and deliver them to our allies, to replace their dead; that they should hunt to pay the expenses of this war, and as a surety of the keeping of their word, they should deliver me six chiefs or children of chiefs, to take with me to M. LA MARQUIS DE VAUDREUIL as hostages, until the entire execution of our treaty, which they did, and I took them with me to Quebec. Besides I have re-united the other nations, at variance among themselves, and have left that country enjoying universal peace."

The scene of DE LOUVIGNY'S engagement was at the Little Butte des Morts, some thirty-seven miles above Green Bay.

In 1725, DE LOUVIGNY, having gone to France, was there appointed governor of Three Rivers, and on his return the same year, lost his life by shipwreck near Louisburg on the night of August 27.

Gov. VAUDREUIL, in a letter to the council, dated October 30, 1716, speaking of "the manner in which the SIEUR DE LOUVIGNY put an end to the war with the Foxes," says of him:

"He has always served his country with much distinction; but in his expedition against the Foxes, he signalized himself still more by his valor, his capacity and his conduct, in which he displayed a great deal of prudence. He made the war short, but the peace which results from it will not be of short duration."

The name, services and memory of the distinguished leader of this formidable military expedition into the very heart of Wisconsin, are necessarily and inseparably associated with its primitive history.

The confident belief of VAUDREUIL, that the expedition had "put an end to the war," and that the peace would "not be of short duration," soon proved to be without warrant.

The Foxes, whom BANCROFT characterizes as "a nation passionate and untamable, springing up into new life from every defeat, and though reduced in the number of their warriors, yet present everywhere, by their ferocious enterprise and savage daring," failed to send deputies to the governor general. He flattered himself for a long time that they would keep their plighted faith; but he was only taught by the renewal of hostilities that an enemy driven to a certain point, is always irreconcilable. During the twelve years that followed DE LOUVIGNY'S expedition, all the peaceable efforts of the French to restrain the hostile conduct of the Foxes were unavailing.

In 1728, the governor of Canada sent a force of four hundred French troops, and eight or nine hundred Indians, principally Iroquois, Hurons, Nepissings and Ottawas, under the command of Sieur MARCHAND DE LIGNERY, who, it is probable, had served under DE LOUVIGNY in his expedition against the Foxes in 1716, and who was now commissioned to go and destroy the Fox nations.

DE LIGNERY had previously, on the 7th of June, 1726, held a council at Green Bay with the Foxes, Sauks and Winnebagoes in the presence of Monsieurs D'AMARITON, CLIGANCOURT and Rev. Father CHARDON, in which the chiefs of the three nations all gave their words that they would maintain peace. But these treacherous and lying savages paid no regard to their plighted faith, and continued their robberies and butcheries as they had done before.

The troops commanded by DE LIGNERY commenced their march on the 5th of June, 1728, and taking the route of the Ottawa river and Lakes Nipissing and Huron, arrived at the fort at the mouth of Fox river on the night of the 17th of August. Father CRESPEL, who accompanied the expedition as almoner of the four hundred Frenchmen, and who wrote an account of it, says:

"Notwithstanding the precautions that had been taken to conceal our arrival, the savages had received information of it, and all had escaped with the exception of four. These were presented to our savages who, after having diverted themselves with them, shot them to death with their arrows."

The expedition continued up the Fox river as far as the portage of the Wisconsin; but none of the enemy could be found, except two women, a girl and an old man, who were killed and burned by the savages. DE LIGNERY learned that the Foxes had fled four days before; that the old men, women and children had embarked in canoes, and the warriors had gone by land. He urged his Indian allies to follow in pursuit; but only a portion would consent, the others saying the enemy had gone so far that any attempt to catch up with them would be useless.

The French had nothing but Indian corn to eat, the season was far advanced, and they had a distance of four hundred leagues to return, so that the safety of half the army was endangered by further pursuit. It was, therefore, decided to burn the Fox villages, their forts and huts, and destroy all that could be found in their fields — corn, peas, beans and gourds, of which they had an abundance. Messrs. BEAU-

HARNOIS and DE ARGEMAIT, from whose letter to the French Minister of War of September 1, 1728, the foregoing facts are taken, add:

"It is certain that half of these natives, who number four thousand souls, will die with hunger, and that they will come in and ask mercy."

The want of success in this expedition of DE LIGNERY was severely criticised by the local authorities of Canada, although he does not appear to have lost the confidence of the French government, which he continued to serve in various commands until 1759, when he led a force of 850 French and 350 Indians to the relief of Fort Niagara, where the party was defeated, and he was wounded and taken prisoner, after which no further mention is made of him.

Subsequently, probably in the autumn of 1729, a party of over two hundred Indians — Ottawas, Chippewas, Menomonees and Winnebagoes — fell on a party of the Foxes, consisting of eighty men and three hundred women and children, who were returning from a buffalo hunt. The party was surprised, and all of the men except three, and all the women and children, were killed and burned, and twenty flat boats were destroyed.

The Sieur PERRIERE MARIN was a native of France of decided and energetic character, and was a prominent trader among the Sauks, and the Indians on the Mississippi. He had a place of deposit for goods and peltries on the left bank of the Mississippi, a short distance below the mouth of the Wisconsin, near what is now called Wyalusing, then called Fort Marin, and another near Mackinaw known by the same designation. Between these two places, MARIN found it necessary to conduct an extensive traffic on the highways of the Fox and Wisconsin rivers; and his boats heavily laden with valuable cargoes were obliged oftentimes to pass the village and fort of the Foxes on the bank of the Fox river at the Little Butte des Morts, and as often to submit to the forced exactions of the Foxes, in the form of tribute.

He was probably in command of the fort of the Folles Avoine or Menomonees in 1730, and it is certain that he had great influence with the French and the Indians who were hostile to the Foxes.

These repeated piratical levies determined MARIN to drive the marauding savages from their position. The traditional and other accounts of his valiant exploits leave some doubt

WARS WITH FOX INDIANS. 37

about the exact date of his first attack, but it was probably as early in the year 1730 as the breaking up of the ice would admit of the passage of boats up the river.

MARIN raised a volunteer force at Mackinaw, which was increased at Green Bay by the friendly Indians. All were embarked in boats, each having a full complement of men well armed, and an oil-cloth or tarpaulin large enough to cover the whole boat and conceal the men, such as was generally used to protect traders' goods from the effects of the weather. Near the Grand Chute, some three miles below, but not within view of the Little Butte des Morts, the party was divided, one portion going by land to the rear of the village to aid and support the attack, which was to be made in front by the others from the boats. The men in the boats, with their guns ready for use, were concealed by the coverings, and only two men to row each boat were in view, thus presenting the appearance of a trader's fleet.

When the Foxes discovered the approach of the boats, they placed out their torch, and posted themselves thickly along the bank, and awaited the landing of the boats and the payment of the customary exactions.

The boats having approached near enough for an effective attack, the tarpaulins were suddenly thrown off, and a deadly volley from the musketry of the soldiers, and the discharge from a swivel gun loaded with grape and canister shot, scattered death and dismay among the unsuspecting savages, to whom the number of their enemies seemed treble the reality. They fled precipitately to their village to prepare for defense, pursued by the troops. Here another horror confronted them. A Menomonee warrior had stealthily entered the village and set on fire the frail bark dwellings on the windward side, which were soon wrapped in a sheet of flame. The Foxes in vain sought safety in the forest; but were met by the party which had flanked their retreat, and they found themselves placed between two hostile fires. Then burst forth one heart-rending, agonized shriek, and the devoted band of free-booting Indians prepared to defend themselves with a courage born of despair. Ball and bayonet now began their bloody work, and the tomahawk and scalping knife were active participants in the terrible work of death. No quarter was asked, and none was given. The time occupied by this bloody tragedy was not long; but in its strategy, surprise and sanguinary execution it probably has no parallel in the annals of Indian warfare. Most of the Foxes were killed or taken prisoners, but a few escaped up the river, and others were absent at the time of the engagement.

The same season the remnant of this savage tribe, having been driven from their village at the Little Butte des Morts, took post about three miles above the Great Butte des Morts, on the southern or opposite side of the river.

From the letter of the Marquis DE BEAUHARNOIS to the French Minister, dated June 25, 1730, it not only appears that the Sieur MARIN had written to the Governor an account "concerning the movement he made last March against the Foxes," but also that he (MARIN) was present at a council held at Mackinaw, when the Menomonees and other friendly Indians invited Monsieur DU BUISSON, who commanded the post, to place himself at their head and fall upon the nation of Foxes and destroy it entirely; that DU BUISSON complied with their request, and that Sieur MARIN went with him. The letter states that

"This officer must have left his post (Mackinaw) the 20th of last May, with six hundred men, among whom are fifty Frenchmen."

The only account of this expedition which is known to exist is the traditionary one, that a severe battle took place at the Great Butte des Morts and many Foxes were killed, though not so many as at the Little Butte des.Morts, and that they were again forced to fly.

On the 2d of November, 1730, Messrs. DE BEAUHARNOIS and HOCQUART addressed a letter to the French Minister, in which they say that

"An affair took place in September under the command of the Sieur DE VILLIERS, commanding at the River St. Josephs, to whom were united the Sieur DE NOYELLE, commanding the Miamis, and the Sieur DE ST. ANGE, father and son, with the French of that distant colony, together with those of our posts, and all the neighboring Indians our allies (we numbered from twelve to thirteen hundred men) which resulted in the almost total defeat of the Foxes. Two hundred of their warriors have been killed on the spot, or burned after being taken as slaves, and six hundred women and children were absolutely destroyed."

They add:

"This is a brilliant action which sheds great honor on Sieur DE VILLIERS."

The surviving Foxes located themselves on the northern bank of the Wisconsin river, about twenty miles above its mouth, and probably not far from the present village of Wauzeka. MARIN was unwilling that they should remain here, where they could still obstruct his great thoroughfare, and collecting his tried and trusted band of French and In-

WARS WITH FOX INDIANS.   39

dians, he made a distant winter expedition against them. The Foxes were taken completely by surprise, and surrounding the place with his followers, MARIN came suddenly upon them, killed twenty warriors, and took all the others prisoners, together with the women and children. Having fully conquered the Foxes, and having the last remnant of them in his power, MARIN gave them their freedom, but required them to retire beyond the Mississippi, which they did.

The Sieur MARIN was in command at Green Bay in 1754, and received repeated evidences of the appreciation of his services by the French government previous to 1759, when he united with DE LIGNERY in the attempt to relieve Fort Niagara, and shared in its defeat, and with him was taken prisoner. The surrender of Canada soon followed, when most likely he retired to the wilds of Wisconsin and resumed his old occupation of a fur trader.

The date of the final expulsion of the Foxes from Wisconsin is involved in some obscurity, but the little light which can now be obtained appears to fix that event in the year of 1746. For thirty years or more the war between the French and the Foxes, with their allies, had been kept up in the heart of Wisconsin with more or less continuity, and with a determination and animosity rarely, if ever equalled.

No apology can be necessary for the time devoted to the detail of the incidents of this long war, which forms so interesting a portion of Wisconsin's primeval history.

The Sacs were the allies of the Foxes in this long French and Indian war, and many years later the two tribes became confederated and formed the nation known as the Sac and Fox Indians.

At the time of the expulsion of the Foxes, the village of the Sacs was on the east side of Fox river, near the present site of Green Bay where they had until that time demeaned themselves well. About that time a difficulty arose between the French and the Sacs, growing out of a demand upon the Sacs to deliver up the few Foxes living among them, and of the delay of the Sacs in complying with it. The result was that Captain DE VELIE, who had been in command of the garrison at Green Bay, shot three of the Sac chiefs, and that the captain was shot in turn by a young Sac only twelve years old, named Ma-kau-Ta-pe-na-se, or the Black Bird, who subsequently became a distinguished chief among his people.

The garrison being reinforced and joined by the French settlers under the lead of CHARLES DE LANGLADE, attacked the Sauk nation at their village, where a severe battle occurred, in which several were killed on both sides, and the Sauks driven away.

The Sauks now retired to the Wisconsin river, and located upon that beautiful plateau of table land, upon which the twin villages of Prairie du Sac and Sauk City are located, where they had a fine village with comfortable houses. They were living here in 1766, when CARVER visited the country, but must have left soon after, as in 1795, according to the authentic statement of AUGUSTIN GRIGNON, the village appeared to have been several years deserted, and there were then only a few remains of fire-places and posts to be seen.

Mr. EDWARD TANNER, in a paper published in the Detroit *Gazette* in January, 1819, states that he visited the Sauks on the Mississippi river about four hundred miles above St. Louis, in August, 1818, and that "they emigrated from the Wisconsin about thirty-five years ago, approximately fixing the period of their migration about 1783.

It seems probable, judging by the dim light to be derived from any authentic history and from tradition, that the Foxes and Sauks having become confederates, wrested from the Illinois their possessions, and incorporating the remnant which they spared of that numerous tribe, with their own, occupied the territory which had been the home of the Illinois. The principal seat of their power was the country about the mouth of Rock river, from whence in 1831, and more formidably and effectively in 1832, they made those forays upon the pioneer settlers of Illinois and Wisconsin, which resulted in what is generally known as the Black Hawk war.

CHAPTER III.

THE LANGLADE FAMILY.

Biography forms no part of the design of this work, except as it tends to present or explain historical facts. But not to give some account of the family that made the first permanent settlement in Wisconsin would be an unjustifiable omission.

The family of the DE LANGLADES was of the nobility of France and had their castle. New France was the great and captivating field of enterprise for the younger nobility of France whose inheritance was limited, and whose ambition for fame or desire for wealth suggested new fields of adventure. AUGUSTIN DE LANGLADE was born in France about 1695. As early as 1720 he was engaged in the Indian trade among the Ottawas, near Mackinaw, and probably had the entire control of the trade at that important point. He was married at Mackinaw, very soon after he came there, to the sister of the head Ottawa chief, King NIS-SO-WA-QUET, or as the French called him, *La Fourche — The Fork*, which alliance contributed largely to his influence among that nation.

Their eldest child was a daughter, born in 1722, named AGATE, whose first husband, SOULIGNY, having died, leaving her no child, she married AMABLE ROY, with whom she lived at Green Bay, where she died at a great age, never having had any children.

Their second child was born in 1724 at the Ottawa village near Mackinaw, and was a son named CHARLES, who became greatly distinguished.

There were two younger sons, who fell with MONTCALM before Quebec, and whose names have not been preserved; also a daughter, who married a Mr. DE VERVILLE, and who had one son named GAUTIER.

While living at Mackinaw, CHARLES DE LANGLADE had a son, the result of a morganatic marriage with an Ottawa woman. He named this son for himself, recognized and educated him; and he had two sons, one of whom was a lieutenant in the British service, and two daughters, but none of them ever lived in Wisconsin.

It is very likely that Sieur AUGUSTIN DE LANGLADE accompanied DE LIGNERY'S expedition against the Foxes in 1728. If he did not, he of course heard the account given by the officers, soldiers and Ottawas on their return, of the country in which they had been, and perhaps was invited to locate and trade there by the Indians residing there. Moreover, being engaged by the government in the Indian department, it is quite likely he was directed to locate west of Lake Michigan, the better to attend to the interests of the Indians. Whether any or all of these reasons prevailed upon him or not, it is well authenticated that in 1745 the Sieur AUGUSTIN LANGLADE, with his wife and son CHARLES, and probably also their younger children, left Mackinaw and migrated to Green Bay, where they remained till they died at advanced ages, and were when they came thither the only persons within the present boundaries of our state whose occupancy acquired any degree of permanency.

When AUGUSTIN DE LANGLADE removed to Green Bay, he was fifty years old; he continued in the pursuit of his agency for and trade with the Indians without any remarkable incidents until 1771, when he died and was buried in the old cemetery at Green Bay.

But a more active, exciting and hazardous career was to attend the life of his energetic, hardy, impulsive but brave and resolute son, CHARLES, whose name deserves to stand high in the roll of the French heroes of the wars in which that nation was engaged near the middle of the eighteenth century.

This son, the Sieur CHARLES DE LANGLADE, was on the 12th of August, 1754, married at Mackinaw to CHARLOTTE BOURASSA, the daughter of RENE BOURASSA, a retired voyageur living at Mackinaw. The marriage certificate is signed by the Roman Catholic priest, Father M. L. LE FRANC, and witnessed by M. HERBIN, commandant of the post and fourteen others. Madam LANGLADE continued to reside at Mackinaw from the time of her marriage until 1760, when she left the comparatively civilized society of Mackinaw, to reside with her husband in the solitudes of Green Bay, where she continued to live until 1818, when she died at the age of seventy-five years.

The French war broke out in 1754; CHARLES DE LANGLADE had only a short time previously led the French settlers against the Sacs, who, aided by re-enforcements from the garrison, had expelled those Indians from the Fox river and driven them to the banks of the Wisconsin. His standing and reputation for bravery and discretion were established. At the commencement of this war, DE LANGLADE was but thirty years of age; but his high character, his experience in border service for twenty years — for his war exploits commenced at the age of ten — his personal relationship to the powerful Ottawas, his knowledge of their language and that of the other neighboring tribes, and his great influence over them, conspired to induce the Marquis VAUDREUIL, governor-general of New France and Louisiana, to select him to raise the tribes of the Northwest and to place him at the head of the partisan forces of the border French and Indians, in the great and savage conflict about to commence. The force under the command of DE LANGLADE, besides the French, was composed of Ottawas, Chippewas, Menomonees, Winnebagoes, Pottawottamies, Hurons or Wyandotts, and perhaps others, among whom were La-Fourche and Pontiac, and numbered not far from fifteen hundred. They repaired at once to Fort Du Quesne for its defense against the English, and also to carry the war against the frontier settlements and forts of the British colonies. The story of BRADDOCK'S defeat and sanguinary repulse in his confident attempt to capture Fort Du Quesne from the French, when his splendid army, freshly imported from England, were within ten miles of the coveted prize, is too well known to all familiar with American history, to justify a detailed repetition of it. While history justly ascribes the result largely, if not chiefly, to the effective aid of the Indian allies of the French, it has nowhere done full justice to the Sieur CHARLES DE LANGLADE, to whose importunities it was due that DE BEAUJEU consented to enter into the fight at all. The English got to the south bank of the Monongahela about noon, halted and prepared for dinner, while the French and Indians were secreted on the opposite side of the river. DE LANGLADE went to DE BEAUJEU and told him no time should be lost, but that the attack should at once be commenced. The French commander made no reply. DE LANGLADE then called the chiefs together, and induced them to demand orders to commence the battle. Still no such orders could be obtained. Again DE LANGLADE went himself and urged the necessity of at once commencing the attack, saying to DE BEAUJEU, that if he did not intend to fight at all, it was well to act as he did, but if fighting was to be done, then was the time to do it, while the English were eating with their arms laid aside, or while attempting to cross the river; that no other so good an opportunity could occur, and that the English were too powerful to be met in open battle. DE BEAUJEU was much disheartened, seeing the strength of the English, and seemed in great doubt what to do, but at length gave orders to commence the attack. The action was at once commenced and the English officers who had their napkins pinned over their breasts, seized their arms and took part in the conflict, and a good many of them were killed with these napkins pinned on their coats, showing how suddenly they rushed into the battle. DE BEAUJEU was killed, but the French and Indian loss was very small.

Of this battle BANCROFT says, speaking of the English:

" Of eighty-six officers, twenty-six were killed, and thirty-seven were wounded. Of the men, one-half were killed or wounded. BRADDOCK braved every danger; he had five horses disabled under him; at last a bullet entered his right side and he fell mortally wounded. His secretary was shot dead; both his English aids were disabled early in the engagement, leaving the American alone to distribute his orders. Of privates, seven hundred and fourteen were killed or wounded, while of the French and Indians only three officers and thirty men fell, and but as many more were wounded."

On the 9th of August, 1756, DE LANGLADE received orders from CHEVALIER DUMAIS, commandant of Du Quesne, to go with a party of French and Indians, and make a strike at Fort Cumberland, and learn whether the English were making any movement in the direction of the Ohio.

In the year 1757, DE LANGLADE was employed in Canada, and served under MONTCALM. With his faithful, but savage Indian followers, he rendered efficient service to that gallant French officer in the investment and final capture on the 9th of August of Fort William Henry at the head of Lake George.

On the 8th of September, 1757, VAUDREUIL issued an order of that date to

" SIEUR LANGLADE, ensign of the troops, detached from the marine, to start from this city (Montreal) immediately for the post of Michilimackinac, there to serve in the capacity of second in command under the orders of M. DE BEAUJEU, commandant at that post."

The following year he returned to Canada at the head of his French and Indian force and shared the dangers and services of that hard campaign. He and his followers formed a large and useful part of the troops stationed at Ticonderoga, when the British under General ABERCROMBIE, passing through Lake George, undertook on the 8th of

July, 1758, to drive the French, in which attempt they met with the most disastrous failure, when, "after losing," according to BANCROFT, "in killed and wounded, nineteen hundred and sixty-seven, chiefly regulars, they fled promiscuously."

After the hard service at Ticonderoga he repaired with his trusty band to Fort Du Quesne, which was then threatened by the enemy, and participated in the defeat of Major GRANT, near the fort, who was attacked on the 14th of September by a large body of French and Indians, under the superior command of the gallant AUBRY.

About two months later the youthful WASHINGTON with a brigade of provincials drew near Du Quesne; when the disheartened garrison, about five hundred in number, set the fort on fire and by the light of the conflagration descended the Ohio. On the 25th of November, 1758, the banners of England floated over the Ohio, and the place was with one voice named Pittsburgh. DE LANGLADE then probably returned to Green Bay, and remained for the winter.

No officer of the French king was more ready to do battle for his sovereign than DE LANGLADE, who participated in all the most important and the final engagements of the campaign of 1759. He aided in the defense of Fort Niagara, and was present at its capitulation on the 25th of July.

In the great and decisive battle before Quebec on the plains of Abraham, on the 13th of September, when MONTCALM and WOLFE each gave his life for the countries they respectively loved and served so well, our hero, in whose veins coursed the mingled blood of the French and the Ottawa, sustained by large numbers of both, devoted his powerful efforts to sustain the expiring dominion of France in his native Canada. He passed through this severe conflict without a wound, while many of his followers were either killed or wounded. Among the killed were his two younger brothers, whose loss he deeply mourned. He was among the number who thought there was no real necessity for the surrender and believing it was effected through bribery, retired from the place with his surviving followers in disgust.

On the 3d of September, 1760, while DE LANGLADE was at Montreal, having received a commission as lieutenant from the king, he received specific instructions from Gov. VAUDREUIL to take charge of and conduct the troops under his command to Mackinaw and the Indians to their villages. Six days later a dispatch was sent to him by VAUDREUIL, notifying him of the surrender of all Canada to the British, under Gen. AMHERST.

The contest between France and Great Britain for dominion in America was now ended. At this day it is difficult to realize the hardships attendant upon such a partisan service as that in which DE LANGLADE was engaged, with such long and constant marches of thousands of miles through a wilderness country, relying mainly upon wild game for a sustenance. Had the French been successful, his name and fame would doubtless have been more conspicuous in history.

DE LANGLADE had but two children by his marriage. The eldest, LALLOTTE, born in 1760 or 1761, was married to Mr. BARCELLOW, but died the next year childless. The other, DOMITELLE, born in 1763, was married to PIERRE GRIGNON, Sen., in 1776.

Upon the breaking out of the Revolutionary war, CHARLES DE LANGLADE, then fifty-two years old, was persuaded by Capt. DE PEYSTER, commanding at Mackinaw, to take an active part in the war should his services be needed, which, DE PEYSTER remarks in his *Miscellanies*, was equivalent to "securing all the Western Indians in our interests." He raised a large body of Indians from several different tribes, and marched for Montreal. He went to Canada with his Indian force several times during the war, and at one time served under Gen. CAMPBELL. In 1779 DE LANGLADE and his followers, with the Indians from Milwaukee, whom he had induced to join him, attended a grand council which DE PEYSTER had called at l'Arbre Croche, near Mackinaw, for the purpose of making a diversion towards Vincennes and Fort Chartres in favor of Gov. HAMILTON at Detroit. After the council, DE LANGLADE with his Indian force embarked upon Lake Michigan, and upon arriving at St. Josephs, they learned of HAMILTON'S surrender, and returned much dissatisfied.

It does not appear that DE LANGLADE was engaged in many, if any battles during the Revolutionary war. Indeed, there was no active service for him to perform in the Northwest, as there were no expeditions by the Americans in that quarter.

From the close of the French war to the end of the Revolutionary war, CHARLES DE LANGLADE by appointment of the British authorities had the superintendency of the Indians of the Green Bay Department. After the close of the Revolutionary war the same superintendency appears to have continued indefinitely. He also had command of the militia composed of the simple hearted people of the settlement, by whom he was most affectionately reverenced and honored. He spent the remainder of his days at Green Bay, receiving an annuity from the British government of eight hundred dollars, as half pay for his services during the American Revolution, and died in January, 1800, at the age of seventy-five years, and was buried beside his father in the cemetery at Green Bay.

PIERRE GRIGNON, Sen., by his marriage with DOMITELLE DE LANGLADE, had seven sons and two daughters. One of the sons was AUGUSTIN GRIGNON, born June 27, 1780, from whose " Recollections," noted down from his lips in 1857 by Mr. DRAPER, secretary of the State Historical Society, most of the foregoing statements in relation to the LANGLADE family, have been literally transcribed.

CHAPTER IV.

JONATHAN CARVER'S EXPLORATIONS

A new era in the history of the West commenced with the year 1763. By the treaty of Paris made in that year, all the claims of the French to the country watered by the Ohio and the Mississippi, and all the French possessions, were ceded to Great Britain. By a secret treaty however, made on the same day the definitive articles of the treaty of Paris had been signed (November 3, 1762), France ceded to Spain all Louisiana west of the Mississippi and the island of Orleans. So that Great Britain, when the treaty was concluded, February 10, 1763, acquired the country east of the Mississippi, which river was to remain equally free to the subjects of Great Britain and France.

Soon after the vast acquisition of territory gained by Great Britain from the French, Capt. JONATHAN CARVER resolved to explore the interior parts of North America and to penetrate to the Pacific ocean, over that broad part of the continent which lies between the 43d and 46th degrees of north latitude, and he hoped to discover a northwest passage from Hudson's Bay to the Pacific. A journal of this exploration was published in 1778. CARVER was born in the town of Canterbury, Connecticut, in the year 1732. He served in the Canadian campaign of 1755, was subsequently with General WOLFE at the taking of Quebec, and the capture of Montreal and conquest of Canada under General AMHERST. He was at the massacre of Fort William Henry in 1757. A battalion of light infantry was raised in Massachusetts in 1758, for the invasion of Canada, in one of the companies of which he served as lieutenant, and in 1760, he was advanced to the captaincy of a company in Col. JOHN WHITCOMB'S regiment of foot. In 1762, he commanded a company of foot in Col. SALTONSTALL'S regiment, and the year after the peace of Versailles, he retired from the service.

In June, 1766, he set out from Boston to carry out his resolution to explore the Northwest, and proceeded by way of Albany and Niagara to Mackinaw, where he arrived the 1st of September. He there made arrangements with Gov. ROGERS for a suitable supply of goods for presents to the Indians on his route, and having received a part, with a promise that the remainder should be sent forward to meet him at the falls of St. Anthony, he proceeded on the 3d of September, and pursuing the usual route to Green Bay, arrived there on the 18th.

Capt. CARVER left Green Bay on the 20th of September, in company with several traders, and ascended Fox river, arriving on the 25th at an island, on which was the great town of the Winnebagoes, now known as Doty's Island. The principal chief of this tribe was a woman, who had married a Frenchman named DE KAURY, who had been mortally wounded at Quebec and died at Montreal; so that the Queen was a widow at this time. Her descendants, the DE KAURY's, have long figured as distinguished chiefs of the Winnebagoes. The town contained fifty houses, which were strongly built with palisades.

Having remained four days, during which he was treated with great civility, and entertained in a distinguished manner, having made some presents to the chiefess, he left on the 29th, and on the 7th of October arrived at the portage of the Fox and Wisconsin rivers.

On the 9th, the party arrived at the great town of the Saukies, now known as Prairie du Sac, which our explorer describes as the largest and best built Indian town he ever saw. It contained, he says, about ninety houses, each large enough for several families, built of hewn plank, neatly jointed and covered so completely with bark, as to keep out the most penetrating rains. Before the doors were placed comfortable sheds in which the inhabitants sat, when the weather would permit, and smoked their pipes. The streets were both regular and spacious, appearing more like a civilized town than the abode of savages. This large and well-built Indian town, the traveler's description of which, it must be confessed, appears somewhat exaggerated, had but a brief existence, for in less than thirty years only a few remains of fire-places and posts were to be seen.

The Sacs had about three hundred warriors who extended their excursions into the territories of the Illinois and Pawnee nations. Capt. CARVER says:

"Whilst I stayed here, I took a view of some mountains, that lie about fifteen miles to the southward, and abound in lead ore (probably the Blue Mounds). I ascended on one of the highest of these, and had an extensive view of the country. For many miles nothing was to be seen but lesser mountains, which appeared at a distance like hay-cocks, they being free from trees. So plentiful is lead here that I saw large quantities of it lying about the streets, in the town belonging to the Saukies, and it seemed to be as good as the produce of other countries.

"On the 10th of October (he says) we proceeded down the river, and the next day reached the first town of the Ottiganmies (Fox Indians). This town contained about fifty houses, but we found most of them deserted, on account of an epidemical disorder that had lately raged among them, and carried off more than one-half of the inhabitants. The greater part of those who survived had retired into the woods to avoid the contagion."

This town is supposed to have been where Muscoda is. When within about five miles of the mouth of the Wisconsin he discovered the ruins of another village, and learned that it had been deserted about thirty years before, and that the inhabitants soon after built a town on the Mississippi river near the mouth of the Wisconsin, at a place called by the French La Prairie des Chiens. It was a large town, and contained about three hundred families. It was the great mart where furs and peltries were annually brought about the last of May from the remote branches of the Mississippi, and where it was determined by a general council of the chiefs whether to dispose of them to traders there, or to transport them either to Mackinaw or to Louisiana.

The traders with CARVER took up their residence for the

4

winter at the mouth of Yellow River, about ten miles above Prairie du Chien, on the opposite bank of the Mississippi, while he with one *voyageur* and a Mohawk Indian, pushed on in his canoe towards the Falls of St. Anthony.

He passed Mount Tremealeau, which he described, and on the first of November arrived at Lake Pepin, where he says he observed the ruins of a French factory, where Capt. ST. PIERRE resided and carried on a very great trade with the Naudowissies, before the reduction of Canada. It was here the first trading houses north of the Illinois River were erected. (As early as 1687, NICHOLAS PERROT was trading in the neighborhood of the Sioux, and according to CHARLEVOIX, he built a fort near the mouth of the lake.)

The pre-historic tumuli, which are found in so many places near the banks of the Mississippi, did not escape the observation of CARVER, and he was the first to call the attention of the civilized world to their existence.

He first made the acquaintance of the Dakota Indians near the mouth of the St. Croix River, probably near Prescott, and had the good fortune to make a treaty of peace between that nation and the Chippewas, at a time when an engagement was imminent, in return for which kindly act the Indians bestowed upon him every possible attention.

In his further progress he came to a remarkable cave on the bank of the Mississippi, about thirty miles below the Falls of St. Anthony, of which he says:

"The entrance is about ten feet wide, with a height of five feet, and a breadth of thirty feet. About twenty feet from the entrance begins a lake which extends to an unsearchable distance."

The walls he describes as being a soft stone, upon which were cut many ancient hieroglyphics, and the cave was believed by the Indians to be the dwelling of the "Great Spirit." It has been materially altered by the action of the elements, the roof has fallen in, and the entrance has been choked up by rock and earth; so that in 1820, SCHOOLCRAFT was led into the error of supposing that the cave near St. Paul, now known as the "Fountain Cave," was the one described by CARVER. The track of a railroad runs along the bank of the river directly in front of the cave, in the construction of which the cave is virtually destroyed, and the stream which flowed through it now supplies a water-tank, while the subterranean lake has disappeared.

On reaching the mouth of the St. Peters river, ten miles

below the falls of St. Anthony, called by the natives Wadda-paw-men-e-so-tor, the ice became so troublesome that he left his canoe, and walked to the Falls of St. Anthony where he arrived November 17th. He gives a very particular description of them, accompanied by a copper-plate engraving, from which it would seem that a constant recession of the rock has been going on, which has gradually reduced the height of the fall, and that in ages long past, this sublime cataract of the Mississippi, thundering in its solitude, was not far from the mural cliffs, upon which were erected the barracks of the garrison at Fort Snelling.

This persevering explorer continued on foot, until he reached the river St. Francis or Elk river, about sixty miles above the falls, but as the season was far advanced, he returned, and on the 25th of November commenced with his canoe the ascent of the St. Peters river, now called the Minnesota, which he found free from ice, and proceeded some two hundred miles to the country of the Naudowissies, or Sioux of the plains, which was the western limit of his travels. With these Indians he spent five months, and was well treated. He learned their language, and acquired all the geographical information they could impart.

Capt. CARVER left his hibernal abode the latter end of April and descended to the Mississippi, escorted by nearly three hundred Indians, among whom were many chiefs. It was the habit of these bands to go annually at this season to the great cave, to hold a grand council with all the other bands. CARVER, on this occasion, was admitted to the grand council, and made a speech which is published in his travels. This was on the 1st of May, 1767.

At this time, as claimed by his heirs and their assignees, two of the chiefs of the Naudowissies gave to Capt. CARVER a deed of a large tract of land lying in Wisconsin and Minnesota, bounded as follows:

"From the Falls of St. Anthony, running on the east bank of the Mississippi nearly southeast as far as the south end of Lake Pepin, where the Chippewa river joins the Mississippi, and from thence eastward, five days' travel, accounting twenty English miles per day, and from thence north six days' travel at twenty English miles per day, and from thence again to the Falls of St. Anthony, on a direct straight line."

These boundaries extend east to the range line between ranges 3 and 4 east, north to the south line of Douglass county and south to the south line of Clark county, and embrace the whole of the counties of Pepin, Pierce, St. Croix,

Barron, Dunn, Eau Claire, Clark, Chippewa, Washburn, Sawyer, Price, and Taylor, with parts of Buffalo, Trempealeau, Jackson, Wood, Marathon, Lincoln, Burnett, Polk and Ashland, with a part of Minnesota, and contain an area of about fourteen thousand square miles.

Whether such a deed was ever made, and is not a mere fiction, has given rise to many well-founded doubts. It is not spoken of by CARVER in his "Journal" of his travels. However the fact may be, it is well known that the Naudowissics, or Sioux of the plains, had no claim to any territory east of the Great River, and as the two Indians by whom this deed purports to have been signed were chiefs of this tribe, they were granting that to which they had no claim.

If the authenticity of the deed be conceded, as well as the validity of the title of the grantors, the transaction was in direct violation of the proclamation of his king, made less than three years before, of which Capt. CARVER was no doubt aware, which strictly enjoined and required that no private person should presume to make any purchase of any land from any Indian.

A petition of the heirs of CARVER and their assignees, for the recognition of the validity of their title under this grant, appears to have been presented to congress as early as 1806, and referred to a committee of the senate, but no report seems to have been made. Subsequently, January 23, 1823, Mr. VAN DYKE, from the committee on public lands, submitted to the senate a report upon a like petition, concluding with a resolution, that the prayer of the petitioners ought not to be granted.

A similar petition was presented to the next congress, and on the 28th of January, 1825, a report was made by Mr. CAMPBELL of Ohio, from the committee on private land claims, which contains a most exhaustive discussion of all the questions involved, and demonstrates most conclusively that there was no foundation for the pretended claim, and that it was utterly worthless.

In a letter from Lord PALMERSTON, dated February 8, 1834, to Hon. AARON VAIL, then charge d'affaires of the United States to Great Britain, is the statement in reference to this claim that

"No trace has been found of any ratification of the grant in question by His Majesty's government."

A claim of somewhat the same kind was made by the

"Illinois and Wabash Land Company," for a large territory in Illinois, under a grant claimed to have been made to WILLIAM MURRAY in 1773, and met a like fate at the hands of congress as the CARVER claim.

The validity of claims founded on actual settlement and improvement, without other pretended title, has been recognized by the United States government. Of this character were all the claims to lands at Green Bay and Prairie du Chien, which, on examination, have been confirmed by the general government.

In continuing the account of the travels of Capt. CARVER, it appears that having first ascertained that the goods which Gov. ROGERS had promised to send to the Falls of St. Anthony for him, had not arrived, he decided to return to Prairie du Chien, abandoning for the present his original plan of proceeding further to the Northwest. Here he obtained from the traders what goods they could spare, but as they were not sufficient, he determined to make his way across the country of the Chippewas to Lake Superior, where he hoped to meet the traders that annually went from Mackinaw to the Northwest, from whom he thought he should be able to obtain what goods he required.

In the month of June CARVER left Prairie du Chien, and leaving the Mississippi River, he ascended the Chippewa, near the head waters of which he found a Chippewa village, composed of forty houses adjacent to a small lake. He left this village in July, and having crossed a number of small lakes and portages that intervened, came to a head branch of the St. Croix River—probably the Namekagon. This branch he descended to a fork, and then ascended another—probably one of the Totogatics—to its source. On both these branches he discovered, as he says, several mines of virgin copper, very pure. That many of the outcrops of rock upon these branches are cupriferous has been shown by the explorations of the late geological survey of the state, but "mines of virgin copper" will be developed only as the result of more labor than has yet been bestowed upon them.

From this last branch he made a portage to a stream which flowed into Lake Superior. Descending this he coasted around the western extremity of the lake, and finally arrived at the Grand Portage on the north shore. Here, although he obtained much information about the lakes and rivers lying to the northwest, he could not procure the goods he wanted, and was compelled to give up the one great object of his travels, and return to Mackinaw, where he arrived the beginning of November. He spent the winter at Mackinaw, and returned to Boston the following year, having been absent two years and five months, and traversed seven thousand miles.

CHAPTER V.

PROGRESS OF SETTLEMENTS IN THE NORTHWEST, AND TRANSFER TO BRITISH JURISDICTION.

The history of the war with the Outagamies on Fox River after their failure to destroy Detroit in 1712, naturally led to an account of the DE LANGLADES and of events intimately connected with them, causing a digression from the chronological narrative which had been attempted and which will now be resumed.

During the first half of the eighteenth century, the progress of settlement and industry in the Wabash country was very considerable. As early as 1705 fifteen thousand skins and hides had been sent to Mobile for the European market. In 1716 the French population of that fertile region kept up a lucrative trade with Mobile, by means of traders and *voyageurs*. Agriculture soon began to flourish, and in 1746, six hundred barrels of flour were manufactured and shipped to New Orleans, besides large quantities of hides, peltry, tallow and beeswax.

In 1730 the Illinois country, not including the Wabash valley, contained one hundred and forty French families, besides about six hundred converted Indians, many traders, *voyageurs* and *couriers du bois*. About twenty years later (1751) it contained six distinct settlements, with their respective villages. These were Cahokia, St. Philip, Fort Chartres, Kaskaskia, Prairie du Rochier, and St. Genevieve. Kaskaskia in its best days, under the French regime, contained two or three thousand inhabitants, but under British dominion the population in 1773 had decreased to four hundred and fifty souls.

The ambition of the French was to preserve the possession

PROGRESS OF SETTLEMENTS IN THE NORTHWEST. 55

of all important points in the Northwest, and to prevent the slightest attempt of the English to occupy any part of the territory west of the Alleghanies, and French commanders had avowed the purpose of seizing every Englishman within the Ohio Valley. In 1753 the Ohio company opened a road into the western valley, and GIST established a plantation near the Youghiogeny, where eleven families settled, and a town and fort were marked out on Shurtee's creek.

Gov. DINWIDDIE, fearful for the safety of these pioneer settlers upon the western dominion of Virginia, in November, 1753, sent WASHINGTON — then twenty-one, to the commander of the French forces on the Ohio river, to know his reasons for invading the British dominions. The commander, GARDEUR DE ST. PERRE, refused to discuss questions of right. "I am here," said he, "by the orders of my general, to which I shall conform with exactness and resolution." WASHINGTON hastened homeward to Virginia, where, after many hardships and dangers, he arrived in January, 1754. WASHINGTON's report was followed by immediate activity. The Virginians had commenced a fort at the forks of the Ohio, which, on the 17th of April, they surrendered to the superior forces of the French, who occupied and fortified it and named it Du Quesne, from the governor of New France. Pittsburg now occupies its site. On the 27th of May, WASHINGTON, followed by only forty raw recruits and a few Mingo allies, coming upon the French, himself fired the first hostile gun, which kindled the world into a flame, and was the signal for the great French war which ensued. The engagement was short. Ten of the French, among them JUMONVILLE, the commander of the party, were killed, and twenty-one made prisoners.

On the first day of July, Washington, not being reinforced as he expected, was compelled to fall back upon Fort Necessity, a rude stockade at Great Meadows. Here for nine hours the fire of the French was returned, when, at last, after thirty of the English and but three of the French were killed, terms of capitulation were accepted. On the 4th day of July, the English garrison, retaining all its effects, withdrew from the basin of the Ohio, and no standard but that of France floated in the whole valley of the Mississippi to its head springs in the Alleghanies.

The next year the contest for the possession of Fort Du

Quesne was renewed, and Gen. BRADDOCK's signal defeat on the banks of the Monongahela occurred on the 9th of July, 1755. From that period to the victory of Gen. WOLFE at Quebec in September 1759, various engagements had taken place between the English and French with various fortunes. At length, on the 8th of September, 1760, Ticonderoga, Crown Point, Niagara and Quebec having previously fallen, Montreal, Detroit and all Canada were given up to the English by the French governor, and the principal posts on the Ohio passed into the possession of the English. The post of Detroit was given by the French into the hands of Major ROGERS on the 25th of November, 1760, and from this period the French power in this region was forever overthrown.

The affection of the Indians for the French was deeply rooted, and by the commingling of blood, created the strong ties of nature between them, which even now continues. Through all the changes in the country that time has wrought, the French language still partially holds its place, and this is especially observable in the vicinity of Green Bay and Prairie du Chien.

The first settlements made by the French on the east side of the Mississippi river were at Cahokia, St. Phillips, La Prairie du Rocher and Kaskaskia. The first is situated nearly opposite to St. Louis, and contained about one hundred and twenty houses; the second became extinct; the third is about twelve miles above Kaskaskia and contained thirty-two houses. Kaskaskia is situated about seven miles up a river of the same name, though not more than three miles from the Mississippi, nearly opposite to St. Genevieve, and about fifty-five miles below Cahokia. This village was once considered as the capital of the country, and was rich and populous and contained two thousand or three thousand inhabitants, but under the British dominion as late as 1772, it contained only five hundred whites and as many blacks, and at a later period it was reduced to forty-five families. This loss of population was occasioned largely by its being transferred to the west side of the Mississippi, principally to St. Louis. Two causes mainly produced this result. The first was the ordinance of 1787 which prohibited slavery in the Northwestern Territory. The slave-holders were disposed to retain their slaves, and to do it effectually, they abandoned their ancient habitations and joined their friends in the then dominions of Spain. The second was the rupture in 1797, when an attack from Canada was projected on the Spanish possessions along the Mississippi river. At this period Spain was bound to evacuate all her military posts on the east side of that river to the north of the 31st degree of north latitude, and Upper Louisiana was the only barrier she had to oppose the descent of the English. The distance of this province from the capital, added to a wilderness of nearly a thousand miles in extent between them, seemed to point out the necessity of strengthening it, and she conceived it good policy to populate it by citizens of the United States.

Additional prospects were therefore held out to settlers, and pains were taken to disseminate them in every direction. Large quantities of land were granted them, with no other cost than office fees and surveys, which were moderate. This accounts for the rapid settlement of Upper Louisiana, three fifths of the population of which, in 1804, consisted of English Americans.

In the time of Father CHARLEVOIX, 1721, Kaskaskia contained a Jesuit college, the ruins of which remained a century later.

All the four villages east of the Mississippi were founded about the year 1683 by LA SALLE or his followers. They were all, as were the intermediate settlements, situated on a fertile bottom, which commences at the mouth of the Kaskaskia river and extends nearly to the Illinois, a distance of about eighty miles, about four to six miles wide, now called the "American Bottom." It is bounded in the rear by a ridge of lime-rock, which in many places is perpendicular and 150 to 200 feet in height.

While the French were in possession of the country they built several forts. One at Kaskaskia, which is wholly destroyed.

They also had one on the Ohio, about thirty-six miles from the Mississippi, which the Indians took by a curious stratagem. A number of them appeared in the day-time on the opposite side of the river, each of whom was disguised with a bear-skin, and walked on all fours. The French supposed them to be bears, and crossed the river in pursuit of them. The troops who did not cross left their quarters and went to the river to see the sport. In the meantime a large body of warriors, who were concealed near the fort, silently entered it without opposition, and very few of the French escaped the carnage. They afterwards built another fort on the same ground, and called it Massac.

Fort Chartres was built in 1720, and much repaired in 1750. It is situated in the neighborhood of Prairie du Rocher, and was orginally about one mile and a half from the Mississippi. Its figure was quadrilateral, with four bastions, the whole of which was composed of limestone well cemented. Each side measured about 340 feet. The walls were fifteen feet high and about three feet thick. There was a spacious square of barracks with stone walls and a capacious magazine and two deep wells. Each port or loop-hole was formed by four solid cliffs or blocks of free stone, worked smooth and into proper shapes. All the cornices and casements about the gates and buildings were of the same material and appeared to great advantage, It was originally intended as a place of refuge for the inhabitants of the adjacent country in time of war. Some years after it was built the Mississippi broke over its banks and formed a channel so near the fort, that one side of it and two of its bastions were thrown down. This circumstance induced its abandonment in 1772, and since that period the inhabitants have taken away great quantities of materials from it to adorn their own buildings, and it became a splendid ruin.

It was on the 10th of October, 1765, that the ensign of France was replaced on the ramparts of Fort Chartres by the flag of Great Britain. For nearly ninety years Illinois had been in the actual occupation of the French, their settlements on the far-off waters of the Kaskaskia, Illinois and Wabash slumbering quietly in colonial dependence, and although for more than one hundred years she had been constructively a part of Florida, no Spaniard had set foot upon her soil or rested his eye upon her beautiful prairies. But the Anglo-Saxon had gained at last a permanent foot-hold on the banks of the great river, and a new life, instinct with energy and progress, was about to be infused into the country.

M. NEYON DE VILLIERS, long the commandant of Fort Chartres, kept from the French and Indians so long as he could a knowledge of the cession of the country to Great Britain, and finally, rather than dwell under the detested flag of the conqueror, he abandoned Illinois in the summer of 1764, and went to New Orleans, followed by many of the inhabitants.

The command of the fort and country then devolved upon M. St. ANGE DE BELLERIVE, a veteran Canadian French officer of rare tact and large experience, who forty years before had escorted CHARLEVOIX through the country, who mentions him with commendation. His position required skill and address to save his feeble colony from a renewed war with the English and from a general massacre by the incensed hordes of savages under PONTIAC, by whom he was surrounded. He had been advised by the home government of the cession to the British and ordered to surrender the country upon their arrival to claim it.

After the evacuation of Fort Chartres, he also retired from the country, conducting his small garrison of twenty-one soldiers to the infant settlement of St. Louis, where in the absence of any Spanish rule as yet, he continued to exercise the functions of his office with great satisfaction to the people until November, 1770, when his authority was superseded by PIERNAS, commandant under the Spanish government.

The civil jurisdiction of Spain west of the Mississippi conferred by the secret treaty of November 3, 1762, was not enforced in Upper Louisiana until 1769.

The exodus of the old Canadian French, induced by the causes already stated for the migration from Kaskaskia, was large just before and during the British occupation. Unwilling to dwell under the flag of their hereditary enemy, many, including some of the wealthiest families, removed with their slaves and other personal effects mostly to Upper Louisiana, just across the Mississippi, and settled in the small hamlet of St. Genevieve. Others joined and aided LECLEDE in founding St. Louis, the site of which had then but just been selected as a depot for the fur company of Louisiana.

The number of inhabitants of foreign lineage at this time in the Illinois settlements was estimated as follows: White men able to bear arms, 700; white women, 500; their children, 850; blacks of both sexes, 900; total, 2,950. By the hegira one-third of the whites and nearly all the blacks migrated, leaving probably less than 1,500 souls at the commencement of the British occupation, and the population was not increased during the possession by the British. Few English or Americans, other than British troops, traders, officers and favored land speculators, were seen there during this time, nor until the conquest by CLARK in 1778.

The first British commandant was Capt. STIRLING of the 42nd Royal Highlanders. He was the bearer of a proclamation made by Gen. GAGE, commander of all the British forces in North America, which bore date in New York, December 30, 1764, and was published by Capt. STIRLING on his arrival in Illinois.

By this proclamation it was delared that:

"His Majesty grants to the inhabitants of the Illinois the liberty of the Catholic religion, and that they may exercise the worship of their religion according to the rites of the Roman Church in the same manner as in Canada."

"That the French inhabitants or others who have been subjects of the Most Christian King (of France) may retire in full safety and freedom, and they may sell their estate, provided it be to subjects of His Majesty, and transport their effects as well as persons upon their emigration.

"That those who choose to retain their lands and become subjects of His Majesty, shall enjoy the same rights and privileges, the same security for their persons and effects and liberty of trade as the old subjects of the king. That they are commanded to take the oath of fidelity and obedience to His Majesty."

It recommended to the inhabitants "to conduct themselves like good and faithful subjects, and act in concert with His Majesty's officers."

Capt. STIRLING died some three months after his arrival, leaving the office of commandant vacant.

Under these circumstances their former beloved commandant, M. ST. ANGE returned to Fort Chartres and discharged the duties of the office until a successor to Capt. STIRLING should be sent out.

Major FRAZER was next sent from Fort Pitt. He exercised a brief but arbitrary power over the settlements, when he was relieved by a Col. REID, who proved for the colonists a bad exchange. For eighteen months he enacted the petty tyrant by a series of military oppressions over these feeble settlements.

Col. REID was at last, however, removed and succeeded by Lieut. Col. WILKINS, who arrived September 5, 1768.

On the 21st of November, 1768, Col. WILKINS issued his proclamation for a civil administration of the laws of the country.

For this purpose, he appointed seven magistrates or judges from among the people as a civil tribunal, to expound the principles of the common law of England. A term of this court was held December 6, 1768, at Fort Chartres, which was the first common law jurisdiction ever exercised in what, within twenty years, became the Northwestern Territory of the United States. The court was a nondescript affair. It was a court of first and last resort—no appeal lay from it. It was the highest as well as the lowest—the only court in the country. The trial by jury, the French mind was unable to appreciate. They thought it very wonderful that the English should refer the determination of nice questions relating to the right of property to a tribunal consisting of tailors, shoemakers or other artisans and trades people, rather than to judges learned in the law. The attempt was a failure.

In 1774, the English parliament restored to the people their ancient laws in civil cases, without the trial by jury; guaranteed the free exercise of their religion and rehabilitated the Roman Catholic clergy with the privileges stipulated in the articles of capitulation of Montreal in 1760. The act was known as the "Quebec Bill." The colonies on the Atlantic seaboard took great umbrage at one portion of this law, which extended the province of Quebec to the Mississippi, including all the French inhabitants at Detroit, Mackinaw, on the Wabash and in the Illinois country, and its enactment was one of the grievances specified in the declaration of independence.

The most noticeable feature of Col. WILKIN's administration, was the wonderful liberality with which he parceled out the domain over which he ruled, in large tracts to his favorites in Illinois, Philadelphia and elsewhere, with no other consideration than requiring them to reconvey an interest to himself.

Settlers now began rapidly to survey the country between the Alleghanies and the Mississippi and prepare for occupation. During the year 1770 a number of persons from Virginia and other British provinces explored and marked out many of the most valuable lands on the Monongahela and along the banks of the Ohio. Pittsburgh was at this time a trading post, about which was clustered a village of some twenty houses, inhabited by Indian traders. The trade from the posts was quite good, and from those in Illinois large quantities of pork and flour found their way to the New Orleans market.

In 1774 Gov. DUNMORE, of Virginia, began to encourage

emigration to the western lands. He appointed magistrates at Fort Pitt, claiming that it was within the jurisdiction of that commonwealth.

The French settlers in the west were predisposed to favor the British government in the war with the colonies, but the early alliance between France and the United States soon brought them to the support of the colonial cause.

At the period of the surrender of the posts to the English there were about fifty cottages on the strait of Detroit with orchards by their side. They were constructed of logs with roof of bark, or thatched with straw. Wheat was sown in rows, potatoes were first introduced by the English, corn was cultivated, while peltries were the chief circulating medium. The first horses used in Detroit were brought from Fort Du Quesne, and these were taken from the English by the Indians at BRADDOCK's defeat.

The succession of authority over the Northwest did not bring with it to the English the friendship of the Algonquin tribes in that quarter. The new masters were regarded as intruders by the Indians, and the long-cherished affection which many of the tribes had for the French produced an opposite feeling in them toward the new people, the enemies of their great French father. This feeling was early exhibited by PONTIAC, and was fully developed in the disastrous events which quickly followed the occupation of the posts by the English, known as the Pontiac war.

PONTIAC had conceived the great design of driving the English at once and effectually from the country by a destruction of their forts and strongholds. His plan was to unite the various tribes in one grand confederacy, and by a simultaneous attack on all the English posts to massacre the garrisons, take possession of these posts, drive out the British from the land, and secure the return of the French.

PONTIAC called a grand council of warriors of the western tribes, the Miamis, Ottawas, Chippewas, Wyandottes, Potawatamies, Mississagas, Shawanese, Outagamies, and the Winnebagoes. These tribes were willing to join the confederacy, and when hostilities were commenced, every energy was bent to their effectual prosecution, in that stern mode of savage warfare, which knows no mercy.

Before any suspicion had been excited on the part of the English, the sanguinary war burst upon them like lightning from the overcharged thunder-cloud. In the month of May,

1763, the attack of the confederated Indians was made mostly at the same time on all the British posts, eight of which were captured, viz.: Ouiatenon, Michillimackinac, St. Josephs, Miami, Sandusky, Presq' isle, Le Beuf, and Venango, and at Presq' isle, St. Josephs and Mackinac, and there was a general slaughter of the garrisons.

The garrison of Michillimackinac at this time consisted of ninety privates, two subalterns and the commandant, and the English merchants at the fort were four in number. Few entertained anxiety concerning the Indians, who had no weapons but small arms. Meanwhile the Indians were daily assembling in unusual numbers, but with every appearance of friendship, frequenting the fort, and disposing of their peltries in such a manner that no fears of danger existed.

The 4th of June was the king's birthday. In order to do honor to the day, and add to the festivities, it was proposed that the game of *baggiteway*, an Indian ball play, generally called by the French *lejeu de la crosse*, should be played between the Chippewas and Sacs for a high wager. The game is played with a bat and ball; two posts are planted in the ground about a mile apart, and each party having its post, the object is to propel the ball, which is placed in the center, toward the post of the adversary. To view this game, Major ETHERINGTON, the commandant, who had wagered on the side of the Chippewas, was not only present himself, but all the garrison who could be induced, were by some pretext drawn outside the pickets, in order to weaken the defenses of the fort. The stratagem of the Indians was soon developed.

The design was to throw the ball over the pickets, which was accomplished, and as in the heat of the game such an event was not liable to excite any extraordinary alarm, so the immediate and promiscuous rushing of the Indians into the fort in pursuit of the ball was for a moment regarded as a mere natural consequence. But in an instant the war-yell was heard within the pickets, and the Indians were seen furiously cutting down and scalping every Englishman whom they could discover. No less than seventy soldiers, together with Lieutenant JEWETTE, had been killed, and but twenty Englishmen, including soldiers, were still alive. Capt. ETHERINGTON and Lieut. LESLIE escaped death by the bold intervention of CHARLES DE LANGLADE, but were held as prisoners by their savage captors.

The fort at Green Bay had received an English garrison in 1761, which consisted of seventeen men, under the command of Lieutenant GORRELL; but although it escaped the fate of Michillimackinac, it was soon abandoned, by orders of Major ETHERINGTON, and the garrison, with Lieutenant GORRELL were afterwards escorted by a band of friendly Indians to L'Arbre Croche, where they met with Major ETHERINGTON and the remnant of his command, who were still detained as prisoners. On the 18th of July, they were liberated, and the whole party reached Montreal by way of the Ottawa river, about the middle of August. Except the garrison of Detroit, not a British soldier now remained in the region of the lakes.

Detroit was then deemed the most important of the northwestern posts. PONTIAC determined to undertake its capture in person. His forces consisted of eight hundred and twenty warriors. The town was garrisoned by one hundred and twenty-two men and eight officers, of whom Major GLADWYN was commandant. PONTIAC having failed to gain possession of the post by stratagem, in consequence of the treachery of a squaw who informed the commandant of his plans, invested the post, and attempted to secure its capitulation by siege. All the means which the savage mind could suggest were employed by PONTIAC to demolish the settlement of Detroit. Blazing arrows were shot; a breach was made in the pickets; floating fire rafts were constructed and sent against the vessels lying in the river, supplies were cut off, and the English were reduced to great distress from the diminution of their rations.

The siege of Detroit continued for about a year. In the month of June, 1764, General BRADSTREET arrived with a force of three thousand men for the purpose of compelling a peace. The tribes of PONTIAC laid down their arms, and, with the exception of the Delawares and Shawanese, concluded a treaty of peace. PONTIAC, however, took no part in the negotiation, and soon after retired to the Illinois, where he was killed in 1767, by a Peoria Indian.

The restoration of peace between the new masters of the country and the Indian tribes, and the natural desire of the English to reap the advantages of their new possessions, were calculated to create expectations of a gradual if not speedy occupation and settlement of the country between the great lakes and the Mississippi, but for a series of years, extending to a period later than the termination of the Revolutionary war, but little account of such improvements is to be found.

When Capt. CARVER visited Green Bay in 1766, there had been at that place no garrison since the fort was abandoned by Lieut. GORRELL, three years before. A few families lived in the fort and opposite to it on the east side of Fox river. There were a few French settlers who cultivated the land and appeared to live comfortably.

At the time Capt. STIRLING, coming by the way of the Ohio, established his headquarters at Fort Chartres, as previously stated, in October, 1765, as commandant of the Illinois country under the orders of Gen. GAGE, commander-in-chief of his Majesty's forces in America, the French population of the whole country, from the Mississippi eastward to the Wabash, was probably not less than five thousand persons, including about five hundred negro slaves. Fort Chartres, subsequently called "Fort Gage," was on the east bank of the Kaskaskia River, opposite the town of Kaskaskia.

The relations between the French settlers in the Illinois country and the neighboring Indian tribes were of the most friendly character. Not so the relations between the Indians and the Americans. At the commencement of the war of the Revolution, and during its continuance, the savages of the Northwest had been associated as allies of Great Britain, and employed by the British commanders to lay waste the whole frontier country.

Virginia claimed that the Illinois country, and of course all the posts within it, including Detroit, were embraced by her three royal charters. PATRICK HENRY was governor of Virginia, and a secret expedition was set on foot for the reduction of these posts under the authority of the governor and executive council, which was prompted and guided by the genius and enterprise of Col. GEORGE ROGERS CLARK.

Col. CLARK assembled his force, consisting of six incomplete companies of fifty men each, at the Falls of the Ohio, about the middle of June, 1778. On the 24th they descended the river in keel-boats as far as Fort Massac. From Fort Massac they crossed the country by land, and on the 4th of July reached a point within two miles of Kaskaskia. In the dead of night, two divisions crossed the river, and were instantly in possession of the town, while Col. CLARK with the remainder of his force with equal success captured the fort, which was unconditionally surrendered to ROCHEBLAVE.

The French inhabitants declared for the American cause, and the Kaskaskians assisted in securing the submission of their neigbors at Kahokia, which was successfully obtained on the 6th of July.

With the exception of Detroit, the post at Vincennes was the most important. M. GIBAULT, the priest of Kaskaskia, with the ready sanction of Col. CLARK, attempted by persuasion alone to induce the inhabitants to throw off their forced connection with England. On the 1st of August he returned with the intelligence that they had taken the oath of allegiance to Virginia. Col. CLARK established courts and placed garrisons at Kaskaskia, Cahokia and Vincennes. Treaties of amity were also entered into by Col. CLARK in the vicinity of all the Northwestern British posts.

In December, 1778, the British commander of Detroit, Lieut.-Gov. HENRY HAMILTON, having collected all the force in his power, arrived at Vincennes, and summoned the garrison to surrender. The only occupants of the fort were Capt. HELM, one private and three citizens. Capt. HELM, making a show of resistance, was offered all the usual honors of war. Gov. HAMILTON took up his winter quarters in the town and fort, with seventy-nine men.

In February, 1779, Col. CLARK, with one hundred and thirty men and forty pack-horseman, marched to Vincennes, where he arrived on the 21st, and immediately invested the fort and demanded its surrender. After a siege of three days, in which only one American was wounded, and seven British soldiers were severely wounded, if not killed, on the 24th of February, Col. HAMILTON capitulated and surrendered the garrison as prisoners of war. He and seven other prisoners were sent to Virginia.

A few days after, Capt. HELM, by order of Col. CLARK, at the head of sixty men, captured a convoy of merchandise and army supplies, amounting to ten thousand pounds in value, which was advancing by way of the Wabash from Detroit, under an escort of forty men.

In the result of the enterprise and success of Col. CLARK, Virginia obtained possession of the territory claimed by her

— the great Northwest — at this day, comprising the states of Ohio, Indiana, Illinois, Michigan, Wisconsin and a large part of Minnesota. Henceforth the Northwest remained in a comparative degree of quiet during the progress of the Revolutionary war, except the predatory excursions of the Indians from this region, on the frontiers of the old states. It exhibits few events worthy of attention, in regard to organized government, production or commerce, and a total barrenness, in relation to settlement and growth of population.

CHAPTER VI.

UNDER AMERICAN JURISDICTION.

The "Ordinance for the government of the territory of the United States, northwest of the river Ohio," adopted by the Continental Congress, July 13, 1787, may be regarded as the fundamental law which led the way to the wonderful growth and prosperity of the states since formed from the "Northwest Territory."

"Slavery or involuntary servitude," notwithstanding the 6th article of this ordinance, continued to exist at Green Bay. During the constant wars of the Indians, the Wisconsin tribes made captives of the Pawnees and other distant tribes who were consigned to servitude. AUGUSTIN GRIGNON says in his "Recollections," that he personally knew fourteen of these slaves, and that his grandfather, CHARLES DE LANGLADE, had two Indian slaves. It also appears quite certain that negroes were held as slaves at Green Bay, one of whom, Mr. GRIGNON says, was a boy, purchased by BAPTIST BRUNETT from a St. Louis Indian trader, and that the negro boy was taken away from BRUNETT as late as 1807, by Mr. CAMPBELL, the Indian agent at Prairie du Chien, in consequence of the cruel treatment inflicted upon him.

The treaty of peace of 1783, was not accompanied by the immediate surrender of the British posts to the American authorities. More than ten years of diplomatic controversy intervened before a great part of the disputes were in a measure settled by JAY's treaty of 1794, and it was not until two years later, that the posts in the Northwest were evacuated by the British and delivered up to the Americans under the stipulations of that treaty. Some of the most cruel and bloody wars with the Indians, which have ever been known in the annals of American history, occurred during the five years immediately preceding the treaty of GREENVILLE, of 1795. In many of these wars, the American forces were signally unsuccessful. They were, however, mostly in that part of the Northwestern Territory, which was so distant from the limits of the present state of Wisconsin, that they are no farther connected with its history, than that history is connected with whatever relates to the Northwestern Territory.

The most signal of these reverses, was the defeat of Gen. HARMAR on the Maumee, in October, 1790, and the route of Gen. ST. CLAIR, on the head-waters of the Wabash, in November, 1791. In these and other engagements, the Indians were undoubtedly aided and abetted by the British.

The subsequent campaigns were entrusted to Major-Gen. ANTHONY WAYNE, and were attended with signal success. In August, 1794, on the Maumee, above Fort Defiance, was fought one of the most successful and decisive battles ever fought with western Indians, and tended more than any other to humble the power and spirit of the hostile tribes. The name of Gen. WAYNE alone was a greater terror to them than any army, for they looked upon him as a chief who never slept and whom no art could surprise. The campaign of 1794 put a close to Indian hostilities in the Northwest, and the tribes soon began to evince a disposition to enter into a permanent treaty of peace and friendship, notwithstanding the opposition urged by the British agents. Preliminary articles were signed at Fort Wayne, January 24th, 1795, by which it was agreed that a definitive treaty should be made the next summer at Greenville. Accordingly there had assembled at the latter place, eleven hundred and thirty chiefs and warriors of the several nations and tribes of the Wyandots, Delawares, Shawanese, Ottawas, Chippewas, Pottawatamies, Miamis, Weas, Eel Rivers, Kickapoos, Piankeshaws and Kaskaskias. The "great and abiding peace document" was finally agreed upon and signed on the 3d of August, 1795, by eighty-four chiefs, representing these nations and tribes, and by Gen. ANTHONY WAYNE, sole commissioner on the part of the United States.

By the treaty of 1783, Great Britain relinquished to the United States all the territory on the east side of the Mississippi, from its sources to the 31st parallel of north latitude, which was the boundary of Florida on the north. The United States claimed the free navigation of the river to its mouth, by virtue of the treaty, as well as by a natural right independent of treaty, to follow the current of their rivers to the sea, as established by the laws of nations.

Great Britain had ceded to Spain all the Floridas, and possessing all the territory on the west side of the river and Florida on the east, the river for the last three hundred miles flowed wholly within the dominions of Spain. His Catholic Majesty therefore denied the right of the United States to the free navigation of the river, and claimed for Spain the exclusive right to the use of the river below the southern limit of the United States. In the exercise of the rights claimed by Spain, heavy duties were exacted of every boat descending the river, which were as arbitrary as they were unjust.

By the treaty of Madrid, which was signed October 20, 1795, boundaries were defined between the territories of the United States and Spain. The treaty provided that the middle of the Mississippi should be the western boundary of the United States, from its source to the intersection of the 31st parallel of north latitude, and that the whole width of said river from its source to the sea should be free to the people of the United States.

By treaty signed at Madrid, March 21, 1801, Spain granted Louisiana to France.

In January, 1803, ROBERT R. LIVINGSTON and JAMES MONROE were appointed ministers to the court of France, and by the last of April in that year concluded a treaty, which was ratified in the following October, which resulted in the purchase, for sixty million francs, in six per cent. bonds, of the whole of the province of Louisiana. Thus the United States became possessed of the whole of the great valley of the Mississippi, while Spain retained Mexico on the west and southwest, and the Floridas on the southeast. The Indian title to the lands in this vast region alone remained to be extinguished.

On the 7th of May, 1800, the Northwest Territory was divided and the new territory of Indiana established, embracing the present states of Indiana, Illinois, Michigan,

Wisconsin and Minnesota, east of the Mississippi, while on the west the boundary was undefined, and the new Indiana territory embraced "all that part of the territory of the United States which lies to the westward of a line beginning at the Ohio, opposite to the mouth of the Kentucky river, and thence north until it shall intersect the territorial line between the United States and Canada."

Gen. WILLIAM HENRY HARRISON was appointed, in 1801, governor of the newly organized territory. He made several treaties on the part of the United States with different Indian tribes, by which their possessory title to extensive tracts of territory was extinguished. But the most important of all the treaties made by him was that with Sacs and Foxes at St. Louis, on the 3d of November, 1804. This treaty was made and signed by only five individuals, on the part of the Indians, and its validity was denied by one band of the Sacs, of which BLACK HAWK was the chief, and the cession of land made by it, and its occupancy by the whites, became twenty-eight years afterward the alleged cause of the Black Hawk war, which in its results materially aided in the settlement of Wisconsin.

The boundaries of the land to which the Indian title was extinguished by this treaty, if valid, are thus described:

"Beginning at a point on the Missouri River, opposite the mouth of Gasconade River; thence in a direct course so as to strike the river Jeffreon (now called Salt River) at the distance of thirty miles from its mouth, and down the said Jeffreon to the Mississippi; thence up the Mississippi to the mouth of the Wisconsin River, and up the same to a point which shall be thirty-six miles in a direct line from the mouth of the said river (this point is about three miles west of Muscoda, in Grant county); thence by a direct line to the point where the Fox River (a branch of the Illinois) leaves the small lake called Sakaegan; thence down the Fox River to the Illinois river, and down the same to the Mississippi."

The "small lake called Sakaegan" is supposed to be Mukwanago lake, a little northeast of the village of Mukwanago in Waukesha county, of which Hon. ANDREW E. ELMORE was an early inhabitant, and which gave to him the title of "Sage of Mukwanago." There are, however, different opinions as to which of the lakes discharging their waters into Fox River was called "Sakaegan." The direct line from the Wisconsin river to the Fox river, where it leaves the Mukwanago lake, forming the northern boundary of this cession, passes about three miles south of Madison, through the Second lake (Waubesa) and crosses Rock river about two miles above Fort Atkinson. These boundaries embrace more than fifty million acres, the purchase price of which was

"Goods in hand to the amount of two thousand, two hundred and fifty-four dollars and fifty cents and a yearly annuity of one thousand dollars, to be paid in goods valued at first cost."

Two separate treaties were made at Portage des Sioux, on the 12th day of September, 1815, by WM. CLARK, NINIAN EDWARDS and AUGUSTE CHOUTEAU, commissioners on the part of the United States. One was with the "chiefs and warriors of that portion of the Sac nation of Indians residing on the Missouri river," in which they "assent" to the treaty between the United States and the Sacs and Foxes, concluded at St. Louis, November 3, 1804, and they "promise to do all in their power to re-establish and enforce the same." The other was with the "king, chiefs and warriors of the Fox tribe or nation" in which they "assent to, recognize, re-establish and confirm" the treaty of 1804 and "promise to fulfill all the stipulations contained in the said treaty, in favor of the said Fox tribe or nation." Neither of these treaties was signed by BLACK HAWK.

On the 13th of May, 1816, a treaty was made at St. Louis, by the same commissioners and the "chiefs and warriors of the Sacs of Rock river and the adjacent country," which recites that the Indians are "anxious to return to the habits of peace and friendship." * * * "Do hereby unconditionally assent to, recognize, re-establish and confirm" the treaty of 1804. This treaty was signed by twenty-two of the "chiefs and warriors," among whom was MUCK-E-TA-MA-CHE-KA-KA, Black Sparrow Hawk. Although BLACK HAWK "touched the quill" to this treaty, he afterward pretended that he was ignorant of what he was doing, and denied its obligatory force upon the Sacs of Rock river, of which he was the head chief.

Soon after the treaty of 1804, Fort Madison was erected by the United States troops, a short distance above the mouth of the Des Moines river.

On the 9th of August, 1805, Lieut. ZEBULON PIKE left St. Louis with a detatchment of soldiers under the orders of government, on an exploring expedition in boats toward the headwaters of the Mississippi. On the 23d of September he held a council at St. Peters with the chiefs of the Mississippi bands, and obtained a grant of one hundred thousand acres for the purpose of military posts at St. Peters, the Falls of St. Anthony and the mouth of the St. Croix.

Predatory excursions by the different Indian tribes were frequently made, resulting in the murder of many of the inhabitants in the Indiana Territory, which were owing greatly to the baneful influence of TECUMTHE and his brother, the Shawanese Prophet, who were active in their efforts to effect a union of all the tribes. But the first blood spilled under public authority since the pacification of Greenville in August, 1795, was at the memorable battle of Tippecanoe, of which Gen. HARRISON was pre-eminently the hero, and in which TECUMTHE fell.

The question "Who killed Tecumpseh?" has been much discussed, but the weight of authority, especially the testimony of Gov. CASS, leaves but little doubt that he was killed by the brave Col. RICHARD M. JOHNSON. This battle was fought on the 7th of November, 1811, near the present city of La Fayette, Indiana. The Americans had not more than seven hundred efficient men, while the Indian force was at least six hundred, and the estimate has been made at from eight hundred to one thousand warriors. The result was a complete route of the savage enemy, who fled in every direction and were pursued by the horsemen into the wood, as far as they could proceed. According to the official returns, the loss of the Americans was thirty-seven killed on the field, among whom were Col. DAVIESS, of Kentucky, and Cols. OWEN and WHITE, of Indiana, twenty-five mortally wounded and one hundred and twenty-six wounded. Of the Indians, forty were left dead on the field, and how many others were killed or wounded, mortally or otherwise, is unknown.

This sanguinary battle was the beginning of the war declared against Great Britain the next year, and the Indian tribes inhabiting the country south and west of the great lakes, immediately flew to arms and sought the aid of their allies, the English in Canada, of which they had previously received assurances, and they now began to threaten all the American border population and the posts in Ohio, Indiana and Michigan territory, as well as the northwestern confines of Pennsylvania and New York.

Previous to the war of 1812, it was the policy of the British government to keep alive the bitter feelings of the Indians against the Americans, which it did by means of the Indian traders without openly violating its peaceful relations to our government.

One of these traders, whose principal trading post was at Prairie du Chien, was a talented Englishman named Col. ROBERT DICKSON. Soon after the congressional declaration of war in 1812, Col. DICKSON arrived at Green Bay with a party of about one hundred Sioux. To this party were joined the Menomonee chief TOMAH and about one hundred of his tribe, and also a larger band of Winnebagoes. The whole body moved forward to Mackinaw, and took part in its capture.

Lieut. HANKS was in command of the American forces at Mackinaw, consisting of only fifty-seven effective men. He had no knowledge that war existed until he was attacked on the 17th of July by a force of British, Canadians and Indians, numbering in all more than one thousand, and was compelled to surrender his men as prisoners of war, who were discharged on parole. The Sioux and Winnebagoes first returned, and TOMAH with his Menomonees in the autumn.

Early in the spring of 1813 the Menomonee chief SOULIGNY and *The White Elk*, with about fifty warriors, were engaged in the hard fighting at Fort Meigs, and soon after returned to Green Bay.

Later in the season, Col. DICKSON assembled a force of Indian warriors, among whom were TOMAH and about fifty of his band; BLACK HAWK, with a band of two hundred Sac warriors, and other Indians consisting of Pottawatamies, Kickapoos, Ottawas and Winnebagoes, the whole force numbering about five hundred. Col. DICKSON, with his Indians, passing Chicago, which had been evacuated, reached Fort Meigs, where little was to be done, and after some slight skirmishing, retired to Detroit. Some portion of DICKSON's forces now returned to Green Bay, and he led the remainder to Sandusky and aided in the attack of the fort, which was so gallantly defended by Maj. GEORGE CROGHAN. BLACK HAWK and his followers then returned to Rock river, and nothing more is heard of Col. DICKSON and his Indian force.

The surrender of Detroit by Gen. HULL, was the crowning misfortune that befell the American cause in this quarter of the seat of war. HULL was afterwards tried by a court martial, found guilty of cowardice, and sentenced to be shot. He was, however, pardoned by the president, but deprived of all military command.

Gen. HULL had informed Capt. HEALD, commander of the post of Fort Dearborn, Chicago, of the loss of Mackinaw, and directed him to retire with his garrison to Fort Wayne. On the 15th of August, Capt. HEALD proceeded to obey these orders with fifty-four regulars and twelve militia, escorted by a guard of about thirty Miamis, under the command of Capt. WELLS, who had been sent from Fort Wayne for that purpose. The evacuating party had proceeded on their way along the lake shore a little more than a mile, when they were attacked by the Pottawatamies, numbering four or five hundred, under BLACK BIRD. Capt. WELLS and other officers, twenty-six regulars, all the militia, with two women and twelve children, were all killed. Capt. HEALD and his wife were severely wounded. TO-PEN-E-BEE, the Grand Sachem of the Pottawatamies, was prevailed upon by JOHN B. CHADANAU and JOSEPH BERTRAND to spare their lives, and they with the few other survivors, were taken back as prisoners to Fort Dearborn, which the Indians burned the next day. During the continuance of the war with Great Britain, Wisconsin presented but a small theatre for action; there was, however, a conflict for the possession of our frontier posts.

The work of repairing the old fort at Prairie du Chien, and its recapture by the British under Col. McKAY, will be described in a chapter devoted to Prairie du Chien.

While Col. McKAY was engaged in capturing the Fort at Prairie du Chien, Major CAMPBELL had ascended the river from St. Louis, with a squadron of boats and a detachment of United States troops, for the purpose of re-enforcing the garrison at that place. When he arrived at Rock Island, he learned that the fort had been captured, and the expedition returned down the river, not, however, until after an attack by the Indians, in which one of the boats was captured, several men were killed, and Major CAMPBELL and several others were wounded.

Soon after this event the British commander at Prairie du Chien, then called Fort McKay, descended the river with a detachment of soldiers and two field-pieces. The guns were placed in position at Rock Island to prevent the passage of the river by any force which might attempt it.

In 1816, the war with Great Britain having terminated in

the treaty of peace, the construction of Fort Armstrong was commenced by United States troops at Rock Island, and a few settlers soon followed, who commenced making improvements, although the Indians had not yet removed.

In the period between 1815 and 1820, Capt. JOHN SHAW made eight trips in a trading boat from St. Louis to Prairie du Chien, and visited the lead mines where the city of Galena now is, and where the Indians smelted the lead in rude furnaces of their own construction, and at one time Mr. SHAW carried away seventy tons, which they had produced from the ores obtained by themselves in their rude and primitive modes. Capt. SHAW afterwards lived in Green Lake county, in this state, where he died August 31, 1871, in his 89th year. He was never married.

The rapids in the Mississippi river immediately above the mouth of Rock river and of the Des Moines river, known as the Rock river rapids and the Des Moines rapids, were a serious obstruction to the navigation of the great river, and until 1824 it was believed that a steamboat could not ascend them. In the spring of that year, the water in the river being high, DAVID G. BATES, who had for several years been engaged in running keel boats on the upper Mississippi, brought over the rapids a boat called the *Putnam*, which was one of the smallest class of boats that run the Ohio river in low water, and was the first to make the through trip from St. Louis to Prairie du Chien and Fort Snelling. In June following, boats of a larger class made the same trip, and since then the river has been navigated to St. Paul and Fort Snelling by steamboats, which have every year increased in size and convenience.

The commanding importance of the pine lumbering interests of Wisconsin is justly calculated to incite inquiry as to their early development and later progress. Lumber in large quantities is manufactured on all the streams that empty into Green Bay; also on the Mississippi at and above the Falls of St. Anthony, and on the Wisconsin, Black, Chippewa, and St. Croix rivers and their tributaries. The construction of the first mills was in the vicinity of Green Bay. The next attempts were on Black river. In 1819, CONSTANT A. ANDREWS, with one DIXON, built a sawmill at the falls of Black river, in which undertaking Col. JOHN SHAW was in some way connected with them. Gov. MCNAIR, of Missouri, who was sutler at Prairie du Chien, and WILFRED OWENS, who had charge of the business, furnished the capital, and were interested in the enterprise.

Authority to build the mill was obtained from the Sioux Indians; but the Winnebagoes claimed that the site was within their domain. By the time the mill was in operation, hundreds of Winnebagoes came there in a starving condition, and took from the adventurers all the food they had to eat, and all their blankets, and they were compelled to leave the mill, and the next year it was burned and abandoned.

About the year 1822 a man by the name of HARDIN PERKINS came to Prairie du Chien from Kentucky, for the purpose of building a saw-mill in the Indian country. He induced JAMES H. LOCKWOOD and JOSEPH ROLETTE to furnish the necessary capital and obtain the consent of the Indians and Indian agent.

The consent of WABASHAW's band of Sioux, who claimed the Chippewa river country, and that of Maj. TALIAFERRO, then agent for the Sioux Indians, having been procured, PERKINS proceeded to the Red Cedar, a branch of the Chippewa, also known as the Menomonee river, and near the mouth of a small stream running into the Menomonee, about fifteen miles above its junction with the Chippewa river, he erected a saw-mill.

The surveys of the public lands, since made, show that the site of this mill was on the northwest quarter of section 26, town 28, range 13 west, in Dunn county, and is identical with the site of the shingle mill of Knapp, Stout & Co., at the village of Menomonee, in Dunn county.

The mill erected by PERKINS was about 150 feet from the mouth of the small stream, which is now known as Wilson creek. The large water-power saw-mill of Knapp, Stout & Co. is on the main (Menomonee) river, about 100 feet below the mouth of Wilson creek, and about seventy-five or eighty yards from the site of the first mill, built by PERKINS.

When the PERKINS mill was nearly completed — so near that he expected to commence sawing in a very few days — a sudden freshet came and swept away the dam, mill, and appendages, and the enterprise was abandoned.

In May, 1830, Messrs. LOCKWOOD and ROLETTE, by permission of the Secretary of War and the consent of the Indians, under the superintendency of a man named ARMSTRONG, rebuilt the mill, with a slight change of the site, but with the dam rebuilt where the first one was.

CHAPTER VII.

GREEN BAY — 1634 TO 1836.

Up to the time when the British took possession of the west there were within the present boundaries of Wisconsin few white inhabitants.

The two settlements, at Green Bay and Prairie du Chien, the one where the Fox river debouches into Green Bay, and the other near the junction of the Wisconsin river with the Mississippi, and being respectively the termini of the great natural highway between the lakes and the Father of Waters, were the earliest abodes of civilization within the limits of the state, the occupation of which became permanent.

The earliest settlement was at Green Bay. NICOLLET, with his voyageurs, was the first white man who trod its soil. He visited Green Bay as early as 1634, ascended Fox river, and was at the Wisconsin river.

As early as 1654, Lake Superior was visited by fur traders from Montreal, and at some time between that date and 1659 they pressed forward to Green Bay, where furs were abundant.

In 1660 Father MESNARD, who was lost in the forests of Lake Superior, had been charged by the bishop of Quebec to visit Green Bay, a mission which his sad fate prevented his fulfilling.

In 1669, Father ALLOUEZ, having previously established a mission at Che-goi-me-gon, exchanged it with Father MARQUETTE for a new mission which he established that year at or near Green Bay, probably at De Pere, and which subsequently was called the mission of St. Francis Xavier.

The precise date of the establishment of the first fortification at Green Bay—which was called St. Francis—is involved in some obscurity. The foundations of the fort at Mackinaw, on the peninsula, were laid by MARQUETTE in 1671, and other fortified posts about this period were established at Green Bay, Chicago, St. Josephs, Sault St. Mary, and Detroit. In 1680 TONTI commanded at Green Bay and had a small detachment of men under him. Soon after him came Lieut. DU LHUT, who had a small troop under his command. It was a dependency of Mackinaw and was easily and speedily re-enforced from that post.

On the 16th of May, 1673, MARQUETTE and JOLIET embarked from the mission station at Green Bay, on their voyage up the Fox and down the Wisconsin, which resulted in the discovery of the Mississippi river; and returned to Green Bay by the route of the Illinois and Chicago rivers, before the end of September of the same year. The ensuing winter and following summer were spent by MARQUETTE, in sickness, at the mission of St. Francis Xavier.

In the autumn of 1680 HENNEPIN and DU LHUT reached the mission near Green Bay, where they spent the winter. It was during this winter that LA SALLE made a journey on foot from Fort Crevecœur, on the Illinois river, to Green Bay.

History is barren of any important events which occurred at Green Bay during the next thirty or forty years. The little garrison was probably there in 1716, at the time of DE LOUVIGNY's expedition against the Foxes, as it certainly was when DE LIGNERY made his fruitless expedition in 1728. In 1746 Capt. DE VELIE was in command of the garrison, and was relieved that year by a new commandant. The garrison was withdrawn before the breaking out of the French war in 1754.

The year 1745 was marked by the permanent settlement at Green Bay of Sieur AUGUSTIN DE LANGLADE and his family. With the DE LANGLADES came but a few settlers besides their own family. M. SOULIGNY and his wife — the daughter of AUGUSTIN DE LANGLADE — came with the family, and they were joined by Mons. CARON, who spent the remainder of his days there. The whole number of which the colony consisted did not exceed eight persons. A blacksmith named LAMMIOT came soon after.

On the 12th October, 1761, Capt. BELFOUR, of the Eightieth Regiment of British infantry, arrived at Green Bay with Lieut. JAMES GORRELL, one sergeant, one corporal, fifteen privates, a French interpreter, and two English traders whose names were MCKAY, from Albany, and GODDARD, from Montreal. On the 14th, Capt. BELFOUR returned, leaving the post — afterward called Fort Edward Augustus — in charge of Lieut. GORRELL, who, with the seventeen men under his charge, busied themselves during the winter in repairing the fort, houses, etc.

On the 26th of June, 1763, Lieut. GORRELL, in pursuance of instructions from Capt. ETHERINGTON, who had been surprised by the Chippewas, at Mackinaw, abandoned his post at Green Bay and set off with all his garrison and the English traders, and a strong guard of friendly Indians, to join Capt. ETHERINGTON, which they did on the 30th of June, at an Ottawa village about thirty miles above Mackinaw.

For forty years after the advent of the DE LANGLADES the settlement at Green Bay made but little progress. In 1785 there were but seven families, who, with their *engages* and others, did not exceed fifty-six souls.

The heads of these seven families were CHARLES DE LANGLADE, PIERRE GRIGNON, Sr., —— LAQRAL, BAPTIST BRUNET, AMABLE ROY, JOSEPH ROY and —— MARCHAND. All the trading was on the east side of the river and was all carried on by Mr. GRIGNON and MARCHAND, and all the residences were on the same side except those of BRUNET, LAQRAL and JOSEPH ROY who lived on the west side.

The first settler who arrived after this date was JACQUES (JAMES) PORLIER from Montreal, who came in 1791. Of him Gen. ELLIS says "of all men of French origin at the Bay, when I arrived there (1822), Judge JAMES PORLIER stood foremost."

The next year, CHARLES REAUME arrived and took up his residence at the Bay. He was a very noted and most singular character. He long held the office of Justice of the Peace, and it has been often said that no person could tell when his official duties first devolved upon him, nor from whence his authority was derived. But it appears reasonably certain that his first commission was derived from the British authorities at Detroit before the surrender of that post in 1796, and that he subsequently received a similar commission from Genl. HARRISON, Governor of Indiana Territory. Many amusing anecdotes are related of the manner in which he discharged his official duties, and it is well authenticated that the only process of the court was the judge's *jack knife,* which served at once as the token and authority by which all defendants were brought under his jurisdiction. In 1818 he was appointed one of the associate justices of the court by Gov. CASS, and the same year moved to Little Kaukalin, about ten miles above Green Bay, where he died in 1822.

In the last years of the last century several other settlers began to arrive, almost invariably from Canada. Among them, JOHN LAWE came in the summer of 1797. The total population in 1812 had increased to as many as two hundred and fifty, among whom the most prominent families not before mentioned were DUCHANO, GRAVEL, CHEVALIER, CHALIFOUX, HOULRICH, FRANKS, BRISQUN, VIEAU, CARDRONE, DOUSMAN, CARBOUNSAU, VAUN, HOULL, JACOBS, GARRIEPY, BAUPREZ, DUCHARME, LANGEVIN, HYOTTE, NORMAN, LAVIGNE, BONNETERRE, BOUCHER, LE BOEUF, THEBEAU, DUMOND, FORTIER, LA ROCK, and JOURDIN.

About 1794 the trading house of Ogilvie, Gillaspie & Co. was established, which three years later gave place to JACOB FRANK'S, of which JOHN LAWE subsequently became proprietor.

It is a great mistake to suppose that the Indian traders— at least those of any character—took what they pleased and kept no account with the natives. As to Judge LAWE'S practice, the Indians, on taking his credit in the fall, high or low, each individual had an account, *bona fide*, opened with him on his books, as formal and precise in all respects as the sharpest white man in which he was debited his blanket, stroud, calico, powder, shot, thread, pipes, tobacco and flints as carefully as possible. On his appearance in the spring with his peltries, he was duly credited with payment, not in the gross, or by the lump, but every skin was counted, separating the prime from the poor, and each kind from the other with exactness, with different prices, according to value, so that the Indian knew exactly how his account stood.

Except the indispensable blacksmith there were no mechanics at Green Bay before 1816, besides AUGUSTIN THIBEAU, a carpenter, who came in 1800.

The earliest mill was erected by JACOB FRANKS about the year 1809. He first built a saw-mill on Devil river, two or three miles east of Depere, and then a grist-mill with one run of stones.

JOHN BOWYER of Virginia, was in 1815, sent as Government Indian Agent and MATTHEW IRWIN of Pennsylvania, as factor, to reside at Green Bay.

In 1816 the government caused a saw-mill to be erected at the Little Kau-kau-lin.

The various kinds of domestic animals were in use from

soon after the settlement by the LANGLADES, and garden vegetables and cereals were also produced in abundance.

Fort Howard was established in 1816, the quarters of the officers and soldiers having been prepared by Gen. (then Major) CHARLES GRATIOT of the engineer corps. On the 16th of July Col. JOHN MILLER in command of a detachment of troops, which it required three schooners to transport, having Major GRATIOT in company, landed with his troops on the west side of Fox River at its junction with Green Bay, to the great wonder and surprise of the inhabitants. The troops pitched their tents near where the fort was subsequently erected, and it was about two months before they got houses and barracks ready for occupation. Col. MILLER returned during that year to Detroit, leaving the post and troops in command of Col. CHAMBERS.

In 1820, the troops under command of Col. JOSEPH L. SMITH were removed two and a half miles up the river, to an eminence on the right bank, which he named Camp Smith, and where he had built a stockade and indifferent barracks.

Col. SMITH was the father of Hon. WINFIELD SMITH, of Milwaukee. He was superseded in command by Col. NINIAN PINKNEY in the fall of 1822, by whose orders the troops were then moved back to Fort Howard, which was fully repaired, and thenceforward made the rendezvous for all the troops and army operations of the upper country.

In the fall of 1823 Col. JOHN McNEILL succeeded Col. PINKNEY, and was himself relieved the next year by Gen. HUGH BRADY.

During the two years that Col. SMITH occupied Camp Smith—which was half a mile back from the river—the followers of the army had ensconced themselves along the river bank, just below and in front of the stockade, where they had erected numerous sheds, or shanties, in which were gathered various articles of trade. This little nondescript village obtained the sobriquet of "Shantytown," which the locality wears to the present time. It had three principal traders — ROBERT IRWIN, Jr., who had built a good residence; DANIEL WHITNEY, the most enterprising trader in the northwest, who had erected a good store and filled it with goods, and WILLIAM DICKINSON, who was a pushing trader, and who built a store and dwelling house.

6

HENRY S. BAIRD, having resided at Mackinaw two years previously, removed with his wife to Green Bay in September, 1824, and soon after built and occupied a house at Shantytown, and a little later Judge JAMES D. DOTY built a fine dwelling just above. A court house and jail—the first west of Lake Michigan—were erected here.

In 1829 the Green Bay mission school, under the fostering care of the Protestant Episcopal Church, was opened under the care of Rev. RICHARD F. CADLE, superintendent, who was the earliest permanent resident missionary of the Episcopal church west of Lake Michigan. By an act of the Legislature of 1833, children could be received by indenture and educated and brought up by the school. Mr. CADLE continued in charge of the mission school until February, 1834, when, feeling aggrieved at some complaints which were made in relation to his punishment of some of the children, he withdrew from its immediate superintendence. The school was devoted principally to the education of the children of the poor, and rendered a valuable service to the community.

By an act of the Legislative Council, approved October 21, 1829, the first Protestant Episcopal church west of Lake Michigan was incorporated. The act prescribed "That RICHARD F. CADLE, as rector; DANIEL WHITNEY and ALBERT G. ELLIS, as wardens; JAMES D. DOTY, WILLIAM DICKINSON, JOHN LAWE, ALEXANDER J. IRWIN, JOHN P. ARNDT, SAMUEL W. BEALE, ROBERT IRWIN, Jr., and HENRY S. BAIRD as vestrymen," be incorporated by the name of "The Rector, Wardens, and Vestry of Christ Church, Green Bay."

Rev. Mr. CADLE rendered his clerical services for a long time to this church gratuitously, and in January, 1834, a vote of thanks was given to him by the wardens and vestry.

The first newspaper printed in the territory which now constitutes the State, was published at Green Bay on the the 11th of December, 1833, by J. V. SUYDAM and ALBERT G. ELLIS. Its title at first was *Green Bay Intelligencer*, and after the twentieth number there was added to its title *Wisconsin Democrat*. The size of the sheet was twelve inches by eighteen, contained four pages with four columns in each page, each column two and one half inches by fifteen. It was published semi-monthly, and the subscription price was two dollars per annum. After the fourth number Mr. SUYDAM withdrew his connection with the paper and it was continued by Mr. ELLIS alone until the twenty-first number, on the 27th of June, 1835, when CHARLES C. P. ARNDT was associated with Mr. ELLIS, and continued the connection through the second volume. Owing mainly to the difficulty of obtaining materials and skilled labor, the publication was suspended from April 16, 1834, to August 2d, and again from August 21, 1834, to April 9, 1835, with the exception of one number, October 9, 1834. The first volume, No. 26, was completed September 5, 1835.

The second volume was commenced as a weekly by Messrs. ELLIS and ARNDT September 12, 1835, and continued with much greater regularity.

About the first of August, 1835, a new weekly paper of somewhat larger dimensions appeared, published by WILLIAM STEVENSON, under the title of *Wisconsin Free Press.*

After the second volume of the *Intelligencer and Democrat,* the paper passed into the control of CHARLES C. SHOLES, by whom it was greatly enlarged, and edited and published under the title of *Wisconsin Democrat.*

Subsequently, commencing in October, 1842, the *Green Bay Republican* was published by HENRY O. SHOLES.

In 1830 the Indian agency was fixed at this place, under Major BREVOORT. The erection of a church edifice and school building by the Roman Catholics in charge of Father GABRIEL RICHARD soon followed. Father RICHARD was afterward the Delegate in Congress for Michigan Territory. A few years subsequently, commencing in 1832, Navarino and Astor below, and Depere above, absorbed the trade, as well as the inhabitants of Shantytown, and its existence was only in name.

Mr. BAIRD in his "Recollections" published in the 4th Vol. of the Coll. of St. Hist. Soc., p. 197, says:

"There were in 1824 at Green Bay but six or eight resident American families, and the families of the officers stationed at Fort Howard, in number about the same. The character of the people was a compound of civilization and primitive simplicity exhibiting the light and lively characteristics of the French and the thoughtlessness and improvidence of the Aborigines. Possessing the virtues of hospitality, and the warmth of heart unknown to residents of cities; untrammelled by the etiquet and conventional rules of modern 'high life,' they were ever ready to receive and entertain their friends and more intent upon the enjoyment of the present than to lay up store or make provision for the future. * * * They deserve to be remembered and placed on the pages of history, as the first real *pioneers of Wisconsin.* "

EBENEZER CHILDS arrived at Green Bay in May, 1820, being then twenty-three years of age. He was a carpenter.

In 1821 he went to St. Louis in a bark canoe by the Fox and Wisconsin Rivers, and returned by the Illinois and Chicago Rivers. JOHN P, ARNDT and family came to the Bay about 1825, and in 1827 he and Col. CHILDS built a saw-mill on the Oconto river. The same year Col. CHILDS with a son of Judge ARNDT, went to the southern part of Illinois, where they bought a drove of 262 cattle, of which they succeeded in driving 210 safely to Green Bay. In 1829 Col. CHILDS was appointed Sheriff of Brown county, and held the office until 1836, when he resigned it and was elected to the Territorial Legislature. He was repeatedly re-elected. In 1852 he removed to La Crosse where he spent the remainder of his days.

Gen. ALBERT G. ELLIS, who was born August 24, 1800, arrived at Green Bay the 1st of September, 1822. For about six years he was engaged in teaching school, at the same time performing the services of the Episcopal church as a lay reader. In 1828 he was appointed Deputy U. S. Surveyor and surveyed the private land claims at the Grand Kaukalin, and the Williams' grant at the Little Kaukalin, and at a future day was largely engaged in surveying the public lands.

Gen. ELLIS, who in connection with JOHN V. SUYDAM commenced the publication of the first newspaper printed within the present limits of Wisconsin, was a member of the first and of several subsequent Territorial Legislatures and was elected speaker in 1842-3. In 1838, he was appointed by President Van Buren, Surveyor General of Wisconsin and Iowa. When a Land Office was established at Stevens Point in 1853, he was appointed Receiver of Public Moneys and removed to that place where he has ever since lived.

JAMES DUANE DOTY came to Detroit in 1818. In 1820 in company with Governor CASS, he went on an expedition to the sources of the Mississippi River. On the 20th of January, 1823, an act of Congress was passed "to provide for the appointment of an additional Judge for the Michigan Territory." Mr. DOTY was appointed to this office by President MONROE. In the fall of 1823 he went to Prairie du Chien for the purpose of making it his residence, and remained there until the following May term of his court. During that time he procured the establishment of a post-office there and was appointed postmaster.

Judge DOTY removed to Green Bay in 1824, and continued to reside there until 1841, when, having been appointed Governor of the Territory, he removed to Madison where he lived until 1844, when he was succeeded by N. P. Tallmadge and removed to Doty's Island, between Neenah and Menasha. In 1861, he was appointed Superintendent of Indian Affairs for Utah, where he immediately removed. He was subsequently appointed Governor of that Territory, and continued to reside there until his death on the 13th of June, 1865.

Judge DOTY was repeatedly elected Delegate in Congress for the Territory of Wisconsin, and was appointed Governor of the Territory in 1841. After the admission of the State into the Union, he was twice elected a member of the House of Representatives. He was a member from Winnebago county of the convention which framed the first constitution.

MORGAN L. MARTIN came to Green Bay in 1827 where he has ever since resided; he was a lawyer of distinction, and more recently Judge of the County Court of Brown county with civil jurisdiction. He was for many years a member of the Territorial Legislature, and in 1845 was elected Delegate in Congress for the Territory. He was a member and President of the convention which framed the present constitution of the State, and has since been a member of the State Legislature.

Green Bay owed much of its progress and prosperity to the citizens whom we have particularly mentioned; as it did also to many others who are not specifically named.

CHAPTER VIII.

PRAIRIE DU CHIEN.

The time of the first settlement, and even of the first visitation, of Prairie du Chien, by any white man, is involved in uncertainty.

It is presumed that HENNEPIN, in 1680, was the first civilized human being to behold this site of rare natural beauty. It could not have escaped his notice; but as he makes no mention of it, the inference is legitimate that it was not then occupied even as an Indian village.

It is not remarkable that MARQUETTE and JOLIET, in their descent of the Wisconsin river into the Mississippi, in 1673, should not have visited or seen it, as it was three or four miles above the route they must have taken, and obscured from their view by the trees and vegetation upon the bank and islands of the Wisconsin river.

It would seem that there was a military post on the Mississippi, near the Wisconsin river, as early as 1689—probably at Prairie du Chien—as the official document of the French taking possession of the Upper Mississippi, by NICHOLAS PERROT, May 8, 1689, has among the witnesses "Monsieur DE BÔRIEGUILLOT, commanding the French in the neighborhood of the Ouiskonche, on the Mississippi."

It is stated by Rev. ALFRED BRUNSON, "as well as I (he) can ascertain," that the first settlement at Prairie du Chien was made by a trader or hunter, whose name was CARDINELLE, who, with his wife, came from Canada in 1726, and made a small farm. The tradition about this settlement, so far as relates to the date, is very questionable.

After the death of this man, the date of which is not known, his wife was again and repeatedly married, and finally died at this place as recently as 1827, and is supposed to have attained the great age of one hundred and thirty years.

The name of the next settler, according to Dr. BRUNSON, was GANIER, whose descendants still remain there.

About the year 1737 a French trading post was established, and a stockade built around the buildings to protect them from the Indians, and occasionally a *voyageur* got married and settled down on a piece of land; but little progress or improvement was made in the place so long as its business was limited to Indian trade; for whatever enterprise the Indian trader possessed in his normal pursuit, he had none which tended to the development and settlement of the country.

It is said in a report made in 1818 to the house of Representatives of the United States, by the committee on public lands, of which Hon. GEORGE ROBERTSON, of Kentucky, a very able and careful writer, was chairman, that in the year 1755 the government of France established a military post near the mouth of the Ouisconsin; that many French families established themselves in the neighborhood and established the village of Prairie du Chien.

But some doubt is cast over this statement by the omission of Capt. CARVER, in his "Travels," to make any mention of there being any white inhabitants at the place when he visited it in 1766, although he describes the large *Indian* town, to which the Indians had removed about thirty years before, from their village on the Wisconsin, about five miles above its mouth, and he says that the traders who had accompanied him, took up their residence for the winter at the Yellow river, on the opposite side of the Mississippi, only about ten miles above Prairie du Chien. This they certainly would not have done if there had been a settlement of whites near the mouth of the Wisconsin river.

It does not appear probable that the trading post and stockade established in 1737—if any such were established—or the military post established in 1755 by the French government, if any was then established, were permanently maintained, or that either had any existence as late as 1780 or 1781. There was a tradition among the old settlers, testified to in 1820, in the testimony taken in relation to private land claims, that the old fort was burned in 1777.

It appears quite certain that in 1781 Gov. PATRICK SINCLAIR, of Mackinaw, at a treaty with the Indians, purchased their right and title to Mackinaw, Green Bay and Prairie du Chien, and a tract at the latter place six leagues up and down the river and six leagues back, and that so far as related to Prairie du Chien, the purchase was made for and in behalf of the traders, by three of whom—BAZIL GUIRD, PIERRE ANTUA and AUGUSTIN ANGE—the payment in goods was made.

MICHAEL BRISBOIS settled at Prairie du Chien in 1781,

where he continued to reside for fifty-six years. He died in 1837, at the age of seventy-seven years, and was buried by his son, in accordance with his request, on a prominent bluff back of Prairie du Chien. He left several children, who continue to reside where their father lived so long.

In his "Early History of Wisconsin," Dr. BRUNSON says that, according to the statements of MICHAEL BRISBOIS, there were twenty or thirty settlers at Prairie du Chien when he went there, and twelve years later (1793) there were forty-three farms and twenty or thirty village lots claimed and occupied, most of which had been built upon. The most of these settlers were hunters, traders, and *voyageurs* who, taking wives of the natives, prosecuted farming upon a small and primitive scale in a way not to interfere with their other employments.

Mr. BRISBOIS, besides being a trader, carried on the business of baking and farming to some extent. He gave to the inhabitants tickets for fifty loaves of bread for each one hundred pounds of flour they brought to him, and these tickets formed a currency with which they carried on trade with the Indians and with each other. None of the inhabitants made their own bread, and BRISBOIS' bake-house was their sole dependence for the staff of life.

About 1807 a trader by the name of CAMPBELL was appointed by the United States government sub-Indian agent, and also justice of the peace by the Governor of Illinois. He was killed at Mackinaw in a duel with one CRAWFORD, about a year afterward, and was succeeded in both offices by NICHOLAS BOILVIN.

The *coutume de Paris* so far prevailed before the laws of Michigan were introduced, about 1819, that a part of the ceremony of marriage was the entering into a contract in writing, generally giving, if no issue, the property to the survivor. When the parties desired to be divorced, they went together before the magistrate and made known their wishes, who, in their presence, tore up the marriage contract, and according to the custom of the country they were then divorced.

JAMES AIRD and DUNCAN GRAHAM had been engaged in the Indian trade from some time during the last century, at as early a period, it is supposed, as during the Revolutionary war. Their trade was with the Sioux or Dacotahs, among whom they spent the winter season, while the summer months were spent at Prairie du Chien.

The most noted character in the history of Prairie du Chien during the first quarter of the present century was JOSEPH ROLETTE. He was born in Canada, of a respectable French family. He was educated for the Roman Catholic church, but, not liking the profession, he quit it, and served a regular apprenticeship to mercantile business.

About the year 1804, having engaged in the Indian trade with Mr. MURDOCH CAMERON, he came to Prairie du Chien, where he continued to reside up to the time of his death in 1841. He was an active merchant and trader, and a hospitable and generous citizen, and for an Indian trader, he had considerable enterprise for the prosperity and improvement of the country. He cultivated quite an extensive farm, and was interested in other improvements. He exercised a very considerable political influence, which he devoted to the interests of his friends, without regard to political considerations. In 1827 or '28 he was appointed Chief Justice of the county court, which office he held until 1830. His wife was a woman of culture and refinement, and he left a daughter who was married to Maj. ALEXANDER S. HOOE, of the United States army.

Before the war of 1812 Prairie du Chien, and the surrounding country, was beginning to attract the attention of settlers, but that event suspended all new settlements.

It was well known in 1813 that the British meditated the occupation of the Illinois Territory, and they had at the portage of the Fox and Wisconsin several cannon for a fort to be erected at Prairie du Chien, where it was stated there were about sixty families, most of whom were engaged in agriculture, and where permanent subsistence could be obtained for one thousand regular troops. For some unknown reason the erection of the fort was not undertaken that year by the British.

In the spring of 1814 the United States government sent from St. Louis a company of regulars, under command of Lieut. PERKINS, and 135 volunteers—dauntless young fellows from Missouri—to Prairie du Chien. They ascended the river in boats, accompanied by Gov. CLARK, who returned to St. Louis in June. He reported that the regulars had taken possession of the house formerly occupied by the old Mackinaw company, and that the volunteers occupied two of the largest armed boats, under command of Aid-de-Camp KENNESLEY and Captains SULLIVAN and YEIZER, and that when he left the new fort was progressing on a most commanding spot. It was finished that month and called Fort Shelby. The site of this fort is nearly opposite the present pontoon railroad bridge, and is where Col. H. L. DOUSMAN, after the removal of the fort to the east side of the *Marais St. Friole*, built an elegant private residence.

From the time of the surrender of the Northwestern posts by the British up to the war of 1812, the feelings of many of the Indian traders had been in sympathy with Great Britain. These traders having learned of the occupation of Prairie du Chien in 1814, by a military force, fitted out at Mackinaw, in conjunction with some British officers, an expedition for its recapture. Lieut.-Col. WILLIAM MCKAY had been originally a trader, and subsequently became a member of the Northwest Fur Company. To him the command of this expedition was confided, and for it he was well fitted.

JOSEPH ROLETTE, who had been active in commanding the Canadians at the capture of Mackinaw from the Americans in 1812, and THOMAS ANDERSON, another trader, each raised a company of militia at Mackinaw among their *engages*. There was a small party of eighteen regulars under Capt. POHLMAN. Col. ROBERT DICKSON, who had commanded a large Indian force in the capture of the fort at Mackinaw, detached a part of his Indian force consisting of two hundred Sioux warriors and one hundred Winnebagoes. With this force and a brass six pounder Colonel MCKAY went in boats from Mackinaw to Green Bay, where he tarried for some time to increase his numbers, and make all necessary preparations. With the accessions obtained at Green Bay the entire force now consisted of one hundred and fifty whites and four hundred Indians. The force was represented in the newspapers of the day to have been much larger but the statement now given is upon the authority of AUGUSTIN GRIGNON, who was a Lieutenant in a company raised at Green Bay, and is undoubtedly correct.

The expedition moved up Fox River being piloted by Capt. ROLETTE; the whites in six barges and the Indians in canoes, and carrying their craft over the "portage" they descended the Wisconsin to the old deserted Fox village about twenty miles above its mouth where the force halted. AUGUSTIN GRIGNON, MICHAEL BRISBOIS and two Indians were sent in the night to reconnoiter and ascertain the situation of the fort and the American forces within it. They brought back with them ANTOINE BRISBOIS, who reported the American strength of the garrison at sixty. The next morning which was Sunday, the 17th of July, 1814, Colonel McKAY, with the white men and Indians composing his force, continued down to the mouth of the Wisconsin, and thence almost up to the garrison, through a bayou, between the islands and the river. They reached the town unperceived. The force made a most formidable display, greatly to the terror of the inhabitants, and the consternation of the garrison.

The gunboat under command of Capt. YEISER, with other boats, were moored to the bank near the garrison. A severe fire was kept up upon the boats, which before sundown of the first day moved down stream out of reach of the guns of the enemy, carrying with them the provisions and ammunition of the garrison. The garrison was then invested. Capt. ROLETTE and ANDERSON, with their companies and the Sioux and Winnebago Indians, took post above the fort, while Col. McKAY, with the Green Bay company, the regulars, and Menomonee and Chippewa Indians encompassed it below. A flag was sent in, borne by Capt. ANDERSON, demanding the surrender of the garrison, which Lieutenant PERKINS the commandant, promptly declined. For four days the gallant little force in possession of the fort successfully resisted the persistent attacks of the enemy, the number of which including Indians was more than nine times larger than the American force. On the fourth day Col. McKAY having become desperate ordered cannon balls heated red hot in a blacksmith's forge, to be fired upon the garrison stockade which was of wood and easily ignited. Lieut. PERKINS perceiving that longer resistance was worse than useless, and would be criminal folly, raised a white flag. Two officers met Col. McKAY and the result was a surrender to him of the fort and public stores, the Americans being permitted to retire unmolested in boats down the river. The formal surrender was postponed until the next morning, the 21st of July.

Several days elapsed before arrangements were completed for sending the prisoners down the river, during which time their lives were in the most imminent danger the utmost exertions of Col. McKAY being necessary to prevent their indiscriminate massacre by the infuriated Indians. At length the Col. succeeded in getting the soldiers on board the large boat—the *Governor Clark*—which a short time before had brought them up the river, and the boat proceeded on its return, under the protection of an escort sent by Col. McKAY. The Indians however pursued the retreating soldiers, and did not relinquish the pursuit until they had passed Rock Island in safety.

Capt. POHLMAN with his regulars remained in command of the garrison, now called Fort McKay, with the two Mackinaw companies one under command of Capt. ANDERSON, and the other of Lieut. GRAHAM, who succeeded Capt. ROLETTE in command, he having been sent to Mackinaw with dispatches, immediately after the surrender. Colonel McKAY with the Green Bay troops and the Indians took their departure soon after.

The British occupation of the fort continued until peace in 1815, and the inhabitants were ordered to do duty in and about the garrison during the war. Upon the advent of peace the fort was evacuated.

Brevet General SMYTHE, Colonel of a Rifle Regiment, came to Prairie du Chien in June, 1816 with a detachment of U. S. troops to erect Fort Crawford. He selected the mound where the stockade had been built, which he repaired and occupied. He also appropriated the ground in front of the stockade, which included the most thickly inhabited part of the village. The arrival of Col. SMYTHE and his troops was very unwelcome to the settlement generally. He arrested MICHAEL BRISBOIS on a charge of treason for having taken up arms against the United States, and sent him to St. Louis.

In the spring of 1817, Col. TALBOT CHAMBERS having assumed command of Fort Crawford, ordered the houses in front of and about the fort to be taken down by their owners, and removed to the lower end of the village, where he pretended to give them lots. The officers, particularly while Col. CHAMBERS was in command, treated the inhabitants as a conquered people, arraigning and trying them by courts martial and sentencing them to ignominious punishment.

CHARLES MENARD was arrested by order of Col. CHAMBERS,

brought five miles from his residence under a guard, tried by a court martial on a charge of selling whiskey to the soldiers, whipped, and with a bottle hung to his neck, marched through the streets with music after him playing the *Rogue's March.*

JOSEPH ROLETTE, charged with some immoral conduct, was banished to an island about seven miles above the fort, where he was obliged to pass the winter; and there were numerous other acts of tyranny perpetrated by the officers upon the inhabitants.

Fort Crawford was continued at the site of the old stockade on the island until the year 1831, when the stone fort was built on the high ground east of the *Marais St. Friole.* The new fort was occupied by U. S. troops until June 9, 1856, when the troops were removed.

On May 27, 1857, the entire military reservation, including the fort and buildings in connection with it, was sold by the United States at auction and the site of the old fort has since been occupied by St. Mary's Institute, as a convent, built in 1872, which is conducted by the School Sisters of Notre Dame.

In the fall of 1815, Capt. JOHN SHAW went up the River from St. Louis to Prairie du Chien with a boat and a stock of merchandise, and there engaged in some little traffic. The next year he returned with a large boat and full load of merchandise. He thought it would be a good locality for a grist mill, and having found a sufficient water power at Fishers' Coulee, four miles above Prairie du Chien, he promised the people he would erect one. He made two other trips in 1816 and also trips every year until 1820, and in 1818 built the grist mill he had promised, which was a great convenience to the people.

In September, 1816, JAMES H. LOCKWOOD arrived at Prairie du Chien via Mackinaw, Green Bay and the Fox and Wisconsin rivers. Judge LOCKWOOD was born at Peru, Clinton County, N. Y., December 7, 1793. He studied law about a year, and then engaged as a merchant clerk. He was clerk in a sutler's store which brought him to Mackinaw in 1815. The transition from clerk to a sutler on the frontier, to engaging in the Indian trade, was easy and natural, and soon resulted in his removal to Prairie du Chien. Here he proved himself a useful citizen; he occupied many positions of trust, both public and private, and was faithful in all. In

1830, he was appointed one of the judges of the county court. When Judge DOTY went to Prairie du Chien in 1823 to hold his first court there were no lawyers, and Mr. LOCKWOOD was induced to commence the practice, but his principal occupation was that of trader and merchant which he continued until nearly the close of his life, which was spent at Prairie du Chien. He died at his home August 24, 1857. In an article prepared by him for the State Historical Society, published in the second volume of its collections, he says, when he arrived at Prairie du Chien

"There were four companies of riflemen under command of Brevet Major MORGAN, building the old fort. * * * JOHN W. JOHNSON, a gentleman from Maryland, was U. S. Factor, with Mr. BELT as assistant and book-keeper, and JOHN P. GATES as interpreter. Col. ALEXANDER MCNAIR, late Governor of Missouri, had the sutling of the fort, and his nephew, THOMAS MCNAIR, and JOHN L. FINDLEY were the clerks in his employ, and had charge of the business. (They were both afterwards superseded by WILFRED OWENS, of Kentucky.)

"There were then of the old traders residing at Prairie du Chien JOSEPH ROLETTE, MICHAEL BRISBOIS, FRANCIS BOUTHILLIER. JEAN BAPTISTE FARRIBAULT and NICHOLAS BOILVIN."

Mr. SHAW in his "Personal Narrative" gives the additional names of ANTOINE BRISBOIS, JEAN B. ST. JEAN. Messrs. TIERCOURT, BENNETT and PALEN. He says:

"ROLETTE was regarded as the largest trader there and reputed wealthy."

To quote further from Judge LOCKWOOD's article.

"Tradition says the place took its name from an Indian chief of the Fox tribe by the name of CHIEN or *Dog*, who had a village somewhere on the Prairie, near where Fort Crawford now stands. CHIEN or *Dog* is a favorite name among the Indians of the Northwest.

There were on the Prairie about forty farms cultivated along under the bluffs where the soil was first-rate, and enclosed in one common field, and the boundaries between them generally marked by a road that afforded them ingress and egress; the plantations running from the bluffs to the Mississippi on the slough of St. Friole, and from three to five arpents wide (35 to 55 rods wide—an arpent is 11 rods). The owners did not generally live immediately on their farms, but clustered together in little villages near their front. * * They were living in Arcadian simplicity, spending a great part of their time in fishing, hunting, horse-racing or trotting, or in dancing and drinking. * * * * They had no aristocracy among them except the traders who were regarded as a privileged class."
* * * * * * * * * * * * * * *

"Prairie du Chien was at this time an important post for Indian trade, and was considered by the Indians as neutral ground, where different tribes, although at war, might visit in safety; but if hostile they had to beware of being caught in the neighborhood, going or returning. Yet I never heard of any hostile movement on the Prairie, after they had safely arrived." * * * * * * * * * * * * * *

"At that time there were generally collected (annually) at Prairie du Chien, by the traders and United States factors, about three hundred packs, of one hundred pounds each, of furs and peltries—mostly fine furs. Of the different Indian tribes that visited and traded more or less at Prairie du Chien, there were the Menomonees from Green Bay, who frequently wintered on the Mississippi; the Chippewas, who resided on the headwaters of the Chippewa and Black rivers; the Foxes, who had a village where Cassville now stands, called Penah. *i. e.*, Turkey; the Sauks, who resided about Galena and Dubuque; the Winnebagoes, who resided on the Wisconsin river; the Iowas, who then had a village on the Upper Iowa river; WABASHAW's band of Sioux, who resided on a beautiful prairie on the Iowa side of the Mississippi, about 120 miles above Prairie du Chien, with occasionally a Kickapoo and Pottowatamie. The Sauks and Foxes brought from Galena a considerable quantity of lead."

The quantity of lead exchanged by the Indians for goods in one season (1810) is stated by NICHOLAS BOILVIN, in a letter to the Secretary of War, to have been four hundred thousand pounds.

In the spring of 1817 a Roman Catholic priest from St. Louis, called Father PRIERE, visited Prairie du Chien, but he did not long remain.

In 1819, the United States government having instructed Col. LEAVENWORTH to establish a military post at or near the mouth of the St. Peters river, on the land purchased in 1806, by Gen. PIKE, Maj. THOMAS FORSYTH, Indian agent, under instructions from the Department of War, left St. Louis on the 8th of June with a keel-boat loaded with goods to be delivered by him to the Sioux Indians above Prairie du Chien. Maj. FORSYTH arrived at the Prairie on the 5th of July, where he remained for more than a month waiting the arrival of the troops. Here RED WING's son was waiting for him, and THE LEAF, the principal chief of the Sioux, arrived that evening. Both begged importunately for goods. Maj. FORSYTH told them he could not give them any goods at that place; that he meant to go up with the troop to the River St. Peters, and would stop at their different villages and speak to them and give them a few goods.

On the 8th of August, a part of the troops having arrived and the remainder being reported on the way, Col. LEAVENWORTH and Maj. FORSYTH set out for St. Peters river with the troops, consisting of ninety-eight rank and file and fourteen batteaux and two large boats, loaded with provisions and ordnance, and stores of different kinds, besides Maj. FORSYTH's boat and goods and the colonel's barge. The whole expedition arrived at their destination on the 24th of August, and the post was established immediately at the mouth of the St. Peters, which was occupied by the government for many years and known as Fort Snelling.

Two companies of the Fifth Infantry accompanied Col. LEAVENWORTH to Prairie du Chien, and occupied Fort Crawford, under command of Maj. MUHLENBERG.

At the session of Congress of 1819-20, an act was passed to take testimony relative to the private land claims at Sault St. Mary, Mackinaw, Green Bay, and Prairie du Chien, which were reserved to subjects of the British government under JAY'S treaty; and in the fall of 1820 commissioners were dispatched to the different places to take testimony.

A Mr. LEE came to Prairie du Chien. Most of the claims here came under JAY'S treaty, but several did not. At a subsequent session of Congress an act was passed giving to every settler who was in possession of land at the date of the declaration of war against Great Britain in 1812, and who had continued to submit to the laws of the United States, the lands he claimed. In consequence of the attitude of some of these settlers toward the government during the war with England, the patents were delayed, to their great annoyance and injury.

On the 17th of September, 1821, an act was adopted by the Governor and Judges of Michigan Territory, to incorporate "The Borough of Prairie des Chiens." It provided for the annual election of a warden, two burgesses, a clerk, treasurer, and marshal. That the borough in legal meeting assembled should have power to levy taxes, to be collected by the marshal. That the wardens and burgesses might lay out highways, streets, and public walks, and should have other specified powers to provide for an effective municipal government.

The borough was duly organized, and JOHN W. JOHNSON was elected the warden, and the first burgesses were M. BRISBOIS and THOMAS MCNAIR. The organization was kept up for three years, and in 1825 it was discontinued by nonuser. The last warden was JOSEPH ROLETTE, and the last burgesses were M. BRISBOIS and JAMES H. LOCKWOOD.

Col. HERCULES L. DOUSMAN came to Prairie du Chien in the autumn of 1827 in the employ of the American Fur Company, where he continued to reside until his death Sept. 12, 1868. He was greatly respected and highly esteemed and accumulated an ample fortune, which he used liberally in promoting the growth and prosperity of his adopted home.

In 1828, Gen. JOSEPH M. STREET came to Prairie du Chien

having been appointed Indian agent. The next year he brought his family, which was the first one settled at that place that made a profession of religion in the Protestant faith.

THOMAS P. BURNETT was appointed sub-Indian agent in October, 1829, under Gen. STREET, and came to Prairie du Chien in June, 1830.

By a proclamation of Gov. CASS, dated October 26, 1818, by virtue of the ordinance of 1787, the county of Michilimackinac was laid out, the southern boundary of which was

"The dividing ground between the rivers which flow into Lake Superior, and those which flow south."

By another proclamation of Gov. CASS, of the same date, all of the Territory of Michigan, south and west of the county of Michilimackinac, was divided into two counties which were separated

"By a line drawn due north from the northern boundary of the State of Illinois through the middle of the portage between the Fox river and Ouissin (Wisconsin) river, to the county of Michilimackinac."

The eastern county was called "Brown" in honor of the then commanding general of the army; the other was called "Crawford" in compliment to the then Secretary of War.

The following day, Oct. 27th, the following appointments were made by Gov. CASS:

For Brown county, MATTHEW IRWIN, Chief Justice, Commissioner and Judge of Probate; CHARLES REAUME, Associate Justice and Justice of the Peace; JOHN BOWYER, Commissioner; ROBERT IRWIN, Jr., Clerk; and GEORGE JOHNSTON, Sheriff. For Crawford county, NICHOLAS BOILVIN and JOHN W. JOHNSON, Justices of the Peace.

The following appointments for Crawford county were made by Gov. CASS May 12th, 1819, viz.: JOHN W. JOHNSON, Chief Justice; MICHAEL BRISBOIS and FRANCIS BOUTHILLIER, Associate Justices; WILFRED OWENS, Judge of Probate; NICHOLAS BOILVIN, JOHN W. JOHNSON and JAMES H. LOCKWOOD, Justices of the Peace; THOMAS McNAIR, Sheriff; JOHN L. FINDLEY, Clerk; HYACINTH ST. CYR and OLIVER SHARRIER, Supervisors of Roads; and JOHN P. GATES, Register of Probate and *ex-officio* Recorder of Deeds.

Gov. CASS sent by Col. LEAVENWORTH, when on his way to the St. Peters River, blank commissions for the different officers of Crawford county, to be filled up with such names as should be selected by the inhabitants. They assembled and selected the persons above named.

The first court held in Brown county of which any record is preserved, was a special session of the county court, held July 12, 1824, JACQUES PORLIER Chief Justice; JOHN LAWE and HENRY B. BREVOORT, Associates. These judges had superseded those first appointed in 1818.

In 1828, JOHN W. JOHNSON and FRANCES BOUTHILLIER having removed away, JOSEPH ROLETTE was appointed Chief Justice and JEAN BRUNET, Associate Justice. Subsequently in 1830, the county court was re-organized and General JOSEPH M. STREET was appointed Chief Justice and JAMES H. LOCKWOOD and HERCULES L. DOUSMAN Associate Justices.

The first term of the county court of Crawford county was held at Prairie du Chien, May 12, 1823, FRANCES BOUTHILLIER and JOSEPH ROLETTE, Judges. A grand jury was impaneled but no indictments were found. No criminal business and but little civil business was done and after granting two tavern licenses and making a decree that "the proceedngs" of JAMES H. LOCKWOOD are legal and proper, adjourned.

The next year, May 11, 1824, the court, composed of the same judges, met and adjourned until the 17th of the same month "for want of juries."

On the 17th a grand jury was impaneled and returned an indictment against J. B. MAYNARD, who was duly called but came not, and the court ordered that

"On his arrival at this place, he do enter in recognizance for his appearance at the next term of this court to answer and plead, etc."

No other term of the court was held until May, 1826, and after that, no other until 1830. In November, 1830, a term was held with JOSEPH ROLETTE as Chief Justice and JEAN BRUNETT, Associate Justice.

THOMAS P. BURNETT, a lawyer from Kentucky, was admitted to practice in the court.

A grand jury was impaneled and found eight indictments for selling liquor by "small measure."

The court adopted rules of practice and thereafter the business in court was transacted more systematically.

The next term of the court was in November, 1831, when JOSEPH M. STREET was Chief Justice and JAMES H. LOCKWOOD and JEAN BRUNETT were Associate Justices. It seems that Mr. DOUSMAN, who had been appointed, did not accept the position.

The history of the settlements at Green Bay and Prairie du Chien is now brought down to a time when they cease to have a purely local interest. As settlements were now beginning to grow up in other parts of the Territory, especially in the lead mines, the subsequent historical events connected with these two principal settlements form a legitimate part of the history of the whole.

CHAPTER IX.

CHEQUAMEGON—PORTAGE—MILWAUKEE.

CHEQUAMEGON.

The early settlement at Chequamegon, on Lake Superior— if it can be called a settlement—earlier, even, than Green Bay, is not especially noticed for the reason that, although it was the field of the first missionary labors within the limits of Wisconsin, as early as 1665, yet its growth was confined to missionary work, which was quite limited, and it has never, until a very recent period, acquired any importance in any other respect.

Very soon after the conquest of Canada by the English, a company of adventurers from England undertook to work the copper mines of Lake Superior. They, however, met with but little success, and soon relinquished their scheme. They had long been preceded by others, as there is abundant evidence of the working of these mines at some far distant period, and by some unknown people. In some cf the old mines not only stone hammers have been found, but a copper gad, much battered; a copper chisel, with a socket for the handle; a copper knife, fragments of a wooden bowl, numerous levers of wood, remnants of charcoal, and pits have been sunk following the course of veins extending in continuous lines, and upon a mound of earth thrown out of one of them, grew a pine tree ten feet in circumference, and upon another a hemlock tree was cut, the annular growths of which counted 395 years. These evidences of a prehistoric people excite our curiosity without satisfying it.

PORTAGE.

The settlement at the "Portage" was so nearly contemporary with that at Green Bay and Prairie du Chien as to be worthy of notice in the same connection. The first white men to visit the "Portage" were JOLIET and MARQUETTE, and their guides and companions, five in number, who "made the portage" in June, 1673, and reached the Mississippi river on the 17th of that month, although NICOLET was at Green Bay in 1634, and ascended the Fox river some distance, probably as far as the portage. Seven years later (1680) HENNEPIN and DU LUTH reached the portage on their return from the falls of St. Anthony. LE SUEUR and his party made the portage in 1683, on his way to the Mississippi.

The first settler at the portage was LAURENT BARTH. He was a trader from Mackinaw. Returning in the spring of 1793, with his family, from the St. Croix river, where he had traded the previous winter in company with JACQUES PORLIER and CHARLES REAUME, of Green Bay, he stopped here and purchased from the Winnebagoes the privilege of transporting goods over the portage. This was the commencement of the settlement at that point. The Indian habitations near there increased immediately, but the settlement was not augmented much by white men for many years. BARTH first built a house on the low ground, but it became overflowed, and he removed the next year to the high ground half a mile above.

The next settler was JEAN L'ECUYER, who went there in 1798, and who also obtained permission to transport goods over the portage. The goods were hauled over in carts. BARTH had at first only a single-horse cart, but when L'ECUYER came he had several teams and carts, and had also a heavy wagon with a long reach, and so constructed as to transport barges.

About 1803 BARTH sold to Mr. CAMPBELL, who was appointed a few years later the first American Indian agent at Prairie du Chien, all his right of transportation, and then removed to Prairie du Chien, where he died before the war of 1812.

CAMPBELL soon after sold out his fixtures to L'ECUYER, who supposed that CAMPBELL intended to relinquish the business; but he placed his two sons, JOHN and DUNCAN, there, and had several teams to convey goods and a large wagon to transport barges. CAMPBELL is the same man who was killed at Mackinaw in a duel with one CRAWFORD, soon after which his business was closed up. In about two years afterwards L'ECUYER sickened and died leaving several children.

After L'ECUYER's death his widow employed LAURENT FILY to carry on the business for her, and he continued it till about 1812, when FRANCIS ROY married a daughter of Mrs. L'ECUYER and took charge of the business and continued it many years.

Sometime after the war with England JOSEPH ROLETTE carried on the transportation business at the portage employing PIERRE PAUQUETTE to manage it for him. The usual charge for transporting goods across the portage was forty cents per 100 pounds, and ten dollars for each boat, but extortions were often practiced upon those who would submit to them.

There was always, after BARTH went to Portage, a considerable Indian trade there. He sold the remnant of the stock which he brought from the St. Croix; and L'ECUYER always kept a large assortment of goods, as did his widow and her son-in-law, ROY. CAMPBELL had goods one year. LAURENT FILY who had been a clerk for L'ECUYER was located there several years as a trader, and died at Grand Kau-kau-lin in 1846, at the age of eighty-three years. AUGUSTIN GRIGNON spent two winters in trade there from 1801 to 1803 and JACQUES PORLIER early spent two or three winters there.

For thirty-five years after BARTH went there, the number of white settlers at the portage did not increase, there being no business except the transportation across the portage and a small Indian trade; but the location and erection of Fort Winnebago at that point effected a very great change.

Previous to the Indian War of 1827, it had been common for RED BIRD's band of Winnebago Indians to levy contributions on the traders while crossing the portage. In consequence of this, and for the protection of the now increasing population from the hostility of the Indians, Major (afterwards General) DAVID E. TWIGGS, was ordered to the portage in the summer of 1828 with three companies of the 1st Infantry to build a fort. The officers of his command were Capt. Brevet Maj. BEALL; Capt. SPENCER; Capt. (afterwards General) HARNEY; 1st Lieut. GAINES MILLER; 1st Lieut. JEFF. DAVIS, who was also quartermaster (President of the Confederate States); 1st Lieut. (afterwards General) ABERCROMBIE; 2nd Lieut. BEALL, afterward General in the Confederate army; 2nd Lieut. (afterwards General) BURBANK and 2nd Lieut. LAMOTTE. A beautiful plateau of ground was selected on the east side of Fox River, which gracefully meandered around three sides of the selected site. It was elevated forty or fifty feet above the river and had a commanding view of the surrounding country for a considerable distance. Upon this plateau was erected Fort Winnebago. The officers and soldiers lived in tents, until temporary log barracks were built, in which they spent the winter of 1828-9. Parties of soldiers were sent up the Wisconsin River where they cut and floated down pine logs, and during the winter they were employed in cutting the logs into lumber and timber with whip-saws, and in making shingles. Brick were made near the Wisconsin River, and lime was obtained at Bellefontaine, about twelve miles northeast. The erection of the buildings was commenced in 1829, but the fort was not completed and enclosed till the summer of 1832. In 1828, the only houses at the portage were a log house in charge of PIERRE PAUQUETTE belonging to the American Fur Co., the Indian agency house occupied by JOHN H. KINZIE, sub-agent, two others occupied by half breeds, and a nice house owned by FRANCIS LeROY.

The 1st Regiment was relieved by four companies of the 5th Infantry in July, 1831.

In 1827, Congress appropriated $2,000 for the purpose of opening a road from Green Bay to the Wisconsin portage. In the year 1830 $5,000 was added to this sum, and the route extended to Fort Crawford; and in 1832 and 1833, an additional sum of $5,000 was appropriated in each year, making a total of $17,000 none of which had yet been expended.

Lieut. W. A. CENTRE and JAMES D. DOTY were appointed commissioners to make a reconnoisance of the country and a survey of the route. They completed their work in September, 1833. The route of the road from Green Bay, was on the east side of Fox River and Lake Winnebago, over the present traveled road through De Pere, Wrightstown, Stockbridge, Brothertown, Calumet, Taycheda, Fond du Lac, Lamartine, Green Lake, and Bellefontaine to Fort Winnebago. From Fort Winnebago the route passed through the present village of Poynette on the railroad from Portage to Madison, and through Cross Plains fourteen miles west of Madison on the railroad to Prairie du Chien. Five miles west of Cross Plains it came to the great dividing ridge, which divides the waters which flow into the Wisconsin River from those which flow southerly. It followed this ridge to within six miles of the mouth of the Wisconsin River, which was then crossed and the road then went to Fort Crawford.

The work of constructing this road was delayed until 1835, when it was opened and so far completed as to admit of travel. The force employed was the U. S. troops. From Green Bay to Fond du Lac, the troops were in charge of Lieut. ALEXANDER, and from Fond du Lac to Fort Crawford, in charge of Capt. HARNEY, Capt. Low and Capt MARTIN SCOTT.

In 1838 another appropriation of $5,000 was made by Congress for the completion of the road, which was mostly expended between Depere and Fond du Lac.

Previous to the settlement of Madison in 1837 and 1838, this was the only travelled route between Fort Winnebago and the western portion of the Territory.

The primitive manner of transporting goods up Fox River in Durham boats is thus described by Mr. HENRY MERRILL:

"It was necessary for them (the freighters) to assemble a large number of Indians at the Rapids to help them over with the boats. At Grand Kau-kau-lin, they had to unload and cart the goods about one mile, and the Indians going into the water pushed, lifted and hauled the boats over the rapids; then reloading them, poled them up to the Grand Chute, where Appleton is now situated. There they had to unload and carry the goods up a hill and down the other side above the Chute, which was a perpendicular fall of three or four feet. The Indians would wade in, as many as could stand around the boat, and lift it over while the others had a long cordelle, with a turn around a tree above, taking up the slack and pulling as much as they could. When the boats were over they were re-loaded and pushed ahead and poled from there to Fort Winnebago. Excepting in low water they would have to make half loads over the Winnebago Rapids at Neenah, and with a fair wind would sail through Lake Winnebago."

In 1834 HENRY MERRILL was offered the post of sutler at Fort Winnebago, which he accepted, went to New York, bought a stock of goods which he had shipped to that place, and entered upon his duties, and conducted a general mercantile business. He resided here from that time until his death, and acquired a handsome fortune. During his long residence in Portage he always commanded the greatest respect. He was a member of the Senate in the first State

Legislature. His name was intimately connected with that of the early settlers of Wisconsin. He died May 5, 1876, after a busy life, without a blemish on his record.

MILWAUKEE.

The settlement of Milwaukee by the whites cannot be said to date back earlier than 1834 or 1835. But, being the metropolis of the State, events connected with its anterior, and especially its very early, history, possess such a general interest as justifies a separate reference to them.

The earliest mention of Milwaukee, that has been found, is in a journal of Lieut. JAMES GORRELL, of the British army, who had command of the military post at Green Bay from October, 1761, to June, 1763. Under date of August 21, 1762, speaking of a party of Indians which had come from Milwaukee, he says:

"They made great complaint of the trader amongst them. * * * He came from Mishamakinak."

From the same journal, under date of March 25, 1763, it appears that—

"One GODDARD, a trader from Montreal, had sent orders to his clerk, a Canadian, to send word to the Milwacky Indians, and desire them not to come here (Green Bay), but stay at home, and he would send goods to them in the spring; the contrary of what he told them last fall."

These extracts furnish very satisfactory evidence that as early as 1762 there was an Indian town at Milwaukee, with an English trader there, who had come from Mackinaw, and was probably the same "GODDARD" who came to Green Bay with Capt. BELFOUR in October, 1761.

AUGUSTIN GRIGNON'S "Recollections," 3 Col. of Hist. So., p. 290-292, contain much information in relation to the early trade at Milwaukee with the Indians. From his statement it appears that ALEXANDER LA FRAMBOISE, from Mackinaw, was located at Milwaukee with a trading establishment at Mr. GRIGNON's earliest recollection—say 1785. After a while he returned to Mackinaw and sent a brother to manage the business for him, who remained there several years and raised a family.

In 1789 JEAN BAPTIST MIREANDEU, a Frenchman, had a blacksmith shop on the spot where the splendid chamber of commerce was erected in 1879-80.

About the year 1800, LA FRAMBOISE having failed, another trader established a post there, and employed as his clerk STANISLAUS CHAPPUE. This trading house was continued until about 1805. CHAPPUE died in 1854, a few miles above Marinet, on the Menomonee river.

While CHAPPUE was thus employed as clerk, and soon after he went there, JOHN B. BEAUBIEN also established a trading post there.

About 1804 or 1805 LAURENT FILY was sent with a supply of goods by JACOB FRANKS, of Green Bay, to carry on a summer trade at Milwaukee.

JACQUES VIEAU, of Green Bay, commenced trading at Milwaukee previous to 1805, and continued it regularly every winter—except that of 1811-12—until 1818, when SOLOMON JUNEAU, who had married his daughter, went there first as his clerk, and then on his own account. JUNEAU erected a permanent dwelling on a site which is now between Michigan and Huron streets, on the east side of East Water street, and became the first permanent and abiding settler, and lived to see the field of his Indian traffic become the theater of an immense commercial trade. He died in 1856.

After the war with Great Britain JAMES KINZIE was sent there by the American Fur Company with a stock of goods, but did not remain long; and HYPOLITE GRIGNON wintered at Milwaukee about the time Mr. JUNEAU went there.

The Green Bay *Intelligencer* of April 16, 1834, contains this editorial:

"The Milwaukee country is attracting much attention. A settlement has commenced near its mouth; and there can be no doubt it will be much visited during the coming season by northern emigrants, and by all who fear the bilious fevers and other diseases of more southern latitudes. Two or three young men from the State of New York have commenced the erection of a *saw-mill* on the first rapid, about three miles above the mouth of the Milwaukee river."

In May, 1835, the fractional township (T. 7, R. 22 E.), in which the city of Milwaukee is situated, was first offered at a public sale, to be held at Green Bay, August 31, 1835. Mr. JUNEAU purchased by right of pre-emption, and the common consent of those attending the land sale, a tract between the Milwaukee river and the lake. BYRON KILBOURN and his associates purchased an extensive tract on the west side of the Milwaukee river, which for some years was called Kilbourntown, and GEORGE H. WALKER made a claim on the south side of the river, for which he ultimately obtained a patent, and which was known as Walker's Point. Some of the most valuable tracts adjoining these were obtained by "floats," and in that mode or by cash purchases, nearly the entire township passed from the government to individuals.

Among those who came to Milwaukee in 1835 were DANIEL WELLS, Jr., W. W. GILMAN, GEORGE D. DOUSMAN, TALBOT C. DOUSMAN, E. W. EDGERTON, J. HATHAWAY, Jr., JAMES SANDERSON, JAMES CLYMAN, OTIS HUBBARD, SAMUEL BROWN, GEORGE O. TIFFANY, DANIEL H. RICHARDS, BENONI W. FINCH, GEORGE REED, ENOCH CHASE, HORACE CHASE, WILLIAM BROWN, Jr., MILO JONES, ENOCH DARLING, ALBERT FOWLER, C. HARMON, B. DOUGLASS, W. MAITLAND, ALANSON SWEET, HENRY WEST, JAMES H. ROGERS, SAMUEL HINMAN, Mr. LOOMIS, Dr. CLARKE, and Mr. CHILDS, and there were many others.

On the 12th of December, 1835, the first public meeting of citizens for public purposes was held at the house of Mr. CHILDS. B. W. FINCH was called to the chair, and Dr. ENOCH CHASE appointed secretary. The object of the meeting was stated by the chairman to be to adopt measures for petitioning Congress for appropriations for internal improvements, etc. Several committees were appointed to draft memorials, petitions, etc., and the meeting adjourned for one week.

On the 19th of December the meeting reassembled and, in the absence of the chairman, B. DOUGLASS was called to the chair. Petitions for the passage of a pre-emption law; for an appropriation for constructing a canal from Milwaukee to Rock river; and another for a light-house and harbor, were reported and adopted.

A committee, consisting of Lieut. CLYMAN, ALBERT FOWLER, ALANSON SWEET, and Drs. CHASE and CLARKE, was appointed to correspond with the settlers of the mining country on the subject of a communication between the two places.

ALANSON SWEET, HENRY WEST, and HORACE CHASE were appointed a committee to draft a petition to Congress for an appropriation to make the Chicago and Green Bay road.

A number of buildings were erected in 1835, and there was a wonderful spirit of speculation in lands, lots, and claims on the public lands.

CHAPTER X.

NEW YORK INDIANS.

From 1818 to 1822, there was a combination of influences dissimilar in motive but perfectly consonant in purpose, all operating simultaneously, which resulted in the removal of a part of the New York Indians, to lands secured for them near Green Bay.

The Holland Land Company, having a pre-emption right of purchasing from the Indians their reservations, which right had been confirmed by the state of New York, sold it in 1810 to DAVID A. OGDEN, who with his associates were known as the "Ogden Land Company." This company, for the purpose of extinguishing the Indian title and thereby perfecting its own, conceived the plan, in 1817-18, of securing in the West, by consent and aid of the general government, an extensive grant of land from the western tribes, as a home or hunting ground for the several tribes of the New York Indians. One of the first steps was to secure the consent and co-operation of the War Department.

The Stockbridge and Brothertown Indians had a small reservation of thirty-five square miles in Oneida county. These Indians, influenced by an educated and eloquent young chief, SOLOMON U. HEDRICK, and their resident missionary, JOHN SEARGEANT, became anxious to obtain a suitable tract of land west of the lakes to which they might remove and where they could have a permanent home. They obtained the influence and aid of the American Board of Missions, by which the late Dr. JEDEDIAH MORSE—whose name is identified with the history of education in America, by the publication of his Geography, Atlas and Gazetteer, and who was the father of S. F. B. MORSE the inventor of the electric telegraph—was induced to undertake the mission of selecting a proper location. Preliminary to this undertaking application was made to the Secretary of War, that he be commissioned to make a general tour among the northwestern Indians, with a view to forming a better understanding between them and the Government.

In 1816-17, ELEAZER WILLIAMS, the same who afterwards advanced the fictitious and preposterous claim to be the Dauphin of France, LOUIS 19th, appeared among the Oneida

Indians. Born among the St. Regis Indians, of which tribe his mother was a native, and with whom he had lived until he was fourteen years old, the Indian language was his native tongue. He spent his boyhood from the age of 14 to 19 in New England schools and acquired a good English education and was tolerably conversant with the Christian system and with theology. He was withal a natural orator and most graceful and powerful speaker. He was commissioned by Bishop HOBART as catechist and lay reader to the Oneida Indians. Great success attended his missionary work, as the result of which the Bishop confirmed about fifty communicants.

But the field for the labors of this missionary confined, as it was to about fifteen hundred Oneidas, was more limited than his ambition. Whether the idea originated with him, or whether it was suggested by the Ogden Land Company, or borrowed from the Stockbridges, he proposed to the Oneidas in 1818, a grand emigration scheme and a confederated Indian Government. This scheme contemplated that the Oneidas, and all other New York Indians, with many of those in Canada and the Senecas at Sandusky, should remove to the neighborhood of Green Bay, and there unite in one grand confederacy of cantons, but all under one federal head. The contemplated government was to be a mixture of civil, military and ecclesiastic, the latter to predominate. The older and more sober minded of the Oneida chiefs lent no favor to the plan, but some of the younger men were more captivated with it, and some of the young hereditary chiefs were drawn into it. He also enticed a few of the young men of each of the other tribes of the Six Nations, to enter into his scheme. He next addressed the War Department, soliciting its countenance and assistance to enable a delegation of twenty, from the several tribes of the Six Nations, to visit the western tribes, for the purpose of obtaining a cession of country for a new home.

The Southern States, and their representatives in Congress and in the executive departments, regarded with extreme jealousy the rapidly advancing power of the free States. By the ordinance of 1787, slavery was forever prohibited in any States to be formed in the Northwest Territory; and the northern boundary of Illinois was by an act of Congress purposely extended more than sixty miles north of the boundary prescribed by the ordinance, in the vain expectation that the country north of it could never acquire sufficient strength in wealth or numbers to claim admission as a State in the Union.

During the administration of Mr. MONROE, JOHN C. CALHOUN was Secretary of War, and lent his sanction to a plan to devote the territory west of Lake Michigan and north of Illinois as an Indian Territory, in which to colonize all the remaining tribes in the Northern States.

It excites no surprise, therefore, that the Secretary of War yielded a ready acquiescence in, and co-operation with, the plans and application of the Ogden Land Company, Dr. MORSE and Mr. WILLIAMS. The application which had been made in behalf of Dr. MORSE was granted, and he spent the summer of 1820 in visiting several of the northwestern tribes, fifteen days of which were spent at Green Bay, where he was the guest of Col. SMITH, and where he devoted his best efforts to securing a western retreat for the Stockbridge and other New York Indians.

In response to the application of Mr. WILLIAMS, the War Department gave orders to the several superintendents of Indian affairs, and commandants of military posts, to issue to the delegates of the different tribes of New York Indians, not exceeding twelve, certain amounts of rations, blankets, powder, lead, etc., and to facilitate their movements on their journey. A requisition also was ordered to be made on the naval officer at Detroit for a vessel to take the delegates from Detroit to Green Bay, if there was any fit for service.

A copy of these orders was furnished Mr. WILLIAMS, and on the 22d of July, 1820, he arrived with the delegation at Detroit and called on Gen. CASS, then Governor of Michigan Territory and superintendent of Indian affairs.

On his arrival at Detroit Mr. WILLIAMS learned that a treaty had been made with the Menomonees a few days before, in which they had ceded to the United States forty miles square of their land in the immediate vicinity of Fort Howard. This purchase of the very land Mr. WILLIAMS most desired, frustrated all his plans, and for the present, at least, defeated all his hopes; and as there was no government vessel there fit for service he, with his delegation of Indians, retraced their steps to the State of New York. That State took the cause of the Indians in its keeping, and the treaty was rejected by the Senate, and this impediment to the emigration project was removed.

The next year a similar order was made by the War Department, and Mr. WILLIAMS, with fourteen delegates from the tribes of Stockbridge, Oneida, Onondaga, Tuscarora, Seneca, and St. Regis Indians, being joined at Detroit by C. C. TROWBRIDGE, deputed by Gov. CASS, proceeded to Green Bay, where they arrived August 5, 1821. A very large portion of the Menomonees, influenced by the French inhabitants, the traders, and many of the half-breeds, were opposed to any cession of lands. But on the 18th of August a treaty was made, signed by some of the chiefs and head men of the Winnebagoes and Menomonees, by which the land was ceded from Grand Kau-kau-lin to the rapids at the Winnebago lake, and extending on each side of the river, up and down, equi-distant with the lands claimed by the Menomonees and Winnebagoes. This treaty was approved by the President of the United States, but its validity was always denied by a large part of the Menomonees.

On returning to New York, Mr. WILLIAMS found a more formidable opposition to his proceedings than he had met at Green Bay. A large part of the Stockbridges, Oneidas, Onondagas, Tuscaroras and all the Senecas were opposed to the treaty.

In 1822 a new order was obtained from the War Department, which still continued to favor the enterprise, providing for another visit to Green Bay. The delegation was larger than that of the previous year, and JOHN SARGEANT, Jr., succeeded Mr. TROWBRIDGE, on the part of the United States. They reached Green Bay the 1st of September. The Winnebagoes and Menomonees were soon assembled at the agency house at Green Bay, but the Winnebagoes refused all further negotiations, and soon retired up the river. After making the payments agreed upon in the treaty of the previous year, followed by feasting, dancing and a general hilarity of two days, there was much negotiation and a conference which continued for several days, the result of all of which was that on the 23rd day of September, 1822, a new treaty was made between the chiefs assuming to represent the Menomonees, and those assuming to represent the Stockbridge, Oneida, Tuscarora, St. Regis and Munsee Indians, by which the former tribe purport to cede to the latter tribes, all their lands, east, north and west of those ceded the previous year.

This treaty was approved by the President, March 13, 1823, with some modifications of the boundaries.

A small party of about fifty Stockbridges located late in the fall of this year, at the Grand Kau-kau-lin on the east side of the river, and were joined the next year by a party of Munsees. A small party of the Brothertowns reached Green Bay the second year (1823) and located at Little Kau-kau-lin on the east side of the river. A small party of Oneidas came at the same time and located at the same place where they remained until 1825, when they removed to Duck Creek.

The treaty of 1822 excited, if possible, more opposition among the Menomonees, than that of the previous year and a large part of the tribe, probably a majority, were determined that they would disregard it. There was no less opposition to the treaty among most of the New York Indians who were resolvod not to emigrate.

On the 11th of August, 1827, a treaty was made at Butte des Morts between Gov. CASS and THOMAS L. McKINNEY, commissioners on the part of the United States, and the Chippewas, Menomonees and Winnebagoes, the chief object of which was to declare the boundaries between these tribes. In the second article of this treaty it is declared that the difficulties between the Menomonee and Winnebago tribes, and the tribes or portions of tribes of the State of New York, and the claims of the respective parties, as well with relation to tenure and boundaries as to the authority of the persons who signed the treaties, be referred to the President of the United States, whose decision should be final. The resolution of the Senate, ratifying this treaty, contained a provision, that it should not affect any right or claim of the New York Indians, which destroyed the effect of the second article of the Cass treaty.

In 1830, ERASTUS ROOT and JAMES MCCALL of New York, and JOHN T. MASON, Secretary of Michigan Territory, were appointed commissioners by the United States to effect an adjustment of the whole matter between the Wisconsin Indians and the New York Indians. Eight days were spent in council and every effort made to reconcile the Menomonees to the claims in whole or in part of the New York Indians. Nothing could be done. The Menomonees were inflexible. They would agree to nothing except that, as the New York Indians were in the country, they might stay during good behavior, but must be regarded as tenants at will and having no interest in the land.

About this time Col. SAMUEL C. STAMBAUGH was appointed Indian agent at Green Bay by General JACKSON. On the 8th of November, 1830, he left Green Bay with a delegation of fourteen Menomonee chiefs to visit Washington with a view to making a treaty there for the sale of a part of their lands to the United States. On their arrival there on the 11th of December, the President appointed Gen. EATON, Secretary of War, and Col. STAMBAUGH, commissioners to make a treaty.

After several delays and much informal negotiation the Commissioners and the Menomonees met and on the 8th of February 1831, agreed upon a treaty, in which it was provided that a tract of land should be set apart as a home for the New York Indians bounded as follows: Beginning on the west side of Fox River, near the little Kau-kau-lin at the 'Old Mill Dam'; then northwest forty miles; then northeast to the Oconto river; then down the Oconto, and up and along Green Bay and Fox River to the place of beginning containing about 500,000 acres, excluding private claims and the military reservation. The treaty in the first article limited the time of the removal and settlement of the New York Indians upon the lands to three years. It further provided in the sixth article, that if the New York Indians then in Wisconsin, should not remove to and settle on the ceded land within three years, the President should direct their immediate removal from the Menomonee country. On the 17th day of February, 1831, a supplementary article was added to the treaty, which provided, that instead of the limitation of three years contained in the first article, the President should prescribe the time for the removal and settlement, and that the removal of the Indians, mentioned in the sixth article, should be left discretionary with the President.

This treaty not having been acted upon at the session which terminated March 4th, 1831, a further stipulation was made on the 15th of March, that it should be laid before the Senate at its next session, with the same effect as at the late session.

The amendments made on the 17th February did not reconcile the New York Indians to the treaty, and they renewed their opposition to it at the next session. The result was that the treaty was ratified by the Senate on the 25th June, 1832, with an amendment in the interest of the New York Indians, which provided that two townships of land on the east side of Winnebago Lake, equal to forty-six thousand and eighty acres, should be laid off for the use of the Stockbridge and Munsee tribes, and one township adjoining, equal to twenty-three thousand and forty acres, should be laid off and granted for the use of the Brothertown Indians; and that the Stockbridge, Munsee and Brothertown Indians should relinquish to the United States all their claims to any other lands, on the east side of Fox River, and that the United States should pay the Indians for their improvements thereon.

The amendment of the Senate also provided that the southwestern boundary of the 500,000 acre tract on the western side of the Fox River, should be extended southwesterly far enough to add to it 200,000 acres, and that the same number of acres should be taken from the northeast side.

On the 27th October, 1832, a council was held at Green Bay, by GEORGE B. PORTER, Governor of Michigan Territory, commissioned for that purpose by the President, with the representatives of the Menomonees, Stockbridges, Munsees, Brothertowns, St. Regis and Six Nations. The Menomonees assented without objection to so much of the Senate amendment as related to the three townships of land on the east side of Lake Winnebago, but proposed a modification of the southwestern boundary line of the 200,000 acres added on the southwest side, not however affecting the quantity of land added. All the New York Indians, including the St. Regis and Six Nations (generally known as Oneidas), accepted and agreed to the Senate amendments, with the modification proposed by the Menomonees, and requested that they might be ratified and approved by the President and Senate of the United States.

The conflict with the Wisconsin Indians, which had its origin in the three separate schemes of the Ogden Land Company to make its pre-emption rights available, of the Stockbridge, Munsee and Brothertown Indians, to obtain a more desirable home, and of ELEAZER WILLIAMS to build up a grand Indian nation, fostered and encouraged as these schemes were by JOHN C. CALHOUN, to render it impossible that more free states should be organized out of the Northwest Territory, by setting it apart for the sole dominion of Indian tribes, was now terminated. This conflict had continued for more than twelve years, and the result had fallen so far short of the grand hopes and castles in the air, built by WILLIAMS, that he abandoned forever his Utopian scheme and devoted his time to the establishment of his more visionary fiction, that he was the Dauphin—the " Lost Prince" of the house of the Bourbons.

The schemes of the Ogden Land Company, of relegating to the wilds of Wisconsin the Indians who occupied the lands in New York, which the company coveted so much, was attended with the same disaster, and the project of obtaining a home for them near Green Bay was abandoned, to be succeeded by a provision for their transfer a few years later to a reservation made west of Missouri, in the southeastern part of what has since become the State of Kansas, where a reservation of nearly two million acres was, by treaty, entered into January 15, 1838, made for—

"A permanent home for all the New York Indians now residing in the State of New York or in Wisconsin, or elsewhere in the United States."

The hopes of the Secretary of War, and of all others who shared them, of abridging the area of freedom, were also disappointed.

The New York Indians, who had removed or desired to remove to Green Bay, were the only parties to the original plan of emigration that were satisfied with the result. The whole of the Stockbridges, Brothertowns, and part of the Munsees, with about eleven hundred Oneidas, moved soon after to their respective locations, and the community of the Oneidas has been continually augmented by the annual accession of small parties from New York.

By a treaty made with the United States, February 3, 1838, the Oneida Indians, in consideration of $33,500, ceded to the United States all their title and interest in the land set apart to them by the treaties of 1831 and 1832, reserving a tract of one hundred acres to each individual of the Oneidas, to be surveyed by the government as soon as practicable, so as to include all their settlements and improvements.

By this treaty the possessions of the Six Nations were reduced to a tract of about eight miles by twelve, containing about sixty-one thousand acres. About two thousand of these people now live on this tract, who are slowly progressing in civilization. There is a missionary church and school in the settlement, under the fostering care of the Protestant Episcopal church. About one hundred and fifty families, comprising about seven hundred and fifty persons, compose the church congregation, of whom about two hundred and fifty are communicants.

The Brothertown Indians had entirely laid aside their aboriginal character, to the extent even of having lost their vernacular, and adopted the English language, and were in a fit situation to abandon their tribal relations and become citizens of the United States. Congress, therefore, by an act approved March 3, 1839, provided that the township of land granted for their use by the Menomonees, should be partitioned and divided among the different individuals composing the Brothertown tribe, and be held by them separately and severally in fee simple. And that thereafter each of them should be citizens of the United States, and their rights as a tribe or a nation should cease and determine. Since then they have been recognized as citizens; have been elected members of the Legislature, and to other offices under the Territorial and State governments, and have become homogeneous with the other inhabitants of the State.

CHAPTER XI.

THE LEAD MINES AND WINNEBAGO WAR.

The history of General SMITH is as complete in relation to the Indian disturbances in Wisconsin, as to the early explorations of the valley of the Mississippi, and this chapter is largely made up of extracts from that rare and valuable work.

Indian wars with their attendant horrors and savage atrocities have ever been concomitants of the primitive permanent settlement of every part of the American continent from those which followed the settlements at Jamestown and Plymouth to the latest conflicts with the savages of the Territories.

Indian traders in the Northwest were suffered to pursue their vocation for nearly two hundred years without molestation, for the reason, doubtless, that the articles of traffic which they exchanged for furs and peltries contributed to the gratification of the tastes of the aborigines and to their success in hunting, fishing and trapping.

Besides the few missionaries who gave no offense to the Indians, and who were the apostles of the gospel of peace, there were no inhabitants who were not directly or remotely connected with the Indian trade, who for reasons already stated were suffered to pursue their vocation during this long period without interruption. Moreover, a large proportion of these traders were Frenchmen, many of whom had intermarried with the Indians of the various tribes, and their hybrid progeny exerted a powerful influence in creating a kindly feeling towards all French people.

But very different feelings pervaded the savage breast towards those who came to occupy the country for agricultural purposes; and, consequently, as they rightly believed, to impair its value for their nomadic use. And most especially were the Winnebago Indians jealous of, and determinedly opposed to, any intrusion upon or occupation of the country, which should threaten to interfere with their exclusive occupancy of the Lead Mine Region, the sole right to which east of the Mississippi, was claimed by that tribe.

Mr. JOHN SHAW has been already mentioned as having been engaged between 1815 and 1820, in running a trading boat between St. Louis and Prairie du Chien. In one of those trips he was anxious to visit the Lead Mines at Galena, with one of his trading boats, but was told by the Indians that the "white man must not see their Lead Mines;" but as he spoke French fluently, he was supposed to be a Frenchman, and was permitted to go up the Fever river with his boat, where he found at least twenty smelting places of which he has given the following description:

"A hole or cavity was dug in the face of a piece of sloping ground, about two feet in depth and as much in width at the top; this hole was made in the shape of a mill-hopper, and lined or faced with flat stones. At the bottom or point of the hopper, which was about 8 or 9 inches square other narrow stones were laid across grate-wise; a channel or eye was dug from the sloping side of the ground inwards to the bottom of the hopper. This channel was about a foot in width and in height, and was filled with dry wood and brush. The hopper being filled with the mineral and the wood ignited, the molten lead fell through the stones at the bottom of the hopper; and this was discharged through the eye, over the earth, in bowl-shaped masses called 'plats,' each of which weighed about seventy pounds.

THE LEAD MINES AND WINNEBAGO WAR. 117

The first occupation of the lead mines by white men was in 1822, when Col. JAMES JOHNSON, brother of the famous RICHARD M. JOHNSON, took possession with a small party of men, under the protection of several detachments of troops sent forward by order of the War Department. A very few persons, probably not more than twenty, spent the ensuing winter at Galena.

Col. MORGAN was then in command at Fort Crawford, and had charge of the troops, and some sort of treaty or agreement was probably made between him and Col. JOHNSON on the one part, and the Indians on the other, by which the occupancy by the whites was assented to; but whatever it was, it does not appear to have been ratified by, if ever submitted to, the Senate.

In 1823, some accessions were made to the population; and in August, by a census then taken, there were seventy-four persons, men, women and children, of whom a number were negroes. The total product of lead shipped that year was 425,000 pounds.*

There was a slight increase of immigration in 1824, and the mines at Hazel Green and New Diggings were discovered, and worked with great profit.

Two officers of the ordinance department—Maj. ANDERSON and Lieut. BURDINE—were sent out to protect the interests of the government; and subsequently Lieut. MARTIN THOMAS was appointed superintendent of the mines.

The fame of the Upper Mississippi lead mines, and their fabulous value and richness, had been spread far and wide throughout the Mississippi Valley; and by the year 1825, the desire for gain and love of adventure and spirit of migration had taken possession of its inhabitants, especially in Illinois, Missouri, Kentucky and Tennessee, so that the determination to occupy and utilize these mines of wealth

---

*"Amount of lead manufactured:

In 1825	439,473 lbs.
1826	1,560,536 lbs.
1827	6,824,389 lbs.
1828	12,957,100 lbs.
1829—first quarter	2,494,441 lbs.

"Estimated number of inhabitants:

In 1825	200
1826	1,000
1827	4,000
1828	10,000

"About one-twentieth are females, and one hundred are free blacks."

could no longer be restrained by any pretensions of the red man to the exclusive right of their possession.

The time had now come when this beautiful country was to be occupied by a hardy, resolute, adventurous and persevering population. The laws which, as a rule, generally confine the migration of the human race to isothermal zones and similarity of climate, were to be set at defiance, and the emigrant from the mild climate of Tennessee, Kentucky, Missouri and southern Illinois was to exchange the balmy and genial atmosphere to which he had been accustomed, for one in which during nearly half the year all nature is bound with icy chains and covered with its robe of snow. But no matter! The migratory spirit stimulated by the greed for suddenly acquired wealth, and the irrepressible love of adventure, had taken possession of the pioneer immigrants to the lead mines, and the years of 1825 and 1826 witnessed a rush of emigration which had never before had its parallel, and the like of which has never since been seen, unless in the migration to California some twenty or more years subsequently.

These pioneers came in search of lead, and nearly all with the expectation of soon getting rich and returning to the homes they left behind them. Many came in the spring and returned upon the approach of winter, thus exhibiting so close a resemblance to some of the piscatory tribe that they received the designation of "suckers," and the results of their temporary and unsystematic labor were known as "sucker holes."

Others, however—some attracted by success and some compelled by the necessities resulting from ill luck — remained, and soon became permanently attached to the country, which they had visited at first only as an adventurous experiment.

Galena was the objective point of all the earliest immigrants, as it was the first point at which their mining and smelting operations were begun. But the mines in the immediate vicinity of Galena were not adequate to meeting the wants and expectations of the thousands of adventurers who were flocking to it, and they sought new fields of discovery, and many with such success that it soon became evident that the extent of the lead district was far greater than their first impressions had led them to suppose. Mines were soon opened at Hardscrabble, Council Hill, Vinegar

THE LEAD MINES AND WINNEBAGO WAR. 119

Hill, East Fork, New Diggings, Buncome, Natches, Gratiot's Grove, Shullsburg, Stump Grove, Wiota, Sinsinniwa, Menomonie, Big Patch, Platteville, Snake Hollow, Beetown, Rattle Snake, Crow Branch, Strawberry, Mineral Point, Dodgeville, Blue Mound, Sugar River and at many other points.

Such was the march of progress in the development of these newly discovered lead mines, that during the first three years of their occupancy, and before the Indian title was extinguished, the lead product exceeded fifteen million pounds, and this, notwithstanding the continued disturbance of the settlers by Indian hostilities, against which they were wholly dependent upon themselves for protection, until, by their own well directed efforts, governmental protection was no longer necessary.

During these first three years of the settlement of the lead mines, the pioneer occupants of the hunting grounds of the Winnebagoes lived in constant apprehension of the resentment of this numerous and savage tribe, who regarded such occupancy as an unwarranted invasion of their country, for which they appeared determined to be revenged.

In the summer of 1825 a grand council, or treaty, was held at Prairie du Chien, with the different tribes of Indians. Gov. CASS, of Michigan, and Gen. CLARK, of Missouri, superintendents of Indian affairs for their respective regions, were commissioners on the part of the United States. The Indian tribes represented were the Sioux, Sauks and Foxes, Chippewas, Winnebagoes, Menomonees, Iowas, and a portion of the Ottawa, Chippewa, and Potawatomie tribes living upon the Illinois. The object of this treaty was to make a general and lasting peace between these tribes, and also to settle the boundaries between them respectively. Gov. CASS, when asked what good he thought would result from it, shrugged his shoulders and smiling, said: "They would have it so at Washington." A treaty of perpetual peace was made, and the boundaries settled between the different tribes, which resulted in keeping the Indians at peace—until they were ready again to go upon the war-path.

In October, 1826, by a positive order from Washington, the troops were removed from Fort Crawford, up the river to Fort Snelling, and Fort Crawford was abandoned, the commandant taking with him two Winnebago Indians who had been confined in the guard-house for some supposed offense of a trivial nature. He left behind, in charge of the sub-Indian agent, a brass swivel, a few wall pieces, all the damaged arms, and some provisions. This removal induced the Winnebagoes to believe that the troops had fled through fear of them.

Several times during the winter of 1826-27, some of the older citizens of Prairie du Chien, who best understood the Indian character, and the peculiarities of the Winnebagoes — and especially Mr. MICHAEL BRISBOIS — expressed serious fears of some outrages from those Indians in the spring, and that they were bent on war. But it was generally thought impossible that, surrounded as they were with Americans and troops in the country, they should for a moment seriously entertain such an idea.

In March, 1827, one of the residents of Prairie du Chien named METHODE, went up Yellow, or Painted Rock creek, about twelve miles above the village, to make sugar. His wife, said to have been a most beautiful woman, accompanied him with her five children. Besides these and his faithful dog, the wolves and the trees were his only companions. The sugar season being over, and he not returning or being heard from, a party of his friends went to look for him. METHODE'S dog was first found, shot with half a score of balls, and yet holding in his dead jaws a piece of scarlet cloth, which he had apparently torn from an Indian legging. After further search the camp was found, consumed by fire. The whole party of seven had been killed, all — Madame METHODE in particular, she being *enceinte* — were shockingly mangled.

It afterward appeared that a party of Winnebagoes had been seen near Yellow creek, after METHODE had gone there, and one of them — Wa-man-doos-ga-ra-ka — having been arrested and examined, is said to have confessed his guilt, and implicated several others.

In the spring of 1827 a rumor was very extensively circulated among the Winnebagoes, and generally believed, that the two prisoners of their tribe who had been removed from Fort Crawford to Fort Snelling, had been turned over to the Chippewas, to run the gauntlet through a party of the latter tribe, armed with clubs and tomahawks, and the race for life had resulted in the killing of both of them. Something like this occurred with reference to some Sioux prisoners at Fort Snelling, but the story had no truth as applied to the Winnebago prisoners.

Hitherto the Winnebago chief, RED BIRD, had not only been well known at Prairie du Chien, but had the confidence and respect of all the inhabitants to such an extent that he was always sought after as a protector; and his presence was looked upon as a pledge of security against any outbreak that might be attempted.

When the unfounded rumors of the killing of the Winnebago prisoners at Fort Snelling were heard and believed, the leading chiefs held a council and resolved upon retaliation; and RED BIRD was called upon to go out and "take meat," as they phrase it. Beckoning to We-kau and another Indian named Chic-hon-sic, he told them to follow him. They proceeded to Prairie du Chien, and on the 26th of June went to the house of Hon. JAMES H. LOCKWOOD, who had left home the previous day, leaving his house in charge of his wife, her brother, a young man of sixteen, and a servant girl. RED BIRD and the other two Indians entered the cellar kitchen, loaded their guns in the presence of the servant girl, and went up through the hall into Mrs. LOCKWOOD's bedroom, where she was sitting alone. The moment they entered her room she believed they came to kill her, and immediately passed into and through the parlor, and crossed the hall into the store to her brother, where she found DUNCAN GRAHAM, who had been in the country about forty years as a trader, and was known by all the Indians as an Englishman. He had formerly been commandant at Prairie du Chien, when under British dominion. The Indians followed Mrs. LOCKWOOD into the store, and Mr. GRAHAM by some means induced them to leave the house.

RED BIRD and his savage accomplices then went the same day to MCNAIR's Coulee, about two miles southeast of the village, where lived RIJESTE GAGNIER and his wife with two small children—a boy three years old, and a daughter aged eleven months; and living with them was an old discharged soldier by the name of SOLOMON LIPCAP. The three Indians entered the cabin, and, such visits being common, were received with the usual civility, and were asked if they would have something to eat. They said yes, and would like some fish and milk. As Mrs. GAGNIER turned to get the fish and milk, she heard the click of RED BIRD's rifle, which was instantly followed by its discharge, and her murdered husband fell dead at her feet. At the same moment the Indian Chic-hon-sic shot and killed old LIPCAP; when Mrs. GAGNIER seeing We-kau, who had lingered about the door, she wrested from him his rifle; but from trepidation or some other cause was unable to use it, "feeling," as she expressed it, "like one in a dream, trying to call or to run, but without the ability to do either." She then, with her oldest child, and bearing the rifle with her, ran to the village and gave the alarm. A party of armed men returned with her, and brought away the two murdered men, and the infant which she had left covered up in the bed, which they found on the floor beneath it. The helpless child had been scalped by We-kau, who had inflicted upon its neck a severe cut to the bone, just below the occiput, from which she afterward recovered, and is still living, the mother of a family, but despoiled of the glory of her sex.

On the same day (June 26th), two keel boats commanded by Capt. ALLEN LINDSAY, which a few days before had ascended the river laden with provisions for the troops at Fort Snelling, passed the mouth of the Bad Axe on their way back to St. Louis. On the upward trip some hostile demonstrations had been made by the Dakotas, which induced Capt. LINDSAY to ask that his crew should be furnished with arms and ammunition. Col. SNELLING, the commanding officer, complied with his request, and the thirty-two men of which the crew consisted, were provided with thirty-two muskets and a barrel of ball cartridges. The Dakotas occupied the right bank of the river, and Capt. LINDSAY and his men were on their guard against any attack from them; but they had no apprehension of any attack from the Winnebagoes who occupied the left bank of the Mississippi.

The village of Wa-ba-shaw, the site of the present town of Winona, was the lowest point on the river at which they expected to encounter the Dakotas. Having passed this point in safety, and a strong wind having sprung up, the boats parted company, and one of them, the O. H. Perry, by the time it reached the mouth of the Bad Axe, was several miles in advance of the other.

In the meantime thirty-seven Winnebagoes, inspired by the same common feelings of vengeance, cruelty and hate, which had led to the murder of METHODE and his family,

THE LEAD MINES AND WINNEBAGO WAR. 123

and which was, on that very day, instigating the invasion of the peaceful home of GAGNIER, and the murder of its inmates by RED BIRD, We-kau and Chic-hon-sic, had, in pursuance doubtless of a common purpose to exterminate the whites, concealed themselves upon an island in the Mississippi near the mouth of the Bad Axe, between which and the left bank of the river, it was known that the two keel-boats would pass on their return from Fort Snelling.

These boats, in model and size, were similar to ordinary canal boats, and furnished considerable protection from exterior attacks with small arms, to those on board, who concealed themselves below the gunwales.

As the "Perry" approached the island where these hostile savages were concealed, and when within thirty yards of the bank, the air suddenly resounded with the blood-chilling and ear piercing cries of the war-whoop, and a volley of rifle balls rained across the deck. Of the sixteen men on board, either from marvellous good luck, or because they were below deck, only one man fell at the first fire. He was a negro named Peter, his leg was dreadfully shattered, and he afterwards died of the wound.

The crew now concealed themselves in the boat below the water line, suffering it to float whithersoever the current and the high east wind might drive it. The second volley resulted in the instant death of one man, an American named Stewart, who had risen to return the first fire, and his musket protruding through a loop-hole, showed some Winnebago where to aim. The bullet passed directly through his heart, and he fell dead with his finger on the trigger of his undischarged gun.

The boat now grounded on a sand bar, and the Indians rushed to their canoes, intending to board it. The crew having recovered from their panic, and seeing that the only escape from savage butchery was vigorous war, seized their arms and prepared to give the enemy a warm reception. In one canoe containing several savages, two were killed, and in their dying struggles upset the canoe, and the rest were obliged to swim ashore, where it was some time before those who were not disabled by wounds could restore their arms to fighting order. Two of the Indians succeeded in getting on board the keel-boat, both of whom were killed. One fell into the water, and the other into the boat, in which he was carried down the river;

but in this hand-to-hand conflict the brave commander of the crew, named BEAUCHAMP, was killed by the first of these two boarders, who in his turn was killed by a daring sailor named JACK MANDEVILLE—called "SAUCY JACK," who shot the rash warrior through the head, and he fell overboard, carrying his gun with him.

MANDEVILLE now assumed command of the crew, whose numbers had been reduced to ten effective men. He sprang into the water on the sand bar for the purpose of shoving off the boat and escaping from their perilous position, and was followed by four resolute men of his crew. The balls flew thick and fast about them, passing through their clothes; but they persisted, and the boat was soon afloat. Seeing their prey escaping, the Winnebagoes raised a yell of mingled rage and despair, and gave the whites a farewell volley. It was returned with three hearty cheers, and ere a gun could be re-loaded, the boat had floated out of shooting distance, and the survivors were safe, arriving at Prairie du Chien about sunset the next day, the 27th of June.

The casualties of this engagement were, two of the crew killed, two mortally and two slightly wounded, while it is supposed that ten or twelve Indians were killed, and a great number wounded.

The other keel-boat, in which was Capt. LINDSAY, had on board Mr. WILLIAM J. SNELLING, a son of Col. SNELLING. Mr. SNELLING, the son, is the putative author of an interesting anonymous article in relation to the "Winnebago Outbreak of 1827," which was republished in the fifth volume of the Reports and Collections of the State Historical Society of Wisconsin, and from which many of the incidents now given are taken. Capt. LINDSAY's boat reached the mouth of the Bad Axe about midnight. The Indians opened a fire upon her, which was promptly returned; one ball only hit the boat, doing no damage; the others passed over harmless in the darkness through which she pursued her way, and arrived safely at Prairie du Chien on the 28th.

A slander upon Capt. LINDSAY and his crew is contained in REYNOLDS' "Life and Times," which ought not to escape contradiction. It is stated in this work that the two keel-boats, in ascending the river,

"Stopped at a large camp of the Winnebago Indians on the river, not far above Prairie du Chien. The boatmen made the Indians drunk—and no doubt were so themselves—

when they captured some six or seven squaws who were also drunk. These captured squaws were forced on the boats for corrupt and brutal purposes. But not satisfied with this outrage on female virtue, the boatmen took the squaws with them in the boats to Fort Snelling, and returned with them. When the Indians became sober and knew the injury done them in this delicate point, they mustered all their forces amounting to several hundred and attacked the boats in which the squaws were confined."

Mr. SNELLING, whose means of knowing the facts were far superior to those of the author of REYNOLDS' "Life and Times," in the paper to which reference has been made, in speaking of the ascent of these keel-boats, says:

"They passed the mouth of Black river with a full sheet, so that a few Winnebagoes who were there encamped, had some difficulty in reaching them with their canoes. They might have taken both boats, for there were but three fire-locks on board; nevertheless, they offered no injury. They sold fish and venison to the boatmen on amicable terms, and suffered them to pursue their journey unmolested. We mention this trifling circumstance merely because it was afterwards reported in the St. Louis papers, that the crews of these boats had abused these Winnebagoes shamefully, which assuredly was not the case."

It is probable that the St. Louis papers were the authority upon which the statement now contradicted was made. Mr. SNELLING also says, that "thirty-seven Indians were engaged in this battle."

The inhabitants in and about Prairie du Chien were generally and very greatly alarmed. They left their houses and farms, and crowded into the now dilapitated fort, and speedily established a very effective discipline. A military company was organized, with THOMAS McNAIR, captain, JOSEPH BRISBOIS, lieutenant, and JEAN BRUNET, ensign, all of whom had previously been commissioned for these offices by Gov. CASS. Mr. SNELLING and Judge LOCKWOOD acted as supernumeraries under Capt. McNAIR, and the force was found, on muster, to number ninety effective men and women who could handle a musket in case of attack. The fort and blockhouse were put in as good state of repair as circumstances and material would admit. The swivel and wall pieces were found and mounted, and all the blacksmiths were put in requisition to repair the condemned muskets. Judge LOCKWOOD, fortunately, had an abundance of powder and lead, which he liberally furnished, so that the old fort and its occupants were in a respectable state of defense.

An old voyageur was engaged to cross the Mississippi, and go back through the country to report the situation to Col. SNELLING at Fort Snelling. He performed his service ; and after considerable delay, Col. SNELLING came down the river with two companies of U. S. infantry.

An express was sent to Galena, and the effect of the alarming news is described by Col. D. M. PARKINSON in these words:

"The reports being spread over the country, a scene of the most alarming and disorderly confusion ensued — their alarm and consternation were depicted in every countenance — thousands flocked to Galena for safety, when, in fact, it was the most exposed and unsafe place in the whole country. All were without arms, order or control. The roads were lined in all directions with frantic and fleeing men, women and children, expecting every moment to be overtaken, tomahawked and scalped by the Indians. It was said, and I presume with truth, that the encampment of fugitives at the head of Apple river, on the first night of the alarm, was four miles in extent, and numbered three thousand persons."

Gov. CASS, who had come to Butte des Morts to hold a treaty with the Winnebagoes, learning from rumor that there was dissatisfaction among them, started in his canoe, and arrived at Prairie du Chien on the morning of the 4th of July. Having ordered into the service of the United States McNAIR'S military company, he proceeded hastily in his canoe to Galena. There he raised a volunteer company, with ABNER FIELDS as captain, WILLIAM S. HAMILTON and one SMITH as lieutenants, in which D. M. PARKINSON was sergeant. The command of Fort Crawford was assigned by Gov. CASS to Capt. FIELDS, who, with his company, immediately proceeded to Prairie du Chien on a keel-boat, and took possession of the barracks. Lieut. MARTIN THOMAS, of the U. S army, went up and mustered the two companies of militia into the service of the government.

In a few days Col. SNELLING arrived with his troops, and assumed command of Fort Crawford. He soon after discharged Capt. FIELD'S company; but Capt. McNAIR'S company was retained in service until some time in the month of August.

Gov. CASS proceeded from Galena to St. Louis to confer with Gen. ATKINSON, then in command of Jefferson Barracks and of the Western military department. This resulted in ATKINSON'S removing up the Mississippi with the disposable force under his command.

During this time the miners in the lead mines had organized a company of mounted volunteers, which numbered over one hundred men, well mounted and armed, and chose Col. HENRY DODGE as their commander. While it was the peculiar duty of this force to protect the settlers of the lead mines against any attack of the savages, they were as ready to pursue them and give battle as to resist attack.

RED BIRD and the other Winnebagoes having, as was supposed, fled up the Wisconsin, it was the plan of General ATKINSON to go up that river in boats; and he also secured the co-operation of Col. DODGE and his mounted volunteers, who marched to the Wisconsin, a detachment going to Prairie du Chien, and the remainder to English Prairie (now Muscoda). This mounted force scoured both sides of the Wisconsin river from its mouth to the Portage, driving every Indian before them.

Major WHISTLER, in command at Fort Howard, had been ordered to proceed up Fox river with any force at his disposal, or which might volunteer to aid him. A company of Oneida and Stockbridge Indians, sixty-two in number, were raised by EBENEZER CHILDS and JOSEPH DICKINSON, which was mustered into Maj. WHISTLER'S detachment at Little Butte des Morts. This force arrived on the 1st day of September, 1827, on the high bluff, where, during the next year, the erection of Fort Winnebago was commenced. Here, in pursuance of orders from Gen. ATKINSON, sent by express announcing the approach of his force and DODGE'S volunteers, Maj. WHISTLER encamped to await the arrival of the General.

The Winnebagoes were now in a desperate plight. With Col. SNELLING in command at Fort Crawford, with a large force of regulars and volunteers, confronted by Maj. WHISTLER and his troops, and with Gen. ATKINSON following their retreat, aided by DODGE and his mounted volunteers, who drove them out of every hiding place, there seemed to be no alternative for them but to appeal to the lenient mercy of their pursuers.

Soon after the arrival of Maj. WHISTLER, it was learned that the Winnebagoes were encamped a little more than a mile distant on the Wisconsin, where Portage City is now located, and were several hundred strong. The Winnebagoes had heard of Gen. ATKINSON'S approach, and of DODGE'S pursuit, before they were known to Maj. WHISTLER, and in a few days a great stir was discovered among the Indians, and a party of thirty warriors was observed by the aid of a field glass, to be approaching his command. The Indian party bore three flags. On two—one in front and one in rear—were the American stars and stripes, while the other, in the center, borne by RED BIRD, was white. They bore no arms. When they had approached near to the Fox river, they stopped, and singing was heard. Those who were familiar with the air, and who recognized the bearer of the white flag, said: "It is RED BIRD singing his death song." When they had reached the margin of the river, Maj. WHISTLER ordered Capt. CHILDS, who was officer of the guard, to take the guard to the river, and ascertain what the Winnebagoes wanted. They replied they had come to deliver up the murderers. They were received by the guard, and taken across the river into the presence of Maj. WHISTLER. In the lead was CAR-I-MAU-NEE, a distinguished chief. He said:

"They are here. Like braves they have come in. Treat them as braves. Do not put them in irons."

The military had been drawn up in line, the Menomonee and Oneida Indians in groups on the left, the band of music on the right. In front of the center stood RED BIRD and his two accomplices in the GAGNIER murder, while those who had accompanied them formed a semi-circle on the right and left. All eyes were fixed on RED BIRD, as well they might be, for of all his tribe he was the most perfect in form, face, and gesture. In height he was about six feet; straight without restraint. His proportions from his head to his feet were those of the most exact symmetry, and even his fingers were models of beauty. His face was full of all the ennobling, and, at the same time, winning expressions; it appeared to be a compound of grace and dignity, of firmness and decision, all tempered with mildness and mercy. It was impossible to conceive that such a face concealed the heart of a murderer.

It was painted, one side red, the other intermixed with green and white. He was clothed in a Yankton suit of dressed elk-skin, perfectly white, and as soft as a kid glove, new and beautiful. It consisted of a jacket, ornamented with fringe of the same material, the sleeves being cut to fit his finely-formed arm, and of leggings, also of dressed elk-skin, the fringe of which was varied and enriched with blue beads. On his feet he wore moccasins. On each shoulder, in place of an epaulette, was fastened a preserved red bird. Around his neck he wore a collar of blue wampum, beautifully mixed with white, which was sewed on to a piece of cloth, whilst the claws of a panther or wild cat, with their points inward, formed the rim of the collar. Around his neck were hanging strands of wampum of various lengths, the circles enlarging as they descended. There was no attempt at ornamenting the hair, after the Indian style; but it was cut after the best fashion of the most civilized. Across his breast, in a diagonal position, and bound tight to it, was his war pipe, at least three feet long, brightly ornamented with dyed horse hair, and the feathers and bills of birds. Other ornaments were displayed with exquisite taste upon his breast and shoulders. In one of his hands he held the white flag, and in the other the calumet or pipe of peace.

There he stood. Not a muscle moved, nor was the expression of his face changed a particle. He appeared conscious that, according to the Indian law, he had done no wrong. His conscience was at repose. Death had no terrors for him. He was there prepared to receive the blow that should send him to the happy hunting grounds to meet his fathers and brothers who had gone before him.

All were told to sit down, when a talk followed between the head men of the Winnebagoes and Maj. WHISTLER, in which the former claimed much credit for bringing in the captives, and hoped their white brothers would accept horses in commutation for the lives of their friends, and earnestly besought that in any event they might not be put in irons. They were answered and told that they had done well thus to come in; were advised to warn their people against killing ours, and were impressed with a proper notion of their own weakness and the extent of our power. They were told that the captives should not be put in irons, that they should have something to eat, and tobacco to smoke.

RED BIRD then stood up, facing the commanding officer, Maj. WHISTLER. After a moment's pause, and a quick survey of the troops, and with a composed observation of his people, he spoke, looking at Maj. WHISTLER, and said:

"I am ready." Then advancing a step or two, he paused and said: "I do not wish to be put in irons. Let me be free. I have given away my life—(stooping and taking some dust between his finger and thumb and blowing it away)—like that," (eyeing the dust as it fell and vanished), then adding: "I would not take it back. It is gone."

Having thus spoken, he threw his hands behind him, indicating that he was leaving all things behind him, and marched briskly up to Maj. WHISTLER, breast to breast. A platoon was wheeled backward from the center of the line when, Maj. WHISTLER stepping aside, the prisoners marched through the line in charge of a file of men, to a tent that had been provided for them in the rear, where a guard was set over them. The other Indians then left the ground by the way they had come, taking with them the advice they had received, and a supply of meat, flour, and tobacco.

Gen. ATKINSON's troops, very soon after the surrender of these captives, arrived at Fort Winnebago, as did also the volunteers in command of Col. DODGE. The Indian prisoners were delivered over to Gen. ATKINSON, by whom they were sent to Fort Crawford. Gen. ATKINSON met the grey-headed DE-KAU-RAY at the Portage, who, in presence of Col. DODGE, disclaimed for himself and the other Winnebagoes any unfriendly feeling toward the United States, and disavowed any connection with the murders on the Mississippi. Gen. ATKINSON then discharged the volunteers, assigning two companies of regulars to the occupation of Fort Crawford, and ordering the other regulars to their respective posts, while he himself returned to Jefferson Barracks. And thus ended the Winnebago outbreak.

It may be thought that the results of this war are very meagre for the amount of force employed in it. If measured by the amount of blood shed after the murders at Prairie du Chien and on the keel-boat, the criticism is very correct. But if it be intended to suggest that there was no sufficient reason for apprehending that the Winnebagoes contemplated a general rising against and massacre of the whites, the thought and suggestion are the results of great ignorance of the intentions of the Winnebagoes, and of the facts of the case. There is satisfactory evidence that the Pottawatamies were allied with the Winnebagoes, and that they were to fall upon and destroy the settlement at Chicago, and it is probable that but for the movements resulting from the efforts of Gen. CASS, who was fortunately near the seat of war, the whole country would have been overrun with a general Indian outbreak.

RED BIRD died in prison at Prairie du Chien; and in September, 1828, his two accomplices, We-kau and Chic-hon-sic, were indicted, tried, and convicted at a term of the United States court held by Judge DOTY, as accomplices of RED BIRD in the murder of GAGNIER and LIPCAP. They were sentenced to be hung on the 26th of December following;

but before that day a pardon arrived from President ADAMS, dated November 3d, and the two Indians were discharged.

CHAPTER XII.

THE BLACK HAWK WAR.

The termination of the Winnebago war brought a temporary restoration of peace, which revived anew the adventurous spirit of immigration, and brought with it a large influx of miners and others to the lead mines, and prosperity and progress constantly attended the increasing settlements of the country, which received no material check until the occurrence of the Black Hawk war in 1832.

The village of BLACK HAWK, or, as he called himself, BLACK SPARROW HAWK, on the left bank of the Mississippi, near the mouth of Rock river, included the site of the present city of Rock Island. This Indian village was all embraced within the limits of the territory ceded by the treaty with the Sauks and Foxes, made at St. Louis on November 3, 1804, by Gen. WILLIAM HENRY HARRISON. The validity of this treaty, which was not signed by BLACK HAWK, was denied by him, and although it was ratified and confirmed by another treaty made in May, 1816, to which BLACK HAWK affixed his mark, he pretended to be ignorant of what he had done, and denied that the second treaty had any more validity than the first.

Previous to 1831 the white settlers were in possession of much of the country east of the Mississippi, around BLACK HAWK'S village, and even of the village itself; and in the spring of that year the chief, driven to desperation in his fruitless attempts to resist what he chose to consider the lawless encroachments of the white settlers, and aggravated by a recent murderous attack of friendly Menomonees, near Prairie du Chien, crossed the Mississippi from the west with his own band of about three hundred warriors, usually called the British band, together with the women and children, with a purpose to regain, if possible, the possession of the home of his people and the burial place of his forefathers.

He ordered the white settlers away, threw down their fences, unroofed their houses, cut up their grain, drove off and killed their cattle, and threatened the people with death if they remained. About the first of June six companies of the United States troops were, upon the application of Gov. REYNOLDS, sent from Jefferson Barracks to the scene of the disturbance; and by the 10th of June fifteen hundred volunteers, on the call of the Governor, assembled at Beardstown, on the Illinois river, and were duly organized under Gen. JOSEPH DUNCAN, of the State militia. On the 26th of June, the volunteer force having united with the regulars under Gen. GAINES, marched, to the Sauk village; but no enemy was found there. The Indians had quietly departed on the approach of the army, and in their canoes had crossed to the western side of the Mississippi, which it was not claimed had been embraced in the territory ceded by the treaties.

The army remained encamped for several days on the site of the town on Rock Island, where BLACK HAWK and his chiefs and braves sued for peace, and a treaty was entered into on June 30th, by which the Indians agreed to remain forever after on the west side of the river, and never to recross it without the permission of the President or the Governor of the State. Gen. GAINES reported that—

"The Sauks were as completely humbled as if they had been chastised in battle, and less disposed to disturb the frontier inhabitants."

In this the General was greatly mistaken; for scarcely a year elapsed before BLACK HAWK, with all the savage forces he could command, again crossed the Mississippi, when the real Black Hawk war ensued.

This war, although originating on a portion of Rock river some distance from the settlements in the lead mines, and inaugurated by a tribe who laid no claim to our territory, justly caused great alarm to the inhabitants. The lead mine region was not so distant from the scene of the first hostile demonstrations, that it could not easily be reached; and the relations between the Sauks and the Winnebagoes were such, that serious fears were entertained that the two tribes would make the war a common one.

These apprehensions induced Col. DODGE, in the month of May, to assemble a company of fifty volunteers, commanded by Captains JAMES H. GENTRY and JOHN H. ROUNTREE, who proceeded to the head of the Four Lakes, where, on the 25th day of that month Col. GRATIOT, the Indian agent for the Winnebagoes, had induced them to meet in council.

Col. DODGE, in his "talk" to the Indians, said:

"My friends: Mr. GRATIOT your father, and myself, have met to have a talk with you. Having identified us both as your friends, in making a sale of your country to the United States, you will not suspect us of deceiving you.

"The Sauks have shed the blood of our people. The Winnebago Prophet, and, as we are told, one hundred of your people, have united with BLACK HAWK and his party. Our people are anxious to know in what relation you stand to us, whether as friends or enemies.

"Your residence being near our settlements, it is necessary and proper that we should explicitly understand from you, the chiefs and warriors, whether or not you intend to aid, harbor, or counsel the Sauks in your country. To do so will be considered as a declaration of war on your part.

"Your great American Father is the friend of the Red Skins; he wishes to make you happy. Your chiefs, who have visited Washington, know him well. He is mild in peace but terrible in war. He will ask of no people what is not right, and he will submit to nothing wrong. His power is great. He commands all the warriors of the American people. If you strike us you strike him. If you make war on us, you will have your country taken from you, your annuity money will be forfeited, and the lives of your people must be lost. We speak the words of truth. We hope they will sink deep into your hearts.

"The Sauks have killed eleven of our people and wounded three. Our people have killed eleven of the Sauks. It was a small detachment of our army who were engaged with the Sauks; when the main body of our army appeared, they ran.

"The Sauks have given you bad counsel. They tell you lies, and no truth. Stop your ears to their words. They know death and destruction follow them, and they want you to unite with them, wishing to place you in the same situation with themselves.

"We have told you the consequences of uniting with our enemies. We hope that the bright chain of friendship will still continue, that we may travel the same road in friendship under a clear sky.

"We have always been your friends. We have said that you would be honest and true to your treaties. Do not let your actions deceive us. So long as you are true and faithful we will extend the hand of friendship to you and your children. If unfaithful to your treaties, you must expect to share the fate of the Sauks."

The Winnebagoes promised to be faithful to their treaties, and remain at peace; but it is well known that their promises were inspired alone by fear, while the desire for revenge was with them the predominant passion.

BLACK HAWK, regardless of the obligations of the treaty into which he had entered the previous year, crossed the Mississippi early in the spring of 1832, with the intention of using all his endeavors, even unto war, to recover possession of his village. Gov. REYNOLDS again called upon the militia of Illinois; and in a few days eighteen hundred men responded to the call. They were organized into four regiments and a spy battalion, under the general command of

Gen. SAMUEL WHITESIDE, of the State militia. The line of march was taken up from Beardstown, on the 27th of April, for the mouth of Rock river. Gen. ATKINSON had left Jefferson Barracks on the 8th of April, and set out for the Upper Mississippi with the regular forces of the United States army; and BLACK HAWK, with his whole tribe of followers, began to move up Rock river. Gen. WHITESIDE, in pursuance of arrangements with Gen. ATKINSON, moved up Rock river to the Prophet's town; and finding that BLACK HAWK was still in advance, they burned the Prophet's village, and moved on about forty miles to Dixon's ferry, where a halt was made to await the arrival of Gen. ATKINSON with the regular forces. At Dixon were found two battalions of mounted volunteers, consisting of about three hundred men, under command of Majors Stillman and Bailey.

Major STILLMAN, with his force, was ordered up Rock river to spy out the Indians. He began his march on the 12th of May; and, about the middle of the afternoon of the 14th, the battalion halted for the purpose of encamping for the night. It has been said, and it is probably true, that many of the men were intoxicated, and the pursuit was generally regarded as a big frolic. Nearly all the horses had been picketed out, turned loose or otherwise disposed of. The men were lazily engaged about camp, some gathering wood, some pitching tents, and others drinking whisky, with which they were abundantly supplied. But suddenly a great commotion arose. The Indians raised the war-whoop, and appeared on the open prairie a short distance in advance. Then the rush began, and a strife ensued as to who should first mount and give chase. Pell-mell was the order of the march, which continued for two or three miles. Two of the Indians were overtaken on the prairie, and killed.

At length the rear of the army reached the Sycamore Creek, where they met the van, in full retreat in the same disgraceful disorder, with the whole body of Indians in hot pursuit. The valiant men, who a few minutes before were so anxious to pursue the enemy, were now more anxious to escape; and they continued their retreat until they reached Dixon. In this confusion Capt. ADAMS, with the company from Peoria, succeeded in crossing the creek, and took a position between the Indians and the fugitives.

This position they held for some time against the whole force of the enemy, and no doubt saved the lives of many; but at the cost of the life of Capt. ADAMS and several of his men. The total casualties in this first and most digraceful encounter with the Indians were eleven of STILLMAN'S battalion killed and three wounded, while only three Indians were known to have been killed. This was the first blood shed in the Black Hawk war. The next day General WHITESIDE, and the volunteers under his command, marched for the scene of the disaster; but the Indians had scattered, and could not be found. The volunteer army buried the dead, and returned to Dixon, where General ATKINSON arrived the following day with the regular forces and supplies of provisions, of which the volunteers stood in much need.

Colonel DODGE, who, by a common intuitive feeling, was regarded as the leader of the people of the lead mines, and commander of all their military forces, as he was also the lawful commander of the militia of that part of Michigan Territory, on the 8th of May addressed a letter from Mineral Point to Governor REYNOLDS, asking for information in relation to the movements of the Illinois forces, expressing fears of a union of the Sauks and Winnebagoes, and requesting that a part of the Illinois forces might be sent across Rock river to co-operate with a mounted force to be brought into the field from the lead mines. This letter was sent by a special embassy, consisting of Judge GENTRY, Col. MOORE and JAMES P. COX.

At the same time, Col. DODGE, with twenty-seven of his neighbors, who were well mounted, among whom was his son AUGUSTUS C., started on an expedition to Rock river to ascertain the position and probable movements of BLACK HAWK and his followers. The small party proceeded by way of Apple river to Buffalo Grove, where an Indian trail was discovered, and followed to a point nearly opposite the Kishwaukee, and within a few miles of the ground from which Maj. STILLMAN was on the same day disastrously beaten, and put to flight. After STILLMAN'S defeat Governor REYNOLDS sent an express at night to Col. DODGE, informing him of the facts, and that his country in the Territory was in imminent danger from the attack of the Indians. Col. DODGE immediately returned home, having been absent about a week, reported the results, and advised the inhabitants to protect themselves by forts and other precautions, and to organize immediately for defense.

The inhabitants of the lead mines were now thoroughly alarmed by constant dread of attack from BLACK HAWK and his warriors, who had small parties scattered all over the country, between the Rock, Mississippi and Wisconsin rivers, which "occupied every grove, waylaid every road, and hung around every little settlement," and induced the most serious fears in the minds of all the inhabitants of the mining region. The bravest hearts thought it no evidence of cowardice to use every precaution against surprise and sudden attack. Forts, block-houses and stockades were erected by the people at numerous places, for the protection and defense of themselves and their families, and into which they removed. Among these were Fort Union, the headquarters of Col. DODGE, near Dodgeville; Fort Defiance, at the farm of D. M. PARKINSON; Fort Hamilton, at Wiota; Fort Jackson, at Mineral Point; Mound Fort, at Blue Mound; and others at Wingville, Cassville, Platteville, Gratiot's Grove, Diamond Grove, Elk Grove, White Oak Springs, and Old Shullsburg, besides many others.

It was soon ascertained that the mode of warfare adopted by the Sauks, was to keep the main body concealed in strongholds, and avoid a conflict with a superior force, while small detached parties should attack the undefended settlements, and any stragglers who could be found away from the protection of the forts and block-houses.

It is difficult to state definitely the number or names of the numerous persons whose lives were sacrificed to the ferocity of the savages.

On the 21st of May, about seventy Indians attacked a party of whites assembled in the house of Mr. DAVIS on Indian Creek, near Ottawa, and killed and scalped fifteen whites, and took two young women named HALL prisoners, who were afterwards surrendered at the Blue Mounds through the agency of a party of Winnebagoes who were inspired by a large reward of $2,000, offered by General ATKINSON, for their restoration.

These female captives were brought to the Mound Fort on the 3rd of June. Col. DODGE, who had returned home only a day or two before, from his "talk" with the Indians on the 25th of May, had been sent for on the 1st of June, on account of an apprehended attack by the Indians. He immediately collected about two hundred mounted men, and was fortunately present with this force when the young women were brought in by the Winnebagoes, of whom there were about fifty, including such distinguished chiefs and braves as WHITE CROW—a famous orator—SPOTTED ARM, LITTLE THUNDER, LITTLE PRIEST and others. Colonel DODGE purchased and furnished them a large beef stew, upon which they feasted sumptuously, furnished them with comfortable quarters in miner's cabins, and in all suitable ways sought to impress on these Winnebagoes that the whites had no other than friendly feelings towards them, and to inspire, if possible, a reciprocal feeling on their part. Their friendship for the Sauks and Foxes was well known, and suspicions and apprehensions of an alliance offensive and defensive between the two tribes had long been generally entertained, which were by no means allayed by their promises of fidelity, friendship and peace made to Colonel DODGE at the talk held only a few days before.

When Col. DODGE retired for the night, no appearance of danger or disaffection could be discovered. But during the night he was awakened, and informed that the Indians had left the quarters assigned them, and gone into the bush; that WHITE CROW, the orator, had been endeavoring to stir up the other Indians to hostility; that they were sulky, moody and stealthy in their conversation and movements; that they had been grinding their knives, tomahawks and spears, and that two athletic young warriors had gone stealthily in the direction of the Four Lakes, where the main body of the Winnebagoes was encamped.

Col. DODGE, taking the officer of the guard, with six men and an interpreter, marched to the "bush" where the Indians were encamped, and took WHITE CROW and five others of the chiefs and braves, and marched them off without ceremony, to a cabin near by, and ordered them to lie down there, and remain there until morning; and then laid down with them, at the same time directing the officer of the guard to place a strong party around the cabin, and a double guard around the whole encampment, which required nearly all the men in the command.

The next day, these captive chiefs and a number of young warriors were marched, much against their will, to Morrison's Grove, fifteen miles west of the Blue Mounds; Col. GRATIOT, the Indian Agent, was sent for at Gratiot's Grove, and on his arrival the next day, another council was held. Col. DODGE told the Indians, frankly and plainly, what were his suspicions and apprehensions in relation to their treacherous intentions. They stoutly denied any such design; but failed to satisfy Col. DODGE, who retained as hostages for the good faith of the Indians, three of their leading chiefs—WHIRLING THUNDER, the principal war chief, SPOTTED ARM and LITTLE PRIEST. These were conveyed to Gratiot's Grove the next day, and all the other Indians were discharged, and the HALL girls were received and restored to their friends. The three hostages were kept in prison until POSEY, HENRY and ALEXANDER arrived with their command, when they were set at liberty.

The detachment of volunteers returned with Col. DODGE to Fort Union (DODGE's residence), and on the 5th of June proceeded to Gratiot's Grove, where they were joined the next day by Capt. STEPHENSON's company of volunteers from Galena.

On the 22d of May the body of one DURLEY was found, murdered and scalped, near Buffalo Grove, and on the next day an Indian agent named ST. VRAIN, together with JOHN FOWLER, WILLIAM HALE, and AARON HAWLEY, met the same fate near the same place.

The object of this assemblage of the volunteers at Gratiot's Grove, was to find and punish the Indians who had been engaged in the perpetration of these murders and to protect the country from the hostilities of the Sauks, in whatever manner they might be directed by the Commandant-in-Chief.

HENRY DODGE was one of the early pioneers of the lead region, to which he had removed in 1826, from Missouri, where he had held the office of United States marshal, and was highly esteemed as a worthy, brave and patriotic citizen. He brought with him a large family of sons and daughters, and was largely engaged in the business of mining and smelting lead, to which his personal efforts were industriously devoted. He was assigned to the command of all the Wisconsin volunteers, as well as those from Galena. He was under the command of Gen. ATKINSON, to whom it was his purpose to report in person at Rock river, with the volunteer forces now under his command.

On the 7th of June Col. DODGE, with his volunteers, marched to KIRKER's farm, at the head of Apple river, where they camped, and Col. DODGE addressed them as follows :

"VOLUNTEERS : We have met to take the field. The tomahawk and scalping knife are drawn over the heads of the weak and defenseless inhabitants of our country. Let us unite, my brethren, in arms; let harmony, union and concert exist; be vigilant, silent and cool. Discipline and obedience to orders will make small bodies of men formidable and invincible; without order and subordination the largest bodies of armed men are no better than armed mobs. Although we have entire confidence in the Government of our choice, knowing, as we all do, that ours is a government of the people, where the equal rights of all are protected, and that the power of our countrymen can crush this savage foe; yet it will take time for the Government to direct a force sufficient to give security and peace to the frontier people.

"I have, as well as yourselves, entire confidence, both in the President of the United States, and the distinguished individual at the head of the War Department; that our Indian relations are better understood by those distinguished men, JACKSON and CASS, than by any two citizens who could be selected to fill their stations. They have often met our savage enemies on the field of battle, where they have conquered them, and have often also met them in council. They understand well all the artifice, cunning, and stratagems for which our enemies are distinguished; they well know our wants and will apply the remedy. In Gen. ATKINSON, in whose protection this frontier is placed, I have the most entire confidence. He is well advised of our situation. You will recollect the responsibility he assumed for the people of this country in 1827, by ascending the Wisconsin with six hundred infantry, and one hundred and fifty mounted men, to demand the murderers of our people. Many of us had the honor of serving under him on that occasion. He has my entire confidence both, as a man of talents in his profession, and as a soldier and a gentleman. If our Government will let him retain his command, he will give us a lasting peace, that will insure us tranquillity for years. He knows the resources as well as the character of the Indians we have to contend with, and if the Government furnishes him the means, our troubles will be of short duration.

"What, my fellow-soldiers, is the character of the foes we have to contend with? They are a faithless banditi of savages, who have violated all treaties. They have left the country and the nation of which they form a part. The policy of these marauders and robbers of our people appears to be, to enlist the disaffected and restless of other nations, which will give them strength and resources, to murder our people and burn their property. They are the enemies of all people, both the whites and Indians. Their thirst for blood is not to be satisfied. They are willing to bring ruin and destruction on other Indians, in order to glut their vengeance on us. The humane policy of the Government will not apply to these deluded people. Like the pirates of the sea, their hand is against every man, and the hand of every man should be against them. Faithless to the Government in everything, it will surely be the policy of the Government to let them receive that kind of chastisement which will quiet them effectually, and make a lasting example for others. The future growth and prosperity of our country is to be decided for years by the policy that is now to be pursued by the Government in relation to the Indians. Our existence as a people is at stake, and great as the resources of our country are, the security of the lives of our people depends on our vigilance, caution, and bravery. The assistance of our Government may be too late for us; let us not then await the arrival of the enemy at our doors, but advance upon them, fight them, watch them, and hold them in check. Let us avoid surprise and ambuscades. Let every volunteer lie with his arms in his hands, so that when he rises to his feet the line of battle will be formed. If attacked in the night, we will charge the enemy at a quick pace and even front. The eyes of the people are upon us; let us endeavor, by our actions, to retain the confidence and support of our countrymen."

The command marched to the scene of the murder of ST. VRAIN, FOWLER, HALE, and HAWLEY, near Buffalo Grove (which is near Polo Station, on the Illinois Central railroad), where they found and buried the bodies of the three former; the body of HAWLEY was never recovered. At this point Capt. STEPHENSON separated from the command, and returned to Galena, with his company. Col. DODGE proceeded with the remainder of the mounted volunteers to the camp of the regular troops, at Dixon's Ferry. Gen. HUGH BRADY was in command here, Gen. ATKINSON's headquarters having been removed to the rapids of the Illinois river (now Ottawa), where he was engaged in organizing three brigades of Illinois volunteers. Col. DODGE, with twenty-five of his mounted volunteers, escorted Gen. BRADY to Gen. ATKINSON's headquarters, where, on the 11th of June, the plan of the campaign was agreed upon, and Col. DODGE received his orders. The whole command of volunteers then returned to Gratiot's Grove, where, on the 14th of June, they were remanded to their respective posts, to hold themselves in readiness for such further services as might be required of them. On the same day Col. DODGE returned to his headquarters at Fort Union, having first communicated to the Winnebago chiefs, WHIRLING THUNDER, SPOTTED ARM, and LITTLE PRIEST, held as hostages, a "talk" sent to them by Gen. ATKINSON.

On the 26th of May, Gen. ATKINSON sent, as an express, Col. WM. S. HAMILTON, from Dixon's to Gen. STREET, Indian Agent at Prairie du Chien, requesting the latter to send forward as many Sioux and Menomonee Indians as could be called within striking distance of Prairie du Chien, to be employed, in conjunction with the troops, against the Sauks and Foxes. A similar message was sent to Col. BOYD, the Indian Agent at Green Bay. Col. STREET sent THOS. P. BURNETT, who was then sub-Indian Agent, up the river, to recruit the Sioux, and whatever Winnebagoes were willing to join them. There were no Menomonees in that quarter. Mr. BURNETT, taking JOHN MARSH with him, went up the river about one hundred and thirty miles; and returned, before the 10th of June, with one hundred Indian warriors, of which eighty were Sioux, and twenty Winnebagoes, and

THE BLACK HAWK WAR. 141

fifty or sixty more were expected to join them. The Indians were placed under command of Col. HAMILTON, who, taking Mr. MARSH and an interpreter with him, proceeded to join the troops under Gen. ATKINSON. Col. BOYD employed Col. S. C. STAMBAUGH, who had recently been the Indian Agent, to recruit the Menomonee Indians, who secured the services of Col. EBENEZER CHILDS, to collect them. Over three hundred were obtained for the service, who were divided into two companies; one commanded by CHARLES L. GRIGNON, the other by GEORGE JOHNSON, and both under command of Col. STAMBAUGH. These Indian allies proceeded to join the pursuing troops. At Blue Mounds they learned that BLACK HAWK with the main body of his followers had crossed the Wisconsin, and that Col. DODGE and his command were in pursuit. They, therefore, went directly to Prairie du Chien. Before reaching there, they learned that a part of the Sauks and Foxes had gone south. They found the trail, and pursued with one company, and overtook the fugitives about fifteen miles north of Cassville, not far back from the Mississippi. There were only two men and a boy, three or four women, and as many children. The Menomonees killed the two men, and the others were taken prisoners.

On the 6th of June JAMES AUBREY was killed at the Blue Mounds, and two weeks later FORCE and GREEN lost their lives by the enemy at the same place. It is probable that AUBREY was murdered by the Winnebagoes, as there is no reason to suppose the Sauks and Foxes had been so near the Blue Mounds as early as the time of his death, and the murder of FORCE and GREEN was more likely the work of the Winnebagoes than of the Sauks and Foxes.

On the 14th of June, five men whose names were SPAFFORD, SPENCER, McILWAIN, MILLION and an Englisman called JOHN BULL, were at work in a cornfield owned by SPAFFORD, situated on the Peckatonica near Spafford's Ford, in what is now the town of Wayne, when they were surprised by a band of Indians, and all except MILLION, who most miraculously escaped, were murdered. The Indians stealthily pursued their way to a place of concealment within four hundred yards of Fort Hamilton, at which place Capt. GENTRY's command of mounted men had by order of Col. DODGE, rendezvoused for the purpose of pursuing and killing them. On the morning of the 16th, at about eight o'clock, as Col. DODGE was approaching the fort to take command of the troops, he heard three guns fired, which proved to be from the hostile Indians, who were lying in ambush, and who killed, in his saddle, a German named APPLE, who was preparing to join in the pursuit, and whom they butchered and scalped. Col. DODGE immediately ordered the mounted men under arms in pursuit of the savage foe. Fortunately they were enabled soon to come upon the Indian trail, and after running their horses about two miles they came in sight of the retreating enemy, who were seeking the low ground where it was difficult to pursue them on horseback. The Indians directed their course to a bend in the Peckatonica covered with a deep swamp, which they reached before their pursuers crossed the stream.

The following account of the action which for daring bravery and cool, undaunted courage, is not excelled in the history of Indian warfare, is from the official report of General DODGE to General ATKINSON:

"After crossing the Peckatonica, in the open ground, I dismounted my command, linked my horses and left four men in charge of them, and sent four men in different directions to watch the movement of the Indians. I formed my men on foot at open order, and at trailed arms, and we proceeded through the swamp to some timber and under-growth where I expected to find the enemy. When I found their trail, I knew they were close at hand. They had got close to the edge of the lake, where the bank was six feet high, which was a complete breast-work for them. They commenced the fire, when three of my men fell, two dangerously wounded, one severely but not dangerously. I instantly ordered a charge made on them by eighteen men, which was promptly obeyed. The Indians being under the bank, our guns were brought within ten or fifteen feet of them before we could fire on them. Their party consisted of thirteen men. Eleven were killed on the spot, and the remaining two were killed in crossing the lake, so they were left without one to carry the news to their friends. The volunteers under my command behaved with great gallantry. It would be impossible for me to discriminate among them. At the word 'charge,' the men rushed forward, and literally shot the Indians to pieces. We were, Indians and whites, on a piece of ground not to exceed sixty feet square."

The precise spot on which this terrific battle occurred is section eleven, town two, range five east, in the town of Wiota.

The following, as near as can now be ascertained, is a complete list of the names of the persons, who in one way or another, as duty was assigned them, took part in the battle of the Peckatonica:

Col. HENRY DODGE commanding; Captain JAMES H. GENTRY; Lieutenants—CHARLES BRACKEN, PASCAL BEQUETTE and ——PORTER; Surgeon ALLEN HILL—doing duty as a private.

Privates—(alphabetically arranged)—ED. BOUCHARD, SAMUEL BLACK, WM. CARNS, ——DEVA, ASA DUNCAN, MATTHEW G. FITCH, ALEXANDER HIGGENBOTHEM, JOHN HOOD, THOMAS JENKINS, R. H. KIRKPATRICK, BENJAMIN LAWHEAD, LEVIN LEACH, DOMINICK MCGRAW, ——MCCONNELL, JOHN MESSERSERSMITH, Jr., ——MORRIS, D. M. PARKINSON, PETER PARKINSON, Jr., SAMUEL PATRICK, THOMAS H. PRICE, ——RANKIN, ——TOWNSEND, ——VAN WAGNER, ——WELLS, and —— WOODBRIDGE. Of these BLACK, MORRIS and WELLS were killed, and JENKINS wounded, while the others escaped without injury.

Col. HAMILTON arrived with the friendly Sioux Indians about an hour after the battle; and some Winnebagoes who professed to be friendly came with them, among whom was the chief DE-KAU-RAY. The friendly Indians went to the ground where the Sauks were killed. They scalped them, and literally cut them to pieces, and appeared to be delighted with the scalps.

On the 18th of June, while a company under the command of Capt. STEPHENSON were engaged in scouting, three of his men were killed and himself wounded by Indians near the Peckatonica, among whom BLACK HAWK was said to have been present.

On the 24th of the month, BLACK HAWK, with a large body of Indians, made an attack on Apple river Fort, near the present village of Elizabeth, which was vigorously defended. The battle lasted fifteen hours. The loss of the Indians was considerable; that of the whites one man killed, and one wounded.

In the *"Life of Black Hawk,"* dictated by himself, and edited by J. B. PATTERSON, of Rock Island, and undoubtedly authentic, BLACK HAWK gives the following account of his attack on this garrison:

"When we arrived in the vicinity of the Fort, we saw four men on horseback; one of my braves fired and wounded a man, when the others set up a yell as if a large force was ready to come against us. We concealed ourselves. No enemy came. The four men ran to the Fort and gave the alarm. We followed them and attacked the Fort, and killed one man who raised his head above the picketing to fire at us. Finding that these people could not all be killed without setting fire to their houses and Fort, I thought it more prudent to be content with what flour, provisions, cattle and horses we could find, than to set fire to their buildings, as the light would be seen at a distance, and the army might suppose we were in the neighborhood, and come upon us with a force too strong. Accordingly we opened a house and filled our bags with flour and provisions, took several horses and drove off some of their cattle."

BLACK HAWK in this marauding raid was accompanied by about two hundred of his warriors. The next day on their return to Rock river, the savages met Maj. JOHN DEMENT in command of a spy battalion, near Kellogg's Grove. A severe contest ensued, in which five whites were killed, and three wounded, while nine Indians were left dead on the field, and five others carried away.

BLACK HAWK in his *"Life"* gives the following account of this engagement :

"We started in a direction toward 'sun-rise.' After marching a considerable time, I discovered some white men coming toward us; we concealed ourselves in the woods, and when they came near enough, we commenced yelling and firing and made a rush upon them. About this time, their chief, with a party of men, rushed up to rescue the men we had fired upon. In a little while they commenced retreating and left their chief and a few braves, who seemed willing and anxious to fight. They acted like braves; but were forced to give way, when I rushed upon them with my braves. In a short time the chief returned with a large party. He seemed determined to fight and anxious for a battle. When he came near enough, I raised a yell, and firing commenced from both sides. The chief (who seemed to be a small man) addressed his warriors in a loud voice; but they soon retreated leaving him and a few braves on the battle field. A great number of my warriors pursued the retreating party, and killed a number of their horses as they ran. The chief and his few braves were unwilling to leave the field. I ordered my braves to rush upon them, and had the mortification of seeing two of my chiefs killed before the enemy retreated. This young chief deserves great praise for his courage and bravery; but fortunately for us, his army was not all composed of such brave men. During this attack we killed several men and about forty horses, and lost two young chiefs and seven warriors."

On the 29th of June, three men were attacked in a field near Sinsinawa Mound, two of whom, JOHN THOMPSON and JAMES BOXLEY, were killed, while the Indians, though pursued by Captain STEPHENSON, made their escape by crossing the Mississippi in a canoe. The Indians were probably a straggling party of Sauks, as the principal body had already returned with BLACK HAWK to Rock river.

During the months of May and June the number of settlers who fell victims to the merciless warfare of BLACK HAWK and his followers, was probably not less than fifty. But by the early part of July, such was the organization and vigorous pursuit by the whites of all straggling bands of marauders, that the great mass of the Indians were concentrated upon Rock river, above Lake Koshkonong, where General ATKINSON was now encamped, and where he had been joined by General ALEXANDER's brigade.

While Maj. DEMENT was engaged with BLACK HAWK at Kellogg's Grove, he sent an express to Gen. POSEY, at Dixon, for relief, who marched with his whole brigade for that purpose; but did not arrive until after the retreat of the Indians. Gen. POSEY awaited the arrival of his baggage wagons, and then proceeded with his brigade to Fort Hamilton, where he was met by Col. DODGE with his entire command of mounted volunteers. In pursuance of the plan of the campaign, as formed at headquarters at Ottawa, on the 17th of June, these two commands composed the left wing of the army. Gen. ALEXANDER'S command formed the center, and Gen. ATKINSON, with Gen. HENRY'S brigade, formed the right wing, and advanced up Rock river.

The left wing marched across the country by the way of the Peckatonica battle ground and Sugar river, to the first of the Four Lakes, being re-enforced at Sugar river by the Galena company of volunteers. At the First Lake they were joined by WHITE CROW and about thirty Winnebago warriors, who avowed their purpose of showing the path of the Sauks to the pursuing army.

Some dissatisfaction existing between Col. DODGE'S command and Gen. POSEY'S brigade, a change of position was made, whereby Gen. ALEXANDER'S command was associated with Col. DODGE'S, while POSEY'S brigade took the place of ALEXANDER'S.

The left wing as reorganized then moved up the right bank of Rock river, accompanied by their volunteer guides, the Winnebagoes. Having marched two days, until Rock river was reached a short distance above the mouth of Bark river, they retraced their steps in consequence of an express from Gen. ATKINSON, and crossed Rock river below the mouth of Bark river, where is the present village of Fort Atkinson. Here they met Gen. ATKINSON.

At this time, and at Gen. ATKINSON'S encampment, Capt. CHARLES DUNN, subsequently appointed Chief Justice, on the organization of the Territory of Wisconsin four years later, while acting as officer of the day, and going around to relieve the guard, was accidentally shot by one of the sentinels, and dangerously wounded. He was so disabled as to be compelled to return home, and was conveyed to Dixon by an escort.

It appeared subsequently, by discovery of the trail and other evidences, that a considerable ambush had been formed on the east bank of Rock river, at a point where the left wing would have been obliged to cross the stream. WHITE CROW had been anxious that Col. DODGE and Gen. ALEXAN-

DER should continue their march up the river, where they had been recalled by Gen. ATKINSON; and it was supposed that this treacherous Indian was acting in concert with BLACK HAWK, and was guiding the army to this point. This suspicion was strengthened by his conduct at the Blue Mounds at the time of the surrender of the Hall girls.

The Indians, in the meantime, finding themselves closely pressed by the advancing troops, had pushed up the river, evidently more anxious to escape their pursuers than to make war upon them.

General ATKINSON being short of provisions, now dispatched DODGE'S command of about two hundred and fifty men, together with HENRY'S and ALEXANDER'S brigades, to Fort Winnebago for supplies, and General POSEY'S brigade was ordered to the Mining Region for the protection of the forts and settlements in that quarter.

The detachment arrived at the Fort on the second day without casualty, and secured the requisite supplies. Colonel DODGE, finding a large number of Winnebagoes at the Fort, and the faithful Pauquette the interpreter, with whom he was well acquainted, and in whom he had the utmost confidence, at once set to work to find out from them the position of the Sauks and Foxes. He soon learned that they were encamped at the Rapids of Rock river, since known as Hustisford. To return by this route would require a divergence to the east of more than thirty miles from the route by which they had come. A council of the officers was held. General ALEXANDER objected that the divergence would be a violation of General ATKINSON'S orders, which required the detachment to return *immediately*. Colonel DODGE insisted that as there was no route specified in the orders, they might return by any route they should deem proper. General HENRY concurred in this opinion, and he and Colonel DODGE agreed to return by way of the Rapids, while General ALEXANDER was to return with the supplies, by the route they had all come.

The worn down horses were sent home, and the forces thereby reduced, so that the effective men which went to the Rapids were about seven hundred, accompanied by Pauquette and twelve Winnebagoes as guides. The command reached its objective point on Rock river the third day; but no indications of the Indians of whom they were in pursuit were found, except some trails that appeared to be several days old. An express was immediately started to go to General ATKINSON, which, after proceeding a few miles down the river, found a fresh trail, evidently bearing towards the Wisconsin river, and immediately returned and reported their discovery. Early the next morning the pursuit of the Sauks and Foxes was commenced on this trail; the express was again sent to General ATKINSON, but this time it did not return. The pursuit was rapid and persevering until it reached the Catfish, near its entrance into the Third Lake, where the force encamped the second night from Rock river. Many Indians were now discovered by the scouts, and the main body of them were on the peninsula between the Third and Fourth Lake, at the time their pursuers were encamped on the Catfish.

In the morning of the 21st, the pursuit was continued over the ground where the city of Madison is now located, with occasional glimpses of straggling Indians—one of whom was shot near the present Capitol, and left dead—until about five o'clock in the afternoon of that day, when the bluffs of the Wisconsin were reached, together with BLACK HAWK and his retreating band, preparing to cross the river with their women and children.

When the army arrived, the Sauks and Foxes were in the low grounds which skirt the river. The immediate commands of Col. DODGE and Col. WILLIAM L. D. EWING were in advance of the main army, and on their arrival at the bluffs they were met by Capt. DIXON's spy company, which had preceded them, with information that the Indians were in sight. These two commands having dismounted, formed the line and advanced to the edge of the bluffs, where they were met by the Indians, who were in pursuit of the spy company. The battle began, and the Sauks and Foxes were repulsed. The position of the advanced commands was maintained under a heavy fire for about an hour, when Col. HENRY's brigade arrived, which, deploying to the right and left, formed the line of battle, leaving Col. DODGE's command in the center. A general charge was now made upon the Indians, in which many of them were killed, and the balance driven into the bottoms of the Wisconsin, where the tall grass was reached, which was wet, and concealed the Indians, and it being nearly dark, the pursuit was continued no further.

The battle began about five o'clock in the afternoon, and

about sundown the firing on both sides had mainly ceased. The American loss was one killed and eight wounded. The loss of the Indians was sixty-eight killed in the battle, and a great many were afterward found dead, on the north side of the Wisconsin river, on the route to the Bad Axe. The number of wounded is unknown. This engagement has ever since been known as the Battle of the Wisconsin Heights.

The morning of the morrow disclosed that the Indians had all crossed the Wisconsin river, and disappeared. The army marched to the Blue Mounds, where Col. DODGE's command, being all near their homes, with worn out horses, were temporarily dismissed to their respective posts, until again called to active duty.

Expresses were sent to Gen. ATKINSON and to Prairie du Chien, and it was a few days before the army could again be brought together to continue the pursuit. Gen. ATKINSON with his army marched by way of the Blue Mounds to Helena. Here the volunteers under Col. DODGE were again assembled, and the whole army crossed the Wisconsin, and soon discovered the trail of the retreating Indians. On the 2d of August—the twelfth day after the battle of the Wisconsin Heights—the army came up with the entire body of the Indians, near the mouth of the Bad Axe, about forty miles above Prairie du Chien. A steamboat, the Warrior, had also been sent up the river, armed with a six-pounder, to prevent their escape across the Mississippi. Thus surrounded, the Indians fell easy victims, and the battle soon terminated in the total destruction of a very large portion of BLACK HAWK's followers, men, women, and children, and the capture and dispersion of the remainder.

Gen. ATKINSON's official report states the loss of the regulars at five killed and four wounded: of the Illinois volunteers at nine killed and wounded, and in HENRY's brigade seven killed and wounded; and this, the final engagement of the Black Hawk war, is known as the battle of the Bad Axe.

Most of the Sauks and Foxes who got safely across the Mississippi, including women and children, were pursued and killed by their implacable enemies, the Sioux. For the proud and haughty BLACK SPARROW HAWK, as he called himself, it was too degrading and humiliating to submit as a prisoner, therefore instant flight became his last and only alternative. He hastily retreated to a neighboring height, accompanied by his faithful adjunct, the Prophet; and giving vent to a loud yell of revenge, he hastily fled to seek a temporary refuge among his *pseudo* friends, the Winnebagoes, in the valley of the Lemonweir—over the bluffs and cliffs of which he had in former days roamed in security and hunted with success.

A large reward had been offered for the capture of BLACK HAWK, and he found now, when he most needed their friendship, that the Winnebagoes were in no way disposed to sympathize with him in his adversity. The fugitives pursued their lonely retreat to the Dalles of the Wisconsin river, and were there captured about two miles above Kilbourn City, by CHA-E-TAR and the ONE-EYED DE-COR-RA, who afterwards brought them to Prairie du Chien, on the 27th of August, and delivered them as prisoners to General STREET, the Indian Agent.

In addition to the regular forces under General ATKINSON, General SCOTT with nine companies of artillery was ordered from the seaboard to the scene of hostilities. These troops left Fortress Monroe on the 20th of June, and arrived at Fort Dearborn on the 8th of July. But the conflict was over before they reached the scene of action. They, however, encountered a more fatal foe. The Asiatic cholera, which for the first time visited America, coming by way of Montreal, seized the troops at Detroit on their way to Chicago. The camp became a hospital, and more than four hundred of these soldiers fell victims of this terrible pestilence.

The loss on the part of the Americans in the Black Hawk war, independent of the ravages of the cholera, and the murders of the settlers, is believed to have been about fifty. The loss of the Sauks was not less than two hundred and thirty killed in battle, and probably a greater number who died of their wounds, and of disease and starvation; while the deaths of the women and children who accompanied the warriors, in the battles, and from their wounds, and by disease, starvation and drowning, cannot be approximately estimated.

The companies of volunteers under the immediate command of Colonel DODGE, at the battle of the Wisconsin Heights, were Captain STEPHENSON's, from Galena; Captain CLARKE's, from White Oak Springs; Captain GENTRY's, from

Mineral Point; Captain PARKINSON'S, from Fort Defiance; Captain JONES', from Blue River; and Captain DICKSON'S, from Platteville. Lieutenant CHARLES BRACKEN was Adjutant to the battalion and aid to Colonel DODGE.

BLACK HAWK knew and feared Colonel DODGE, and said:

"If it had not been for that chief, DODGE, 'the hairy face,' I could easily have whipped the whites; I could have gone anywhere my people pleased in the mining country."

BLACK HAWK was sent as a prisoner from Prairie du Chien to Jefferson Barracks, under charge of Lieut. JEFFERSON DAVIS—then in the United States Army at Prairie du Chien, and thirty years later, President of the Confederate States. BLACK HAWK was kept a close prisoner until April, 1833, when he was taken to Washington, together with some of his family, and the Prophet. After an interview with President JACKSON, and being emphatically told by him that the Government would compel the red men to be at peace, they were sent as prisoners to Fortress Monroe, for "levying war," as DAVIS was, thirty-two years later, for the same offense. On June 4th, 1833, by order of the President, BLACK HAWK and his fellow prisoners were liberated and sent home under officers appointed to conduct them through the principal cities of the Union, in order to impress them with a proper sense of the power of the whites, and of the hopelessness of any conflict, on the part of the Indians, with the Government of the United States. BLACK HAWK ever after remained quiet. He died October 3, 1838, and was buried on the banks of the Mississippi, in the State of Iowa, near the head of the Des Moines Rapids, where the village of Montrose is located.

This was the last of Indian wars upon the soil of the present State of Wisconsin.

CHAPTER XIII.

CIVIL GOVERNMENT—1512 TO 1834.

The domain which constitutes the State of Wisconsin has been successively claimed as within the dominion of Spain, of France, of England, of Virginia, and finally of the United States, until, on the 29th of May, 1848, it was "admitted into the Union on an equal footing with the original States in all respects whatever."

This claim of dominion carried with it the uncontested right of civil jurisdiction.

In the earlier periods, the military and civil jurisdiction exercised by the governors and others, upon whom power was conferred, were so blended together, that if the government was not that of martial law, civil rights were recognized only through the channels of military authority; and it was not until the ordinance of 1787 "for the government of the territory of the United States northwest of the River Ohio," that the distinct civil rights of the inhabitants were recognized, and civil remedies for their enforcement provided.

Florida was claimed by Spain to extend as far as Newfoundland on the sea coast, and westerly and northwesterly indefinitely, by virtue of the discovery of PONCE DE LEON in 1512, who was appointed governor of the country, and so continued until 1521.

In 1537 CHARLES V. conceded to FERDINAND DE SOTO the government of the Isle of Cuba, with absolute power over the immense territory to which the name of Florida was still vaguely applied. DE SOTO died on the 21st of May, 1542, and wrapped in a mantle was buried in the Mississippi, which he had been the first to discover.

On the 20th of March, 1563, a compact was framed and confirmed between King PHILIP II. and PEDRO MELENDEZ DE AVILES, by which, in consideration of the promise of MELENDEZ to invade Florida, complete its conquest, and establish a colony, he was constituted its governor for life, with the right of naming his son-in-law as his successor.

The history of civil government in Florida, previous to the seventeenth century, possesses no interest so far as applicable to Wisconsin, whose soil was probably never pressed by the foot of a white man until the advent of NICOLLET, in 1634. We must therefore turn to the claims of dominion set up by France for the earliest pretensions of the right to establish civil government upon our domain.

The charter grant of New France, made to the "hundred associates," among whom were RICHELIEU, CHAMPLAIN, RESZILLY, and a number of opulent merchants of France, was referred to in the first chapter, and the fact stated that the government of the province was not entered upon until after the restoration of Quebec by the English in 1632.

At this time CHAMPLAIN was governor of Canada.

In 1663 the company of the hundred associates resigned the colony to the king, and immediately, under the auspices of COLBERT, it was conceded to the new company of the West Indies.

In 1665 the colony was protected by a royal regiment, with TRACY as viceroy, COURCELLES as governor, and TALON as intendant and representative of the King in civil affairs.

In May, 1671, at the Sault St. Mary, the French, represented by ST. LUSSON as the delegate of TALON, at an assembled congress of Indian tribes, raised a cross of cedar, and planted by the side of it a cedar column, marked with the lilies of the Bourbons. Thus were the authority and the faith of France uplifted in the presence of the aboriginal races of America, in the heart of our continent.

It was eleven years later (1682) that LA SALLE, having descended the Mississippi to its mouth, formally took possession for France of all the country watered by the Father of Waters, and named it Louisiana.

During the war in America between France and England declared by France in 1689 and terminated by the peace of Ryswick in September, 1697, Count FRONTENAC was governor of Canada. As a result of the war, France retained possession of all the territory which she claimed at the beginning of it, including Canada and the valley of the Mississippi; and the military occupation of Illinois continued without interruption.

The territorial claims of the English colonists on the Atlantic coast, to an extension of their limits westward, whatever they might have been under the terms of their respective charters, did not, during the seventeenth century, practically interfere with the French claims west of the great lakes and in the Mississippi valley.

Soon after the war, as early at least as 1700, DE CALLIERS became governor-general of Canada.

Previous to 1711 the settlements of Louisana had been a dependence on New France or Canada. In this year it was made an independent government, responsible only to the crown and comprising all the "Illinois country" under its jurisdiction. The seat of the colonial government was established at Mobile. DE MUYS, who had been appointed the governor-general, died on the voyage and DIRON D'ARTAQUETTE, early in the year, entered upon his duties as commissary *ordonnateur*.

In 1712, DE LA MOTTE CADILLAC, who eleven years previously had made the first permanent settlement at Detroit, was the royal governor of Louisiana.

The Marquis DE VAUDREUIL was governor of Canada from 1704 until his death, April 10, 1725. His salary was the modest sum of £272—1s—8d.

He was succeeded by the Marquis DE BEAUHARNOIS who held the office until 1745.

In that year Admiral DE LA JONQUIERE was sent from France, as governor, with a naval expedition to capture Nova Scotia; but on the 3rd of May, 1746, they fell in with a British fleet under Admiral ANSON and Rear Admiral WARREN and were compelled to surrender.

As soon as the capture of the Governor was known in France, Compte DE LA GALISSONERE was appointed to fill the vacancy, but the Admiral (JONQUIERE) being shortly released from captivity and conveyed to Canada the Count (GALISSONERE) returned to France. Admiral JONQUIERE, before his successor could be appointed, died at Quebec, May 17, 1752.

The Marquis DU QUESNE DE MENNEVILLE was appointed Governor of Canada, Louisiana, Cape Breton, St. Johns and their dependencies.

The Marquis DU QUESNE resigned and returned to the marine service and the Marquis DE VAUDREUIL DE CAVAGNAC, son of the former governor, was appointed to succeed him. His commission was registered July 10, 1755, and he continued in office until the conquest by Great Britain in 1763.

Major General JAMES MURRAY was commissioned November 21, 1763, as Captain General and Governor-in-Chief of the province of Quebec.

The claim of France to dominion over the whole of the Northwest Territory continued until it was successfully disputed by Great Britain, and finally relinquished as the result of the war which ensued between those two powerful rival nations.

This claim of dominion in the entire valley of the Mississippi was practically evidenced by its settlements on the head waters of the Alleghany, which in 1753 led Governor DINWIDDIE of Virginia to assert civil jurisdiction over those settlements, by sending young WASHINGTON, to demand of the commander of the French forces the reason for invading the British dominions in a time of peace.

This was soon followed by the war between France and England, which after varying fortunes resulted in the signing of the preliminaries of peace on the third day of November, 1762, and their ratification by treaty on the tenth of February, 1763.

By this treaty, the West Indies, Florida, Louisiana to the Mississippi (but without the island of New Orleans), all Canada, Acadia, and Cape Breton, with its dependent islands, were all ceded to England; while New Orleans and all Louisiana west of the Mississippi, with boundaries undefined, were at the same time ceded to Spain.

Virginia was the representative of the British claim to jurisdiction in the valley of the Ohio River and the civil jurisdiction was represented in the person of the Governor of that colony.

In October, 1776, the general Assembly of Virginia divided the district of West Augusta (then comprising all the northwestern part of the State) into three distinct counties with the names of "Ohio, Yohogany and Monongahela."

On Monday, the 6th January, 1777, the first court for the county of Ohio was held at Black's cabin.

There is every reason to believe that this was the first civil court held in the valley of the Mississippi.

The French posts in the "Illinois Country," having in 1778 surrendered to Virginia, the inhabitants, upon learning of the alliance between France and the United States, readily joined the latter in the war against Great Britain, and acknowledged the jurisdiction of the United States and Virginia over the country.

The legislature of Virginia, in October 1778, formally extended its jurisdiction over all the settlements on the Wabash and the upper Mississippi by establishing the county of Illinois, and appointing JOHN TODD Lieutenant Colonel and civil commandant.

The new county of Illinois embraced all of the territory within the limits of the present State of Wisconsin.

Few events in the progress of civil government in the Northwest, worthy of record, transpired during the Revolutionary war, nor until the adoption by the Continental Congress of the ordinance of 1787.

This ordinance was the fundamental as well as the organic law—the MAGNA CHARTA of the great Northwest— and was adopted by the Continental Congress July 13, 1787. The territory to which its provisions applied was not otherwise defined than in the title, which was "The territory of the United States northwest of the River Ohio."

The boundaries were well understood to be the Ohio river on the south, the Mississippi river on the west, while on the north the territorial limits were the undefined and unsettled, if not disputed boundary line, between the British possessions and the United States.

This magnificent territory, vast in area, but destitute of civilized occupancy, except at the few points already mentioned, was destined within a century to exercise a great, if not a controlling, influence upon the affairs of the nation.

The first census, taken in 1790, does not show the population of the Northwest Territory, but in the census of 1800, in stating the population of Indiana Territory, it is said: "On the 1st of August, 1800, at Prairie du Chien were sixty-five souls; at Green Bay there were fifty souls."

The population of the six States which have been formed out of it, by the census of 1880, was 12,989,571, being more than one fourth of the entire population of the United States.

The present and future interest of the people of Wisconsin in this ordinance, aside from its historical interest, arises from the fact that they are entitled to all the rights and privileges granted and secured to the people of the Northwestern Territory by the articles of compact contained in it.

The ordinance contained two distinct characteristics:

One was the legislative feature, by which rules of inheritance were prescribed; the appointment of territorial officers —governor, secretary, judges, and inferior officers—was provided for, as well as the modes by which the functions of local legislation might be exercised. These provisions, and some others of a cognate character, were like any other legislative act, subject to be modified or repealed by the old Congress, or by that to which it gave place about twenty months later, organized under the Constitution of the United States.

The other characteristic was the "articles of compact" which it contained, "between the original States and the people and States of the said territory," and which were to "forever remain unalterable unless by common consent."

There were six of these "articles."

By the fifth of them, the southern boundary of the States of Michigan and Wisconsin, it was declared, should be an "east and west line drawn through the southerly bend or extreme of Lake Michigan."

The sixth has been styled the "charter of freedom," and prohibited "slavery and involuntary servitude in the said territory otherwise than in the punishment of crimes, whereof the party shall have been duly convicted."

The ordinance was published at length in the Revised Statutes of 1839.

On the 15th of October, 1787, Gen. ARTHUR ST. CLAIR was elected by the Continental Congress the first governor of the Northwestern Territory, and WINTHROP SARGEANT, secretary. On the 16th of October SAMUEL HOLDEN PARSONS, JOHN ARMSTRONG, and JAMES MITCHELL VARNUM were elected the first judges of the Territory.

ARMSTRONG declined, and JOHN CLEVES SYMMES was appointed to the vacancy in February, 1788. VARNUM died in 1789, and WILLIAM BARTON was appointed his successor, but declined, and GEORGE TURNER was appointed in 1789, to fill the vacancy, and accepted.

Judge PARSONS was drowned November 10, 1789, in attempting to cross Big Beaver creek, and RUFUS PUTNAM became his successor March 31, 1790.

In 1796 Judge PUTNAM resigned and was succeeded by JOSEPH GILMAN.

On the 29th of October, 1798, Gov. St. CLAIR issued a proclamation directing an election on the third Monday of December, 1798, of members of the House of Representatives.

The five persons selected by Congress to constitute the council were JACOB BURNETT, HENRY VANDENBERG, ROBERT OLIVER, JAMES FINDLAY and DAVID VANCE.

CIVIL GOVERNMENT — 1512 TO 1834.   157

The Council and House of Representatives met at Cincinnati September 16, 1799, and elected WILLIAM H. HARRISON delegate in Congress from the Northwest Territory, who was the first delegate from a Territory ever admitted on the floor of the House of Representatives.

General HARRISON also succeeded WINTHROP SARGEANT as Secretary in 1798, and in 1799 was succeeded by CHARLES WILLING BYRD.

JOHN ARMSTRONG was Treasurer from 1792 to 1803.

WM. MCMILLAN was elected delegate as the successor of General HARRISON and served in 1800 and 1801, and in turn was succeeded by PAUL FEARING who held the office from 1801 to 1803.

On the 4th of January, 1803, a resolution was introduced that, Ohio having formed a state government, Mr. FEARING was no longer entitled to a seat as a delegate from the Northwestern Territory. The resolution, however, does not appear to have been acted upon.

BENJAMIN PARKE took his seat as delegate from the Territory of Indiana, December 12, 1805, and continued as such during that and the two next sessions when he resigned and JESSE B. THOMAS was elected as his successor and took his seat December 1, 1808.

In 1809 JONATHAN JENNINGS was elected, and took his seat November 27, 1809. A memorial against his right to the seat was presented to the committee on elections who reported adversely to his right. The House, however, overruled the report and Mr. JENNINGS retained his seat during that and the next session.

The Territory of Illinois was created February 3rd, 1809, and embraced the territory now forming Wisconsin.

During the period from January, 1805, when the Territory of Michigan was created embracing Wisconsin, until February, 1809, Michigan had no delegate in Congress.

Neither did the Territory of Illinois have any until the year 1812, when SHADRACK BOND was elected delegate and took his seat December 3, 1812. A petition of BENJAMIN M. PIATT, protesting against the election of Mr. BOND was presented, but was never acted upon, and he held the seat during that and the two subsequent sessions when he resigned.

In 1814 BENJAMIN STEPHENSON was elected in place of Mr. BOND resigned, and continued to hold the office until 1816, when NATHANIEL POPE was elected delegate and took his seat December 2, 1816, which he continued to hold until Illinois was admitted as a State in the Union.

The first delegate elected from Michigan Territory was in 1819 when WM. W. WOODBRIDGE was chosen and held the office until the next year, when he resigned and SOLOMON SIBLEY was elected his successor and took his seat November 20, 1820.

In 1823 GABRIEL RICHARD was elected delegate as the successor of Mr. SIBLEY and took his seat December 8, 1823. A petition representing that Mr. RICHARD was ineligible was presented by JOHN BIDDLE, but it was withdrawn and no action taken on it, and Mr. RICHARD held the office during that and the next session

In 1825 AUSTIN E. WING was elected, and re-elected in 1827, serving the entire terms of the 19th and 20th Congresses.

In 1829 JOHN BIDDLE was elected and served until February 21, 1831, about ten days before the expiration of his term when he resigned.

In 1831 AUSTIN E. WING was again elected. He took his seat December 8, 1831, and served until the expiration of his term, March 3, 1833.

LUCIUS LYON was elected in 1833, and took his seat December 2d, 1833, and held it until March 3d, 1835.

The inhabitants of Michigan, east of Lake Michigan, having in 1835 adopted a State constitution, although not yet admitted into the Union, did not elect a delegate in Congress but claimed to be represented in both houses of Congress as a sovereign State. The voters cf Michigan Territory, however, not within the boundaries of the new State, together with a few within it, held an election in 1835, which resulted in the choice of GEORGE W. JONES, who took his seat December 7th, 1835.

An act of Congress passed in 1789, provided that the President of the United States by and with the advice and consent of the Senate, should have all the power and authority and perform all the duties, in relation to the appointment and removal of officers, which by the ordinance were to have been appointed by the United States in Congress assembled. And that the President of the United States, instead of Congress, should be the organ of communication with the Governor and other officers of the Territory.

And that in case of the death, removal, resignation or necessary absence of the Governor, the Secretary should execute the powers and perform the duties of the Governor during such vacancy.

In 1792, an act of Congress was passed which authorized the Governor and judges to repeal laws made by them, whenever the same might be found to be improper. That one of the judges in the absence of the others should be authorized to hold a court. And that the Secretary of State provide seals for the public officers in the territory.

By act of December 15, 1800, the franking privilege was extended to the delegate, and his compensation fixed the same as members of the House.

On the 7th of May, 1800, INDIANA TERRITORY was organized, embracing all of the Northwestern Territory which lies to the westward of a line " beginning at the Ohio, opposite to the mouth of the Kentucky river, and running thence to Fort Recovery, and thence north until it shall intersect the territorial line between the United States and Canada."

The act organizing the new territory created a government in all respects similar to that provided by the ordinance of 1787.

The powers, duties, and compensation of territorial officers were the same as those of the " Northwestern Territory" under the ordinance of 1787.

Saint Vincennes, on the Wabash river, was made the seat of the government for the new Indiana Territory.

On the 30th of April, 1802, Congress passed an act to enable the inhabitants of the eastern division to form a constitution and State government; the western boundary of which should be a line drawn north from the mouth of the Great Miami; which provided that the territory west of that line should be part of the Indiana Territory.

On the 29th day of November, 1802, the constitution was adopted and State government created under the name of the "State of Ohio."

By act of Congress passed February 19, 1803, it was declared that "the said State has become one of the United States of America."

According to the census of 1800, the eastern division of the Northwestern Territory (Ohio) contained a population of 45,365, and the new Indiana Territory 5,641, of which 135 were returned as slaves.

An act to divide the Indiana Territory into two separate governments, approved January 11, 1805, prescribed that —

"All that part of the Indiana Territory which lies north of a line drawn east from the southerly bend or extreme of Lake Michigan, until it shall intersect Lake Erie, and east of a line drawn from the said southerly bend through the middle of said lake to its northern extremity, and thence due north to the northern boundary of the United States, shall, for the purpose of temporary government, constitute a separate Territory, and be called Michigan."

The provisions of government prescribed by the ordinance of 1787 were extended over the Territory of Michigan, as by the act of May 7, 1800, they had been over the Indiana Territory. Detroit was established as the seat of government until Congress should otherwise direct.

On the 3d of February, 1809 "an act for dividing the Indiana Territory into two separate governments," was passed, by which the civil jurisdiction in that portion of the territory which is now Wisconsin, was conferred upon the government of the newly created Territory of Illinois.

The boundaries of the "Separate Territory" were by the act defined to be "all that part of the Indiana Territory, which lies west of the Wabash river and Post Vincennes, due north to the territorial line between the United States and Canada."

The terms in which the powers of the territorial government were conferred upon its officers, and the appointment of officers provided for, were nearly identical with those used in the act of 1805 conferring like powers, and in the appointment of like officers in the Territory of Michigan.

Kaskaskia was established as the seat of government until it should be otherwise ordered by the legislature of the Illinois Territory.

By an act of Congress, approved March 3d, 1815, Illinois was divided into three judicial circuits, and one of the three judges was assigned by allotment to each circuit. The judges were required to hold two terms annually in each county. The county of Madison was in the first circuit, and embraced all of the northern part of Illinois, and what is now Wisconsin.

The courts had general, civil and criminal jurisdiction and their judges or a majority of them constituted a court of appeals, and was required to hold two sessions annually at Kaskaskia.

St. Clair county, organized April 28, 1809, included the

whole territory of Illinois and Wisconsin, to the British possessions, and St. Clair and Randolph counties were the only counties in the Territory.

Madison county was erected from St. Clair September 14, 1812, and comprised all the territory north of the line of the second township south, to the line of the British possessions.

Bond county, organized January 4, 1817, extended in a strip about thirty miles wide, on each side of the third principal meridian, to the northern boundary of the territory.

The time had now arrived for Illinois to take her place as one of the states in the Union, and by an act of Congress passed April 18, 1818, the inhabitants of the Territory were authorized to form for themselves a constitution and state Government and to be admitted into the Union.

The north boundary of the state was the parallel of north latitude of forty-two degrees and thirty minutes.

It is noticeable that Congress in fixing the northern boundary of the new state, disregarded the *fifth* of the " articles of compact between the original states and the people and states in the said territory" contained in the Ordinance of 1787, and which were to " forever remain unalterable, unless by common consent," and which contemplated that the northern boundary should be " an east and west line drawn through the southerly bend or extreme of Lake Michigan."

There is a semblance of an attempt, however, to obtain this common consent in a *proviso*, which immediately follows the designation of boundaries, in these words:

"*Provided*, that the convention hereinafter provided for, when formed, shall ratify the boundaries aforesaid; otherwise, they shall remain as now prescribed by the ordinance for the government of the territory, northwest of the river Ohio."

The " people " of the fifth state (Wisconsin) were not consulted, and had no opportunity to " ratify " this transfer to Illinois of 8,400 square miles of the choicest part of that state as contemplated by the ordinance; an area extending sixty miles north and south, and from Lake Michigan to the Mississippi River.

The act authorized the election of thirty-three representatives apportioned among the fifteen counties, to form a convention, which should meet at the seat of government on the first Monday of August, with authority to form a constitution and state government, if it should deem it expedient: *Provided,* that it should not be repugnant to the

Ordinance of 1787 "*excepting so much of said articles as relate to the boundaries of states therein to be formed.*"

The convention met and on the 26th day of August completed the formation of a constitution and state government, and, on the 3rd day of December, 1818, by a joint resolution of the two houses of Congress, Illinois was declared to be one of the states of the Union.

Civil government of the remaining portion of the Northwestern Territory lying west of Lake Michigan was transferred from Illinois Territory to Michigan Territory by the *seventh* section of said enabling act of April 18, 1818.

An act passed February 16, 1819, authorized the citizens of Michigan Territory to elect a delegate to Congress who should possess the qualifications and exercise the privileges required of and granted to the delegates from the several territories of the United States.

The elective franchise was conferred upon and limited to the free white male citizens of the Territory above the age of twenty-one years who had resided therein one year and paid a county or territorial tax.

On the 30th day of January, 1823, an act was passed to take effect from and after the 20th of March, by the provisions of which an additional judge for the Michigan Territory was required to be appointed

"Who should possess and exercise within the counties of Michilimackinac, Brown and Crawford, the jurisdiction and powers possessed and exercised by the Supreme Court of the said Territory, and by the County Courts of said counties respectively, within the said counties, and to the exclusion of the original jurisdiction of the said Supreme Court."

Appeals were allowed from the County Court to the court established by this act, and writs of error to this court, from the Supreme Court, and appeals in suits in equity.

This court was required to hold one term annually in each county; at Prairie du Chien on the second Monday in May; at Green Bay on the second Monday in June, and at Mackinaw on the third Monday in July.

The clerks of the court were the clerks of the County Courts and the officers appointed to execute the process of the County Courts, were authorized and required to execute the process of this court.

The judge was required by the act to reside in one of the counties, and was paid the same salary and in the same manner as the judges of the Supreme Court.

The first judge appointed under this act was JAMES D.

DOTY, only twenty-four years of age at the time of his appointment. He first resided at Prairie du Chien for a short time and afterwards permanently at Green Bay. He was succeeded by DAVID IRVIN, who was appointed April 26, 1832, by President ANDREW JACKSON, and continued to hold the office until the organization of the Territory of Wisconsin in 1836, having been appointed one of the three judges of the Supreme Court of Wisconsin Territory.

A radical alteration of the mode in which the affairs of civil government were to be administered in the Territory of Michigan was made by an act of Congress passed March 3, 1823.

It was provided by this act that the same powers which were granted to the Governor, Legislative Council, and House of Representatives of the Northwestern Territory by the ordinance of 1787, and which were transferred to the Territory of Michigan by the act of January 11, 1805, were thereby conferred upon, and should be exercised by the Governor and a Legislative Council; that the Council should consist of nine persons, to serve for two years, of whom five should be a quorum, and be appointed as follows: The qualified electors of the Territory were to chose by ballot eighteen persons, whose names were to be transmitted by the Governor to the President of the United States, who was to nominate, and by and with the advice and consent of the Senate, appoint therefrom nine, who should constitute the Legislative Council.

The power of disapproval of any act passed by the Governor and Legislative Council was reserved to Congress.

The act provided that the Legislature should have power to submit at any time to the people the question whether a general assembly should be organized, agreeably to the provisions of the ordinance of 1787, and for the mode of such organization if a majority of the qualified electors should be in favor of it.

The tenure of office of the judges of the Territory was declared by the act to be limited to four years, and that the office should become vacant on the first day of February, 1824, and every four years thereafter. It was enacted that the judges should possess a chancery as well as a common law jurisdiction, and that their powers and duties should be regulated by such laws as were or might be in force in the Territory.

Two years subsequently the number of persons to be chosen by the people and transmitted to the President, from whom the members of the Legislative Council were to be appointed, was, by an act of Congress passed February 5, 1825, increased from eighteen to twenty-six, and the number to be appointed from nine to thirteen, and their compensation was increased from two to three dollars per day.

By the same act the Governor and Legislative Council were authorized to divide the Territory into townships and provide for the election of township officers; and also to provide for the election of all county officers, except judges of courts of record and clerk thereof, sheriffs, judges of probate, and justices of the peace; and that all other non-elective civil officers in the Territory, except such as are appointed by the President and Senate, should be appointed by the Governor and Legislative Council.

The act also prescribed that not less than two judges of the Supreme, or Superior Court of the Territory should hold, or transact the business of a court.

Such was the progress of the idea of popular government, that at the next Congress, by an act passed January 29, 1827, it was provided that the electors of the Territory, instead of choosing twenty-six, should " elect thirteen fit persons as their representatives," who should constitute the Legislative Council. The Governor and Legislative Council were to apportion the representatives among the several counties or districts in proportion to the number of inhabitants in each.

But the reluctance to intrusting the people of a Territory with the power of electing their own representatives, in their own legislature, was such, that Congress, although it had the reserved power of disapproving of any act of the Territorial Legislature, inserted a section "that Congress have the right, at any time, to alter or repeal this act."

The settlement of that part of Michigan Territory known as the " Lead Mines," had so increased by 1830, that an act of Congress was passed on the 2d of April, in that year, which provided "that the term of the court appointed to be held annually on the second Monday of May, at the village of Prairie du Chien, by the additional judge of the United States for the Territory of Michigan, shall be held on the first Monday of October, annually, at Mineral Point, in the county of Iowa," and the clerk and sheriff of that county were to be the clerk and sheriff of the court.

The domain of the Territory of Michigan was more than doubled by an act of Congress passed June 28, 1834, which added to it the territory now embraced in the states of Iowa, Minnesota, and that part of Dakota which lies east of the Missouri River. It was provided that "the inhabitants therein shall be entitled to the same privileges and immunities as the other citizens of Michigan Territory."

CHAPTER XIV.

LEGISLATION PREVIOUS TO 1835.

The last chapter was devoted to an account of civil government for a period of 322 years, during which Wisconsin was successively under the dominion of Spain, of France, of Great Britain, Virginia, and the United States.

To present in a connected way that feature of civil government, which consists of its legislation, during the same period — or more correctly the latter half of it — is the purpose of this chapter.

The first actual occupation of the Northwest Territory, as has been seen, was by the French.

During this possession which continued until 1763, when it was succeeded by British occupancy, the customs of Paris and the ordinances of the Kingdom with certain arrets and decrees of the Canadian authorities, constituted the rule of civil conduct in that extensive region of country.

The administration of justice however seems to have been limited to the more densely settled portions of the country. There only, courts of justice were established.

These laws were never enforced at any of the northern posts, or in the settlements which grew up in their vicinity. The parish priest and a few intelligent Frenchmen might have been provided with a copy of the "*Coutume de Paris,*" but there was no judicial officer to administer it.

The only civil officer located at any of these posts, was a notary public duly commissioned by the governor. He was an educated man, versed in the "*Coutume*" and a very important official, in view of the duties which devolved upon him. He was required to keep a register, in which he recorded all the legal instruments drawn by him. It was his duty to keep the original document, and to furnish the parties interested with certified copies. Some of these instruments have been the subject of litigation in modern times.

In all matters of controversy between the inhabitants, justice was administered by the commandant of the post in a summary manner. The party complaining obtained a notification to his adversary of his complaint accompanied by a command to render justice. If this had no effect he was notified to appear before the commandant on a particular day and answer the complaint; and if the last notice was neglected, a sergeant and file of men were sent to bring him. The recusant was fined and kept in prison until he did his adversary justice. There was no sheriff and no costs.

But the practical administration of laws during this period was exceedingly limited in its effects, in that portion of the Northwest now constituting Wisconsin. The only inhabitants to be affected by it were at Green Bay, and possibly at Prairie du Chien. We have seen that as late as 1745 the colony at Green Bay did not exceed eight persons, and it is not probable that it was materially increased before the post was occupied by British troops in 1761. It is a matter of serious doubt whether there were any inhabitants at Prairie du Chien until after the jurisdiction passed to Great Britain.

On the 7th of October, 1763, immediately after the transfer of the country, the British King established by proclamation four separate and distinct governments, called Quebec, East and West Florida and Grenada, and at the same time introduced into these provinces the civil and criminal laws of England, but no part of the territory north of the Ohio river was embraced within the limits of either, and for a period of eleven years that portion of the country appeared to be without the pale of civil government.

In 1774 a bill was introduced into Parliament as a government measure to make "more effectual provisions for the Government of Quebec in North America." Upon motion of Burke the bill was amended so as to embrace the whole Northwest Territory which was declared to be "annexed to and made a part of the Province of Quebec."

The bill was passed and the domain which is now Wisconsin was subjected to its provisions by which

"Canadian subjects were to hold and enjoy their property and possessions, with all customs and usages relative thereto, and all their civil rights in as large, ample and beneficial manner as if the proclamation, ordinances and other acts had not been passed; and it is declared that in all matters of controversy, relative to property and civil rights resort should be had to the laws of Canada, as the rule for the decisions of the same. All suits relative to such property and rights, were to be determined agreeably to such laws and customs until altered by the Governor and Legislative Council. The owner of lands, goods or credits had a right to alienate the same in his life-time, by deed of sale, gift or otherwise or to devise or bequeath the same, at his death, by last will or testament to be executed either according to the laws of Canada or the laws of England. The criminal law of England was to be continued in force in the Province. The King might appoint a council, who should have power and authority to make ordinances for the peace, welfare and good government of the Province, with the consent of the Governor, and which were to be also approved by the King; but no ordinance should be made touching religion, or by which any punishment might be inflicted greater than fine and imprisonment for three months, until approved by the King."

Such were the principal provisions of the act, which the Old Congress in 1774 denounced as unjust, because it

"Extended the Province, so as to border on the western frontier of the colonies, establishing an arbitrary government therein, and discouraged the settlement of British subjects in that wide extended country — thus by the influence of evil principles and ancient prejudices, to dispose the inhabitants to act with hostility to the Protestant Colonies whenever a wicked ministry shall choose to direct them."

This is the law which in the Declaration of Independence is referred to as one of those "acts of pretended legislation" to which the King had given his assent, in these words:

"For abolishing the free system of English laws in a neighboring province, establishing therein an arbitrary government, and enlarging its boundaries, so as to render it at once an example and fit instrument for introducing the same absolute rule into these colonies."

Notwithstanding the adoption of this law the inhabitants of the district of country "annexed to and made a part of the province of Quebec" were not yet destined to realize the benefit of a civil government. A few justices of the peace were commissioned but this was all.

A citizen of Detroit, who went there in 1778, relates that in 1779, the governor

"Getting tired of administering justice, proposed to the merchants to establish a court of trustees, with jurisdiction extending to £10 Halifax currency. Eighteen of these entered into a bond that three of them should be a weekly court, in rotation, and that they should defend any appeal which might be taken from their decision. They rendered judgment and issued execution, and imprisoned the defendant in the guard house."

Neither the change of sovereigns or of laws seems to have

resulted in any benefit to the inhabitants of that portion of the annexed country, which now constitutes Michigan or Wisconsin. No courts had been established, no competent judge appointed, or jail erected. The settlements were still too remote from the provincial capital, and intercourse difficult, and at times impracticable. The fostering care of these governments was almost entirely withheld from the early settlers.

At length the Captain-General of the Province, by proclamation in 1788, laid out the province into separate districts; and that which embraces Michigan and Wisconsin was called "Hesse."

On the 25th of November, 1790, the Imperial Parliament passed another act, by which it divided the Province of Quebec into two provinces, to be called the Province of Upper and Lower Canada respectively, each of which was to have a Legislative Council and General Assembly to make all laws not repugnant to that act, and to be approved by the King or the Governor,

The Governor with the Executive Council (appointed by the King) were, in each of the Provinces, created a court of civil jurisdiction for hearing and determining appeals. The act declares that the lands in Upper Canada (comprising Michigan and Wisconsin) should be granted in fee and common socage as in England, and that any person holding lands should be entitled to a fresh grant if desired.

The Legislature of Upper Canada by an act passed October 15, 1792

"Repealed the law of Canada and every part thereof, as forming a rule of decision in all matters of controversy relative to property and civil rights, but this was "not to affect existing rights, claims on real property, contracts or securities already executed."

From the passing of this act, in all matters of controversy relative to property and civil rights, it is declared that resort should be had to the laws of England as the rule for the decision of the same, and further

"That all matters relative to testimony and legal proof in the investigation of fact and the forms thereof, in the several courts of law and equity, should be regulated by the rules of evidence in England."

Further legislation introduced jury trial, established a court of request in each district, and provided for the building of a court-house and jail in every district.

Among the acts passed in 1793 was one fixing the terms and places of holding the Courts of General Quarter Sessions of the Peace, and another establishing a Court of Probate, and also a Surrogate Court in all the districts.

An act was also passed the same year to prevent the further introduction of slaves, and to limit the term of contracts for servitude within the province. The term was restricted to nine years from the date of the contract.

"The owners of slaves at that time were confirmed in their property therein. The children that should be born of female slaves were to remain in the service of the owner of their mother until the age of twenty-five years, when they were to be discharged. In case any issue should be born of children during their infant servitude or after, such issue were entitled to all the rights and privileges of free-born subjects."

In 1794 an act was passed for the regulation of juries. Also in the same year an act "to establish a Superior Court of civil and criminal jurisdiction, and to regulate the Court of Appeal."

The Court of King's Bench was required to be held by the Chief Justice and two Puisne judges; and its sessions were to be held "in the city, town, or place where the Governor or Lieutenant Governor should usually reside." The act is very minute in detailing the proceedings and practice of the court.

The Court of Appeals was to consist of the Governor, Lieutenant Governor, or the Chief Justice, together with any two or more members of the executive council. The judges below might assign their reasons, but not give their votes on the appeal.

An act to establish a court for the cognizance of small causes in each district was passed. By this act "the court for the Western District is required to be holden in the town of Detroit."

In this year the Governor was authorized by law to license practitioners in the law. These were to be —

"Liege subjects, not exceeding sixteen in number, as he should deem, from their education, probity, and condition in life, best qualified to act as advocates and attorneys;" they were then "holden as duly authorized to receive fees for practicing in any of the courts."

In 1795 a law was enacted "for the public registering of deeds, conveyances, wills, and other incumbrances which might be made or affect real estate." It prescribes the manner of making up a memorial of these instruments for record in the county where the lands lie.

On the 3d of June, 1796, the law which required the Quarter Sessions to be held at Mackinac was repealed, and as to the District Court which had been held at Detroit, it is declared that —

"As it seems not to be any longer expedient to hold the said court in the town of Detroit, it should thereafter be held where the General Quarter Sessions might be held."

The last term of this court was held at Detroit on the 29th of January, 1796.

Early in the month of July, 1796, in accordance with the provisions of JAY's treaty, all jurisdiction over and occupancy by the British government of the territory now constituting Michigan and Wisconsin, was formally surrendered to the United States.

On the 15th day of the same month a proclamation was issued by Governor ST. CLAIR, by which the county of Wayne was organized. It included the northwest part of Ohio, the northeast part of Indiana, and the whole of Wisconsin, and part of Minnesota, and annexed the same by a mere executive act to the United States Territory northwest of the River Ohio.

That the laws, usages and customs of a conquered or ceded country, continue in force till altered by the new sovereign, is a principle of jurisprudence which is universally recognized by the Supreme Court of the United States.

This principle was applicable to the Northwest Territory after the transfer of jurisdiction from Great Britain to the United States. The laws and rights of the inhabitants under them were left as they had been.

These laws were very materially modified by the action of the Governor and Judges of the Northwest Territory.

In 1795 the Governor and Judges adopted an act from Virginia, by which it is declared that

"The common law of England, all the statutes or acts of the British Parliament, made in aid of the common law prior to the fourth year of the reign of King James the First (and which are cf a general nature, not local to the Kingdom), and also the several laws in force in the Territory, shall be the rule of decision, and shall be considered of full force, until re pealed by legislative authority or disapproved of by Congress."

It was a contested question whether it was competent for the Governor and Judges to adopt this act, because it adopted as law in a new and thinly populated district, the whole jurisprudence of a foreign country, and because it was not an existing law of Virginia or of any original state. Upon this question the Judges were equally divided in opinion.

During the year 1805, thirty-four different acts were adopted and published together, at Detroit, by the Governor and Judges of the Territory of Michigan, which was called the "Woodward Code," Hon. AUGUSTUS B. WOODWARD being then Chief Justice of the Territory.

This code embraced nearly the entire scope of the civil polity of the newly created territorial government.

Among the subjects to which the acts composing this code related stated in the order of their adoption were the following: a territorial seal; the Marshal; oaths; courts; juries; notaries; recovery of debts; marriages; holding of lands by aliens; appeals; recording deeds; ferries; tavern-keepers and retailers; auctions; militia; compensation of officers; wills and intestacies; the territorial treasurer; literature; taxes; inquests; highways; imprisonment for debt and poor prisoners, paupers and some others.

None of these acts were local, but the scope of their operation embraced the entire limits of the territory; nor were any of them applicable exclusively to the Territory west of Lake Michigan.

From February 3, 1809, until December 3, 1818, the territory now embraced within the State of Wisconsin was under the jurisdiction of the Territory of Illinois.

In 1816, a compilation was published containing the titles, with a digest or a copy of the Acts of the Territory of Michigan, which could then be ascertained to be in force.

Hon. LEWIS CASS was then Governor of Michigan and the compilation appears to have been made by the Governor and Judges, and was called the "CASS CODE."

As the territory west of Lake Michigan was, at this time, a part of the Territory of Illinois, no alteration or repeal of former laws, nor any enactment of new ones, could have any effect upon its inhabitants until December 3, 1818, when upon the admission of Illinois into the Union, that portion of the Territory north of the new State of Illinois, was remanded to the jurisdiction of Michigan Territory.

On the 16th of September, 1810, an act of considerable importance was adopted by the Governor and Judges which continued in force in 1818 and subsequently was and may still be operative in Wisconsin. As it is nearly out of print, it is given entire — omitting the States from whose laws the several sections were adopted.

"WHEREAS, The good people of the Territory of Michigan may be ensnared by ignorance of acts of the parliament of England, and of acts of the parliament of Great Britain, which are not published among the laws of the territory, and it has been thought advisable by the governor and the judges of the territory of Michigan, hereafter specially to enact such of the said acts as shall appear worthy of adoption:

"*Be it therefore enacted by the Governor and Judges of the Territory of Michigan*: That no act of the parliament of England, and no act of the parliament of Great Britain shall have any force within the Territory of Michigan; Provided, that all rights arising under any such act, shall remain as if this act had not been made.

"SECTION 2. AND WHEREAS, the good people of the Territory of Michigan may be ensnared by ignorance of the laws of other governments under which this territory has heretofore been, that is to say, of the *Coutume de Paris*, or common law of France, the laws, acts, ordinances, arrets and decrees of the ancient kings of France, and the laws, acts, ordinances, arrets and decrees of the governors or other authority of the province of Canada, and the province of Louisiana, under the ancient French crown and of the governors, parliaments or other authorities of the province of Canada generally, and of the province of Upper Canada particularly, under the British crown, which laws, acts, ordinances, arrets and decrees do not exist of record, nor in manuscript or print in this country and have never been formally repealed or annulled.

Be it enacted by the Governor and Judges of the Territory of Michigan: That the *Coutume de Paris*, or ancient French common law, existing in this country, the laws, acts, ordinances, arrets and decrees of the governors or other authorities of the province of Canada and the province of Louisiana, under the ancient French crown, and of the governors, parliaments or other authorities of the province of Canada generally and of the province of Upper Canada particularly under the British crown are hereby formally annulled, and the same shall be of no force within the Territory of Michigan; *Provided*, That all rights accruing under them, or any of them shall remain valid.

"SECTION 3. AND, WHEREAS, The good people of the Territory of Michigan may be ensnared by ignorance of laws adopted and made by the Governor and the judges of the ancient territory of the United States northwest of the River Ohio (it was then twenty-three years old), and of laws made by the General Assembly of the said territory, and of laws adopted and made by the Governor and the judges of the Territory of Indiana, under all of which respective governments this territory has heretofore been, and which said laws do not exist of record or in manuscript in this country, and are also out of print, as well as intermingled with a multiplicity of laws which do not concern or apply to this country, and therefore may not be expected to be reprinted in a body, and may not be expected to be selected and reprinted in a detached form without much uncertainty, delay and difficulty, and it has been thought advisable by the Governor and the judges of the Territory of Michigan, heretofore, specially to re-enact such of the said laws as appeared worthy of adoption, and hereafter also to re-enact such of the said laws as shall appear worthy of adoption:

"*Be it therefore enacted by the Governor and Judges of the Territory of Michigan:* That the laws adopted and made by the Governor and judges of the territory of the United States northwest of the River Ohio, and the laws made by the General Assembly of the said territory, and the laws adopted and made by the Governor and judges of the Territory of Indiana, shall be of no force within the Territory of Michigan; *provided*, that all rights accruing under the said laws, or any of them, shall remain valid.

"SECTION 4. *And be it enacted*, That all the laws passed between the second day of June 1807, and the first day of September, 1810, be repealed, saving all legal rights heretofore accruing under them."

In 1821 a compilation of the laws in force in the Territory of Michigan was published, which was called the Code of 1820, and comprehended all such laws as were essential to the successful administration of civil government within the Territory.

The Governor of Michigan, in October, 1818, as already mentioned, laid out that part of the Territory west of Lake Michigan into three counties, viz.: Michilimackinac, Brown, and Crawford.

An act adopted by the Governor and Judges on the 27th day of October, 1818, provided that the County Court for the counties of Brown and Crawford should be held on the second Monday of July in each year. In 1821, the time in Crawford county was changed to the second Monday of May.

The act of Congress of March 3d, 1823, creating a Legislative Assembly, provided that the first Legislative Council should be assembled, at such time and place, as the Governor should by proclamation designate. By virtue of that provision Governor CASS issued his proclamation on the 15th of April, 1824, designating the Council House in Detroit as the place, and the first Monday of June, 1824, as the time for the assembling of the first Legislative Council of the Territory. ROBERT IRWIN, Jr., was a member from Brown county during the years 1824 to 1827 inclusive.

On the 3d of July, 1824, an act was passed by the Governor and Legislative Council of the Territory of Michigan, convened in pursuance of the act of Congress of March 3d, 1823, the preamble of which recited that "The judges of the County Court" of the county of Brown have neglected to comply with the requisitions contained in said proclamation of October 26, 1818, "to the great and manifest inconvenience of the people of said county;" and that no particular place within the village of Prairie du Chien was designated where the public buildings should be erected, and it appearing doubtful by said proclamation which of the said villages upon the said prairie were alluded to; and said act prescribed as follows:

"SECTION 1. That the County Commissioners of the county of Brown, or a majority of them, shall have power and they are hereby required, on or before the first day of October next ensuing, to establish the seat of justice of said county of Brown, at any point they may deem expedient within six miles of the mouth of Fox River.

"SECTION 2. That the seat of justice of the county of Crawford shall be and the same is established upon the farm lots situated at Prairie du Chien numbered 34 and 35 upon the map or sketch of the claims to lands at said place, submitted to the commissioners in the year 1820, and entered in the names of Pierre Lessard and Strange Pass, or upon whichever of the said lots the three high mounds, lying immediately below the village of Ferriole (so called) and above the lot claimed by FRANCIS LA'POINT, Sen., may be found to be situated when the boundary lines of said lots are run by the surveyor, or may be otherwise ascertained; and the County Commissioners are hereby required to erect the Court House upon the highest or center mound of said three mounds, and all the other public buildings of said county in the immediate vicinity thereof whenever the person who is the owner of said mounds and the lands adjacent shall execute to the commissioners of said county for the time being, for the use of said county, a quit-claim deed of a lot which shall include the said three mounds, bounded in front by a certain road leading from the village of St. Ferriole to the old French Trading Fort (so called) and extending in the rear of said mound thirteen rods."

It is observable that at the next session of the Legislative Council, held on the third Monday in January, 1825, the style of the acts was changed so as to read, " Be it enacted by the Legislative Council of the Territory of Michigan," the " Governor," which had previously been inserted, being dropped.

In illustration of the great length of time required to convey information to Prairie du Chien of legislation had at Detroit, especially in the winter, it is worthy of note, that, by an act passed February 4, 1825, the time for the election of a delegate to Congress was changed from the first Monday in April to the last Tuesday in May, 1825, and bi-ennially thereafter; and that it was also enacted —

"That should an election be held at Prairie du Chien on the first Monday of April, such election shall be valid to all intents and purposes, any law to the contrary notwithstanding."

By an act of the Legislative Council, approved April 21, 1825, the act of July 3, 1824, "to establish the seats of justice within the counties of Brown and Crawford," was amended, so that the duties required by that act to be performed by the commissioners of the county of Brown might

" Be performed by the said commissioners, together with the justices of the county court of said county and the Territorial judge for the counties of Brown, Crawford, and Michilimacinac, or a majority of them,"

who were required to perform the said duties within one year from the passage of the act.

The boundaries of the county of Michilimacinac, as established by the Governor's proclamation of October 26, 1818, were essentially altered by an act of the Legislative Council, approved December 22, 1826, to organize the county of Chippewa, which was made to embrace the entire southern shore of Lake Superior, as well as a vast domain west and northwest of that lake.

The county seat of the new county was established at Sault de St. Marie.

On the 12th of April, 1827, an act was passed "to divide the several counties in this Territory into Townships." In

LEGISLATION PREVIOUS TO 1835.

that portion of the Territory which is now Wisconsin, but two townships were formed. One was in Crawford county called "St. Anthony," which was bounded on the north by the parallel of north latitude, 43° 30', on the east by a line running parallel with and ten miles easterly from the Mississippi river, on the south by the parallel of north latitude 42° 30', and on the west by the Mississippi river.

The other was in Brown County, and was called Green Bay. Its southwestern boundary was a line running southeast and northwest through the head of the rapids of the Grand Kaukaulin, and extending ten miles on such line each way therefrom. The northeastern boundary was a line drawn northwest and southeast through Point au Sable of Green Bay, and extending ten miles on such line, each way therefrom. The southeast and northwest boundaries were parallel lines, twenty miles apart, connecting the other boundaries. Fox river consequently run through nearly the center of the township.

An act approved April 12, 1827, provided for taking a census of the inhabitants of the Territory, by the assessors in the several townships in the Territory, at the time they make the assessment for that year.

Another act approved April 13, 1827, required that as soon as might be after the census returns were received at the office of the Secretary of the Territory it should be the duty of the Governor to apportion the thirteen members composing the Legislative Council, among the several counties, in a mode specified in the act.

The act also provided that in the counties of Brown and Crawford the census should be taken by the sheriffs of those counties instead of the assessors.

In pursuance of the requirements of this act Governor LEWIS CASS, on the 3d day of October, 1827, issued his proclamation, announcing the number of members of the council apportioned to the different counties, among which it was announced that the counties of Crawford, Brown, Michilimacinac and Chippewa should form one district which was entitled to elect two members of the council.

It was further provided by the act, that the election for members of the council, should be held on the first Monday of November, 1827.

At that election HENRY R. SCHOOLCRAFT, of Chippewa

county, and ROBERT IRWIN, Jr., were elected members of the council.

It was provided by an act approved June 3, 1828

"That the additional judge for the Michigan Territory in the counties of Michilimacinac, Brown and Crawford, be authorized to hold a special session of the circuit court for the county of Crawford on Monday, the 25th day of August next, and so long a time thereafter as may be necessary for the trial of all such criminal cases as shall then and there be moved and prosecuted in said court."

The object of this special term, was the trial of RED BIRD, WE-KAU and CHIC-HON-SIC for the murders perpetrated at the breaking out of the Winnebago war.

By an act approved June 18, 1828, all civil and criminal jurisdiction of the county courts in the counties of Michilimacinac, Brown and Crawford was transferred to the circuit court of the United States, to be held in each of the said counties.

This jurisdiction was restored to the county of Crawford by an act passed July 31, 1830.

The Legislative Council consisted of thirteen members, and by an act approved July 3, 1828, they were apportioned among the several counties. The counties of Michilimacinac, Brown, Crawford and Chippewa, constituted the sixth district which was entitled to two members.

The act provided that the next election should be held on the second Monday of July, 1829, and on the same day in every second year thereafter.

Messrs. SCHOOLCRAFT and IRWIN were elected. Two sessions of the council were held, one commencing May 11, 1830, which adjourned July 31. The other commenced January 4, 1831, and adjourned March 4. Mr. IRWIN did not attend the second session.

The county of Iowa was organized by an act approved October 9, 1829.

The boundaries, as prescribed by this act, were as follows:

"Beginning at the mouth of Ouisconsin River and following the course of the same so as to include all the islands in said river, to the portage between the said Ouisconsin and the Fox River; thence east until it intersects the line between the counties of Brown and Crawford, as established by the proclamation of the Governor of this Territory, bearing date the 26th day of October, 1818; thence south with said line to the northern boundary of Illinois; thence west with said boundary to the Mississippi River; thence up said river with the boundary of this Territory to the place of beginning."

SAMUEL W. BEALE and LEWIS GRIGNON of the county of Brown and JOSEPH M. STREET of the county of Crawford were appointed commissioners to fix the seat of justice of the county, which was temporarily established at Mineral Point.

The 5th section of the act provided that there should be two terms of the county court of said county annually on the first Mondays of June and December.

It was provided by the seventh section that the organization of Iowa county should not affect suits, prosecutions, and other matters pending in the United States circuit court or the county court, or before any justice of the peace in Crawford county, nor the levy or collection of taxes.

An act was passed July 27, 1830, to legalize the proceedings of officers within the county of Iowa.

The next day an act was passed excepting the counties of Chippewa and Iowa from the operation of the law requiring freehold security to be given for any purpose, or as a qualification for office.

The third section of the act authorized the judges of the county court of Iowa county to order the sitting of said court at such place in the county as to them might seem most convenient for the public interest, until the necessary public buildings were erected at the county seat.

The fourth section provided for annexing unorganized townships in Iowa county to organized townships.

The fifth and sixth sections authorized the sheriffs of Brown, Crawford, Chippewa and Iowa counties to provide for the security and health of prisoners until sufficient and secure gaols were provided. And the eighth section authorized the sheriffs to employ convicts, sentenced to hard labor, in work on the public highways or on the public buildings.

The 7th section provided that until a treasurer should be elected in Iowa county, bonds and other securities required to be approved and filed with him should be approved and remain with the justices of the county court, until a treasurer be appointed.

The *Miners' Journal,* of Galena, August 7, 1830, says:

"LUCIUS LYON, Esq., of Detroit, is now engaged, under instructions from the Secretary of War, in surveying and marking the boundary between the ceded and unceded lands west of Lake Michigan, and east of the Mississippi, agreeably to the stipulations of the treaty of Prairie du Chien, of 1829.

"The survey of the boundaries of the Pottawattamies, etc., commencing on Lake Michigan, about twelve miles north of Chicago and running west to Rock river, has been finished. The distance from the lake to Rock river is eighty-four miles, and the boundary strikes the river forty miles below the mouth of the Peck-a-ton-o-kee.

"Mr. LYON and Mr. KERCHEVAL arrived at Galena in a light pleasure wagon, which was the first that ever came through from Detroit by way of Chicago and the branches of Rock river. The distance is about five hundred miles."

A new apportionment of members of the Legislative Council was made by an act approved March 4th, 1831. But no change in the representation of the sixth district as fixed by the act of July 3, 1828, except that the county of Iowa — organized in 1829 — was named as constituting a part of the district, and the numbering of it was changed from sixth to seventh.

It is also observable, as showing that the organization of Wisconsin Territory was contemplated more than five years before its occurrence, that the act provided, that if the counties constituting the seventh district, should "at the present session of Congress" — which expired on that day — be set off into a separate territory, to what districts its two members should be assigned.

The act also provided in contemplation that the number of members should be increased by act of Congress; that in that event the Governor should apportion them to each of the districts according to population as shown by the census of 1830.

The tenth section of the act fixed the first session of the fifth legislative council on the first Tuesday of May, 1832, at Detroit.

The members elected to the fifth Legislative Assembly were HENRY DODGE of Iowa county and MORGAN L. MARTIN of Brown county. The first session convened at Detroit, May 1, 1832, and adjourned June 29th. The second session convened January 1, 1833, and adjourned April 23. Mr. DODGE did not attend either session.

It was provided by an act approved June 29, 1832, that the electors of the several townships in the Territory should express by their votes on the first Tuesday of October, 1832, "whether it be expedient for the people of this Territory to form a State Government; yea or nay."

Owing to the paucity of newspapers in the counties of Brown, Iowa and Crawford, an act was passed February 1, 1833, substituting the posting of notices in legal proceedings "on the door of the house, where the circuit court was last held," for the publication in newspapers, required by law.

The additional Judge for the Michigan Territory was authorized by act approved April 6, 1833, to hold special sessions of the circuit court for the counties of Brown or Iowa, at such time and place as he may deem expedient for the trial of criminal cases.

The judges of the county court of Iowa county were authorized by an act approved April 20, 1833,

" To designate as many several places in said county in addition to those provided by law, as they shall deem expedient, where the electors of said county may meet for the purpose of voting for delegate to Congress and members of the Legislative Council."

The supervisors of the county of Iowa were authorized and required by an act approved April 23d, 1833, to locate the seat of justice of said county, at some point therein which shall be most convenient.

They were required to do so on or before the 1st day of July, 1833, and if they failed the county seat should continue at Mineral Point.

The time and place of the meeting of the sixth Legislative Council was fixed for the first Tuesday of January, 1834, at Detroit.

It was provided by act of April 23, 1833, that the election districts established by act of March 4, 1831, should remain unchanged.

At the election of 1833, the official returns forwarded showed that JAMES D. DOTY was elected a member of the sixth Council, and that WM. S. HAMILTON was elected over MORGAN L. MARTIN; but the returns from Crawford county, which changed the result, were not forwarded, and Col. HAMILTON did not claim the seat and Mr. MARTIN was admitted. The first session convened January 7, 1834, and adjourned March 7. An extra session met September 1, 1834, and adjourned September 8. An adjourned session met November 11, 1834, and adjourned December 31. The second regular annual session convened January 12, 1835, and adjourned March 28. MORGAN L. MARTIN was elected President. A special session met August 17, 1835, and adjourned August 25.

No act affecting that part of the territory west of Lake Michigan appears to have been passed at the January session 1834.

An act of Congress, of June 30, 1834, authorized an extra session of the Legislative Council. In pursuance of this act, Acting Governor MASON, on the 14th of July, issued his proclamation for the extra session, held at Detroit, September 1, 1834.

Resolutions were adopted, declaring the right of the inhabitants under the Ordinance of 1787 to form a state government bounded on the south by an east and west line, through the southern bend or extreme of Lake Michigan, and requesting the state of Virginia to require of the government of the United States a strict compliance with the Ordinance of 1787.

On the 6th of September, 1834, an act was passed entitled "An Act to establish the boundaries of the counties of Brown and Iowa, and to lay off the county of Milwaukee." The act was as follows:

"SECTION 1. That all that district of country bounded north by the county of Michilimacinac, west by the Wisconsin river, south by the line between townships eleven and twelve north in the Green Bay land district, and east by a line drawn due north, through the middle of Lake Michigan, until it strikes the southern boundary of the county of Michilimacinac, shall constitute the county of Brown.

SECTION 2. All that district of country bounded north by the middle of the Wisconsin river, west by the Mississippi, south by the north boundary of Illinois, and east by the principal meridian dividing the Green Bay and Wisconsin land district (this was the range line between ranges eight and nine east) shall constitute the county of Iowa.

SECTION 3. All that district of country bounded north by the county of Brown, east by the eastern boundary of Illinois extended, south by the state of Illinois and west by the county of Iowa, shall constitute the county of Milwaukie.

SECTION 4. The county of Milwaukie is hereby attached to the county of Brown for judicial purposes."

It remained attached to Brown county, until August 25, 1835, when an act was passed giving it an independent organization.

Another act was passed, by which all of the territory west of the Mississippi river, which had been attached to Michigan Territory by act of Congress approved June 28, 1834, was divided into two counties which were laid out and organized; the northern one by the name of Dubuque, and the southern one by the name of Demoine.

The division line between the two counties was

"A line to be drawn due west from the lower end of Rock Island to the Missouri river."

The sixth section of the act provided that

"Process, civil and criminal, issued by the Circuit Court of the United States for the county of Iowa, shall run into all parts of said counties of Dubuque and Demoine. That writs of error shall lie from the Circuit Court for the county of Iowa to the County Courts established by this act."

It was provided by an act approved September 6, 1834, that a census of the inhabitants of the territory east of the Mississippi river, should be taken by the sheriffs of the several counties, between the second Monday of October, and the first Monday of November, 1834.

The first act incorporating a bank west of Lake Michigan was passed January 23, 1835, the title of which was "An act to incorporate the stockholders of the Bank of Wisconsin."

The act provided that a bank should be established in the county of Brown or Iowa, at such place as a majority of the stockholders should determine; the capital stock whereof should be $100,000, in shares of $50 each. Subscriptions toward the stock were to be opened at Green Bay and Mineral Point, of which two months' notice was to be given in a newspaper printed at Detroit, under the superintendence of JOHN D. ANSLEY, JOHN P. ARNDT, CHARLES TULLAR, WILLIAM DICKINSON, GEORGE D. RUGGLES, HENRY MERRILL, and NATHAN GOODELL.

The bank was put in operation at Green Bay, and had a history, which will be adverted to in subsequent pages.

A dam across Fox river at the head of a rapid in said river, called the Rapide des Peres, was, by an act approved January 26, 1835, authorized to be built by WILLIAM DICKINSON, CHARLES TULLAR and JOHN P. ARNDT. The dam was subsequently built, and the village of Des Peres grew up at that point.

The first effective step toward the formation of a State government in Michigan was taken January 26, 1835, by an act of the Legislative Council approved that day, entitled "An act to enable the people of Michigan to form a constitution and State government."

The Territory as established by the act of Congress, entitled "An act to divide Indiana Territory into two separate governments," approved January 11, 1805, was by the act divided into sixteen districts, among which were apportioned eighty-nine delegates, to be elected by the several districts on the 4th day of April, 1835.

The delegates were elected April 4, 1835, and were to meet at the capitol, in the city of Detroit, on the second Monday of May, 1835.

There were eighty-seven delegates, and as political parties were then divided, there were about seven eighths Democrats and one eighth Whigs. JOHN BIDDLE, who had previously been delegate in Congress, was president of the convention.

The constitution was adopted by a vote of the people in

October, 1835, there being 6,299 yeas and 1,359 nays. It remained in force as the fundamental law of the State until the constitution of 1850 went into operation.

On the 11th day of July, Secretary and Acting Governor STEVENS T. MASON issued his proclamation for a special session of the Legislative Council at Detroit on the 17th day of August, 1835. No reason for this session was assigned in the proclamation, except that —

"Matters of import involving the rights and interests of the Territory require the consideration of the Legislative Council."

The Council met at the time named in the proclamation, JAMES D. DOTY being the sole representative of that part of the Territory west of Lake Michigan. It was disclosed by the message of the Acting Governor that the principal "matter of import" was the southern boundary controversy with Ohio. Some other matters, however, received the attention of the Council. Of those affecting Wisconsin were the following:

An act changing the time of electing delegate to Congress and members of the Council from the first Monday of November to the first Monday of October, and changing the officers who were to canvass the votes for delegate to Congress and certify the result.

An act to organize the county of Milwaukee; and an act to incorporate the Wisconsin Internal Improvement Company. This related to the Fox and Wisconsin rivers.

The Council was in session only about ten days.

The following appointments for the newly-organized county of Milwaukee were made by the Governor and Council:

Chief Justice, WILLIAM CLARK; Associate Justices, JOEL SAGE and JAMES GRIFFIN; County Clerk, ALBERT FOWLER; Sheriff, BENONI FINCH; Judge of Probate, GILBERT KNAPP; Justices of the Peace, BENJAMIN FINCH, JOHN BULLEN, Jr., WILLIAM SEE, JOEL SAGE, SYMMES BUTLER, HENRY SANDERSON, and WILLIAM CLARK.

The laws of the Territory of Michigan, so far as the same were applicable to the counties of Brown, Crawford, Iowa, and Milwaukee, were the laws governing those counties from the time they were respectively organized until they were altered or repealed by the Legislative Assembly of Wisconsin after its organization on the 4th of July, 1836.

And after that time the laws of Michigan, not incompatible with the organic act of Wisconsin Territory, were extended over it, subject to alteration, modification, or repeal.

The most important of these laws were those affecting the rights of persons and property.

The judicial system of Michigan Territory consisted of a Supreme Court, Circuit Courts, County Courts, Probate Courts, and justices of the peace.

The Supreme Court consisted of three judges appointed by the President of the United States.

This court had original and exclusive jurisdiction in all civil actions at law, where the matter in controversy exceeded one thousand dollars; all cases of divorce, all actions of ejectment, all criminal cases when the punishment was capital, and of all cases not made cognizable before some other court. It had concurrent jurisdiction with the county court of all other crimes and offenses; and appellate jurisdiction from the county courts in all civil cases in which those courts had original jurisdiction.

The Supreme Court had power to issue writs of habeas corpus, mandamus, prohibition, error, supersedeas, procedendo, certiorari, scire facias, and all other writs which might be necessary to enforce the administration of right and justice. It held one term annually at Detroit on the third Monday in September.

The laws prescribed with much particularity the mode of proceeding and the practice in the court, and clothed it with all authority essential to the complete and effective exercise of its judicial powers.

In 1825 the Territory, except the counties of Brown, Crawford and Michilimacinac was divided into five circuits, and one of the judges of the supreme court was required to hold a circuit court in each circuit. But the act of Congress passed in 1823, by which an additional judge for the Michigan Territory was required to be appointed for the counties of Brown, Crawford and Michilimacinac, rendered it unnecessary, if not incongruous that the circuit court system of eastern Michigan, should be extended to these counties, and they were therefor excepted from the operation of the circuit court system established in 1825.

The county court system of jurisprudence, although it had previously existed, was revised and re-organized by an act of the Governor and judges adopted on the 21st of December, 1820.

It was provided by this act that a court should be established in every county of the Territory, to consist of one chief justice and two associate justices, any two of whom should form a quorum. It had original jurisdiction in all civil cases where the matter in controversy was not within the jurisdiction of a justice of the peace, and did not exceed the sum of one thousand dollars; and appellate jurisdiction from any judgment or decision of justices of the peace. It also had cognizance of all crimes and offenses the punishment whereof is not capital, concurrent with the Supreme Court.

It is, however, to be borne in mind, that in the counties of Michilimacinac, Brown and Crawford, and subsequently in Iowa and Milwaukee counties, the additional judge for those counties was substituted for the Supreme Court.

Clerks of the County Court were appointed by the Governor.

The terms of the court were limited to two weeks.

The practice, pleadings and proceedings in the court were most minutely provided for by the act; even to the extent of providing that paper instead of parchment should be used in all proceedings in the court.

An act passed April 21, 1825, provided that the county court in Brown county should be held on the second Monday in January, and in Crawford county on the second Monday in May.

By an act approved April 12, 1827, it was provided that the county courts should have jurisdiction in all matters properly cognizable in chancery, where the sum or matter in dispute does not exceed one thousand dollars, with a right of appeal in all cases.

The probate court consisted of a judge in each county, appointed by the Governor, and possessed the power and jurisdiction ordinarily exercised by probate courts.

The judicial powers vested in justices of the peace were similar to those ordinarily exercised by like officers, except that they were restricted to matters where the subject in controversy did not exceed one hundred dollars.

As intimately connected with and essential to the proper administration of justice, suitable provision was made by law in reference to attorneys, the marshal of the Territory, sheriffs, coroners, constables, grand and petit juries, as well as notaries public, and in relation to the compensation of officers.

As incidental thereto, proper laws were enacted in reference to amendments and jeoffails, attachments, executions depositions, arbitrations, marriages, divorce, bastardy, wills and intestacies, executors and administrators, settlement and descent of estates, insolvent estates, and guardians as well as to the execution and recording of deeds, fraudulent conveyances, forcible entry and detainer, partition of lands and surveyors, also providing for the punishment of crimes and the trial of accused persons, and prohibiting gaming.

The duties of the treasurer of the Territory and county treasurers, and the levying and collection of taxes were all regulated by law.

Imprisonment for debt not having been abolished, proper laws were passed in relation to poor debtors and their discharge.

The subject of slavery not having been much agitated as early as 1827, an act was passed in that year which provided, that no black or mulatto person should settle or reside in the Territory without a certificate of freedom; and made it a penal offense to harbor or secrete any such person, the property of another, or to hinder or prevent the owner from recapturing him or her. All blacks and mulattoes were required to enter bonds for good behavior, and that they should not become a public charge, as a condition of residence.

Laws were passed to enforce the observance of the Sabbath and concerning religious societies, as well as for the establisment of common schools.

Interest was regulated by law, six per centum being the established lawful rate.

An organized militia was provided for.

The support of paupers was provided for by contract with the lowest bidder.

The appointment of auctioneers was provided for.

Laws were passed in relation to highways and fences and many other subjects affecting the civil and criminal polity of the Territory.

CHAPTER XV.

WISCONSIN IN A TRANSITION STATE — 1835-6.

In 1825, to a very limited extent, but more generally in 1826, 1827, and 1828, the country known as the Upper Mississippi lead mines, as contra-distinguished from the Missouri mines, was occupied in numerous localities by adventurers from every part of the country. This occupancy at first was confined to the immediate vicinity of Galena, but soon extended to Grant, La Fayette, and Iowa counties, and to the western part of Dane and Green counties. It was not, however, until after the "Winnebago war" of 1827, and the Black Hawk war in 1832, and the Indian treaties which were the result, that such a feeling of security attended the inhabitants as was essential to the permanent and secure growth and prosperity of the country.

By the treaties of Prairie du Chien, of July 29th and August 1, 1829, and of Rock Island of September 15th and 21st of that year, and of September 21st, 1832, the Indian title to much territory was extinguished, its boundaries defined, the removal of the Indians secured, and occupancy by the whites divested of its hazards.

Col. WILLIAM S. HAMILTON was a son of Gen. ALEXANDER HAMILTON, of Revolutionary fame. He had been engaged in surveying the public lands in Illinois, and in 1825, having entered into a contract to supply the garrison at Fort Howard with provisions, he left the southern part of Illinois with seven hundred head of cattle, and proceeded with his whole drove by the way of Chicago, coasting the lake by the mouths of the Milwaukee, Sheboygan and Manitowoc rivers to Green Bay, where he arrived in safety on the 27th of June, without any material loss of his cattle. On reaching Milwaukee he found SOLOMON JUNEAU, who had a trading house on the east side of the river, near where Wisconsin street is now laid out. Mr. JUNEAU was the only civilized human being then living near the lake shore between Chicago and Green Bay. Col. HAMILTON, in 1828, removed to what is now Wiota, in La Fayette county, where he lived about twenty years, when he removed to California, and died there in 1851.

From 1825 to 1830, although the settlements in Wisconsin were limited to those in the lead mines and the older ones near Green Bay and Prairie du· Chien, the wants of the people for a nearer local self-government than that provided for Michigan Territory, the seat of which was at Detroit, were seriously felt, and exhibited in numerous ways. Public attention was called to the subject by the inhabitants of Green Bay, and in February, 1829, Gen. HENRY DODGE, in behalf of the inhabitants of the lead mines, in a letter to Hon. AUSTIN E. WING, then delegate in Congress from Michigan Territory, with great force presented the "claims the people have on the National Legislature for a division of the Territory."

On the 6th of January, 1830, the committee on the Territories in the House, reported "A Bill establishing the Territory of Huron." It was bounded southwardly by the states of Illinois and Missouri; westwardly by the Missouri river and the White Earth river; northwardly by the northern boundary of the United States and eastwardly

"By a line running from the northeast corner of the state of Illinois, down Lake Michigan east of the Fox and Beaver islands, through the straits to the southern extremity of Bois Blanc island and south of said island, thence due east to the boundary of the United States in Lake Huron."

This boundary would have cut off from the Territory of Michigan, and perhaps the future state, all of its upper peninsula on Lake Superior, the Sault St. Marie and even the island of Mackinac.

The bill vested the legislative power of the Territory in the Governor and a Legislative Council to consist of five persons, one from each of the counties of Brown, Crawford, Iowa, Chippewa and Michilimacinac.

The bill provided that the seat of government of the Territory should be established at the village of Munnomonee on the Fox river, but subject to be changed by the Governor and Legislative Council with the approbation of Congress. Ten thousand acres of land to be located by the Governor, below the Grand Kau-kau-nah on the said river were given to the Territory to defray the expenses of erecting public buildings at the seat of government.

The bill did not become a law and Michigan Territory for the time being remained intact.

In 1831 a bill to create a new Territory in the western part of Michigan passed the House of Representatives, but did not pass the Senate. In 1832 another bill for the same purpose was reported in the House and remained over among the unfinished business. In October of that year under authority of an act of the Legislative Council, a vote of the inhabitants was taken in favor of the formation of a state government for Michigan.

On the 14th of December, 1833, at a public meeting at Green Bay, resolutions were adopted in favor of a new Territory, and a memorial to Congress for its creation was prepared and presented.

Jealousy existed between the people of the mines and those of the Green Bay country, as to the location of the seat of government; whether it should be at Mineral Point or near Green Bay. This jealousy was one of the causes which had previously prevented the passage of either of the bills on this subject.

On the 14th of February, 1834, a bill establishing the Territory of Wisconsin, by which the location of the seat of government was left to the decision of the Governor and Legislative Council was reported in the Senate. This bill did not pass, but instead of it the act of June 28, 1834, was passed, which, by attaching to the Territory of Michigan all the territory of the United States west of the Mississippi River and north of the State of Missouri, increased the necessity for a new territorial government.

On the 15th of June, 1836, Congress provided by an act for that purpose for the admission of Michigan as a state in the Union, upon certain conditions contained in the act, relating chiefly to its boundaries, but in consequence of the difficulties existing and arising out of the boundary questions, Michigan was not admitted as a state until January 26, 1837.

With the exception of some private land claims at and near Green Bay and Prairie du Chien, which had been confirmed by the general government, none of the public lands within the limits of Wisconsin had previous to 1834 been disposed of. By an act of Congress approved June 26, 1834, it was enacted that

"All that tract north of the State of Illinois, west of Lake Michigan, south and southeast of the Wisconsin and Fox Rivers, included in the present Territory of Michigan, shall be divided by a north and south line drawn from the northern boundary of Illinois along the range of township line next west of Fort Winnebago, to the Wisconsin River, and be called, the one on the west side the Wisconsin, and that on the east side the Green Bay land districts."

Two years later, the Green Bay district was
'Divided by a line commencing on the western boundary of said district, and running thence east, between townships ten and eleven, to the line between ranges seventeen and eighteen east; thence north to the line between townships twelve and thirteen; thence east to Lake Michigan,"
and the country south of this line was called the Milwaukee land district. Some of the public domain had been surveyed previous to 1834 and the surveys were afterwards rapidly prosecuted, and the permanent ownership of the country speedily passed from the government to individuals, and settlements extended in every direction.

To provide for the election of a delegate to Congress and members of the Legislative Council in that portion of the Territory of Michigan not embraced within the limits of the state of Michigan, in the contingency that the constitution to be framed for the state should not take effect previous to the first day of November, 1835, an act was passed on the 30th of March, 1835, which provided that the election of a delegate to Congress and members of the Legislative Council, should be postponed until the first Monday of November, 1835, on which day it should be held, provided that if the constitution to be framed for the state should not take effect previous to that day, it should be the duty of the Governor to fix the time of holding said election by proclamation on such day as he might deem expedient subsequent to the taking effect of said constitution.

The previous acts of the Territory regulating elections were declared to be applicable to the elections provided for by this act, and it was made the duty of the governor to make such apportionment of the members of the Legislative Council to the several counties in the district not embraced in the state, as he might deem expedient. The Legislative Council was to meet at such time and place as the Governor by proclamation might appoint.

The act also provided for the contingency that a constitution should not be adopted, so as to enable the people of Michigan to enjoy the benefits of state government previous to January 1, 1836; in which case the provisions of the act for a meeting of the Legislative Council in that district of the Territory not within the State, and for the election of members thereto, were to be nugatory; and it was made the duty of the governor in that event by proclamation to apportion the members which the several districts east of Lake Michigan are entitled to elect, to the said districts respectively in proportion to population as ascertained by the census in the year 1834, and the counties in the seventh district lying east of the principal meridian should be entitled to one member at the session which should commence at Detroit on the 1st Monday of January, 1836.

By another provision of this act it was declared that all laws which might be in force on the 1st day of May, 1835, and not locally inapplicable to the district of the Territory not embraced within the state, should be and continue in full force and effect in said district after said first day of May.

At the session of the Legislative Council of the Territory of Michigan, held at Detroit on the 17th of August, 1835, STEVENS T. MASON, Secretary and acting Governor, in his message, referring to the act of March 30, 1835, said

"The anticipated contingency will arise by the organization of the contemplated state government in November next. The general law regulating these elections requires the returns of elections to be made to the secretary of the Territory who with the attorney general and treasurer, constitutes the board of canvassers, who are authorized to give a certificate of election to the delegate elect. The election, however, occurring before the appointment of these officers under the territorial government of Wisconsin, it will be necessary to create some other board of canvassers to meet the emergency and to em power them to issue a certificate of election. Such an amendment of the act of March 30, 1835, is respectfully suggested for your consideration."

In accordance with this suggestion of the Governor, an act was passed on the 22d of August, fixing the first Monday of October as the time for holding the election of delegate to Congress and members of the Legislative Council.

The act also changed the mode of canvassing, by providing that the returns from the other counties west of Lake Michigan should be made to the clerk of the county of Brown, who should make return thereof to the clerk of the Supreme Court of the Territory, at Detroit.

In pursuance of the act of March 30, 1835, as thus amended, Secretary and acting Governor MASON issued a proclamation, bearing date August 25, 1835, making a new apportionment of —

"The members of the Legislative Council to the several counties in that district of country, not embraced within the limits of the State of Michigan." It was proclaimed that—

"The counties of Brown and Milwaukee shall constitute the *first district*, and shall be entitled to elect *five* members of the Legislative Council.

"The county of Iowa shall constitute the *second district*, and shall be entitled to elect *three* members.

"The county of Crawford shall constitute the *third district*, and shall be entitled to elect *one* member.

"The county of Dubuque shall constitute the *fourth district*, and shall be entitled to elect *two* members.

"The county of Demoine shall constitute the *fifth district*, and shall be entitled to elect *two* members."

The proclamation also contained the following :

" And I do further appoint Friday. the 1st day of January, next, for the meeting of the said Legislative Council; and the members thereof are hereby required to convene on that day at Green Bay, in the county of Brown, or such other place as may be hereafter directed by law, in order to proceed in the execution of their official duties."

Peninsular Michigan had adopted a State constitution and formed a State government, with all its branches — executive, legislative, and judicial — ready to discharge their several official functions; and although it was not admitted into the Union until January, 1837, in consequence of its boundary troubles, yet it chose to abandon its Territorial form of government and assume the powers of a sovereign State, as it clearly had a right to under the ordinance of 1787. A State in the Union if the difficulties with the State of Ohio could be satisfactorily settled — at all events a State.

That portion of Michigan Territory not within the limits of the new State of Michigan, still remained vested with all the governmental powers of the Territory of Michigan, which embraced the powers of electing a delegate to Congress, and a Legislative Council of thirteen members.

STEVENS T. MASON continued to remain Secretary of the Territory of Michigan, and *ex-officio* acting Governor until his election as Governor of the State of Michigan, when JOHN S. HORNER was appointed by the President of the United States as his successor.

The "contingent remainder" of the ancient Territory of Michigan consisted of the counties of Brown, Milwaukee, Iowa, Crawford, Dubuque, and Des Moines, containing a population probably not exceeding fifteen thousand.

Everything was now in readiness for the inhabitants of these counties to elect from among themselves a delegate to Congress, and to assume to themselves the legislative powers of the government of the Territory of Michigan. A very lively interest in the elections existed throughout these counties, especially in Brown, Iowa, and Dubuque. Although great interest in the election of members of the Territorial Council existed, the overshadowing interest and excitement was in the election of delegate.

Gen. JACKSON was then President of the United States, and democracy was supposed to be very largely predominant in all the counties.

The friends of JAMES DUANE DOTY were the first in the field. As early as the 19th of May, 1835, "a large and general meeting of the democratic republicans" was held at Green Bay, which determined to organize the democratic party, and for that purpose appointed a committee to call a general meeting at a future day.

On the 28th of May the committee issued a call for such a meeting, to be held on the 10th of June. At that time a meeting was held, at which JAMES DUANE DOTY was unanimously nominated as the democratic candidate for delegate to Congress.

The meeting declared, that

"In the life and service of the Hon. J. D. DOTY, this meeting finds abundant guaranties that in the future he will not abandon the principles he has hitherto advocated."

Soon after the nomination of Judge DOTY, a number of the citizens of Brown county, made a call upon MORGAN L. MARTIN, of Green Bay, to become a Democratic candidate for delegate which call he accepted and was announced as a candidate.

In pursuance of a call previously published in the Galena newspapers (there were no others in the lead mines), a meeting of the citizens of Iowa county was held at Mineral Point on the 23d day of May, at which GEORGE WALLACE JONES was nominated as a candidate for delegate. The meeting did not profess to be representative of any political party. The resolutions which were adopted, however, one of which nominated General JONES, were introduced by AUGUSTUS C. DODGE, who prided himself upon his democracy, as it was well known that General JONES did.

The following also appeared in a Galena paper:

"We are authorized to announce Hon. DAVID IRVIN of Green Bay as the JACKSON candidate for Delegate to Congress from the Territory of Michigan.—MANY VOTERS."

It was denied that this announcement was with Judge IRVIN'S sanction. At any rate he received but few votes.

The nomination of Col. GEO. W. JONES was ratified by a very large meeting held at Dubuque.

THOMAS PENDLETON BURNETT of Prairie du Chien was nominated as a candidate for the Legislative Council at the Mineral Point meeting of May 23d, at which General JONES was nominated. Subsequently Mr. BURNETT was nominated as candidate for Delegate by a large number of the citizens of Iowa county. On the 15th of September, Mr. BURNETT published in the Galena papers a card, in which he accepted the position as a candidate for the Legislative Council and refused to be a candidate for Delegate.

Notwithstanding the action of the Legislative Council of Michigan Territory, of the acting Governor and of the people there was an insignificant minority within the new state of Michigan, who persisted in the exercise of what they claimed to be their rights as citizens of the Territory of Michigan.

WILLIAM WOODBRIDGE was the candidate for delegate of this minority.

At the time of the election the principal candidates for the delegacy were JAMES DUANE DOTY and MORGAN LEWIS MARTIN of Green Bay; GEORGE WALLACE JONES of Iowa county and WILLIAM WOODBRIDGE of Detroit, all professing to be democrats. The result was that GEORGE W. JONES was elected.

For members of the Legislative Council there were rival candidates in most of the counties, and the election excited great interest. The result was that the following members were elected:

Brown and Milwaukee: JOHN LAWE and WM. B. SLAUGHTER of Brown county; GEORGE H. WALKER, GILBERT KNAPP and BENJAMIN H. EDGERTON of Milwaukee county.

Iowa: WM. S. HAMILTON, JAMES R. VINEYARD and ROBERT C. HOARD.

Crawford: THOMAS P. BURNETT.

Dubuque: ALLEN HILL and JOHN PARKER.

Demoine: JOSEPH B. TEAS and JEREMIAH SMITH.

After the election the newly appointed secretary, JOHN S. HORNER, successor of Gov. MASON, thought it proper to issue a proclamation as secretary and acting governor, which was a cause of great confusion and misunderstanding and resulted in an abortive session of the Legislative Council.

The proclamation " for divers good causes and considerations," changed the time of the meeting of the Legislative Council from the first day of January, 1836, to the first day of December, 1835. The proclamation was dated the ninth day of November, only twenty-one days before the time fixed in it for the meeting. From the nature of the country, the season of the year, the tardy and uncertain movements of the mails, it was impossible for the members to receive the necessary information to reach Green Bay by the time fixed in the proclamation. The members from Des Moines did not learn of the change of time until they arrived at Galena about the 20th of December, when on their way to Green Bay to attend the session on the 1st of January.

This action of Secretary HORNER evoked severe criticism of the people and the press, and gave to the Legislative Council, at the January session, a theme for severe animadversion.

None of the members-elect went to Green Bay on the first of December, nor did Secretary HORNER go there, and if his proclamation was intended to prevent a session at that time, it was a complete success.

On Friday, the 1st day of January, 1836, a quorum of the members-elect of the Seventh Legislative Council met at Green Bay, and organized temporarily by electing JOSEPH B. TEAS, President *pro tem.*; A. G. ELLIS, Secretary *pro tem.*; and LEVI STERLING, Sergeant-at-Arms *pro tem.*

A committee was appointed which examined and reported upon the credentials. The oath of office was administered to the members present by the Secretary *pro tem.*, acting in his capacity as justice of the peace of Brown county.

Nine members were present—Messrs. LAWE, SLAUGHTER, KNAPP, EDGERTON, HAMILTON, VINEYARD, BURNETT, TEAS, and SMITH. The absentees were: Messrs. WALKER, of Milwaukee, HOARD, of Iowa, and HILL and PARKER, of Dubuque.

The first business of the second day was the election of permanent officers. Col. WILLIAM S. HAMILTON was elected President, having received eight out of the nine votes. The President-elect, in returning his acknowledgments for the honor, referred to —

"The delicate relations we bear to the General Government, and to the Peninsula; the numerous and varied interests of our country; its rapidly increasing population, and our own peculiar political existence,"

and counselled the exercise of moderation and caution, at the same time firmness.

Messrs. ELLIS and STERLING were elected to fill permanently the offices to which they had been temporarily elected, and THOMAS A. B. BOYD, WILLIAM B. LONG, W. H.

BRUCE, CHARLES GREEN, and GEORGE W. LAWE were elected to subordinate offices.

Messrs. BURNETT and KNAPP were appointed a committee to wait on JOHN S. HORNER, Secretary and acting Governor, and inform him that the Council was organized and ready to receive any communication he might have to make.

At the next session, January 4th, the committee reported that they had not been able to perform the duty assigned them in consequence of the absence of the acting Governor from Green Bay. That they had not been able to ascertain whether he would arrive, nor did they know of any reasonable apology for his absence, except a communication dated at Detroit, December 14th, published in a Green Bay paper, which seemed to bear the sanction of his authority, and which the committee submitted with their report.

The substance of the communication is that —

"No returns of the Wisconsin election (for delegate) have as yet been furnished to the clerk of the Supreme Court, at Detroit, according to law. Upon a lean vote of 730 in the Peninsula, WILLIAM WOODBRIDGE, Esq., has demanded the certificate of election as delegate.

"Being satisfied from inofficial, though credible, evidence, that the Wisconsin delegate has received a greater number of votes, the returns of which are now, from some unknown cause, outstanding, the acting Governor has hitherto declined giving a certificate to Mr. WOODBRIDGE, until the receipt of the Wisconsin poll.

"The people of Wisconsin will at once perceive the necessity of the Acting Governor's remaining at Detroit until the delegate-elect is furnished with his certificate.

"He deems it of vital interest to them that GEORGE W. JONES, Esq., their delegate, should obtain his seat in Congress at the earliest day practicable. It is decidedly more important, in his opinion, to Wisconsin, that she should at this particular crisis be represented in Congress than that there should be a session of the Legislative Council."

On the same day Mr. BURNETT offered a resolution

"That a committee of three be appointed to inquire into the obstructions which prevent the Council from proceeding in the regular course of legislation, to the enactment of laws for the good government of the Territory, with instructions to report by resolution or otherwise."

Subsequently, on the 6th of January, the resolution was adopted and Messrs. BURNETT, TEAS and EDGERTON appointed the committee.

On the 8th of January, the committee submitted a unanimous report, which, after considering the evils endured by the inhabitants of that portion of Michigan Territory west of Lake Michigan for many years, during which time they were ruled "rather as a distant colony than as an integral portion of the same government," and commenting upon the satisfaction with which they regarded the prospect of a session of a Legislative Council composed exclusively of representatives elected by the several counties in that portion of the Territory, refers to the proclamation of Acting Governor MASON, appointing the 1st day of January, for the assembling at Green Bay of the Legislative Council. The report states that the regular and extra sessions of the Council of 1835 had consumed the whole sixty days, which it is authorized by law to sit, during any one year, so that the Council could not lawfully hold another session during the year 1835, and that Acting Governor MASON in naming the 1st day of January, 1836, appointed the earliest day at which the Council could by law commence a session.

The report characterizes the proclamation of Acting Governor HORNER directing the Council to assemble on the 1st of December

"As most unwise in its character, and one that could not have been adopted by a man who had any correct knowledge of the laws of the land and the circumstances of the country and who felt the least regard for the rights and interests of the people." * * * * "The proclamation was wholly nugatory, and only exhibited the folly of attempting that which the executive had no power to perform."

It was impossible for the members to meet on the 1st of December, and the report continues

"The members of the Council very justly disregarded this proclamation and assembled and organized on the 1st day of January, 1836, and have been met by a letter written by authority of the Acting Governor to a newspaper editor, in which he tells the people of the country that he considers it a matter of more importance that they should be represented in Congress than that the Legislative Council should assemble, and that he is remaining at Detroit for the purpose of giving to the Delegate elect a certificate of his election."

The extra session of the Council

"Passed a law making it the duty of the County Clerks to forward the returns of that election to the Clerk of the Supreme Court, who should give a certificate of the whole vote given; so that whether the returns had been made in due time or not, his excellency had no lawful business with the subject, and his apology intended to excuse his absence, appears to the committee to be frivolous and insufficient. And the committee can not forbear to remark the extraordinary circumstance, of the Governor tendering such an apology to the editor of a newspaper instead of the Legislative body which he had called upon to meet him at Green Bay. As a co-ordinate branch of the government, without whose presence and sanction no law can be passed for the benefit of the people, it is a matter of unfeigned regret that the executive officer for no better reasons, determined to remain at Detroit and dissappoint all hope of benefit from the present session of the Council."

"The Acting Governor seems to have failed in every legal measure proper, to continue and carry on the operations of the Territorial government for the benefit of the people. He himself remains with all the records, books and documents belonging to the executive office, within the bounds and jurisdiction of another state, where the laws of the Territory are no longer regarded."

"In the absence of the Governor the Council can do nothing more than to adopt such resolutions, memorials, etc., as the circumstances and situation of the country require.

Having done this, they will have exerted the extent of their power, and the responsibility of having done nothing more will not rest upon them. That responsibility, weighty and serious as it is, will be thrown where it ought to be, upon the Acting Governor of the Territory: and the committee consider that the Council would not be true to the high trust reposed in it, if it did not represent the facts, and in the name of the people, request the President of the United States to relieve the country from the authority of a man who seems to be only calculated to bring evil upon it. Entertaining this opinion, the committee would respectfully submit to the Council the following preamble and resolution which they recommend for its adoption."

Omitting the preamble, the substance of which is contained in the report, the resolutions declare

"That JOHN S. HORNER, Secretary and Acting Governor of the Territory, has forfeited all just claims to the confidence of the people, and from his incapacity and disregard of his official obligations and duties to the country, he is, in the opinion of this Council, unworthy of the high office which he fills.

"That the President of the United States be and is hereby requested in behalf of the people of the Territory, to revoke the commission of the said JOHN S. HORNER, and to appoint some other person better qualified to fulfill the duties of the office."

The resolutions were immediately considered in committee of the whole and debated at great length by Mr. SLAUGHTER in opposition and Messrs. BURNETT and HAMILTON in favor, when they were adopted by a vote of 8 to 1.

The resolutions had no effect upon General JACKSON. The expressed wishes of HORNER'S wife having, it was said, more weight with "Old Hickory" than any resolutions the Legislative Council could adopt.

GEORGE H. WALKER, of Milwaukee, one of the members elect of the Council who did not attend the session, published in the *Chicago American,* about the first of February, the following communication:

"Having just seen a copy of the proceedings of the Legislative Council of Michigan Territory, I perceive that the Council have passed strong censures on J. S. HORNER. Acting Governor and Secretary of said Territory.

In justice to Gov. HORNER, I feel it my duty to state my belief of his intention to have gone to Green Bay, for on my passing through Detroit, Mr. HORNER communicated to me his intention of meeting the Council as soon as possible. He then expressed a desire that I should remain if convenient at Chicago or Milwaukee until his arrival. I have accordingly remained here in the daily expectation of seeing him, and with the design of affording him such facilities on the route as my knowledge of the country would afford, but have just learned of a gentleman from Detroit that Gov. H. has been prevented from coming on by sickness which no human ingenuity could foresee.

These observations I make public, not with a view to throw the least blame on the council for passing a vote of censure. For, had I taken my place at the Council, I would have added my own vote to their resolutions, having no other information than such as was before them; but I am desirous that all the facts should be known, so that the citizens of the Territory may be able to view impartially the explanation which Governor HORNER will undoubtedly feel it his duty to make.   Respectfully,

Your Obedient Servant,
GEORGE H. WALKER."

It is not known that Acting Governor HORNER ever published any explanation.

A select committee was appointed by resolution to prepare a memorial to Congress praying that a separate territorial government in the country west of Lake Michigan, commonly called Wisconsin Territory, might be established.

Mr. VINEYARD moved that the committee be instructed

"To embrace as a part of the wishes of the inhabitants, that the seat of government be established on the east bank of the Mississippi River south of the Wisconsin River."

The resolution and amendment were considered in committee of the whole, where Mr. HAMILTON (Pres't) moved to strike out all after the word "established" and insert the words "at Cassville."

The location of the seat of government for the Territory had, ever since the prospect of an independent territorial government seemed favorable, excited more interest among the few and widely separated communities for which it was intended, than any other, and this interest did not cease to exist until some time after the erection of the capitol at Madison.

The excitement and intensity of this feeling was developed by the introduction of Col. HAMILTON's amendment, which elicited an animated discussion conducted, however, in the best of temper.

Col. HAMILTON in describing the natural beauty of the site proposed by him said:

"Cassville stands on the east bank of the Mississippi surrounded by very pretty scenery. The eye can rest on the soft and soothing, the grand and sublime. There, will be found everything necessary for the promotion of man's comfort, and the exercise of his energies. In a word nature has done all in her power to make it one of the most delightful spots in the 'far West'."

He described its central location, on the supposition that the new Territory, and the future state to be formed from it would embrace both sides of the Mississippi River, which he argued to be probable in order to preserve

"The happy balance of power which now exists in the Senate of the United States between the slave and non-slave-holding states, and so long as our land is affected with the evil of slavery, it should be the first wish of every patriot and true American, that this balance of power should never be broken. Divide the proposed Territory into two governments, and the United States will be driven to the necessity of violating its faith pledged to the several tribes of Indians they are now removing to the west side of the Mississippi in order to make another government where slavery will be admitted, to balance the two thus created. (Texas had not then been annexed.) Now Michigan stands opposed to Arkansas, and Wisconsin that is to be ere long, will be to Florida."

How mistaken are the predictions of the wisest of political prophets liable to prove! Col. HAMILTON but gave voice to the general opinion of politicians at that time, and in thirty-one months from the time of this session at Green Bay, Wisconsin Territory was divided, Iowa Territory organized, followed a few years later by the admission of both as states in the Union, and the "happy balance of power," was destroyed forever.

To return to the debate: Mr. SLAUGHTER opposed the amendment, because it was doubtful whether any new Territory would be organized, and if organized we did not know what would be its boundaries; and because the late elections were not conducted with reference to this subject, and the Council was incapable of representing the views and wishes of the people upon it. He thought the people the only tribunal competent to judge and decide upon the question. He said he had no local influences to prejudice him; he was opposed equally to all locations, but would place the subject upon the broad principle that it was the people's right and interest, and it should be their privilege to decide it.

Mr. BURNETT said that if

"Left to him to fix the seat of government and he could feel at liberty to consult his own interests and that of his constituents he would establish it at Prairie du Chien."

He described the eligibility and centrality of that point. In reply to Col. SLAUGHTER he said

"If he should postpone the question until the counties on Lake Michigan should have a majority in the Council it would never be settled. Those counties have now a greater voice here than they can ever again have upon any equal principle of representation. Look at the number of votes given in the different counties and compare them with the members elected. Brown and Milwaukee with about three hundred votes have elected five members, while Iowa with five hundred votes has elected but three members. Can the gentleman then in reason expect, that the counties on the Lake will ever have a stronger voice upon this question than they have now? I think not."

If that portion of the present state which in 1835 was in the counties of Brown or Milwaukee be called the eastern part, and that which was then a part of Iowa or Crawford be called the western part, it will be found that by the census of 1880 the eastern part contained a population of 803,808, and the western part 511,672.

The amendment was adopted by a vote of 7 to 2, all the members voting for it except Messrs. LAWE and SLAUGHTER, from Brown county.

Mr. SLAUGHTER then moved to postpone the resolution indefinitely, and expressed disappointment at the votes of the members from Milwaukee county.

Mr. KNAPP, in reply, said that he was conscious of having not only acted for the best, but in perfect accord with the wishes of his constituents, whose minds and feelings he believed himself well acquainted with. He believed that the general good was always to be preferred before any private or local consideration. The site proposed was *central*, and would accommodate the greatest number of the whole; he felt no regrets for voting as he had.

The motion to postpone was lost, and the resolution as amended was adopted by the same vote as the amendment.

On the 9th of January Mr. SLAUGHTER, from the committee to which the subject had been referred, reported a memorial to Congress on the subject of a new territorial government. It gave a graphic description of the country west of Lake Michigan and north of the States of Illinois and Missouri, and represented it as being unsurpassed for fertility of soil, salubrity of climate and commercial facilities. It represented the population at that time at twenty-five thousand, and predicted that in two years it would have sufficient population to be entitled, under the ordinance of 1787, to admission into the Union as a state.

It speaks of Cassville as among the most prominent of the several flourishing villages on the banks of the Mississippi river, and recommends it as the most eligible for the seat of government for the proposed Territory.

It states that —

"Already have a large portion of our citizens (those west of the Mississippi), upon the trial of one for the murder of another, been adjudged to be beyond the jurisdiction of the courts of the United States.   *   *   *   *   *   *   *   *   *   *   *

"That ten or twelve thousand freemen, citizens of the United States, living within its territory, should be unprotected in their lives and their property by its courts of civil and criminal jurisdiction is an anomaly unparalleled in the annals of republican legislation."

It was recommended that twenty-five instead of thirteen members be authorized to be elected to the Legislative Council.

The extinguishment of the Indian title to, further surveys of, and pre-emption rights upon the public land were favorably alluded to in the memorial, in which the Council state —

"We have deemed it our last and best policy to ask the intervention of the National aid, to give us a new, efficient political existence."

The memorial was immediately considered in committee of the whole, when, on motion of Mr. HAMILTON, some amendments were adopted, presenting more prominently the interests of the people west of the Mississippi river, as well also as those of the lead mines. The chief interest developed in the discussion of the memorial was upon an amendment offered by Mr. BURNETT, and an amendment thereto offered by Col. HAMILTON.

Mr. BURNETT moved to amend the memorial by inserting —

"That in the organization of the Territorial government the offices of Governor and Superintendent of Indian Affairs may be separated, *and that the people of said Territory be permitted to elect their Governor and Secretary.*"

Col. HAMILTON moved to strike out all after the word "separated," (the words in italics).

In support of his amendment to the amendment, Col. HAMILTON said:

"He had taken this course, not because he did not think the people would act correctly in choosing a proper person to fill this office. We are the property of the Government, and it is not reasonable to suppose that they will give up all control of us. If the office is made elective, then all authority of the General Government is at an end, and he thought that by asking that which he deemed unreasonable, we were endangering the whole."

Mr. BURNETT, in reply, said:

"The gentleman says we are the property of the United States, and they have the right to do with us as they please. I deny the correctness of this doctrine; I never can subscribe to its principles. I deny that the people are lawfully the subjects of property in any government. The gentleman has referred to the clause in the Constitution, which authorizes Congress to make needful rules and regulations respecting the territory and other property of the United States, and says that it is the only constitutional authority for establishing territorial governments; and because the word property is there used, in conjunction with territory, the people of the territory are the property of the United States. Sir, territory and property never can be made to mean the people. Territory has a geographical meaning and relates to the soil of the country; but because the United States have the property of the soil, it does not therefore follow that they have unlimited jurisdiction over the people also. Property and jurisdiction are not co-relevant terms. * * *

"This country was a part of the confederacy before the adoption of the Constitution. Its rights have never been forfeited. Those rights are secured by the ordinance of 1787 so firmly that Congress itself can not take them away."

In his rejoinder, Col. HAMILTON said

"I come not here to engage in phillipics against any individual or to court the people— *I came to do my duty.* When the gentleman denies we are the property of the United States he denies our very existence. He forgets the only clause of the constitution which gives Congress power to possess and provide a government for the country, the language of which is 'Territory and other property.' We are therefore the property of the United States, and are we to suppose that the government will divest itself of the power over its property. If the people elect the governor, the government have no right to remove him. He may violate the laws, sacrifice the interest of the general government and they have no power to control him."

The memorial was then adopted.

On the 11th of January a memorial to Congress was adopted asking for the division of the Green Bay land district and the establishment of a new land district.

On the 12th of January an animated debate took place upon a resolution offered on the previous day by Mr. VINEYARD, that the governor be requested to call the next Legislative Council to meet at Cassville.

Mr. SLAUGHTER moved to strike out "Cassville" and insert "Fond du Lac."

Mr. BURNETT and Col. HAMILTON opposed the amendment, and on taking the question it was lost.

Mr. KNAPP proposed to substitute "Racine" for Cassville, which was sustained by Mr. SLAUGHTER, but the amendment was not agreed to.

Mr. SLAUGHTER now suggested that the law required the Council to meet *at Green Bay*. He did not think it competent for the executive to alter the place.

Mr. HAMILTON concurred with Mr. SLAUGHTER and moved that the committee rise and report against the resolution, which was done and the resolution lost.

On the 13th of January Mr. EDGERTON from the committee on internal improvements, reported a memorial to Congress asking for

"An appropriation sufficient to cover the expense of surveying all the necessary harbors on the western shore of Lake Michigan, and also for the construction of two light houses; one at Milwaukee and the other at Root River."

Also " for the survey and examination of the Fox and Wisconsin Rivers, and for the removal of the obstructions at the rapids in the Mississippi River."

The attention of Congress was also called to

"The opening and building of the road from Chicago to Green Bay, the surveys of which were completed last season."

The memorial set forth that

"The subject of constructing a railroad from Lake Michigan, passing through the mining district, terminating at or near Cassville on the Mississippi River, is one which claims the attention of all who take an interest in the prosperity and growth of our country; and we would pray your honorable body to make provision for the survey and examination of the route."

It also asked Congress

" To declare Navarino at the head of Green Bay, and Cassville on the Mississippi River, ports of entry."

Mr. SLAUGHTER made an ineffectual effort to have inserted among the surveys asked for

"A survey of the Manitowoc river to its source, with a view to ascertain the practicability of connecting Lake Michigan and Lake Winnebago by slack-water navigation, and a canal of about two and a half miles."

The memorial was adopted without material amendment.

A resolution introduced by Mr. VINEYARD, that the printers to the Council be instructed to print five hundred copies of the journal was adopted.

At an early day of the session, Hon. JAMES D. DOTY had been appointed Fiscal Agent of the Territory without any express understanding as to the extent to which he was to provide for the expenses of the Council. As the close of the session was approaching, it appeared that some members of the Council supposed that Judge DOTY was to defray all of the expenses, which would probably be $2,000 or $3,000, while he had expected only to defray the necessary contingent expenses, amounting to about $500.

On the last day of the session, Judge DOTY addressed a communication to the Council stating his understanding of the extent of expenses he was to defray, and his perfect willingness to make the advance, as originally proposed by him, or to decline the situation.

A resolution was then introduced

"That the terms proposed by JAMES D. DOTY, upon which he will perform the duties of Fiscal Agent for the Council, are satisfactory; and that it is the wish of the Council that he may accept the appointment of Fiscal Agent."

After considerable debate, in which Judge DOTY's motives were assailed and defended the resolution was adopted.

On the 7th of January, Mr. VINEYARD introduced a resolution that the Council adjourn *sine die,* on Saturday the 9th of January. It was laid on the table.

On the 11th of January, Mr. VINEYARD again offered a resolution that the Council adjourn on the 12th. This resolution was also laid on the table.

On the next day, the 12th, he again offered a resolution that the Council adjourn on the 14th. On motion of Mr. SLAUGHTER it was amended by substituting Friday the 15th.

After a resolution had been reported by the committee on expenses, and adopted by the Council, that there should be paid by the Fiscal Agent, from the sum appropriated by Congress for defraying the contingent expenses of the Legislative Council for the year 1836, various specific sums to the members, printers, officers etc., amounting to the aggregate sum of $2,371.72;

And after the report of the committee on enrollment as correctly enrolled of the memorials and resolutions adopted by the Council;

And after the introduction, discussion and passage of the resolution in relation to the Fiscal Agent, the seventh and last session of the Legislative Council of Michigan Territory, on Friday the 15th day of January, 1836, adjourned *sine die.*

CHAPTER XVI.

ORGANIZATION OF WISCONSIN TERRITORY.

The Indian possessory right of occupancy of that part of the Territory south and east of the Wisconsin and Fox Rivers having been extinguished by treaty, the surveys of the public lands were prosecuted with vigor soon after the close of the Black Hawk war, and that part of the Territory became subject to settlement.

As previously stated, this part of the Territory was in June, 1834, divided into two land districts the "Wisconsin" district, with land office at Mineral Point, and the "Green Bay" district, with land office at Green Bay. The Green Bay district was subsequently divided and the "Milwaukee" district established with land office at Milwaukee, containing the ten southern townships west of range eighteen, and the twelve east of range seventeen.

The first public sale of lands was at Mineral Point on the 10th day of November, 1834, in pursuance of the proclamation of the President, dated July 7, 1834, by which all the lands south of the Wisconsin River and west of the fourth principal meridian, were offered for sale, corresponding with the townships now forming Grant county.

On the 6th of May, 1835, the President issued two other proclamations for public land sales; one for sales at Green Bay on the 17th and the 31st days of August, the other for sales at Mineral Point on the 7th and 21st days of September, 1835.

These sales brought into market all the lands in the present counties of Iowa, La Fayette, Green, Dane, Manitowoc,

Kewaunee, Calumet, so much of Brown, Outagamie and Winnebago as is east of the Fox River and north of Lake Winnebago; Rock county, except seven towns on the eastern side of it; the towns of Lowville, Wyocena, Marcellon, Portage, Pacific, Dekorra and Arlington in Columbia county; the towns of Kingston and Marquette in Green Lake county and that small part of Marquette county south of Fox River. Fractional townships seven, eight, nine and ten, of range 22, in Milwaukee and Ozaukee counties, embracing almost the entire city of Milwaukee, were also offered at the sale held at Green Bay on the 31st of August.

The lands south of Fox river, which were not offered at these sales, embraced the entire counties of Kenosha, Racine, Walworth, Waukesha, Jefferson, Washington, Dodge, Fond du Lac, and Sheboygan, and a part of the counties of Winnebago, Green Lake, Columbia, and Rock.

By a proclamation of the President of August 15, 1835, another sale was held at Green Bay on the 16th day of November, at which all the lands in Sheboygan county, five townships in Fond du Lac, two in Washington, and four in Ozaukee counties were offered for sale.

By the second section of an act of Congress, approved May 29, 1830, it was provided that when two or more persons were settled on the same quarter section it was to be equally divided between the two first actual settlers, and each should be entitled to a pre-emption of eighty acres of land elsewhere in the same land district, so as not to interfere with other settlers having a right of preference.

Such rights of pre-emption "elsewhere" were called "floats," and were in very great demand by speculators in lands, for the purpose of securing desirable locations in advance of the public sales, and many town sites, supposed at the time to be very valuable, were entered with these "floats."

The pre-emption laws in force at the time of these land sales in August and September, 1835, required that the settler, to entitle him to a pre-emption right, should have cultivated some part of his land in the year 1833.

In a great many instances, settlers had gone upon lands offered by these proclamations, with their families, in good faith, to make homes for themselves and their children, in the hope that the pre-emption laws would be extended to them. But as the bill for this purpose had failed they were without the protection of any pre-emption law, and a serious and widespread fear existed that they would be deprived of their hard-earned possessions by the greed of heartless speculators.

But when the time for action arrived at the Green Bay sales, a spirit of justice and honorable dealing proved to be paramount to the demands of grasping rapacity. A meeting of the settlers was held, a committee appointed to determine the justice and good faith of the claims of settlers to their respective "claims," and in every case the decision of the committee was respected by the speculators, many of whom had come from the eastern cities to purchase lands offered at the public sales, and some probably expecting to bid upon the "claims" of some of these settlers; but all the settlers were allowed to purchase their "claims" at the minimum price. The good feeling which resulted was evidenced by the following card, published at the time:

"The settlers of Milwaukee tender their most cordial acknowledgments to the gentlemen who attended the land sales for the handsome manner in which their claims were regarded. And they take pleasure in saying that no case occurred which was not justly entitled to the consideration which it received.

JAMES SANDERSON,   B. W. FINCH,
JAMES CLYMAN,   T. C. DOUSMAN,
GEORGE H. WALKER,   SAMUEL BROWN,
                         OTIS HUBBARD."

There was but little conflict between the settlers and speculators at the Mineral Point land sales, and in all cases the just rights of the settlers were respected.

It is difficult for those of a generation living half a century after these events to appreciate the importance attached to them by those whose interests and feelings were so deeply involved.

The land sales being over, the next subjects to attract the attention and excite the interest of the early settlers were territorial and congressional legislation.

The last authoritative legislation affecting the inhabitants of the territory west of Lake Michigan and prior to the organization of the Territory of Wisconsin, July 4, 1836, was that of the sixth Legislative Council of Michigan Territory at Detroit in January, 1835, and at the special session in August of that year.

The seventh Legislative Council, which met at Green Bay on the 1st of January, 1836, in pursuance of the proclamation of Acting Governor MASON, was unable, owing to the non-appearance of Secretary HORNER, acting governor who had succeeded Governor MASON, to transact any legislative business except to adopt resolutions and memorials. After being most pleasantly entertained for two weeks by the citizens of Green Bay, who have ever been famous for their hospitality, the council adjourned *sine die*, and the members wended their way in the midst of winter; over a country where settlements were so infrequent that " camping out " was a necessity; to their respective homes in the counties of Milwaukee, Iowa, Crawford, and Des Moines.

While Acting Governor HORNER was remaining at Detroit to see that GEORGE W. JONES, the delegate in Congress elect, was not prevented from obtaining his seat by the efforts of Mr. WOODBRIDGE, as stated in Governor HORNER's communication to a Green Bay paper bearing date December 14, Gen. JONES was at Washington representing his constituents.

Upon the assembling of Congress on the 7th of December, Mr. JONES appeared with the delegates from the other territories, was qualified and took his seat without opposition or even any question as to his right to it.

On the 18th of January, 1836, Mr. STORER of Ohio presented sundry affidavits and certificates relative to the late election of delegate for the Territory of Michigan which were referred to the committee of elections.

On the 1st of March he presented documents relating to the same election which had the same reference.

These " affidavits and certificates " and these " documents" are supposed to have related to the right of Mr. WOODBRIDGE to the seat, although it is not so stated, and it does not appear from the journal of that session that he ever formally presented any claim to the seat.

The committee of elections made no report and Mr. JONES continued to occupy the seat through the entire session without any question having been made as to his right to it.

The most important measure of the session, so far as concerned the interests of the inhabitants of Michigan Territory west of Lake Michigan, was an act " establishing the Territorial Government of Wisconsin."

This bill having passed the senate, where it originated, was read the first and second times in the house of Representatives on the 30th of March and referred to the committee of the whole on the state of the Union.

On the 2nd of April, on motion of Mr. PATTON of Virginia, the rules in relation to the priority of business were suspended, for the purpose of considering the bill, and the house then resolved itself into committee of the whole on the state of the Union, and reported that they had come to no resolution thereon.

On the 7th of April it was again considered and reported to the House with amendments, when on motion of Mr. JONES, the delegate, it was ordered postponed until to-morrow and made the special order from 11 o'clock A. M. until 1 o'clock P. M.

When the bill came up for consideration the next day (April 8th) the first question was upon concurring in the first amendment reported by the committee of the whole on the state of the Union, which was to strike out an appropriation of ten thousand acres of the public lands for the purpose of building a capitol, which was in the bill as it passed the Senate and inserting in lieu of it twenty thousand dollars for the same purpose.

Mr. BOND of Ohio moved to amend the amendment by reducing the amount from twenty thousand to twelve thousand five hundred dollars which was lost by a vote of 60 to 117, and the amendment for twenty thousand dollars was then adopted.

Mr. CAVE JOHNSON of Tennessee then moved to amend the bill by striking out the 17th section, which appropriated five thousand dollars for "the purchase of a library for the accommodation of the Assembly and of the Supreme Court." The motion was lost.

The bill as it passed the Senate provided that the salary of the Governor should be two thousand dollars, and fifteen hundred dollars as Superintendent of Indian Affairs. Mr. UNDERWOOD of Kentucky moved to strike out this provision and insert that the Governor should receive an annual salary of two thousand five hundred dollars for his services as Governor and as Superintendent of Indian Affairs.

Mr. VINTON of Ohio moved to amend by reducing the amount from two thousand five hundred to two thousand. This was lost and the amendment offered by Mr. UNDERWOOD was agreed to, which was the second amendment adopted to the Senate bill.

Mr. HARDIN of Kentucky moved to strike out five thousand in the appropriation for a library and insert two thousand, which motion was decided in the negative.

The boundary of the Territory as described in the Senate bill after running north from the northeast corner of the state of Illinois through the middle of Lake Michigan to a point in the middle of said lake and opposite the main channel of Green Bay, run thence "through said channel and Green Bay to the mouth of the Menomonee river," and thence up that river, etc.

Mr. HOWELL of Ohio offered an amendment to strike out "Green Bay to the mouth of the Menomonee river, etc.," and insert

"From the middle of Green Bay to the head of Chocolate river thence down said river to Lake Superior, thence due north to the territorial line and thence with said line, etc."

The effect of this amendment, if it had been adopted, would have been to deprive Michigan of a principal part of its northern peninsula, and leave it a part of the proposed Territory of Wisconsin. The amendment of Mr. HOWEL was, however, lost and the boundaries contained in the Senate bill remained intact.

A third amendment of the Senate bill was adopted, which as it was proposed by a committee of the whole on the state of the Union, does not appear in the journal. It was probably unimportant as it was concurred in by the Senate.

The bill was then read a third time and passed and sent to the Senate for concurrence in the three amendments.

It came up in the Senate, on the 12th of April, when the first and the third amendments were concurred in, and the second, in relation to the compensation of the Governor was disagreed to, and the bill returned to the House.

Mr. PATTON moved on the 14th of April, that the House recede from its second amendment. This motion was lost by a vote of 58 to 135.

MR. CAVE JOHNSON moved that the House insist upon this amendment, which was agreed to.

A committee of conference was then appointed by the request of the Senate, consisting of Messrs. BUCHANAN, WEBSTER and SHEPLEY on the part of the Senate and Messrs. PATTON, KENNON and CASEY on the part of the House.

The result was that the Senate on the 18th of April, receded from its disagreement to the second amendment, the effect of which was the final passage of the bill by both

Houses. It was approved by President ANDREW JACKSON on the 20th of April, when it became a law.

Although the few and widely separated inhabitants of that portion of the country which was organized into the Territory of Wisconsin, could not be said to have ever been without some kind of civil government, it was not until the 4th day of July, 1836, when this act of Congress passed April 20, 1836, took effect, that the advantages and protection of civil government were practically brought within their reach. The due exercise of the three essential, and only important elements of civil power — legislative, judicial and executive —was adequately provided for; and in a republican form, except to the extent that it was limited by the reserved power of the disapproval of laws, by Congress.

BOUNDARIES — The Territory was bounded east by a line drawn from the northeast corner of the State of Illinois, through the middle of Lake Michigan, to a point in the middle of said lake and opposite the main channel of Green Bay, and through said channel and Green Bay to the mouth of the Menomonee river; thence through the middle of the main channel of said river, to that head of said river nearest to the Lake of the Desert; thence in a direct line to the middle of said lake; thence through the middle of the main channel of the Montreal river to its mouth; thence with a direct line across Lake Superior to where the territorial line of the United States touches said lake northwest; thence on the north with the said territorial line, to the White Earth river; on the west, by a line from the said boundary line, following down the middle of the main channel of White Earth river, to the Missouri river, and down the middle of the main channel of the Missouri river, to a point due west from the northwest corner of the State of Missouri (at that time the western boundary of Missouri was the "meridian line passing through the middle of the mouth of the Kansas river," but by an act passed subsequently at the same session, it was extended to the Missouri river); and on the south from said point due east to the northwest corner of the State of Missouri, and thence with the boundaries of the States of Missouri and Illinois, as already fixed by acts of Congress.

The executive power was vested in a *Governor,* who held his office for three years, subject to removal by the President, was required to reside in the Territory, was commander-in-chief of the militia, was to perform the duties and receive the emoluments of Superintendent of Indian Affairs, was required to approve all laws before they should take effect, had the pardoning power for offenses against the laws of the Territory, and might reprieve for offenses against the laws of the United States, until the decision of the President could be made known; he was to commission all territorial officers and take care that the laws were faithfully executed. His salary as Governor and Superintendent of Indian Affairs was two thousand five hundred dollars annually.

A SECRETARY of the Territory was provided for who was to reside in the Territory; his term of office was four years, subject to removal by the President. His duties were to record and preserve all the laws and proceedings of the Legislative Assembly, and all the acts and proceedings of the Governor in his executive department, and transmit one copy to the President of the United States, and two copies to the Speaker of the House of Representatives for the use of Congress. He was authorized and required to execute and perform all the duties and powers of the Governor, during any vacancy caused by his death, removal or resignation or during his necessary absence. The annual salary of the Secretary was twelve hundred dollars.

The legislative power was vested in the Governor and a Legislative Assembly. The Legislative Assembly consisted of a Council and House of Representatives elected by the qualified voters. The council consisted of thirteen members whose terms of service were four years. The House of Representatives consisted of twenty-six members whose term of service was two years. The compensation of each was three dollars per day and three dollars for every twenty miles travel both ways.

The first election was to be held at such time and place as the Governor should appoint and direct. Previous to the first election the Governor was to cause a census to be made by the sheriffs of the several counties of the inhabitants of each. The Governor was to declare the number of members of the Council and House of Representatives to which each of the counties were entitled and declare who was elected. The persons thus elected were to meet at such place on such day as the Governor should appoint, and thereafter the time, place and manner of holding and conducting all elections, and the apportioning of the representatives in the several counties to the Council and House of Representatives, was to be prescribed by law, as well as the day of the annual commencement of the sessions of the Legislative Assembly, but no session in any year could exceed the term of seventy-five days.

Every free, white male citizen of the United States above the age of twenty-one years, who was an inhabitant of the Territory at the time of its organization, was entitled to vote at the first election, and was eligible to any office in the Territory; but the qualifications of voters at all subsequent elections was to be such as should be determined by the Legislative Assembly; *Provided*, that the right of suffrage should be exercised only by citizens of the United States.

The sixth section of the organic act declared

"That the *legislative power* of the Territory shall extend to all rightful subjects of legislation, but no law shall be passed interfering with the primary disposal of the soil; no tax shall be imposed upon the property of the United States, nor shall the lands or other property of non-residents be taxed higher than the lands or other property of residents. All the laws of the Governor and Legislative Assembly shall be submitted to, and, if disapproved by the Congress of the United States, the same shall be null and of no effect."

The governor was to nominate and by and with the advice and consent of the Legislative Council, appoint all judicial officers, justices of the peace, sheriffs and all militia officers, except those of the staff. Clerks of the courts were to be appointed by the judges thereof, but township officers and all other county officers, were to be elected by the people in such manner as might be provided by the Governor and Legislative Assembly.

The *judicial power* of the Territory was vested in a Supreme Court, District Courts, Probate Courts, and justices of the peace. The Supreme Court was to consist of a chief justice and two associate justices, to hold their offices during good behavior, and were each to receive an annual salary of eighteen hundred dollars. The Territory was to be divided into three judicial districts, and a district court to be held in each by one of the judges of the Supreme Court at such times and places as might be prescribed by law. The jurisdiction of all the courts was to be as limited by law, except that justices of the peace should not have jurisdiction in any matter where the title or boundaries of land might be in dispute, nor where the debt or sum claimed exceeded fifty dollars. Writs of error and appeals in chancery causes were allowed in all cases from the district courts to the Supreme Court, and from the Supreme Court to the Supreme Court of the United States, when the amount in controversy exceeded one thousand dollars. The district courts were to have and exercise the same jurisdiction in all cases arising under the Constitution and laws of the United States as is vested in the circuit and district courts of the United States. An attorney and a marshal for the Territory were to be appointed, each for the term of four years, subject to removal by the President.

The Governor, Secretary, judges, attorney, and marshal were to be nominated, and by and with the consent of the Senate appointed by the President of the United States. Each was to take an official oath, which was to be filed with the Secretary of the Territory.

There was to be appropriated annually three hundred and fifty dollars to defray the contingent expenses of the Territory, to be expended by the Governor, and a sufficient sum to be expended by the Secretary of the Territory, to defray the expenses of the Legislative Assembly, the printing of the laws, and other incidental expenses.

Not only did the organic act provide, as has been previously mentioned, that the inhabitants of the Territory should be entitled to enjoy all the rights, privileges and advantages granted and secured to the people of the territory northwest of the River Ohio by the articles of compact contained in the ordinance of 1787, but that they should also be entitled to all the rights, privileges, and immunities theretofore granted and secured to the Territory of Michigan and its inhabitants. It also provided that the laws of the Territory of Michigan should be extended over it, so far as the same should not be incompatible with the organic act, subject, however, to alteration, modification, and repeal. And further, that the laws of the United States be extended over, and should be in force in the Territory of Wisconsin so far as they might be applicable.

The Legislative Assembly was to hold its first session at such time and place as the Governor should appoint, and that the Governor and Legislative Assembly should thereafter locate and establish the seat of government at such place as they might deem eligible, subject thereafter to be by them changed. Twenty thousand dollars were appropriated to defray the expenses of erecting public buildings at the seat of government.

The act provided for the election of a delegate to the House of Representatives, to serve for the term of two years, who should be entitled to the same rights and privileges as had been granted to the delegates from the several Territories to the House of Representatives. The first election was to be held at such time and place or places as the Governor should appoint, who was to give a certificate to the person elected.

Suitable provision was made for the transfer of pending judicial proceedings from the courts of Michigan to those of Wisconsin.

An appropriation of five thousand dollars was made for the purchase of a library for the accommodation of the Assembly and of the Supreme Court.

With these provisions of the organic act and the subsequent action of the President in the appointment of the territorial officers for which it provided, the civil government of the Territory of Wisconsin was in complete readiness to be set in operation on the 4th day of July, the day on which by the act, it was to be organized.

To summarize the several different periods of time from the early part of the sixteenth century to the organization of the Territory of Wisconsin in 1836, during which the right of civil government has been claimed or exercised by different powers, the facts stated in this and the preceding chapter, present these results.

For more than a century, from 1512 to 1627, the only claim to the right of civil jurisdiction over the domain of the present state of Wisconsin, which any governmental power pretended to possess, was the claim of Spain derived from the discovery of Florida by PONCE DE LEON. This claim was, however, entirely ideal, as during that period no subject of Spain ever saw any portion of this domain.

From 1627 to 1762, civil jurisdiction over the Territory was claimed, and to a considerable extent exercised by France.

By the treaty of February 10, 1763, resulting from the war between France and England, the right of civil jurisdiction passed from the former to the latter, and civil jurisdiction accompanied by actual occupancy of the posts on the northern frontier was maintained by Great Britain until 1796, although the last thirteen years of this jurisdiction was in open violation of the treaty of 1783.

During the Revolutionary war and thereafter until the formation of the Northwest Territory in 1787, jurisdiction was claimed by Virginia. This claim was practically exercised over and acquiesced in by the inhabitants of that portion of the territory now forming the states of Ohio, Indiana and Illinois while those in the remaining portion were compelled to recognize the power of Great Britain.

From 1787 to 1800 the right of civil government was vested by the Ordinance of 1787 in the territorial government which it established; but owing to the jurisdiction which was maintained by Great Britain, the right was not practically exercised within the present state of Wisconsin until 1796.

From May 7, 1800, to January 11, 1805, jurisdiction over the domain of the state of Wisconsin was vested in and exercised by the Territory of Indiana.

From January 11, 1805, until February 3, 1809, by the Territory of Michigan.

From February 3, 1809, until December 3, 1818, by the Territory of Illinois.

From December 3, 1818, until July 4, 1836, the Territory of Michigan again had and exercised the jurisdiction.

Hitherto our attempts at historiography have resulted only in the exposition of the history of Florida, Louisiana, Virginia, the Northwestern Territory, and the Territories of Indiana, Illinois and Michigan, so far as that portion of them which is now known as Wisconsin, was affected.

An epoch is now reached from which a new historical departure is to be taken, and the story is to be told of the settlement, development and progress of the Territory of Wisconsin, from its organization as a distinct territorial government in 1836, to its admission into the Union as a sovereign independent state in 1848. This period of twelve years is highly interesting, as being that in which the political character and material features of the future State were molded and crystallized.

CHAPTER XVII.

TERRITORY OF WISCONSIN IN 1833.

The early organization of the new Territory of Wisconsin was, during the years 1835 and the early part of 1836, clearly foreseen as one of the inevitable results of the formation of the independent *State* of Michigan. The fragmentary *Territory* of Michigan thus left, was not designed and was illy adapted to the wants of the inhabitants of the country west of the lake.

The organization of the new Territory was delayed until the question of the boundaries of the State of Michigan could be acted upon by Congress, and so soon as it was known what that action would be, it was anticipated by the act to organize the Territory of Wisconsin, which was passed April 20, 1836, although the act to provide for the admission of the State of Michigan into the Union was not passed until twenty-five days later.

The scenes and events successively occurring during the twelve years of the existence of the Territory of Wisconsin, which were so commonplace at the time of their occurrence as to make but little impression upon those immediately connected with them, may now possess some historic interest to those who had no personal knowledge of them, if not create a revived interest in those who participated in them; which can only be gratified by a reference to the archives of the State Historical Society.

The spirit of migration, the desire for change, is believed to be the fundamental element, the inspiring cause of and chief reason for the wonderful progress which has marked the advance of American civilization, especially in the states formed out of the Northwest Territory.

Whatever the cause, the historical fact is now acknowledged, that the rapidity of settlement in Wisconsin for the fifteen years next succeeding 1835, was almost, if not quite, unprecedented in the settlement of new states. Previous to 1835 much the largest proportion—about two thirds—of the population of the Territory was to be found in Iowa county. They had, however, generally come in search of lead, and nearly all with the expectation of soon getting rich and returning to the homes they had left behind them. It was emphatically a *floating* population. Many, however —some attracted by success, and some compelled by the necessities resulting from ill-luck—remained, and became permanent inhabitants of the country, which they had visited only as an adventurous experiment.

After the Indian right of occupancy on the lands south and east of the Wisconsin and Fox rivers had been extinguished, the lands had been surveyed and offered for sale, which to a limited extent occurred in November, 1834, and more extensively in August and September, 1835, the purposes of most of those who came with no fixed intention of remaining became changed. They purchased land and became permanently identified with the country; and the same influences which were thus operating upon those who were already here, produced a like effect upon large numbers possessed of the migratory spirit, but whose feet had never trod the soil west of Lake Michigan, and induced them also to become permanent inhabitants of the new Territory.

Another class, who were characterized by the settlers as "speculators," visited the country, either personally or by agents, in great numbers and purchased very large quantities of the choicest of the public lands, which had been offered for sale in 1834 and 1835. These purchases were almost exclusively made on speculation, and with no purpose of occupancy, but solely with the expectation of selling the lands at a future period at a greatly increased price. The effect of these speculations was greatly to retard and prevent the occupancy of the country by permanent inhabitants.

Some idea may be formed of the magnitude of this land speculation from the fact, which the records of the General Land Office show, that the total sales of the Government lands in Wisconsin previous to December, 31, 1836, amounted to 878,014 acres, of which as much as 600,000 acres were probably sold to speculators.

The correctness of this estimate is confirmed by the fact that the total amount of sales during the years 1837 and 1838, after the spirit of speculation had ceased, amounted to only 360,919 acres, although the population during that period had more than doubled.

The wild spirit of speculation which pervaded the whole

country in 1836 is within the present recollection of the older persons of the present generation. The currency of the country, which consisted mainly of the notes of state banks, was abnormally expanded. The Receivers of the Land offices were authorized to receive the notes of many of the state banks in payment for the public lands, and appearances seemed to indicate that the entire body of the public domain would soon be exchanged for bank credits and paper money, and would be absorbed by speculators to the serious injury of actual settlers and emigrants.

In this condition of things, the specie circular, as it was called, of LEVI WOODBURY, Secretary of the Treasury, was issued by the direction of President ANDREW JACKSON, which had the effect to soon arrest the land speculating mania.

This circular was issued on the 11th July, 1836, and recited, that —

"In consequence of complaints which had been made of frauds, speculations and monopolies in the purchase of the public land, and the aid which was said to effect these objects by excessive bank credits and through bank drafts and bank deposits, and in consequence of the general evil influence likely to result to the public interests, and especially the safety of the great amount of money in the Treasury, and the sound condition of the currency of the country from the further exchange of the national domain in this manner, and chiefly for bank credits and paper money;"

and then instructed the Receivers of Public Money,—

"After the 15th day of August next to receive in payment of the public lands nothing except what is directed by the existing laws, viz.: GOLD AND SILVER and in the proper cases Virginia land scrip; *provided*, that till the 15th day of December next the same indulgences heretofore extended, as to the kind of money received, may be continued for any quantity of land not exceeding three hundred and twenty acres, to each purchaser who is an actual settler or *bona fide* resident of the State when the sales are made."

The circular further stated that —

"The principal object of the President in adopting this measure was to repress alleged frauds, and to withhold any countenance or facilities in the power of the Government, from the monopoly of the public lands in the hands of speculators to the injury of the actual settlers of the new States, and of emigrants in search of new homes, as well as to discourage the ruinous extension of bank issues and bank credits, by which those results are supposed to be prompted."

The specie circular, considered with reference to its effects subsequent to the time when it went into operation, produced all the beneficial results which had been hoped for it by General JACKSON, but so far as related to southwestern Wisconsin, embracing the present counties of Grant, Iowa, La Fayette, Dane, Green, and the west half of Rock and Columbia, its wisdom was analagous to that of the old adage of locking the stable after the horse was stolen. A very large proportion of the most valuable lands in that portion of the State had before the 15th of August, 1836, passed from the control of the government to that of speculators.

The result was that the great mass "of emigrants in search of new homes," during the years 1836, 1837, and 1838, avoided those counties which had been affected by the mildew of speculation, and swarmed upon the counties of Kenosha, Racine, Waukesha, Dodge, Jefferson, Walworth and the eastern parts of Rock and Columbia, where the lands were not offered for sale until 1839, and where a choice of location was open to them, and into which the blight of land monopoly had not yet entered. "Claims" were made and when accompanied by such visible acts as indicated the good faith of the claim and the intention of occupancy, were always respected.

These immigrants, thus locating upon the public lands, though called not inaptly "squatters," were not, and were never regarded, either by the Government, by themselves or by the community of which they formed a part, as trespassers. The pre-emption acts of 1830, 1832, 1833 and 1834, although limited in the period of their operation which expired in June, 1836, encouraged such "squatting" as well as a just expectation that the pre-emption right would be revived, which, however, was not realized until the act of June 22, 1838, by which this right was extended for a further period of two years.

A community of interest and a spirit of justice which demanded that the pioneer immigrant should not be robbed of the fruits of his honest toil, gave to these squatters' claims all the practical security which belonged to a patent from the government, and as a consequence the inhabitants pursued their ordinary avocations in peace and safety and devoted the same time and attention to the interests of the public as was the case in older communities.

In the last chapter was given in detail the features of the organic act of the Territory. The first appointments made by the President and Senate of the several officers provided for by that act were:

Governor — HENRY DODGE of Dodgeville, Wisconsin.
Secretary — JOHN S. HORNER of Virginia.
Chief Justice — CHARLES DUNN of Illinois.
Associate Judges — DAVID IRVIN of Virginia and WM. C. FRAZER of Pennsylvania.

Attorney — W. W. CHAPMAN of Burlington, Iowa.
Marshal — FRANCIS GEHON of Dubuque, Iowa.

On the 4th of July the Governor and Secretary took the prescribed oath of office at Mineral Point, which event contributed a novel and interesting element to a grand celebration of the national jubilee, which was very generally participated in by the inhabitants of the lead mine region, of which that hamlet was then the recognized metropolis.

The first important thing to be done to complete the organization of the embryo territorial government was the convening of the Legislative Assembly. Preliminary to this a census was to be taken by the sheriffs, and an apportionment of members of the two branches made by the Governor among the several counties.

The population of the Territory in August, 1836, as exhibited by the census was as follows:

Brown county	2,706
Crawford county	854
Des Moines county	6,257
Du Buque county	4,274
Iowa county	5,234
Milwaukee county	2,893
Total	22,218

On the 9th of September, Governor DODGE issued a proclamation to the effect that he had apportioned the members of the Council and House of Representatives amongst the several counties of the Territory as follows:

Brown, ... 2 members of the Council and 3 of the House of Representatives.
Crawford .... 0 members of the Council and 2 of the House of Representatives.
Milwaukee ...... 2 members of the Council and 3 of the House of Representatives.
Iowa .... 3 members of the Council and 6 of the House of Representatives.
Du Buque .... 3 members of the Council and 5 of the House of Representatives.
Des Moines ..... 3 members of the Council and 7 of the House of Representatives.
      13   26

The proclamation further ordered and directed that the first election should be held on the second Monday of October, and that the electors present, on the day and at the place of election, might elect three persons to preside at and conduct said election, and provided for the return and canvass of the votes.

It further ordered and directed that the members elected from the several counties should convene at Belmont in the county of Iowa on the 25th of October, for the purpose of organizing the first session of the Legislative Assembly.

It also directed and appointed that at the same time and places specified for electing members of the legislature, there should be elected a delegate to Congress for the term of two years.

The election campaign was quite brief, hardly one month, but it excited very considerable interest.

GEORGE W. JONES of Sinsinawa Mound in Iowa (now Grant) county had been the delegate during the first session of the 24th Congress, 1835-6, from the fragment of Michigan Territory remaining after the creation of the State of Michigan. He had rendered himself very acceptable to the people of the new Territory of Wisconsin, especially by his zealous and successful efforts in securing the passage of the act of April 20, for its organization. It appeared to be very generally thought that an election as the first delegate from the new Territory was due to him as a recognition of his valuable services, while it would at the same time promote the best interests of the infant Territory. Expression was given to this general feeling at a public meeting held at Belmont on the 23d of September, in pursuance of very extensive notice, for the purpose of nominating candidates for the Legislature; when Col. JONES was recommended as a suitable person for Delegate, and as "possessed of integrity, untiring zeal, perseverance, industry and weight of character." His election, however, was not destined to be entirely unanimous.

MOSES MEEKER, one of the earliest settlers of the lead mines, who first came to Galena in November, 1822, and permanently located there in June, 1823, with his family and several others, all of whom came in a keel boat from Cincinnati, announced himself as a candidate in a card dated "Blue River, Iowa Co., September 21, 1836." His candidacy was indorsed by a meeting subsequently held at Mineral Point, called for the purpose of nominating candidates for the Legislature.

The following is the result of the vote:

	JONES.	MEEKER.
Brown County	314	11
Crawford County	56	10
Des Moines County	860	8
Dubuque County	930	49
Iowa County	612	617
Milwaukee County	750	1
	3,522	696

The result in Iowa county is thus explained by the *Belmont Gazette*:

"A temporary excitement with regard to the seat of government was made to operate against him (JONES); gratuitous and unfounded reports of his being interested in a particular place were circulated and to this, and this alone, is to be ascribed his loss of votes."

The elections for members of the Legislature were conducted on personal and local grounds, and aside from mere personal preferences, the questions affecting the results were those which were supposed to affect local interests, especially the division of counties, creating new counties and locating county seats.

In *Iowa county* two tickets were put in nomination, supposed to represent different local interests; one by a meeting held at Belmont on the 23rd of September, the other by a meeting subsequently held at Mineral Point.

The candidates nominated at Belmont were:

For the Council: JAMES R. VINEYARD, JOHN W. BLACKSTONE and JAMES GILMORE.

For the House of Representatives: THOMAS CRUSON, THOMAS J. PARISH, JAMES H. GENTRY, JAMES COLLINS, JOHN BEVANS and BENONI R. GILLETT.

Those nominated at Mineral Point were:

For the Council: EBENEZER BRIGHAM, JOHN B. TERRY and GLENDOWER M. PRICE.

For the House of Representatives: JAMES P. COX, THOMAS MCKNIGHT, THOMAS SHANLY, WILLIAM BOYLES, DANIEL M. PARKINSON and GEORGE F. SMITH.

The candidates nominated at Mineral Point were all elected except Mr. PRICE for the Council, in place of whom Mr. VINEYARD was chosen.

The "Mineral Point" ticket was supposed to be in favor of the division of Iowa county in the mode adopted by the Legislature, with county seats at Mineral Point and on Boice Prairie (Lancaster). The candidates nominated on the "Belmont" ticket were supposed to favor a division which should create one county out of ranges one and two east, with one and two west, with the county seat at Belmont or Platteville, and another county west of that, comprising ranges three, four, five, and six west, with a county seat at Cassville.

In *Brown county* the candidates for the *Council* were HENRY S. BAIRD, JOHN P. ARNDT, and MORGAN L. MARTIN, of whom Messrs. BAIRD and ARNDT were elected. The candidates for the *House of Representatives* were EBENEZER CHILDS, ALBERT G. ELLIS, ALEXANDER J. IRWIN, JOSEPH DICKINSON, and GEORGE MCWILLIAMS. Messrs. CHILDS, ELLIS, and IRWIN were declared by the returns to be elected, but the seat of Mr. IRWIN was subsequently vacated by the House, and Mr. MCWILLIAMS was admitted to it.

In *Milwaukee county* ALANSON SWEET and GILBERT KNAPP were elected to the *Council*, and to the *House of Representatives*, WILLIAM B. SHELDON, MADISON W. CORNWALL, and CHARLES DURKEE were elected.

In *Crawford county* JAMES H. LOCKWOOD, and JAMES B. DALLAM were elected members of the *House of Representatives*.

No member of the Council was apportioned to this county by the Governor, whereat a public meeting was held, said to have been "the largest ever held in the county upon any public occasion," at which resolutions were adopted, among which was the following:

"*Resolved*, That in the exercise of our lawful rights, secured to us by the act organizing the Territory, we will at the approaching election vote for and elect a member to represent the county of Crawford in the Council, and demand that he be admitted to his seat as such, relying upon the patriotism and intelligence of our fellow-citizens in the other counties of the Territory, and of their representatives, with the confident belief that the 'majesty of truth will triumph,' that equal and impartial justice will be maintained, and the laws of our country vindicated."

THOMAS P. BURNETT received almost the entire vote of the county.

The petition of Mr. BURNETT, claiming a seat in the Council, was presented and referred to a select committee, which reported that —

"The Council have no control of the case, the power to declare the number of members of the Council to which each county is entitled belonging exclusively to the executive as prescribed by the act of Congress for establishing the Territory of Wisconsin."

The report was accepted and the committee discharged, and nothing more was heard of the matter.

The names and place of nativity of the first Legislative Assembly, as organized, were as follows:

COUNCIL.

Brown county — Henry S. Baird, Dublin, Ireland.
Brown county — John P. Arndt, Northampton county, Pennsylvania.
Des Moines county — Jeremiah Smith, Jr., Pickaway county, Ohio.
Des Moines county — Joseph B. Teas, Knox county, Tennessee.
Des Moines county — Arthur B. Inghram, Washington county, Pennsylvania
Dubuque county — Thomas McCraney, Delaware county, New York.

Dubuque county — Thomas McKnight, Augusta, Virginia.
Dubuque county — John Foley, Waterford county, Ireland.
Iowa county — Ebenezer Brigham, Worcester county, Massachusetts.
Iowa county — John B. Terry, Duchess county, New York.
Iowa county — James R. Vineyard, Caldwell county, Kentucky.
Milwaukee county — Gilbert Knapp, Barnstable county, Massachusetts.
Milwaukee county — Alanson Sweet, Genesee county, New York.

HOUSE OF REPRESENTATIVES.

Brown county — Ebenezer Childs, Worcester county, Massachusetts.
Brown county — Albert G. Ellis, Oneida county, New York.
Brown county — Alexander J. Irwin, Westmoreland county, Pennsylvania.
Crawford county — James H. Lockwood, Peru, Clinton county, New York.
Crawford county — James B. Dallam, Hartford county, Maryland.
Des Moines county — Isaac Leffler, Washington county, Pennsylvania.
Des Moines county — Thomas Blair, Bourbon county, Kentucky.
Des Moines county — John Box, Claiborne county, Tennessee.
Des Moines county — George W. Teas, White county, Tennessee.
Des Moines county — David R. Chance, Madison county, Kentucky.
Des Moines county — Warren S. Jenkins, Hardin county, Kentucky.
Des Moines county — Eli Reynolds, Washington county, Pennsylvania.
Dubuque county — Loring Wheeler, Cheshire county, New Hampshire.
Dubuque county — Hardin Nowlin, Monroe county, Illinois.
Dubuque county — Hosea T. Camp, Jackson county, Georgia.
Dubuque county — Peter Hill Engle, Delaware county, Pennsylvania.
Dubuque county — Patrick Quigley, Londonderry, Ireland.
Iowa county — William Boyles, Green county, Pennsylvania.
Iowa county — George F. Smith, Wilkes county, North Carolina.
Iowa county — Daniel M. Parkinson, Carter county, Tennessee.
Iowa county — Thomas McKnight, Spartenberg county, South Carolina.
Iowa county — Thomas Shanley, South Carolina.
Iowa county — James P. Cox, Philadelphia county, Pennsylvania.
Milwaukee county — William B. Sheldon, Providence, Rhode Island.
Milwaukee county — Madison W Cornwall, Monroe county, Virginia.
Milwaukee county — Charles Durkee, Royalton, Windsor county, Vermont.

Both houses convened on the day appointed by the Governor (October 25), and a quorum being present in each house they were duly organized, the oath having been administered by the Governor.

In the council HENRY S. BAIRD was elected President, EDWARD MCSHERRY, of Mineral Point, was elected Secretary, and WILLIAM HENRY, of Mineral Point, Sergeant-at-Arms.

In the House of Representatives, PETER HILL ENGLE was elected Speaker, WARNER LEWIS, of Dubuque, Chief Clerk, and JESSE M. HARRISON, Sergeant-at-Arms.

On the second day of the session the Governor delivered his message in person, to the two houses jointly assembled.

The message recommended early action in defining the jurisdiction and powers of the several courts, dividing the territory into judicial districts and prescribing the times and places of holding courts.

It recommended a memorial to Congress for extending the right of pre-emption to settlers on the public lands, and to miners for their mineral lots, and expressed the opinion that the "price of the public lands should be reduced and graduated according to the value of the land" and that "the public interest would be greatly promoted by the establishment of a Surveyor General's office within the Territory."

It recommended a memorial to Congress asking an appropriation of two hundred and fifty thousand dollars for the completion of the work of the removal of the obstructions in the rapids of the Upper Mississippi for which forty thousand dollars had been appropriated at the last session of Congress. Also an appropriation sufficient to cover the expense of surveying all the necessary harbors on Lake Michigan and the construction of such habors and light-houses at the most eligible situations for the security and protection of our lake trade. Also for the survey of the Fox river from Green Bay to Fort Winnebago.

The following passage is interesting, as showing the ideas of the Governor at that day on the subject of internal improvements in the Territory:

"The improvement of the navigation of the Rock river I consider a subject of vital importance to the future prosperity of this Territory. This river waters a large extent of fertile country; a small appropriation by Congress would be sufficient to remove the obstructions in its navigation. It is known that from the outlet of the Four Lakes, that discharges itself into the Rock, the distance to Rock river does not exceed twelve miles by land, and from the Fourth Lake it is not more than sixteen miles to the Wisconsin river. Indians have frequently descended in canoes, in high water, from the Fourth Lake to the Wisconsin river. The great advantage of this inland communication must be apparent; it would greatly enhance the value of the national domain in that part of the Territory, and increase the value of lands purchased by individuals from the government.

The construction of a railroad, commencing at some suitable point on the Mississippi, in this Territory, passing through the mining country to Rock river and direct to Lake Michigan, is a subject of great interest to the citizens of this Territory, who have strong claims on the patronage of the government in granting a donation in land for that important purpose."

The message recommended

"The propriety of asking from Congress a donation of one township of land, to be sold and the proceeds of the sale placed under the direction of the Legislative Assembly, for the establishment of an academy for the education of youth."

A considerable portion of the message was devoted to the subject of "organizing and arming the militia," which the Governor regarded as "of great interest to the future peace of the people of the Territory."

Mounted riflemen were recommended as "the most efficient troops for the protection and defense of our frontier settlements;" one company composed of sixty men besides officers, was recommended to be organized by law in each county, to be uniformed and required to muster once during each month, and held at all times in readiness to take the field. The justice and propriety of asking of Congress a deposit of three thousand stand of arms—one half rifles and the remainder muskets—for the use of the citizens in the event of an Indian war, with fixed ammunition prepared sufficient for a campaign of four months, was recommended. Also four light brass field pieces (three pounders) fixed on carriages, with a supply of fixed ammunition for them.

No law was passed for "organizing and arming the militia," no companies of mounted riflemen were organized, no "arms" or "field pieces" were deposited by the Government, and no "Indian war" occurred to demonstrate the wisdom of these preparations for such an event.

The Governor voluntarily divested himself of the absolute negative given him by the organic act, so far as related to the permanent location of the seat of government, by the declaration with which his message concluded, in these words:

"I deem it proper to state that my assent will be given to its location at any point where a majority of the representatives of the people agree it will best promote the public good."

The appropriation "to defray the expenses of the Legislative Assembly," approved May 9, 1836, was only $9,400. It was estimated by the finance committee that the actual expenses of the session would be $18,980, leaving a deficit of $9,580. The actual deficit was $15,730.16.

To meet this deficit an act was passed November 15, 1836, authorizing the Secretary of the Territory to borrow such sum as might be wanted to defray the expenses of the session, not to exceed $10,000. The Secretary was not able to make the loan, and the act was repealed December 8th. In the meantime, a joint resolution adopted December 3rd, by which JOHN ATCHINSON, Esq., was appointed Fiscal Agent, contained a pledge

"That all advances of money made by him, should be refunded to him out of such money as might thereafter be appropriated by Congress."

The first act of this session was one which privileged the members from arrest and conferred upon them authority to punish for contempt.

The next act divided the Territory into three judicial districts, and made an assignment of one of the three judges to each district. Crawford and Iowa counties constituted the first district, to which the chief justice was assigned; Dubuque and Des Moines the second to which Judge IRVIN was assigned, and Judge FRAZER was assigned to the third, consisting of Milwaukee and Brown counties, The act provided that two terms of the district courts should be held annually in each of the counties, and prescribed the times for the commencement of the terms in the several counties. Subsequently another act was passed authorizing the judges to appoint clerks of the courts previous to the holding of the first term.

Three banks were incorporated — the Miners' Bank of Dubuque, the Bank of Mineral Point and the Bank of Milwaukee, all of which were organized and went into operation, and all failed and became utterly bankrupt, as did also the Bank of Wisconsin at Green Bay, which was incorporated in 1835 by the Legislative Council of Michigan Territory. The loss sustained by the community by the failure of the Bank of Mineral Point was over $200,000.

All the territory south and east of the Wisconsin and Fox Rivers was subdivided into counties, the boundaries of which were mainly like those of the existing counties, except that Kenosha has been formed from Racine; Waukesha from Milwaukee; Ozaukee from Washington; Green Lake from Marquette and La Fayette from Iowa. Columbia county was called Portage. In most of the counties the county seats were established at the same session. These questions, however, did not create much discussion or excitement in the Legislative Assembly, as the questions, where any existed, had been mainly decided at the elections, and the members had only to give effect to the expressed will of those citizens by whom they had been elected.

The great and paramount question of the session was the location of the seat of government. To this all others were subordinate and made subservient. The wild spirit of speculation, which in the earlier part of the year 1836 had, like a tornado, swept over the whole country, and which, having invaded and unsettled the prices of every species of personal property, seized upon the unsold public domain, which was transferred by millions of acres from the control of the Government and the occupation of the settler, to the dominion of the speculator, although on the wane in the last months of that year, was still omnipotent, and exerted a marked influence upon many of the members of the Belmont Legislature.

Numerous speculators were in attendance with beautiful maps of prospective cities, whose future greatness was portrayed with all the fervor and eloquence which the excited imaginations of their proprietors could display. Madison, Belmont, Fond du Lac, and Cassville were the points which were most prominently urged upon the consideration of the members. Hon. JAMES DUANE DOTY, afterward a delegate in Congress and Governor of the Territory, and more recently Governor of Utah, where he died, had resided many years at Green Bay as additional Judge of Michigan Territory. His frequent journeys in discharge of his judicial duties, in the different parts of the Territory, had rendered him familiar with its geography and topography, and had given him superior advantages for judging of the eligibility of different points as sites for the capital of the Territory and future State. Judge DOTY fixed upon the isthmus between the third and fourth of the Four Lakes, and in conjunction with STEVENS T. MASON, the Governor of Michigan Territory, purchased from the Government about one thousand acres in sections 13, 14, 23, and 24, upon the common corner of which the capital now stands. Upon this tract of land a town plat was laid out, called Madison, and under the auspices of its founder became a formidable competitor for the honor and advantages of being selected as the seat of government. Madison town lots in large numbers were freely distributed among members, their friends, and others who were supposed to possess influence with them.

Nearly four weeks were spent in skirmishing outside the legislative halls, when on the 21st of November, the battle was formally opened in the Council, and the bill considered in committee of the whole until the 23d, when it was reported back, in the form in which it became a law, fixing upon Madison as the seat of government, and providing that the sessions of the Legislative Assembly should be held at Burlington, in Des Moines county, until March 4, 1839, unless the public buildings at Madison should be sooner completed. When the bill was reported back by the committee of the whole, and was under consideration in the Council, where the ayes and noes could be called, a spirited attack was made upon it, and motions to strike out Madison and insert some other place were successively made in favor of Fond du Lac, Dubuque, Portage, Helena, Milwaukee, Racine, Belmont, Mineral Point, Platteville, Green Bay, Cassville, Belleview, Koshkonong, Wisconsinapolis, Peru, and Wisconsin City; but all with one uniform result—ayes 6, noes 7; and the bill was by the same vote ordered engrossed, and the next day passed the Council.

The members of the Council who had voted for the bill, and, of course, in favor of Madison as the permanent seat of government, were Messrs. ARNDT, BRIGHAM, INGHRAM, SWEET, SMITH, TERRY and TEAS; and those who voted against it were Messrs. FOLEY, KNAPP, McKNIGHT, McCRANEY, VINEYARD and BAIRD (Pres't).

A protest signed by all who voted against it, except Mr. VINEYARD, was afterwards presented, but the Council refused to receive it.

In the House of Representatives the opposition was not so formidable, and on the 28th the bill was ordered to a third reading by a vote of 16 to 10 and passed the same day. Those who voted for the passage of the bill were Messrs. BLAIR, BOX, BOYLES, CHANCE, CORNWALL, COX, DURKEE JENKINS, LEFFLER, LOCKWOOD, McKNIGHT, PARKINSON REYNOLDS, SHANLEY and TEAS. Those who voted against it were Messrs. CAMP, CHILDS, DALLAM, ELLIS, IRWIN, NOWLIN, QUIGLEY, SHELDON, SMITH, WHEELER and ENGLE, (Speaker).

The speaker, in his farewell address to the House, thus alluded to this measure:

"There has been one subject settled of more than ordinary interest—it has elicited all the ingenuity, tact and talent of the House in debate, and some asperity of feeling. It has been a measure of such absorbing interest, as to color, in a degree, the other proceedings of this body. I have been in the minority on this question; my votes will be found on the side of those who ardently resisted the course that question has taken."

On the 31st of October the President laid before the Council a communication from the Secretary of the Territory accompanied with "a great seal of Wisconsin Territory" and an impression thereof.

The seal was $2\frac{1}{4}$ inches in diameter. Upon the scroll, surmounting the seal are the words "Great Seal of Wisconsin."

A miner's arm projects from the left, grasping a pick and suspending it over a pile of lead ore. Under the base line are the words " 4th day of July, Anno Domino, 1836."

Memorials to Congress were adopted asking for aid to construct a railroad from Lake Michigan to the Mississippi River; requesting that three thousand stand of arms — half rifles and half muskets — one thousand pistols, and four light field pieces, be deposited within the Territory for the use of the citizens; asking a small appropriation to defray the expense of surveying a canal from the mouth of the Sheboygan River to the head of Lake Winnebago; also for an appropriation of eight thousand dollars

" For the purpose of opening a road from Fort Winnebago to intersect the military road leading from Green Bay to Chicago, at the most eligible point between the mouth of the Milwaukee River and the northern boundary line of the State of Illinois;"

to complete the opening and building of which military road already surveyed, an appropriation of the necessary sum was asked. An appropriation was also asked for a wagon road from Milwaukee *via* Madison to the Mississippi River. Another memorial was adopted asking the following appropriations for internal improvements:

For the improvement of the harbor and construction of a light house at Milwaukee, thirty thousand dollars;

At Racine twenty-six thousand dollars;

At the mouth of Pike River (Kenosha) six thousand five hundred dollars;

At the mouth of Sheboygan River, twenty-five thousand dollars;

At the mouth of Manitowoc River, twenty-five thousand dollars;

At the mouth of Kewaunee River, twelve thousand dollars;

At the mouth of Twin Rivers, six thousand, four hundred dollars;

For the construction of a pier and beacon light at Long Tail Point at the head of Green Bay, twenty thousand dollars, and six hundred dollars for buoys to mark the ship channel from thence to the mouth of Fox River; the sum of twenty-five thousand dollars for the improvement of Fox River; and the sum of two thousand dollars for the survey of the Wisconsin River, and the sum of one thousand dollars for the survey of Rock River. An appropriation of two hundred and fifty thousand dollars was asked for the improvement of the rapids of the Mississippi River.

A memorial was also adopted asking far the passage of a pre-emption law.

An act prescribing the manner of approving sheriffs' bonds and one defining the duties of coroners were passed.

A general law was passed to provide for the incorporation of towns and villages.

A law authorizing the construction of a bridge across the Milwaukee River from Oneida to Wells street was passed which encountered much opposition in Milwaukee.

An act was passed which provided that the county seat of Brown county should be established either at Navarino, Astor, or Depere as might be decided by a vote of the qualified electors.

The supervisors were empowered to grant licenses in their respective counties for the sale of intoxicating liquors.

Three territorial roads were authorized to be laid out at the expense of the several counties through which they run:

From Janes's ferry through Rockford, Centerville, New Mexico and White Oak Springs to the Mississippi river.

From Milwaukee *via* Madison to the Blue Mounds.

From the mouth of Pike Creek by way of the fork of White and Fox rivers to the Rock river at Janesville.

The only railroad charter granted out of the many that were desired was one for the construction of a railroad from "Belmont in Iowa county to the nearest and most eligible point on the Mississippi river," with "power to extend the railroad from Belmont to Mineral Point and from thence to Dodgeville."

The act establishing the seat of government provided that three commissioners should be elected by joint ballot of the Council and House of Representatives, whose duty it was to cause the necessary public buildings to be erected at Madison. In pursuance of this law, JAMES D. DOTY, JOHN F. O'NEIL and AUGUSTUS A. BIRD were elected.

By a joint resolution, JOHN M. CLAYTON and LEWIS F. LINN, senators, GEORGE W. JONES, delegate in Congress, and PETER HILL ENGLE, speaker, were appointed a committee to select and purchase a library for the use of the Territory, and for that purpose were authorized to draw the money appropriated therefor by the organic act.

A proposition was made for a commission to codify the

laws, but the opinion was prevalent that the Territory would soon be divided, so that this and other propositions of a kindred character, met with but little favor.

The first Legislative Assembly, having enacted that the annual sessions should thereafter be held on the first Monday of November, adjourned *sine die* on the 9th day of December, having been in session 46 days, and passed 42 laws, about one-half of which were of a private nature.

It was provided by the organic act that "the Governor shall nominate and by and with the advice and consent of the Council shall appoint all judicial officers, justices of the peace, sheriffs and all militia officers (except those of the staff), and all civil officers not herein provided for." A large number of appointments were made by the Governor and Council, of which a few are mentioned:

Brown county. BARLOW SHACKLEFORD, District Attorney.

Crawford county. WILLIAM WILSON, sheriff; JAMES H. LOCKWOOD, Judge of Probate.

Iowa county. JUSTUS DE'SEELHORST, Sheriff; HUGH R. COLTER, Judge of Probate.

Grant county. JOSEPH H. D. STREET, Sheriff; JOHN H. ROUNTREE, Judge of Probate.

Milwaukee county. OWEN ALDRIDGE, Sheriff; WILLIAM CAMPBELL, Judge of Probate.

Racine county. EDGAR R. HUGUNIN, Sheriff; WILLIAM BULLEN, Judge of Probate.

Surveyors, masters in chancery, supreme court commissioners, auctioneers, numerous justices of the peace and notaries public were appointed in all the counties; as well those newly organized as the six old counties.

No attempt to preserve the debates in either House on any subject is made, but it is thought the following extracts from the verbatim report in the *Belmont Gazette,* of the remarks of Mr. CHANCE, a member of the House from Des Moines county, justify a reproduction. He is reported as having said

"MR. CHAIRMAN: I have waited patiently, till the doctors and lawyers got through, to make a speech on the location of the seat of government. I was raised in the wiles of Ellinois, and us't to wear a leather huntin' shirt and sleep under a buffalo rug. I was edicated in the woods. The yearly part of my life was spent in trackin' Ingens; but it is harder tracken these gentlemen. We have envited the gentlemen to come up to the troft, and argy the question on its merits, but as the Yankee said, they squerm, and won't come up to the rack.

Mr. Chairman, we are honest men from Des Moines; we are not to be bought or sold.

I have no town property in the Territory of Wisconsin, only some marked out in the town of Wapello and want to sell them. We are willin' to meet the opposers of this bill on this floor, on its merits, and at the bar of the great day.

Mr. Chairman, in all legislative bodies there is a majority and a minority; the minority, unfortunit critters, are sure to kick up and bellow. It puts me in mind of the little boy's swearin. The cattle came up one evening bellowin; the little boy ran to his mother and said, "Mother let me swear at the cattle?" "Begone you little rascal," was the reply. He came the second time and the mother, becoming desirous to hear what he would say, gave him liberty. He ran out, got on the fence and said "bellow on you devils."

The Supreme Court of the Territory held its first session at Belmont on the 8th of December. Present, CHARLES DUNN, Chief Justice, and DAVID IRVIN, Associate Justice. Judge FRAZER was not present.

JOHN CATLIN was appointed clerk and THOMAS P. BURNETT, reporter.

The following gentlemen were admitted to the bar: HENRY S. BAIRD, PETER HILL ENGLE, DAVID G. FENTON, JAMES DUANE DOTY, JAMES B. DALLAM, THOMAS P. BURNETT, WILLIAM W. CHAPMAN, LYMAN I. DANIELS, BARLOW SHACKLEFORD, WM. N. GARDNER, HANS CROCKER, JOSEPH TEAS, WILLIAM SMITH, JAMES H. LOCKWOOD, JAMES NAGLE and JOHN S. HORNER.

The first newspaper in Milwaukee — the *Milwaukee Advertiser* — was established at Milwaukee July 14, 1836, by DANIEL H. RICHARDS, publisher and editor. It was a six-column paper of four pages, the form being 18½ inches by 14 inches. The terms of subscription were $3.00 per annum, payable in advance.

The *Belmont Gazette* was published at Belmont by JAMES CLARKE and JOHN B. RUSSELL; the first number appeared October 25, 1836. It had four pages 21 inches by 14 inches, six columns to a page. After the adjournment of the Legislature its size was reduced to 16½ inches by 10 inches, with only four columns to a page. Its publication was continued at Belmont until April, 1837, when it was removed to Burlington.

This, it is believed, presents a compendium of the most important events occurring in 1836, the first year of the existence of the new Territory of Wisconsin.

CHAPTER XVIII.

TERRITORY OF WISCONSIN IN 1837.

During the twelve years of the political existence of Wisconsin under its new and final territorial form of government, the proceedings of the Congress of the United States, in relation to matters affecting its welfare, were of especial interest to its inhabitants.

It is true that by the organic law a local legislature was provided, the power of which extended to all rightful subjects of legislation, but with the qualification that—

"All the laws of the Governor and Legislative Assembly shall be submitted to, and if disapproved by the Congress of the United States, the same shall be null and of no effect."

A further limitation was that no session in any year should exceed seventy-five days.

The expenses of the Legislative Assembly, as well as the compensation of the Governor, Secretary, Judges, and all United States officers of the Territory were to be paid by appropriations made by Congress, and the chief interest in its proceedings was directed to bills making appropriations for these objects as well also as for the survey and improvement of harbors, the erection of light-houses, and the survey, opening, and construction of roads.

Another subject of congressional action in which the early settlers, especially those between Rock river and the lake, felt an interest paramount to any other, was the renewal and extension to them of the provisions of the pre-emption laws.

It was in the twenty-fourth Congress that the great advantage to the inhabitants of the newly established Territory of Wisconsin of being represented by a delegate elected by themselves, and from among themselves, whose thoughts, feelings, interests, and pioneer experiences were homogeneous with theirs, was first manifested.

GEORGE WALLACE JONES was born near the beginning of the nineteenth century in the State of Missouri. His father was a prominent member of the convention which framed the first constitution of that State, and one of the judges of the Supreme Court. The son having been graduated at the

Transylvania University of Kentucky, studied law, and was admitted to the bar in 1826. But the slow-going town of Cape Girardeau, and the limited opportunities which it furnished in the practice of law for the exercise of his energetic faculties, could not long retain the genius it had reared. In 1827 he migrated to the lead mines of the Upper Mississippi, and located at Sinsinawa Mound, in the southwestern township of Wisconsin, where he successfully engaged in mining and smelting. He took an active part in the Black Hawk war in 1832 as the aid de camp of Gen. HENRY DODGE, and filled various civil offices, among which was that of judge of the county court of Iowa county.

Gen. JONES having in 1835 been elected delegate in Congress to represent the "contingent remainder" of the old Michigan Territory, served as such during the first session of the twenty-fourth Congress, and was elected as the first delegate from the new Territory of Wisconsin, by a vote nearly unanimous in every county except Iowa, where, for reasons already given, the vote was divided nearly equally between him and MOSES MEEKER, his only opponent.

The commencement of the year 1837 found the newly-elected delegate at his post in the House of Representatives, fortified in the successful discharge of his duties by a fresh indorsement of a newly-created constituency. His opportunities, which he had well improved during the preceding session, had given him an extensive acquaintance with the members of that Congress, and he was able, not by his much speaking, nor by rhetoric or oratory, but by a kind and amiable temper, a fascinating and persuasive manner, an untiring industry and perseverance, a clear and forcible presentation of the wants and needs, as well as the just claims of his constituents, to secure an early and favorable consideration of the various measures proposed to promote their welfare.

One of the most important and effective means to secure such favorable action; especially when such a continuous contest for the precedence of business is ever going on; and which was largely due to his indefatigable labors, was to induce the House to set apart a specific time for the consideration of bills affecting the territories.

Of all the members of the 24th Congress none was more devoted to the interests of Wisconsin than LEWIS F. LINN, one of the senators from Missouri. He was the half brother of Gov. DODGE, and upon all occasions was watchful for and attentive to every measure affecting the Territory of which his kinsman was the chief executive officer.

On the 19th of December, he introduced a series of resolutions which were adopted by the Senate, giving instructions to different committees as follows:

The committee on public land to inquire into the expediency of establishing a Surveyor General's office for Wisconsin Territory; also of appropriating for the purpose of constructing roads and bridges in the Territory, the value of all rent lead received at the United States lead mines on the upper Mississippi river; also of making appropriations in land and in money for the construction of roads in the Territory of Wisconsin from Lake Michigan to the Mississippi river through the United States lead mines.

The committee on commerce to inquire into the expediency of improving harbors and constructing light houses on the coast of Lake Michigan, in the counties of Milwaukee and Brown, and of constructing a pier and beacon light at the head of Green Bay, and of placing buoys in its channel; also of amending the act of July 2, 1836, laying off certain towns in Wisconsin.

The committee on Indian affairs to inquire into the expediency of appropriating money to hold treaties with and the purchase of the land belonging to the Sac and Fox, Sioux, and Winnebago Indians and to provide for their removal west of the Mississippi River.

Several of these measures received the favorable action of Congress.

The first act of the second session of the 24th Congress possessing any special interest to the people of Wisconsin, was "An act to admit the state of Michigan into the Union, upon an equal footing with the original states" approved January 26, 1837.

This act was the final consummation of the compromise of the serious question of boundary between Ohio and Michigan. A compromise which was a flagrant violation of the fifth of the "articles of compact," which by the ordinance of July 13, 1787 (older than the constitution itself) were to "forever remain unalterable, unless by common consent." By this compromise, the northern peninsula (so called) lying between Lakes Superior and Michigan and bounded on the southwest by the Menomonee river of Green

Bay and the Montreal river of Lake Superior, and containing about one third of the territory naturally and properly belonging to Wisconsin (the fifth state of the Northwest Territory), was given to the state of Michigan, as a compensation for the small strip, "north of an east and west line drawn through the southerly bend or extreme of Lake Michigan" of which she had been robbed in the establishment of the boundaries of the state of Ohio.

The act recited, that whereas in pursuance of an act of Congress of June 15, 1836,

"A convention of delegates elected by the people of the said state of Michigan for the sole purpose of giving their assent to the boundaries of the said state of Michigan as described, declared and established in and by the said act, did on the 15th day of December, 1836, assent to the provisions of said act, therefore" it was enacted " that the said state of Michigan shall be one and is hereby declared to be one of the United States of America, and admitted into the Union on an equal footing with the original states, in all respects whatever."

This act was an outrage upon all geographical propriety and upon the inchoate rights of boundary which the people of the State of Wisconsin were in the near future to possess. But these considerations were of no avail, and this unjust measure of infringement upon the boundaries of the future State of Wisconsin was consummated.

On the 3d day of September, 1836, a treaty was negotiated at Cedar Point, on Fox River, near Green Bay, between HENRY DODGE, Governor of the Territory and Commissioner on the part of the United States, on the one part, and the chiefs and head men of the Menomonee nation of Indians of the other part, which was ratified by the President of the United States, by and with the advice and consent of the Senate, on the 15th day of February, 1837.

By this treaty the Menomonee nation ceded to the United States two separate tracts of territory. One embraced all the country between Green Bay and Fox River on the east and southeast, and the Wolf River on the south, southwest and west, the northern portion of the boundary being a line extended northeastwardly from the Wolf to the upper forks of the Menomonee River. The northern boundary extended from the upper forks of the Menomonee River to the Escanaba River, thence following that river to its mouth in the Bay de Noquet. This tract was estimated in the treaty at four million acres, and embraced a portion of Michigan as well as Wisconsin.

The other tract ceded began at a point on the Wisconsin River a short distance below Grand Rapids, in Wood county,—

"Thence running up and along said river forty-eight miles in a direct line, and being three miles in width on each side of the river."

The Indians agreed to remove from the ceded country within one year after the ratification of the treaty.

In consideration of this cession the United States agreed to pay to the Menomonees annually for the term of twenty years, the sum of twenty thousand dollars in money, three thousand dollars worth of provisions, five hundred dollars per year for farming utensils, cattle or implements of husbandry, two thousand pounds of tobacco and thirty barrels of salt per annum; to appoint and pay two blacksmiths, erect two blacksmiths' shops, and supply them with the necessary iron, steel and tools. Also to pay the debts of the Indians according to a schedule annexed to the treaty, amounting to about one hundred thousand dollars.

To the "relatives and friends of mixed blood" of the Indians, eighty thousand dollars.

And the further sum of seventy-six thousand dollars in consideration of the release of the United States from certain provisions of certain former treaties.

The total amount of the sums agreed to be paid by the United States would amount, during twenty years, to but little, if any, less than eight hundred thousand dollars.

There was appropriated by act of Congress of March 3, 1837, for carrying this treaty into effect the sum of two hundred eighty-eight thousand, five hundred and forty dollars.

Some other Indian treaties were negotiated during the year 1837, but as they were not ratified until the subsequent year, they are not here noticed.

The civil and diplomatic appropriation act, of March 3, 1837, contained an appropriation "for arrearages for the expenses of the Legislative Assembly for the year 1836, fifteen thousand, seven hundred and thirty dollars and sixteen cents," which discharged all the obligations of the territorial government.

The same contained an appropriation of nine thousand, one hundred dollars "for compensation of the Governor, Judges and Secretary."

It also contained in different parts of the act, two separate appropriations for apparently similar objects. One is

"For contingent expenses and compensation of the members of the Legislative Assembly and printing of the laws, nine thousand, seven hundred and fifty dollars."

The other is "for the expenses of the Legislative Assembly for the year one thousand, eight hundred and thirty-seven, thirty-six thousand, seven hundred and sixty-five dollars."

It was provided by an act of Congress approved July 2, 1836, that the tracts of land, not to exceed one entire section, including the towns of Fort Madison, Burlington, Belleview, Dubuque, Peru and Mineral Point, should under the direction of the Surveyor General, be laid off into lots, streets, avenues and public squares, and into out lots, and offered at public sale to the highest bidder. The lots were to be classified into three classes, the minimum price of which was to be forty dollars per acre for the first class, twenty for the second and ten for the third, and no lot to be sold for less than five dollars. Occupants of lots were to have a right of pre-emption.

By an amendatory act passed at the next session, approved March 3, 1837, it was provided that the acts and duties required to be done and performed by the Surveyor General, should be done by a board of three commissioners to be appointed by the President. They were to hear and determine all pre-emption claims and to receive a compensation of six dollars per day, to be paid out of the proceeds of the sales of lots. All the residue of the money arising from the sales of lots, after paying the commissioners and the other expenses incident to the survey and sale, was to be paid over to the trustees of the respective towns.

It was under this act that titles to lots in the city of Mineral Point are held, except to certain portions, which had been sold by the United States before the passsage of the act of July 2, 1836.

While it was provided by the law organizing the Territory that laws of the Territory should be submitted to, "and if disapproved by Congress, should be null and of no effect," there was another act of Congress approved July 1, 1836, which prescribed in affirmative terms—

"That no act of the Territorial Legislature of any of the territories of the United States incorporating any bank or any institution, with banking powers or privileges hereafter passed, shall have any force or effect whatever, until approved and confirmed by Congress."

To comply with the requirements of this act, the delegate obtained the passage of an act which then appeared to be in accordance with the general desire of the people, that the three acts of the Territorial Legislature, incorporating the Bank of Milwaukee, the Miners' Bank of Dubuque, and the Bank of Mineral Point, be approved and confirmed on certain conditions expressed in the act which was passed March 3, 1837.

In the act making appropriations for building light houses, light boats, beacon lights, etc., for the year 1837, were inserted the following appropriations for the Territory of Wisconsin:

"For erecting a light house at the mouth of Milwaukee River, five thousand dollars; for erecting a light house at the mouth of the Manitowoc River, five thousand dollars; for a light house at Chipewagan (Sheboygan), five thousand dollars; for erecting a light house at the entrance of Green Bay, five thousand dollars; for erecting a light house at Root River, five thousand dollars."

The pre-pemption laws were not extended or renewed. A bill for this purpose passed the Senate and was defeated in the House, but even this bill required occupancy of and residence on the tract before the 1st of December, 1836, and cultivation within the year 1836, so that if it had passed it would have been practically valueless to the great mass of those who had made "claims" in the district of lands subject to sale at Milwaukee. This land district included the present counties of Kenosha, Racine, Milwaukee, Ozaukee, Washington, Waukesha, Jefferson, Walworth, Rock, the east range of townships in Green county, the four east ranges in Dane county, the southern tier of towns in Columbia county, and the two southern tiers in Dodge county, in all about one hundred and fifty townships.

Twelve months before the adjournment of the 24th Congress the population of this district probably did not amount to five hundred. By the census taken in August, 1836, it was nearly three thousand, and it is estimated that during the next six months it had nearly doubled, and that by the 1st of March, 1837, it was but little, if any, less than six thousand.

On the 27th of February, an anonymous notice was given in the *Milwaukee Advertiser* and in hand-bills, that a meeting of the people of Milwaukee, Washington, Jefferson and Dodge counties would be held at the court house in

Milwaukee on the 13th of March, "for the purpose of adopting such rules as will secure to actual settlers their claims on principles of justice and equity" and stating that in the absence of pre-emption laws it was the duty of the settlers "to unite for their own protection when the lands shall be brought into market."

Before noon of the appointed day the number of settlers assembled in response to this notice, astonished every one present, and no one more than the settlers themselves. The most reliable estimates placed the number at not less than one thousand, while many thought it was much greater.

Nor was the meeting any less remarkable for the elevated character of the men composing it, than for the magnitude of its numbers. It was not a rabble of lawless "squatters," but the men who have assisted in laying the foundation and rearing the superstructure of our state, and who are entitled to a large share of credit for its growth and prosperity, were those who were assembled on this occasion to devise measures to protect their "claims" and improvements from being sacrificed to the unconscionable greed of avaricious speculators.

The very presence and determined resolution of this assemblage was an admonition to all such speculators that any attempt to interfere with the rights of the settler would be futile if not hazardous to personal safety, while the rules and regulations adopted, whereby the right of occupancy might be determined, were so well adapted to the end in view that security of the occupancy of the public domain for the purpose of permanent settlement and improvement, appeared to be placed beyond doubt; and the inviolability of settlers' claims made in good faith was made as certain as it could have been by any pre-emption law.

The meeting was organized by the election of SAMUEL HINMAN. President; SAMUEL SANBURN and SYLVESTER PETTIBONE, Vice-Presidents and A. O. T. BREED and I. A. LAPHAM, Secretaries.

A committee of twenty-one was appointed to report rules and regulations for the consideration of the meeting. The committee was composed of BYRON KILBOURN, SOLOMON JUNEAU, ALFRED MORGAN, ALFRED ORENDORFF, HENRY SHEW, LUTHER PARKER, CHARLES EVERETT, ENOCH CHASE, N. F. HYER, JOHN MANDERVILLE, ROBERT MASTERS, JOHN S. ROCKWELL, JOHN HOWARD, DWIGHT FOSTER, ALVA HARRINGTON,

Thomas H. Olin, Nicholas Whalen, James Sanderson, Jeremiah Putney and A. L. Barber.

After a recess of two hours the committee, by Byron Kilbourn, reported rules and regulations for the consideration of the meeting.

They were prefaced by a preamble which recited that the settlers of Milwaukee county and the several counties thereto attached had removed to and settled in that section of country for the purpose of bettering their condition by agricultural pursuits.

That the Congress of the United States, by the repeated passage of pre-emption laws, had impressed them with a reasonable belief that the same policy would continue to be pursued for their benefit.

That the settlements in that section of the country had been in great part so recently formed that a pre-emption law containing such provisions as that reported during the late session of Congress would not embrace the case of a large number of meritorious settlers. That they could not witness without emotion the sacrifice of their property and improvements.

That in order to secure the fruits of their labors in a peaceable and equitable manner it was necessary that certain fixed rules and regulations should be adopted by the settlers, whereby the right of occupancy should be determined. Therefore it was resolved that they adopt and would to the best of their ability sustain in full force of obligation the rules and regulations adopted.

These rules and regulations prescribed that any person who had prior to that date made a claim on one or more quarter sections, not exceeding in the whole one section, and made improvements thereon equal to fifty dollars for each quarter section, should have the right to retain such claims, and the future right to make such claims was also recognized; but such rights were subject to the right of improvement and cultivation in the mode and within the time prescribed by the rules, which also contained definitions of what constituted cultivation and improvement.

The rules provided for the appointment by the meeting of a central executive committee of fifteen, whose duty it was to fix the limits of the different precincts, the people in each of which precincts were to appoint a judicial committee.

Also for the appointment of a clerk of the committee and a register of claims.

Eight or more members constituted a quorum of the committee, and a vote of a majority of the members present decided all questions, including appeals.

The judicial committee in each precinct was to decide all disputes between claimants in each precinct to the same tract of land, subject to an appeal to the central executive committee. All trials by either of said committees were to be governed by the rules and regulations, and by the principles of justice and equity.

It was provided that all existing claims should be entered with the register of claims, and that any one not entered by the first day of May should be considered as no claim, and might be occupied by any person who might choose to take it; and that all claims thereafter made should be entered with the register within ten days, or be considered vacant and subject to be entered by any other person.

If any claimant neglected to make the improvements required by the rules within the time limited therefor, he forfeited his rights, and any person might take possession thereof in his own right.

When any person purchased a claim from another he was required to give immediate notice thereof to the register, and have the transfer made in his name.

The party in whose favor any decision was made by any judicial committee, or by the central committee on appeal, was to receive a certificate thereof, on presenting which, to the register of claims, he was to enter the tract of land therein described in the name of such party, any previous entry to the contrary notwithstanding, and such party was thereupon entitled to take possession of such tract without any further judicial proceedings.

The essence of all these rules and regulations was contained in the *ninth* rule, which was as follows :

"Whenever the lands shall be brought into market, the executive committee shall appoint an agent to bid off the lands in behalf of the settlers whose claims are entered on the book of registry, and *no person shall in any case be countenanced in bidding in opposition to such agent.*"

The moral sentiment of that whole community was all in one direction, and it was well known and felt by all to be abundantly adequate to protect the agent against any competition in bidding at the land sale, and to secure to the settler his claim at the government minimum price.

Not to be "countenanced" was a mild mode of expressing the deep seated determination of the pioneer settlers, but it was quite as effective as if it had been in the form of a threat of lynching, which would have been an unseemly mode of publishing an unlawful combination and conspiracy, to prevent competitive bidding at a public sale of the lands of the United States.

The central executive committee appointed by the meeting consisted of A. A. BIRD, SOLOMON JUNEAU, N. F. HYER, SAMUEL BROWN, ALBERT FOWLER, D. H. RICHARDS, A. O. T. BREED, SAMUEL HINMAN, WILLIAM R. LONGSTREET, H. M. HUBBARD, JAMES SANDERSON, C. H. PEAKE, DANIEL WELLS, Jr., BYRON KILBOURN and ENOCH CHASE.

At a meeting of this committee the next day, the following officers were elected: A. A. BIRD, President; BYRON KILBOURN and SAMUEL HINMAN, Vice-Presidents; WM. A. PRENTISS, Clerk; and ALLEN O. T. BREED, Register of Claims. It was ordered that in deciding appeals from precinct committees, the central committee would proceed according to the practice of courts of equity, and that it would meet on the first Monday of every month.

It was also ordered that the territory to which the rules and regulations were applicable, be divided into ten precincts, which were called Washington, Dodge, Jefferson, Prairie Village, Muckwanago, Muskego, Oak Creek, Poplar Creek, Chase's Point and Menomonee, the townships in each of which were definitely specified. The time fixed for the election of a judicial committee in each precinct was Monday, March 27, and a convenient place was designated in each, and the result of the election was required to be reported to the clerk of the central committee.

At a meeting of the central committee held on the 10th of April, Jefferson county was divided into three precincts, called respectively, Watertown, Jefferson and Fort Atkinson, and the last Monday of April designated as the time for holding elections of judicial committees in each precinct.

At the same meeting I. A. LAPHAM was appointed Register of Claims, *vice* A. O. T. BREED, resigned.

The mode provided for determining disputed claims between settlers and its administration appeared to give great satisfaction to all parties interested. This organization did not embrace Racine county (of which Kenosha was then a part) nor Walworth or Rock, but another similar organization existed for the settlers in these counties.

The press is justly regarded as the handmaid, if not the precursor of civilization. Previous to the year 1837 there were two newspapers at Green Bay, the *Intelligencer and Democrat* and the *Free Press*, at Milwaukee the *Advertiser*, and at Belmont the *Gazette*. About the first of the year or the last of the preceding, the two Green Bay papers were consolidated into one, called the "*Wisconsin Democrat*," which was well conducted and ably edited by Hon. CHARLES C. SHOLES, who subsequently attained marked political distinction in the State.

In the month of April the *Belmont Gazette* was discontinued, and its material removed to Mineral Point, and used in the publication of the *Miners' Free Press*, while the proprietors of the *Gazette*, JAMES CLARKE & Co., established at Burlington the *Wisconsin Territorial Gazette and Burlington Advertiser*.

No small portion of the columns of these newspapers was occupied with articles in relation to the comparative importance and growth of the different towns. While Green Bay and Prairie du Chien were the oldest, and Mineral Point had been a town of considerable importance for seven or eight years when Milwaukee first made metropolitan pretensions, yet its superior advantages soon placed it beyond all questions of rivalry and it became the acknowledged metropolis of the Territory.

But there were local jealousies and rivalries within its own borders which resulted in the organization of two municipal corporations. One was called "Milwaukee on the West side of the River," the other " Milwaukee on the East side of the River." On the west side an election for five trustees was held on the 4th of February and resulted in the election of W. R. LONGSTREET, BYRON KILBOURN, LUCIUS I. BARBER, B. W. FINCH and S. D. COWLES.

BYRON KILBOURN was elected president, N. F. HYER, clerk, W. P. PROUDFIT, assessor, PAUL BURDICK, marshal and I. A. LAPHAM, surveyor and engineer, and thus was organized the first municipal corporation in the city of Milwaukee.

On the 16th of February, SOLOMON JUNEAU, G. D. DOUSMAN, SAMUEL HINMAN, A. A. BIRD and WILLIAM A. PREN-

TISS were elected trustees for the town of Milwaukee on the east side of the river. SOLOMON JUNEAU was elected president.

On the 28th of January, the "Milwaukee County Agricultural Society" was formed, a constitution adopted, and the following officers elected:

BYRON KILBOURN, President; SOLOMON JUNEAU, 1st Vice-President; SYLVESTER PETTIBONE, 2nd Vice-President; HUGH WEDGE, 3rd Vice-President; I. A. LAPHAM, Secretary; WM. A. PRENTISS, Cor. Secretary; SAMUEL HINMAN, Treasurer; JAMES H. ROGERS, GEORGE D. DOUSMAN, JOHN MANDERVILLE, JOHN OGDEN, DAVID S. HOLLISTER, W. R. LONGSTREET, and HENRY M. HUBBARD, Directors.

The first Tuesday in October was fixed as the time of holding the first fair, and premiums to the amount of one hundred and sixty-eight dollars were offered.

The year 1837 witnessed an unusual activity in the business of mining for copper ore. As early as 1829 copper ore was discovered by Mr. HENRY LANDER in section 9, town 4, range 3 east, about three miles southeasterly from Mineral Point, and soon after another discovery was made by Mr. HUGHLETT on the southeast part of section 5, about half a mile from the first. Mr. HUGHLETT observed particles of copper ore mingled with the mass of earth which had been drawn out by a badger in making his burrow, and following up this indication he found a large body of valuable ore, and about the same period similar discoveries were made by Mr. ROBINSON still further north. All these and other discoveries were supposed to be parts of one common range, the extent of which had already been demonstrated to exceed three miles in length. Much work had been done at different times and a large amount of copper ore had been raised. There were no facilities for smelting the ore nearer than Baltimore. Some of the ore was sent to England to be reduced and tested, and it was ascertained that it contained from 30 to 50 per cent. of pure copper.

At the Belmont session of the Legislature an act incorporating the "Pekatonica Copper Mining Company" was passed. The company was organized and the practical value of the copper mine was demonstrated by the production of a large amount of copper ingots. Litigation ensued and the mines have since then been unworked, but no doubt exists that a large amount of valuable ore still remains there and that it possesses large economic value.

The location of county seats in all newly organized territories or states is always a question that excites much interest and is often prolific of heated controversies.

Questions of this character, during the year 1837, were confined to three counties, Brown, Grant and Green.

By "An act to change the seat of justice in Brown county" approved December 9, 1836, it was provided that the qualified voters of the county should on the 3d Monday of January, 1837, vote for Navarino, Astor or Depere as the future seat of justice. That the returns should be certified to the Governor, who should issue a proclamation declaring the result.

The election was held and on the 1st day of February, the Governor issued a proclamation "that the town of Depere has received a large majority of the votes" and "establishing the seat of justice of said county of Brown at Depere from and after the first day of April next."

In the "Act to divide the county of Iowa" approved December 8, 1836, it was enacted that all that part of Iowa county west of the fourth principal meridian should be a separate county to be called Grant.

By the same act it was provided that HENRY W. HODGES, JAMES GILMORE, E. E. BROCK, DENNIS MCCARTNEY, and FRANCIS MCCARTNEY, should be commissioners to fix the seat of justice of said county of Grant, on or before the first day of February, and that the place designated by them should be considered the seat of justice of said county. Courts were required to be held at Cassville until the necessary public buildings should be erected at the seat of justice.

The commissioners met at the prescribed time and selected and agreed upon the southeast quarter of section 3, town 4, range 3 west, which they fixed and designated as the county seat of Grant county.

Soon after Hon. G. M. PRICE laid out a town on the tract so selected, which was called Lancaster, and it has hitherto remained the undisturbed county seat of that county. Mr. PRICE advertised "an extensive sale of lots," to take place on the 1st of May. The town immediately commenced to grow, and its progress has been continued and uninterrupted.

The same "act to divide the county of Iowa," prescribed that towns 1, 2, 3 and 4, of ranges 6, 7, 8 and 9, should constitute the county of Green, and the seat of justice be established at the town of New Mexico.

The difficulty in determining where the county seat was, grew out of the doubt as to where "New Mexico" was. Mr. JACOB ANDRICK claimed that he had laid off a town in the summer of 1836 which he called New Mexico, and he charged that Mr. JOSEPH PAYNE, owning other land a quarter of a mile distant, finding that a bill was about to pass fixing the seat of justice at New Mexico, laid off a town on his land which he called by the same name — New Mexico. Mr. PAYNE denied that Mr. ANDRICK had ever had any town plat recorded, and claimed that the town which he had laid out in the summer, but had not recorded, was called "Mexico," and not "New Mexico," and that the only genuine New Mexico" was the plat recorded by him (PAYNE) November 29, 1836. The controversy remained undetermined for about two years, when in pursuance of a special law, a vote of the people determined that neither place should be the county seat, and selected the present site, which was called Monroe.

In the subdivision of the county of Milwaukee into other counties, towns 1, 2, 3 and 4, of range 10, constituting the towns of Avon, Spring Valley, Magnolia and Union, did not form a part of any county, but remained an isolated range of towns between the counties of Green and Rock, until subsequently attached to Rock county by an act approved June 21, 1838.

Early in this year JOHN S. HORNER, Secretary of the Territory, and WILLIAM B. SLAUGHTER, Register of the Land Office at Green Bay, made a mutual arrangement with each other to swap offices. They went to Washington, and both being Virginians and in favor with General JACKSON, they had no difficulty in obtaining his assent to the arrangement, in accordance with which WILLIAM B. SLAUGHTER was appointed Secretary of the Territory and JOHN S. HORNER, Register of the Green Bay Land Office.

In consequence of the absence of the new Register, the Land Office was not opened until about the 1st of June, when the land sales were resumed and large amounts of the public lands were sold.

Numerous post routes had been established by Congress in different parts of the Territory, but the postal facilities were not great.

On the 7th of June proposals were invited by the Postmaster-General (AMOS KENDALL) for carrying the mail from January 1, 1838, to June 30, 1842, on the different post routes, but most of them were to be carried but once a week. On three of the routes the mail was to be carried twice a week. These were, Mineral Point to Cassville, Elk Grove to Prairie du Chien, and Prairie du Chien to Galena. On five of the routes it was to be carried tri-weekly. These were Milwaukee to Green Bay, Green Bay to Fort Winnebago, Fort Winnebago to Mineral Point, Mineral Point to Galena—the three last in stages, and from Chicago to Milwaukee in four-horse post coaches—and there was not to be a daily mail throughout the Territory.

In February, 1837, postoffices were established at Chase's Point, HORACE CHASE, postmaster; Moundville, JOHN C. KELLOGG, postmaster; Madison, JOHN CATLIN, postmaster; Elk Grove, JOSEPH PERRY, postmaster, and Cassville, RICHARD RAY, postmaster, and during the summer a postoffice was established at Watertown, and WILLIAM M. DENNIS appointed postmaster.

On the 22d of May Judge WILLIAM C. FRAZER held at Depere his first term of court, which continued until the 30th of May. No civil cases were tried in consequence of the disarrangement of records and papers. The criminal calendar, however, was generally disposed of. Maw-zaw-mon-nee-hah, a Winnebago Indian, was indicted for the murder of PIERRE PAUQUETTE at Fort Winnebago the previous October. The prisoner was defended by JOHN S. HORNER, who was appointed by the court for that purpose. The evidence left no doubt of the guilt of the accused, who was found guilty of murder, and sentenced to be hung on the first day of September.

The cases of AMABLE CARBONNO, for the murder of his wife, and of two Indians for the murder of ELLSWORTH BURNETT, were transferred to Milwaukee county for trial. JOSEPH DUTCHER was convicted of burglary and sentenced to seven years' solitary imprisonment in the county jail at hard labor and a fine of one hundred dollars.

JOHN O'DONNELL was convicted of keeping a disorderly

house and selling liquor to an Indian, and was fined fifty dollars for the first offense, and one hundred for the second.

Judging by newspaper comments, Judge FRAZER'S first appearance on the bench in Brown county was highly creditable, and in marked contrast with the manner in which his judicial functions were subsequently performed.

Judge FRAZER'S first term of court at Milwaukee was held on 14th June.

The two Menomonee Indians, Ash-e-co-bo-ma and Ash-o-wa, indicted in Brown county for the murder of ELLSWORTH BURNETT, on the bank of Rock river in the month of November, 1835, were tried. Their trials were separate. The counsel for the prosecution was W. N. GARDNER, district attorney, and HANS CROCKER; for the defense, H. N. WELLS and J. E. ARNOLD. The jury returned a verdict of guilty against Ash-e-co-bo-ma, the father, who was sentenced to be hung on the first day of September. A *nol pros.* was entered by the district attorney, by the advice of the court, in the case of the younger Indian.

AMABLE CARBONNO, indicted for the murder of his wife in Brown county, was so reduced by sickness and long confinement that he had to be brought into court upon a bed, in which condition he was tried. The prosecution was conducted by F. PERRIN and J. E. ARNOLD, and the defense by HENRY S. BAIRD. He was found guilty of manslaughter and sentenced to ten years' imprisonment in the common jail of Brown county, and to pay a fine of one thousand dollars.

The sentence was superseded by his death, which resulted from his disease, within twenty-four hours after the rendition of the verdict.

On the 31st of May, 1837, AUGUSTUS A. BIRD, one of the commissioners for the erection of public buildings at Madison, left Milwaukee with thirty-six workmen with six yoke of oxen, and all the necessary mechanical tools, provisions, cooking utensils, etc., to enable operations at the capital to be commenced immediately. There was no road at that time from Milwaukee to Madison, and the party were compelled to make one for their teams and wagons as they went along. It rained incessantly and the obstructions to their progress presented by the drenched ground, fallen trees, unbridged streams, including Rock River at Watertown and the Crawfish at Milford, hills, ravines and marshes, and the devious course which they necessarily pursued, so delayed them that they did not reach Madison until the 10th of June.

Notwithstanding all these and other embarrassments, they made such progress that they were able to lay the corner stone of the capitol on the 4th of July, but by the end of the year 1837, the only progress made was the erection of the walls of the basement.

PETER HILL ENGLE was the acting and active member of the committee appointed to select and purchase a library for the use of the Territory with the money ($5,000) appropriated by Congress for that purpose. In the performance of that duty he went to the eastern cities, where he could best execute his mission as well as consult his colleagues. Before the 1st of July he returned to Burlington with a well-selected assortment of valuable books, the selection of which was approved by Senators CLAYTON and LINN and Delegate JONES who were associated with him on the committee.

The books were delivered to JAMES CLARKE, who had been appointed librarian, and who opened and arranged them in a convenient and handsome style in a commodious room procured for that purpose. The library cost nearly the whole amount appropriated for its purchase and contained about twelve hundred volumes of law and miscellany, about two-thirds of which were law books, including valuable state papers, and the remainder standard miscellaneous works.

The event of the year 1837, which had a more marked effect upon the business of the whole country than any other, was beyond question the suspension of specie payment by nearly all the banks throughout the whole country in the months of May and June. The effect was as visible in Wisconsin as elsewhere, although it had as yet no banks organized and in operation. Its tendency was to check immigration to a considerable degree and to affect injuriously for a time the prosperity of those who had already established themselves in their new homes.

But the recuperative powers and energy of the indefatigable pioneers of the new Territory could not long be restrained as was demonstrated by the successful progress which they soon exhibited.

The second session of the first Legislative Assembly of the Territory convened at Burlington on the 6th day of November, 1837.

Some changes in the membership of both Houses had taken place since the adjournment of the first session; in the Council by resignation and in the House of Representatives by death as well as resignations.

In the Council, HENRY S. BAIRD, a member from Brown county, resigned, and on the first day of the session the certificate of JOSEPH DICKINSON was presented as his successor, and he was admitted to the seat.

The seat of Mr. DICKINSON was contested by ALEXANDER J. IRWIN, on the ground that Mr. DICKINSON was postmaster at Green Bay. On the 21st the seat was declared vacant by the Council, and it was resolved that ALEXANDER J. IRWIN is entitled to the vacant seat, and the Sergeant-at-Arms was directed to proceed forthwith to Green Bay, and inform Mr. IRWIN of the action of the Council, which he did, and on the 26th of December, more than a month afterward, Mr. IRWIN appeared and took the seat.

This result he regarded as retributive justice, he having at the previous session been deprived of his seat as member of the House, on the same ground, although he had resigned his office before the commencement of the session.

Mr. VINEYARD, one of the members from Iowa county, did not take his seat until the 18th of January, two days before the adjournment of the session.

In the House of Represensatives, the seat of Col. HOSEA T. CAMP, a member from Dubuque county, was rendered vacant by his death. On the 5th of March he was returning to his home, a short distance from Dubuque, in the night, on horse-back, when the horse fell, threw him and caused his death.

A. W. McGREGGOR, who resided opposite Prairie du Chien, and for whom the town of McGreggor was named, was elected to fill the vacancy which Col. CAMP's death created.

Gen. ALBERT G. ELLIS, a member of the House from Brown county, resigned his seat and CHARLES C. SHOLES was elected his successor.

Messrs. JAMES H. LOCKWOOD and JAMES B. DALLAM, the two members from Crawford county, both resigned their seats, and that of the first was filled by JEAN BRUNETT, and of the last by IRA B. BRONSON.

The Council was organized by the election of ARTHUR B. INGHRAM of Demoines county, president, and GEORGE BEATTY of Mineral Point, secretary.

In the House ISAAC LEFFLER of Demoines county was elected speaker and JOHN CATLIN of Madison, chief clerk.

The Governor's message was delivered in person on the second day of the session to the two Houses assembled in the Representatives' Hall. It was marked by those features of sound, practical, common-sense which pervaded all his official utterances as well as his official acts.

In recommending to the Legislature to memorialize Congress to pass a pre-emption law, he said

"Land was the immediate gift of God to man, and from the earliest history of the world was designed for cultivation and improvement, and should cease to be an object of speculation. The just and proper policy of the government would be to reduce the price of the public lands and sell them to the actual settler alone. The public domain would be sold in a short period of time. Indian wars would cease to exist. The frontiers would be settled by a brave and hardy race of men who would be a barrier to Indian encroachment, and there would be no necessity of maintaining military posts for the protection of our frontiers."

This session of the Legislative Assembly was not marked by any events of peculiar interest. The Governor, in his message, recommended, as he had at the previous session, a codification of the laws, but nothing was done in that direction, except to provide, by resolution, for the printing, as an appendix to the pamphlet laws of the session, of one hundred and twenty-five acts specified by their titles, selected from those then in force. The provisions of this resolution, however, were never complied with.

The whole number of acts passed at this session was one hundred and six.

Of these, eighteen related to the laying out and organization of counties, locating county seats, and to town, village and city organization; ten to the establishment of eighteen different seminaries and universities; nine to the location of roads; and thirty-six to the general conduct of the public affairs of the Territory. There were also passed thirty-two private acts, of which one was to incorporate a bank at Prairie du Chien, which was disapproved by Congress and never went into effect; six to grant divorces, all of which took effect immediately after, and some, perhaps, before their passage.

Of the public acts, the two most important were the act providing for taking another census, and the act abolishing imprisonment for debt, which relic of barbarism had continued in force, by operation of the laws of Michigan, upon the organization of the Territory. Among the eighteen universities and seminaries established was the "University of the Territory of Wisconsin" at Madison, to which Congress was by joint resolution urged to make an appropriation of $20,000 in money, and two townships of land. The money was not appropriated. But on the 12th of June, 1838, Congress made an appropriation of the amount of land asked for, which was the fundamental endowment of that noble University, whose spacious buildings now adorn the capital of our state, and whose facilities and capacity for educating its youth reflect much credit upon those who have manifested so great an interest, and such untiring perseverance in promoting its welfare.

It was at this session that an act was passed "to incorporate the Milwaukee and Rock River Canal Company," which contained, among other things, an authority to the company to apply to Congress for an appropriation in money or lands to aid in the construction of its works. In pursuance of this authority application was made, and an appropriation obtained in June, 1838, of the odd-numbered sections on a belt of territory five miles in width on each side of the line of the proposed canal. This grant of land, if it had been judiciously managed, would have produced a fund adequate for the construction of a canal connecting Rock River with Lake Michigan, which would have been followed, no doubt, by slack water navigation on Rock River, providing a cheap means of transit to market of the bulky agricultural products of the extensive and fertile valley of Rock River, and of other parts of the state and of Illinois. But instead of the blessing it might have been, it proved a curse and a blight upon the early prosperity of the Territory, owing mainly to the antagonisms which grew up between the officers of the canal company and the territorial officers entrusted with the disposition of the lands granted by Congress, and of their proceeds, and to the conflicts between the beneficiaries of the land grant and some of the leading politicians of the times.

It is intended to devote the last chapter of this work exclusively to the history of the Milwaukee and Rock

River canal and its incidents, and therefore it is not necessary to say more in this connection.

On the 20th of January, 1838, in pursuance of a resolution adopted on the 17th, the Legislative Assembly adjourned to meet at the same place on the second Monday of June.

CHAPTER XIX.

TERRITORY OF WISCONSIN IN 1838.

The second session of the first Legislative Assembly which commenced in November, 1837, was extended twenty days into January, 1838, but to preserve the continuity of its proceedings, they were all referred to in the last chapter.

For the same reason the proceedings of the second session of the 25th Congress, which commenced on the first Monday of December, 1837, so far as they affect Wisconsin, will be collated in this chapter.

The 24th of February of this year will ever be memorable as that upon which was enacted one of the most heart-rending tragedies that ever resulted from the barbarous practice of duelling. It was the sacrifice of the life of Hon. JONATHAN CILLEY, a member of the House of Representatives from the State of Maine, in an "affair of honor" with Hon. WM. J. GRAVES, a member from the State of Kentucky.

This duel derives its interest for the people of Wisconsin from the fact that Hon. GEORGE W. JONES, then the delegate in Congress from Wisconsin, was the "friend" and second of Mr. CILLEY in the terrible tragedy, which is a sufficient reason for giving a detailed account of the events which led to, and the circumstances which attended the fatal meeting.

JAMES WATSON WEBB was the editor of the New York *Courier and Enquirer*. In a discussion in the House on the 12th February, Mr. CILLEY was reported in the *Globe*, while speaking of the *Courier and Enquirer*, to have made remarks to the following effect: He knew nothing of the editor, but if he is the same who once brought grave charges against an institution (Bank of the United States) from which he was said to have received afterwards $52,000 in facilities, he (Mr. CILLEY) did not think that anything which the editor had said deserved to be noticed by Congress.

On the 21st of February Mr. GRAVES had a friendly interview with Mr. CILLEY, in which he presented to the latter a note from J. W. WEBB, which Mr. CILLEY declined to receive. There were no witnesses to the conversation between Messrs. GRAVES and CILLEY in that interview.

Subsequently on the same day Mr. GRAVES addressed the following note to Mr. CILLEY—

"In the interview which I had with you this morning, when you declined receiving from me the note of Colonel J. W. WEBB, asking whether you were correctly reported in the *Globe*, in what you are there represented to have said of him in this House on the 12th inst., you will please say whether you did not remark in substance, that in declining to receive the note, you hoped I would not consider it in any respect, disrespectful to me, and that the ground on which you rested your declining to receive the note was distinctly this: That you could not consent to get yourself into personal difficulties with conductors of public journals for what you might think proper to say in debate, and that you did not rest your objection in our interview upon any personal objections to Colonel WEBB as a gentleman."

Mr. CILLEY immediately made the following reply:

"The note which you just placed in my hand has been received. In reply I have to state that in your interview with me this morning, when you proposed to deliver a communication from Col. WEBB, of the New York *Courier and Enquirer*, I declined to receive it because I chose to be drawn into no controversy with him. I neither affirmed or denied anything in regard to his character, but when you remarked that this course on my part might place you in an unpleasant situation, I stated to you, and now repeat, that I intended by the refusal no disrespect to you."

On the next day (22d) Mr. GRAVES addressed to Mr. CILLEY the following note:

"Your note of yesterday, in reply to mine of that date, is inexplicit, unsatisfactory, and insufficient; among other things in this: that in declining to receive Col. WEBB's communication, it does not *disclaim* any exception to him personally as a gentleman. I have therefore to inquire *whether you declined to receive his communication on the ground of any personal exception to him as a gentleman, or a man of honor?* A categorical answer is expected."

To this note, Mr. CILLEY on the same day, made the following reply:

"Your note of this date has just been placed in my hands. I regret that mine of yesterday was not satisfactory to you, but I cannot admit the right on your part to propound the question to which you ask a categorical answer, and therefore decline any further response to it."

The next day (23d) at a few minutes before noon, no further communication between the parties having intervened, a challenge from Mr. GRAVES was presented by Hon. HENRY A. WISE to Mr. CILLEY, in the following words:

"As you have declined accepting a communication which I bore to you from Col. WEBB, and as by your note of yesterday you have refused to decline on grounds which would exonerate me from all responsibility growing out of the affair, I am left no other alternative but to ask that satisfaction which is recognized among gentlemen. My friend, Hon. H. A. WISE, is authorized by me to make the arrangements suitable to the occasion."

Mr. CILLEY, after some delay, secured the friendly services of Hon. GEORGE W. JONES as the bearer of his acceptance of the challenge. Mr. JONES, however, in a published letter to the people of Wisconsin, dated June 20th, says:

"It is now known that I came into the controversy at a very late period (only twenty-three hours before the fatal meeting), after all the terms as to time, weapon, distance, etc., had been agreed upon."

Mr. CILLEY'S letter, accepting the challenge, was delivered by Mr. JONES at the hour of 5 P. M. on the same day the challenge was received, and was in these brief terms:

"Your note of this morning has been received. My friend, Gen. JONES, will 'make the arrangements suitable to the occasion.'"

The following terms of meeting were then agreed upon between the seconds, Messrs. WISE and JONES, in conformity with those already agreed upon between Mr. CILLEY and his friends: the place to be such as might be agreed upon between them at 12 M. the next day, the 24th. The weapons to be rifles. The parties placed side to side at eighty yards distance from each other; to hold the rifles at arms length downward; the rifles to be cocked and triggers set; the words to be "Gentlemen are you ready?" After which, neither answering "No," the words shall be in regular succession "Fire-one, two, three, four." Neither party is to raise his weapon from the downward position until the word "fire" and neither shall fire before the word "fire" nor after the word "four." The position of the parties at the end of the line to be determined by lot. The second of the party losing the choice of position, shall have the giving of the word. Each party may have on the ground, besides his second, a surgeon and two other friends. The rifles to be loaded in presence of the seconds.

It was then agreed between the seconds, at about noon of the 24th, and after some correspondence and delay in relation to a rifle for Mr. GRAVES, that the meeting should take place at 3 P. M. of that day; that they should meet at the Anacosta bridge on the road to Marlborough, Md., between the hours of 1½ and 2½ P. M., and that if either got there first he should wait for the other, and that they would thence proceed out of the District. The parties met at the bridge, Mr. CILLEY and his party arriving first; and all proceeded about 2 P. M. to the place of meeting. The seconds marked off the ground and decided the choice of positions. Mr. WISE won the choice, and Mr. JONES had the giving of the word.

Shortly after 3 o'clock P. M., the rifles were loaded in the presence of the seconds; the parties were called together; they were fully instructed by Mr. JONES as to their positions, and the words twice repeated to them as they would be and as they were delivered to them in the exchange of shots. After this they were ordered to their respective positions, the seconds assuming their places and the friends accompanying the seconds, were disposed along the line of fire to observe that each obeyed the terms of meeting.

Mr. JONES gave the words distinctly, audibly and in regular succession, and the parties exchanged shots without violating in the least a single instruction. They both missed.

The friends generally, then assembled to hear what was to be said. Mr. JONES then inquired of Mr. WISE whether his friend (Mr. GRAVES) was satisfied. Mr. WISE replied

"These gentlemen have come here without animosity towards each other, they are fighting merely upon a point of honor. Cannot Mr. CILLEY assign some reason for not receiving Col. WEBB's communication or make some disclaimer which will relieve Mr. GRAVES from his position."

After Mr. JONES was informed by Mr. WISE that the challenge was suspended for the purpose of explanation, he went to Mr. CILLEY, his principal, and then said to Mr. WISE, as Mr. JONES remembered a few hours afterwards what he said:

"I am authorized by my friend Mr. CILLEY to say that in declining to receive the note from Mr. GRAVES, purporting to be from Col. WEBB, he meant no disrespect to Mr. GRAVES, because he entertained for him then as he now does the highest respect and most kindly feelings, but that he declined to receive the note because he chose not to be dragged into any controversy with Col. WEBB."

The recollection of Mr. WISE in regard to the answer of Mr. JONES was, that Mr. JONES also said in his answer:

"My friend refuses to disclaim disrespect for Col. WEBB, because he does not choose to be drawn into an expression of opinion as to him."

Much conversation then ensued between the seconds and their friends, but no nearer approach to reconciliation being made, the challenge was renewed, another shot was exchanged and both missed.

After this the seconds and the friends again assembled, the challenge was again withdrawn, and a very similar conversation to that after the first exchange of shots ensued.

Mr. JONES then remarked:

"Mr. WISE, my friend, in coming to the ground and exchanging shots with Mr. GRAVES, has shown to the world, that in declining to receive the note of Col. WEBB, he did not do so because he dreaded a controversy. He has shown himself a brave man and disposed to render satisfaction to Mr. GRAVES. I do think that he has done so and that the matter should end here."

To this Mr. WISE replied

"Mr. CILLEY has already expressed his respect for Mr. GRAVES in the *written correspondence*, and Mr. GRAVES does not require of Mr. CILLEY a certificate of character for Col. WEBB; he considers himself about not only to deserve the respect due to himself, but to defend the honor of his friend Col. WEBB."

Mr. WISE thinks, he added,

"Mr. GRAVES only insists that he has not borne the note of a man who is not a man of honor and not a gentleman."

These last words Mr. JONES does not recollect.

After much more conversation and ineffectual attempts to adjust the matter, the challenge was again renewed; and while the friends were again loading the rifles for the third exchange of shots, Mr. JONES and Mr. WISE walked apart and each proposed to the other anxiously to settle the affair.

Mr. WISE asked Mr. JONES

"If Mr. CILLEY could not assign the reason for declining to receive the note of Col. WEBB that he did not hold himself accountable to Col. WEBB for words spoken in debate?"

Mr. JONES replied that

"Mr. CILLEY would not wish to be understood as expressing the opinion whether he was or was not accountable for words spoken in debate."

Mr. WISE then asked Mr. JONES whether

"Mr. CILLEY would not say that in declining to receive the note of Col. WEBB, he meant no disrespect to Mr. GRAVES either *directly or indirectly.*"

To this Mr. JONES replied affirmatively, adding

"Mr. CILLEY entertains the highest respect for Mr. GRAVES, but declined to receive the note because he chose not to be drawn into a controversy with Col. WEBB."

In further explanatory conversation, Mr. WISE said to Mr. JONES:

"If this matter is not determined this shot, and is not settled, I will propose to shorten the distance."

To which Mr. JONES replied

"After this shot without effect I will entertain the proposition."

The parties then exchanged the third shot. It was fatal.

The bullet from Mr. GRAVES rifle struck Mr. CILLEY in the left *iliac* region, and passed through the right *lumbar* region, completely severing the *aorta* or main artery of the heart. The only words he spoke were "I'm wounded", and instantly died.

Mr. GRAVES, through Mr. WISE, expressed to Mr. JONES a desire to see Mr. CILLEY. When Mr. JONES approached Mr. GRAVES to inform him that his request would be granted, he asked Mr. JONES, "How is he?" Mr. JONES replied, "My friend is dead, sir." Mr. GRAVES then went to his carriage.

On the 28th of February, 1838, a committee was appointed by the House of Representatives, to investigate the causes which led to the death of Mr. CILLEY and the circumstances connected therewith. The committee on the 21st of April submitted a report accompanied by a large amount of testimony.

The report concluded with resolutions that Mr. GRAVES be expelled from the House, and that Messrs. WISE and JONES be censured.

Two minority reports were also presented.

The reports of the committee and the resolutions occupied the attention of the House from the 21st of April to the 10th of May, when by a vote of 103 to 78, the whole subject was laid on the table, and the reports and documents were ordered to be printed.

On the 4th of July a motion was made that the House do proceed to the consideration of the report when the motion to consider was ordered to lie on the table, and nothing further was done on the subject, except that the Senate passed a bill to prohibit the giving or accepting within the District of Columbia of a challenge to fight a duel, which was not acted upon by the House.

The act of December 3, 1836, fixing the seat of government at Madison, prescribed that the commissioners should —

"Agree upon a plan of said buildings and issue proposals, giving due notice thereof. and contract for the erection of said buildings without delay."

No "proposals" were issued during the year 1837, but the expenditures were made by the commissioners according to their own discretion, and amounted at the end of that year to the sum of $17,900.12, and the walls of the basement were erected, but none of the superstructure.

On the 20th of February, 1838, notice was published that

sealed proposals would be received until the 15th day of April, for the completion of the capitol above the basement story. The contract was let to JAMES MORRISON, and work progressed under the contract.

By an act of Congress approved June 18, 1838, a further appropriation of twenty thousand dollars was made—

"To defray the expenses of completing the public buildings in the Territory of Wisconsin, which are now commenced and partially completed."

The annual civil service appropriation bill approved April 6, 1838, contained an appropriation of $9,100 for compensation of the Governor, Judges, and Secretary, and of $29,625 for contingent expenses, pay and mileage of the members of the Legislative Assembly, officers of the Council, taking census, printing, and furniture and rent of buildings.

During the year 1837 three separate treaties with Indian tribes had been made, which were destined within a few years to be of the greatest interest and advantage to Wisconsin. They were submitted by the President to the Senate for their consideration at its next session, commencing in December of that year.

The tribes with which these treaties were made were the Chippewas, the Sioux, and the Winnebagoes.

Gov. DODGE, Governor and Superintendent of Indian Affairs, together with Gen. WILLIAM R. SMITH, then residing at Huntingdon, Pa., but immediately after and, until his death in Wisconsin, were appointed commissioners to effect a treaty with the Chippewa Indians for a cession of their lands to the United States.

The month of July was appointed as the time, and Saint Peters (the confluence of the St. Peters and Mississippi rivers) as the place for having a "talk" with the Chippewas with a view to the cession.

Unavoidable delays prevented Gen. SMITH from reaching the ground in season, and Gen. DODGE was the sole representative of the United States in conducting the negotiations.

The treaty with the Chippewas was concluded on the 29th day of July, 1837.

In the treaty with the Sioux the United States was represented by JOEL R. POINSETT, then Secretary of War, and the negotiations were conducted at Washington, where the chiefs and braves of the Sioux nation had gone for the purpose of having a "talk" with their "Great Father." The treaty was signed at Washington on the 29th day of September, 1837.

CAREY A. HARRIS, Commissioner of Indian Affairs, acting for the United States, concluded a treaty at Washington with the Winnebagoes on the first day of November, 1837.

By these treaties, and those previously made, the Indian title to all the land in the present State of Wisconsin, and a considerable part of Minnesota, was extinguished, except a portion occupied by the Menomonees and a few small reservations.

One of the minor effects of these treaties was to extinguish forever the hopes of the heirs of JONATHAN CARVER and their assigns, that their claim to the so-called "Carver grant" might in some unknown way be made available.

But the most important effect was that the extinguishment of the Indian title opened to settlement and occupation, and to the application of the subsequently enacted pre-emption and homestead laws, all that extensive region, the waters of which form those great arteries of commerce in lumber, the Wisconsin, Black, Chippewa, and St. Croix rivers, with the Wolf and others which empty into Green Bay.

Although these treaties were submitted to the Senate at an early period of the session, yet their ratification was so long delayed that apprehensions arose in the minds of those interested in them that possibly they might not be ratified.

Such was the extent of these fears, that in the message of Governor DODGE to the Legislative Assembly, at the extra session held in June, 1838, he deemed it his duty earnestly to recommend to the Legislative Assembly to adopt a memorial—

"Asking the ratification by the United States Senate of the treaties made with the Winnebagoes, Sioux and Chippewa Indians, for the extinguishment of their title to country within the limits of this territory. Until recently, no doubts were entertained of the ratification of the treaties in question."

Such a memorial was adopted.

The message of Governor DODGE was delivered on the 11th day of June, and it is a noteworthy coincidence that all three of the treaties were ratified by the Senate on the same day, and perhaps in the same hour in which the Governor's message was being read.

Previous to the 12th of June, 1838, the jurisdiction of the

Surveyor General of Ohio embraced Michigan and Wisconsin. An act of Congress approved on that day, created the office of Surveyor General for Wisconsin, comprehending all of Wisconsin, as bounded by the act of 1836, establishing the Territory.

The office was located at Dubuque, and ALBERT G. ELLIS was appointed the first Surveyor General, with a salary of fifteen hundred dollars, and three hundred and fifty dollars for office rent, fuel and other incidental expenses.

By an act of Congress approved June 12, 1838, the Secretary of the Treasury was authorized to set apart and reserve from sale, two entire townships of land for the use and support of a university, to be located in tracts of not less than an entire section.

An act had already been passed by the Territorial Legislature, approved January 19, 1838, to establish at or near Madison a university, the name of which should be "The University of Wisconsin." It was to—

"Be under the government of a board of visitors, not exceeding twenty-one in number, of whom the Governor, Secretary of the Territory, Judges of the Supreme Court, and the President of the University shall be part, and BUSHNELL B. CARY, MARSHALL M. STRONG, BYRON KILBOURN, WILLIAM N. GARDNER, HENRY STRINGHAM, CHARLES R. BRUSH, CHARLES C. P. ARNDT, JOHN CATLIN, GEORGE H. SLAUGHTER, DAVID BRIGHAM, JOHN F. SCHERMERHORN, WILLIAM W. CORIELL, GEORGE BEATTY, HENRY L. DODGE and AUGUSTUS A.' BIRD the remainder."

The act provided that the first meeting should be held on the first Monday in July, and might be adjourned from time to time.

The first meeting of the board of visitors was adjourned from the first to the third Monday of July, when Hon. CHARLES DUNN and WM. C. FRAZER, Judges of the Supreme Court, A. A. BIRD, JOHN CATLIN and WM. N. GARDNER were present. Judge FRAZER was appointed Chairman and WILLIAM N. GARDNER, Secretary. There being no quorum present, the board adjourned until Monday of the second week of the next session of the Legislative Assembly.

The next meeting of the Board was held in December pursuant to adjournment. Officers and committees were appointed and steps taken for the selection of a site, and to have the lands donated by Congress selected, and specifically appropriated for the use of the university.

At the second session of the 24th Congress there were fifteen new post routes established, and in June, 1838, there were eighty post-offices in the Territory east of the Mississippi.

These were Green Bay, Menomonee, Grand Kakalin, La'Fontain, Nashoto, Twin Rivers, Duck Creek, Butte de Morts and Depere in Brown county; City of Winnebago and Pipe Village in Calumet county; Prairie du Chien in Crawford county; Madison in Dane county; Cassville, Plattville, Lancaster, Sinsinawa Mound, Van Buren, Blast Furnace, Brooklyn, Port Hudson, Sinipee, Menomonee, Hazel Green and Gibraltar in Grant county; Centreville and New Mexico in Green county; Fond du Lac in Fond du Lac county; Mineral Point, Belmont, Elk Grove, Dodgeville, Helena, Moundville, Arena, Mill Seat Bend, Diamond Grove, Blue River, Wingville, English Prairie, Wisconsin, Gratiot's Grove, Wiota, Otterburn, White Oak Springs, New Diggings, Ridgeway and Willow Springs in Iowa county; Jefferson and Watertown in Jefferson county; Manitowoc in Manitowoc county; Milwaukee, Prairie Village, Belleterre, New Berlin and Oak Creek in Milwaukee county; Dekorre and Fort Winnebago in Portage county; Racine, Southport, Mount Pleasant, Aurora, Pleasant Prairie, Rochester Pike and Foxville in Racine county; Turtle Creek, Hume, Janesville and Outlet Koshkonong in Rock county; Sheboygan in Sheboygan county; Fox Lake in Dodge county; Washington in Washington county and Delavan, Elkhorn, Troy, Springfield, Geneva and Franklin in Walworth county. Of these twenty-seven have been discontinued or have different names.

There was appropriated by Congress at this session the sum of four thousand dollars for the construction of a lighthouse on Grassy Island at the head of Green Bay, The President was authorized to appoint one or more naval officers upon whom was devolved various duties with reference to light-houses, among which was to examine and determine whether it was expedient to construct lighthouses or beacon lights, at nearly fifty designated points. Three of these points were Southport, and the mouth of Sauk River and Kewaunee River.

Thirty thousand dollars was appropriated for the construction of roads, viz.: From Fort Howard, *via* Milwaukee and Racine, to the state line, fifteen thousand dollars; from

Milwaukee *via* Madison to a point opposite Dubuque, ten thousand dollars, and from Fort Crawford *via* Fort Winnebago to Fort Howard, five thousand dollars.

The surveying, marking and designating of the boundary line between the State of Michigan and Territory of Wisconsin, was provided for by act of Congress, and an appropriation of three thousand dollars made for that purpose.

There was granted to the Territory, by an act approved June 18, 1838, for the purpose of aiding in opening a canal to unite the waters of Lake Michigan at Milwaukee, with those of Rock River, all the land not theretofore disposed of in the odd numbered sections within the breadth of five full sections on each side of said canal.

A joint resolution was adopted June 12, 1838,

"That Congress do hereby dissent from, disapprove and disaffirm an act of the Legislative Council of Wisconsin entitled 'An act to incorporate the stockholders of the State Bank of Wisconsin at Prairie du Chien,' and the said act, is hereby declared to be null and void and to have no force or effect whatsoever."

Of all the legislation at this session of Congress none had been contemplated with more interest by the settlers upon that portion of the public domain in Wisconsin, which had not yet been offered at public sale, than an effective preemption law.

The measure which they had hoped for, and which was generally advocated by the representatives from those states in which the public lands were situated, was one which would confine the sales of the lands to actual settlers, thus preventing their absorption by speculators; provide homesteads to all actual *bona fide* settlers, and secure a permanent pre-emption right upon any of the public lands before they were offered for public sale.

An act entitled "An act to grant pre-emption rights to settlers on the public land" was passed June 22, 1838, which, while it did not meet the hopes of the settlers, secured to such of them as had resided on their "claims" four months next preceding its passage, the right to enter their claims and obtain a title to them.

The act of Congress of May 29, 1830, authorized every settler or occupant of the public lands prior to its passage and who was then in possession and cultivated any part thereof in the year 1829, to enter not more than one hundred and sixty acres or a quarter section, to include his improvement, upon paying to the United States the then minimum price of said land.

The act of June 22, 1838, declared

"That every actual settler of the public lands, being the head of a family, or over twenty-one years of age, who was in possession and a housekeeper, by personal residence thereon, at the time of the passage of this act and for four months next preceding, shall be entitled to all the benefits and privileges of an act entitled 'An act to grant pre-emption rights to settlers on the public lands, approved May 29, 1830,' and the said act is hereby revived and continued in force two years."

It had been foreseen from the time of the establishment of the Territory of Wisconsin, that it would at some time be divided into two or more Territories. The division came, however, sooner than had been generally anticipated.

By an act approved June 12, 1838, it was enacted

"That from and after the third day of July next, all that part of the present Territory of Wisconsin, which lies west of the Mississippi River, and west of a line drawn due north from the headwaters or sources of the Mississippi to the Territorial line, shall for the purposes of temporary government, be and constitute a separate Territorial government by the name of Iowa; and after the said third day of July next, all power and authority of the government of Wisconsin in and over the Territory hereby constituted shall cease."

The act further provided

"That from and after the 3rd day of July the terms of the members of the Council and House of Representatives of the Territory of Wisconsin shall be deemed to have expired and an entirely new organization shall take place."

It provided that the Governor should apportion the members of the Legislative Assembly among the several counties, and appoint the time of election and of the first meeting of the Legislature at Madison.

The United States Marshal and Attorney for the Territory of Wisconsin, resided west of the Mississippi, and their offices therefore became vacant, and EDWARD JAMES was appointed Marshal and MOSES M. STRONG Attorney for the reorganized Territory of Wisconsin.

A proclamation of the President of the United States was issued, bearing date July 6, 1838, declaring and making known that public sales would be held at Green Bay on the 22d October and 5th November, for the disposal of the public lands east of the Indian boundary, which had not previously been offered for sale, and within the boundaries of the present counties of Columbia, Marquette, Green Lake, northern part of Dodge, Fond du Lac, Winnebago and Door.

And also at Milwaukee on the 19th day of November and the 3d day of December, for the lands not previously offered in the south part of Dodge county, and in the counties of Jefferson, Rock, Walworth, Kenosha, Racine, Milwaukee, Waukesha, Washington and Ozaukee, except such sections as were within the limits of the grant for the Milwaukee and Rock River canal.

The sales to have been held in Milwaukee were postponed until the next year by a proclamation of the President in October.

The Legislative Assembly convened in special session at Burlington, on the second Monday (11th) of June, pursuant to a joint resolution adopted in the preceding January.

No change had taken place in the membership of the council, but some changes had taken place in the composition of the House of Representatives. At the previous session a charge had been made that ALEXANDER MCGREGOR, a member from Dubuque county, had accepted a bribe from one JOHN WILSON, to procure a certain ferry charter at or near Rock Island. The matter was referred to a committee, which reported that the charge was true, and that WILSON be brought to the bar and reprimanded, and that MCGREGOR be expelled.

Upon the consideration of the resolution in relation to WILSON, W. HENRY STARR, ESQ., an attorney, was permitted to appear for WILSON. Mr. STARR having used language toward Mr. QUIGLEY which the latter regarded as personally offensive, and the House having refused to adopt a resolution to punish Mr. STARR, Mr. QUIGLEY, on the 17th of January, resigned his seat. He was re-elected to fill the vacancy created by his own resignation.

The consideration of the resolution for the expulsion of ALEXANDER MCGREGOR, was postponed until the first day of the special session, and in the meantime, soon after the adjournment, he resigned his seat, and LUCIUS H. LANGWORTHY was elected as his successor.

JAMES COLLINS was elected to fill the vacancy occasioned by the resignation of GEORGE F. SMITH.

The two houses were organized by the election of ARTHUR B. INGRAM, President, and GEORGE BEATTY, Secretary of the the Council, and WILLIAM B. SHELDON, Speaker, and JOHN CATLIN, Chief Clerk of the House. The Governor's message was delivered in the afternoon of the first day of the session. The session was a short one, lasting only two weeks, having been held mainly for the purpose of making a new apportionment of members of the House of Representatives, based upon the census taken in May. Thirty-one acts were passed, of which six related to counties, five to roads, seven to the conduct of public affairs, and the remaining thirteen to private matters, of which four were to grant divorces. Among the public acts was one postponing the general election from the first Monday of August to the second Monday of September; and another making a new apportionment of the members of the House of Representatives to be then elected. Of the twenty-six members, twelve were apportioned among the counties east of the Mississippi river, and fourteen among those west. This apportionment was, however, to be contingent upon the division of the Territory; upon which contingency, it was made the duty of the Governor to make an apportionment. Having provided that the next session should be held at Madison, the first Legislative Assembly of Wisconsin Territory adjourned *sine die* on the 25th of June, 1838.

The population of the Territory in May, 1838, as shown by the census, was as follows:

Brown county	3,048
Crawford county	1,220
Dane county	172
Dodge county	18
Green county	494
Grant county	2,763
Iowa county	3,218
Jefferson county	468
Milwaukee county	3,131
Racine county	2,054
Rock county	480
Walworth county	1,019
Washington county	64
Total	18,149

On the 13th of July the Governor issued his proclamation, making the following apportionment:

Crawford county	1 member of Council,	2 members of House.
Iowa county	2 members of Council,	5 members of House.
Grant county	2 members of Council,	4 members of House.
Brown county, etc.	2 members of Council,	4 members of House.
Milwaukee county, etc.	2 members of Council,	5 members of House.
Racine county	2 members of Council,	3 members of House.
Rock and Walworth counties	1 member of Council,	2 members of House.
Green, Dane, Jefferson, and Dodge counties	1 member of Council,	1 member of House.

The time fixed for the election was the second Monday in September, and that for the meeting of the Legislative Assembly was the fourth Monday in November.

Party lines had not yet been drawn, and the members were chosen without reference to, and perhaps without a knowledge of, their views upon national politics. Among those elected were some who have since held public positions of distinction.

The members elect were as follows:

CRAWFORD COUNTY—*Council*, GEORGE WILSON; *House of Representatives*, ALEXANDER MCGREGOR and IRA B. BRUNSON.

IOWA COUNTY—*Council*, JAMES COLLINS and LEVI STERLING; *House of Representatives*, RUSSELL BALDWIN, JOHN W. BLACKSTONE, HENRY M. BILLINGS, THOMAS JENKINS and CHARLES BRACKEN.

GRANT COUNTY—*Council*, JAMES R. VINEYARD and JOHN H. ROUNTREE; *House of Representatives*, THOMAS CRUSON, NELSON DEWEY, RALPH CARVER, and JOSEPH H. D. STREET.

BROWN COUNTY, and the counties attached to it—*Council*, ALEXANDER J. IRWIN and MORGAN L. MARTIN; *House of Representatives*, EBENEZER CHILDS, CHARLES C. SHOLES, BARLOW SHACKELFORD and JACOB W. CONROE.

MILWAUKEE AND WASHINGTON COUNTIES—*Council*, DANIEL WELLS Jr., and WILLIAM A. PRENTISS; *House of Representatives*, LUCIUS I. BARBER, WILLIAM SHEW, HENRY C. SKINNER, EZEKIEL CHURCHILL and AUGUSTUS STORY.

ROCK AND WALWORTH COUNTIES—*Council*, JAMES MAXWELL; *House of Representatives*, EDWARD V. WHITON and OTHNI BEARDSLEY.

GREEN, DANE, JEFFERSON AND DODGE COUNTIES—*Council*, EBENEZER BRIGHAM; *House of Representatives*, DANIEL S. SUTHERLAND.

RACINE County—*Council*, WILLIAM BULLEN and MARSHALL M. STRONG; *House of Representatives*, ORRIN R. STEVENS, ZADOC NEWMAN and TRISTRAM C. HOYT.

At the time of the election of members of the Legislature an election was also had for Delegate in Congress for the Territory, as changed by the establishment of Iowa Territory.

Under date of Washington, June 20, Hon. GEORGE W. JONES addressed a circular letter to the people of Wisconsin, in which he says that he has yielded to the solicitations of his friends to become a candidate for delegate. The act changing the time of election from the first Monday of August to the second Monday of September, was not passed until the 23d of June, and the address was written on the supposition that the election would occur on the first Monday of August. For this reason Mr. JONES said—

"I fear that I shall not be able to reach home before the day set apart for the election, which will prevent my communing with you face to face, instead of through the medium of a printed circular."

He however arrived at Racine on the 24th July, on his return from Washington, and started the next day in a private carriage across the Territory for his home at Sinsinawa Mound, and had a few weeks before the election in which to make a personal canvass. Colonel JONES was also nominated at public meetings held at Milwaukee and Mineral Point on the 11th day of July.

In the early part of July the name of THOMAS P. BURNETT was announced as an independent candidate for delegate. He canvassed the Territory very generally and made public addresses in many places. At two different meetings held in Brown county, MORGAN L. MARTIN was nominated and renominated as candidate for delegate, but before the election he withdrew from the canvass and became a candidate for member of the Council and was elected.

At a meeting of citizens of Brown county on the 26th July, JAMES D. DOTY was nominated as candidate for delegate, and on the 1st August addressed a letter to the chairman of that meeting, in which he declined that nomination because it was local, and said—

"I hope therefore my friends will permit me to decline the acceptance of their nomination, as the nomination of a single county, and to express my desire, if it accords with their wishes, that they should submit my name to a general convention, and to tender them my thanks for the honor they have done me."

At a subsequent meeting on the 8th of August, six delegates were elected to a Territorial convention to be held at Madison on the 29th of August,

Delegates were elected from several other counties, and the assemblage met at Madison on the 29th of August and put Mr. DOTY in nomination as a candidate for delegate. The contest assumed a triangular form, the three candidates being GEORGE W. JONES, THOMAS P. BURNETT and JAMES D. DOTY.

Judge DOTY was elected, having received 1,758 votes. Mr. JONES received 1,174, and Mr. BURNETT 920. More than seven hundred of the votes for Mr. BURNETT were from the western part of the Territory, and would probably have been cast for Mr. JONES if Mr. BURNETT had not been a canditate. The odium of the GRAVES-CILLEY duel was a great embarrassment to Mr. JONES in the eastern part of the Territory and cost him many votes.

The following is the vote by counties in detail:

COUNTIES.	DOTY.	JONES.	BURNETT.
Brown	442	35	18
Milwaukee	562	193	35
Racine	325	14	98
Walworth	133	3	43
Rock	83	15	14
Iowa	36	457	327
Grant	105	302	307
Crawford	18	93	26
Green		37	52
Dane	54	25	
Total	1,758	1,174	920

On the 26th of October, EDWARD E. OLIVER suffered the extreme penalty of the law — death by hanging. He was executed at Lancaster in Grant county, by the sheriff of that county for the unprovoked murder of JOHN RUSSELL at Cassville about six months previously.

By the fourth article of the treaty with the Winnebagoes, made at Washington November 1, 1837, in consideration of the cession and relinquishment of all their lands east of the Mississippi, there was set apart by the United States the sum of two hundred thousand dollars , of which fifty thousand dollars was to be paid specifically to certain individuals named in the treaty, and the remaining one hundred and fifty thousand dollars were to be applied to the debts of the nation, which might be ascertained to be justly due, and which might be admitted by the Indians. If the debts amounted to more than that sum, the creditors were to be paid *pro rata.*

There was also set apart the further sum of one hundred thousand dollars, to be paid under the direction of the President to the relatives and friends of said Indians having not less than one quarter of Winnebago blood.

SIMON CAMERON, of Pennsylvania, and JAMES MURRAY, of Maryland, were appointed by the President commissioners to adjust and pay the debts of the Winnebagoes, and to distribute among their relatives and friends of mixed blood the sum so set apart for them. GEORGE W. FEATHERSTONHAUGH was appointed secretary of the commission.

The determination of the question who were the creditors of the Indians, and what was the amount of their credits— the admission of the Indians having been obtained — as well also as the other question of what persons were to be allowed a share of the fund for those of mixed Winnebago blood, were left to the uncontrolled discretion and decision of the commissioners.

The commissioners gave public notice that their office would be open for business at Prairie du Chien on the 6th of September, when they would adjudicate upon all claims filed with the secretary in the order in which they were filed.

The whole Winnebago nation was assembled, amounting to about four thousand souls, men, women, and children, and "relatives and friends of mixed blood" innumerable. A large number of creditors was in attendance, and a proportionately large number and amount of claims were filed and acted upon.

It would be only natural that the action of the commissioners should subject them to censorious remarks. It was openly charged that collusion existed between a Mr. BRODHEAD, of Pennsylvania, and the commissioners. He was there in the capacity of attorney for claimants and persons of mixed blood, and it was alleged that he was always successful, and it was said that he received large commissions, which he divided with the commissioners.

At the first session of the Legislative Assembly, WILLIAM BULLEN was chosen President of the Council, and JOHN W. BLACKSTONE, Speaker of the House.

It met at Madison, on the 26th of November.

Upon convening, it was found that the capital was in an unfinished state, and so much dissatisfaction existed with the accommodations at Madison, that it was a matter of doubt for two weeks, whether a temporary adjournment to Milwaukee would not be had. A committee appointed for the purpose of investigating the extent of the accommodations, reported "that at the Madison House there was one room that would accommodate six persons, at the Madison Hotel two rooms that would accommodate four persons, and at the American Hotel eight rooms, sufficient to accommodate twenty-six persons. But they could not ascertain that more than fifty persons could be accommodated with sufficient rooms for the transaction of business."

A resolution to remove the session to some other place passed one House, and would probably have passed the other, if there had been any satisfactory evidence that the accommodations at any other place in the Territory were any better. Under the circumstances, the Legislative Assembly remained at Madison about four weeks, when they adjourned from the 22d of December to the 21st of January.

During this short session a committee of three members from each of the two branches was appointed to make a revision of the laws; and two other committees, of three members each, to investigate the banks of the Territory, which they were required to visit in person. The duty of serving upon these committees was practically a removal of twelve of the thirty-nine members from the scene of their labors on the floor of their respective houses, and was the ostensible reason for the recess.

A special messenger was appointed by joint resolution to proceed to Burlington and procure the quota of the laws of the last session, belonging to the Territory of Wisconsin.

A joint resolution was also adopted, that JAMES E. EDWARDS, with whom a contract had been entered into on the 30th of January, for printing and binding certain laws, and with which he had failed to comply, be directed not to proceed any further with the printing and binding of said laws.

The District Attorney of the United States was requested by joint resolution to examine and report whether the Territory had a title to the ground on which the Capitol stands.

MOSES M. STRONG was appointed fiscal agent with authority to adjust all accounts for any money appropriated by law to defray the expenses of that session of the Legislative Assembly, and to borrow for the use of the Legislature fifteen thousand dollars, in coin or in notes of the banks of Illinois or Missouri.

At this December session, twenty acts were passed nearly all of which were of a purely local or private nature.

The county of Walworth was organized and the county seat located at Elkhorn, and the counties of Manitowoc and Sheboygan were organized for county purposes, continuing attached to Brown county for judicial purposes.

The proceedings of the board of commissioners of Milwaukee county were declared legal and valid, and the commissioners were also authorized to prepare copies of the record of deeds, etc., from Brown county. Commissioners were appointed to locate the seat of justice of Green county.

Eleven of the twenty acts related to the locating, authorizing or establishing roads, bridges and ferries, two incorporated mining companies.

One changed the name of the Wisconsin University of Green Bay to Hobart University of Green Bay, while the only other and the last act of this short session, approved on the 22d December, was "to provide for the compensation of the officers of the Legislative Assembly and for other purposes." The appropriation made by this act amounted to $6,454.14.

After adopting a joint resolution—

"That E. CHILDS, Chairman of the Committee on Arrangements of the House of Representatives, be instructed to procure, during the vacation, such articles as may be necessary for the accommodation of the Legislature during the next session,"

this first and necessarily short session was adjourned, and such of the members as were not engaged in committee work returned to their homes.

CHAPTER XX.

TERRITORY OF WISCONSIN IN 1839.

The proceedings of the third session of the twenty-fith Congress, commencing December 3, 1838, and ending March 3, 1839, so far as they affected the Territory of Wisconsin, were not subordinate in interest to those of any preceding session.

The first question which arose, affecting those interests, was, which of the two gentlemen claiming the right to represent the Territory during that session—GEORGE W. JONES or JAMES D. DOTY — was lawfully entitled to the seat?

It was claimed by Mr. JONES that by virtue of his election in October, 1836, and in accordance with the provisions of an act of Congress passed March 3, 1817, his term did not expire until March 3, 1839.

He took his seat at the opening of the third session, as members of the House did, having taken the oath and occupied the seat at the first (special) and second sessions of that Congress.

Mr. DOTY presented the certificate showing that on the 10th of September, 1838, he had been duly elected, and claimed the seat occupied by Mr. JONES, contesting his right to hold it.

The matter was referred to the committee on elections.

The first section of the act of March 3, 1817, which was still in force, prescribed:

"That in every Territory of the United States, in which a temporary government has been, or hereafter shall be, established, and which, by virtue of the ordinance of Congress of 13th July, 1787, or of any subsequent act of Congress, passed or to be passed, now hath or hereafter shall have the right to send a delegate to Congress; such delegate shall be elected every second year for the same term of two years for which members of the House of Representatives of the United States are elected."

It was claimed by Mr. JONES that under the act of 1817, a delegate must be elected only for one Congress, and not for parts of two congressional terms; that his term as a delegate from Wisconsin did not commence until the 4th of March, 1837, and consequently would not expire until the 4th of March, 1839. Of course, upon this hypothesis, it was claimed that his service as delegate previous to March, 1837, was as a delegate from Michigan Territory, by virtue of his election as such in 1835.

It was claimed by Mr. Doty that the act of 1817 was controlled by the organic act of the Territory of Wisconsin, passed April 20, 1836, which gives the power to its citizens to elect a delegate to represent them in Congress, without fixing any time for the commencement of his services, and that the term of service commenced instanter upon the election of the delegate, and that Mr. Jones's duties as a delegate from Wisconsin commenced with his election in October, 1836, and terminated with Mr. Doty's election in 1838.

On the 21st of December, 1838, Mr. Buchanan, from the committee on elections, submitted a report, in which the committee say—

.. "After all the consideration which the committee have been able to bestow on the subject, they have no hesitation in saying that considerable difficulty exists in reconciling the different acts which may be supposed to have a bearing on the matter; yet they feel a great degree of confidence in two positions; first, that it was the intention of Congress by the act of April, 1836, organizing the Territory, to afford the people of the Territory the privilege of an immediate representation in Congress by a delegate to be elected by themselves; and second, that the people of the Territory acted with a view to the enjoyment of that privilege in electing a delegate in October, 1836, and that Mr. Doty is entitled to a seat under his election in 1838."

The committee reported the following resolution:

"*Resolved*, That James Duane Doty is entitled to a seat in this House as a delegate from Wisconsin Territory, and that George W. Jones is not so entitled."

On the 3d of January, 1839, the resolution reported by the committee being under consideration, its adoption was advocated by Mr. Craig, Mr. Randolph of New Jersey and Mr. Cary of Michigan. Mr. Jones's right to the seat was advocated by Mr. Thomas of Maryland and Mr. Cushing of Massachusetts, when the previous question having been ordered, the resolution was adopted by a vote of 165 to 25, and Mr. Doty was qualified and took his seat.

On the 5th of January, Mr. Mason, of Ohio, offered a resolution that Mr. Jones was not entitled to mileage or *per diem*, which after a long debate was defeated by a vote of 96 to 89. So that he received his mileage and *per diem*, up to the 3d of January.

The Graves and Cilley duel, to the details of which so much space was devoted in the preceding chapter, led to the passage of the act of Congress of February 20, 1839,

"To prohibit the giving or accepting within the District of Columbia of a challenge to fight a duel, and for the punishment thereof."

This act has ever since been in force.

By its provisions the giving, accepting or the carrying of a challenge to fight a duel, or a message intended as such, within the District of Columbia, is made punishable by imprisonment to hard labor in the penitentiary, not exceeding ten years if the duel is fought, and either party is slain or mortally wounded, and not exceeding five years, whether the duel is fought or not.

The act also prescribes penalties for minor offenses incidental to a challenge.

The beneficial results to the Territory of the legislation of this session of congress, measured by the appropriations made, were meagre, when compared with the demands made upon Congress as exhibited by the bills introduced in the Senate and House.

This was attributable in a large degree to the state of the finances of the country at that time, and the embarrassed condition of the country, which was such that it was so difficult to procure funds for the ordinary operations of the Government, that the President recommended that no appropriations be made which could properly be avoided.

To this cause may be added the fact, that the contest for the seat of Delegate consumed one month of the short session, and the legislation affecting the Territory was postponed until near the close of the session.

In addition to the appropriation of $9,100 for compensation of Governor, Judges and Secretary, and of $25,000 for contingent expenses, pay and mileage of members of Legislative Assembly, printing, etc., the only appropriations made were the following :

"For the security of the commerce of the United States" there was appropriated ; "For building a pier at the northern extremity of Winnebago Lake," five hundred dollars;

"For placing buoys at the mouth of Neenah river at the head of Green Bay, to mark the channel thereof," five hundred dollars;

"For the survey and estimate of the cost of improving the navigation of the Neenah and Wisconsin Rivers," two thousand dollars;

"For the construction of a road from Racine by Janesville to Sinipee on the Mississippi River," ten thousand dollars;

"For the survey and construction of a road from Sauk harbor on Lake Michigan to Dekorree on the Wisconsin River," five thousand dollars.

"For the construction of a road from Fond du Lac on Lake Winnebago by Fox Lake to the Wisconsin River," five thousand dollars;

That the sum of two thousand dollars, appropriated by act of July 7, 1838, for a railroad. shall be applied by the

Secretary of War to the survey of a railroad from the town of Milwaukee to the Mississippi River.

Being a total of twenty-three thousand dollars for internal improvements in the Territory at this session.

A private act was also passed authorizing JOHN DOUGHERTY, a well-known Indian trader, to enter at the land office at Mineral Point, section 12, town 3, range 3 east, at the minimum price ($1.25 per acre).

Besides these acts making appropriations but three others affecting Wisconsin were passed at this session.

One of these modified the absolute veto power of the Governor upon the laws passed by the Legislature, contained in the organic act, to a qualified veto, and provided that bills might become laws if passed by a majority of two-thirds after being returned by the Governor without his signature.

Another act passed was one which provided for the partition and division of the township of land owned by the Brothertown Indians, among the different individuals composing said tribe and declaring that they should be citizens of the United States.

The other of the three acts alluded to, was to make the "middle or center of the main channel" of the Mississippi River, the common boundary line between the Territories of Wisconsin and Iowa and to give both territories concurrent jurisdiction upon the river.

The several bills which were introduced and which failed to pass, contemplated legislation of vastly more importance than any or all which did pass.

Their importance demands a brief reference to them.

The most important of these, and the most dangerous in its possible consequences, was entitled: "A bill to establish a system of internal improvements in Wisconsin." It provided that the Legislative Assembly of the Territory might authorize by law a loan upon the credit of the Territory of such unlimited sum as might be required for the improvement of the navigation of the Fox and Wisconsin Rivers; for the improvement of the Rock River and its branches — the Pecatonica, River of the Four Lakes, the eastern branch of Rock River—to connect with the Milwaukee River, and of the latter stream to the lake, and the construction of a canal to connect Rock River with Winnebago Lake at Fond du Lac, and for the construction of such roads and canals as might thereafter be designated.

It authorized the Legislative Assembly to pass such laws as might be necessary to establish a board of public works; to create separate loans for each of said separate objects of improvements, and for the sale and negotiation of the stock for said loans, and to pledge the faith of the Territory and future State for the redemption of the loans at the periods stipulated, being not less than thirty years.

The net proceeds of the tolls to be received from the works, and all donations of land which might be made to the Territory in aid of said improvements, were to be and remain pledged for the redemption of the loans.

The board of public works was to consist of three citizens of the Territory, to be elected by the Legislative Assembly, on joint ballot, under whose direction the several proposed routes for improvement were to be surveyed and constructed, under the control and direction of the Legislative Assembly.

A survey of the route of any work, with a general plan and estimate of its cost, was to be made under the direction of the Chief of the Topographical Engineers and approved by him before such work could be commenced.

The money obtained from loans was to have been in the custody of the board of public works, subject to the control and management of the Legislative Assembly. No act creating a loan was to take effect until approved by Congress.

There were many other minor provisions.

A most plausible letter to Hon. J. H. BRUNSON, chairman of the committee on territories, was written by Judge DOTY February 2d, in support of this bill, which was laid upon the table to accompany the bill.

A kindred measure and an essential part of the "system" was "A bill making a grant of land in aid of certain internal improvements in Wisconsin," which was reported in the Senate on the 11th February by Mr. LYON, from the committee on roads and canals.

The bill granted to the Territory alternate sections of land along and on each side of the Fox and Wisconsin rivers, and of the canal to connect them, in aid of the improvement of said rivers and of the construction of said canal, which were to be disposed of for the redemption of such loans as might be made by the Legislative Assembly, for the purpose of constructing said improvements.

It also granted the alternate sections along and on each side of Rock River within the limits of Wisconsin, and of its branches — the Peckatonica to Mineral Point, and River of the Four Lakes to the Fourth Lake,— and of a canal from Rock River to Fond du Lac, to aid in the improvement of the navigation of said river and its branches, and of the construction of said canal, which lands were in like manner to be disposed of for the redemption of loans.

The act also granted compensatory lands, to be selected in lieu of such of the granted lands as had been previously disposed of.

Another bill which was defeated, was one amending the organic act, so as to limit the tenure of the offices of Governor, Secretary, Marshal and Attorney to two years; Judges to four years, members of the Council to two years, members of the House to one year, and requiring executive officers to reside at the seat of government.

". A bill to approve and confirm an act of the Legislative Assembly of Wisconsin" (incorporating banks) passed the House but did not pass the Senate.

The other measures which were pending but failed to become laws, were:

A joint resolution which passed the Senate and was sent to the House, appropriating the sum of fifteen thousand dollars for a survey and examination of the lake coast for the purpose of obtaining the necessary information to make accurate charts thereof.

A bill granting the proceeds of the sale of lots in Southport (Kenosha) for the construction of a harbor at Southport; and another for a road from Southport to Rock River; both failed.

The bills making Milwaukee and Green Bay ports of entry, making an appropriation of thirty thousand dollars for a harbor at Milwaukee and an appropriation for a like purpose at Racine, all failed to become laws.

The second Legislative Assembly commenced its second session at Madison on the 21st day of January, to which time it had adjourned on the 22d of the preceding December.

There was no change in the membership of either house, but JAMES COLLINS of Iowa county was elected President of the Council, in the place of WILLIAM BULLEN, and LUCIUS I. BARBER of Milwaukee was elected Speaker of the House, in place of JOHN W. BLACKSTONE. The Secretary of the

Council, Chief Clerk of the House and Sergeant-at-Arms of both houses were re-elected.

The message of the Governor was delivered on the second day of the session, in which he said:

"I deem it not necessary at this time to call your attention to any other subjects except those embraced in my last message, with the exception of our relations with the Winnebago Indians, to which I would respectfully invite the attention of the Legislative Assembly."

After describing the recent depredations and threatening demonstrations of the Indians, and his correspondence with the war department, and recommending a memorial to the Secretary of War for four companies of dragoons for the purpose of removing the Indians, the Governor in his message said:

"Unless the Government takes the proper steps to effect their removal early in the spring, I will assume the responsibility of raising a mounted volunteer corps of riflemen (and head them in person) sufficient to effect their removal from this Territory, with those who are advising and instigating the Winnebago Indians to remain east of the Mississippi, from no regard they have for the Indians themselves, but for the purpose of defrauding them out of their annuities."

The resolution adopted at the first session in December authorized the fiscal agent to borrow fifteen thousand dollars

"In gold or silver or the notes of the Bank of Illinois, or its branches, or the notes of the bank of Missouri for the use of the legislature."

On the first day of the second session, the fiscal agent reported to the Legislative Assembly that he had made a loan from COLLIER & PETTIS of St. Louis, of fifteen thousand dollars, a large part of which was in notes of a bank in Cincinnati; whereupon a resolution was immediately adopted by both houses, reciting that

"WHEREAS a large portion of the money received by the said fiscal agent from the said COLLIER & PETTIS was of a kind not authorized by the resolution of the Legislative Assembly;"

Resolved, "That the Legislative Assembly approves of said loan and hereby ratifies and agrees to the contract made on the 26th day of December, 1838, by MOSES M. STRONG, fiscal agent of the Legislative Assembly, with Messrs. COLLIER & PETTIS.

On the third day of the session, the speaker laid before the House a report of the United States Attorney, in pursuance of a resolution adopted at the preceding session requesting him

"To examine and report to the Legislative Assembly as soon as practicable, whether the Territory has a title to the ground on which the capitol stands; and if not, in whom the title thereof is, together with such other facts in relation thereto, as to him may seem expedient."

The report states that the land was entered in the joint names of JAMES DUANE DOTY and STEVENS T. MASON, and that DOTY conveyed all his right, title and interest to MASON, and after setting forth all the conveyances with particularity, and stating the reason, for the conclusion, states

"That the result of the whole enquiry seems to be, that Mr. MASON acquired the title to half these lands by the original entry; that he acquired the title to the other half by virtue of the deed from Mr. DOTY; thus vesting in him the whole title. That he has never so far as we have examined, parted with that title; the only deed which purports to convey any part of it (the deed from TILLOU and MASON to DOTY) being void for the reasons already stated; and therefore that neither of the acknowledgments of either of the town plats by by Mr. DOTY vests any title to the public square in the Territory."

Mr. MASON afterward conveyed half of his interest to KINTZING PRITCHETTE.

The United States attorney, in concluding his report, says:

"Considering that the interests of the Territory imperatively required that the title to the ground on which the Capitol stands, together with such ground adjacent thereto as might be convenient, should be speedily secured to them, or that it should be known with certainty at an early day that it would not be; I lost no time in writing to Messrs. MASON and PRITCHETTE, and on the 7th of January, instant, I received from them a power of attorney authorizing me to convey the title to the Territory, accompanied by a request that I would execute a conveyance agreeably to the authority given in the letter of attorney. Accordingly, on the 16th of January, inst., I executed to the Territory of Wisconsin a deed of the tract known and described upon the plat acknowledged by Mr. DOTY as the public square, to be held by the Territory until the organization of a State government, with a reversion to the State when organized, which secures to the Territory 'a title to the ground on which the Capitol now stands.'"

A joint resolution was adopted February 8, 1839, in pursuance of which a committee of three members from each House was appointed to investigate the affairs of the commissioners for the building of the Capitol, with power to send for persons and papers, and administer oaths, and report to the Legislative Assembly the manner in which the public building had been conducted and in which the money appropriated by Congress had been paid out.

The committee, after an investigation and an examination of witnesses, submitted a report, accompanied by the evidence before it, written and oral, from which it appears that the commissioners elected on the 7th of December, 1836, held no meeting until the 4th of the following May, when only Messrs. DOTY and O'NEILL were present. Mr. BIRD was appointed acting commissioner, with authority to purchase materials, employ mechanics and laborers, and to do whatever else was requisite to construct the buildings.

The act to locate the seat of government, by which the commissioners were appointed, provided that they should—

"Agree upon a plan, issue proposals, giving due notice thereof, and contract for the erection of said buildings without delay."

The report of the committee states—

" That the commissioners, instead of entering upon the discharge of their duties agreeably to the requirements of the law under which the board were created, and in which their duties were plainly marked out, boldly assumed the power of purchasing materials, employing mechanics and laborers, and proceeding in the construction of the buildings on their own account. The acting commissioner in the month of May, 1837, commenced operations at Madison, having previously engaged a number of mechanics, purchased provisions, etc. The construction of the work was continued by him until the month of September following, when a notice for proposals was issued for the first time. Three bids were received, but none were accepted by the commissioners, and the work was continued by them until April 25, 1838."

A contract was let to JAMES MORRISON April 17, 1838, to complete the buildings for the sum of $26,200.

The committee submitted the evidence—

"Without expressing an opinion in relation to the proper measures to be adopted by the Legislature."

The report was submitted in the House on 4th March by Mr. BLACKSTONE, one of the members of the joint committee. It was read and referred back to the committee appointed on the part of the House, with instructions to report by bill or otherwise.

Mr. BLACKSTONE in behalf of the committee, on the same day reported—

"That the commissioners have acted from the commencement of their duties in direct violation of the laws under which they were appointed. Under a conviction of this fact your committee would respectfully report the following bill—"

The bill without material amendment became a law on the 8th of March. It repealed the 3d section of the act of December 3, 1836, which provided for the election of commissioners, to cause the necessary buildings to be erected.

It further provided that three commissioners should be elected by joint ballot, who should be styled Commissioners of Public Buildings, and that an annual election should be held, the commissioners to hold their offices until the termination of the next regular session of the Legislative Assembly after their election.

The act prescribed that the old commissioners should immediately settle their accounts with the new commissioners and pay over to them all money or evidences of debt in their hands, and books, papers, etc., and if they should neglect or refuse it was made the duty of the new commissioners to cause suit to be instituted against them in the name of the Territory.

It was made the duty of the new commissioners under this act, to cause the public buildings which had been commenced to be completed and finished according to the contract with MORRISON.

JAMES L. THAYER, NATHANIEL C. PRENTICE and LESTER H. COTTON were elected commissioners.

The efforts of the new commissioners to effect a settlement with the old ones or to obtain from them any money, evidences of debt, books or papers, having proved unavailing, they instituted a suit in the name of the Territory against the former commissioners for the recovery of the money in their hands.

The contract of MORRISON for completing the Capitol expired on the 20th of September, at which time it was entirely unfinished, almost no work having been done since the adjournment of the Legislative Assembly, although the contractor had been overpaid by the old commissioners $7,460.70, according to the estimate of the new commissioners.

Suit was commenced against him and his sureties for a breach of the contract and for the recovery of the public money in his hands.

The new commissioners having no public funds, advanced of their own over $230, with which they did such work on the Capitol, as enabled the Legislative Assembly to occupy it, at the next session.

The reason assigned by Judge DOTY in several communications in the newspapers, for refusing to account with and pay over to the new commissioners the funds in his hands was that Congress, by the act of June 18, 1838, making a second appropriation of $20,000 for completing the public buildings, had enacted that the money should

"Be expended according to the act of the Legislative Assembly, entitled 'An Act to establish the seat of Government of the Territory of Wisconsin and to provide for the erection of public buildings,' approved December 3, 1836;"

and that the Legislature had not the

"Power to cause the sum appropriated by Congress to be expended by any other persons than the commissioners elected in pursuance of the third section of the act of December 3, 1836."

The financial condition of the whole country during the winter of 1838-9, resulting from the crash of 1837, and the general suspension of specie payments, affected the infant Territory of Wisconsin no less disastrously than the longer settled portions of the country.

Two banks—one at Green Bay and one at Mineral Point,—were in active operation at this time, and the charter of another was in existence—the Bank of Milwaukee—the franchises of which were claimed by two different boards of directors, but were not practically exercised by either.

At the December session separate joint committees had been appointed to investigate the affairs of the Bank of Wisconsin at Green Bay, and the Bank of Mineral Point.

The first named committee went to Green Bay and commenced their duties on the 1st of January. The only officers of the Bank were H. STRINGHAM, Cashier, and H. W. WELLS, Clerk. They each presented sworn statements of the affairs of the Bank, but refused to be examined or to answer any questions under oath, and would not exhibit to the committee the books of the bank for their inspection. The committee reported such statements as the officers had volunteered to give, and expressing their regret that circumstances beyond their control had prevented them from fully and satisfactorily making such an investigation and report as the resolution under which they acted contemplated; they reported that the refusal of the officers of the bank to allow the committee to examine into the doings of the corporation is, in the opinion of the committee, a direct abuse and violation of the provisions of its charter.

Thereupon the Legislative Assembly passed an act that the Attorney General of the Territory commence and prosecute a suit by injunction to close up all proceedings of said Bank and annul its charter, and authorizing the court to appoint a receiver to take charge of its property, collect its debts and pay its creditors the proportions due to them.

Upon the passage of this act HENRY S. BAIRD, the Attorney General, resigned his office, and on the 30th March the Governor appointed HORATIO N. WELLS his successor, who commenced and prosecuted the suit against the bank and obtained the appointment of a receiver, under whose charge the affairs of the bank were wound up.

The committee appointed to investigate the affairs of the Bank of Mineral Point met there on the 4th and 5th of January. Every facility for making the examination was furnished by the cashier, who presented a statement of the affairs of the bank, prepared and sworn to by him, which the committee compared with the funds in the bank and with the books, and which they reported to be a fair and correct statement of the affairs of the institution.

The report concludes:

"From a full and particular investigation of its books and funds, and from the statement of its cashier under oath, as well as from the general confidence of the community in which it is placed, your committee unhesitatingly express their belief that the Bank of Mineral Point is in a safe and solvent condition,"

when the experience of a short time demonstrated its utter insolvency.

The Legislative Assembly made short work of disposing of the Bank of Milwaukee, by the unconditional repeal of the act of November 30, 1836, incorporating it, and declaring that the charter granted by said act be annulled, vacated and made void.

It would seem that the action of the Legislative Assembly was not prompted by any spirit of hostility to banks as such, as at the same session an act was passed to incorporate the State Bank of Wisconsin, with a capital of one million dollars, which was to be procured in this wise:

The stockholders were to make subscriptions for stock, which were to be guaranteed and secured by mortgages on real estate, and the directors were to obtain the capital by the issue of the bonds of the bank, payable at the expiration of its charter, for the payment of which the mortgages given by the stockholders were to remain a perpetual pledge to the holder of the bonds of the bank.

The Governor was authorized to subscribe for over half of the capital, and pay for it in bonds of the Territory bearing 7 per cent. interest payable in 1863.

There was to be a mother bank and branches, not exceeding five, located where the directors might determine.

This act could not go into effect until approved by Congress, which approval was never given, and the "State Bank of Wisconsin" died still-born.

Another abortive act of this session, under which it was contemplated that a banking business would be done at Sinipee in Grant county, was "An act to incorporate the Mississippi Marine and Fire Insurance Company." But Sinipee failed to justify the sanguine hopes of its progenitors, who were alike unsuccessful in giving vitality to the "Insurance Company" charter.

But far different was the fate of "An act to incorporate the Wisconsin Fire and Marine Insurance Company," passed at this session. Its authorized capital was five hundred thousand dollars, and was controlled by some wealthy Scotch gentlemen, who organized it, and who, under the power contained in the charter, to "receive money on deposit, and loan the same," filled all the channels for money circulation in the valley of the Mississippi for years, with its certificates of deposit, in the similitude of, and which supplied the place of, bank notes, although the charter expressly provided that nothing therein contained should give the company banking privileges. This is a striking illustration of the futility of legislative restrictions upon the exercise of corporate powers, especially when sustained, as that company undoubtedly was, by popular sentiment.

Three acts incorporating mining companies, and two incorporating manufacturing companies, were passed at this session.

The "Pekatonica and Mississippi Railroad Company," to construct a railroad from Mineral Point to the Mississippi River, and the "Pekatonica Navigation Company," to construct a canal or slack-water navigation along the valley of the Pekatonica River, from the Illinois state line to Mineral Point, were the only internal improvement corporations of the session.

Acts were passed appointing commissioners to lay out territorial roads from Rochester to Madison, from the Illinois line near Fox River to Prairie Village, from Geneva to Milwaukee, from Geneva to Fond du Lac, from Mineral Point to English Prairie, from Janesville to White Oak Springs, from Mineral Point to Sinipee, from Southport to Madison, from Manitowoc to Green Bay, from Southport to Beloit, from Manitowoc Rapids to Sheboygan Falls, from Mineral Point to Brewster's Ferry, from Plum Creek to Manitowoc Rapids, from Prairie du Chien to Fort Winnebago, from Sac Creek to Fort Winnebago, from Milwaukee to Watertown, and from Sheboygan to Madison.

These matters at that early day were regarded as of great local importance.

Two acts were passed authorizing private parties to erect dams across Rock River. One "at a place known as Johnson's Rapids, on section 4, town 8, range 15;" so little was the present city of Watertown then known. The other was in section 6 or 7, in town 11, range 16, where Horicon now is.

Several acts organizing municipal corporations passed.

One of these incorporated "The President and Trustees of the town of Green Bay," consisting of the north ward and the south ward.

Another incorporated "The President and Trustees of the town of Milwaukee," consisting of the east ward and the west ward.

The only other act of importance in relation to municipal corporations, was an act to establish certain towns in Milwaukee, Brown, Racine and Walworth counties.

The towns established by this act were Lake, Kinnikenick, Milwaukee, Vernon, Prairie Village, Muskego, Lisbon, Mequanego, Brookfield, Gennessee, Summit, Washington, Dodge, Bark River, Finch, Jefferson, Watertown, Racine, Mount Pleasant, Rochester, Salem, Burlington, Troy, Spring Prairie, Elk Horn, Delavan, Geneva, Southport, Pleasant Prairie, Rock, Sheboygan, Manitowoc, Oconto, Pasaukie, Howard, Kakalin, Winnebago, Butte des Morts, Calumet, Fond du Lac, Depere, Green Bay, Bay Settlement, Portage and Kewaunee.

The organization of the counties of Rock, Dane, Jefferson and Fond du Lac was authorized by laws passed at this session.

Commissioners having been appointed at the December session to locate the seat of justice of Green county, they performed that duty and in pursuance of the act by which they were appointed, the Governor on the 20th of February issued his proclamation announcing the result.

This action was unsatisfactory to a large number of the citizens of the county, who expressed their dissatisfaction at a public meeting held on the 23rd of February, and as a result another act was passed March 9th, providing for an election by the male residents of the county on the first Monday of May. This election resulted in a *tie* vote. There were 130 votes polled, which were equally divided between "New Mexico" and the other location.

An act of considerable importance to the citizens of Racine and relating to the origin of the titles of many lots in that city was passed at this session. On the 2nd of January, 1838, an act had been passed which appeared to contemplate that GILBERT KNAPP should loan to the board of supervisors of Racine county, a sufficient sum to enable them to enter the east fractional half of section 9, town 3, range 23, as the county seat of Racine county, in pursuance of the act of Congress of 1824, authorizing them to do so, and that the supervisors should re-sell the lands so entered, to Mr. KNAPP at ten dollars per acre.

By an act passed February 2, 1839, the foregoing act was repealed, and the Board of County Commissioners were authorized to convey said lands for a gross sum of $8,000, or a part thereof — if they only obtained title to part — for a proportionate part of that sum.

By a resolution adopted at this session, JOHN V. SUYDAM, FRANCIS C. KIRKPATRICK and JEREMIAH B. ZANDER were appointed commissioners to locate a portion — not exceeding two thirds — of the lands donated by Congress for the use and support of a university. No selections were made under this appointment and the act became obsolete.

Acts were passed to incorporate the "Southport Academy" and the "Platteville Academy," the objects of which were entirely educational.

The "Jefferson Institute," to be located at or near Aztalan, was also incorporated, the object of which was :

" The instruction of young men in practical and scientific agriculture, and the promotion of the general interest of education."

And another act was passed to incorporate " The Milwaukee Lyceum," the objects of which were :

"The advancement and general diffusion of useful knowledge, by discourses or lectures, by the formation of a library, and also the collection and preservation of such facts and specimens as will tend to illustrate the antiquities, the civil and natural history of Wisconsin."

An act was passed relating to judicial districts by which the counties of Crawford, Grant and Iowa were made to constitute the first district ; Walworth. Rock, Green and Dane the second, and Brown, Milwaukee and Racine the third. It provided that CHARLES DUNN should be judge of the first district, DAVID IRVIN of the second, and ANDREW G. MILLER of the third, and fixed the times for holding courts in the several counties.

It was provided by law that the regular sessions of the Legislative Assembly should commence on the first Monday of December, annually.

The appropriations made by the Legislative Assembly, for the pay of members, printing, and all incidental expenses of this session amounted to $25,614.80, and those of the December session amounted to $6,450.14, making a total of $32,064.94, being an excess of $7,064.94 over the appropriation made by Congress.

The most important work of this session was the revision of the laws, which was perfected during the recess, and submitted to the two Houses at their second meeting.

The committee for this purpose consisted of Messrs. MARTIN, MARSHALL M. STRONG, and COLLINS, of the Council, and Messrs. WHITON, STORY, and SHACKELFORD, of the House of Representatives. They were required by the resolution to make a division of the labor of revision, and the portion allotted to each branch of the committee was to be reported to the House of which they were members. The committee, during the recess of the Legislative Assembly, prepared, and at the succeeding session reported, numerous bills, which were passed by that body, and compose the principal part of the laws contained in the volume of the Revised Statutes published in 1839, and which took effect the 4th of July of that year.

Hon. EDWARD V. WHITON, the late able and upright Chief Justice of the State, was entrusted by the Legislative Assembly with the care of the printing and publication of this volume, and the preparation of marginal notes and index. The manner in which he discharged these duties was such as might have been expected, and did great credit to his comprehension of the subject, and to his carefulness and industry. The volume itself was a most valuable one to all classes, but especially to the courts and lawyers, during the ten years of Territorial life in which it was the *vade mecum* of statutory law.

Other questions, of more or less temporary interest, occupied the attention of the Legislative Assembly during its long and laborious session, which cannot be referred to in detail; and it may with truth be said that, as a whole, no session during the existence of the Territorial government ever performed more labor, or in a more satisfactory manner.

To avoid a recurrence of the question as to the beginning and end of the term of service of the delegate in Congress from Wisconsin, which was the cause of the contest between Messrs. JONES and DOTY, it was provided in an act "to provide for and regulate general elections," embodied in the new Revised Statutes, that "an election for a delegate to serve in the Twenty-sixth Congress (or so much thereof as may remain after the term of the present delegate shall have expired) shall take place on the first Monday in August, 1839, and on the same day in every second year thereafter."

Although this act did not take effect until the 4th of July, it was approved March 7th, and it was well known that an election for delegate to Congress would be held on the first Monday of August, and public sentiment commenced at once to take shape with reference to that event.

Hitherto national politics had not been an important factor in Territorial elections, but now a large number thought it wise that party lines should be drawn.

The first demonstration in this direction was a public meeting at Mineral Point on the 13th of April, which, after setting forth several reasons why the democrats of Wisconsin ought to unite for the purpose of effecting a permanent organization, adopted resolutions recommending to their democratic fellow citizens in the several counties, to appoint delegates for the purpose of meeting in general convention at Madison on the first Monday of June, "for the purpose of deliberating on measures for the general good," and calling upon all democrats in the several counties to organize, to appoint all necessary committees for that purpose, and to correspond frequently with each other to promote general harmony and concert.

A few days later a call for a "Territorial Convention" was issued signed by 36 voters of Brown county and 30 of Dane county, who

"Believing that in the selection and election of a candidate (for delegate in Congress) there should be a general understanding and unity of action on the subject, recommended that meetings be held throughout the several counties for the purpose of appointing delegates to attend a *Territorial Convention* to nominate a proper person to represent the *people* in Congress."

The call recommended the 18th day of June, at Madison, as the proper time and place for holding the "Territorial Convention."

On the 3d of June, agreeably to the request of the meeting held at Mineral Point on the 13th of April, delegates met at Madison, from Dane, Iowa, Rock and Green counties and organized a democratic convention.

A committee on credentials was appointed and reported a list of delegates elect, and a committee on resolutions having been appointed made a report recommending that the convention adjourn until the 19th of June, which was adopted.

On the 1st day of June a meeting was held at Green Bay, at which six delegates were appointed to attend the "Territorial Convention," at Madison on the 18th of June, and instructed the delegates to use every fair and honorable means to secure the nomination of JAMES DUANE DOTY.

One of these delegates was Hon. MORGAN L. MARTIN who published a card on the 4th of June, announcing his determination not to act in that capacity, in which he says:

"That the proceedings of that meeting do not accord with the sentiments of a large, and perhaps the larger portion of this community, and that its design was to secure a packed convention for particular purposes. It should, I think, be condemned by every one who has the interest of our country at heart."

The "Territorial Convention" met at Madison on the 18th of June. Twenty-six delegates were in attendance of whom six were from Brown county, five from Racine, seven from Milwaukee, five from Dane, one from Walworth, one from Rock and one from Dodge. GILBERT KNAPP was elected President and SAT. CLARK and A. A. BIRD, secretaries.

A committee appointed for that purpose reported the following resolutions which were unanimously adopted:

"*Resolved*, That this convention do nominate JAMES DUANE DOTY of Brown county as a candidate for election to the office of delegate in Congress in August next.

Resolved, That we deprecate the bitter course of his enemies in endeavoring unjustly to deprive him of his seat in Congress in violation of the express wishes of a large portion of the electors, thus delaying the business of the Territory and crippling his efforts to procure appropriations.

Resolved, That we believe that those who are hostile to him, are moved by feelings of prejudice and a greedy desire to obtain the crumbs of office.

Resolved, That we call on his friends in the east and west, north and south, to rally at the polls in August next, in such numbers as to silence forever the clamor and abuse of his enemies.

Resolved, That the ridiculous assemblage of Whigs and Administration men under the banner of Democracy which convenes at Madison on the 19th for the purpose of nominating an available candidate, is calculated to excite the disgust and contempt of every true party man.

Resolved, That we will use all fair and honorable means to secure the election of JAMES DUANE DOTY as delegate to Congress — that we will not give sleep to our eyes nor slumber to our eyelids till we can say that we have met the enemy and they are ours."

The convention also resolved:

"That H. N. WELLS of Milwaukee, THOMAS P. BURNETT of Grant county, and JOHN LAWE of Green Bay, be appointed a committee for the purpose of calling future conventions."

And further: "That any attempt to effect a party organization in the election of Delegate for this Territory at this time, will be calculated to injure the true interests of the Territory and greatly lessen the influence of such Delegate in the councils of the nation."

The *Democratic* Territorial convention which had met at Madison, on the 3d of June, and adjourned to the 19th, reassembled at that time.

WILLIAM B. SHELDON was President; WM. H. BANKS and WM. N. SEYMOUR, Secretaries.

There were thirty-five delegates in attendance, of whom 10 were from Iowa county, 7 from Dane, 7 from Brown, 7 from Milwaukee, 1 from Rock, 2 from Portage and 1 from Dodge.

An informal ballot was had for a candidate for the delegacy, the result of which was as follows:

BYRON KILBOURN..18 votes.
MORGAN L. MARTIN... 7 votes.
JOHN P. SHELDON.. 8 votes.
GEORGE W. JONES.. 2 votes.

Some of the persons who were acting as delegates were of Whig antecedents, and as a consequence, a discussion ensued, as to the political character of the convention, which resulted in the adoption of the following resolution:

"*Resolved*, That this be considered a Democratic convention, and that we are in favor of drawing the party lines."

Thereupon a formal ballot was taken, as follows:

BYRON KILBOURN..24 votes.
MORGAN L. MARTIN...10 votes.
GEORGE W. JONES.. 1 vote.

And Mr. KILBOURN was decided duly nominated.

The convention adopted this preamble and resolution—

"WHEREAS, the intentions and feelings of the members of this convention in relation to the objects of their meeting on this day, have been assailed with a wantonness and illiberality as unexampled as it was unexpected, and inasmuch as certain citizens assembled ostensibly in convention at this place yesterday, have by their proceedings endeavored to give countenance to those assaults, and to misrepresentations of a malignant character; therefore—

Resolved, That we feel it to be a duty due to our fellow citizens generally and to our own characters, to deny, as false and groundless, the assertion and intimation that we are here to carry into effect any sectional project, or to give our aid to promote the aspirations or interests of any particular individual."

Other resolutions were adopted discountenancing and rebuking attempts to create or foster sectional jealousies, and calling upon the citizens of the Territory to aid in the organization of the parties to which they have honestly attached themselves, be they democratic, whig or conservative.

The "citizen" and his consort with "bank speculators," alluded to in the following resolutions, was so well understood to be Judge Doty, that a more pointed reference to him was not thought necessary. These were the resolutions:

Resolved, That whenever a citizen by his own exertions, or through the labors of those who have placed themselves under his dictation, attempts to aggrandize himself by promoting sectional jealousies and prejudices, or by injuring by misrepresentations the reputation and public character of those who will not administer to his ambitious cravings, that individual should be divested of the public confidence and receive the open condemnation of his fellow citizens.

Resolved, That we will unite our individual exertions, and urge our fellow-citizens throughout the Territory, to unite in opposing all candidates for the suffrages of the people of Wisconsin who may have willfully, at any time, consorted with reckless bank speculators for the purpose of defrauding the public by means of fraudulent and insolvent banks."

The Democratic candidate was spoken of in resolutions as —

"In every respect well qualified to discharge the various and arduous duties devolving upon a Representative in Congress." It was said "That his general information in regard to the wants of the Territory, will enable him, if elected, to secure to each portion its proper share of the benefits of appropriations which may reasonably be expected from Congress."

A committee of five was appointed to prepare an address to the people; and a "central corresponding committee" was appointed in each county.

Immediately after his nomination Judge Doty addressed "To the Public" a communication containing an explanation and defense of his transactions in relation to the title to lots in Madison, which was first published in the *Wisconsin Enquirer,* and copied into other papers.

In reply to this communication Gov. Mason of Detroit had published a communication in the *Enquirer* of July 29th, in which he says

"That the publication of Doty is a tissue of fabrications from beginning to end, as false as the man is base."

On the 19th of July, Judge DOTY published another communication " To the Public " in the *Enquirer* in defense of his neglect to meet the new board of commissioners of public buildings and settle with them his accounts as treasurer of the old board. The essence of this defense is in the following extract:

"The appointment of the first board of commissioners having been sanctioned by Congress, it is not very probable they (the commissioners) will, without due authority, surrender the interests of the seat of government to its political enemies. When Congress approves of the law superseding the first board, I shall willingly surrender my place."

Judge DOTY made as thorough a personal canvass of the Territory as the limit of time before election would admit, and his easy, familiar intercourse with the people, prepossessing personal presence and wonderful suavity of manner, were very effective in removing prejudices which existed against him and in making and attaching to him new supporters.

As no accusations which demanded defense or explanation had been made against Mr. KILBOURN, he was not required to offer any.

Instead of this he presented to the people a very able and somewhat elaborate address of considerable length, containing a statement of his views in relation to the course which ought to be pursued by the Delegate, and which he should consider it his duty to pursue, if elected.

After adverting to the natural features of the country, and the natural means and capabilities for its improvement, embracing the Mississippi on the west, the chain of inland seas on the north and east, and Rock River in the interior, with its tributaries—the River of the Four Lakes and the Peckatonica—and also the Fox and Wisconsin Rivers; the statement continues that Congress has placed in the hands of the Territory a grant of lands, which will secure, beyond a doubt, the successful completion of the Milwaukee and Rock River canal.

The address states that public interest demands that government aid should be secured for completing the connection between the Fox and Wisconsin Rivers, and for the improvement of those streams from Green Bay to the Mississippi, and continues :—

"Suitable aid for this and the Peckatonica improvement, either in land or money, ought to be sedulously sought for by our Representative ; and I would not seek the support nor ask the confidence of my fellow-citizens, if I could not freely and frankly pledge myself to the active support of these essential measures."

The address advocates the improvement of the *rapids* of the Mississippi River, and devotes much space to the subject of harbor improvements on the western coast of Lake Michigan.

The danger of asking for too much at once is suggested, and the policy advised of—.

"Asking at the next session of Congress appropriations for two or perhaps three harbors (not to exceed the latter number). Those harbors would thenceforth come up in connection with the 'old harbor bill,' and would in no wise interfere with the introduction of a new bill at the next succeeding session for two or three new harbor appropriations, and in this manner we should probably secure to the country the object so long sought for in vain."

The three points for which the address suggests that appropriations should be first asked, are Milwaukee; Southport (or Pike River) and Sheboygan, and in that order. The next in importance are stated to be Racine and Manitowoc (or Twin Rivers). The other points along the lake being (in the present state of the country) of minor importance, will not immediately claim the attention of the government.

The address further says—

"In order to render these (harbors) of the greatest possible value to the country, simultaneous appropriations ought to be secured for the construction of roads leading from these several points (Milwaukee, Southport and Sheboygan) to the interior."

"It can be urged" (says the address) " with great force and propriety upon Congress that the government have already drawn from this Territory near $3,000,000 in the shape of land revenues, and more than a quarter of a million from the mineral region by a direct tax on their labor and industry " (rent lead) —

"We ought in justice to receive an appropriation not less than $100,000 per annum to be expended in works of primary importance in the mineral district, and a like amount to be expended along the lake border, in the interior for the next five years, and this sum would but little, if any, exceed the amount of direct taxation drawn from the mineral country and five per cent. on the land revenues drawn from the Territory up to the close of that period."

In relation to political questions the address says:

" All who know me are aware that I have been a steadfast friend and supporter of the present administration and of the Democratic party.

I am, nevertheless, free to state, that so far as regards parties within the Territory, my opinion is decidedly that the interests of this country would not be promoted by fixing now the rule of party lines as a test for support or opposition to our candidates for offices and public trusts."

"While, therefore, I assert my full adhesion to Democratic principles and republican government, I must be permitted to state distinctly that if the people shall select me as their delegate in Congress, it must be with the full understanding that I cannot consent to occupy that station as a partisan politician. My politics will be to secure ' the greatest good to the greatest number ' of the people of our Territory."

Mr. KILBOURN also visited different parts of the Territory, but his canvass was by no means so thorough as that of his principal competitor.

The aspect of the contest for the election of delegate to Congress was materially affected, and involved in increased uncertainty, by the self-assumed candidacy of THOMAS P. BURNETT, which was announced on the 29th of June, in the following card:

TO THE PEOPLE OF WISCONSIN:

Fellow-Citizens — At the request of numerous friends, I have concluded again to become a candidate to represent you as delegate in Congress. In presenting myself a second time before you to solicit your suffrages, I do so without reference to any party, either local or national, and independently of caucus nominations. If elected I shall devote my labors with zeal and fidelity to promote the best interests of the *whole* Territory, without regard to parties or sectional interests. The period of time which will elapse between this and the day of the election is too short to allow me to visit the different parts of the Territory for the purpose of making myself more generally known, and I hope this will be considered as sufficient apology for this short address.

Respectfully, your fellow-citizen,

THOMAS P. BURNETT.

Grant County, June 29, 1839.

Mr. BURNETT, however, found time to visit the people of Milwaukee and Racine counties, and made as thorough a canvass as was practicable under the circumstances.

The following is the official result:

COUNTIES.	DOTY.	KILLBOURN.	BURNETT.
Brown	274	27	22
Milwaukee	379	362	51
Racine	384	83	13
Jefferson	83	13	30
Dane	40	27	6
Walworth	159	42	9
Iowa	145	295	221
Rock	126	81	12
Manitowoc	29	1	9
Sheboygan	14	1	4
Grant	266	161	425
Crawford	148	2	30
Green	57	63	29
Fond du Lac	21	00	00
Totals	2,125	1,158	861

Under the organic law the term of office of the Governor was three years. Governor DODGE was appointed in April, 1836, and his term of service commenced on the 4th of July. Shortly before the expiration of his term he was re-appointed for another term of three years.

The public sales of the Government land in the Milwaukee land district first proclaimed to take place at Milwaukee on the 19th of November, and 3d day of December, 1838, were in accordance with the general wish of the settlers, as expressed in their petitions, postponed by the proclamation of the President of the United States, until the 18th of February, and the 4th of March, 1839.

The sales took place at the times to which they were postponed, and during the first week averaged $25,000 per day. There was no competition at the sales, nor any attempt by "greedy speculators" to interfere with the claims of the settlers, who adjusted all conflicting disputes by arbitration, and the capitalists found it more for their interest to loan money to the settlers on the security of the land purchased by them, than to invest it in the lands themselves.

Thus all apprehensions on the part of the settlers in obtaining title to their claims, proved to be groundless, notwithstanding they had not been in possession of them on the 22d of June, 1838, as required by the pre-emption act passed on that day.

Very few lands were bought on speculation, and consequently a great portion of the best lands in the district were subject to entry at $1.25 per acre by the throng of emigrants that soon after occupied the entire country.

Complaints were forwarded to Washington of the manner in which Messrs. CAMERON and MURRAY had executed their duties as commissioners, for distributing the funds provided by the treaty with the Winnebago Indians of November 1, 1837, for the payment of their debts and for distribution among their relatives of mixed blood, of the large sum set apart by the treaty for their benefit. It was represented that of $52,300 awarded to sixteen half-breeds, $31,700 was retained by BRODHEAD as their attorney, and only $20,600 paid over to the half-breeds.

A full report of the proceedings of the board of commissioners was sent to the Secretary of War (Hon. JOEL R.

POINSETT), and he annulled all that was done by the former board of commissioners, and appointed Judge FLEMING, of the State of New York, to make the necessary awards and distribution of the money set apart under the treaty.

The new commissioner met the persons having claims upon the Winnebagoes and those of mixed blood claiming a distributive share of the fund provided for their benefit, at Prairie du Chien in the month of September, 1839, and discharged his duties in a satisfactory manner.

CHAPTER XXI.

TERRITORY OF WISCONSIN IN 1840.

Unlike the preceding session, the interests of Wisconsin in the action of the first session of the twenty-sixth Congress were not affected by any contest in relation to the seat of its delegate.

But if the bills and resolutions which were introduced by the delegate, and at his instance, are contrasted with the results, it will be seen that it was barren of affirmative action.

These measures were:

First. "A bill concerning the judiciary of Wisconsin." It provided that the tenure of office of the Chief Justice and assistant judges should be limited to four years, and that it should be lawful for the President of the United States to revoke their commissions whenever it should be made to appear to him that they were unqualified, intemperate, incompetent, or neglected to perform the duties of their offices.

Second. A bill to amend the organic act; the first section of which provided, that the secretary, attorney, and marshal of the Territory should hold their offices, respectively, for the term of two years, unless sooner removed by the President, and that on the third day of July, 1840, and every two years thereafter the said offices should become vacant.

The second section provided that the term of service of the members of the Legislative Council should be limited to two years, and that of members of the House to one year, to be computed from the 1st of January, 1841. That the

Legislative Assembly should hold one session annually, commencing on 1st Monday in October. The Governor might convene the Assembly whenever, in his opinion, the public interests rendered it necessary; but its session or sessions should in no one year exceed the term of forty days, nor should any law passed by the Legislative Assembly take effect until submitted to Congress.

The third section, restricted the authority of the Legislative Assembly to levy taxes, to three mills on the dollar of assessed valuation for all purposes whatever.

The fourth section related to the right of redeeming lands sold for taxes.

The fifth section provided that the Secretary, Marshal and Attorney should reside at the seat of Government of the Territory; and the judges in the judicial districts, to which they might respectively have been assigned.

Third. A joint resolution, declaring that certain laws of the Territory, designated by their titles,

"Shall be and the same are hereby disapproved by the Congress of the United States, from the date of the passage of said laws."

There were twenty-one of these laws and resolutions of which nine laws created private corporations; two related to the corporation of the borough of Green Bay, one to the corporation of the town of Milwaukee; one legalized the proceedings of commissioners of Milwaukee county; one for the relief of the county officers of Brown county; one authorized the erection of a dam across Rock River; the other law, and the one in which the delegate was supposed to have a personal interest, was the act of March 8, 1839, which removed the commissioners of public buildings, passed December 3, 1836, and provided for the election of new commissioners.

Of the resolutions specified, two related to the transportation of the mail between Madison and Milwaukee, and three in relation to fiscal agencies.

Fourth. A bill concerning the southern boundary of Wisconsin.

Fifth. A bill to provide for the construction of harbors in Wisconsin.

Sixth. A bill to continue the duty on lead imported into the United States. This bill provided that in lieu of the duties then imposed by law on lead, the duty should be three cents per pound on lead in pigs, bars, pipes, sheets and scrap lead; three and one-half cents on leaden shot or balls and four cents on red or white lead.

Seventh. A bill to authorize the erection of a penitentiary, which granted and appropriated ten thousand dollars to the Territory for the purpose of constructing a penitentiary at such place as the Legislative Assembly should select, to be drawn and expended by that body after the location, plans, and estimates should have been made and contracts entered into for its erection, and satisfactory evidence thereof should have been exhibited to the Secretary of the Treasury.

None of these seven measures were adopted by Congress. No appropriation was made for harbors, light-houses, roads, or for any internal improvements whatever, nor for any object of direct interest to the Territory, except the annual appropriation for the salaries of the Governor, Secretary, and Judges, which was the usual amount of $9,100; for contingent expenses, $350, and for the pay and mileage of the members of the Legislative Assembly, pay of officers, printing, furniture, stationery, fuel, and other incidental expenses, the sum of $34,075.

The subject of appropriations by Congress for harbors on the western coast of Lake Michigan, and for roads into the interior, was of great importance to the people, and a harbor at Milwaukee and roads from that point were, by common consent, regarded as of the first importance. Public meetings at Milwaukee, Madison, and other points were held, pressing these measures upon the favorable consideration of Congress, and petitions for the same purpose were presented to Congress, signed very generally by the inhabitants of all parts of the Territory, and great disappointment was felt at the result.

An act was passed, approved June 1, 1840, which extended the provisions of the pre-emption act of 1838, until June 22, 1842, to all settlers on the public lands at the date of its passage.

A general law was also passed, to the effect that whenever the surveys and records in any district for which surveyors-general had been or might be appointed, should be completed, the surveyor-general thereof should be required to deliver over to the Secretary of State of the respective States, including such surveys, all the field notes, maps, records, and other papers appertaining to land titles within the same; and that the office of surveyor-general in every such district should thereafter cease and be discontinued.

The other section of this law provided that whenever the quantity of public land remaining unsold in any land district should be reduced to one hundred thousand acres, it should be the duty of the Secretary of the Treasury to discontinue the land offices of such district, and that the unsold lands in such district should be subject to sale at the most convenient of the other land districts, of which the Secretary of the Treasury shall give notice.

The third session of the second Legislative Assembly convened at Madison on the second day of December, 1839. The terms for which the members were elected had not yet expired, but there were several changes of membership caused by resignations.

In the Council ALEXANDER J. IRWIN of Brown county had resigned and CHARLES C. P. ARNDT elected to fill the vacancy; MARSHALL M. STRONG of Racine county had resigned and LORENZO JANES elected to supply the vacancy, and in Crawford county JOSEPH BRISBOIS was elected in place of GEORGE WILSON, resigned.

In the House, Messrs. LUCIUS I. BARBER, HENRY C. SKINNER and EZEKIEL CHURCHILL of Milwaukee county resigned in pursuance of pledges given at the time of their election and ADAM E. RAY, WILLIAM R. LONGSTREET and HORATIO N. WELLS were elected to fill their unexpired terms, and in Grant county JONATHAN CRAIG was elected in place of RALPH CARVER.

JAMES COLLINS of Iowa county was re-elected president of the council on the nineteenth ballot, the balloting having been protracted until the sixth day of the session.

EDWARD V. WHITON of Rock county was elected speaker on the fourth day of the session and on the fifth ballot.

In the meantime both houses had been temporarily organized by the election of WILLIAM BULLEN, president *pro tem.* of the Council, and EBENEZER CHILDS, Speaker *pro tem.* of the House.

The following table of the places of the nativity of the members of the two Houses, their residence and occupation is supposed to possess some historic interest.

TERRITORY OF WISCONSIN IN 1840.

MEMBERS OF THE COUNCIL.

Names of Members.	County of Residence.	State of Nativity.	Occupation.
Morgan L. Martin	Brown	New York	Lawyer.
Charles C. P. Arndt	Brown	Pennsylvania	Lawyer.
Joseph Brisbois	Crawford	Wisconsin	Farmer.
Ebenezer Brigham	Dane	Massachusetts	Farmer.
John H. Rountree	Grant	Kentucky	Farmer.
James R. Vineyard	Grant	Kentucky	Farmer.
James Collins	Iowa	Virginia	Mechanic.
Levi Sterling	Iowa	Kentucky	Farmer.
William A. Prentiss	Milwaukee	Massachusetts	Merchant.
Daniel Wells, Jr.	Milwaukee	Maine	Farmer.
William Bullen	Racine	New York	Merchant.
Lorenzo Janes	Racine	Vermont	Lawyer.
James Maxwell	Walworth	Vermont	Farmer.

MEMBERS OF THE HOUSE OF REPRESENTATIVES.

Name of Member.	County of Residence.	State of Nativity.	Occupation.
Ebenezer Childs	Brown	Massachusetts	Mechanic.
Charles C. Sholes	Brown	Connecticut	Printer.
Barlow Shackleford	Brown	Virginia	Lawyer.
Jacob W. Conroe	Manitowoc	Vermont	Mechanic
Ira B. Brunson	Crawford	Ohio	Lawyer.
Alexander McGreggor	Crawford	New York	Farmer.
Daniel S. Sutherland	Green	New York	Farmer.
Nelson Dewey	Grant	Connecticut	Lawyer.
Thomas Cruson	Grant	Virginia	Farmer and Miner.
Joseph H. D. Street	Grant	Kentucky	Farmer.
Jonathan Craig	Grant	Virginia	Merchant.
Russell Baldwin	Iowa	New York	Smelter.
John W. Blackstone	Iowa	New York	Farmer and Miner.
Henry M. Billings	Iowa	New York	Miner.
Thomas Jenkins	Iowa	South Carolina	Farmer and Miner.
Charles Bracken	Iowa	Pennsylvania	Farmer.
William Shew	Milwaukee	New York	Farmer.
Augustus Story	Milwaukee	Massachusetts	Farmer.
Adam E. Ray	Milwaukee	New York	Farmer.

MEMBERS OF THE HOUSE OF REPRESENTATIVES — Continued.

Name of Member.	County of Residence.	State of Nativity.	Occupation.
William R. Longstreet	Milwaukee	Pennsylvania	Farmer.
Horatio N. Wells	Milwaukee	New York	Lawyer.
Orrin R. Stevens	Racine	New Hampshire	Farmer.
Zadoc Newman	Racine	Connecticut	Farmer.
Tristram C. Hoyt	Racine	New Hampshire	Farmer.
Edward V. Whiton	Rock	Massachusetts	Lawyer.
Othni Beardsley	Walworth	New York	Farmer.

The Governor having been notified of the organization of the two Houses, delivered his message in person on the second day of the session.

The message suggested the propriety of the passage of a resolution, recommending to the electors to determine by their votes at the next election, whether they were for or against the organization of a state government.

It recommended the propriety of memorializing Congress for an appropriation of $30,000 for the erection of a penitentiary in the Territory; also for suitable appropriations for the improvement of the navigation of the Fox River of Green Bay, the Wisconsin, Rock, Peckatonica and Platte Rivers and the river of the Four Lakes; for the construction of harbors on Lake Michigan; for additional appropriations for the construction of the Territorial road from Milwaukee by way of Madison to a point opposite Dubuque, and from Racine by Janesville to Sinipee, and for a further appropriation for the survey of a railroad from the town of Milwaukee to the Mississippi river.

The message presented for the serious consideration of the Legislative Assembly the embarrassed state of the currency, and that a forced sale of property under the existing execution laws, would deprive the debtor of the means of support, and in many cases prevent the creditor from the recovery of his debt, and suggested that if a stay of twelve months could be given on execution, upon proper security, that no injustice would be done to the plaintiff; while in legislative action between debtor and creditor, a due regard should be had for the rights of both.

It recommended to the Legislative Assembly the propriety of taking such legal measures as they might deem necessary to ascertain the true state and condition of the Bank of Mineral Point.

The propriety of again memorializing Congress for an extension of the right of pre-emption to miners in possession of mineral lots, was called to the attention of the Legislative Assembly.

It also stated that the commissioners appointed to locate a portion of the University lands, not having been officially notified of their appointment, their duties remained unperformed, and it recommended the propriety of adopting such measures as would ensure an early location of these lands.

The various parts of the message were referred in each house to different committees.

The excitements and animosities developed in the election campaign of the preceding August were visible in their effects during the winter of 1839-40.

During that campaign the conduct of Judge DOTY in relation to land titles at Madison, as well as that in relation to his office as one of the commissioners of public buildings and treasurer had been assailed.

In defending himself in the newspapers against the charge in relation to the land titles he imputed to Gov. STEVENS T. MASON of Detroit, who with Judge DOTY had originally made a joint purchase from the United States of the land in question, a disposition to swindle the public and the Judge out of the property.

Gov. MASON on the eve of his departure from Detroit, on what proved to be an extended absence, characterized the publication of Judge DOTY in opprobrious terms and stated that at an early day an explicit statement of the transaction between DOTY and himself would be submitted, and in conclusion asked

" A suspension of judgment by a public who are too intelligent to be misled by the misrepresentations of a designing knave."

On his return to Detroit in November, Gov. MASON published another card in the papers in which he stated that his promised reply had been prepared, but before its publication the controversy had assumed a judicial character, and that a proper respect for the court induced him to refrain from any publication of the facts in the case. He had, however, he stated, placed on the records of the court a full reply to DOTY's allegations and he hoped at a becoming time his attorney would

"Lay it before the people of Wisconsin that they may see reflected in the person of their delegate in Congress the features of a liar, a calumniator and a swindler."

The controversy about the land titles was in some manner settled, so that it never reached a judicial determination, but in connection with the troubles growing out of the erection of public buildings at Madison, had a marked effect upon the action of the Legislative Assembly at its session of 1839–40. Indeed the investigation of matters connected with the building of the capitol occupied much of the time of that session.

Comparatively little work had been done upon the Capitol after the adjournment of the second session in March and the commencement of the third session in December. The new commissioners had no public funds, and the total expenditures on the Capitol to fit it for the reception of the Legislature was only $231, and this was advanced by the new commissioners.

The commissioners elected at the preceding session of the Legislative Assemby submitted to the Governor a report, dated July 16, which stated that the board met on the 8th of May, and elected N. C. PRENTISS acting commissioner, and J. L. THAYER, treasurer; that they had been assiduous in their efforts to settle the accounts of the former board, which had all proved unavailing, and they had been unable to obtain a meeting with them, or with the contractor, who was doing nothing in execution of his contract to complete the Capitol by the 20th of September.

Another report was made by the new commissioners to the Legislative Assembly on the 2d of December, in which the statement of their unavailing efforts at settlement is repeated, followed by a statement that in September a suit was instituted in the name of the Territory against the former commissioners for the recovery of the public moneys in their hands. The suit was still pending, and the commissioners predicted that the Territory would be debarred from the use of the money in the hands of the late treasurer and contractor until it should be recovered by the force of an execution.

A suit, they state, had also been commenced against

JAMES MORRISON, the contractor, for a breach of contract, and for the recovery of the public moneys in his hands.

This report further states that the contract of JAMES MORRISON for completing the Capitol expired on the 20th of September. That on the 23d of September the commissioners took possession of the building after having been refused by the agent of the contractor. That soon after MORRISON broke the lock of the door and took forcible possession of the building. That they commenced an action of forcible entry and detainer, obtained a writ of restitution, by means of which they regained possession of the Capitol, which they had ever since retained, and commenced fitting it up for the reception of the Legislature.

The report further states that from a continued chain of circumstances and a variety of facts

"We are unhesitatingly of the opinion that a co-partnership has existed and does still exist between the late board of commissioners and the contractor, and that the late board have been during their continuance in office acting in the double capacity of commissioners and contractor, showing a fraudulent design to speculate and trade upon the funds of the Territory without regard to its best interests."

The report gives a statement of the receipts of the old board of commissioners, and an estimate of their expenditures and shows the sum of $21,345.40, in the hands of the former commissioners and contractor, the prospect of collecting which is such (they state)

"That we believe the Capitol must remain for some time to come in its present unfinished condition and the Territory in the unfortunate situation of a party in suits that have already been commenced and are now pending."

The first report of the commissioners to the Governor was submitted by him to the Legislative Assembly with his annual message and a statement that it was due to the people

"That proper measures should be adopted to ascertain what disposition had been made of that part of the appropriation which had not been accounted for."

During the first week of the session a resolution was offered in the House instructing a committee to inquire into the expediency of bringing in a bill to provide for the removal of the seat of government, which having been amended by adding "and of converting the present public buildings into a penitentiary" it was lost by a vote of 9 to 16.

So much of the Governor's message as relates to the public buildings, having been referred in the House to a select committee consisting of Messrs. CRUSON, SHEW and JENKINS;

the reports of the commissioners of public buildings were referred to the same committee which was authorized to send for persons and papers and administer oaths, and by the subsequent action of both houses was made a joint committee, and Messrs. MAXWELL and VINEYARD of the Council added to the committee.

On the 3d of January, Mr. CRUSON, from the majority of the joint select committee, and Mr. SHOLES, in behalf of Mr. MAXWELL, from the minority, submitted reports.

The report of the majority states that

"Although more than two years had elapsed from the time the commissioners were elected, until they were superseded, and although they were supplied with funds that were more than ample for the erection of suitable buildings, yet at the time of the election of new commissioners, they had done little more than erect a shell of a capitol, which is scarcely capable of sustaining its own weight, and which, unless it is speedily secured by extensive repairs must become a heap of ruins."

The report states that the Treasurer of the Commissioners, Mr. DOTY, received from the Treasurer of the United States, the whole of both the appropriations made by Congress ($40,000.)

"That the unaccountable and unprecedented refusal of these agents of the people to submit their accounts for examination and settlement has deprived your committee of the only correct means of ascertaining with any degree of certainty, in what manner that money has been expended. A very slight examination of the results of the doings of these commissioners, is sufficient to satisfy any one, that it has not been expended where the law intended it should be, to wit : in the erection of the public buildings. Upon the most liberal estimate of the buildings which have been erected at Madison, they cannot have expended more than $19,000 in the erection of them, which would leave in their hands a balance of $21,000 unexpended." * * * * * * * *

"The former commissioners not content with having withheld a large proportion of the money which properly belonged to the Territory, denied the right of the Legislature to pass any law which should operate to remove them from office and refused to settle with the new board of commissioners, or to pay over to them any money in their hands." * * * * * * * * * * * * * *

"Your committee look upon the conduct of the commissioners as reprehensible in the highest degree, and such as should justly bring upon them the censure of all who desire to see the laws of our country upheld and enforced. That sensible men should assume the position that the same power which created their office could not destroy it, appears to your committee so perfectly preposterous that they cannot avoid the conclusion that the commissioners must have been actuated, in taking that ground, by a design to keep the people in ignorance of their doings, and indeed their whole proceedings from the time they first entered upon the discharge of their duties seems to support that conclusion, and taken in connection with other facts to which your committee will presently advert, cannot fail to convince the unbiased that there has been for a long time past a secret co-partnership existing between JAMES D. DOTY, J. F. O'NEILL and AUGUSTUS A. BIRD, the late commissioners, and JAMES MORRISON, the contractor, by which they were to share in the profits or loss resulting from MORRISON'S contract, as well also as of the mercantile and other business at Madison that was conducted ostensibly by MORRISON."

The report concludes with a complimentary reference to the manner in which the new board have discharged their duties, and says—

"The disposition they have evinced upon all occasions to promote the interest of the Territory, entitles them in the opinion of your committee, to the approbation of all."

A large amount of evidence was taken by the committee, which is submitted with their report, which appears to fully sustain its conclusions.

The committee reported a bill and recommended its passage, which was subsequently passed by both houses without material amendment.

The only important feature of this law was to provide for the annual election of *one* commissioner of public buildings instead of *three*.

The minority report of Mr. MAXWELL, the only member of the committee who dissented from the report of the majority was very brief, and presented these points:

First. That he deems—

"The report of a similar committee amply sufficient to satisfy the most sceptical that the former board of commissioners of public buildings had not acted in conformity to law in the discharge of their duties, and that any further investigation could in no way change the results of said former report."

Second. "Because on the suggestion of the former report a new board of commissioners were elected, authorized to adjust and settle the accounts of the old board, and acting under that authority have commenced suits against the old board in the name of the Territory."

Third. "That the majority of your committee assumed the powers of a grand inquest and went into the forms of an *ex parte* trial, all of which I deem a work of supererogation, and one calculated to act prematurely and improperly on the prejudices of the public while such suit or suits are pending."

And further that the investigation of the majority of your committee, of matters anterior to the report of a former committee (before alluded to) with the accompanying documents would, in the opinion of a minority of your committee be too apparent of a design for effect, rather than for any beneficial results to the best interests of this Territory.

The minority of your committee cheerfully concurs in that part of the majority report which approves of the doings of the present board of commissioners of public buildings, and also in the principles of the bill submitted for the consideration of the Legislature.

There was no subject which excited a more lively and general interest among the people of the Territory at that time, and the omission of anything material to it would be a failure to portray a faithful history of that period.

After the reports of the committee had been made, the speaker laid before the House on the 7th of January a statement of AUGUSTUS A. BIRD, which admits the co-partnership between the commissioners and the contractor in the erection of the hotel and in the mercantile concern, and gives copies of the written agreements in relation to such co-partnership, but denies that there was any agreement of co-partnership in MORRISON'S contract for completing the capitol. This statement of Mr. BIRD was afterwards sworn to and then referred to a committee with instructions to report next day as to the genuineness of the contracts and the allegations set forth in the statement.

The committee had no evidence before it, nor any authority to obtain any, and upon that statement alone, submitted on the next day the following report:

"That from the facts before us no reason appears why full faith and credit should not be attached to the statements of Mr. BIRD. That there can be no doubt as to the genuineness of the contracts and that they have no evidence before them to induce the belief, nor the slightest reason of any kind to believe that there are any other contracts in existence between the parties implicated in the report of the majority of the committee on public buildings."

Mr. CONROE of the committee, dissented from the report.

The bill reported by the committee on public buildings became a law by the approval of the Governor on the 11th of January, and on the same day, NATHANIEL C. PRENTISS was elected Commissioner of Public Buildings on a joint ballot of the two Houses.

Some weeks after the adjournment of the Legislature, a letter appeared in the newspapers from JAMES D. DOTY, to Hon. JOHN POPE, chairman of the committee on territories in H. of R.—which bore the date, Washington, February 20, 1840.

This letter professed to give a statement of all the facts in relation to the action of Congress, the Territorial Legislature, the old and the new board of commissioners in relation to the public buildings at Madison, the appropriations for their erection and the conduct of the commissioners in their expenditure.

The letter contained many statements, which were fully supported by the facts, and many which were not.

It presents the idea that the action of Congress of June

18, 1838, making a second appropriation for completing the capitol, was

"An affirmance of the proceedings of the Legislature and of the Commissioners," and "that the act to establish the seat of government at Madison, was not subject to be repealed by the Territorial Legislature, without the assent of Congress."

The object of this letter appeared to be to obtain the disapproval by Congress of the act of March 9, 1839 (by virtue of which the old commissioners were removed and new ones appointed); which, the letter states, was now first submitted to Congress ; and of all laws on this subject passed subseqent thereto.

Messrs. M. M. STRONG and F. J. DUNN, attorneys for the Territory, in the suits which were pending against the old board of commissioners, the treasurer and his sureties, and the contractor, believing, as they stated,

"That Mr. DOTY was prompted in the effort which he was making to procure the disapproval of the act of March 9, 1839, by a desire to affect the decision of those suits, considered it their duty to make a brief statement of facts in relation to the matters adverted to in Mr. DOTY's letter,"

and addressed a letter to Mr. POPE, chairman of the committee, dated March 29, 1840.

The letter corrected the misrepresentations which, they stated, were contained in DOTY's letter, and set forth other facts which were not stated in it, and concluded with the expression of the confident hope —

"That Congress would take no action on the subject, which would tend to confer authority upon men whom the representatives of the people of Wisconsin have rejected, and to divert it from those whom the same representatives have selected as agents, in whom they could repose confidence, and more especially when such action would affect the rights of the Territory in relation to matters which were then the subject of judicial investigation."

The act of March 9, 1839, removed the old commissioners and treasurer, and on the 4th of April, 1840, Mr. DOTY performed the idle ceremony of addressing a communication to the Legislative Assembly, offering his resignation of the office of commissioner of public buildings and treasurer of the board — offices from which he had been removed nearly thirteen months previously, and which during that time he had not held.

Mr. DOTY's only defense of his conduct, and that of his co-commissioners and the contractor, was based upon the assumption that the acts of the Legislative Assembly did not become effective until submitted to Congress, and that the act of March 9, 1839, not having been submitted to Congress before the new commissioners were elected, that the old ones were not superseded.

This assumption was judicially determined by the Chief Justice to be erroneous, who held that the sixth section of the organic act, having declared :

"That the legislative power of the Territory shall extend to all rightful subjects of legislation," and that "all the *laws* of the Governor and Legislative Assembly shall be submitted to, and if disapproved by the Congress of the United States, shall be null and of no effect;"

All *laws*, when enacted by the Governor and Legislative Assembly, became effective, subject to being annulled and rendered of no effect by the subsequent disapproval of Congress, when they should be submitted to that body.

The citizens of Madison felt perhaps a deeper interest than any others in the question raised by Judge DOTY, and J. A. NOONAN and JOHN CATLIN of that place, addressed letters to H. N. WELLS, Attorney General, MOSES M. STRONG, United States Attorney, EDWARD V. WHITON, late Chief Justice, HANS CROCKER and MORGAN L. MARTIN, eminent and able lawyers, asking their opinions on the question, each of whom wrote very able opinions, some of which, especially that of Judge WHITON, were entirely exhaustive of the subject, and all of which fully sustained the authoritative opinion of Chief Justice DUNN.

The matter of the southern boundary and the formation of a State Government were subjects which did not fail to attract much of the attention of this session of the Legislative Assembly.

So much of the Governor's message as related to these subjects was referred in each house. In the Council to the committee on Territorial affairs, consisting of Messrs. BRIGHAM, VINEYARD and WELLS, and in the House to a select committee consisting of one from each election district, composed of Messrs. SHACKELFORD, LONGSTREET, HOYT, BEARDSLEY, SUTHERLAND, JENKINS, STREET and BRUNSON. Various propositions were submitted, entertained, reported upon and considered in each house, and all resulted in adopting the following joint resolutions—

"WHEREAS, the southern boundary of this Territory and of the State to be formed therein, is fixed and established by the ordinance of July 13, 1787, on a line running due west from the southerly bend or extreme of Lake Michigan to the Mississippi River.

AND WHEREAS, although said ordinance is declared to be forever unalterable, unless by common consent, a large and valuable tract of country is now held by the State of Illinois, contrary to the manifest right and consent of the people of this Territory.

AND WHEREAS, it is inexpedient for the people of this Territory to form a constitution and State Government, or to ask admission in the Union as an independent State, until the southern boundary to which they are so justly entitled by said ordinance shall be fully recognized by the parties to the original compact; therefore—

"*Resolved*, That the inhabitants of this Territory qualified to vote for delegate in Congress, be requested at the next general election, to be held on the fourth Monday of September next, to vote for or against the formation of a state government, including all that district of country north of a line running due west from the most southerly bend or extreme of Lake Michigan to the Mississippi River, over which the State of Illinois exercises jurisdiction, and if a majority of such electors vote in favor of said measure, the Governor is hereby authorized to issue his proclamation requesting the electors aforesaid to meet in their respective precincts on such a day as he may appoint and choose delegates from their respective districts equal to the number of representatives in both branches of the Legislative Assembly, to assemble at the capitol in Madison on the third Monday of November *for the purpose of deliberating upon and adopting such lawful and constitutional measures as may seem to be necessary and proper for the early adjustment of the southern boundary, and admission into the Union of the State of Wisconsin on an equal footing with the original states in all respects whatever.*

Resolved further, That the inhabitants of the district of country now claimed by Illinois lying north of the line running due west from the southern extreme of Lake Michigan to the Mississippi River be, and are hereby invited to furnish the executive of this Territory as early as may be convenient, and in such manner as they may deem proper, an expression of their sentiments in relation to the formation of a state government as contemplated by the foregoing resolution, and in the event of an election being ordered by the proclamation of the Governor, for the election of delegates to a convention as above provided for, to choose delegates to the convention aforesaid, proportionate to the ratio of representation in the Legislative Assembly of this Territory, to act on the business of said convention on an equal footing with the other delegates."

The resolutions provided for the manner of conducting the elections and determining the results.

By a resolution subsequently adopted at the August session, it was declared that the words in the first resolution which are *italicised*, should—

"Not be so construed as to authorize the said convention to adopt a State Constitution and form of government, or to declare themselves an independent State."

The passage of these resolutions aroused considerable feeling among those on the "disputed territory," who were in favor of becoming a part of the State of Wisconsin, and public meetings to give expression to this feeling were held at Galena, Belvidere, and Rockford, which culminated in a general convention of delegates from Jo Davies, Stephenson, Winnebago, Boone, McHenry, Ogle, Carroll, Whitesides, and Rock Island counties, held at Rockford on the 6th of July.

This convention adopted resolutions declaring the right of Wisconsin to the "disputed territory," and recommended to the citizens to elect delegates to the convention to form a State government should one be held.

But the resolutions of the Wisconsin Legislature did not elicit the exhibition of much feeling within the Territory, and that feeling was mostly one of opposition to the objects of the resolutions.

At a public meeting held at Green Bay on the 24th of April, it was declared that they had seen the resolutions with concern and regret, and that the members of the Legislature be requested to vote to rescind them.

There was but a very light vote upon the question submitted by the resolutions themselves, and that vote was almost unanimously "against State Government."

This vote, it is believed, was more the result of an apprehension that a majority vote "for State Government" would lead to the premature formation of a State government, than of any objection to embracing the "disputed territory" within the boundaries, when the proper time for its formation should have arrived.

In the House of Representatives at the session of 1839-40, so much of the Governor's message as relates to banks was referred to the committee on corporations, which consisted of Messrs. STREET, SHEW, SHOLES, BLACKSTONE and JENKINS.

The committee reported that the Bank of Mineral Point was—

"The only legal banking institution now in the Territory; and your committee are of opinion from the best information in their possession, that it is in a sound and solvent condition."

A bill for the election of a bank commissioner was recommended, but is met with no favor.

The conduct of the Wisconsin Marine and Fire Insurance Company in conducting banking business in alleged violation of the restrictions of its charter, was discussed, but no definite action taken.

Notwithstanding the recommendation of the message of the Governor, no law was passed granting any stay upon executions, or to relieve debtors from forced sales upon execution.

The expenditure of the appropriations by Congress for the construction of roads in Wisconsin made previous to 1840, was placed in charge of Captain THOS. J. CRAM, of the

United States Engineer Corps. In his report to the Chief of the Bureau, that officer recommended the following additional appropriations:

1. From Green Bay *via* Milwaukee and Racine to the State line $33,381.00
2. For the completion of the road from Sauk Harbor to Dekorre 12,700.00
3. From Fond du Lac *via* Fox Lake to Wisconsin River, nothing, the first appropriation being sufficient.
4. From Milwaukee *via* Madison to a point on the Mississippi River, opposite Dubuque 15,000.00
5. From Racine *via* Janesville to Sinnipee 22,620.00
6. From Fort Howard to Fort Crawford 35,267.00
7. For the completion of the *right kind* of a survey of a railroad from Lake Michigan to the Mississippi River 11,250.00

Total additional appropriations recommended $130,218.00

None of these appropriations, however, nor any other for improvements in Wisconsin, were made by Congress.

An act was passed prescribing the manner in which Territorial roads should be laid out, surveyed and recorded. It also prescribed that

"No part of the expense of laying out and establishing any Territorial road, or of the damages sustained by any person or persons in consequence of laying out any Territorial road, shall be paid out of the Territorial or County Treasury."

The effect of this provision was that all such expenses and damages had to be provided for by individual personal contributions, and the only advantage of an act to provide for locating a Territorial road, was that if laid out according to the requirements of the law, a legal highway could be established.

Notwithstanding this provision, acts were passed for laying out twenty-eight Territorial roads in the various portions of the Territory, at the winter session, and for two others at the August session.

The peaceable removal west of the Mississippi of the Winnebago Indians, whose presence had given the frontier setlers so much annoyance, was effected in the early part of the year 1840, and was a subject of congratulation in the message of the Governor at the August special session. The message said:

"The removal of the Winnebagoes will enable our enterprizing citizens to extend their settlements to a desirable and interesting country north of the Wisconsin River."

A public sale of land was held at Green Bay on the 6th of April, 1840, at which all that part of Winnebago county between Winnebago Lake and Fox and Wolf Rivers was offered for sale, embracing the towns of Winchester, Clayton, Vineland, and that part of the towns of Wolf River and Winneconne east of those rivers, and the cities and towns of Menasha and Neenah, and that part of Oshkosh north of Fox River.

On the 13th of April a public sale was held at Milwaukee of that part of the towns of Beloit, Rock, Janesville, Fulton and Milton in the county of Rock which lie east of Rock River, embracing the cities of Beloit and Janesville and the village of Milton.

An act was passed January 11, 1840, which authorized the Governor to contract with the Marshal of the Territory, at a sum not exceeding six hundred dollars, to furnish to the Governor on or before the 1st day of August, a transcript of the census of the Territory taken by him in pursuance of the act of Congress authorizing the taking of the sixth census.

The act also provided that there should be an extra session of the Legislative Assembly on the first Monday of August.

The two houses adjourned on the 13th of January and the extra session — the fourth of the second Legislative Assembly — convened on the third day of August.

But one change in the composition of the Legislature occurred during the recess. JOSEPH BRISBOIS, member of the Council from Crawford county, had resigned and CHARLES J. LEARNED was elected as his successor and took his seat on the first day of the session.

MORGAN L. MARTIN was elected President *pro tem.*, and on the second day WILLIAM A. PRENTISS, of Milwaukee, was, on the first ballot, elected permanent President.

In the House of Representatives EDWARD V. WHITON was elected Speaker *pro tem.*, and on the second day a ballot was had for Speaker for the session, on which NELSON DEWEY received 9 votes, CHARLES C. SHOLES 7, BARLOW SHACKELFORD 4, and there were 3 scattering, when Messrs. SHOLES and SHACKELFORD declined being candidates, and NELSON DEWEY received 21 of the 23 votes cast, and was elected on the second ballot.

The message of the Governor was brief, and confined mainly to the special object of the session — the apportion-

TERRITORY OF WISCONSIN IN 1840. 317

ment — but tendered his co-operation in such acts of legislation as "have for their object the good of our constituents." Attention was invited by the message to the failure on the part of the contractor in printing the laws of the late session, which was criticised. The propriety of investigating the condition of the Bank of Mineral Point was recommended, and the advisability of appointing by law a bank commissioner was suggested.

The following is the official census:

Brown county	2,107
Calumet county	270
Crawford county	1,508
Dane county	315
Dodge county	67
Fond du Lac county	139
Green county	933
Grant county	3,923
Iowa county	3,977
Jefferson county	914
Manitowoc county	235
Marquette county	18
Milwaukee county	5,001
Portage county	1,623
Racine county	3,475
Rock county	1,701
Sauk county	102
Sheboygan county	133
St. Croix county	618
Walworth county	2,610
Washington county	343
Winnebago county	135
Total	30,747

Under the organic act members of the Council had been elected for four years, and could not be affected by any new apportionment, as one half of the term for which they were elected was unexpired. Members of the House of Representatives having been elected for only two years, about half of which had expired, an entire new apportionment was not practicable.

The plan of apportionment of the members of the House of Representatives was to distribute them among the existing districts for members of the council.

By this plan the following apportionment was made:

The district composed of the county of Brown and the counties thereto attached, had three members.

The district composed of the counties of Milwaukee and Washington, had five members.

Racine county had three members

The district composed of Walworth and Rock counties had four members.

The district composed of the counties of Dane, Dodge, Green, Jefferson and Sauk, had two members.

Iowa county had four members.

Grant county had three members.

And the district composed of Crawford and St. Croix counties, had two members.

Three districts lost one member each. These were Brown and the counties attached, Iowa and Grant. The districts which gained were Rock and Walworth, two members; Dane, Dodge, Green, Jefferson and Sauk, one member. The number of representatives in the other districts was unchanged.

At the winter session of 1840, the following towns were created or names changed. Franklin, Menomonee, Wauwatoosa, Pewaukee (spelled in the published act by mistake, Peraukee) and Granville, in Milwaukee county, were established; Prairie Village changed to Prairieville, and Mentor changed to New Berlin. The town of Delavan, in Walworth county, was divided and Darien established. Pleasant Prairie, in Racine county, was divided and Bristol established, and in Jefferson county the town of Aztalan was created out of the towns of Jefferson and Watertown.

The act of March 9, 1839, incorporating the town of Green Bay, was conditionally repealed, subject to a vote of the electors of the town.

At the August session the town of Oak Creek, in Milwaukee county, was organized out of the town of Lake, and the town of Whitewater was created out of the town of Elkhorn, in Walworth county.

By an act approved January 6, 1840, Calumet county was organized for the purpose of county government, and that part of the county lying south of the Indian Reservation, comprised in town 17, of ranges 18 and 19, was detached from Calumet county and attached to Fond du Lac county, and the remainder of Calumet county remained attached to Brown county for judicial purposes.

By the same act the county of Winnebago was laid off, and NATHANIEL PERRY, ROBERT GRIGNON and MORGAN L.

MARTIN were appointed commissioners, with authority to locate the county seat and enter for the use of the county the quarter section of land upon which the county seat might be located and to borrow money for that purpose.

On the 9th of January, 1840, the county of St. Croix was laid off by natural boundaries and fully organized for all purposes.

At the same session the county of Sauk was laid off and attached to Dane county for county and judicial purposes.

The county of Dodge at this session was organized for county purposes, and attached to Jefferson county for judicial purposes.

By an act approved August 13, 1840, the county of Washington was organized for county purposes, and continued attached to Milwaukee county for judicial purposes.

So much of any act or acts as establishes or locates the county seat were repealed, and the question of the selection of the county seat was submitted to a vote of the inhabitants.

The same act, which the title declared was "for other purposes," repealed the act of the previous session organizing Calumet county, and remanded it back to its former union with Brown county for all purposes.

The "Bridge War" in Milwaukee first assumed practical shape by the enactment at the winter session, 1840, of a law which authorized and required the county commissioners of Milwaukee county to locate and construct a drawbridge across the Milwaukee River from the foot of Chestnut street to the foot of Division street.

At the same session HOEL S. WRIGHT was authorized to erect a toll bridge across Fox River at the mouth of Plum Creek, where "Wrightstown" now is.

A special act passed at that session authorized WM. H. BRUCE and others to build and maintain a dam across the Manitowoc River at the point where the village of Manitowoc Rapids has since grown up.

An act to incorporate the Michigan and Rock River Railroad Company was passed at that session which authorized the corporation to construct a railroad

"From the Rock River, at a point at or near where the line of the State of Illinois crosses the same (being where Beloit now is) to such point near Lake Michigan in the township of Southport (now Kenosha) as shall be determined on by a majority of the board of directors."

"The Wisconsin Lead Mining, Smelting and Manufacturing Company" was incorporated with a capital of one million dollars and the operations of the company in mining and smelting were to be confined to the counties of Grant and Iowa.

The time for holding general elections was at this session changed from the first Monday in August to the fourth Monday of September.

A very anomalous divorce act was passed at this session, which recited that

"JOSEPH R. BROWN (who was the next year elected a member of the House of Representatives from St. Croix county) and MARGARET BROWN, a half-breed Chippewa woman, were legally married and were mutually desirous of dissolving the marriage contract in consequence of the danger they both incur of the destruction of their lives and property by continuing to live together, at the place where they have been accustomed to and now reside, on account of the hostile incursions of the Sioux Indians."

That it should be lawful for them by a written article of separation, under their hands and seals, to dissolve the marriage contract existing between them, provided that the articles of separation should contain a provision for her of one third of all his property.

A joint resolution was adopted making further provision for the location of a portion, not exceeding two thirds, of all the lands granted by Congress in 1838, for the use and support of a university.

The appropriations made by the Legislative Assembly, for the pay and mileage of members, printing, and all incidental expenses of the two sessions held in 1840, amounted to a total sum of $27,892.65. The excess of the expenses of the preceding year over the appropriation by Congress was $7,064.94, which two sums made $34,957.59. The appropriation by Congress for 1840 was $34,075, which still left a small sum of $882.59, while the appropriations of the Legislative Assembly for the two years of 1839 and 1840 exceeded the amounts appropriated by Congress during those two years for their liquidation.

An important act was passed at the winter session, which prescribed that the term of all officers of the Territory, whose terms were not limited by law (except militia officers), should be two years, and should terminate on the first day of January, 1842.

About the first of October JOHN P. SHELDON was removed from the office of Register of the Land Office, at Mineral Point, and JOHN V. INGERSOLL appointed as his successor.

Maj. SHELDON, previous to his appointment to this office by Gen. JACKSON, had been an editor of a democratic paper at Detroit. He was a zealous and effective partisan, with warm and devoted friends, and brought upon himself the serious and determined opposition of many opponents, which finally culminated in his removal.

A large public meeting was held at Mineral Point, in which he was highly eulogized, and surprise and regret at his removal expressed.

The presidential election of 1840 will long be remembered by those who were on the stage of action at that day, and will stand recorded in history as having been attended by a more exciting campaign than any which ever preceded it. Mr. VAN BUREN was the candidate of the democratic party for re-election, and Gen. WILLIAM HENRY HARRISON was the whig candidate, with JOHN TYLER as the candidate for Vice-President.

The Whig candidates were euphoniously designated in the political songs as "Tippecanoe and Tyler too." The campaign as the "Log-cabin," "Hard Cider," "Coon skin," etc., campaign, arising from the free use made in public processions and meetings of these supposed emblems of General HARRISON'S early life.

As Wisconsin had no vote in the presidential election, the excitement in the Territory was only sympathetic and secondary, and was exhibited in a partial and fragmentary organization of the democractic party for the nomination of candidates for the election held in September, for members of the House of Representatives. Such organizations were formed in Brown and Iowa counties, but were not perfect, personal considerations entering largely into the elections, while the canvass in other counties was conducted entirely upon the personal characteristics of the candidates.

The excitement in the Territory was largely augmented by the publication of a paper, signed by the Delegate in Congress, bearing date New York, September 7, 1840, under the title of "The voice of an injured Territory." It was gotten up in a style similar to the statement of grievances of the American colonies, at the conduct of the King of Great

Britain, contained in the Declaration of Independence. It was extensively circulated throughout the United States, as a campaign document, and undoubtedly contributed considerably to the election of the Whig candidates.

Its great length forbids its entire reproduction here, and only a few extracts can be given.

It commenced as follows:

To the People of the United States—

"In the administration of the Territorial Government of Wiskonsin the Executive of the United States has not consulted or regarded the feelings, interests or wishes of the people. Being entitled to no vote in the election of President, they are compelled to appeal to the citizens of the states. That appeal as their delegate and representative I now make.

"He has refused to cause harbors and light houses to be constructed on the shore of Lake Michigan, for the protection of commerce and of the lives and property of our citizens.

"He has taken the sum of $34,000, which was appropriated specifically for the erection of *light houses*, and applied it towards the construction of the SUB-TREASURY BUILDING in Washington.

"He has suddenly abandoned the system of internal improvement within the Territory, leaving the roads, which have been commenced, in an unfinished state, and the navigation of the rivers, which are the great thoroughfares throughout the country, unimproved.

"He has thus and by other measures prevented the sale and settlement of the public lands within the Territory, by which he has diminished the revenues of the government and deprived Wiskonsin of an accession to her population, which would have entitled her to admission into the Union.

"He has endangered the peace of the frontier by compelling by a military force the Winnebago Indians to remove from the country, and before the Government had fulfilled on its own part, the stipulations of the treaties with that tribe.

"He has appointed men to the offices of the Territory who were not citizens of the Territory and who were unqualified and incompetent, and has refused to remove them after their unfitness was proved."

The remainder of this long campaign document is taken up with specific allegations of neglect, disregard and abuse of the interests of the Territory in the appointment of, and the neglect or refusal to remove the Governor, Judges, District Attorney, Surveyor General and Register of the Land Office at Mineral Point; and with a long array of reasons, why these officers ought not to have been appointed, or why, having been appointed, they ought to have been removed.

It closes as follows:—

"These facts, which were duly laid before the President, are now submitted to you, that you may determine whether he faithfully performed his duty.

"For this neglect and disregard of the interests of the Territory and of the General Government, and for these gross acts of mal-administration, the Executive alone is responsible. Disfranchised as we are, we cannot forget that we are still American freemen. When our petitions have been spurned by the rulers you have set over us, because we have no voice in the party politics of the country — when those rulers have filled those offices with political mendicants from other states, having no knowledge of or interests in common with us, it is our right to address ourselves to you, the only source of power, and ask a redress of grievance.

"New York, September 7, 1840. J. D. DOTY."

In states remote from Wisconsin this "Voice of an Injured Territory," was well calculated to augment the opposition to Mr. VAN BUREN, which had already attained a magnitude which indicated the defeat which in less than two months proved disastrously overwhelming.

But in Wisconsin the absurdity of charging upon the executive, responsibility for the non-construction of harbors and light-houses, and of abandoning a system of internal improvements, and thus (and by other measures not stated) depriving " Wiskonsin of an accession to her population," when it was well-known that the responsibility rested with Congress alone, was fully met and exposed.

There too, it was well-known that the removal of the Winnebago Indians, so far from endangering "the peace of the frontier" was the most effective means of securing it.

The covert attack upon the Governor, Judges, Attorney, Surveyor-General and Register of the Land Office, under the pretense of assailing the President of the United States, produced no damaging effect upon those officers in the Territory where they were well-known. The Governor was the next year elected delegate. Again appointed Governor in 1844 — elected the first United States Senator and subsequently re-elected. The Surveyor-General (GEO. W. JONES) was for a long time United States Senator from Iowa, and represented the United States, as its Minister, at a foreign court. The Judges and Attorney often received marked and convincing evidence of the confidence which the people reposed in them, and there is no doubt if the voters of Wisconsin could then have voted for President, that the vote of Mr. VAN BUREN would have been increased rather than diminished by these charges of the delegate.

CHAPTER XXII.

TERRITORY OF WISCONSIN IN 1841.

So long as its political dependence upon the United States continued, the interest of the inhabitants of the Territory in the proceedings of Congress was unabated.

The second session of the 26th Congress, commencing on the 7th of December, 1840, and ending on the 3d of March, 1841, was barren of any results of interest to the Territory, with the exception of the ordinary appropriations for the salaries of the Governor, judges and secretary, and for the expenses of the Legislative Assembly.

The appropriations for salaries ($9,100) and contingent expenses ($350) were the same as in former years, while the appropriation for the pay and mileage of members and other expenses of the Legislative Assembly, was reduced from the sum $34,075, appropriated at the previous session, to the unprecedentedly small sum of $20,000.

This reduction was made in the face of the fact that the Legislative Assembly had, during this same session of Congress, been compelled to anticipate the appropriation by a resort to certificates of indebtedness, in payment of its expenses.

No appropriations were made for any of the numerous harbors on the lake shore, for territorial roads, or internal improvements of any description nor for any of the numerous objects for which they were so greatly needed.

Judge DOTY was the Territorial Delegate during this session.

The first session of the third Legislative Assembly convened at Madison on the 7th day of December, 1840.

The members of the Council elected in 1838 to the second Legislative Assembly were, under the provisions of the organic act, elected for four years, and continued, with two exceptions, to hold their offices during the terms of both the second and third Assemblies.

The exceptions were WILLIAM A. PRENTISS and DANIEL WELLS, Jr., from the district of Milwaukee and Washington who had resigned, in place of whom JONATHAN E. ARNOLD and DON A. J. UPHAM were elected.

In the House of Representatives, however, there was almost an entire change in the *personnel* of its members, elected under the new apportionment made at the previous August session, but three of the members of the previous House having been elected to this. These were, Messrs. DEWEY of Grant, RAY of Milwaukee, and WHITON of Rock.

The new House of Representatives consisted of the following members:

Brown, Fond du Lac, Manitowoc, Portage, and Sheboygan—WILLIAM H. BRUCE (whose seat was successfully contested by ALBERT G. ELLIS), MASON C. DARLING, and DAVID GIDDINGS.

Crawford and St. Croix—JOSEPH R. BROWN and ALFRED BRUNSON.

Dane, Dodge, Green, Jefferson, and Sauk—LUCIUS I. BARBER and JAMES SUTHERLAND.

Grant—DANIEL R. BURT, NELSON DEWEY, and NEELEY GRAY.

Iowa—FRANCIS J. DUNN (who resigned on the last day but one of the session), EPHRAIM F. OGDEN, DAVID NEWLAND, and DANIEL M. PARKINSON.

Milwaukee and Washington — JOSEPH BOND, JACOB BRAZELTON, ADAM E. RAY, JOHN S. ROCKWELL, and WILLIAM F. SHEPHARD.

Racine — GEORGE BATCHELDER, REUBEN H. DEMING, and THOMAS E. PARMELEE.

Rock and Walworth; JOHN HACKETT, HUGH LONG, JESSE C. MILLS and EDWARD V. WHITON.

In the Council, Hon. JAMES MAXWELL of Walworth county was elected President on the third ballot, and GEORGE BEATTY of Iowa county, was unanimously re-elected Secretary.

In the House of Representatives, Hon. DAVID NEWLAND of Iowa county was on the first ballot elected Speaker and JOHN CATLIN of Dane county was unanimously re-elected Clerk.

On the second day of the session Governor DODGE delivered his annual message to the two houses jointly assembled in the Representatives' hall.

The Governor renewed the recommendation of his message of 1838, of memorializing Congress to amend the organic law so that the members of the Council be elected every second year, and members of the House annually, and also recommended that Congress be asked so to amend the organic law as to permit the qualified electors in each county, to elect all their county officers, civil and military, which, as provided by that law, were appointable by the Governor.

The attention of the Legislative Assembly was again called to the dangers threatened by the course pursued in the management of its affairs by the Bank of Mineral Point, especially in its issue of what were denominated *post-notes*, payable at a future day.

He said :

"This is a violation of all judicious banking; it is certainly a dangerous power to be exercised by any banking institution. The time of redeeming her notes might be extended to twelve or eighteen months as well as for three or four months. If a bank is permitted to leave her legitimate business and enter the field of speculation by dealing in the staple commodity of the country, her capital will always enable her to prostrate individual enterprise, to the great injury of the people. Banks are created for the benefit of the people and should be confined to the legitimate purposes for which they were chartered."

The Governor recommended the enactment of so much of the New York Safety Fund law as provided for the appointment of bank-commissioners, with the power of examination and the other powers conferred by that law, the charter of the bank containing a provision that it should be subject so far to be amended as to make it conform to such a safety fund system.

The opinion was expressed that corporations of a private nature ought not to be increased.

It was recommended that Congress be asked to extend the right of pre-emption to the settlers on the even-numbered sections of land reserved by Congress in the act making appropriations for the Milwaukee and Rock River canal.

Also to grant the miners pre-emption rights to their mineral lots, where they were held by discovery or purchase, under permission of the Superintendent of the United States lead mines, as well as to extend the right of pre-emption to actual settlers who are located on reservations made by the superintendent for smelting purposes, and also to settlers on lands located for the half-breed Winnebagoes under the treaty of 1829.

The message stated that in conformity with a resolution

of the Legislative Assembly the Governor had appointed three commissioners to make location of the University lands. That the commissioner for the Green Bay district had selected from that district 10,248 acres, which had been approved by the Treasury Department and reserved from sale. That no reports had been received from the other two commissioners appointed in the Milwaukee and Wisconsin districts.

The appointment of a Territorial geologist was recommended.

The justice and propriety of asking Congress for appropriations for the improvement of the navigation of Rock River and of the Fox and Wisconsin rivers, and uniting the waters of those rivers by a short canal at the Portage, as well as for the improvement of the Pecatonica and Platte rivers, was repeated in this message.

Memorials asking appropriations from Congress for the construction of harbors on the shores of Lake Michigan, although they had been annually forwarded since the organization of the Territorial government, were again recommended.

The message stated that the Indians on our extended frontier appeared peaceably disposed. That the Winnebagoes were removed to the west bank of the Mississippi in the preceding June, but that a great unwillingness to occupy their country, generally called the neutral country, was discovered; that they appeared to entertain a dread from attacks of the Sac and Fox Indians, and it would require a strong, mounted force to keep them from returning to the country east of the Mississippi and north of the Wisconsin Rivers.

The report of the Adjutant General in relation to the state of the militia was referred to in the message as were some other minor subjects.

One of the most interesting questions which occupied the attention of the Legislative Assembly at this session arose in the contested election case of ALBERT G. ELLIS against WILLIAM H. BRUCE. It was the question whether the Brothertown Indians were so far citizens of the United States as to be entitled to the right of suffrage.

The certificate of election had been given in due form to Mr. BRUCE, upon which he was sworn in with other members and took his seat.

On the third day of the session the petition and remonstrance of ALBERT G. ELLIS was presented contesting the seat of Mr. BRUCE. On the next day an affidavit of Mr. BRUCE concerning his right to a seat was presented. The petition and remonstrance of Mr. ELLIS and affidavit of Mr. BRUCE were then referred to a select committee of five members (afterwards increased to seven) with powers to send for persons and papers, and instructions to report to the House as soon as practicable the facts in the case.

HORATIO N. WELLS, Attorney General of the Territory, was retained as counsel for Mr. BRUCE, and MOSES M. STRONG, United States District Attorney, as counsel for Mr. ELLIS.

The following resolution was reported by the committee and adopted.

Resolved, That HORATIO N. WELLS and MOSES M. STRONG be appointed commissioners to take testimony relative to the contested election between ALBERT G. ELLIS and WILLIAM H. BRUCE, and that they each be authorized to administer oaths and compel the attendance of witnesses, and that the said WELLS and STRONG shall each be allowed such per diem compensation and mileage as is allowed to the members of this House, and such sum for their necessary expenses as the Legislative Assembly may allow.

The commissioners immediately entered upon the work imposed upon them by this resolution. They visited the counties of Sheboygan, Manitowoc, Brown,.Calumet, Fond du Lac and Portage and took testimony in each of these counties. They were absent on this business from the 16th December until the 9th of January, and on the 11th of January submitted to the House the testimony taken by them, consisting of over seventy depositions and copies of election returns, which was referred to the select committee.

On the 26th of January the committee made its report, from which it appeared that by the official canvass there were three more votes canvassed for Mr. BRUCE than for Mr. ELLIS.

That there were illegal votes cast in several precints, of which seventeen were cast for Mr. BRUCE and thirteen for Mr. ELLIS, deducting which, left a majority of one in favor of Mr. ELLIS, independent of the votes cast in the Pinery (Portage county), and by the Brothertown Indians.

In the Pinery three votes were given to Mr. ELLIS and seventeen to Mr. BRUCE, all of which, it was claimed by Mr. ELLIS, should be rejected. At Manchester thirty-four votes were given for Mr. ELLIS by Brothertown Indians, which it was claimed by Mr. BRUCE should be rejected.

In regard to the Pinery precint, in Portage county, the committee reported that the election was held at a place not authorized by law, where the polls were opened after twelve o'clock (noon), that it did not appear that either the judges or clerks were sworn; that one of the judges did not possess the qualifications of a voter in Portage county, and that it did not appear that any poll books were ever made or returned.

In regard to the Brothertown Indians, the committee reported:

"It appears from an act of Congress (passed March 3, 1839), that the Brothertown Indians, upon certain conditions set forth in the act, were made citizens of the United States."

The committee expressed no opinions of the legality of these votes, but reported as a fact that the Brothertown Indians had long since adopted and did then pursue the habits of civilized life.

The report of the committee was taken up on the 27th of January, when by a vote of the House, both parties were to be heard by counsel, and the counsel of the party in relation to whom the pending question affirmed a favorable proposition, was to have the opening and close.

The first question considered by the House and argued by counsel related to the votes in the Pinery precinct. It was discussed a large part of two days and on the 28th a resolution was adopted, by a vote of twenty-three to two, that those votes, for the reasons stated by the committee were

"Not an expression of the wishes of the legal voters of that precinct and therefore ought not to be received or allowed."

Mr. BRUCE, the contestee, was excused from voting and all the other members except Messrs. BRUNSON and GIDDINGS voted in favor of the resolution.

The important question remained of the right of the Brothertown Indians to vote. This question was presented by the following resolution:

"*Resolved*, That the votes of the Brothertown Indians given at Manchester precinct ought to be received and allowed, excepting those which have been rejected by the committee."

This resolution was debated at great length by counsel and by members, and on the second day of the debate (29th) a vote was reached when the resolution was adopted by a vote of fourteen to ten.

Ayes: Messrs. BATCHELDER, BRAZELTON, DARLING, DEM-
ING, DUNN, HACKETT, LONG, OGDEN, PARKINSON, PARMELEE,
RAY, ROCKWELL, SHEPARD, and NEWLAND, speaker.

Noes: BARBER, BOND, BROWN, BRUNSON, BURT, DEWEY,
GIDDINGS, GRAY, MILLS and WHITON.

On the same day a resolution was adopted that WILLIAM
H. BRUCE was not entitled to a seat in the House, and on
the 30th that ALBERT G. ELLIS was, and he was then sworn
in and occupied the seat during the remaining nineteen days
of the session.

Pending this serious contest an episode of a less serious
nature occurred in the presentation of a petition on the 25th
of January of EBENEZER CHILDS claiming the seat occupied
by MASON C. DARLING. The petition and a counter statement of Dr. DARLING were referred to a select committee.

On the 2nd of February Mr. CHILDS withdrew his petition
which ended the farce, except that a resolution introduced
on the last day but one of the session, that he was entitled
to his per diem and mileage was rejected by a vote of five
to seventeen.

Another contest of a serious nature was developed at a
late period of the session.

On the 6th of February the memorial of THEOPHALUS LA
CHAPPELLE, contesting the seat of ALFRED BRUNSON, was
presented, praying the appointment of a commissioner to
take testimony and report at the next session of the Legislature. It was referred to the committee on elections, as
was a statement in reply made by Mr. BRUNSON.

The committee subsequently, on the 13th February, reported a resolution that Hon. JOSEPH R. BROWN, a member
from the same district, be authorized as commissioner to
take testimony in the county of St. Croix, in the case, to
send for persons and papers, administer oaths, and report at
the commencement of the next session, and that the parties
be authorized to take testimony in Crawford county, as provided by law for taking depositions in civil cases.

The resolution was adopted, and thus ended for the session
the contest of LA'CHAPPELLE *vs.* BRUNSON.

The Capitol remained in about the same unfinished condition at the commencement of this session of the Legislative
Assembly as that in which it had been left at the close of
the preceding session.

No provision had been made for means to pay for any improvements on the public buildings except the collection of money from the old commissioners and treasurer by means of the suits which had been commenced, and the opinion was expressed by the commissioner in his report to the Legislative Assembly in January, 1841, that it would —

"Require great exertion and much time to recover the money belonging to the Territory, so as to apply the funds to the purposes for which they were originally designed."

The same unfinished rooms which had been occupied by the Council and House of Representatives at the previous session, although uncomfortable and but poorly adapted to the use of the two branches of the Legislative Assembly, were made to supply the place of better. There was, however, much dissatisfaction felt and expressed by several members, and a disposition existed in some quarters to change the location of the seat of government. This feeling exhibited itself in a most marked manner in Jefferson county. Propositions were made by the citizens of Jefferson, Watertown and Aztlan to remove the seat of government from Madison to their several localities.

These propositions were referred to committees, but none met with any favor, except that a minority of one committee reported a bill to remove the seat of government to Aztlan, which, however, never progressed beyond a second reading.

The committee on Territorial affairs of the Council, submitted a report upon the subject in which they say:

"It does not appear that a removal of the seat of government is petitioned for or even desired by any considerable portion of the people of the Territory, and no measures ought to be adopted by the Legislature affecting the removal of it, without satisfactory proof that a majority of the people are in favor of the measure. No objections have been urged against the present site and no reasons exist in the mind of your committee in favor of a removal, except the present unfinished state of the Capitol, and the want of good accommodations at this place. The present Capitol can be finished easier and sooner than one could be built in any other part of the Territory, and it is highly probable that no other site would be selected that would afford better accommodations than are now to be found at Madison. * * * * * * * It appears from the report of the commissioner of public buildings, as well as from an inspection of the building, that it is in a very unsafe and dilapidated condition, and that unless it is soon completed or repaired, the expenditure already laid out upon the Capitol will be wholly lost."

In the house the committee on Territorial affairs reported that by an examination of the building in its present condition, and comparing it with the original designs and draughts, they have estimated the probable cost of its completion at $6,758.86.

A bill was introduced into the House, which after some amendments was passed by a vote of 17 to 7, which provided that the Treasurer of the Territory be authorized to issue Territorial bonds of $100 each to the amount of $7,000, payable in two years with interest at seven per centum; that the Treasurer, after public notice, should cause the bonds to be sold at not less than par for specie or its equivalent; that when one half of the bonds should be sold the commissioner of public buildings should immediately let the contract for the completion of the Capitol to the lowest and best bidder, upon the original plan and specifications in the contract with MORRISON, to be finished on or before the next meeting of the Legislature. It provided that the contractor should be paid on monthly estimates one half in money and one half in bonds, if not previously sold, and that the money to be collected from the old board of commissioners or Treasurer should be applied to the extinguishment of the bonds, and if the same should be insufficient or not received when the bonds should become due, such further provision for the redemption thereof should be made as might be deemed expedient.

In the Council the bill was concurred in by a vote of 7 to 5,— Mr. JANES of Racine not voting — with two very material amendments.

The first amendment provided, in three sections, that the commissioner of public buildings should first give MORRISON, the original contractor, the privilege at any time before the 25th day of March next of renewing his bonds for the completion of the public buildings, according to his original contract, and if he did so the commissioner was authorized to fulfill the contract on the part of the Territory, and give the contractor until the first day of November to complete the buildings, and to pay the contractor by orders on Mr. DOTY, the late treasurer of the board of commissioners, who was authorized and required to pay the same in the manner provided for in the act creating said office of treasurer. This amendment further provided that in case of refusal or neglect on the part of MORRISON to renew his said bonds, then the Territorial bonds might be issued, as provided in the House bill.

The second amendment provided that in case the provisions of the act should not be carried into effect, and it should appear to the satisfaction of the Governor that the Capitol would not be completed agreeably to its provisions, the Governor was authorized to issue his proclamation, thirty days at least, previous to the next annual session, convening the Legislative Assembly at Milwaukee. *Provided*, suitable rooms are furnished in the said town of Milwaukee for the accommodation of the two branches of the Legislative Assembly when holding their sessions, and for committee rooms; also, an office for the executive, and offices for the accommodation of the several Territorial officers, free from any charge or expense to the Territory or general government.

These amendments were not adopted by the Council, especially the first, without the most serious opposition. It was said in support of this amendment that if it was embodied in the law MORRISON would resume his contract, give new bonds, and that DOTY would pay *him* and the Capitol would be finished without incurring any debt. On the other hand it was said that to pass the law with this amendment was to undo all that had been done at the previous session. The Legislature upon a strict examination had come to the conclusion that the public money, which was fully ample to build the Capitol, had been squandered for objects foreign from what was intended, and they turned out the old board of commissioners, and suits had been brought against the old commissioners and contractor.

One member (Mr. COLLINS of Iowa county) said

"Are we now to say that all this has been wrong and provide for the withdrawal of the suits. He thought it the bounden duty of the Territory to proceed with the suits. It may be the fact that this is the only way in which we can get the money, but he would rather it would be lost than that the Territory should thus compromise its dignity and honor and the Legislature descend to such child's play. He would rather see the capitol burned to the ground than to give the completion of the work into the hands of the old commissioners or the contract again to JAMES MORRISON."

The first amendment was, however, adopted by a vote of nine to four— Messrs. COLLINS, MARTIN, ROUNTREE and VINEYARD voting against it— and the second without a division, and so the bill passed the Council.

The House at first disagreed to all the amendments and the Council insisted upon them and again returned the bill to the House, when on motion of Mr. WHITON the House receded from its disagreement to the second amendment and insisted upon its disagreement to the first amendment and for the third time returned the bill to the Council.

A committee of conference was then appointed upon the disagreement to the first amendment, consisting of Messrs. MARTIN and LEARNED of the Council and Messrs. BURT and HACKETT of the House.

This committee reported that the cost of completing the Capitol under the MORRISON contract would be $14,000, and that it need not exceed $9,000, if given out according to the plan proposed in the House bill, and that if the amendment should be adopted the Territory must lose at least $50,00, which would otherwise be saved, and recommended that the Council do recede from its first amendment.

The report of the committee was adopted and the Council receded without a division and thus the bill became a law with the second but without the first amendment.

The act was approved on the 19th of February, and on the 25th the Treasurer gave notice that the bonds would be for sale at his office on the 25th of March. On the 26th of March one half of them were sold at par.

The commissioners immediately gave notice that proposals would be received until the 26th of April, for completing the Capitol, according to the published specifications. The proposal of DANIEL BAXTER for $7,000 was accepted and a contract made with him to complete the Capitol according to the specifications by the 1st day of December. The work was not fully completed according to the contract, but was so far completed that the Governor did not feel warranted in issuing a proclamation for the meeting of the Legislative Assembly at Milwaukee which under the law he was in his discretion authorized to do.

N. C. PRENTISS was re-elected Commissioner of Public Buildings.

Every obstacle which the defendants could interpose to prevent a speedy trial of the Territorial suits was resorted to. The suits were pending in Iowa county, where a trial was expected at the April term and was urged by the attorneys for the Territory, but the defendants obtained a continuance until the September term, for the reason that one of the defendants (DOTY) who was delegate in Congress, had not returned from Washington, although Congress had adjourned on the 4th March.

At the September term the venue was changed to Walworth county, on the alleged ground of the prejudice of the inhabitants of Iowa county.

The court met at Elkhorn, in Walworth county, on the fourth Monday of October, where, after some preliminary questions had been decided in favor of the Territory, the suits were, on the application of the defendants, again continued for the alleged reason that the record sent from Iowa county was imperfect, in that it did not contain a certain bill of exceptions which the defendants said was taken by them to the decision of the judge, and signed by him. It afterwards was ascertained that no such bill had been signed by the judge, which statement was made by one of the attorneys for the Territory, in opposing the application for a continuance.

The question of the formation of a State Government was not agitated at this session of the Legislative Assembly.

A memorial to Congress relative to the southern boundary of the Territory was introduced by Mr. BRUNSON, which, on motion of Mr. ELLIS, was laid on the table by a vote of 16 to 9, and was not again brought up during the session.

A resolution relative to the northeastern boundary was adopted by both houses, which authorized the Governor to open a correspondence with the Governor of the State of Michigan, to ascertain, if possible, the terms on which that part of the State of Michigan south of Lake Superior and west of Green Bay and Lake Michigan, might be restored to the jurisdiction of the Territory of Wisconsin.

By the act of Congress providing for the admission of Michigan into the Union, approved June 15, 1836, the boundary line, after reaching the mouth of the Montreal River, was thus described:

"Thence through the middle of the main channel of the said Montreal River, to the middle of the Lake of the Desert; thence in a direct line to the nearest head-waters of the Menomonee River; thence through the middle of that fork of the said river first touched by the said line, to the main channel of the said Menomonee River; thence down the center of the main channel of the same, to the center of the most usual ship channel of the Green Bay of Lake Michigan, etc."

The Surveyor-General was authorized and required by an act approved June 12, 1838, to cause this boundary line to be "surveyed, marked and designated," and the sum of $3,000 was appropriated for that purpose.

This was not done and the same sum was re-appropriated to be expended under the direction of the Secretary of War, by the second section of the act making appropriations for the support of the army, approved July 20, 1840.

The appropriation was inadequate to the work, and by the third section of the army appropriation act, approved March 3, 1841, there was

"Appropriated $6,000 to be expended under the direction of the Secretary of War, in the *survey and examination of the country* situated between the mouths of the Menomonee and Montreal rivers, who is hereby directed to cause to be made a plat or plan of such survey and examination, which shall be returned to Congress with all convenient dispatch."

The time was so short after the appropriation of July, 1840, and the appropriation so small, that but little was done that year. A reconnoisance of the wild country between the Montreal and Menomonee rivers was made by Capt. T. J. CRAM of U. S. Top. Eng., who submitted a report, December, 1840, to be found in Senate Ex. Docs., No. 151, 26th Congress, 2d Session, in which he says :

"It was ascertained that Lac Vieux Desert or 'Lake of the Desert,' has no connection whatever with the Montreal river ; and that the nearest distance between said lake and this river is such, that an Indian requires eight days, without a pack, to pass from one to the other ; and it is also believed with much confidence, that the Montreal river does not head in a lake, but takes its rise in an extensive swamp. Neither is Lac Vieux Desert, or Lake of the Desert, at all connected with the Menomonee river ; but this lake was found, contrary to the opinions of all except the Indians, to be the principal head of the Wisconsin river."

Capt. CRAM in this report further says :

"It would be exceedingly difficult, yea, utterly impossible, to run the boundary in complete accordance with the present reading of the description in the act of Congress ; particularly on that part of the ground between the Montreal river and the head of the Menomonee (the Brulè river), which comes nearest to 'Lake of the Desert.'"

He suggested modifications in the description of the boundary to the following effect :

"To the mouth of the Montreal River (of Lake Superior) thence (in ascending) through the centre of the extreme right hand channel, that the said Montreal River may be found to have, so far up the same as where the said channel shall be found to be intersected by a direct line drawn from the highest point of ground on Middle Island of Lac Vieux Desert north —⁰ west; thence (from the said intersection) along the just described direct line, to the said point of Middle Island; thence in a direct line to the centre of the channel of the outlet of Brulè River; thence following the center of the extreme left hand channel of Brulè River down to the middle of the channel of the Menomonee River."

This suggestion was subsequently so far adopted by Congress in the "enabling act" of August 6, 1846, as to remove the practical physical difficulty of delineating the boundary line. That act prescribed that the boundary, after running through Lake Michigan to the Menomonee River, should run

"Up the channel of that river to the Brulè River; thence up said last mentioned river to Lake Brulè; thence along the southern shore of Lake Brulè in a direct line to the center of the channel between Middle and South islands in the Lake of the Desert; thence in a direct line to the head waters of the Montreal River, as marked upon the survey made by Capt. CRAM."

In the summer of 1841 another reconnoisance, with many astronomical observations and instrumental surveys, was made by Capt. CRAM, whose report can be found in Senate Ex. Documents, No. 170, 27th Congress, 2nd session.

This reconnoisance and survey embraced the whole distance from the mouth of the Menomonee River at Green Bay to the mouth of the Montreal River at Lake Superior.

The report says—

"The length of the surveyed line from the head of the Montreal to eastern extremity of Trout Lake is 43 miles 3,188 feet."

"The length of the line from Trout Lake to Lac Vieux Desert is 35 miles 2,987 feet."

The sum of these two lines is 79 miles 795 feet, but this distance is not on a straight line.

The report further says—

"The length of the surveyed line from Lac Vieux Desert to Lac Brulè is 15 miles 143 feet."

"The whole length of the survey from the head of the Montreal to the head of the Brulè therefore becomes 100 miles 2,199 feet.

Speaking of Lake Vieux Desert, Captain CRAM in his first report says—

"The country in the vicinity of this beautiful lake is called in Chippewa language Ka–ta–kit–te–kon, and the lake bears the same name. On South Island there is an old potato planting ground, hence the appellation of Vieux Desert, which in mongrel French means old planting ground. There is certainly more reason for calling it "Lac Vieux Desert" than for the appellation "Lake of the Desert."

In the House of Representatives so much of the Governor's message as relates to the Bank of Mineral Point was referred to the committee on corporations, of which Hon. E. V. WHITON was chairman.

At an early period of the session Mr. WHITON reported from the committee a bill to establish the New York safety fund system.

The principal object which it was expected the passage of the bill would accomplish was the election of a bank commissioner, with power at all times to examine the affairs of the bank, and to cause it to be wound up whenever the public welfare demanded it.

The passage of the bill was vigorously opposed by those interested in the bank, with all the influence they could bring to bear upon it, and the cashier had the assurance to send a communication to the House, asking to be heard before it by counsel.

On motion of Mr. WHITON it was resolved that the bill be referred to the committee on the judiciary, and that the stockholders be allowed to appear before that committee by counsel, and be heard relative to the bill.

After this the bill was before the House for more than a month, and on the 13th of February it passed that body by a vote of 16 to 10.

In the Council several amendments were adopted to the bill, which its friends in the House regarded as defeating its beneficial objects and proposed amendments to the Council amendments calculated to prevent such an effect. The Council refused to concur and the House refused to recede, and the disagreement resulted in the defeat of the bill.

After the defeat of the bill, Mr. COLLINS, of Iowa county, who had reported the amendment adopted by the Council, on the last day of the session, introduced on leave a resolution that the President of the Council appoint a committee of three members, to make a thorough examination of the state and condition of the Bank of Mineral Point, and to cause the result of their examinations to be published in a newspaper at the seat of government and to make a report to the Council at its next session.

The resolution was adopted and Messrs. ARNOLD, LEARNED and MARTIN appointed the committee.

In about a month the committee caused their report to be published which bore date March 23, 1841.

The report was of course based upon information derived from the officers of the bank and showed that the immediate liabilities of the bank (not including stock) were $250,295.34, and the available resources were $246,132.95, in addition to which the bank had "paper which is not considered immediately available, but which may be deemed ultimately good," amounting to $86,877.69 and that the remaining property consisting mainly of real estate amounted to $17,723.46, making a sum total of assets $350,734.10.

That it further appeared from the statement of the cashier that $100,000 of the capital stock was paid in, which if added to the liabilities would increase them to $350,295.34.

The report stated that of the immediate liabilities $208,820, consisted of its outstanding bank note circulation, which was an increase of $118,515, since the 25th of September 1840, when an examining committee of the Council reported the circulation to be $90,305. The remaining liabilities consisted of drafts on New York $27,400, and deposits $14,075.34.

This examination was made about three weeks after a published announcement "to the public" over the signature of the cashier, bearing date March 5, 1841, that the bank had suspended specie payments and would pay her liabilities by drafts on St. Louis at sight, payable in Illinois, Kentucky or Indiana bank notes.

In the early part of August, 1841, the affairs of the bank were placed in the custody of the law. An injunction was issued to restrain the bank from continuing its operations and receivers were appointed to take charge of its assets. They found the vaults empty. The specie, of which the committee reported March 23d, there was $26,507.25 on hand, had been clandestinely removed. The cashier, S. B. KNAPP, his brother, R. C. KNAPP, and the teller, PORTER BRACE, had absconded and taken with them the currency and other portable assets of the bank. They were pursued by the receivers, and the cashier and his brother were overtaken at Rockford and made prisoners. They had attempted to conceal a large amount of bank notes and drafts by sealing them up between the fly leaves and covers of some books, which they had left with a friend and acquaintance, and who delivered them up to the receivers. Upon "breaking the seals" in the presence of several Rockford gentlemen they found $1,500 of Illinois Bank notes and over $70,000 in certificates of deposit and drafts on Galena, St. Louis, New York and Boston, and bills of lading for 12,901 pigs of lead (903,070 lbs.).

The culprits escaped, and many of the parties upon whom the drafts were drawn interposed defenses or offsets, so that very little was ever realized from them.

The most mysterious thing about the whole affair was the unaccountable disappearance of WILLIAM H. BANKS, Esq., one of the receivers. He was a lawyer at Mineral Point of high standing; a native of Virginia of unimpeachable character in every respect. He went to St. Louis in the discharge of his duties as receiver, when he mysteriously disappeared and was never afterwards seen or heard of, notwithstanding the most diligent search and inquiry. The mystery can only be solved on the theory of murder or suicide.

Reports were made by the Attorney General and the Receiver of the Bank of Wisconsin showing that the suit to forfeit the charter of that bank was still pending and that the affairs of the bank were in process of liquidation.

The committee on corporations was instructed, on motion of Mr. WHITON, to inquire into the expediency of memorializing Congress to disapprove of an act of the Legislature of the Territory incorporating the Wisconsin Marine and Fire Insurance Company.

Near the close of the session (February 18) Mr. WHITON from the committee on corporations, reported that

"No memorial which the Legislature could adopt would reach Congress in season to receive the attention of that body at its present session. Without expressing any opinion as to the expediency of the measure, the committee recommend that no action be had relative to the subject."

An act was passed at this session incorporating two distinct fire insurance companies, one called the "Western Mutual Fire Insurance Company," located at Prairie du Chien and the other the "Howard Mutual Insurance Company" located at Green Bay. Neither of these companies, however, it is supposed, were ever organized; at least they never went into active operation.

A memorial to Congress was adopted, asking an appropriation for the Fox and Wisconsin rivers, and calling the attention of Congress to the importance of improving the navigation of the Rock and Peckatonica rivers, and also stating the importance of the improvement of the Grant river, known as the "Grant Slue" and of the Platte river, which contained the questionable statement that

"The Little Platte river is navigable for the largest class of steamboats to within nine miles of Platteville."

Another memorial requested Congress to make an appropriation of money for the construction of harbors on the western shore of Lake Michigan.

An act was passed to incorporate the "Fox and Wisconsin Steamboat Company." The incorporators were mostly citizens of Green Bay. It was a small affair with an authorized capital of only $10,000, and it is not known that any thing was ever done by virtue of the charter.

At this session of the Legislative Assembly two acts were passed granting divorces from the bonds of matrimony, and annulling the marriage contract. One of these annulled and made void the marriage contract between PETER HOWARD of Iowa county and SARAH HOWARD his wife, and changed the name of PETER HOWARD to ROBERT C. HOARD. The other, the marriage contract between JOSIAH MOORE of the county of Milwaukee and LEVISEE his wife.

These acts were passed as expressly exceptional, and in the first case the judiciary committee which reported the bill, say:

"The power by law being invested in the courts, for wise reasons that jurisdiction should not be disturbed except in extreme and peculiar cases ;. such as where every one may, in their own minds, be satisfied that the causes exist, yet the person applying for divorce may be unable to establish the fact by legal testimony. Such case would warrant the interference by the Legislature, and such appears to be the case that your committee have had under consideration."

The select committee to which was referred so much of the Governor's message as related to the appointment of a Territorial geologist, after referring to the extent, richness and value of the mines of lead and copper so long known to exist in the Territory, expresses the opinion that the entire Territory abounds in the most valuable minerals. That on Black River, and near its principal falls, iron ore of a superior quality and inexhaustible in quantity had recently been discovered, which was nothing short of an *iron mountain*, only two miles above the falls, the base of which was washed by the river, on which its products could be conveyed by boats, and —

"It is believed," the report says, "that this one spot is capable of supplying with iron all the States and Territories along the 'Father of Waters' lying above the Des Moines Rapids for centuries to come."

That in the vicinity of Prairie du Chien are found blocks for mill-stones, equal in quality to the best importations from France, inexhaustible in quantity, while gypsum or plaster Paris, used for cementing these blocks, is said to be found at Green Bay in abundance.

The probability of finding bituminous coal is discussed and opinions advanced entirely in conflict with geological facts, which are now well known.

The conclusion to which the committee arrived was —

"That from the want of funds in the Territorial treasury, it is inexpedient at present to appoint a Territorial geologist."

The subject of common schools received special attention at this session of the Legislative Assembly, and an act was passed condensing and consolidating the previous laws upon this subject, and introducing some new features, which were calculated to give efficiency to the common school system of education.

The "Prairieville Academy" was incorporated and "The Trustees of the Milwaukee Educational Institute."

Probably the most important act of the session so far as it affected local self-government, was the—

"Act to provide for the government of the several towns in this Territory, and for the revision of county government."

The New England and New York system of local self-government is what may be called the *town* system, while that of the western and southern states was what may be called the *county* system.

The great mass of the inhabitants of the lead mine region prior to this period, came from the western and southwestern states, and brought with them prejudices in favor of the county system, which therefore became the recognized system of municipal government. Their number was greater than that of all other parts of the Territory at the time of its organization.

The eastern portion of the Territory during the first four or five years of the Territorial existence rapidly became settled with a population largely imbued with the ideas of New England and New York, in which they had been educated, and a corresponding desire was manifested that the system of local government should be changed to conform to their ideas.

This conflict of ideas resulted in the passage of this act, approved February 18, 1841.

It contained a complete system for the organization of towns, and specified all the details of town government, and provided that the legal voters should at the next general election vote for or against the provisions of the act, and if a majority of the electors in any county should vote in favor of the adoption of the act, the county so voting should be governed by and be subject to the provisions of the act, on and after the first Tuesday of April, 1842.

The result was that in some counties the *town* system was adopted, and in others the *county* system continued to exist.

TERRITORY OF WISCONSIN IN 1841. 343

The creation of towns by Legislative enactment continued and at the same session, that part of the town of Watertown comprised in townships number seven and eight in range sixteen, was set off into a separate town by the name of Union.

That part of the town of Whitewater comprised in township three, range fifteen was set off into a separate town by the name of Richmond.

The territory included in township five, range seventeen, was created into a separate town by the name of Eagle.

And the name of the town of Kinnikinnick was changed to Greenfield.

The towns of Potosi and Platteville in Grant county and Southport and Racine in Racine county, were incorporated with all the municipal powers of incorporated villages.

Commissioners were appointed with authority to lay out the following Territorial roads:

From Marine Mills on the St. Croix River to Grey Cloud island on the Mississippi River.

From the Falls of St. Croix to the Marine Mills.

From Prescott's ferry to Grey Cloud island.

From English Prairie on the Wisconsin River (Muscoda) to Whitney's Mills (Wood County).

From the Fox River of Green Bay, opposite the mouth of Plumb Creek, to Smithfield north of the grist-mill in the Oneida reservation.

From the United States road near the house of SEYMOUR WILCOX in Fond du Lac county (Waupun) and to intersect the same again near the bridge where the said road crosses the Fox River in Portage county, and running on the north side of Fox Lake.

From Fond du Lac to Oshkosh.

From Fort Winnebago to the Plover Rapids on the Wisconsin River.

From Madison *via* Columbus, to the house of SEYMOUR WILCOX in Fond du Lac county.

From Fort Howard to Whitney's Mills.

From Monroe, Green county to Jefferson, Jefferson county.

From Milwaukee *via* Watertown to Fond du Lac.

From state line in section thirty-one, town one, range nine east, to Monroe and thence to Mineral Point.

From Sheboygan to Manchester.

From state line in section thirty-one, town one, range nine east to Madison.

From Haneys' Ferry on Wisconsin River to Hickox's Mills in Iowa county, thence to the military road.

From Haneys' Ferry to the Dalles on Wisconsin River.

From Madison to Rowins' Rapids on Baraboo River.

From Racine to Prairieville.

From Sauk Prairie to Whitney's Mills.

From Stockbridge to Sheboygan.

From Prairieville to northeast corner of section twenty-nine, town four, range sixteen, thence to United States road in town three, range sixteen.

From northeast corner of section 29, town four, range sixteen to Janesville.

From Beloit to southwest corner of section sixteen, town four, range ten east, thence northerly to intersect road to Madison.

A supplemental act was passed in relation to the militia.

An act was passed to provide for the support of illegitimate children and regulate the mode of proceedings.

Peddlers were required to obtain license.

The law in relation to assessing and collecting county revenue was materially changed.

The northern boundary of Portage county, as established in 1836, was the line between towns fourteen and fifteen, but by an act passed at this session all that district of country lying north of such boundary and comprised in ranges two, three, four, five, six, seven, eight and nine east, and extending to the northern boundary of the Territory (except fractional townships fourteen and fifteen, range nine, east), was annexed to Portage county, so that Portage county thus became forty-eight miles (eight ranges) in width east and west and extended north from Dane county to the boundary line between Michigan and Wisconsin, a distance of more than two hundred miles.

The county was organized for all purposes of county government, and the county officers were required to hold their offices at Wisconsin Portage, and for judicial purposes it was attached to the county of Dane.

The north and south boundary lines of all counties bordering upon Lake Michigan were extended east to the eastern boundary line of the Territory (in Lake Michigan) which was declared to be the eastern boundary line of such counties; and the north and south boundary lines of all counties bordering on the Mississippi River was extended west to the western boundary line of the Territory, and jurisdiction was conferred upon said counties co-extensive with the jurisdiction of the Territory.

SAMUEL H. FARNSWORTH was authorized to build a dam across the south branch or channel of the Menomonee River, in the county of Brown, and WILLIAM P. OWEN was authorized to build a dam across Rock River, on section 19, town 8, range 16 (town of Ixonia).

The Governor was authorized by joint resolution to appoint a competent person in the room of the one heretofore appointed for the Wisconsin land district, to locate 10,248 acres of University lands and advertise and make return thereof to the Governor.

A selection of 10,248 53-100 acres had previously been made in the Milwaukee land district by WM. B. SHELDON, the agent appointed for that purpose, and advertised November 25, 1840.

The annual expenses of the Legislative Assembly had grown to proportions greatly in excess of the appropriations made by Congress for their liquidation. To mitigate in some measure the embarrassments arising from this condition of affairs, the Legislative Assembly provided in February, 1841, that the Secretary of the Territory, or in his absence the Governor, be authorized to issue to the several creditors of the Territory, certificates of the amounts due them respectively, setting forth the amount due and for what purpose, and bearing interest at ten per cent. per annum, which certificates should be transferable by indorsement, and for the redemption of which the faith of the Territory and the several sums appropriated by Congress for the payment of the expenses of the Legislative Assembly were irrevocably pledged.

The creditors were to execute duplicate receipts for the amount of their claims, which were to be forwarded to the proper accounting officers of the Treasury department, and the amount received thereupon was to be applied in the redemption of the certificates.

The President of the United States — WILLIAM HENRY HARRISON — died at Washington on the 4th of April, 1841, one month after his inauguration.

The Vice-President, JOHN TYLER, immediately succeeded not only to the honors but to the responsibilities and duties of the Presidential office.

In Wisconsin a very extensive system of removals from, and appointments to, office was soon developed.

HENRY DODGE was removed from the office of Governor and JAMES D. DOTY appointed his successor.

FRANCIS J. DUNN was removed from the office of Secretary of the Territory and ALEXANDER P. FIELD appointed his successor.

MOSES M. STRONG was removed from the office of United States Attorney, and THOMAS W. SUTHERLAND appointed his successor.

GEORGE W. JONES was removed from the office of Surveyor-General of Wisconsin and Iowa, and JAMES WILSON, of New Hampshire, appointed his successor.

EDWARD JAMES was removed from the office of United States Marshal and DANIEL HUGUNIN appointed his successor.

PASCAL BEQUETTE, Receiver, and JOHN V. INGERSOLL, Register of the Wisconsin land district, were removed and LEVI STERLING and JOSIAH D. WESTON appointed their respective successors, and the land office itself was removed from Mineral Point to Muscoda.

L. S. PEASE was removed from the office of Receiver of Public Moneys in the Green Bay land district and STODDARD JUDD appointed his successor.

A. B. MORTON was removed from the office of Register of the Land Office at Milwaukee and PARACLETE POTTER was appointed his successor.

Numerous other changes were made in United States officers and the removals of postmasters for political and party reasons were innumerable.

Political proscription was not confined to the United States government, but was practiced in a small way in the Territory. Necessarily in a small way as the patronage of the governor was limited.

H. N. WELLS was removed from the office of attorney general and M. M. JACKSON appointed his successor. WILLIAM T. STERLING was removed from the office of librarian and ALMON LULL appointed his successor.

N. T. PARKINSON was removed from the office of sheriff of Dane county and A. A. BIRD appointed his successor. JOHN CATLIN was removed from the office of district attorney of Dane county and BARLOW SHACKELFORD appointed.

GEORGE MESSERSMITH was appointed sheriff of Iowa county and ENOS S. BAKER of Grant county.

The *Wisconsin Enquirer* published at Madison announced in its issue of June 9th

"That all difficulties between Ex-Governor MASON and Governor DOTY, involving the title of this town, have been settled, and that a deed from the former to the latter of the whole property has been placed upon record. The settlement of the title will considerably enhance the value of property and we may calculate now with some certainty on great improvements being made in the town during the present season."

Previous to 1841, spasmodic efforts had been made to organize political parties for the selection and election of members of the Legislature and Delegate to Congress. Such efforts, however, had never been completely successful.

The overwhelming success of the Whigs at the presidential election in 1840, appeared to have aroused the zeal and given strength to the courage of the Whigs of the Territory.

On the first day of January, the Whigs, in pursuance of previous arrangements, assembled at Milwaukee to celebrate the

"Brilliant victory achieved by the hardy yeomanry of our country in the late presidential contest."

This meeting was large, jubilant and enthusiastic and many representative men from every part of the Territory participated in it.

Among other proceedings was an agreement upon a complete and thorough organization of the Whig party of Wisconsin. To this end a central committee was appointed.

The committee issued the following notice:

WHIG CONVENTION.

The undersigned, members of the Whig Central Committee in this Territory, in pursuance of a resolution passed at a meeting of the Whigs, in attendance at the celebration held at Milwaukee on the first day of January, 1841, hereby give notice that a convention of the Whigs of the Territory will be held at Madison, in the county of Dane, on the 4th day of February next, to take into consideration the expediency of an efficient organization of the Whig party throughout the Territory, and to transact such other business as may be thought proper. The Whigs in the several counties are requested to send delegates equal to the number of Representatives to which they are entitled in both branches of the Legislature.

A. BRUNSON,
WILLIAM A. PRENTISS,
E. CHILDS,
JAMES COLLINS,
JOHN H. ROUNTREE,
EDWARD V. WHITON,
GILBERT KNAPP.

MADISON, January 9, 1841.

On the 4th of February the convention assembled at Madison. A committee on credentials reported the names of sixty-one persons entitled to seats in the convention. No regard was paid by the committee to the apportiontment of delegates among the several counties, but they reported the delegates in attendance and entitled to seats from the several counties, as follows: Crawford and St. Croix, 4; Dane, 3; Jefferson, 3; Sauk, 3; Brown and the counties attached, 9; Milwaukee, 10; Walworth, 5; Rock, 2; Iowa, 13, and Grant, 9.

It was further resolved:

"That all Whig citizens of the territory who are present and friendly to the objects of the convention be invited to seats within the bar and to participate in the deliberations of the convention."

Under this resolution the names of twenty other persons were presented as members of the convention, increasing the number to eighty-one.

A preamble and series of resolutions, reported by a committee appointed for that purpose, were adopted; and a plan of organization was also adopted in pursuance of a report of a committee.

The plan provided for the appointment of a central committee of five, whose duty it should be to call Territorial conventions at such time and place as they might think the interests of the party require; in which the representation should be limited to double the number to which each election district shall be entitled in the House of Representatives. The plan also provided for the appointment on the nomination of the delegates then present a committee of five in each of the election districts, whose duty it should be to call conventions in their districts and to correspond with the Whigs of the Territory in relation to the general interests of the party.

The committees were all appointed and the convention adjourned, and thus the Whig party of the Territory was fully organized for any subsequent political contests.

The Democrats were not slow to accept the gage thrown down by the Whigs.

On the 14th of January a meeting of Democrats was held at Madison, which, after appointing a committee to report resolutions upon the subject of party organization, adjourned until the next day.

On the 15th the meeting re-assembled, and recommended that a Territorial convention be held at Madison on Thursday, the 11th of February, to be composed of delegates to be chosen from each county, or from each election precinct, as may suit the views and convenience of the citizens.

A central corresponding committee was appointed temporarily, to continue until a permanent one should be appointed by the contemplated convention, and a committee of three for each county in the Territory to secure from their respective counties full delegations to the proposed Democratic Territorial convention.

The proceedings of the meeting were indorsed by the signature of the names of sixty-two of the leading Democratic citizens of the Territory.

The central committee immediately issued a stirring appeal to their Democratic fellow citizens throughout the Territory to organize and send full delegations to the proposed Territorial convention.

On the 11th of February the Democratic Territorial convention assembled, consisting of one hundred and thirty-four delegates, and five others admitted to seats through courtesy. The delegates represented the county of Brown and the counties attached, and the counties of Dane, Grant, Green, Iowa, Jefferson, Milwaukee, Racine, Rock, Sauk, St. Croix, and Walworth, comprising every organized county except Crawford (which elected delegates who sent a letter stating their inability to attend), and some counties (Sauk and St. Croix) which were not organized.

Hon. MORGAN L. MARTIN was chosen President, with eight vice-presidents, and NELSON DEWEY and B. H. EDGERTON, Secretaries.

Committees on resolutions, to draft an address to the people, and to report a plan for organizing the Democratic party were appointed.

The committee on resolutions reported a lengthy platform which was adopted; and in accordance with the report of the committee on organization a central committee of five was appointed whose duty it was to call Territorial conventions at the Capitol at such times as they might think the interest of the party required, and to designate the number of delegates thereto; which should be apportioned to each election district according to population.

The Democrats of the different counties were requested to appoint county committees, and to take speedy and efficient measures for the organization of the Democratic party.

Having thus met the challenge of the Whig party, and placed the Democratic party in an attitude of readiness for any subsequent political contests, the convention adjourned *sine die.*

On the 25th of May the Whig central committee issued a call for a convention of *Democratic Whig* delegates to be held at Madison on the first day of July. The representation under the call was double the number to which each election district was entitled in the House of Representatives, so that the convention, if fully represented, would consist of fifty-two delegates.

The convention assembled at the time fixed and the election districts were all nearly fully represented.

JOHN P. ARNDT of Green Bay was elected President, and THOMAS WRIGHT of Racine and C. J. LEARNED of Prairie du Chien were elected Secretaries.

A series of resolutions was reported and adopted after which the convention proceeded to ballot for a candidate for delegate. The result was:

For JONATHAN E. ARNOLD..29 votes.
For WILLIAM S. HAMILTON...14 votes.
For JAMES COLLINS... 7 votes.
For WILLIAM A. PRENTISS.. 1 vote.
For Blank... 1 vote.

And JONATHAN E. ARNOLD was declared the candidate of the Whig party for delegate to Congress.

A committee of five — EDWARD V. WHITON, WILLIAM S. HAMILTON, WM. A. PRENTISS, DAVID BRIGHAM and CHARLES J. LEARNED — was appointed to prepare an address to the people of the Territory.

A central committee of three — A. A. BIRD, DAVID BRIGHAM and JAMES MORRISON — was appointed and the convention adjourned *sine die.*

On the 2d of June the Democratic central committee made a call for a Democratic Territorial convention, to be held at Madison on the 19th day of July, and designated the number of delegates thereto, to which each district should be entitled according to population, and was as follows: Brown and the counties attached 8, Milwaukee and Washington 13, Racine 8, Rock and Walworth 9, Green, Dane, Jefferson, Dodge and Sauk 5, Iowa 9, Grant 9, Crawford and St. Croix 5; total 66.

The convention assembled on the 19th of July with 57 delegates in attendance; the vacancies were from the district of Brown, etc., 2, Milwaukee and Washington 1, Grant 2, and Crawford and St. Croix 4.

HORATIO N. WELLS of Milwaukee was appointed President of the convention, and JOHN CATLIN of Madison and C. LATHAM SHOLES of Southport were appointed Secretaries.

A resolution was adopted that the convention now proceed to vote *viva voce* for a Democratic candidate for delegate to Congress, that the vote be taken by districts, and that each district cast the number of votes to which it is entitled.

The result was that every district cast its entire vote for HENRY DODGE, being a total of 66 votes.

The names of the delegates were then severally called over and each voted *viva voce* for HENRY DODGE, and the President declared that he was unanimously nominated.

A committee was appointed to inform the nominee, who soon reported that he accepted the nomination.

Governor DODGE was also nominated as the Democratic candidate to fill the vacancy in the office in the event that any election should be held to fill such vacancy.

After the adoption of a very long series of resolutions and the appointment of a committee to draft an address to the citizens of the Territory, the convention adjourned *sine die*.

The election was held on the 4th Monday (27th) of September and resulted in a majority of 507 in favor of Governor DODGE.

The following is the official canvass:

COUNTIES.	HENRY DODGE.	J. E. ARNOLD.
Brown	195	125
Crawford	76	57
Dane and Sauk	73	99
Dodge	10	11
Fond du Lac	13	11
Grant	502	633
Green	135	98
Iowa	547	347
Jefferson	120	101
Manitowoc	27	19
Milwaukee	656	535
Racine	483	307
Rock	203	229
Sheboygan	12	23
St. Croix	17	10
Walworth	340	311
Washington	26	12
Total	3,435	2,928
Majority for HENRY DODGE		507

CHAPTER XXIII.

TERRITORY OF WISCONSIN IN 1842.

The second session of the 27th Congress, which commenced on the sixth day of December, 1841 and terminated on the thirty-first day of August, 1842, was looked to by the people of Wisconsin with no less interest than were the sessions which preceded it.

The expenditures of the Legislative Assembly at every session since the organization of the Territory had been in excess of the appropriations by Congress for their payment, so that a large arrearage had accumulated which was represented by certificates of indebtedness and scrip, which, though depreciated, served to a great extent as a substitute for currency.

The act making appropriations for the civil and diplomatic expenses of the government for the year 1842, approved May 18, 1842, besides the ordinary annual appropriation of $9,100 for the compensation of the Governor, Judges and Secretary and $350 for contingent expenses, contained an appropriation of $20,000 for the expenses of the Legislative Assembly. It also contained appropriations for the expenses of Iowa and Florida Territories, as well as this proviso:

"That the Legislative Assembly of no Territory shall hereafter, in any instance or under any pretext whatever, exceed the amount appropriated by Congress for its annual expenses."

Another act was subsequently passed at the same session, approved August 29th,

"To provide for the settlement of certain accounts for the support of government in the Territory of Wisconsin and for other purposes."

This enacted, "That the proper accounting officers of the treasury department be directed to audit and settle the accounts for the expenses of the Legislative Assembly of the Territory of Wisconsin, including the printing of the laws and other incidental expenses, which have not heretofore been closed at the treasury department."

The act contained many restrictions upon the allowances to be made by the accounting officers, but the effect was to substantially expunge the indebtedness of the Territory.

It also contained another provision which at the next session of the Legislative Assembly was assigned by the Governor as a reason for refusing to have official intercourse with it. This provision was in the following words:

"No session of the Legislature of a Territory shall be held until the appropriation for its expenses shall have been made."

The appropriations made by the Legislative Assembly in 1842, payable out of the moneys appropriated by Congress for defraying its expenses, amounted to $24,073.58, besides the per diem and mileage of members (about $10,000 more), for which certificates were issued by the presiding officers of each house.

The appropriation bill was vetoed by the Governor, but passed the Council by a vote of 9 to 2, and the House of Representatives by a vote of 19 to 6, and thus became a law.

Certificates of indebtedness or scrip were issued in pursuance of an act of the Legislative Assembly approved February 15, 1842. The act provided that the Treasurer of the Territory be authorized and required to issue to the several creditors whose demands were properly chargeable to the fund appropriated by Congress, drafts or bills for the amounts due them respectively, drawn upon the Secretary of the Territory in denominations of five and ten dollars, or in such amount as might be desired by the creditor, payable to the person to whom issued or bearer and transferable by delivery, for the payment of which the moneys to be thereafter appropriated by Congress were pledged.

In response to a resolution of the Council, the Secretary of the Territory (A. P. FIELD) submitted a report stating the amount of certificates issued in conformity with the act of the previous session, authorizing the Secretary of the Territory to issue certificates of the amounts due to the creditors of the Territory bearing ten per cent. interest for the expenses of that session and the unpaid expenses of previous sessions.

This report showed that the certificates issued by his predecessor (F. J. DUNN) amounted to $33,754.57, of which $28,105.00, were for appropriations of the last session and $5,649.57, for appropriations of previous sessions and that those issued by himself amounted to $2,015.75, all for previous sessions and that the whole amount issued by him and his predecessors was $35,768.32.

Secretary FIELD further stated that this amount did not include the whole amount of indebtedness of the Territory on account of appropriations made by previous Legislatures but as far as he could learn there was some $4,000 due for which certificates had not been issued, and he states that the whole may be fairly estimated at $40,000.

Whenever certificates were issued, a receipt for a corresponding amount was taken by the Secretary, which receipts upon being forwarded to the proper accounting officers at Washington, served as vouchers showing the disbursements of the appropriations made by Congress. The vouchers thus taken and forwarded by Mr. DUNN, amounting to $33,754.57, were with the exception of a few items placed to his credit in the first auditor's office.

But a new difficulty now arose which created great embarrassment, and a serious injury to the holders of these certificates. Mr. DUNN who had been credited with the vouchers had been removed and Mr. FIELD had been appointed his successor, and it was months before the Secretary of the Treasury could or would decide to which of these two officers the appropriation should be paid over.

In this condition of affairs a resolution was submitted by the delegate calling on the Secretary of the Treasury to report to the House of Representatives the causes which had prevented the payment of the appropriation to the Territory. The resolution was adopted, and soon after, in the month of June, the sum of $44,963 was paid over to Mr. Secretary FIELD.

Under the pre-emption act of 1834, a number of settlers on the public lands in the district of lands subject to sale at Mineral Point, who would otherwise have been entitled to enter 160 acres, by pre-emption, were refused the privileges granted by such act in consequence of the mineral character of the land claimed by them. For the relief of such persons an act of Congress was passed August 23, 1842, by virtue of which all such settlers were permitted to enter at the rate of one dollar and twenty-five cents per acre, one complete quarter section of land, of any lands in said district which had not then been offered at public sale, and which did not contain mines or discoveries of lead ore, and upon which there was no improvement or residence, and which had not been reserved from sale.

At this session of Congress the following post-routes were established in Wisconsin, viz.:

From Patch Grove, in Grant county, to Blue River.

From Fort Winnebago, *via* Grand Rapids, to Plover Portage.

From Delavan, by Darien, to Beloit.

From Fort Atkinson, by Cold Spring and Whitewater, to Elkhorn.

From Summit, in Milwaukee county, *via* Piperville and Watertown, to Washara (or Fox Lake).

From Southport *via* Aurora post-office, to Burlington.

From Madison, by Monroe, to Freeport, Illinois.

From Milwaukie, *via* Muskeego, Rochester, and Burlington, to Geneva.

On the 29th of January, 1842, the delegate in Congress (Gen. DODGE) called the attention of the Commissioner of Pensions to the great delay that had occurred in the payment of pensioners in Wisconsin. On the 31st of January the Commissioner informed Gen. DODGE that CHARLES DOTY, Esq., of Madison, was appointed agent for paying pensioners on the 28th of December, and that his bond was daily expected, and that as soon as received he would be instructed to enter on the duties of the office.

Governor DODGE immediately replied, stating—

"I am informed by a gentleman of high respectability now in this city (Washington), that CHARLES DOTY is the son of Governor DOTY of Wisconsin, and that he is a minor, not to exceed nineteen years of age. If such is the fact no official bonds he may sign would be binding."

On the 16th of February Governor DODGE authorized the commissioner to furnish Governor DOTY with a copy of the above letter of 1st inst.

On the 5th of May the commissioner, in a letter to Governor DODGE, stated—

"So soon as you informed me that Mr. CHARLES DOTY was under twenty-one years of age, I immediately wrote to him and his father, and on receipt of the answer to my inquiry another agent was appointed. That agent was Mr. PARACLETE POTTER, Register of the Land Office at Milwaukee. He was appointed on the 31st of March last. His bond as agent may be expected daily."

The bond of Mr. POTTER was received on the 10th of May and his instructions were immediately sent to him with the necessary funds.

In the recess between the first and second sessions of the third Legislative Assembly some changes occurred in the *personnel* of both houses.

In the Council JOHN H. TWEEDY of Milwaukee was elected in place of JONATHAN E. ARNOLD, resigned, and MOSES M. STRONG of Iowa county in place of LEVI STERLING, resigned.

In the House of Representatives JONATHAN EASTMAN was elected from Racine county in place of REUBEN H. DEMING, resigned.

JAMES TRIPP from Walworth county in place of HUGH LONG, resigned, and THOMAS JENKINS in Iowa county in place of FRANCIS J. DUNN resigned.

In the county of Racine Messrs. GEORGE BATCHELDER and REUBEN H. DEMING resigned their seats and their resignations were received at the executive office in due season. THOMAS E. PARMELEE resigned his seat by a note addressed twelve days before the election to the board of county commissioners of Racine county. An election was ordered by proclamation of the governor to fill *two* vacancies in that county and four persons were voted for. GEORGE BATCHEL-

DER received 395 votes, JONATHAN EASTMAN 378, ELISHA S. SILL 366 and PHILO BELDEN 357.

Mr. PARMELEE claimed that as his resignation was not acted upon, and no election held to fill the vacancy, he was entitled to retain the seat.

Mr. SILL contested the right of Mr. PARMELEE to the seat and claimed to be entitled to it himself.

The contest was referred to the committee on privileges and elections which made a majority and minority report.

The majority reported a resolution that Mr. PARMELEE

"Is not entitled to a seat in this House and that the seat now occupied by said PARMELEE be declared vacant."

The report of the minority was that he was entitled to the seat.

The resolution having been amended so as to read

"That THOMAS E. PARMELEE has resigned his seat in this house, and that thereby said seat became vacant,"

was adopted by a vote 19 to 5, those who voted in the negative being Messrs. BOND, BRUNSON, OGDEN, PARKINSON and WHITON.

In the contest of THEOPHALUS LA'CHAPPELLE for the seat occupied by ALFRED BRUNSON at the previous session, the commissioner, JOSEPH R. BROWN, on the second day of this session submitted his report containing the testimony of twenty-two persons.

The matters in controversy were referred to the committee on privilege and elections, which reported the facts in the case but made no report as to who was entitled to the seat. Both parties were heard by very able counsel, the contestant being represented by Hon. ALEX. P. FIELD, and the contestee by Hon. THOMAS P. BURNETT.

The contest depended largely upon the question whether the testimony taken by the commissioner was taken in accordance with the resolution of the House, by which the taking of it was authorized. A result was reached on the 20th of January, when it was decided by a vote of 13 to 11 that Mr. BRUNSON was not entitled to the seat, and that Mr. LA'CHAPPELLE was, who then appeared and took the oath of office as a member.

But few of the members of either House had been elected with reference to their party affiliations, yet in the organization of both the spirit of party which had distinctly marked the election of Delegate in the previous September, dominated in the election of presiding officer.

Mr. ROUNTREE of Grant, a Whig, was on the first day elected President *pro tem.* of the Council without opposition, but it was not until the ninth day of the session that the permanent President was elected. Upon a party division there were seven Whigs and six Democrats. Mr. ROUNTREE was the Whig candidate, but he could not be elected without voting for himself, which he persistently refused to do. The Democrats sometimes voted for one of their number and sometimes for another. They finally proposed to the Whigs to elect one of their number, but for several days the proposition was declined until the twenty-second ballot, when they acceded to it, and JAMES COLLINS received three Democratic and six Whig votes, M. L. MARTIN three Democratic votes — Mr. COLLINS'S vote being cast blank — and he was elected.

GEORGE BEATTY was re-elected Secretary without opposition.

In the House of Representatives there were sixteen Democrats, counting Mr. PARMELEE, and ten Whigs. Mr. ELLIS was elected Speaker *pro tem.*, after which the Democrats in caucus agreed upon Mr. NEWLAND, who was elected on the first ballot.

JOHN CATLIN was elected Chief Clerk without opposition.

In the Council on the first day and about the first business, Mr. JANES of Racine offered a resolution that the standing rules of the last session be adopted. Mr. STRONG of Iowa moved to amend so as to exclude the 48th rule, which required executive sessions to be held with closed doors. After some slight opposition the amendment was adopted.

The Legislative Assembly met on the 6th day of December, 1841, but owing to delays in the organization the Governor was not officially notified until the 9th, and on the 10th he met the two houses jointly assembled, and addressed them—

"Upon such subjects affecting the public good as in his opinion are entitled to the consideration of the representatives of the people."

It was the longest paper of that kind which had ever been submitted by any Governor of the Territory.

It commenced with the expression of the opinion that it was

"Expedient to adopt measures preparatory to a change in the government of Wisconsin from a Territory to a State,"

and several reasons were given for this opinion.

The Governor's address deprecated the Territorial debt which had been created by former Legislatures, and was in the shape of bonds or certificates, and he said that it appeared to him that the power to create it was not intended to be granted — and was not granted — to the Governor and Assembly.

"The holders of the bonds," he said, "can have no other remedy than by application to Congress."

The address said:

"Excessive legislation is an evil of the greatest magnitude; and rapid changes in the "laws are injurious to the private rights and to the public interests. Mr. JEFFERSON said: "'the instability is really a very serious inconvenience. I think we ought to have obviated "it by deciding that a whole year should always be allowed to elapse between bringing in "a bill and the final passing of it. It should afterwards be discussed and put to the vote "without the possibility of making any alteration in it; and if the circumstances of the "case required a more speedy decision, the question should not be decided by a simple "majority, but by a majority of at least two-thirds of both Houses.'"

The Governor expressed the opinion that the provisions of the act organizing the Territory, required the laws to be actually submitted to Congress before they take effect. This opinion had, as will be seen, a very consequential effect upon his administration of the executive department of the Territorial Government.

The address disapproved in strong language the laws by which *monopolies* — acts of incorporation granting exclusive privileges to certain individuals — "The offspring of the last four years" had been created, and also those incorporating villages.

Attention was called to the state of the currency, and a question was suggested whether the people of the Territory had been benefited by the destruction of the banks and the introduction of foreign depreciated paper. He thought an effort ought to be made to secure specie and the notes of specie paying banks for a circulating medium, by prohibiting the use of depreciated bank paper. A favorable allusion was made to the establishment by Wisconsin

"Of an institution which may be hereafter created by herself, whose circulation shall be based upon specie, and whose privileges shall be so few and so closely guarded that the public interests will be entirely protected.

The address recommended that to encourage the *growth*

of wool, sheep and their fleeces be exempt from taxation for a term of years.

The protection of the business of *mining and smelting* and of the *fur trade* were favorably mentioned.

The improvement of the navigation of the Fox and Wisconsin Rivers was strongly recommended and that of the Rock and Peckatonica when Illinois shall have rendered the Rock navigable from the present boundary to its mouth, and the hope is expressed that appropriations will be obtained from Congress to improve the navigation of the Platte and Grant Rivers and the River of the Four Lakes.

A rail or macadamized road ought, he said, to be constructed on the most practicable route from Lake Michigan to the Mississippi River, and turnpike or macadamized roads are much required through the timbered as well as some other sections of the Territory.

Complaint was made of the *system of taxation* and the opinion was expressed that county officers ought

"To render such services as are required on behalf of the public without compensation. 'That the honor of the office is its reward'."

A more effective system for the support of common schools was recommended, and the establishment of a high school.

The militia did not escape consideration

The address recommended —

"That the removal of all Indians within our limits, except those who are settled as agriculturists, be urged upon Government as an act of humanity to them, and as the only safe protection which it can give to this frontier."

Complaint was made that the public offices had not been held at the seat of government, and that the public records of the executive department were not at that place.

The Governor closed with the assurance to the members of both houses that he should—

"Earnestly endeavor to co-operate with them in all such measures as may be proposed by them to correct the evils of government, to secure the civil and political rights of individuals, to strengthen the foundations of society, or to render more permanent the institutions of freedom."

The question of the expediency of forming a State government was one that occupied the attention of the inhabitants of the Territory for six years or more previous to the admission of the State into the Union. The year 1842 was not an exception, although the population had not reached fifty thousand, while sixty thousand was the minimum number which, under the ordinance of 1787, entitled the "fifth State" to a place in the Union of States.

During the administration of Gov. DOTY the interest of the people in the question was intensified and extended over the northern portion of Illinois, by the aggressive efforts of the Governor to unite the "free inhabitants" of the district west of Lake Michigan and north of an east and west line running through its southern bend, in the formation of the "fifth State" contemplated by that ordinance.

So much of the Governor's address to the two Houses as related to the formation of a State government was referred to a committee in each House.

In the Council, Mr. UPHAM, from the committee on Territorial affairs (consisting of Messrs. UPHAM, MARTIN and BRIGHAM) submitted a report on the 8th of February. It said:

"The right of forming a State government with that Territory (northern Illinois) when the population amounts to sixty thousand or upwards, and claiming an admission into the Union under the Ordinance of 1787, is one question, the expediency of doing it is another."

The committee had little difficulty in coming to the conclusion that the inhabitants of the "fifth state" had the *right* to adopt the east and west line running through the southern bend of Lake Michigan and form a state north of it, and west of the Lake and demand its admission into the Union with that boundary, provided it contained sixty thousand free inhabitants.

Upon the question of *expediency*, the committee expressed no opinion, but proposed that the people of Wisconsin should decide it. For that purpose they reported a bill providing for referring the question of forming a State government to the people at the next general election, and also a resolution recommending to the people of the territory under the jurisdiction of Illinois, to hold an election at the same time on the question of uniting with us in forming a State government.

In the House of Representatives, Hon. A. G. ELLIS from the committee on Territorial Affairs to which the same subjects had been referred, submitted a report on the 11th of January.

The report was very pronounced in opposition to the formation of a State government, as also to embracing the "disputed territory;" and submitted the following resolutions:

"That the time has *not* arrived when it is expedient to adopt measures preparatory to a change in the form of government of Wisconsin.

"That our present Territorial Government is suited to our condition; that we ought to adhere to it till we have population sufficient in our present limits to entitle us to one representative on the floor of Congress.

"That the question of annexation of that part of the State of Illinois generally known as the 'disputed tract' to this Territory, ought not to be submitted to and settled by the vote of the inhabitants of that tract alone, but should be decided only with the advice and consent of the people of Wisconsin."

"That such annexation ought never to be made until the tract is discharged from its share of the public debt, as a part of the State of Illinois, nor until the population of Wisconsin shall be equal to that of said tract."

The bill and resolution reported in the Council were both passed by that body and sent to the House of Representatives, where they were laid on the table and no attempt was afterwards made to take them up for consideration.

The resolutions reported in the House were never taken up or considered by that body, and no act or resolution on the subject met with the concurrent action of both branches of the Legislative Assembly.

On the 19th of February a meeting of the citizens of Stephenson county, Illinois, was held at Freeport, at which resolutions were adopted asserting the right of the inhabitants of the Territory west of Lake Michigan and north of an east and west line through its southern bend, to become the "Fifth State," under the ordinance of '87, and that an election be held on the 5th day of March, in the several election precincts in that county, for or against the organization of such state. Judges of election were also appointed by the meeting for each precinct.

The elections were held and 570 votes were cast, of which all but one were in favor of the proposed State government.

On the 28th of June, Governor DOTY addressed to the Governor of Illinois an official letter, calling his attention to the fact that the commissioners appointed to locate the lands granted by the United States to the State of Illinois, had made the principal part of their selections, in the "disputed territory," and protesting against such selections,

"Because they are within the limits of the fifth of the Northwestern States, established by the Ordinance of 1787, and not, therefore, within the constitutional boundaries of the State of Illinois."

In concluding this protest Governor DOTY said :

"I cannot but remark the impropriety of permitting Illinois to become so extensive a landholder within a district which it is believed does not belong to her, and over which she can only be regarded as exercising accidentally and temporarily her jurisdiction."

At the August (general) election held in Boon county, where 496 votes were cast, a voluntary election was held for or against being attached to Wisconsin, when there were 485 in favor of it, and 11 not voting.

On the 13th of August, Gov. DOTY issued and had extensively published, a proclamation, under the Great Seal of the Territory, reciting that whereas, it was the opinion of many citizens that the Ordinance of 1787 and subsequent acts of Congress, guarantee to the people west of Lake Michigan and north of the line west from its southern bend, the right to form a permanent constitution and government; and whereas, it was desirable that it should be known whether it is the wish of the people to form such constitution: Therefore, it was recommended to the said "free inhabitants" that they do each, on the 4th Monday of September, vote "yea" or "nay," as the vote may be in favor of or against *the formation of a permanent government for the State of Wiskonsan.*" Provision was made in the proclamation for the return and canvassing the votes.

Only nine of the twenty counties then organized made any returns of elections under the proclamation.

These are here tabulated, showing that less than twenty-five hundred of the "free inhabitants" paid any attention to the proclamation, of which more than three fourths were against the formation of a State government.

COUNTIES.	FOR.	AGAINST.
Dane and Sauk	42	44
Fond du Lac	1	47
Green	98	15
Iowa	98	610
Jefferson	79	65
Milwaukee	95	634
Racine	136	206
Rock	70	193
Sheboygan	...	29
Total	619	1,843

On the 14th of January a resolution was adopted by the House of Representatives requesting the delegate in Congress to ascertain what progress had been made in the survey of the boundary between the State of Michigan and Wisconsin, and to obtain copies of the reports of the officer in charge of that work.

On the 16th of February, near the close of the session, the Governor sent a special message to the Legislative Assembly in which he said:

"It is ascertained that a part of the western boundary of the State of Michigan as prescribed by the act of Congress of the 15th of June, 1836, is an impracticable line, there being no such natural boundary as is therein described. The Lake of the Desert does not discharge its waters into the Montreal River.

It having, therefore, become necessary to designate a new line, I avail myself of the occasion to present the subject to the notice of the Assembly, that such measures as are proper may be adopted to procure the recognition by the government of the United States of the boundary which was established between Michigan and Wisconsin in 1805."

The message was referred to the committee on Territorial affairs which reported resolutions concurring with the Governor, stating that the

"New line" ought to be "a line drawn through the middle of Lake Michigan to its northern extremity."

And protesting against any other boundary, and that our delegate in Congress be requested to use his influence to procure the establishment of such a boundary.

The resolutions were adopted without a division.

The several parts of the Governor's address were referred in each House to appropriate committees.

Among other resolutions adopted by the House was this:

"That so much of the message of the Governor as relates to excessive legislation, and what Mr. JEFFERSON said, be referred to the committee on the judiciary."

The committee consisted of Messrs. WHITON, DEWEY, BARBER, ELLIS, and PARKINSON.

Mr. WHITON, chairman of the committee, made the following report:

"The committee on the judiciary, to whom was referred so much of the message of his Excellency, the Governor, as relates to excessive legislation, and what Mr. JEFFERSON said, report: That they fully concur with the Governor in the opinion that excessive legislation is a great evil, and that rapid changes in the laws are injurious to private rights and to public interests. But as the Governor has recommended no specific measures in relation to the subject, unless it be the one which seems to have received the approbation of Mr. JEFFERSON, the committee would confine their observations to the one which that great statesman deemed a salutary one.

"The committee are of the opinion that the measure recommended, however proper in older states, where great changes in the condition of the people seldom take place, would be found very inconvenient and indeed almost impracticable in a community as new as ours, where the population increases with such great rapidity, where wealth is accumulated with so much facility by almost every class of society, and where consequently great changes are constantly occurring. Where these changes take place new interests are consequently springing up which require the speedy attention of the Legislature, and if a year was allowed to elapse between the bringing in of a bill and the final passing of it, great injury might result. Nor do the committee think it would be politic or proper to require a majority of two-thirds to pass a law. They have arrived at the conclusion that sufficient checks now exist to prevent hasty legislation. The Territory has a Legislature consisting of three branches, one of which is not chosen or appointed by the people of the Territory.

"If all these branches concur in passing a law, it afterwards is subject to be negatived by Congress and becomes null and void, and acts incorporating banks do not take effect until approved by Congress. It is true that two-thirds of both houses can pass an act without the assent of the Governor, but the negative of Congress is absolute. If Congress had no power to negative our acts it might be well to require a majority of two-thirds to pass acts creating corporations, especially banking institutions, as is required in the State of New York, but as the Territory is now situated in relation to laws passed by its Legislature, we think the requirement unnecessary. The committee entertain in common with all classes in society, a very great respect for the opinions which Mr. JEFFERSON expressed on all subjects connected with government, but cannot bring themselves to the conclusion that they ought in this particular instance to govern us in our legislative action. The evil complained of must be corrected by the Legislature taking care to pass no laws which will not subserve the interests of the people."

In the Council, so much of the Governor's address as relates to banks and other incorporations was referred to the committee on incorporations, which consisted of Messrs. STRONG, LEARNED and BRIGHAM.

Mr. STRONG, chairman of that committee, submitted a report, in which after expressing the concurrence of the committee in the opinions expressed by the Governor in relation to *monopolies,* says:

"They are, however, of the opinion that these corporations, which have yielded the *bitterest* 'fruit for the people,' are not the 'offspring' of the last four years,"

and that the Bank of Wisconsin chartered seven years ago, and the Bank of Mineral Point chartered five years ago, pre-eminently demand the attention of the Legislature, and that these acts appear as clearly as any others "to have been granted to favor particular persons," and that "They are incorporations to aid speculation."

The committee did not concur with the Governor in the idea which he seemed to convey, that the banks had been *destroyed* by the Legislature, but conceived that "They had destroyed themselves."

The report further says:

"Your committee entertain no doubt but that the Legislature possesses the power to prohibit the circulation, and the buying and selling of depreciated bank paper, within the limits of the Territory, and that, too, without placing them, as the Governor does, on the footing of counterfeit notes; but the experience of other States, which have made the experiment, admonishes them, that a law, having that for the object, would never be carried into practical operation; that it would remain a dead letter upon our statute-book; or at best serve but as an instrument in the hands of the malicious, to injure or annoy their more honest and undesigning neighbors, and they are therefore of the opinion that such a law would be unwise and impolitic. The other suggestion in relation to 'an institution to be hereafter created' your committee conceive (if it is a recommendation of any thing) is a recommendation for the incorporation of another bank, and the committee cannot perceive why it is not justly open to the same objections which the Governor has so forcibly and clearly pointed out as existing against monopolies generally; and — applying the language of the Governor to such an institution — the committee conceive it would be an incorporation 'granting exclusive privileges to certain individuals'; 'that it would justly excite alarm in the minds of all men who are friendly to equal rights, and to the establishment of all such institutions as are most favorable to Democracy'; that it would be a combination of 'political power and wealth,' a 'petty aristocracy'; the offspring of the year that brought it forth; and in whatever neighborhood it might be planted, although it 'might now give temporary benefits to a few individuals, we may expect the time will soon arrive when it would yield only bitter fruit for the people'; it would be an 'incorporation to aid speculation.' Your committee cannot, therefore, recommend the passage of such an act of incorporation."

In the House the committee on mining and smelting, to which was referred by resolution that part of the Governor's message relating to the duties on lead, by Mr. JENKINS, the chairman, reported :

"That they have in vain examined the message of His Excellency, for the purpose of finding any portion having any particular bearing upon the subject submitted, and that they are unable to make a report based upon any recommendation in the message.

"The Governor has not in any manner, at least in a direct way, alluded to the particular interests of the miner and smelter of the Territory. Although, in general terms, he has stated what everybody knows, viz.: 'That the protection of the business of mining and smelting lead ore, which has heretofore been afforded by the United States, by the duty on lead, has enabled the miners of Wisconsin to supply chiefly the consumption of the United States,' etc. Yet, there he leaves the matter, so far as the interests of the mining portions of the Territory are concerned, without any specific recommendation or expression of opinion, and concludes his only paragraph on the subject by paying a high compliment to the Boston merchants, which exhibits more solicitude on the part of the executive for the enterprise of the 'enterprising merchants' of the city alluded to, than for the interests of the enterprising miners and smelters of his own Territory, whose claims upon his attention were certainly greater than those of any foreign class."

A reference was made in both Houses to so much of the Governor's address as relates to the prosecution of the inland trade, the Milwaukee and Rock River canal, the improvement of rivers, the construction of rail, turnpike and McAdamized roads.

Able reports upon these subjects were made in both Houses. So much of these reports as relates to the canal and cognate matters will be considered in a future chapter devoted to that particular subject.

The substance of the reports in both houses is contained in the report of the committee on Internal Improvements in the Council, which consisted of Messrs. TWEEDY, JANES and BRIGHAM.

The report of this committee submitted by Mr. TWEEDY its chairman, stated in reference to a railroad from the Mississippi river to Lake Michigan, that:

"Measures designed to carry into effect these recommendations were some time since presented for the action of the Council."

The only measure, however, which was adopted by the legislature, in this report was a joint resolution

"That the Congress of the United States be urgently requested to make an appropriation of ten thousand dollars, to be expended under the direction of the Territorial engineer for the survey of a railroad from Potosi in Grant county on the Mississippi river to Lake Michigan, to form a part of the chain of internal improvements, from the Atlantic to the Mississippi river."

Congress did not respond to the "urgent request" and no appropriation for that purpose was made. The report continues:

"The improvement of the Rock and Peckatonica rivers and of the river of the Four Lakes has from year to year engaged the attention of the legislature, and been recommended to the favor of Congress.

It is believed that further action on this subject is not advisable at the present session of the Legislative Assembly.

Your committee concur in opinion with His Excellency that turnpike and McAdamized roads are much required through the timbered and other sections of the Territory. They do not conceive, however, that any company should be incorporated or that taxes in any of the several counties should be appropriated by law, for the prosecution of such improvements in any case, until such legislative aid is demanded by the people of the districts which will be affected thereby."

Mr. WHITON, from the judiciary committee of the House, to which that part of the message of the Governor was referred relative to taxes and tax titles, submitted a very able and lucid report, such as might have been expected from the pen of that great jurist.

After demonstrating that every government possesses the power of determining what property shall be taxed and what shall be exempt, and that a wise exercise of that power is expedient and just, the report proceeds at considerable length, to consider the objections of the Governor to the system of taxation then in existence in the Territory. These objections, the report said, appeared to be five in number.

First. That the taxes are too high.

Second. That property is exempt from taxation which ought not to be.

Third. That the taxes are illegal.

Fourth. That the land upon which taxes are assessed and not paid is sold; and

Fifth. That the law which limits the right of bringing an action to recover back land sold for taxes to three years is wrong.

The refutation of all these objections is so complete that no abbreviation of it could do it justice, and only a reference to it in the journal of the House of that session (page 133) can be made.

The *removal of the Indians* from Wisconsin, recommended by the Governor, received the favorable consideration of the Legislative Assembly by the adoption of joint resolutions, that the delegate in Congress be requested to urge upon the general government the necessity of freeing the Territory from the Indian population within her limits, and their permanent location in a district of country west of the Mississippi, to which the white settlements shall not extend and where the energies of the government may be directed to the improvement of their condition.

So much of the Governor's address as relates to schools and to the University was referred in the House to the committee on schools, and the Rev. ALFRED BRONSON, chairman of that committee, before the adoption of a resolution that he was not entitled to a seat, made very elaborate reports accompanied by two bills, one in relation to schools, the other in relation to the University.

The first after being emasculated so as to limit its operation to the protection of school lands was passed into a law and the other was indefinitely postponed in the House.

Acts were passed to incorporate academies at Platteville and at Delavan.

The subjects of exempting sheep and their fleeces from taxation for the purpose of encouraging the *growth of wool*, the *fur trade* and the holding of *public offices* away from the seat of government, brought to the attention of the Legislative Assembly by the Governor, did not make a favorable impression upon either house, and were not even considered by either.

One of the most important subjects which demanded legislative action, appears to have entirely escaped the attention of the Governor and was not referred to in his address.

This was a new apportionment of members for the fourth Legislative Assembly.

A resolution was adopted by the Council that a select committee be appointed on apportionment. The committee consisted of Messrs. TWEEDY, BRIGHAM and STRONG.

Mr. TWEEDY in behalf of the committee submitted a report which stated that several bases had been suggested, (1) The votes cast at the late general election in the several districts. (2) A conjectural estimate of the increase of population. (3) A new census to be ordered to be taken during the ensuing summer. (4) The census of 1840. Of these several bases, they say:

"The two first mentioned are liable to numerous fatal objections too obvious to require notice.

"A new census would furnish the true basis. But the expense attending the enumeration of the inhabitants, and of an extra session of the Legislature presents an objection of policy, which in the opinion of your committee, should deter the Legislature from providing for another census at the present time.

"This objection may be avoided in part by authorizing the Governor to make an apportionment upon the basis of a census to be taken, upon principles to be prescribed by law."

The committee, therefore, adopted the fourth of the above bases — the census of 1840.

Having decided that the existing arrangement of the election districts should not be disturbed they reported a bill with the following apportionment:

NAMES OF ELECTION DISTRICTS.	Members of Council.	Members of House of Representatives.
Milwaukee and Washington counties................................	2	6
Grant county...	2	3
Iowa county..	2	3
Rock and Walworth counties.....................................	2	4
Crawford and St. Croix counties.................................	1	2
Green, Dane, Jefferson, Dodge, and Sauk counties................	1	2
Brown county and counties attached, including Portage...........	1	4
Racine county..	2	2
Totals..	13	26

Subsequently Mr. BULLEN, on leave, introduced a bill to provide for the taking of the census of the inhabitants, and to authorize the Governor to apportion the members of the Council and House of Representatives. After much discussion, the bill reported by the select committee was laid on the table, and the bill introduced by Mr. BULLEN was passed. In the House it was at first negatived, and afterward reconsidered and passed.

The law as passed provided for an enumeration of the inhabitants of the Territory, omitting Indians not citizens and officers and soldiers of the army. It was to commence on the first day of June and be completed in fifty days, by the sheriffs and their deputies. The returns were to be made in duplicate to the Register of Deeds and Secretary of the Territory. The Secretary was to make and file an abstract of the returns and furnish the Governor with a copy of it.

The Governor was then to make an apportionment of the members of the Council and House of Representatives among the several election districts, in a mode particularly prescribed by the act; and at least thirty days preceding the annual election to be held in September (fourth Monday), he was to make proclamation declaring the apportionment made under the act.

The number of inhabitants in each county and the apportionment is shown in the following table:

Name of Counties.	No. of Inhabitants in County.	No. of Inhabitants in District.	Members of Council.	Members of House.
Milwaukee	9,565			
Washington	965	10,530	3	6
Racine	6,318	6,318	2	3
Brown	2,146			
Winnebago	143			
Marquette	59			
Sheboygan	221			
Manitowoc	263			
Calumet	407			
Fond du Lac	295			
Portage	646	4,180	1	3

TERRITORY OF WISCONSIN IN 1842. 371

Name of Counties.	No. of Inhabitants in County.	No. of Inhabitants in District.	Members of Council.	Members of House.
Walworth	4,618			
Rock	2,867	7,485	2	4
Dane	776			
Green	1,594			
Jefferson	1,638			
Dodge	239			
Sauk	303	4,550		
Iowa	5,029	5 029	1	3
Grant	5,937	5,937	1	3
Crawford	1,449		2	3
St Croix (estimated)	1,200	2,649	1	1
Totals	46,678	46,678		

At this session the county of Richland was formed out of the county of Crawford and attached temporarily to the county of Iowa.

The counties of Calumet and Winnebago were organized for all purposes of county government.

It appeared from the report of a committee appointed to examine the returns that the counties in which a majority of the votes cast on the question were in favor of the act, approved February 18, 1841,

"For the government of the several towns in this Territory and for the revision of county government,"

were Jefferson, Milwaukee, Walworth, Racine, Fond du Lac, Rock, Crawford and Brown; in Green and Iowa counties the majorities were against the act; and from the counties of Dane, Sauk, Portage, Dodge, St. Croix, Sheboygan, Manitowoc, Washington and Grant, no returns were received.

An act was passed in 1842, declaring that said act had been adopted by the people of the counties of Milwaukee, Racine, Walworth, Rock, Jefferson, Brown and Fond du Lac, and should be in force in those counties on the first Tuesday of April next; and its taking effect in all other counties in which it had been adopted should be postponed to the first Tuesday of April, 1843.

A number of towns were organized by act of the Legislative Assembly at this session: Wheatland, Paris, Mount Pleasant, Yorkville and Caledonia, in Racine county; Fond du lac, Calumet and Waupun, in the county of Fond du Lac; Warren, in Milwaukee county; Clinton, Beloit, Rock, Union, Center, Janesville and Milton in the county of Rock, and the name of the town of Finch in Jefferson county was changed to Koshkonong.

Four acts were passed at this session to amend acts of previous legislatures, incorporating villages, each of which was vetoed by the Governor, and passed by a majority of two thirds of each House, notwithstanding the objections of the Governor. One of these vetoes is a fair sample of all and is as follows:

"I consider the original charter to have been passed without authority, and that it contains provisions which are in violation of the act of Congress establishing the Territorial government of Wisconsin.

"All laws passed in this Territory must, according to the requirement of that act, be submitted to Congress. If the Legislature had the power to create this corporation, it could not confer upon the corporation greater powers than itself possessed, nor authority to exercise them in a manner different from that prescribed for the Legislature by the act of Congress.

"The provisions of this bill, in my opinion, conflict with those of the act of Congress, and I must, therefore, decline signing it. J. D. DOTY."

The act amending the charter of Southport was passed over the veto by a vote of 9 to 1 in the Council and 21 to 0 in the House (unanimous).

That to amend the charter of Racine by a vote of 9 to 2 in the Council and 23 to 2 in the House.

That to amend the charter of Milwaukee by a vote of 9 to 1 in the Council and 23 to 1 in the House.

That to amend the charter of Green Bay by a vote of 9 to 1 in the Council and 24 to 0 in the House.

Two other acts were passed over the Governor's veto:

One was an act to incorporate the Janesville Bridge Company, which passed the Council by a vote of 9 to 2 and the House unanimously — ayes 25, noes 0.

The other was "An act to provide for the payment of the expenses of the Legislative Assembly" (Session Laws, p. 85).

This passed the Council, notwithstanding the veto, by a vote of 9 to 2, and the House by a vote of 19 to 6.

An act of great importance to the inhabitants of Fond du Lac was passed at this session. In November, 1835, at Green Bay, a number of persons voluntarily associated themselves together under the name of the "Fond du Lac" company, and purchased about two thousand acres of land embracing the area of the present city of Fond du Lac. The company laid out a town into lots and blocks and sold numerous lots, the conveyances being executed by the president of the company.

The act set forth at length the "articles of association" and recited that *"whereas* doubts are entertained of the legality of such conveyance, and also as to the nature and degree of the estate which the members of an incorporated joint stock company may have therein; Therefore, for the purpose of perfecting the title of purchasers and to prevent difficulty and litigation in relation thereto, it was enacted that the stockholders of said association should be an incorporation with all appropriate corporate powers.

An act was passed to repeal the act of December 2d, 1836, "to incorporate the stockholders of the Bank of Mineral Point."

On the 10th of January, ALEX. MITCHELL, secretary of the Wisconsin Marine and Fire Insurance Company, in response to a resolution of the Council, submitted a statement sworn to by him, showing the financial condition of that corporation.

The statement gave the assets at $299,893.31 and the liabilities, exclusive of capital stock, at $75,418.31 of which $34,028, were one, three and five dollar evidences of debt issued and outstanding (currency).

At the fall term of the Circuit Court for Brown county, held by Judge MILLER, in a proceeding commenced by the Attorney General, the charter of the Bank of Wisconsin was vacated.

The provisions of the act of February 19, 1841, "to incorporate the Western Mutual Fire Insurance Company, at Prairie du Chien and the Howard Fire Insurance Company of Brown county," not having been complied with, another act was passed declaring that said act was revived and continued in force.

Divorces were for the first time in the history of Wisconsin legislation refused to be granted.

A brief but important act in the interest of humanity was passed in these words:

"That so much of any law of this Territory as authorizes the issuing an execution against the body of the defendant, in any civil cause, excepting in action of trespass or tort, is hereby repealed."

An act was passed "to incorporate the Fox River Improvement Company."

The following special acts were passed authorizing the building and maintaining of dams.

By ASA CLARK, at the outlet of Pewaukee Lake.

By D. G. KENDALL and GILMORE KENDALL and their associates, across the Rock River, in sections two and eleven in town six, range fourteen, in Jefferson county.

By OLIVER C. HUBBARD and his associates, across the Manitowoc River, on section twenty-three, town nineteen, range twenty-three, in Manitowoc county.

By LUCIUS I. BARBER and ENOCH G. DARLING and their associates across Rock River, on section eleven, town six, range fourteen, in Jefferson county.

By GEORGE LURWICK and his associates, across the Oconto River, on section twenty-four, town twenty-eight, range twenty-one.

Special acts were passed authorizing the keeping and maintaining two ferries:

One by WEBSTER STANLEY, across Fox River, on section twenty-three, town eigteen, range sixteen east — the site of the present city of Oshkosh.

The other by CHRISTOPHER CARR, across the Mississippi River, within the military reserve of Fort Snelling, about one mile above the mouth of St. Peters River. This ferry site is now in the State of Minnesota.

Besides the act to incorporate the Janesville Bridge Company, passed over the Governor's veto, two acts for the erection of bridges were passed and approved by the Governor; one to incorporate the Beloit and Rock River Bridge Company, and "an act to authorize JAMES H. ROGERS and others to construct, at their own expense, a free floating bridge across the Milwaukee River."

The annual demand for the appointment by law of commissioners to locate Territorial roads, existed in an undiminished degree, and the location of the following Territorial roads was provided for:

From Mineral Point to Milwaukee.

From Menomonee Mills, in Crawford county, to Dacotah, in St. Croix county.

From Rock River, in section 24, town 11, range 15, by Closson's settlement, in Dodge county, to Dickason's Mills, in Portage county.

From Prairie Village, in Milwaukee county, to Fort Atkinson, in Jefferson county.

From Fond du Lac to intersect Territorial road from Depere to Knapp's Ferry, crossing Fox River at or near Oshkosh.

From the Wisconsin River, opposite Helena, to the Dells of the Wisconsin River.

From the Fox River, opposite Green Bay, to the Wisconsin River between Plover Portage and Big Bull Falls.

From Beloit, in Rock county, to Monroe, in Green county.

From Platteville, in Grant county, *via* New Diggings and White Oak Springs, in Iowa county, and thence to the State line.

From Belmont, in Iowa county, to a point on the Mississippi River in Grant county, opposite Dubuque.

From Sauk Prairie, in Sauk county, *via* Arena and Hicox's Mills, to the military road.

From Watertown, in Dodge county, to Washara, in Dodge county.

From Whitewater, in Walworth county, to Monroe, in Green county.

From Prairie du Sauk, in Sauk county, *via* Helena and Hicox's Mills, to the military road.

On the assembling of the Legislative Assembly an accrimonious controversy was in existence as to who was lawful Treasurer of the Territory. The matter was investigated by a committee of the House of Representatives, with power to send for persons and papers and examine witnesses on oath, from whose report the following facts appear:

That on the 17th of December, 1839, ROBERT L. REAM was duly appointed Treasurer for the term of two years, and that under the law he would hold his office until his successor was lawfully appointed.

The office being created by the laws of the Territory, the incumbent was not subject to removal by the Governor.

That on the 3d of September, 1841, Gov. DOTY, assuming

that the office was vacant for the alleged reason that Mr. REAM had not filed his official bond, appointed JAMES MORRISON treasurer.

That, in fact, Mr. REAM executed his official bond, which was approved by the Governor on the 6th of January, 1840, and took the oath of office, and performed all that the law required to constitute him the legal Treasurer.

That after the appointment of Mr. MORRISON, Mr. REAM refused to surrender the official books and papers in his possession, and continued such refusal after two years from the date of his appointment, claiming that his successor had not been legally appointed.

Mr. MORRISON was afterwards nominated by the Governor, and the nomination was confirmed on the 24th of January, 1842.

The principal importance of this controversy was the possession of the funds of the Territory, and particularly the sum of $1,758.28 which had been paid into the treasury of the United States by J. D. DOTY as treasurer of the commissioner of public buildings, which he claimed to be the balance in his hands of the funds received by him from the United States of the $40,000 appropriated by Congress for the public buildings.

This sum was received by Mr. MORRISON about the 1st of January, 1840, and under the law was applicable alone to payments for the completion of the Capitol.

At the meeting of the Legislative Assembly the Capitol was not yet completed even to the extent required by the contract made under the act passed at the previous session; but it was far better adapted to the necessities and even the convenience of the legislators than it had before been.

On the 7th of January the commissioner of public buildings — N. C. PRENTISS — submitted his report to the Legislative Assembly.

It stated that in pursuance of the act of February 19, 1841, he let a contract on the 27th of April to DANIEL BAXTER for seven thousand dollars for the completion of the Capitol by the 1st of December, 1841. It states that the work is not completed and shows the progress which had been made and expresses the opinion that the balance of one thousand dollars of the fund applicable to the payment for the work, remaining in the hands of the treasurer is sufficient protection to the Territory for the completion of the contract.

In relation to the pending suits in favor of the Territory, one against J. D. DOTY, J. F. O'NEILL and A. A. BIRD, the other against JAMES MORRISON and his sureties, the commissioner stated the reasons which had prevented their being brought to trial.

JOHN Y. SMITH was elected by the two houses on the 18th of February commissioner of public buildings, as the successor of Mr. PRENTISS.

Two acts were passed by both branches of the Legislative Assembly, having for their object the completion of the Capitol and the payment of the contractor, which were presented to the Governor in the forenoon of the day before the adjournment and retained by him, neither of which were approved by him or returned with his objections. He afterwards caused to be published in the newspapers a statement of his objections to the acts, which he was prevented by want of time from sending to the House of Representatives, where they originated.

One of these acts extended the time for the completion of the Capitol until November 1, 1842, and the other directed the Treasurer to pay for the work out of whatever moneys were in his hands or should come to his possession, of the money donated by Congress for the purpose of erecting the Capitol — except $250 — provided the sum paid by the Treasurer should not exceed $1,750.

The approval of these two acts by the Governor would seem to have placed the completion of the Capitol at an early day beyond peradventure, while the failure of the Governor to approve them created great embarrassment in the consummation of that desirable result.

In a few days after the commissioner — Mr. SMITH — was elected, he took possession of the Capitol and made efforts to induce BAXTER to proceed with its completion. The dome was in a sad condition, leaking very badly, and the rains were seriously injuring the interior of the building. The contractor was willing to proceed with the work if funds for the purpose could be furnished him.

The commissioner applied to the Treasurer for the small sum of $100 to repair the dome, but was unable to obtain it.

The Treasurer refused to consent to pay any part of the funds in his hands applicable to the completion of the Capitol without the approval of the Governor. The Governor refused to give any such approval except upon one condition, which was, that the suits pending against the commissioners and the Treasurer and his sureties *should be discontinued.*

The commissioner in his report says:

"He (the Governor) admitted that finishing the Capitol and settling the suits had no necessary connection, but said he thought the whole matter had better be settled together; and in this position he remained invincible."

The commissioner submitted this proposition:

"That the defendants should pay the costs of the suits and five thousand dollars in Territorial liabilities in addition to the $1,758.38, in the treasury."

The proposition was rejected.

The commissioner said:

"For the Territory to be *compelled* by an executive usurpation of her treasury, to abandon a just claim, was what your commissioner could by no means consent to, but was of the opinion that she had better see her Capitol sunk in the middle of the Fourth Lake than submit to terms so unjust and humiliating."

The only remaining resource of the commissioner was to prevail upon the contractor to raise the means from his private resources, and finish the building complete before the meeting of the Legislature. In this he was in some degree successful. The dome and roof were put in such condition as to prevent leaking and such other work was done as seemed indispensable.

Previous to the April term of court in Walworth county, the counsel for the Territory, at the solicitation of the defendant's counsel, consented to a continuance of the Territorial suits, upon their agreement to a peremptory trial at the fall term. At the October term the cases were reached, and after a series of lengthy arguments, the suits against MORRISON were withdrawn on account of a defect in the declaration. In the other suit it was thought advisable to amend the declaration which involved the continuance of the suit.

"No question " (the commissioner said in his report) " has as yet been decided, which at all militates against the right of the Territory to recover heavy judgments against the defendants. These judgments, however, can never be reached while the court is confined to one week at a session."

The Legislative Assembly adopted a resolution approved January 21, 1842,

"That the Legislature of the State of New York be requested to abolish all toll, imposed by the laws or canal regulations of that state upon the transportation of pig and bar lead through the Erie canal on its passage eastward."

The policy of the United States Government which had been adopted as early as 1807 of *leasing* the lead mines, continued to be enforced for more than ten years after the discovery of the lead deposits of the Upper Mississippi. So long as the title of the entire domain in which these mines were situated was in the United States, the system worked without much friction or dissatisfaction. But so soon as a portion of the lands were sold, and lead mines were discovered upon the lands of individuals, there arose an inequality in the condition of those who were working upon government lease and paying rents, and those working on other lands who paid no rents.

This condition of things resulted in a practical abandonment by the government in 1834 of the policy of leasing the lead mines and it was not attempted to be revived until 1842.

The matter had always been in charge of the ordnance bureau of the war department, and an officer of the regular army detailed to take charge of the business. But in 1841 in some manner, a civilian named JOHN FLANIGAN had procured himself appointed "Superintendent of the United States Lead Mines," and opened an office at Galena. By the terms of his appointment he was to be entitled to ten per cent. of all such collections as he might make, besides his salary.

He assumed that all lands containing lead ore had been reserved from sale, and the sale by the government of any tract upon which known deposits existed at the time of the sale was void, and that all the lead mines, as well those upon lands which had been purchased by individuals as upon unsold lands, were subject to be leased.

These pretensions and assumptions of this "Superintendent" would be harmless if they had not been sanctioned by the officials from whom he derived his pretended authority. But the Ordnance Bureau, the Commissioner of the General Land Office, the Secretary of War, and even the President ratified and approved his acts in proposing to grant leases of lead mines without regard to the rights of individuals, acquired by their purchase from the Government.

This "Superintendent" issued, and caused to be generally published, a "notice to miners," that on the 15th of February, 1842, he would be prepared at his office, in Galena, to grant leases for the lead mines of the United States in the State of Illinois and Territories of Wisconsin and Iowa.

On the 10th of January Mr. STRONG offered a resolution in the Council, reciting this "notice," and that, whereas, there was reason to believe that the "Superintendent" intended to lease all lands containing lead mines, whether the same had been entered or not. Therefore —

"That a select committee be appointed, with instructions to prepare a *memorial* to the Secretary of War, asking him to rescind any instructions that may have emanated from his department, or any bureau thereof, authorizing the said Superintendent to lease any lead mines in this Territory."

The resolution was adopted, and Messrs. STRONG, VINEYARD, and ROUNTREE appointed the committee, which presented the memorial in conformity with the instructions, which was adopted.

The notice proved a great attraction to the miners of the country who were not owners of land, to the floating landless population, and to all affected with *communistic* notions; so that in October it was reported that the number of leases granted by the —

"Superintendent up to that time was about 500, and averaged about twenty-five acres in extent, with five hands to each lease."

On the other hand, the permanent, substantial population of the lead mines regarded the course pursued by the "Superintendent" as a gross outrage upon their rights, against which they were swift to enter their protest.

Mr. YOUNG, one of the Senators from Illinois, introduced a bill for the survey of the unsold mineral lands into ten acre lots, with the pre-emption right to occupants of them to purchase such lots. The bill failed to pass Congress. But at the opening of the next session the message of the President contained this recommendation :

"For several years angry contentions have grown out of the dispositions directed by law to be made of the mineral lands held by the government in several of the States. The government is constituted the landlord, and the citizens of the States wherein lie the lands, are its tenants. The relation is an unwise one and it would be much more conducive to the public interest that a sale of the lands should be made, than that they should remain in their present condition."

Would that fidelity to the work in hand admitted the closing of this chapter of the events of 1842, without reference to the most painful tragedy, growing out of personal conflict, which occurred during the existence of the Territorial government of Wisconsin. But it cannot be. The sad tale must be told ; and the truth presented regarding the terrible homicide by which in the Legislative Halls of the Territory, CHARLES C. P. ARNDT, a member of the Council, was fatally shot by a fellow member, JAMES R. VINEYARD.

The consideration of executive nominations to office was a matter which, in cases of contest, created a considerable degree of feeling. Mr. ARNDT was a zealous partisan, and a faithful and devoted friend of Governor DOTY, and with a single exception, gave his vote to advise and consent to all of the contested nominations of the Governor. Party allegiance sat more lightly on Mr. VINEYARD. Sometimes he voted for the questionable nominations, and sometimes against them, and it was generally thought by his fellow members that his votes were influenced more by policy than principle.

The personal relations between Messrs. ARNDT and VINEYARD had always during their acquaintance been of the most friendly character.

At an early period of the session the Governor submitted the nomination of ENOS S. BAKER to be Sheriff of Grant county.

On the 24th of January the consideration of the nomination was on motion of Mr. VINEYARD postponed until the 5th of February, when it came up, and after a protracted discussion was rejected.

On Monday, the 7th of February, Mr. UPHAM moved a reconsideration of the vote of the previous Saturday, by which the nomination was rejected.

The motion was for the time laid on the table.

On the 11th of February the Governor sent to the Council the following communication:

"The nomination of ENOS S. BAKER, Esq,, to be Sheriff of Grant county being still before the Council on a motion to reconsider the vote of Saturday last, it is my duty to submit to the Council a paper which I have received in relation to that nomination, which is signed by nineteen members of the House of Representatives.

"EXECUTIVE OFFICE, February 10, 1842. "J. D. DOTY."

The paper thus submitted was dated February 7th and addressed to the Governor, the nineteen members who signed it being as nearly as possible divided between the political parties, and after giving the reasons of the signers at length, said in conclusion:

"We cannot approbate the course that has been taken against Mr. BAKER, and hoping that some portion of the Council at least who voted against him will, upon reflection, see the propriety of sustaining him, we earnestly request your Excellency to renominate Mr. BAKER to the office of Sheriff of Grant County."

It was said and is probable, that the feeling which

prompted this paper influenced Mr. UPHAM to move the reconsideration. It is certain that an intense feeling in relation to the nomination pervaded both houses and extended outside the Capitol.

Soon after this communication from the Governor was received and on the same day, Mr. ARNDT moved to take up the motion to reconsider, which motion was opposed by Mr. VINEYARD. What then occurred is best described in the testimony of witnesses upon the preliminary examination of VINEYARD on the charge of murder.

"J. H. TWEEDY sworn: The difficulty grew out of a debate on motion to lay on the table the nomination of E. S. BAKER. Mr. ARNDT opposed it, because the gentleman from Grant (alluding to Mr. VINEYARD, I suppose), 'had given the highest testimonials as to the character of the nominee.' I think, upon his making that remark, Mr. VINEYARD turned partly round in his seat, and said it was a falsehood. Some words passed and order was restored. Soon after a motion to adjourn was made, and a division had thereon; and immediately after the members had arisen in the negative, before announcement by the chair, most of the members and by-standers rose and I saw deceased and Mr. VINEYARD, and I believe one or two others, close together at the corner of Mr. VINEYARD's desk. Many words in a high key passed; heard deceased demand of Mr. VINEYARD an explanation. Then Mr. STRONG called aloud 'order,' twice; and the president arose and called the House to order. VINEYARD and deceased were parted by one or two by-standers. Saw deceased then move about eight feet towards the fire-place. He stood there, and Mr. VINEYARD at his desk, until the chair announced an adjournment. Mr. ARNDT then came up to Mr. VINEYARD's desk. Mr. V. was standing at the corner of it. Deceased asked Mr. VINEYARD if he imputed to him falsehood in his remarks. Mr. VINEYARD answered 'yes,' or that 'they were false,' I do not remember which. Think I then saw deceased strike at Mr. V's face, or forehead — they were about three feet apart. Rose to go to them. Did not see distinctly, but thought one or two blows had passed; then heard an explosion. Deceased partly reeled around and moved several steps towards the fire-place, with his hands on his breast. I believe next moment saw him in the arms of Mr. DEERING. I believe in about five minutes saw him die. He said nothing, and did not appear to be conscious of anything."

"JAMES COLLINS sworn: After Mr. VINEYARD made the motion to postpone the nomination, Mr. ARNDT rose and opposed it and said something like this: 'He must oppose the motion of the gentleman from Grant for the reason that he was not willing to give him an opportunity to introduce evidence to *belie* the statement he had before made on the floor.' I think at this time VINEYARD arose for the purpose of explanation. Mr. ARNDT did not give way, and both were speaking at the same time, and I saw Mr. ARNDT wave his hand toward Mr. VINEYARD and said, 'That difference will be accommodated at some other time.' They had some private conversation together, and I called to order. They separated. Before the vote on the adjournment was announced I saw them together again. High words passed between them. Mr. ARNDT then walked to the fire-place and Mr. VINEYARD stepped to his seat. I then paused for a short time, and announced the vote on adjournment and left my seat. Mr. ARNDT approached Mr. VINEYARD. High words again passed between them, and I was reaching forward my hand to lay hold of Mr. ARNDT, when he struck Mr. VINEYARD with his right hand. Mr. VINEYARD seemed to recede a little, and I very soon heard the report of a pistol. I did not know who fired it at the moment, and supposed some one had let off a pistol in attempting to draw it from his pocket. ARNDT reeled around and soon fell. I then turned to VINEYARD, and for the first time saw what I supposed to be a pistol in his hand. He had it clasped round the lock. I was of the impression and still am that it was a six-shooter pistol. It is possible I may be mistaken. Some one called out 'arrest him!' He replied, 'I'm not going away.' I walked over with him to the American and left him in the hall or on the stoop."

JOHN H. ROUNTREE, called for the defense, being sworn, testified as follows:

"The deceased and Mr. VINEYARD have always manifested friendship for each other during the session. I have frequently seen them in each other's room. I noticed them during the morning session standing before the fire in very friendly conversation. Each had an arm around the other's neck. I think this was during a call of the house. I have known Mr. VINEYARD for fifteen or sixteen years; intimately for fourteen or fifteen years. He has lived for fourteen years within half a mile of me. I have ever esteemed him as a kind and benevolent man. I have never known any revengeful act in him, or disposition to seek revenge. He is very warm and ardent in his feelings. From my acquaintance with him I should say that he did not bear malice. He is excitable, but his passions soon subside, and kind feelings quickly return."

The testimony of the other witnesses was substantially the same, all agreeing that the deceased was the assailing party, and that VINEYARD was defending himself against the assault.

He immediately surrendered himself to the sheriff and was committed to jail, where his wife remained with him until he was released.

The next day the death of Mr. ARNDT was announced in each house and appropriate resolutions were adopted in both. The body of the deceased was conveyed to his friends at Green Bay at the expense of the Legislative Assembly, the members of which accompanied it in a body for several miles.

At the next meeting of the Council on Monday the 14th, the President stated that he had received a communication on the subject of which there was doubt whether this body had any control. The communication is signed by JAMES R. VINEYARD, a member of the Council from the county of Grant, tendering his resignation of his seat in this body, and asked if it was the pleasure of the Council to receive for consideration the communication?

Mr. STRONG requested that it be read.

Mr. BRIGHAM then moved that the communication be returned to its author without reading, which was agreed to.

Mr. BRIGHAM then, by leave, offered a preamble and resolution.

The preamble recited the fatal shooting of Mr. ARNDT,

and that VINEYARD was unworthy to be a member of the body, and therefore

Resolved, That he be expelled and his seat declared vacant.

Mr. STRONG said he would cheerfully vote for the preamble, but could not vote for the resolution. He felt the deepest, the warmest indignation at the outrage which had been perpetrated and would unite with any member in expressing those feelings in any appropriate manner, but he could not bring his mind to the conclusion that the Council had any right to reject the resignation. He considered that every member, so long as he was such, had the control of his own seat, and that he could resign it or not, at his pleasure; but as soon as he did resign it, the Council had no power to reject the resignation. His connection with the body had ceased, and they had no further control over it or him, not even the power to expel him, for he had no seat to be expelled from.

The preamble was adopted unanimously and the resolution by a vote of 10 to 1, all the members present voting in the affirmative except Mr. STRONG, who called for the ayes and noes and voted against the resolution.

About the 10th of March, VINEYARD was taken from the jail at Madison to Mineral Point, by virtue of a writ of *habeas corpus* issued by Chief Justice DUNN. A long and thorough examination was had, and all the facts connected with the tragedy fully exposed. The State was ably represented by M. M. JACKSON, the Attorney General, and the defendant by Col. A. P. FIELD, who was assisted by MOSES M. STRONG, and after an exhaustive argument, the Chief Justice took the matter under consideration from Saturday until Monday, the 14th of March, when he decided that VINEYARD should be admitted to bail in the sum of $10,000, for his appearance at the next term of the district court for Dane county. The bail was at once given by several of the most responsible and wealthy citizens of Grant county.

The court met at Madison May 9th, Hon. DAVID IRVIN presiding. The grand jury was about to be impaneled when the counsel for VINEYARD objected to EBENEZER BRIGHAM being sworn upon the jury for the reason that he had been recognized as a witness in the VINEYARD case. The objection was sustained by the court and Mr. BRIGHAM excluded. The counsel for VINEYARD then attempted to exclude for cause others of the panel from being sworn as grand jurors for the reason that they had expressed opinions, but were not sustained by the court.

The jury on the 13th May returned a bill for manslaughter, the defendant entered into new bonds, and the cause was adjourned until the next term.

The venue was afterwards changed to Green county on the affidavit of the defendant of prejudice of the people of Dane county, and in October, 1843, he was acquitted by verdict of the jury.

The Legislative Assembly, after taking a recess from December 27th to January 7th, adjourned *sine die* on the 19th of February, being seventy-six days from the first to the last day of the session.

CHAPTER XXIV.

TERRITORY OF WISCONSIN—1843.

There was no subject in relation to which the inhabitants of Wisconsin in the earlier years of its Territorial existence, had looked to Congress for aid with as great anxiety, as they had to the protection of the infant commerce of Lake Michigan. Not a session of the Legislature had passed from 1836 to 1842 that a memorial was not sent to Congress asking appropriations for harbors of refuge at the more important ports on the Wisconsin shore of Lake Michigan. These memorials were supplemented by numerous petitions from the people, but until 1843, all efforts to obtain such appropriations had been unavailing, except that on the 4th day of July, 1836, the day on which the act organizing the Territory took effect, an act making appropriations for harbors was approved which contained an appropriation of four hundred dollars

"For the survey of the mouth of Milwaukee river, to determine the practicability of making a harbor by deepening the channel."

The same act appropriated twenty thousand dollars for a harbor at Michigan City and the same sum for a pier or breakwater at St. Joseph, which were the only appropriations for Lake Michigan.

Appropriations were also made in 1837 and in 1838, not only for Michigan City and St. Joseph, but also for Chicago, which were the only points on either shore of Lake Michigan for which any appropriation was made until 1843.

During the years 1839, '40, '41 and '42, the policy of the government of making appropriations for the improvements of rivers and harbors appears to have been entirely suspended.

Such suspensions also continued during the year 1843 as to all the rivers and harbors in the United States, except that an act

"For the protection of commerce on Lake Michigan," was passed which appropriated thirty thousand dollars "for the construction of a harbor at the most suitable situation at or near Milwaukee," and enacted that before the money should be expended "the corps of topographical engineers shall select from actual examination and survey the point of location of said harbor."

The same act provided for the survey and selection of "the most suitable site for a light house at or near Southport" (now Kenosha).

It also contained an appropriation of twenty-five thousand dollars for each of the harbors of Chicago and St. Joseph.

Two separate appropriation bills for the civil and diplomatic expenses of goverment were passed at the session of Congress for 1842-3, one approved December 24, 1842, for the half calendar year ending June 30, 1843. The other for the fiscal year ending June 30, 1844, approved March 3, 1843.

The first appropriated for compensation for the Governor, judges and secretary for the half year and for contingent expenses, the sum of four thousand seven hundred and twenty-five dollars. The other for the same objects for a full fiscal year, the sum of nine thousand four hundred and fifty dollars.

The first appropriated—

"For compensation and mileage of the members of the Legislative Assembly, pay of officers, printing, stationery, fuel, furniture and other incidental and miscellaneous objects, nineteen thousand two hundred and seventy-five dollars."

for the half calendar year.

The other appropriated for the same objects and for postage, the sum of seventeen thousand two hundred and seventy-five dollars for the full fiscal year.

Another act was passed at this session of Congress conferring upon the people further powers of self-government, by authorizing the Legislature—

"To provide by law for the election or appointment of sheriffs, judges of probate, justices of the peace and county surveyors."

These offices were under the organic act appointable by the Governor and Council.

The second section of this act prescribed—

"That the members of both houses of the Legislative Assembly shall, upon the expiration of the terms of service for which the present members have been elected, be hereafter elected to serve for the same terms of service as that for which the members of the Legislative Assembly in Iowa are now elected."

Such "terms of service" in Iowa were two years for members of the Council and one year for members of the House of Representatives.

Another act was passed at this session of much local importance, by which the township of land on the east side of Winnebago Lake, which was reserved for the use of the Stockbridge tribe of Indians, might be partitioned and divided among the different individuals composing said tribe, and might be held by them separately and severally in fee simple.

The act prescribed particularly the mode of making the partition by commissioners to be elected by themselves under the supervision of a United States officer.

The fourth Legislative Assembly convened at Madison on the fifth day of December, 1842 — the day prescribed by law — for the purpose of holding its first session.

The members of both houses had been elected at the preceding September election upon a new apportionment, and there was an almost entire change of membership in both Houses.

In the Council only three members had been members of the preceding Council. These were Messrs. MARTIN of Brown county, ROUNTREE of Grant, and STRONG of Iowa. Five others had been members of the House of Representatives the preceding year. These were Messrs. WHITON of Rock, BARBER of Jefferson, DEWEY of Grant, LA'CHAPPEL of Crawford, and NEWLAND of Milwaukee, the last of whom had represented Iowa county, was the speaker and on the adjournment of the previous session had removed to Milwaukee county where he was elected to the Council. The other five members were Messes. HEATH and HUGUNIN of Racine, BAKER of Walworth, CROCKER and WHITE of Milwaukee, neither of whom had previously been members of the Legislature.

All the members of the Council were present on the first day of the session, except Messrs. HEATH and HUGUNIN, who did not take their seats until the 6th of March.

The Council was organized by the election of MOSES M. STRONG, President; JOHN V. INGERSOLL, Secretary; and CHARLES E. BROWN, Sergeant-at-Arms.

The House of Representatives was composed of the following members:

Brown and the counties attached— ALBERT G. ELLIS, MASON C. DARLING, and DAVID AGRY.

Crawford and St. Croix— JOHN H. MANAHAN.

Dane, Dodge, Green, Jefferson, and Sauk— ISAAC H. PALMER, LYMAN CROSSMAN and ROBERT MASTERS.

Grant— FRANKLIN Z. HICKS, ALONZO PLATT and GLENDOWER M. PRICE.

Iowa— ROBERT M. LONG, MOSES MEEKER, and WILLIAM S. HAMILTON.

Milwaukee and Washington— ANDREW E. ELMORE, BENJAMIN HUNKINS, THOMAS H. OLIN, JONATHAN PARSONS, JARED THOMPSON, and GEORGE H. WALKER.

Racine— PHILANDER JUDSON, JOHN T. TROWBRIDGE, and PETER VAN VLEIT.

Rock and Walworth— JOHN HOPKINS, JAMES TRIPP, JOHN M. CAPRON, and WILLIAM A. BARTLETT.

Of these, Messrs. ELLIS and DARLING had been members of the preceding Legislature; Mr. HAMILTON was elected, in 1835, a member of the Michigan Legislature, which met at Green Bay in January, 1836, while all the others were without legislative experience.

All the members were present at the December session except Messrs. JUDSON and TROWBRIDGE, who did not take their seats until the 30th of January, and Mr. AGRY, who took his seat on the 4th of February, and Messrs. BARTLETT and VAN VLIET, who took their seats on the 6th of March.

The House was organized by the election of ALBERT G. ELLIS, Speaker, JOHN CATLIN, Chief Clerk, and WILLIAM S. ANDERSON, Sergeant-at-Arms.

Each house was notified of the organization of the other.

A joint committee of two from each house was then appointed to wait on the Governor and inform him that the two houses were organized *pro tempore* and ready to receive any communication he might have to make to them.

The committee consisted of Messrs. MARTIN and WHITON

on the part of the Council, and Messrs. WALKER and HOPKINS on the part of the House.

The joint committee submitted a report to each house, on the first day of the session —

"That they have discharged the duty assigned them, and that the Governor informed the committee that, 'not conceiving that the Legislative Assembly had authority by law to meet at the present time, he had no communication to make to them.'"

On the same day a resolution was introduced by Dr. DARLING, which on the next day was agreed upon by both houses, in the following words:

"*Resolved by the Council and House of Representatives:* that the report of the joint committee appointed to wait upon his Excellency the Governor, and inform him that the two houses were organized *pro tempore*, and ready to receive any communication he might have to make to them, be referred to a joint committee, consisting of three members of each house, to report whether there is any valid objection to the Legislative Assembly holding its annual session at this time; whether it is expedient to adjourn the session of said Legislative Assembly to some other day; whether the Legislative Assembly ought to take any, and if any, what action, expressive of their views relative to the course pursued by the executive, as exhibited in said report; and generally to report as they may think the circumstances of the case may require in relation to the said report of the said joint committee."

The committee consisted of Messrs. CROCKER, MARTIN and LA'CHAPPELLE on the part of the Council, and Messrs. DARLING, TRIPP and MEEKER on the part of the House.

The Governor did not, in his response to the committee appointed to wait on him, give any reasons why he thought the Legislative Assembly had no right to meet at that time or why he had no communication to make to them. But soon after the report of the joint committee, of which Col. CROCKER was chairman, there appeared in the newspapers a paper addressed to the members elect of the Legislative Assembly, over the signature of the Governor, and which he adopted as his own, in a communication to the two houses of Congress.

It was said in the newspapers accompanying this paper, that it was prepared by Gov. DOTY, with the intention of submitting it to the members, if they called upon the executive, as had been the custom to administer to them the oath of office.

Such a custom had to some extent prevailed, but not uniformly, and the newly elected members, upon assembling, ascertained that the Governor was not authorized by law to administer oaths, and took the oath of office before one of the Judges of the Supreme Court.

In justice to the Governor, with reference to this important subject, the paper is given at length:

TO THE MEMBERS ELECT OF THE LEGISLATIVE ASSEMBLY OF WISKONSAN:

The acts of Congress provide,

1st. That " No session " [of the Assembly] " *in any year* shall exceed the *term* of seventy-five days."

2d. That "The Legislative Assembly of no Territory shall hereafter, in any instance, or under any pretext whatever, exceed the amount appropriated by Congress for its annual expenses."

3d. That "No session of the Legislature of a Territory shall be held until an appropriation for its expenses shall have been made."

The Territorial act authorizing "a regular session" to be held on the first Monday of December annually, if it was ever valid, was suspended or annulled by these acts and by the failure of Congress to make an appropriation after the passage of the latter act.

The Legislature held a session in the year 1842, which terminated on the nineteenth day of February last.

On the eighteenth day of May following Congress appropriated twenty thousand dollars for the expenses of the Assembly during the year 1842, which sum was drawn from the Treasury in June last *and expended according to the direction of the act of the Assembly* of the 19th of February, to defray the expenses of a session held in the year 1842.

The whole of the appropriation for the year 1841 having been thus expended, and no additional appropriation made, no session can now be held under the authority of the laws of the United States, or indeed without violating them. If a session is held it must be *at the expense of the people of the Territory*; and all laws passed by an unauthorized and prohibited Assembly would be void and of no effect.

It is believed that a session is neither expected nor desired at this time by the people; and that as there is no money to pay the expenses, there ought to be no session.

Wiskonsan is yet under a Terrritorial form of government, and while this is continued by the people, the acts of Congress are supreme over this government and over the people and must be obeyed.

When a session of the Assembly has reached the amount appropriated for the year it must terminate; and no new session can commence, or expense be incurred, until an appropriation has been made.

If the expenses of an unauthorized session are not paid by Congress, they must be paid by the people of the Territory. This would greatly increase the taxes, without any corresponding benefit to the country; for it is believed to be the sentiment of the tax-paying part of the community that there has been already too much legislation; and that the taxes now levied are excessive and ought to be diminished.

To protect the people therefore from further taxation, and to maintain their right to a strict and economical administration of this government, and to preserve the authority of the laws of the United States and avoid the possibility of an increase of the public debt, it is deemed to be the duty of the Executive to decline meeting the members elect of the Legislature, to hold a session, until an appropriation shall have been made for its expenses by Congress.

J. D. DOTY.

Madison, Wiskonsan, December 5, 1842.

This paper was accompanied by some correspondence between the Governor and the Secretary of the Treasury, and between the Governor and the Secretary of the Territory, the material part of which is the statement of the Secretary of the Treasury, bearing date November 21, 1842.

" That the amount appropriated by the act of Congress of the 18th day of May, 1842, for the compensation of members and expenses, etc., of the Legislative Assembly of the Territory of Wiskonsan, having been paid to A. P. FIELD, Esq., the Secretary of the Territory, no further amount can be expected, until an appropriation for this object is made at the approaching session of Congress."

And also the statement of Col. FIELD, Secretary of the Territory, under date of November 25, 1842, that

"The appropriation of twenty thousand dollars made by Congress in May last to which you alluded has been received and applied by me to the payment of the liabilities incurred by the last Legislature."

The report of the joint committee of three from each house was unanimous, and was signed by all the six members of the committee. It was presented on the 8th day of May in the Council by Col. CROCKER, and in the House by Dr. DARLING, and is very exhaustive of the questions at issue between the Governor and the Legislature. Its great length precludes its insertion entire but such extracts are given as present the substance of the views of the committee.

In reference to the inquiry whether there is any law of Congress or of this Territory which would prevent the holding of a session of the Legislature at this time, the committee say:

"The law of Congress organizing the Territory provides that 'the time, place and manner of holding and conducting all elections by the people and the apportionment of the representation in the several counties to the Council and House of Representatives according to the population shall be prescribed by law, as well as the *day of the annual commencement of the session of the Legislative Assembly*' (organic act, section 4). Accordingly the Legislative Assembly have '*prescribed by law*' that 'the regular sessions of the Legislative Assembly shall commence on the first Monday of December, in each and every year.' (R. S. page 157.)"

In pursuance of that law the members of the Council and House of Representatives did meet in their respective halls at the Capitol, on the first Monday of December, 1842, and commenced the session of the Legislative Assembly, by organizing their respective houses in the usual manner.

In conformity to the long established usage, they adopted a joint resolution appointing a committee to wait upon the Governor and inform him of the organization of the two houses and that they were ready to receive any communication he might have to make to them. To this customary message of courtesy to a co-ordinate branch of the Legislature the Governor made the following reply: 'Not conceiving that the Legislative Assembly had authority by law to meet at the present time, he had no communication to make to them.'

He refuses to make any communication to the Legislature *because* he says he conceives they have no authority to meet at the *present time*.

* * * * * * * * * * * *

The Governor, no doubt with some object in view, has seen fit to withhold from the Legislature and the public his reasons for so extraordinary a course of conduct. And as your committee can imagine no other, they have presumed that if the Legislative Assembly has not the authority by law to meet at the present time, the only reason is the one that rumor and the public press has assigned viz.: that in a law passed at the last session of Congress occurs the following paragraph: 'No session of the Legislature of a territory shall be held until the appropriation for its expenses shall have been made.'

* * * * * * * * * * * *

"The act of Congress 'making appropriations for the civil and diplomatic expenses of the Government for the year 1842,' approved May 18, 1842, contains the usual appropriation for the payment of the expenses of the annual session of the Legislative Assembly of the Territory of Wisconsin. The amount thus appropriated is $20,000.

* * * * * * * * * * * *

"The title of the act last referred to is in itself convincing proof to your committee, that the amount appropriated was for the express purpose of defraying the expenses of the session which we are now holding; but to remove all doubt, the committee will briefly refer to the several appropriations made by Congress for defraying the expenses of the Legislature of this Territory.

"The appropriation for the first session of the Legislative Assembly, which was held in the fall of 1836, was but nine thousand dollars, the estimate being predicated upon the usual expenses of the Territorial Legislature of Michigan, a body of but thirteen members. To meet the deficiency caused by this inadequate appropriation, Congress, by the act of 3d of March, 1837, appropriated the further sum of $15,765.16 'for the payment of *arrearages*' due for the expenses of the first Legislative Assembly. By the same act was appropriated the further sum of $36,765 for the expenses of the second session of the first Legislative Assembly.

By the act of 6th of April, 1838, $25,000 were appropriated for the first session and by the act of 3d March, 1839, $25,000 for the second session of the second Legislative Assembly. The act of the 8th May, 1840, appropriated $34,075 for the first session, and the act of 3d March, 1841, $20,000 for the second session of the Legislative Assembly. And the act of 18th May, 1842, appropriates $20,000 for the expense of the present, being the first session of the fourth Legislative Assembly.

If it be supposed that the $20,000 last appropriated, were intended to meet the payment of arrearages, created by a deficiency in the appropriation of previous sessions of the Legislature, the impression will be removed by reference to another part of the same act, making an appropriation 'for the arrearages and expenses for the Legislative Assembly of the Territory of Iowa.'. An appropriation for a similar purpose for Wisconsin, would have been expressed in like words. That territory was similarly situated with Wisconsin, the expenses of the Legislature exceeding the amount of appropriations, but the exact amount of the arrearages of the expenses of that Territory being known, a definite sum was appropriated for their discharge. A portion of the arrearages of expenses of Wisconsin, consisting of disputed items, and the amount not being ascertained, no definite sum could be appropriated. It was attempted when the act making appropriations for the civil and diplomatic expenses of the government for the year 1842 (in which the above appropriation of $20,000 is included) was before the House of Representatives, to appropriate the further sum of $24,000 to cover the arrearages of expenses of our Legislature, for previous years, but their extent not being known, as we have above stated, the last item was omitted, and the chairman of the committee of ways and means declaring his intention of introducing a bill for the purpose of providing for the payment of such arrearages as were chargeable to the Treasury of the United States. Accordingly, on the 29th day of August last Congress passed a law, 'for the settlement of certain accounts for the support of the government of the Territory of Wisconsin.'

By this law, no definite sum was appropriated, but the accounting officers of the Treasury Department were directed to audit and settle those accounts. By the act of 18th May, 1842, the sum of $27,125 was appropriated to defray the expenses of the Legislative Council of the Territory of Florida, and by the act of 29th August, the accounts and arrearages of expenses of that Territory were directed to be audited and settled, in the same manner as those of the Territory of Wisconsin.

Yet, so far as has come to the knowledge of your committee, no doubt has ever been entertained in either of the Territories of Iowa or Florida, but that their Legislatures have the undoubted right to hold their annual sessions without any further act or appropriation by Congress. By reference to that part of the act of 18th May, making appropriations for the Territory of Iowa it will be seen that no part of the sum appropriated for *arrearages* shall be used for any other purpose, than for the payment of those arrearages. Now if, as it is possible the Governor may suppose, the $20,000 last appropriated, was 'for arrearages of expenses,' why was it not limited and restricted to that specific object as was done in the appropriation for Iowa ?

No money shall be drawn from the Treasury of the United States, but in consequence of appropriations made by law, and in such law must be expressed the precise nature and object of such appropriation. And your committee believe that since the organization of the Government, no instance can be found, where Congress has made an appropriation for arrearages of expenses in any branch or department of the Government, unless it be so expressed in the law making such appropriation. Had such been the object of the appropriation now in question, your committee can not but think it would have been so expressed.

The mere fact that Congress has every year since the organization of our Territory appropriated what they thought would be a sufficient amount to defray the annual expenses of the Legislature, previous to the holding of the annual session thereof, is conclusive evidence to your committee that the appropriation of $20,000 contained in the act of the 18th of May was intended to defray the expenses of the *present session* of the Legislature. But if any doubt could exist it would be removed by reference to the act of the 29th of August, the object and intention of which was to pay and discharge all arrearages of expenses of the Legislature of Wisconsin, owing to the Legislature having incurred an annual debt greater than the annual appropriations of Congress.

The object of the act last referred to was to relieve the Territory from its pecuniary embarrassments, not to crush it by depriving it of the invaluable privileges of Legislation.

It cannot be supposed by any honest and rational mind, that it was the intention of Congress to deprive the people of Wisconsin of all the rights of Legislation, or that having failed to include—as it is possible the Governor may suppose—an appropriation to defray the expenses of the present Legislature, in the usual law, they would afterwards, on the last day of the session pass another law prohibiting a session of the Legislature because they had failed or neglected to make such appropriation. In looking at the usual course of Congress in defraying the expenses of our Legislature, no doubt exists in the minds of your committee that in passing the act of the 29th of August it was their belief that the appropriation of $20,000 previously made was to cover the expenses of the present Legislature.

By the 11th section of the Organic Act, there is 'to be appropriated *annually* a sufficient sum to defray the expenses of the Legislative Assembly,' and by the act of the Territory already quoted, 'the regular session of the Legislative Assembly shall commence on the first Monday of December in each and every year.'

These acts are plain, explicit and unrepealed, and if it be true that Congress have not 'appropriated *annually* a sufficient sum to defray the expenses of the Legislative Assembly,' and if true, that *for that reason* 'the regular session of the Legislative Assembly' cannot 'convene on the first Monday of December,' then are both those laws to that extent repealed. But can it be believed that Congress ever intended by, to say the most of it, so strained and remote an inference, to repeal laws which lay at the very foundation of our political existence? Such a construction would be an insult to the understanding and the good faith of the Congress of the United States.

But it is said that whatever may have been the intention of Congress in making the appropriation, it has in point of fact been received by the Secretary of the Territory and paid out by him in defraying the expenses of the last session of the Legislative Assembly.

Assuming such to be the fact, does it affect in any degree our right to sit as a Legislative Assembly? It must be borne in mind that the restriction upon our Legislative powers arises only from the *want of an appropriation*, not for the *want of money* in the Treasury of the United States, nor from the misapplication of that money to any other purpose, nor even the refusal of the officers of the Treasury Department to pay it out when made, nor from any circumstances whatever, except the *want of an appropriation.*

* * * * * * * * * * * * *

If the appropriation has been made we have clearly the right to hold a session of the Legislature.

* * * * * * * * * * * * *

"If, as we contend, the appropriation has been made, there was on the 29th of August last in the Treasury of the United States to the credit of Wisconsin at least $40,000, being the amount of the appropriation and a sufficient sum to defray arrearages of expenses of former sessions; and if the sum of $20,000 has been misapplied in the payment of arrearages, it leaves an equal amount in the Treasury to be applied as originally intended, to defray the expenses of the present session.

* * * * * * * * * * * * *

"In examining this part of the subject referred to us in every light in which it has presented itself to our minds, we can not hesitate to give it as our decided opinion, that there is no valid objection to the Legislative Assembly holding its annual session at the present time, by reason of *no appropriation having been made by Congress.*"

The committee further reported that they were —

" Aware that there are many important subjects, deeply affecting the interests of the people, upon which they are now anxiously desiring legislative action.

" 'A few of the most important of these' were stated to be:

"The acts and condition of the Milwaukee and Rock River Canal Company.

"The extension of the term of court in Walworth county, in which the suits in favor of the Territory against the Governor as a public defaulter, were pending;

" The re-election of the commissioner of public buildings, who is the agent of the Territory in conducting those suits;

" The unfinished and exposed condition of the Capitol, and the securing of the money appropriated for its completion; and,

" Many other subjects constantly occurring in a newly settled and rapidly growing country."

The committee add: " Yet, notwithstanding this pressing necessity, and the important subjects ready to be brought before the Legislature, your committee are constrained by a sense of duty, to report that, in their opinion, it is *inexpedient* to hold a session of the Legislature at the present time. To this conclusion your committee are forced by the action of the Governor himself, who, in violation of all law, has refused, for reasons which may be apparent, to hold communication with the Legislature. Your committee have not thought it necessary to enter upon a discussion of the question whether the Legislature can enact laws without the concurrence of the Governor, but inasmuch as serious doubts are entertained upon this subject, they are led to the conclusion above stated.

"The Legislature have done all that the law, duty to their constituents, or courtesy to the Governor, a co-ordinate branch of the Legislature, have required. If consequences injurious to the Territory result from the course which we recommend, let the responsibility rest upon the head of him who invoked it."

As to whether the Legislative Assembly ought to take any, and if any, what action, expressive of their views relative to the course pursued by the executive, the committee say:

"They can not but consider the conduct of the Governor, in refusing to meet the Legislature, as extraordinary, unwarranted by any principle of reason or law, evincing a disposition to bid defiance to the will of the people, and a total disregard of their interests. Such conduct deserves the reprobation of the Legislature, as it will most assuredly receive the condemnation of an injured and insulted Territory.

"Courtesy to the representatives of the people, similar to that extended by them to him, should have induced the Governor to have assigned, in respectful terms, his reasons for not meeting or recognizing the Legislature. These reasons he has withheld, and standing in an attitude independent of the will of the people he treats their representatives with insolence and contempt, and disregards the laws of the Territory which he is sworn to obey."

The committee came to the conclusion that it was expedient that the Legislature adjourn *sine die,* but recommended the adoption of a memorial to Congress, asking the passage of some law that would enable the Legislature to convene before the first Monday of December.

Resolutions were reported in conformity with the views expressed in the report.

No serious difference of opinion existed in either house, in relation to any of the views expressed by the committee, except as to whether it was expedient to adjourn *sine die,* or to some definite time so remote as to give Congress time to act.

In the Council, a motion was made to amend the resolution so that the adjournment should be until the third Monday in January. This was lost by a vote of four to seven, Messrs. BARBER, NEWLAND, WHITON and STRONG voting in the affirmative; and then the resolutions were adopted unanimously.

In the House the resolution was amended without division so as to provide that the adjournment should be until the last Monday in January, and the resolutions were then unanimously adopted; Mr. CAPRON, however, the next day, on leave changed his vote to the negative.

The following are the resolutions as agreed to by both houses:

"*Resolved by the Council and House of Representatives of the Territory of Wisconsin*: That, in their opinion, the Congress of the United States did, on the eighteenth day of May last, appropriate the sum of $20,000 to defray the expenses of the Legislative Assembly of the Territory of Wisconsin, commencing on the first Monday of December, 1842; and that there is no law either of Congress or of the Territory which would prevent the holding of a session of the Legislature at the present time or would render invalid or nugatory any law which it might enact.

"*Resolved*, That while we entertain the opinion that there can be no objection to continue the present session of the Legislature by reason of no appropriation having been made to defray its expenses, or any other legal disability, yet inasmuch as doubts are entertained as to the expediency of proceeding with business at the present time, because the Governor refuses to act with us, we deem it prudent that the Legislative Assembly adjourn their session until the last Monday in January, 1843.

"*Resolved*, That the conduct of the Governor in refusing to meet the Legislature at the present session, thereby attempting to concentrate all power in his own hands is unparalleled in the history of this government and a gross violation of all law — evincing an utter disregard of the will and interests of the people, and of those laws which as Governor of the Territory he is sworn to support, and that his 'refusal to assign reasons for so extraordinary a course is an insult to the Legislature and the people of Wisconsin.

"*Resolved*, That copies of the report of the committee and resolutions, together with a transcript of the ayes and noes of both houses upon the passage of these resolutions, be transmitted to the President of the Senate and Speaker of the House of Representatives of the United States, to be laid before the bodies over which they respectively preside, that such relief may be granted by Congress as the nature of the case may require, and the wants of the people of the Territory demand."

A joint committee of the two houses was appointed to draft a memorial to the President of the United States, praying the removal of the Governor. The committee consisted of Messrs. WHITON, BARBER and ROUNTREE, of the Council, and HAMILTON, HOPKINS and WALKER, of the House.

Mr. WHITON, chairman of the committee, reported a memorial, which was adopted by a unanimous vote of the Council, and by the House with two votes (Messrs. CAPRON and PALMER) in the negative. It was as follows:

"MEMORIAL

Of the Council and House of Representatives of the Territory of Wisconsin, to the President of the United States, praying for the removal of JAMES D. DOTY *from the office of Governor of said Territory.*

To his Excellency JOHN TYLER, *President of the United States—*

"Your memorialists beg leave most respectfully to represent that they find themselves placed in a most extraordinary and embarrassing situation. The members of the Council and House of Representatives were elected by the people of the Territory at a general election, held pursuant to law on the fourth Monday of September last, and on the 5th day of December instant, the day appointed by law for the meeting of the Legislature, assembled at the Capitol in Madison to transact the usual business of the Legislature. The two houses proceeded to organize in the usual mode, and then chose a joint committee to wait on his Excellency the Governor and inform him of our organization, and that we were ready to receive any communication which he might have to make to us. The committee proceeded to discharge the duty assigned them and were informed by the Governor 'that not conceiving the Legislature had any right by law to meet at the present time, he had no communication to make to them.' The committee reported this fact to the two houses, and your memorialists found themselves in the extraordinary position of two branches of a Legislature attempting to hold a session, and the third branch — the Governor — refusing his co-operation."

"In the opinion of many members of the two houses, the legislative functions of your memorialists are suspended, by the refusal of the Governor to act with them, and that no business can be transacted.

Your memorialists need not enlarge upon the embarrassment and confusion which will be created by reason of not holding a session of the Legislature at the usual time, nor upon the great increase of executive power, which that circumstance will occasion.

If the facts above set forth constituted the only cause of complaint, which your memorialists and the people of the Territory have against their Governor, your memorialists might not have addressed your Excellency on the present occasion, but might have borne with whatever patience they could bring to their aid this abuse of power. But your memorialists represent that his conduct both before and since his appointment to the office he now fills, has been such as to destroy, in almost the entire population of the Territory, all confidence in him as a man and a public officer.

Your memorialists are informed that numerous charges have been made against him which, with the proof to sustain them, are now in the possession of your Excellency.

Your memorialists would most respectfully call your Excellency's attention to those charges and proofs, and also to his recent attempt to corrupt the commissioner of public buildings, in order to get that officer to dismiss the suits at law now pending against him, to recover large sums of money which he has received on behalf of the Territory and refuses to pay, as that fact is set forth in the report of the commissioner herewith submitted, and to which we respectfully call the attention of your Excellency.

For the reasons above set forth we respectfully, yet earnestly, request your Excellency to remove JAMES D. DOTY from the office of Governor of the Territory of Wisconsin.

It is with extreme regret that your memorialists have been forced to the extremity of making this representation and request ; and we assure your Excellency that nothing short of the belief that our duty requires us to take the course we have adopted, would have induced us to address this memorial to your Excellency; we assure your Excellency, further, that the removal of the Governor is demanded by almost the entire population of the Territory, and is the only measure which can restore peace and harmony to the people.

And your memorialists, as in duty bound, will ever pray."

On the 14th of February, the delegate — Gov. DODGE — addressed an official letter to the President, asking for the removal of JAMES D. DOTY from the office of Governor of the Territory. Numerous reasons were assigned for this request, among which were : That he had

"In violation of and contempt for the laws of the United States and of the Territory, refused to co-operate with the Legislative Assembly at their annual meeting begun on the 5th day of December last."

That having accepted the appointment of Governor in April, 1841, he did not resign his office as delegate, nor issue a proclamation ordering an election of a delegate in Congress, and permitted them thereby to go unrepresented in the then next session of Congress, and the belief is expressed:

"That his dereliction of duty in this respect was in consequence of a determination on his part to return and occupy the seat as delegate himself, should his nomination as Governor be rejected by the Senate, which was confidently expected.

"That the Governor (DOTY) made use of every device in his power to induce the commissioner (of public buildings) to favor his schemes to defraud the Territory, and indirectly offered to bribe him to dismiss the suits then and still pending in the United States Court of the Territory, for the recovery of several thousand dollars, for which the said DOTY still remains a defaulter.

"That he recommended and procured the appointment of his own son, CHARLES DOTY, to the office of paying pensioners in the Territory, knowing that he was a minor in his nineteenth year, contrary to the laws of the United States."

The letter further states that "petitions from the people in every county, numerously signed, have been sent to your Excellency, urging the removal of Gov. DOTY from office. These petitions, sir, emanate from the people without respect to either of the great parties of the country, and show that a large majority of the voters of the Territory desire the removal of the Governor."

A popular representative Democratic assemblage convened at Madison on the twenty-second day of March, to the number of nearly one hundred, appointed at primary meetings. There were in attendance from Brown county 5 delegates, Crawford 3, Dane 25, Fond du Lac 1, Grant 2, Green 5, Iowa 18, Jefferson 1, Milwaukee 17, Racine 5, Rock 3, Sauk 4 and Walworth 9. Total 98.

The convention resolved "That we view with feelings of surprise and disgust, the recent attempts on the part of the Governor to destroy the powers which by the free and honest suffrages of the citizens of Wisconsin were entrusted to the members of the fourth Legislature."

Also "That the history of the present Governor of this Territory is a history of repeated injuries and usurpations, all having in direct object the establishment of an absolute tyranny over the people of Wisconsin."

The Governor was not removed by the President.

On the tenth day of December both houses adjourned until the last Monday in January, 1843, at 12 o'clock M.

An act "making appropriations for the civil and diplomatic expenses of government for the half calendar year ending the thirtieth day of June, 1843," which was passed December 24, 1842, contained an appropriation of $19,275 for the expenses of the Legislative Assembly.

On the 30th of January, which was the fourth Monday, the Governor issued a proclamation for a special session of the Legislative Assembly.

It recited that no appropriation had been made for a session to be held on the first Monday of December, and that an appropriation of $19,275 was made on the 24th of December; and that it was provided by law that the Governor might appoint special sessions which should not exceed *twenty* days and that a majority of the members had declared

"That there were many important subjects deeply affecting the interests of the people upon which they are now anxiously desiring legislative action."

Therefore, he appointed a special ssssion of the Legislative Assembly to be held on Monday, the sixth day of March next, at twelve o'clock M.

The House of Representatives met on Monday, the 30th of January, the day to which both houses had adjourned, but in the Council no quorum was present until Saturday, the 4th of February.

On that day a joint committee was appointed to wait upon the Governor, and inform him that the two houses were in session pursuant to their adjournment, and ready to receive any communication which he might be pleased to make. The committee immediately reported that they had

"Discharged the duty imposed upon them, and were informed by his Excellency that he was still of the opinion he had formerly expressed, and had no communication to make to the Legislative Assembly, except a copy of his proclamation convening the Legislature on the 6th day of March next, which he requested your committee to lay before the Legislature."

Joint resolutions were then adopted, unanimously in the Council, and by a vote of 11 to 6 in the House, which, after reciting in detail all that had previously occurred in reference to the efforts of the two houses to hold a session of the Legislature and of the Governor to prevent it, concluded as follows:

"*Resolved*, That the Congress of the United States be requested to provide, by law, for the election of Governor by the people of the Territory.

Resolved, That the only reason heretofore assigned by the Governor, for refusing to meet the Legislature, having been removed by the appropriation of 24th December last, leaves no other excuse for his singular and unwarrantable conduct, than such as can be found in his determination to prevent all legislation, and sacrifice for his own private purposes, the welfare of the Territory and the interests of the people.

Resolved, That the conduct of Gov. DOTY, in again refusing to meet the Legislature, after he has been officially informed that an appropriation has been made by Congress to defray its expenses, is another evidence of his violation of law, and utter disregard of the duties of his station, and of the wishes and interests of the people.

Resolved, That a copy of the foregoing preamble and resolutions be forwarded to the President of the United States, and to the presiding officers of the Senate and House of Representatives of Congress."

A joint resolution was then offered in the Council by Mr. CROCKER, with a preamble reciting the reasons, and concluding that inasmuch as the Governor had refused to co-operate with the Legislature, it was advisable to adjourn to meet on the 6th day of March next.

To this Mr. WHITON offered an amendment—

"That the Legislative Assembly will now proceed to discharge its duties without regard to any course that has been or may be pursued by the Governor."

This amendment was supported by Messrs. LA'CHAPELLE, WHITON and STRONG, but was not carried, and the resolution offered by Mr. CROCKER was adopted by the Council and concurred in by the House, and on the 6th of February both houses adjourned to meet on the 6th March at 10 o'clock, A. M.

Both houses assembled on the 6th of March, there being a full attendance of members in each.

There was some discrepancy in the hour of assembling, as specified in the resolution of adjournment and as prescribed by the Governor's proclamation. By the former the hour was fixed at 10 o'clock A. M., and by the latter at 12 M.

The journal of the Council stated that it "met pursuant to adjournment" and that of the House stated that it "was called to order at 10 o'clock A. M. by the Speaker."

A resolution was offered in the House—

"That a committee be appointed to act jointly with a committee on the part of the Council, to wait upon the Governor and inform him that quorums of the two houses have assembled, and that they are now ready to receive any communication he may be pleased to make to them."

Motions were successively made to lie on the table until after 12 o'clock M., to adjourn until 12 o'clock M., to insert after the word "assembled" the words "pursuant to his proclamation," and also to insert the words "again pursuant to adjournment," but they were all lost, and the resolution as originally introduced was adopted and concurred in by the Council. The committee was appointed and immediately reported to the Council that they had performed the duty assigned them, and were informed by his Excellency that he would send a written message to each house at 2 o'clock, to which hour both houses adjourned.

The message of the Governor, after opening with a statement of his reasons for appointing a *special session* of the Legislature contained a sentence the ambiguity of which was the occasion of severe censure in both houses.

In the Council, Mr. CROCKER, the chairman of the committee to wait on the Governor; when the message had been read, called the attention of the Council to a passage in it, which he said

"The author must know, which every member of the committee knows, and which he would now assure the Council was entirely false." The passage is in these words: "I therefore meet you on this occasion, being informed by your committee that the two houses are convened for the purpose of holding a special session."

"This allusion of the Governor to the information which he derived from the joint committee who waited upon him," Mr. CROCKER pronounced to be "an unqualified falsehood, and in this declaration he knew he would be sustained by every member of the committee."

No further notice was taken of the matter in the Council.

In the House the message was referred to a select committee of which Dr. DARLING was chairman, who reported that the discrepancy of statement between the Governor and the committee

"Must have arisen from an error of punctuation in the reading of the message by the clerk" * * * * * "The idea intended to be conveyed by his Excellency in this passage might have been that the committee merely communicated the fact, that the two houses had now convened, and that 'he,' therefore, met them for the purpose of holding a special session."

The report of the committee states that this conclusion is confirmed by

"The fact that the Governor must have known that the Assembly adjourned from the 6th day of February to meet again on the 6th day of March, at a *previous hour* to the one named in the proclamation and consequently had *not* met under that proclamation."

This charitable excuse for the offensive passage was not satisfactory to a large minority of the members of the House, and Mr. ELMORE, a member of the committee to wait on the Governor, offered a preamble which recited the facts, and the following resolutions:

"*Resolved*, That the statement made by the Governor of 'his being informed by your committee that the two Houses are now convened for the purpose of holding a special session' is wholly unwarranted and without excuse.

"*Resolved*, That the message of the Governor be prefaced with the foregoing preamble and resolution."

On motion of Mr. DARLING the preamble and resolutions were indefinitely postponed by a vote of 14 to 10.

The message recommended the submission to the people of the question of the adoption of a State government, and that a law should be passed authorizing a vote to be annually taken upon the question.

The adjustment and payment of the Territorial debt, economy in public expenditures, reduction in the fees of officers, expense of courts, and of town and county government, reform in the system of taxation, and a reduction of the cost of public printing were recommended.

The distributive share of Wisconsin of the net proceeds of the public lands was stated to have amounted, June 1, 1842, to $1,082.45, and the application of it to the repairs which are required on the Territorial roads leading west from Astor, Milwaukee, Racine, and Southport was recommended.

The improvement of the navigation of the Wisconsin River and the establishment of a Territorial road from Prairie du Chien, by the mills on the Black and Chippewa rivers to the shores of Lake Superior, at the mouth of the Montreal River, comprised the measures recommended by the message, with the concluding advice—

"That we should hold a short term and confine our labors chiefly to the *amendment* of the laws now in force rather than the enactment of new ones."

The several parts of the Governor's message were referred to appropriate committees in both houses; the customary communications between the two houses and the Governor had been made; on the 7th inst., a joint resolution to authorize the purchase of stationery was presented to the Governor for his approval, which on the 10th of March in a message dated the 9th, was returned to the House with his objections, which were confined to its expediency, and everything indicated that entire harmony existed in the official relations between the Governor and the Legislature.

The conflicts as to whether the session was a "special" or an "adjourned" one, were dying away; a motion to amend the journal of the Council of the 6th of March by striking out the words "the Council met pursuant to adjournment" and inserting in lieu thereof the words "the Council was called to order at ten o'clock A. M., by the President," had been adopted, and both houses appeared to be in the full tide of co-operative legislative work.

But a new movement of the Governor within one short week of the commencement of this session of ambiguous origin, was now to destroy this harmony and again renew the contest between him and the representatives of the people.

On the 13th of March, the Governor returned without his approval to the House of Representatives, in which it originated, a bill to amend a ferry charter. The message did not state any objections to the bill itself, but says:

"When I met you on the 6th instant I stated in my message that it was for the purpose of holding a *special session*. It appears by your journals that you are holding a session which commenced on the first Monday in December last, and which has continued to the present time by adjournment or otherwise.

"I met you on the sixth to hold a term which is styled by the law a 'special session,' and I can take no part or lot in any other. * * * * * * * * *

"I therefore return the bill and must decline receiving it or any other bill until advised that the members are holding the 'special session' appointed by the proclamation of the 31st of January last."

The two houses continued during the whole of that week their ordinary work of legislation.

The following report of the committee on enrollment presented March 17, by Mr. WHITON, the chairman, gives a correct idea of the official relations between the Governor and the Legislature.

"The committee on enrollment report, that the said committee did, on this day, present to his Excellency, the Governor, for his approval, a bill entitled 'An act to annex certain fractions or lots of land in the town of Rock, in the county of Rock.' That his Excellency immediately took the bill from the table, where it had been placed by the chairman of the committee, and placed it in the hat of the chairman, and said : 'I must decline to receive it.' The chairman then asked his Excellency if he could leave it. His Excellency answered, 'No, you can not leave it.' The chairman then said, 'The bill has been presented.' His Excellency then replied, 'Yes, the bill has been presented.' The committee then retired with the bill in the hat of the chairman, where it had been placed by his Excellency.

All of which is respectfully submitted.

      EDWARD V. WHITON,
      H. CROCKER,
      ROBERT M. LONG,
      JOHN M. CAPRON.
      JOHN H. MANAHAN."

On the 17th of March the House adopted the following joint resolution, by a vote of 20 to 6 :

"That a committee of three from each house be appointed to confer with the executive relative to the disagreement between the executive and Legislative Assembly."

In the Council on the same day the resolution was rejected by a vote of 8 to 5.

On the 18th of March, a preamble and resolution were offered by Mr. MARTIN, which after slight verbal amendments were adopted by the Council in the following terms :

WHEREAS, The Governor of the Territory has informed the two houses of the Legislative Assembly, that he declines any further communication with them until advised that the members are holding the special session appointed by the proclamation of the 31st of January last; and

"WHEREAS, The public good imperiously demands the enactment of various laws at the present time, and more especially such laws as may have a tendency to relieve the people of the Territory from the evils which now exist in consequence of the accumulation of power in the hands of the present executive;

"The Legislative Assembly, therefore, for the sole purpose of satisfying the scruples of the Governor, and thereby enabling all the branches of the Legislature to proceed harmoniously in the business of their session; yet protesting against the right of the executive to demand the information sought, and declaring that the resolutions hereto annexed shall not be taken or considered as expressing the opinions of the members of the Assembly in regard to the question 'Whether the present is an adjourned or a special session?' resolves as follows:

"*Resolved*, The House of Representatives concurring:

"1st. That the Legislative Assembly is now holding the 'special session appointed by the proclamation of the Governor, dated January 31st, 1843.'

"2d. That the present officers of the two houses shall continue in office until further order of their respective houses; and the presiding officer of each house is hereby authorized to make such alteration in the journal of the proceedings of the 6th of March inst., kept by them respectively, as shall make it correspond with the resolution first above written.

"3. That the committee on enrollment be directed to communicate to the Governor the information expressed in these resolutions."

After the passage of these resolutions and their transmission to the House, the Council took a recess to await the action of the House.

The House concurred in the resolutions by a vote of 13 to 11, and at 9 o'clock P. M. the result was announced to the Council by the President, who then resigned his office, saying—

"I cannot make the alterations which the resolutions require me to without becoming the instrument of the Council in placing upon the journal what I deem to be a falsehood, and of making myself appear in the character of an usurper of authority that I did not possess. Neither of these things can I consent to do. It appears to me therefore that the only course left for me to pursue is to resign to your hands the office you have conferred upon me."

On Monday, the 20th March, MORGAN L. MARTIN was elected President, but it does not appear from the printed journal that any alteration to it was ever made.

On the same day the Governor sent to each house a message as follows—

"I have the honor to acknowledge the receipt this morning of a joint resolution of the Assembly passed on the 18th inst., relative to the present session of the Assembly, and to express my entire willingness to co-operate with the Council and House of Representatives in the dispatch of the public business.

EXECUTIVE DEPARTMENT, Madison, March 20, 1843.   J. D. DOTY."

The thirty days to which the special session was limited by law would expire on the 25th of March, and it only remained to provide for the contingency now quite certain to occur, that the expiration of the time would find the business of the session unfinished.

For that purpose a bill had been introduced in the Council on the 13th of March and passed on the 16th. It passed the House on the 20th, and was approved by the Governor on the 23d.

The act provided that the session then being held should terminate on the 25th of March, and that there should be a session held at the Capitol to commence on the 27th day of March, at 10 o'clock A. M., which should continue until terminated by joint resolution of the Assembly, at which the Council and House of Representatives might proceed to complete the unfinished business remaining in their respective houses at the termination of the session then being held.

A joint resolution was adopted on the 23d March, that the session to commence on the 27th March, should terminate on or before the 17th April.

Both houses formally adjourned their sessions *sine die* on the 25th March, and re-assembled on the 27th, and a resolution was passed in each house, that the organization of the last session stand for the present session and that all the officers then chosen be continued for this session.

A joint committee was appointed to wait on the Governor who immediately sent to each house a brief message, which

"Invited attention to the various subjects presented in his message of the 6th instant which had not already received their consideration and renewed his assurance that he should cheerfully co-operate with the Assembly in all such measures as might be proposed for the public good, and upon which by the acts of Congress we have the right to legislate."

The Governor said in conclusion—

"I avail myself of the occasion to remark that I consider the appointment of *civil officers* of the Territory by the Council and House of Representatives the exercise of an authority not granted by the acts of Congress, and being an encroachment upon the powers of the Executive it will become my duty to resist it by such means as the constitution has provided for the Executive to protect itself."

JOHN V. INGERSOLL resigned the office of Secretary of the Council and JOHN P. SHELDON was appointed as his successor.

Notwithstanding the embarrassments which the Legislative Assembly encountered from the causes already stated, quite a number of laws were passed, which were regarded by the members as of importance to the Territory. Many of these were passed by two thirds of each house, after having been returned by the Governor without his approval.

It had been found that the time allowed by law (one week) for holding court in Walworth county, where the Territorial suits were pending, was not long enough to admit of the trial of those cases, and the time was extended at this session to three weeks.

An act was also passed over the Governor's veto to provide for the election by joint ballot of the Council and House of Representatives, of an agent of the Legislative Assembly to be styled "Superintendent of Territorial Property." The act provided that all the duties which devolved by law upon the commissioner of public buildings and those which devolved by law upon the librarian, should devolve upon and be performed by the Superintendent of Territorial Property. JOHN Y. SMITH was elected superintendent under this law.

It was by the act made the duty of this new officer to bring to as speedy a termination as possible the several suits pending in favor of the Territory in the county of Walworth, and he was vested with full power and authority to compromise, settle, and discharge said suits.

The board of commissioners of Dane county submitted to the Legislative Assembly a proposition to put a new roof upon the Capitol in consideration of being permitted to use suitable rooms in it as offices for county purposes; whereupon an act was passed authorizing the superintendent to contract with the county to that effect.

Under these laws the principal duties devolved upon the "superintendent" as successor of the commissioner were such as related to the Territorial suits and the care of the Capitol.

In relation to the Capitol, BAXTER claimed that he had completed his contract and that a large amount was due to him for extra work, which the Superintendent was not authorized to adjust, much less to pay, and which could only be settled by the Legislature, and which they were annually called upon to investigate for a series of years.

In pursuance of the provisions of the foregoing act a contract was made with the commissioners of Dane county, for new shingling the roof of the Capitol and covering the hips of the main roof with sheet lead, in consideration of which the use of suitable rooms in the Capitol as offices for county purposes was granted to the county.

The county officers also by the authority of the Superintendent did additional work to the amount of $485 in re-tinning the dome and finishing the back piazza, with the understanding that the Legislature would be at perfect liberty to pay the expense or not.

In relation to the Territorial suits the report of the superintendent makes the following statements:

"The suit against the building commissioners, J. D. DOTY, JOHN F. O'NEILL, AUGUSTUS A. BIRD, and their sureties, came on for trial at the April term, 1842, for Walworth county.

"The substance of the evidence on the part of the Territory was, that the defendants had received from the Treasury of the United States, by authority from the Territory, forty thousand dollars, which they were bound to expend according to the provisions of law, in the erection of the Capitol at Madison. It was also shown in evidence by two of the most competent builders in the Territory, that up to the time the work was taken out of the hands of these commissioners, there could not have been expended upon the building to exceed eighteen or nineteen thousand dollars, making sufficient allowance for the circumstances under which the work was commenced and prosecuted. It was further shown that the money had been expended for other purposes than building the Capitol.

"The evidence chiefly relied on by the defense, and, indeed, the only evidence having any bearing on the case so far as related to the first $20,000, was a memorial to Congress, adopted by the Legislature of the Territory, asking for an additional appropriation of $20,000 to complete the building.

"This memorial contains what was claimed to be a tacit admission that the money had been properly expended according to law, in the following extract: 'These commissioners, in the exercise of the authority vested in them, immediately proceeded in the performance of the duties assigned to them, having, however, at the outset, difficulties of no ordinary nature to contend with, arising from the scarcity of the proper materials, and the scarcity also of mechanics and laborers—the former of which could not be purchased, and the latter not employed but at very high prices. At a great but not unreasonable expense (taking the situation and resources of the Territory into consideration), the public buildings were commenced, and have progressed as far as, under the pressure of adverse rcicumstances, could reasonably have been anticipated.'

"The following resolution adopted by both houses of the Assembly at the same session, but a few days after the adoption of the memorial, shows in express language that the Legislature did not intend to justify the commissioners in any of their acts—

'*Resolved* by the Council and House of Representatives of the Territory of Wisconsin, that the report of the commissioners appointed to agree upon a plan of the public buildings and to superintend the erection of the same at Madison, dated at Mineral Point November 29, 1837, be approved; *provided*, that nothing herein contained shall go to excuse the commissioners for any misconduct or for acting contrary to the act above recited.'

"I have made these extracts," the superintendent in his report continues, "for the purpose of presenting a condensed view of the nature of the evidence which procured, or rather furnished an excuse for a verdict against the Territory, in order that the Legislature may be better able to judge as to the propriety of further prosecuting those suits.

"There was no definite testimony of any sort to show what disposition had been made of the second appropriation of $20,000. One of the witnesses (Mr. MORRISON) stated in general terms that certain items of work and materials cost *him* certain sums; when asked how much had been paid him by the commissioners on his contract he declined giving an answer, and was excused by the court from doing so.

"With this view of the testimony, which I believe is fairly stated, it may appear strange to any one unacquainted with other circumstances attending the trial that such a verdict should have been rendered, but to every one present at the Walworth court in April last, it must have been apparent that no amount of testimony nor any array of professional talent could possibly have produced a different result from the jury which tried the cause."

"From an examination of the list of jurors summoned for that term of court, it was manifest that there had been foul play, and that the jury had been selected to meet the emergency. Of the thirty-six jurors drawn for that term of the court, all but three or four were attached to the political party known to be, in that county, particularly favorable to the executive of the Territory, and the whole seventy-two selected for the year, were about in the same proportion.

"When the case was called for trial, it was found that but about half the full panel of jurors were present. The counsel for the Territory insisted that the panel should be filled, before drawing from the box, which was refused by the court. Several of the jurors were put upon their *voire dire*, who uniformly swore that they had not formed or expressed any opinion in relation to the case. In the case of one of these jurors it was proven in court, in the face of his oath to the contrary, that he had repeatedly expressed such an opinion; and the same might have been proven of some others, who testified upon their *voire dire*, but owing to the limited number of jurors present, the counsel for the Territory did not deem it prudent. It is also a fact that at least half the jury who tried the case boarded, during the four days occupied in the trial, with one of the defendants (Governor Doty) at a private house; and I am creditably informed that some of them changed their boarding places and took lodgings with his Excellency after they were sworn upon the jury."

"The counsel for the Territory moved for a new trial, on the ground that the verdict was contrary to law and evidence; which motion was sustained, and a new trial ordered, on condition that the Territory pay the costs already incurred, *instanter*, and in less than twenty-four hours after this decision was made, judgment was entered against the Territory for costs in consequence of the order of the previous day not having been complied with. The costs amounted to $150, and no provision has been made by the Legislature to meet such an emergency.

"The case has been brought up to the Supreme Court, by writ of error. The defendants at the July term of the Supreme Court, alleged a defect in the records, and obtained an order to perfect the same, which prevented the case being argued at that term of the court. It is the opinion of good judges of law that there are strong points of error in the case, and that an order for a new trial is sure to be obtained."

BAXTER presented his claim against the Territory, and the whole subject, together with that of the bonds issued, for the completion of the Capitol, was referred to a joint committee, who submitted the following propositions for consideration:

"First. To abandon forever the purpose of ever having, building, or finishing a capitol at Madison.

"Second. To change the place of meeting of the Legislature to Prairie du Chien, Green

Bay, or Milwaukee, or wherever buildings and accommodations might be had free of expense to the Territory.

"Third. To settle, on as reasonable terms as possible, with BAXTER, and dissolve by mutual consent, and cancel the contract for finishing the capitol.

"Fourth. To raise a revenue from the several counties which will be sufficient in a short time to redeem the bonds, and abolish the office of Attorney-General as a useless burden to the Territory, and apply the salary appertaining to that office to the liquidation of said bonds.

"Fifth. To authorize the Superintendent of Territorial Property to commence suit forthwith against JAMES MORRISON, to recover the money now in his hands belonging to the Territory."

No action was taken in relation to either of these propositions except the third, as to which a resolution was adopted by both houses —

"That a joint committee of two from each house be appointed to settle with DANIEL BAXTER for work done on the capitol."

The committee submitted a report, but it did not result in any action by the Legislature.

Mr. CAPRON, of Walworth county, on the 12th of April — two days before the close of the session — offered a resolution,

"That ———— ———— be and they are hereby appointed commissioners to examine and finally settle the accounts, vouchers, and all claims and matters in dispute, in relation to the public buildings at Madison, between the Territory of Wisconsin and JAMES D. DOTY and his sureties, and JOHN F. O'NEILL, A. A. BIRD, JAMES MORRISON and DANIEL BAXTER and his sureties, or with either of said parties, and that the commissioners report the result of their proceedings to the Legislature at the next session."

The resolution was laid on the table and not called up during the remaining two days of the session.

The librarian appointed by the Governor was his brother-in-law, Mr. BARLOW SHACKELFORD, who seems to have become involved in a conflict with the Legislature.

His predecessor, Mr. LULL, contracted with Messrs. J. & L. WARD for the stationery for the use of the Legislature for the year 1842–3, as it was his duty by law to do, and it appears to have come to the possession of Mr. SHACKELFORD before the first of February, 1843. The law made it the duty of the librarian to deliver the stationery to the Secretary of the Council and Clerk of the House. But on that day in reply to a request from the Clerk for the delivery of the stationery for the use of the House, the librarian replied that he had just received word from Mr. WARD not to deliver the stationery until the commencement of a *legal* session of the Legislature, and that none could be delivered at present.

The Clerk reported the facts to the House which appointed

a committee to examine the library and ascertain the facts in relation to the stationery.

The committee on the second of February addressed a letter to the librarian enclosing a copy of the resolution, and inquiring when it would be convenient for him that they should proceed to examine the library and to answer the inquiries made by the resolution.

To this letter the librarian made the following reply:

MADISON, February 3, 1843.
" To Messrs. HAMILTON, DARLING and HUNKINS:

Gentlemen: Your favor of 2nd inst. has been received, in which you desire to be informed when it will be convenient for me that you should proceed to examine the library, and hand you an answer, etc.

In reply, I have only to say that it will afford me great pleasure and be entirely convenient to give the information desired on the *sixth* day of March, eighteen hundred and forty-three. I am with great respect,

B. SHACKELFORD,
Librarian."

The Legislative Assembly on the 7th of March, passed a joint resolution

"That the Secretary of the Council and Chief Clerk of the House of Representatives be authorized to purchase the stationery necessary for the use of the Legislature during the present session."

The resolution was sent to the Governor for his approval, and on the 10th of March he returned it to the House with his objections, and on the same day it passed the House by a vote of 23 to 1 (Mr. PALMER in the negative). Absent, Messrs. AGRY and MANAHAN. It passed the Council by 12 to 0. Absent, Mr. DEWEY.

The auditor appointed by Governor DOTY was Mr. JULIUS T. CLARK. He had been suffered to use for his office one of the committee rooms of the Capitol.

Mr. CLARK being unwilling to vacate the room the House passed a resolution

"That the Sergeant-at-Arms be directed to notify the Auditor that the exclusive use of said room must be given to the use of the Legislative Assembly, and the key thereof placed in the hands of the Sergeant-at-Arms."

This having been done, the Auditor on the same day addressed a communication to the House, which it characterized as "insolent." He stated that

"Under ordinary circumstances he should not have hesitated to comply with a *request* of the House covering the grounds embraced in the resolution; but in this instance he was constrained to believe that more was meant by the resolution than at first meets the eye."

This latent meaning of the resolution the Auditor believed to be, as he plainly intimated, that the House desired

"To remove the records and papers, etc., of his office from the room," and said he deemed it his duty to guard them, and if such is the object, he said, "I do not feel at liberty to surrender it (the room)."

Thereupon the House by a vote of 15 to 7 adopted a resolution

"That the Sergeant-at-Arms be directed to remove the effects of the said CLARK from the said room and take possession of the same for the use of the Legislature, *peaceably* if he can, *forcibly* if he must."

It was found that *force* was necessary to obtain possession of the room.

A resolution was adopted by the House on the 6th day of December

"That the editors and reporters of the different newspapers published in the Territory be allowed to occupy seats within the bar of this House."

Under this resolution the reporter of the *Wisconsin Enquirer*, the reputed organ of Governor DOTY, had occupied a seat until the 24th of March.

Many complaints of the unfairness of his reports had from time to time been made, and on that day Dr. DARLING offered a preamble which recited specific instances of false reports and suppressions, as well as slanders and libels of a member of the House and a resolution

"That the reporter and editor of the *Wisconsin Enquirer* be expelled from seats within the bar of this House."

The preamble and resolutions were adopted in a full House by a vote of 24 to 2, Messrs. CAPRON and PALMER alone voting against them.

The recommendation of the Governor that provision be made by law for a vote of the people on the question of the formation of State government did not meet with a favorable response by the Legislative Assembly. In the Council no notice was taken of it except to refer it to a committee, which made no report, and in the House a joint resolution was introduced, which, after being amended, was indefinitely postponed.

The Governor however on the 23rd of August, issued his proclamation, reciting that as no provision had been made by law for such vote—

"Therefore, in order that the public voice may not be stifled by this failure, but that it may be clearly expressed to the Congress of the United States and the Legislature of this

Territory be thereby instructed, I do recommend to each of the inhabitants to deposit with the judges of the election precincts on the day of the general election, to-wit: the fourth Monday of September next, a ballot with the word "yea" or "nay" thereon, as the voter may be in favor of or against the formation of a permanent government for the State of Wisconsin."

This proclamation of the Governor elicited less interest than that of the previous year. Only five of the counties which then made returns made any this year, while five others made returns this year which made none the preceding year. The total vote was only 1,817, although the total vote of the Territory for delegate was over eight thousand.

The following table shows the vote as returned—

Counties.	For.	Against.
Brown	5	110
Dane and Sauk	88	21
Fond du Lac	1	35
Iowa	164	562
Manitowoc	5	6
Milwaukee	126	169
Rock	37	158
Walworth	85	175
Washington	28	10
Winnebago	2	30
Totals	541	1,276

This inharmonious session of the Legislature called out from the Governor ten vetoes of its acts and joint resolutions; being more than one sixth of the whole number passed, of which all but two were on re-consideration passed by two thirds of each house.

Of these vetoed measures, incidental mention has already been made of the joint resolution authorizing the purchase of stationery; of the bill to amend a ferry charter, the vote on the reconsideration of which was 10 to 2 in the Council and 19 to 6 in the House, and of the bill to elect a superintendent of territorial property, which on re-consideration received the votes of every member of the Council (13) while in the House the vote was 24 to 2.

The other seven of these measures with the vote in each House on re-consideration were as follows:

"An act to abolish certain offices therein named," (Laws of 1843, p. 28) — vote in Council 10 to 2; in House 17 to 8.

"An act to amend an act entitled 'an act to change the time of holding courts in certain counties in the second judicial district" (Laws of 1843, p. 73) — vote in Council 11 to 0; in the House 25 to 0.

"An act concerning removals from office." (Laws of 1843, p. 76.) Vote in Council, 9 to 1; in House, 24 to 1.

"An act to provide for the payment of the expenses of the Legislative Assembly." (Laws of 1843, p. 76.) Vote in Council, 9 to 1; in House, 20 to 5.

"Joint resolutions relative to the distributive share of Wisconsin in the net proceeds of the public lands." (Laws of 1843, p. 84). Vote in Council, 8 to 3; in House, 21 to 4.

The two measures that did not pass over the vetoes, and the votes thereon, were:

"An act to provide for the election of a Territorial printer." The vote in the Council was 7 to 5, which, not being two thirds, it was not sent to the House.

And "an act to amend an act to prevent trespass and other injuries being done to the possessions of settlers on public lands, and to define the right of possession on said lands, approved January 4, 1842." The vote in the Council was unanimous in favor of the passage on reconsideration, but in the House the vote was 15 to 10 — not two thirds.

In compliance with a resolution of the Council, the Governor, on the 30th of March, sent to the Council a copy of the estimate submitted by him September 26, 1842, to the Register of the United States Treasury, of appropriations for the support of the government of Wisconsin for the half year ending June 30, 1843, and for the year ending June 30, 1844, which were referred to the committee on Territorial affairs.

The next day Mr. CROCKER, chairman of the committee on Territorial affairs, submitted the report of that committee, which exposed some grave errors in the estimates of the Governor. The estimates were in tabular form, and were repeated separately for each of the two periods. They each contained the following:

For pay of members, 75 days each, at $3 per day	$6,750 00
For mileage	400 00
	$7,150 00

The committee call attention to the fact that there are 39 members, and that
a correct estimate for 75 days each, at $3 per day would be.................. .... $8,775 00
That the act of Congress allows $3 for every twenty miles travel, that the amount
of mileage allowed at the present session is $1,035 80, and about the same sum
has been allowed at every session........ .... 1,035 80

True sum for per diem and mileage of members................................... $9,810 80
Deduct estimate of Governor........ .... 7,150 00

Under-estimate on these items......................, ... $2,660 80

A difference for both periods of $5,321.60.

The estimates of the Governor were the guide of Congress in the two appropriations of December 24, 1842, and March 3, 1843, and the appropriations correspond literally with the estimates.

There are other items in which the committee think the estimates are too low, which may result from error in judgment, but in reference to the items for mileage and pay of members, they say —

"The committee would be happy, out of charity to his Excellency, to consider this error as unintentional on his part and the result of ignorance of the simple rules of arithmetic. They might adopt this conclusion had this *error* occurred but once, but when it occurs a second time they can attribute it to no other intention or object on the part of his Excellency than a desire to again plunge the Territory into all the difficulties attending expenditures exceeding the appropriations.

"The committee cannot forbear to express their opinion that the attempt to mislead the Treasury Department and thereby prevent the requisite appropriations by Congress, is a part of the scheme devised by his Excellency to prevent as far as possible, the sessions of the Legislative Assembly and involve in confusion and difficulty the financial affairs of the Territory.

"The committee would cheerfully avoid the necessity of speaking in terms of condemnation of the Governor in this instance, having so often in the discharge of their duties as members of the Legislature, been called upon to censure his official conduct. It is humiliating to the members of this body that they are so often compelled to hold up to the public gaze the errors and imperfections of the Executive of their Territory, yet it is necessary that they be exposed, that he may be prevented from committing similar offences in future."

The annual report of the Territorial Treasurer (JAMES MORRISON) was laid before the House of Representatives on the 1st day of April, 1843.

It showed disbursements during a period extending from September 18, 1841, to March 7, 1843, amounting in the aggregate to $5,895.75, the means to pay which had been the Territorial revenue from the several counties.

The Capitol Fund account showed that the Treasurer had received
from the United States... $1,758.28

That the expenses of collection were.................................. $42.00
Paid for fifteen bonds of $100 each, issued to DANIEL BAXTER and
  interest.. 1,710.00
Balance of specie on hand... 6.28
                                                                          ——— $1,758.28

That he had received from his predecessor ten of the BAXTER bonds of
  $100 each, and had then on hand...................................... $1,000

The system of levying and collecting Territorial revenue was radically changed by the Legislature at this session, by providing that there should be annually levied in each county a Territorial tax of such per cent. on the assessment roll as the Legislative Assembly shall have prescribed at its next preceding annual session.

The rate prescribed for the year 1843, was three eights of a mill on the dollar in Milwaukee, Racine, Jefferson and Crawford counties, and five eights of a mill on the dollar in all the other counties.

The President of the Council, on the 8th of March, called Mr. NEWLAND to the chair, and from the floor offered certain joint resolutions relative to the northwestern boundary of the Territory.

The resolutions declared that the treaty commonly called the "Ashburton treaty," concluded at Washington, August 9th, 1842, between DANIEL WEBSTER and Lord ASHBURTON, by the boundary therein defined from Lake Superior to the Lake of the Woods, by the way of Pigeon river, surrenders to the British government without the slighest equivalent, the extensive tract of country lying between that boundary and the water communication from Lake Superior to Rainy Lake, by way of the Kamanistiquia River and the Long Lake; which was clearly within the limits of the United States as defined by the treaty of 1783, and within the limits of the Territory of Wisconsin.

The resolutions specified other violations of the rights of the people of Wisconsin by the treaty, and requested the government of the United States by treaty with Great Britain or otherwise to restore the boundary defined by the treaty of 1783.

The temporary occupant of the chair decided that the President had no right to offer resolutions as a member, and that the resolutions were not in order.

From this decision Mr. STRONG appealed, claiming that his

election to the Presidency had not deprived him of any of his rights as a member.

The decision of the chair was overruled and the resolutions were received. They were considered at a subsequent day, and indefinitely postponed.

One bill granting a divorce passed the House without a division, but in the Council it was refused a third reading by a vote of 4 to 8.

One bill was passed to change a person's name from HENRY SAUNDERS BROWN to HENRY BROWN SAUNDERS.

The question of the division of Grant and Iowa counties, and the creation of a new county, of which Platteville should be the county seat, was one that excited much interest in the localities immediately affected by it.

Numerous petitions were presented which were referred to the committee on corporations, which reported that there was a remonstrance of 1,398 names against any division of said counties, and that the petitions in favor of the division contained 1,147 names, leaving a majority of 251 against any division, and a majority of the committee reported a resolution that the prayer of the petition be not granted and the committee be discharged.

The minority of the committee submitted a report, in which they concurred with the majority as to the division of Iowa county, but introduced a bill for the division of Grant county, which provided that the people should approve or disapprove of the same at the ballot box.

This bill was indefinitely postponed by a vote of 16 to 9.

Mr. PLATT (of Platteville) then offered a resolution that the voters of Grant county, at the next general election, be authorized to vote for or against a division of said county from north to south. But the House refused to pass the resolution by a vote of 11 to 14.

By "an act relative to Dodge county" (laws of 1843, p. 54) an election of a judge of probate was provided for. The voters were also authorized to determine by ballot the place at which the county commissioners should hold their sessions, and thereafter the sessions of the county board should be held at the place so determined upon.

The fourth section of the act of January 9, 1840, which authorized the holding of courts in the county of St. Croix was repealed, and the county was attached to the county of Crawford.

A number of laws were passed creating and changing the boundaries of towns.

These are stated as a matter of historical interest to the different localities.

In Walworth county the original town of Troy embraced town 4, ranges 17 and 18. It was divided, the west half being called Meacham and the east half retaining the name of Troy. At the same session, in less than three weeks, such was the dissatisfaction that another law was passed giving to Meacham the name of Troy, and to Troy that of East Troy. The towns of La'Fayette La'Grange and Sharon in the same county were created.

In Milwaukee county the towns of Nemahbin and Ottawa were organized.

In Rock county the towns of Johnstown and Fulton were organized; the north half of town three, range eleven, was annexed to Union; fractional sections one and two lying north and west of Rock River in town two, range twelve, were attached to the town of Rock; five sections in the town of Beloit were attached to the town of Clinton, and that part of town three, range twelve, west of Rock River was annexed to the town of Janesville.

In Jefferson county the town of Oakland was detached from the town of Jefferson and organized separately, and the north half of town 6, and the two southern tiers of sections in town 7, ranges 15 and 16, were annexed to the town of Jefferson.

The county of Calumet was incorporated into one town with the name of Manchester.

The county of Marquette was created into a town with the name of Marquette.

The county of Winnebago was formed into one town, the name of which was changed from Butte des Morts to Winnebago.

In Brown county the boundaries of the towns of Depere, Green Bay and Kaukaulin were defined and prescribed.

In Racine county the town of Pike was organized out of town 2, range 22, into a separate town; that part of the town of Pleasant Prairie comprised in fractional town 1, range 23 east, was annexed to the town of Southport; section 31, town 3, range 22, was set off from the town of Paris and annexed to the town of Mount Pleasant; and lot 5, in section 9, town 3, range 23, was excluded from the village of Racine.

Acts were passed authorizing the laying out and establishing eighteen different Territorial roads to and from the several points named in such acts.

Acts were passed authorizing the construction of dams on navigable rivers as follows:

On the Fox River in the county of Racine, on sections 2 and 11, town 3, range 19, in the town of Rochester; and in section 32, same town and range, in the town of Burlington.

On Rock River in section 36, town 3, range 12, in town of Janesville, and on section 21 or 16 in town 4, range 12, in the town of Fulton.

On the Milwaukee River, in section 23, town 9, range 21 east, in Washington county.

Also, amendments of laws heretofore passed, authorizing dams on the Manitowoc and Menomonee rivers.

The trustees of the village of Racine were empowered to levy and collect a special tax not exceeding five thousand dollars annually, for three years, for the purpose of constructing a harbor at the mouth of Root River.

Congress having authorized the Legislature to provide by law that the offices of sheriffs, judges of probate, and justices of the peace might be made elective by the people, an act was passed that there should be a general special election on Monday, the first day of May, 1843, for the election of those officers.

An act was passed to incorporate the Prairieville Manufacturing Company, for the purpose of manufacturing flour and other commodities for market.

The act passed in 1839 to incorporate "The State Bank of Wisconsin" was repealed.

As showing the feeling of opposition to agitation of the question of slavery, which then existed, mention is made of the fact that a resolution granting the use of the Council Chamber to the Rev. Mr. MATTHEWS to deliver an anti-slavery address, received but three votes (Messrs. BAKER,

CROCKER, and HUGUNIN), while the other ten members all voted against it. A like resolution, granting the Representatives' Hall for the same purpose, was the next day defeated in the House by a vote of 7 to 18.

The receivers of the Bank of Mineral Point, appointed in 1841, submitted their report to the court in January, 1843, which showed that nearly all the assets, consisting of liabilities of foreign debtors, in Saint Louis, New York, and Boston, had been absorbed by attaching creditors, and that there was little or nothing left for the less fortunate creditors.

In the latter part of the year 1843, the village of Platteville, was visited with that terrible scourge, the small pox, in its most virulent form. Quite a number of its most prominent citizens, in the full vigor of matured manhood, were victims of the terrible disease, and in numerous instances with fatal results. The whole number of cases was 153, of which nine proved fatal.

Hon. STEVENS T. MASON, the last Governor of the Territory of Michigan, while Wisconsin was under its jurisdiction, and the first Governor of the State of Michigan, and whose name is inseparably connected with titles to lots in the city of Madison, died in the city of New York on the 4th of January, 1843, of suppressed scarlet fever, after a sickness of four days.

The election for Delegate in Congress, in 1843, was conducted on party grounds, so far as nominations by party conventions could make it political.

The Democratic convention assembled at Madison on the 19th of July, and placed in nomination General HENRY DODGE, with entire unanimity. MARSHALL M. STRONG, presided.

The Whig convention assembled at Madison on the 25th of July, and resulted in 27 votes for GEORGE W. HICKCOX and 17 votes for WILLIAM S. HAMILTON — Col. HAMILTON withdrew his name, and GEN. HICKCOX was nominated without opposition.

The canvass was animated and resulted in 4,685 votes for General DODGE and 3,184 for General HICKCOX.

The following is the official canvass in detail by counties:

Counties.	Henry Dodge.	Geo. W. Hickcox.	Jonathan Spooner.	Scattering
Brown	81	117	1	....
Calumet	49	35	....	....
Crawford	123	52	....	....
Dane	157	152	2	....
Dodge	41	32	....	....
Fond du Lac	49	17	....	....
Grant	670	560	....	2
Iowa	585	483	....	....
Jefferson	184	155	11	....
Manitowoc	29	3	....	....
Milwaukee	930	351	115	2
Portage	85	52	....	....
Racine	748	490	11	....
Rock	280	222	12	....
St. Croix	171	61	....	2
Sheboygan	21	27	....	....
Walworth	468	355	1	19
Winnebago	14	20	....	....
Totals	4,685	3,184	153	25

CHAPTER XXV.

TERRITORY OF WISCONSIN — 1844.

The legislation of the paternal government at the first session of the twenty-eighth Congress, between December, 1843, and June, 1844, resulted in greater good to the Territory, than that of any former session, or of all the three next preceding it.

An appropriation of twenty thousand dollars was made "for continuing the works at the harbor at Milwaukee, Wisconsin" which had been commenced under an appropriation made at the preceding session. This appropriation was placed in the general river and harbor bill, which association secured for it in the future its proper share of the fostering care of the government, which might be bestowed upon other works of a like character.

Two separate and special acts were also passed, each having a single object. One appropriated twelve thousand five hundred dollars "for the construction of a harbor at the town of Southport" and the other appropriated a like sum "to aid in the completion of a harbor already commenced by the citizens of Racine at the mouth of Root river."

The annual appropriation "for compensation and mileage of the members of the Legislative Assembly, pay of their clerk, librarian and superintendent of public buildings, printing, stationery, fuel, lights, arrearages of previous sessions and all other incidental and miscellaneous objects" was only seventeen thousand two hundred and fifty dollars, that being the amount of the estimate furnished by the Governor. This was for the fiscal year ending June 30th, 1845, and was in the general civil and diplomatic appropriation bill.

Another act was passed of great importance to the town of Potosi, and to the improvement of the approaches to the banks of the Mississippi River, near that place.

Section 34, town 3, range 3 west, containing 640 acres of valuable land, was one of the numerous tracts which had been reserved from sale by the Government in consequence of its supposed mineral character. Numerous settlements had been made upon it, and a large portion of it, probably the whole, was "claimed" by "squatters," some claiming only a small lot for a residence, and others, several acres, and a large part of the town of Potosi was built upon it.

An act was passed, in conformity with a memorial of the Legislative Assembly, granting this section to the Territory "for the purpose of improving Grant River, known as the Grant Slue at the town of Potosi." It provided that the land should be surveyed and divided into lots and be sold and disposed of in such manner, and under such regulations and restrictions as the Legislature should establish; provided, that pre-emption rights should be granted to actual settlers and occupants.

This act was approved June 15, 1844, and practical effect could not be given to it until the Legislative Assembly, at its next session, should establish the necessary "regulations and restrictions."

Another act was passed by Congress at the same time which provided "that it should be competent to the Legislatures of the several Territories to re-adjust and apportion the representation in the two branches of their respective bodies, in such manner from time to time as may seem to them just and proper. And that justices of the peace and all general officers of the militia, in the several Territories, shall be elected by the people in such manner as the respective legislatures thereof may provide."

The second session of the fourth Legislative Assembly convened at Madison on the 4th of December, 1843.

There were two changes in the membership of the Council and three in the House of Representatives. Messrs. HEATH and HUGUNIN, of Racine county, had resigned their seats in the Council, and MARSHALL M. STRONG and MICHAEL FRANK were elected as their successors.

In the House, Col. HAMILTON, of Iowa county, resigned, and GEORGE MESSERSMITH was elected to succeed him. Messrs. JUDSON and VAN VLIET, of Racine county, resigned, and LEVI GRANT and EZRA BIRCHARD were elected to fill the vacancies.

In the Council all the members were present on the first day except Dr. BARBER of Jefferson who appeared on the fourth. In the House there was a full attendance at the opening of the session except that Mr. HICKS of Grant county did not take his seat until the 11th of December, and Mr. LONG of Iowa until the 5th of January.

In the Council, after a temporary organization, MARSHALL M. STRONG of Racine was elected President, BEN C. EASTMAN of Grant, Secretary, and GEO. C. S. VAIL of Milwaukee, Sergeant-at-Arms.

In the House GEORGE H. WALKER of Milwaukee was appointed Speaker *pro tem.* on its assembling, and on the second day was elected permanent Speaker. JOHN CATLIN was re-elected Clerk, and JOHN W. TROWBRIDGE of Racine was elected Sergeant-at-Arms.

RICHARD F. CADLE, who for several years had been a missionary of the Episcopal church at Green Bay, was elected Chaplain of the Council, and JESSE L. BENNETT was elected Chaplain of the House.

On the 26th of January, Mr. LA'CHAPPELLE of Crawford county resigned his seat as a member of the Council.

Hon. LEWIS F. LINN, senator in Congress from Missouri, from 1833 until his death in 1843, had taken a lively and effective interest in every measure designed to promote the interests of Wisconsin.

On the morning of the first day of the session, and before the delivery of the Governor's message, the following resolutions were adopted by the Council:

"*Resolved*, by the Council (if the House of Representatives concur) that the Legislative Assembly of the Territory of Wisconsin have learned with feelings of deepest regret the death of Hon. L. F. LINN, late a Senator in Congress from the State of Missouri; that by his death his family have been deprived of a most affectionate and amiable head; Congress of a true patriot and able statesman; his own state of a most able and efficient representative; the whole west of a firm and ever ready advocate of its best interests; and the Territory of Wisconsin in particular of one who has been on all occasions its resolute and devoted friend, and to whom it is deeply indebted for his zealous activity in its behalf in the body of which he was a member.

"*Resolved*, that as a testimony of the respect which the Legislative Assembly entertain for the memory of the Hon. LEWIS F. LINN, both houses will immediately adjourn."

The Council then adjourned.

The resolutions were on the same day adopted by the House of Representatives, which then immediately adjourned.

The Governor's message opened with the expression of his opinion that

"The people, only in the exercise of their sovereign power as an independent State, can correct the evils which appear to be incidental to this colonial form of government, in its judicial, legislative nd executive departments."

It next informs the Legislative Assembly of what they already knew too well, that

"The appropriation by Congress for the fiscal year 1844, to defray the expenses of the Assembly, will not allow a session to be held the usual term of seventy-five days," and expresses "the hope that your present session may be as short as the public interests will permit."

Attention is called to the indebtedness of the Territory and provision for its payment recommended.

The revision of the laws in relation to taxation and the reduction of taxes are recommended.

The remainder of the message, being more than five sixths of the whole of it, is devoted to the expression of the opinions of the Governor, that the "Fifth State" to be formed under the ordinance of 1787, has the right, notwithstanding the action of Congress in the admission of Illinois and Michigan into the Union, to insist that its southern boundary shall be an east and west line running through the southern bend or extreme of Lake Michigan; to an able argument in support of his opinions on that subject, and to the recommendation of

"The passage of a law appointing a day for the free inhabitants of this district to vote upon the question, whether a permanent government shall be formed according to the articles of compact of 1787."

The message further says:

"There are now, it is admitted by every person acquainted with our settlements, more than sixty thousand inhabitants within the limits of this Territory; and within the limits fixed by the ordinance and subsequent acts of Congress, for the fifth state in the Northwestern territory, there is estimated to be over one hundred and twenty thousand."

The message recommended, that if there shall be a majority in favor of state government, the taking of preliminary measures for the formation of a state government without the intervention of Congress. It claims that

"The Ordinance of 1787 grants *to the people* the right to form states within certain districts and *to Congress* the right to admit such states into the Union. The constitutions of the states of Tennessee and Michigan were formed under this provision; *the right* cannot therefore now be questioned."

The message further says:

"In relation to the right of a state *to enter the Union with a contested boundary*, there were several instances of unsettled boundaries between the thirteen original states when they joined the Union, some of which are yet undetermined, and it is not perceived why a new state has not the privilege to adjust her boundaries, or have them settled, in the same manner as an old state. It may be taken for granted, therefore, from the example of those states as well as that of Michigan, that this state has the right to be admitted, although her boundaries may be contested by other states. A state *out of the Union* has as good a right to her established boundaries, as a state *in it*. The form of government to which she may at any period of her existence be subject, neither increases nor diminishes this right. It cannot be conceded that the right to *admit* can control the right to *form* a constitution, further than to require that the constitution is republican and in conformity to the principles contained in the articles of compact."

So much of the Governor's message as relates to the expediency of forming a State government was referred to a joint select committee composed of Messrs. MARTIN and CROCKER of the Council, and Messrs. ELLIS, PRICE and GRANT of the House.

While the subject was under consideration another question arose, intimately connected with the question of the wisdom of changing the form of government from Territorial to State, a question which excited great interest among the people of the Territory, which was reflected by their representatives, and which was in a great measure similar to the questions out of which the political party known as "Know Nothings," or as it styled itself "American" had its origin.

The fifth section of the organic act of the Territory contained a proviso

"That the right of suffrage shall be exercised only by citizens of the United States."

About the time of the meeting of the Legislative Assembly and for some time after, the justice and propriety of extending to the residents of the Territory, who under this proviso were denied the right of suffrage, authority to vote upon the preliminary question of forming a State government, and of participating in the election of delegates to form a State constitution, called out much feeling in Milwaukee which to a considerable degree extended to other parts of the State. The expressions at Milwaukee were almost unanimous in favor of the measure, and the same feeling was exhibited to a less extent in other parts of the State.

On the other hand there were many demonstrations of opposition to the measure, one of the most marked of which was a public meeting of citizens of Jefferson, Koshkonong and Oakland, held at Fort Atkinson on the 15th of January, 1844, which resolved that they

"Solemnly protested against the passage of any law that would extend the elective franchise to foreigners."

In Grant county the opposition to the passage of the law was quite extensive and very decided.

On the 4th of January, as the journal reads—

"The Speaker laid before the House the petition of SOLOMON JUNEAU and JOHN WHITE, Esquires, and twelve hundred and eighteen others, relative to State Government and the right of foreign born citizens to vote."

A struggle immediately ensued between the friends of the measure and its opponents on the question of the reference of the petition, the former desiring its reference to the committee on Territorial affairs and the latter opposing it. The result soon exhibited the strength of the opposing forces, and the proposed reference was carried by a vote of 15 to 7, with four absent.

A strong lobby was present advocating the measure, the acknowledged leaders of which were ISAAC P. WALKER, FRANCIS HUEBSCHMANN and JOHN WHITE. There was no organized outside opposition to the bill.

The committee on Territorial affairs was composed of Messrs. DARLING, ELMORE, CROSSMAN, PARSONS and HUNKINS.

The committee on Territorial affairs by Dr. DARLING, its chairman, on the 9th of January, reported —

"A bill in relation to the qualification of voters for State Government, and for the election of delegates to form a State constitution."

The following is the text of the bill:

"SECTION 1. That whenever the question of forming a State Government in Wisconsin Territory shall be submitted to the people thereof, all the free white male inhabitants above the age of twenty-one years who shall have resided in said Territory three months shall be deemed qualified and shall be permitted to vote upon said question.

"SECTION 2. That at any election hereafter to be held in this Territory for the purpose of choosing delegates to form a constitution and State Government for the people of said Territory, all the free white male inhabitants thereof above the age of twenty-one years, who shall have resided in said Territory three months next preceding such election, shall be deemed qualified and shall be permitted to vote for such delegates."

All the members of the committee concurred in the report except Mr. ELMORE, who was understood to be opposed to the bill, and voted against it on its final passage, although he made no minority report.

Several amendments were offered to the bill and a motion to indefinitely postpone, all of which were defeated by large majorities, one of which amendments, in view of subsequent events, is worthy of being preserved. It was offered by Mr. BARTLETT, and was to strike out the word *white* wherever it occurs. The only votes in favor of it were those of Messrs. BARTLETT, ELMORE, HOPKINS, OLIN, and THOMPSON, and there were twenty-one against it. The bill was then ordered to be engrossed, and on the next day — January 16th — it passed in a full House by a vote of 22 to 4 — the negative votes being given by Messrs. ELMORE, HICKS, THOMPSON, and TRIPP.

In the Council several amendments were offered, all of which were defeated; one of which was, that the residence of the voter preceding the election should be six months instead of three. The amendment to strike out the word "white" was made by Mr. WHITON, and obtained five votes to six against it.

Mr. WHITON also offered the following amendment:

"*Provided*, That the subjects of any foreign state with which the United States may be at war, shall not be entitled to vote on said question."

This was voted down by five to six.

Another amendment offered by Mr. WHITON was:

"*Provided*, That the said inhabitants who shall be allowed to vote, shall be able to speak the English language."

This was lost, one to ten, Mr. WHITON alone voting for it.

An amendment offered by Dr. BARBER to strike out the second section was lost, without a division.

The bill was then ordered to a third reading, and on the next day — January 18 — was passed by a vote of 8 to 3 in the same words in which it was originally reported in the House. Those who voted in the affirmative were Messrs. FRANK, LA'CHAPPELLE, MARTIN, NEWLAND, ROUNTREE, MARSHALL M. STRONG, MOSES M. STRONG and WHITE. Those who voted in the negative were Messrs. BARBER, DEWEY and WHITON. Messrs. BAKER and CROCKER were excused from attendance.

The joint select committee appointed on the 8th of December, to which the subject of State government had been referred, had not yet made any report, when on the 15th of January, Mr. LA'CHAPPELLE introduced a bill to submit the question to the people.

The bill provided for an election to be held on the first Monday of April, for or against State government, and if a majority should vote in favor of it, the Governor was to issue a proclamation as soon as might be, for delegates corresponding with the number of members of the Legislature from the several districts, to a convention for the formation of a State Constitution. If the bill had become a law, and a majority had voted in favor of a State government, the constitution would probably have been formed and submitted to the people by midsummer.

The bill was referred to a select committee, consisting of Messrs. MOSES M. STRONG, LA'CHAPPELLE and FRANK, which on the next day was reported back by a majority of the committee, with the following substitute:

"That at the general election to be held in this Territory on the fourth Monday of September next, all persons who shall be authorized by any law of the Territory, which has been or which may be hereafter passed, to vote on the question of forming a State government, shall be authorized to vote on that question at said election, by depositing with the judges of election a ballot, upon which shall be written or printed 'For State Government' or 'Against State Government'; and all such votes shall be canvassed, certified and returned, in the same manner as is required by law for the canvassing, certifying and returning of votes for Delegate to Congress, and the Secretary of the Territory is hereby required to certify to the Legislative Assembly, at its next session, the result of such vote."

Mr. LA'CHAPPELLE dissented from this report and submitted a minority report, and insisted in vigorous language upon an earlier submission of the question.

The next day (January 16th) the joint select committee submitted a report which took up and combatted the reasons of the Governor in his message in favor of a change in our form of government, and adopted the report of a committee of the House of Representatives submitted on the 11th of January, 1842, and desired that it might be received as a part of their report.

The result arrived at in the report was, that in the opinion of a majority of the committee—

"It is inexpedient to take any measures for the formation of a State Government at present."

A resolution had been introduced in the House requesting the delegate to procure, if possible, the passage by Congress of an "enabling act." This was laid on the table at the time of its introduction, and subsequently was indefinitely postponed by a vote of 16 to 7.

The bill introduced by Mr. LA'CHAPPELLE, in contrast with the substitute for it recommended by the select committee, met with so little favor in the Council that the substitute was adopted without a division.

The only remaining question was the passage of the substitute, or the adoption of the views of the majority of the joint select committee that it was "inexpedient to take any measures."

The bill came up in the Council for a test vote on the 19th January. Mr. CROCKER moved to strike out all after the enacting clause and insert the following: "WHEREAS, at the general election in the years 1841, 1842 and 1843, the voters of this Territory by decided majorities voted against the expediency of forming a State government;

"AND WHEREAS, since the last election there have been no petitions presented to the Legislature desiring any action on this subject; therefore,

"*Resolved* by the Council and House of Representatives of the Territory of Wisconsin, that it is inexpedient at this time to adopt any measures or take any action in relation to the formation of a State Government."

This amendment was lost, Messrs. CROCKER, DEWEY, MARTIN, NEWLAND and WHITE voting for it and the other eight against it.

As an evidence of the feeling of opposition to the bill to allow foreigners to vote, which passed the Council on the previous day, the following amendment offered by Mr. WHITON is referred to:

"*Provided*, That when a person shall offer his vote on said question who can not speak or understand the English language, it shall be the duty of the supervisors or judges of election (as the case may be) to procure some competent interpreter to interpret the Declaration of Independence, the Constitution of the United States, the ordinance enacted by the Congress of the United States for the government of the territory of the United States northwest of the River Ohio, and also an act of the Congress of the United States establishing the Territorial government of Wisconsin, who shall interpret said Declaration and acts to said person who may offer to vote."

Mr. WHITE demanded the previous question, which was sustained by a majority, and, under the rules of the Council at that time, cut off the amendment and brought it to a direct vote on the engrossment of the bill for a third reading, which was carried by the following vote: Ayes—Messrs. BAKER, BARBER, FRANK, ROUNTREE, MARSHALL M. STRONG, MOSES M. STRONG, and WHITON; noes — Messrs. CROCKER, DEWEY, LA'CHAPPELLE, MARTIN, NEWLAND, and WHITE. On the next day it passed the Council and was sent to the House.

On the same day of the passage of the bill by the Council Mr. ELLIS introduced in the House a resolution —

"That the time has not yet arrived in Wisconsin when 'the happiness of the people or the prosperity of the country will be advanced by the adoption of a State government.'"

The resolution was preceded by an able, argumentative preamble; but it was ordered, without a division, that the preamble and resolution be laid on the table.

When the bill came up for action in the House, an amendment, that if a majority of the votes should be against State government, the same question should be annually submitted, was voted down — 6 to 18.

An amendment was offered by Dr. DARLING to the effect that if a majority of votes were for State government, that

Congress should be requested to pass an enabling act, make provision for a census, and other necessary measures. The amendment was lost by a vote of 7 to 17. The bill was then ordered to a third. reading, under the operation of the previous question, by a vote of 17 to 6. Those absent or not voting were Messrs. ELMORE, MANAHAN, and PALMER. The other members voted for the bill, except Messrs. DARLING, ELLIS, HICKS, HUNKINS, MEEKER, and PRICE.

On the 25th of January the bill was passed by the same vote, with the addition of Mr. PALMER to the affirmative vote and Mr. ELMORE to the negative — Mr. MANAHAN being the only member not voting.

It was approved by the Governor on the 26th of January, in the words of the substitute reported by the select committee of the Council, except an amendment offered by the chairman of the committee that the votes should be deposited in a separate box.

Notwithstanding the requirement of the act that the votes should be returned to the Secretary of the Territory in the same manner as required by law for returning votes for delegate to Congress, and that the Secretary was required to certify the result to the Legislative Assembly at its next session, it appears from the certificate of the Secretary, that only one half of the counties made any returns. The counties which held no election, or if, they held any, made no returns, were Calumet, Crawford, Fond du Lac, Green, Manitowoc, Marquette, Portage, Racine, Saint Croix, Walworth and Washington.

The total vote as certified by the Secretary of the Territory is 6,846, of which the footings show (in which there is an error of 57 votes) 1,503 for State government and 5,343 against State government.

The following table gives the votes of the counties which made returns:

COUNTIES.	FOR.	AGAINST.
Brown	10	54
Dane	92	184
Dodge	21	89
Grant	176	1,324
Iowa	215	637
Jefferson	302	219

COUNTIES.	FOR.	AGAINST.
Milwaukee	459	2,115
Rock	199	523
Sauk	12	76
Sheboygan	10	55
Winnebago	4	19
Totals	1,503	5,343

The consideration of these questions and especially of the question who should have a right to vote, brought to the surface the question of negro suffrage for the first time in the history of the Territory.

Mr. WHITON presented the petition of six colored men praying that the right of suffrage might be extended to all persons holding real estate in the Territory or taxable property to the value of one hundred dollars. The Council refused by a vote of 3 to 9 to lay the petition on the table and it was referred to a select committee, consisting of Messrs. WHITON, BAKER and BARBER.

Mr. WHITON from the select committee, reported a bill to amend an act to provide for and regulate general elections and on his motion the bill was amended by adding the following proviso:

"Provided that when a person shall offer his vote, who is in whole or in part of the negro blood, such person shall not be allowed to vote unless he shall be a freeholder, or shall possess and own personal property of the value of one hundred dollars."

The bill with the amendment was ordered engrossed by a vote of 6 to 5, but subsequently on the same day, the enacting clause was stricken out by a vote of 6 to 4, Mr. FRANK having changed his vote, and Mr. MARTIN not voting.

In the House a similar petition had been presented by Mr. OLIN from inhabitants of Milwaukee, which was laid on the table. Subsequently two ineffectual efforts were made to take the petition from the table; the last failed by a tie vote of 12 to 12. The next day it was referred to the committee on the judiciary, and after about two weeks the committee reported that "it is not expedient to legislate on the subject." The report was accepted and the committee discharged without a division.

Much of the Governor's message was devoted to the subject of the infringement of the boundaries of the future

State. So much of the message as related to that subject was referred to a select committee, consisting of Messrs. MOSES M. STRONG, NEWLAND and WHITON, with instructions to report:

First. Whether the boundaries prescribed for the fifth State by the ordinance of 1787 have been infringed by the Government of the United States, and in what respect.

Second. If there has been any such infringement, what measures ought to be taken by the people of Wisconsin in relation thereto, and what effect it should have on the formation of a State government in Wisconsin.

A report was prepared by the chairman of the committee which was approved by the other members and submitted to the Council.

The report presents the views of the committee upon the questions submitted to it, in the order in which they are stated in the resolution.

It presents the conclusion that the boundaries of the fifth State have been infringed by the Government of the United States upon three different occasions and in three different particulars.

First. By the admission of Illinois into the Union, with the boundaries defined in the act of admission approved April 18, 1818.

Second. By the act of June 15, 1836, for the admission of Michigan into the Union, by which the Montreal and the Menomonee Rivers are declared to be the southwestern boundary of Michigan.

Third. By the 'treaty to settle and define the boundaries between the territories of the United States and the possessions of her Britanic Majesty in North America,' etc., entered into at Washington, August 9, 1842.

It then attempts to show that the conclusions of the report are justified by the facts and arguments which it presents.

The facts and arguments collated in the report to show the infringement by granting to Illinois a portion of the Territory rightfully belonging to the fifth State, sixty-one and a quarter miles in width, extending from Lake Michigan to the Mississippi River, while they lacked the charm of novelty were exhaustive of the question, and it is believed are unanswerable. However interesting they might be, the space they would occupy precludes their statement at length.

In reference to the second particular, the report states

that the southwestern boundary of Michigan between Lake Superior and Lake Michigan—

"If it embraces any territory whatever is an infringement of our boundaries; if not by the words of the ordinance, at least by what was understood at the time of its adoption as its true spirit and fair intent and by what all candid men would say should be its construction."

The boundary from Lake Superior to Green Bay has been heretofore described.

"This boundary," the report states, "assumes the fact, which at the time was supposed by Congress to exist, that the Lake of the Desert discharged its waters into the Montreal River; subsequent survey and exploration have proved that this is not the case, but that it discharges into the Wisconsin River, and is located far south of where it was supposed to be, and that the boundary line fixed by Congress is an impossible one, and that Congress have really given to Michigan no western or southwestern boundary. There is no boundary between Michigan and Wisconsin, and it is to be hereafter adjusted by the concurrent action of Congress and those States."

In reply to what may be said

"That the Montreal and Menomonee Rivers, through their main channels, are fixed and unalterable boundaries and that all that remains is to unite them by a suitable line," the report says "that such a boundary violates, if not the words, at least the spirit and intent of the ordinance."

The report further says:

"If the country should become inhabited, as it now is to some extent, and as it is reasonable to suppose it soon will be to a much greater, the convenience of its inhabitants would be much better consulted by uniting them with Wisconsin than with Michigan. Their facilities of intercourse with Wisconsin would be much greater, and they would enjoy their civil and political rights to a much greater extent by being united with a people to whom at all times they would be contiguous, than by being connected with those from whom all communication would be absolutely cut off for nearly half the year."

The report makes the following quotation from the communication of the Senators and Representatives of Michigan to the judiciary committee of the Senate:

"Its limits (boundaries of Michigan), are fixed and immutable without the consent of the people. They have never claimed anything beyond those limits; they have never transcended them; they have in all their proceedings adhered to them with punctillious fidelity. A due regard to the 'natural boundaries' and to the rights, political and territorial, of another people, whom she hopes at an early day to hail as another accession to this great confederacy of States, would forbid her to accept any acquisition of territory north and west of her, as a consideration for the serious loss alluded to."

The report concludes the second branch of the inquiry, as follows:

"To review this matter then, it appears that the boundary between Michigan and Wisconsin is still open, and must so remain until settled by competent authority. That the boundary which Congress attempted to establish, violates the spirit, intent and fair construction of the ordinance, is not the most natural one, productive of great inconvenience to all parties interested in it, and (as Michigan herself admits), one to which she had no claim and that 'operates injuriously and unjustly upon their fellow citizens west of Lake Michigan, both in a political and territorial point of view,' and one which upon every consideration that has a bearing on the question. ought not to be established as the permanent boundary between the two States."

The third particular relates to the infringement of boundaries by the treaty made at Washington, August 9, 1842, and then generally called the "Ashburton Treaty."

The report, after stating that the northern boundary of the fifth State, was defined by the ordinance of 1787 to be "the territorial line between the United States and Canada", and that this line was the one which, by the treaty of peace of September 3, 1783, was thus described after entering Lake Superior:

"Thence through Lake Superior, northward of the Isles Royal and Philipeaux to the Long Lake; thence through the middle of said Long Lake and the water communications between it and the Lake of the Woods," etc.;

proceeds to consider the only question which could have been in controversy between Mr. WEBSTER and LORD ASHBURTON in 1842, to wit: what and where was the "Long Lake" called for by the treaty of 1783? What water, whether lake, bay, estuary or river was in 1783 known and designated as Long Lake?

The Ashburton treaty designates "Pigeon River" as the point at which the boundary line leaves Lake Superior, and it defines the line thence to the Lake of the Woods.

The report states that —

"What was known in 1783 as 'the Long Lake,' is what is now known as the Kamanistaquia, or Dog River, and that its entrance into Lake Superior is about sixty miles northeast of Pigeon River. After the two boundaries separate on this coast they do not unite again until they unite in Rainy Lake, embracing between the two a superficies of about ten thousand square miles, which, by the treaty of 1842, is given to the British government."

The report of the committee is quite voluminous on this subject, and is made up largely of extracts from the report of the commissioners (Mr. BARCLAY on the part of Great Britain, and Mr. PETER B. PORTER on the part of the United States), under the sixth and seventh articles of the treaty of Ghent, contained in the eleventh volume of "Executive Documents," 1837-8 — No. 451.

It demonstrates most clearly and incontestably that the boundary defined by the treaty of 1783, was the Kamanistaquia or Dog River, and that the treaty of 1842, by adopting the Pigeon River route, creates a new boundary, "giving," to quote from the report,—

" To the British government about ten thousand square miles of the territory, and about sixty miles of the lake coast, which rightfully belongs to the fifth State, and which can not be lawfully taken from her without her consent, which she has never given or been asked to give, and is an infringement of the boundary of the fifth State, as prescribed by the Ordinance of 1787."

It is difficult at this comparatively remote period to appreciate the interest which was felt in these questions at that time, and the statement of the remedial measures recommended by the committee can not be abbreviated without a failure to give an accurate idea of that feeling. It is therefore quoted at length :

"It follows as a necessary consequence, if the committee are correct in their conclusions, and our boundaries have been abridged as has been attempted to be shown, and that without any authority on the part of the government of the United States; that such action on the part of the United States government is not to any extent obligatory on the people of Wisconsin, but they may, whenever they think proper to form a State government for themselves, do so, and adopt as the boundaries of the State those prescribed for it by the ordinance, and it will be the duty of Congress to admit the State, with those boundaries, into the Union on an equal footing with the original States.

"The committee, however, can not shut their eyes to the consequences which would follow such a course. It can not for a moment be supposed that the state of Illinois will relinquish without a struggle 8,000 square miles of the most beautiful part of the territory embraced within its boundaries, as fixed by the act of Congress, notwithstanding it is probable that the people living on the tract in question would be nearly unanimous in favor of it, and perhaps those of the extreme south part of the state, jealous of the growing importance and political weight of the north, might consent to it; yet the vast majority of the state, embracing the whole central portion of it, it may well be supposed would adhere with inflexible tenacity to their boundaries as fixed by the act of Congress.

"And although Michigan, while struggling to enforce her claim to the territory on her south border claimed by Ohio, disavowed in the most emphatic terms any claim or pretensions to any territory west of a line drawn north and south through the straights of Michilimacinac, yet it is not in the nature of political communities to surrender any rights, especially rights of territory to which any circumstances have given them the color of claim, and it is not reasonable to expect that Michigan will voluntarily surrender to us any claims she may have to territory west of Lake Michigan, derived by virtue of the act admitting her into the Union.

"And least of all is it to be expected that the British government, ever ambitious of extending her empire, will consent to surrender to us any portion of our territory which the United States have undertaken to cede to them, although the United States did what they had no right to do, and the treaty so far as it affects our rights is void.

" What then would be our attitude if we insist upon our boundaries as defined by the ordinance, and form a state government embracing all the territory within them? We should at the very threshhold of our political existence find ourselves involved in a controversy of the most serious character with the States of Illinois and Michigan and the Kingdom of Great Britain — a controversy in relation to boundary, which of all others is the most difficult to be amicably adjusted. What would be the result of those controversies it is impossible to foresee and unnecessary to speculate upon, for whether they should terminate favorably or not to our claims, the consequences could not be otherwise than disastrous to our prosperity. Our first duty, of course, would be to appeal to the

United States government for its aid in protecting us in our rights and to sustain us in those controversies which were brought upon us by its unauthorized interference in parceling out our territory among the adjoining sovereignties. We cannot predict what would be the result of that appeal, but have we any very good reason to suppose that a government which ought to have been the guardian of our rights in our infancy, but which on the contrary has continued to disregard them and trample them under foot, will retrace her steps and restore to us that of which we have been so unjustly deprived, when she cannot now do it without danger of involving herself in a controversy with those states to whom she has given our Territory? Most certainly not.

"It appears to the committee then that the most politic course to be pursued under these circumstances is, instead of involving ourselves in a controversy in the first instance with Illinois, Michigan and Great Britain, to appeal to the nation's sense of justice, to address ourselves to the Congress of the United States, and while we retain our present form of government, obtain if possible from the United States government redress for the injuries they have from time to time inflicted upon us.

"For that purpose the committee recommend that an address be passed by the Council and House of Representatives to Congress, couched in respectful and conciliatory, but firm and decided language, setting forth in a plain, clear manner, the numerous unauthorized infringements of our boundaries, and calling upon the National Legislature to declare whether they are disposed to redress the wrongs they have done us and in what manner.

"It is within the power and constitutional authority of Congress to make an atonement for those wrongs in a manner which will at the same time promote our welfare and future prosperity and benefit the general government and the general interests of the Union to an extent nearly, if not quite corresponding, with any liabilities she may incur on our account.

"We are in our infancy, just on the point of emerging from a Territorial to a State government; our people are comparatively poor, although they cultivate a rich soil and are surrounded by rich mines, and will after a few years become as prosperous and wealthy as any other, and they cannot for several years spare from their present means a sum sufficient to effect those internal improvements which their necessities so imperiously require.

"A railroad across the Territory, connecting Lake Michigan with the Mississippi River, a distance of about one hundred and fifty miles, is a work the necessity of which is daily felt and the value and importance of which to the people of this Territory and of the whole Union would be incalculable. Within a very few years we may calculate that Michigan will have completed her railroad across the peninsula, and the only remaining link to be completed in the chain of steam communication from the Atlantic to the Mississippi, would be the short distance across this Territory, and the day would not be distant when such a road would be found extending itself to the Rocky Mountains and over them to the Pacific Ocean, opening a direct trade to that ocean and its islands and to the Celestial Empire.

"The improvement of the navigation of the Fox and Wisconsin Rivers, and as connected with that, also a connection by means of a short canal with Rock River, and the improvement of the latter stream by slack water navigation, are projects, the importance and feasibility of which, especially the former, have been so often, so forcibly, and so correctly set forth, that it is unnecessary to consume time by a repetition. The propriety of making an appropriation for the improvement of the Fox and Wisconsin, as a matter of national concernment, has been repeatedly pressed upon the attention of Congress by the Legislative Assembly, as well as by the officers of the United States; and it is hoped the day is not distant when, independent of all other considerations, it will receive that attention at the hands of Congress, which it so well merits.

"Another improvement which Congress owes it to the commerce of the world to effect, is the construction of a harbor at the mouth of every considerable river on the western shore of Lake Michigan. At the towns of Southport, Racine, Milwaukee, Sauk Harbor, Sheboygan and Manitowoc, harbors can be constructed at a moderate expense, which will at all times afford shelter to the exposed commerce of the lakes; and while their benefit in a national point of view would be incalculable, the benefit to the citizens of the Territory would be very great.

"The committee can not for a moment entertain the idea that an appeal of that kind would be made in vain, but they firmly believe, if made in such a spirit, the Congress, well knowing that if not met in a corresponding spirit, that the most deplorable state of things imaginable must arise, would hasten to make all the atonement in its power, and that they would guaranty the construction by the general government of the improvements before mentioned, or such other reasonable equivalents as might be mutually agreed upon by the general government and Wisconsin.

"Should we be disappointed in these reasonable expectations, we shall continue to occupy the same position that we now do, with this advantage, that we shall have shown to the world that we exhibited to the United States government a disposition in the first instance amicably to arrange the difficulties in which we are involved by their action, and we shall then have but to satisfy civilized communities that we are right in our claims and pretensions to secure their sympathy and kind feeling, if not kind action ; and we could then safely entrench ourselves behind the Ordinance of 1787, fortified by the doctrine, well understood in this country, that all political communities have the right to govern themselves in their own way, within their lawful boundaries, and take for ourselves and our State the boundaries fixed by that ordinance, form our state constitution, which should be republican, apply for admission into the Union with those boundaries, and if refused, so that we could not be a state in the Union, we would be a *State out of the Union*, and possess, exercise and enjoy all the rights, privileges and powers of the *sovereign, independent State of Wisconsin*, and if difficulties must ensue, we could appeal with confidence to the Great Umpire of nations to adjust them."

In regard to the remaining branch of the inquiry:

"What effect this infringement should have on the formation of state government in Wisconsin," the report states that "Her wisest policy is to continue under her present form of government, until a sufficient opportunity has been afforded Congress to do her justice."

The committee submitted with their report an address to Congress, which contained a summary of the facts and arguments which were presented more elaborately in their report, a printed copy of which was appended to and made a part of the address.

The address was adopted by a small majority in each House, but it does not appear to have elicited any action by Congress. It was the opinion of those members of the Legislature, who opposed the adoption of the address, and of some others, that its tone, as well as some part of the report, were too beligerent to be best calculated to obtain concessions from Congress.

The report of JOSHUA HATHAWAY, appointed by an act of the last session of the Legislature a special agent to receive and disburse the distributive share of Wisconsin in the net proceeds of the public lands, under an act of Congress passed September 4, 1841, was on the third day of the session presented by Mr. CROCKER, and referred to the committee on Territorial exependitures. It showed that the agent had received from the United States $1,082.45, which he had disbursed in conformity with the directions of the resolution by which he was appointed.

In harmony with the views expressed by the Governor in his message, a bill was very early introduced in the Council (No. 1) " To provide the means for paying the public debt of the Territory." The bill contemplated giving practical effect to the act of the precedingsession "to provide for levying and colleting a territorial revenue" by fixing a certain percentage upon the assessment roll which should be levied in each county. By an oversight the act had been passed without any enacting clause.

That act fixed the amount of territorial tax for the year 1843, at three eights of a mill, and provided that the tax to be thereafter annually levied should be such a per cent. as the Legislative Assembly shall have prescribed at the next preceding annual session, and the object of this bill was to fix the per cent. for the year 1844. It was referred to the committee on territorial expenditures which reported it back with a tabular statement of the assessments in each county, partly from returns and partly estimated, and showing the effect of different ratios of taxation.

The following is the table so far as it exhibited the gross assessment in each county of all descriptions of property:

NAME OF COUNTY.	GROSS ASSESSMENT.
Brown	$500,000 00
Calumet	70,000 00
Crawford	269,000 00
Dane	386,200 00
Dodge	70,100 00
Fond du Lac	100,000 00
Grant	606,500 00
Green	300,800 00
Iowa (including Richland)	996,800 00

Name of County.	Gross Assessment.
Jefferson	273,300 00
Manitowoc	127,500 00
Marquette	10,000 00
Milwaukee	1,373,200 00
Portage	69,800 00
Racine	1,000,000 00
Rock	516,000 00
Saint Croix	70,000 00
Sauk	70,000 00
Sheboygan	109,500 00
Walworth	789,300 00
Washington	359,000 00
Winnebago	10,200 00
Total	$8,077,200 00

A practical objection to the passage of any bill for the levy of a direct tax grew out of the difficulty amounting to a practical impossibility, of ascertaining the amount of the debt and which of the claims of the creditors were proper subjects for allowance and payment by the United States; and which must be paid by the Territory.

When the bill (No. 1) came up for consideration in the Council a majority refused to pass it or to levy any tax whatever.

Another bill, "to ascertain the indebtedness and the taxable property of the Territory," had been introduced in the House, which finally passed both houses and was approved by the Governor.

This law provided for the presentation to the Auditor of the Territory by creditors, of any claims against the Territory which they had, and that the Auditor should make a record of the same and put some mark or device on them which would prevent a second registration. And further, that claims so registered should have a preference in payment over any not registered.

Another section required clerks of counties and towns to transmit to the Auditor an abstract of the assessments in their several counties or towns, and the Auditor to report such abstract to the Legislative Assembly.

A joint resolution was also adopted, by which CHARLES M.

BAKER, a member of the Council from Walworth county, was appointed a special agent for the adjustment and settlement of all claims upon the United States for arrearages of the expenses of the Legislative Assembly, under the act of Congress of August 29, 1842, "to provide for the settlement of certain accounts for the support of government in the Territory of Wisconsin." The agent was also required to ascertain and report to the Legislative Assembly the total amount of all outstanding and unpaid claims against the United States.

At the same session the following appropriations were made, payable out of the Territorial treasury:

For fees of witnesses and others in suit against the Bank of Wisconsin	$124 91
Against DOTY and others	311 45
Commissioner of public buildings	261 67
For apprehending fugitive from justice	102 23
Miscellaneous	34 35
Total	$834 61

The report of the Treasurer was submitted December 16, 1843, which stated a balance due him on April 1, 1843, of		$1,081 31
Payments made by him April 1 to December 15	$1,404 25	
Receipts by him April 1 to December 15	890 97	
		513 28
Balance due Treasurer December 15, 1843		$1,594 59
A supplemental report made by the Treasurer January 5, 1844, stated his receipts since December 15, 1843, at	$879 84	
And his payments since December 15, 1843, at	135 52	
		744 32
And a balance due the Treasurer January 5, 1844, of		$850 27

A few days before the close of the session a paper was submitted by the Auditor and Treasurer, jointly, being an attempt to report the amount and nature of the indebtedness of the Territory. These officers state that —

" There are no records in our offices by which we can arrive at any accurate estimate of the debts outstanding against the Territory."

But they believe their report was correct.

The report of these officers shows a manifest purpose to swell the debt of the Territory to the highest possible figures. An accurate footing of the several items of indebtedness stated in the report, shows an aggregate amount of liabilities beyond assets of $57,252.17, besides the further sum of $27,148 on account of the Milwaukee and Rock River Canal Company.

The report was so full of errors and exaggerations that it failed to be of any use to the Legislative Assembly.

A bill passed both houses to abolish the offices of Auditor and Treasurer. It was vetoed by the Governor, and failed on reconsideration to receive a majority of two thirds in the House, where it originated.

ALEXANDER BOTKIN was appointed Auditor October 18, 1843, in the recess of the Council, and continued to act under that appointment until the end of the session (January 31). He had been nominated by the Governor at an early day of the session for the full term, and on the 12th of December the nomination was rejected, all of the thirteen members voting against it.

On the 25th of January, JAMES MORRISON was nominated for Treasurer of the Territory, and on the same day the nomination was rejected by a unanimous vote, all the members voting.

A resolution to discontinue the prosecution of the Territorial suits was introduced in the Council by Mr. LA'CHAPPELLE, which the Council refused to consider. A similar resolution was introduced in the House by Mr. TROWBRIDGE, and, after consideration, was laid on the table.

The case of the Territory against the old commissioners of public buildings (DOTY, O'NEILL, and BIRD), in which judgment had been rendered against the Territory at the April term of court, in 1843, in Walworth county, and in which a writ of error was brought in the Supreme Court, was decided at the July term of the Supreme Court, 1844, when the judgment was reversed and the case remanded for further proceedings. (The case is reported in 1 Pinney's R., p. 396.) Several errors were assigned, upon three of which the judgment was reversed. One was that a witness — MORRISON — was asked:

"How much money he had received from the commissioners, and the time of its reception."

Which question the witness declined answering for the reason that the answer might tend to establish a civil liability from him to the the Territory of Wisconsin, in a suit that might be brought against him for a breach of his contract; the court decided that the witness should not be required to answer the question. The supreme court held this decision was error, and decide

"That the reason given by the witness for his refusal to answer the question is not in law sufficient to excuse him, and that the court should have required the witness to answer."

The second is, that the court having sustained a motion for a new trial, on the ground that the verdict was contrary to law and evidence, granted the new trial only on condition of the payment of all costs by the plaintiff, and held that if a new trial was granted on these grounds, it should be granted unconditionally.

The third and radical error, because it totally invalidated the judgment was, the rendition of judgment against the Territory for costs.

"It is a general rule," the court say, "that a judgment can not be entered against a sovereignty." By the organic act "a government was established or created composed of executive, legislative and judicial branches. * * * It is apparent that by this law, a municipal corporation or government is created subject to the control of and immediately connected with the government of the United States. By virtue of its incorporation and as a necessary means of protecting its rights in all contracts, the Territory can maintain an action in the courts within its limits. By virtue of its incorporation all the powers and functions of sovereignty exist — subject to the supervision and control of the general government. * * * For all necessary purposes of government, Wisconsin is a sovereignty and should be entitled to the same immunities. It is a Territory of the United States, and therefore is considered a part of the United States, or immediately connected therewith. For these reasons we come to the conclusion that the Territory of Wisconsin cannot be sued in the courts of the Territory in the absence of express authority of law for the purpose, and that the judgment against the Territory for the costs expended by the defendants in this case must be reversed."

Soon after this decision, the Superintendent of Public Property applied to Judge IRVIN, at Chambers, for a change of venue, on the grounds (supported by the Superintendent's affidavit) of prejudice in the people of Walworth county, and that the defendants, or some of them, possessed an undue influence over the inhabitants of said county. The application was entertained and the cause removed to Milwaukee county for trial. At the November term of the court in that county, the case being called, the court (Judge MILLER) decided that he had no jurisdiction of the case and ordered it back to Walworth county. The court virtually held that there could be but one change of venue. The Judge says:

"This cause legally belonged to the jurisdiction of the District Court of Iowa county and was there pending until the judge of that court ordered it to be transmitted to Walworth county for trial. The court of Walworth county was by law authorized to try the cause, but not to order it to be transmitted to another county for trial. The statute does not authorize this court to try this cause."

The suit against J. D. DOTY, as treasurer of the board of building commissioners was continued by consent of parties, without costs, during the pendency of the principal suit against the commissioners.

The suit against JAMES MORRISON, as contractor for building the Capitol, was ready for trial on the part of the Territory at the spring term, 1844, of the Court of Iowa county. JAMES D. DOTY, an important witness in the case, had been duly subpœnaed, but failed to appear, and the trial was put over. At the fall term of the court Mr. DOTY, though he had again been subpœnaed, again failed to appear, and in addition to this untoward circumstance, the pleadings in the case could not be found by the counsel among the papers filed. New pleadings were prepared, and the case again continued. The first pleadings were soon afterward found.

About the first of July, the commissioners of Dane county applied to the Superintendent of Public Property for permission to finish the Capitol. He consented to the proposition on condition that he should have the control and direction of the work, and that the Territory should not be considered as placed under any obligations to pay the expenses incurred. The commissioners received proposals for doing the work, according to specifications furnished by the Superintendent, and the contract was let to AUGUSTUS A. BIRD, and was promptly, and, with but few exceptions, properly executed, at an expense to the county of about two thousand dollars.

On the 20th of January a joint convention of the two houses was held, when JOHN Y. SMITH was re-elected superintendent of territorial property, having received twenty votes out of the thirty-one cast by the members in attendance.

At the commencement of the second week of the session a petition of DANIEL BAXTER, relative to his account with the Territory was presented in the House and referred to a select committee consisting of Messrs. MASTERS, CROSSMAN and PALMER. After an investigation of about a week a majority of the committee (Messrs. MASTERS and CROSSMAN) submitted a report that there was a balance due from the Territory to BAXTER of $899.88, and that he was entitled to $108.67 for interest, being a total of $1,008.55, and the committee reported a joint resolution that he be paid the last named sum.

Mr. PALMER, two days later, submitted a minority report,

in which he arrived at the conclusion that BAXTER had been overpaid $847.76 for all work done on the Capitol. The resolution reported by the committee was adopted by the House and sent to the Council.

In the Council the resolution elicited much debate on several different days, when finally on the 23rd of January those who were in favor of its adoption having become satisfied that it could not pass, moved that the further consideration of it be postponed until the first Monday of January, 1845, which motion prevailed by a vote of 10 to 3.

Nearly six years had elapsed since the passage by Congress, June 12, 1838, of the act granting lands for the foundation of a University fund, and these lands had not yet been all selected and set apart.

At an early day of the session a resolution was adopted by the Council, on motion of Mr. CROCKER, that the committee on Territorial affairs, of which he was chairman, be instructed to ascertain and report what portion of these lands had been selected by authority of the Territory, and whether it was expedient to provide for selecting the remainder.

The committee through its chairman reported that the lands granted were two entire townships, amounting to 46,080 acres. That there had been selected and approved by the secretary of the treasury in the Green Bay district 10,248 82-100 acres, and in the Milwaukee district 10,248 53-100 and that in the Mineral Point district 10,250 75-100 had been selected, the approval of which had been suspended because some of them were supposed to have been reserved by the president for mining and smelting purposes.

That there remained to be selected 15,331 90-100 acres and if the suspended selections in the Mineral Point district were added, the whole amount to be selected and approved would be 25,582 65-100.

A bill was reported to provide for the selection of these lands, which when it came up for consideration in the Council was transformed into a joint resolution, appointing JOHN T. HAIGHT of Jefferson county, who was a surveyor, and eminently fitted by his judgment integrity and special knowledge of the subject, to make the selection. In this form it passed the Council and was sent to the House of Representatives.

In the House the resolution was amended by providing that three commissioners should be appointed to select all the lands which should be selected in equal quantities as near as might be within the three land districts, and that THEODORE CONKEY should be the commissioner in the Green Bay district, JOHN T. HAIGHT in the Milwaukee district and GEORGE W. LAKIN in the Mineral Point district, and so amended, the resolution was adopted.

The Council refused to concur in the amendment of the House; the House insisted upon its amendments and two committees of conference were appointed, neither of which could agree and the result was the defeat of the resolution.

Much interest had been spasmodically exhibited in the construction of a railroad between Lake Michigan and the Mississippi River, but subsequent events demonstrated that it was even yet too early for practical effect to be given to that interest.

In the light of subsequent experience, the ideas that were presented in responsible and authentic form at that early period of railroad history, in reference to routes, feasibility, cost, business and profits possess such value as to demand their re-production.

A select committee of the House, consisting of Messrs. PRICE, MESSERSMITH and THOMPSON was appointed to inquire into the expediency of constructing a railroad from Potosi on the Mississippi River to Lake Michigan.

This committee had not the advantage of any experimental survey to aid them in the suggestion of any feasible route, and yet one of the routes pointed out in the report is identical with one upon which a railroad has since been constructed, with the exception of a short distance between Potosi and Lancaster.

This route was described as commencing at Potosi on the Mississippi River, and following the course of a small rill, about three miles to its source near the summit of a ridge which divides the waters of the Platte River from those of the Mississippi, and which further north divides those of the Platte and Grant Rivers.

"After this ascent is overcome" the route, the report continues, "would follow in a northerly direction, the ridge before alluded to, dividing the waters of the Platte and Grant Rivers, to its intersection at the Fennimore Grove, in town six, range two west, with the main dividing ridge, which divides the waters which flow into the Wisconsin from those which flow into the Platte, Peckatonica and Sugar Rivers, and thence after intersecting the main ridge it would follow it in an easterly direction a distance of about fifty miles to the head waters of Sugar River, in range seven east."

"From the head waters of Sugar River the line of the railroad could continue in an easterly direction, crossing the Catfish or Four Lake River, or if it was highly desirable to continue a more level route, keeping north of the Fourth Lake; and after getting upon the eastern side of the Catfish only two impediments exist to the continuation of the route to Lake Michigan, without expensive grading, to wit: The Fox and Rock Rivers; and the features of the country are such that each of these streams can be approached from either direction, through the vallies of their respective tributaries without such ascent or descent as will be to any extent objectionable," * * * "And the committee are of the opinion that the entire route is not only practicable but that no route can be found in the United States of the same extent, giving the same promise of profit, upon which a road can be built cheaper than upon this route."

The estimate of the first cost of the road and equipments, made by the commmittee, was $4,000,000.

The following estimate of probable receipts from the species of freight specified was made by the committee, and is presented as showing the over-estimates upon some items and the under-estimates on others:

25,000,000 lbs. lead at 37½ cts. per 100 lbs.	$93,750
1,000,000 lbs. copper at 37½ cts. per 100 lbs.	3,750
10,000 tons merchandize and return freights at $10	100,000
100,000 bushels grain at 12½ cents per bushel	12,500
4,000,000 feet pine lumber at $2.50 per M	10,000
Total	$220,000

No estimate was made for freight on live stock, the raising of which for market was not then supposed to be among the possibilities, nor of zinc ores, which although then abundant had no practical value.

It was estimated that the receipts from unenumerated freights and from passengers would pay operating expenses, and that $220,000 would be a dividend fund.

At the preceding session of the Legislative Assembly (April, 1843) a joint committee was appointed to investigate the Wisconsin Marine and Fire Insurance Company. At an early day of the session of 1843-4 Dr. DARLING, a member of the committee, submitted a report, which exhibited in detail the liabilities and resources of the company, the names of its stockholders and amount of stock paid in and the nature and methods of the business of the company.

One of these methods of business was the issue of certificates of deposit, in sums of one, three and five dollars each, in the form and similitude of bank bills, and apparently designed to circulate as currency. The amount of these certificates outstanding at the time of the investigation was over $52,000.

The committee state that the financial concerns of the company at the time of the examination were in a favorable condition, but that the issue of these certificates, intended to circulate and circulating as money was the exercise of a banking privilege and was unequivocally prohibited by the charter of the company, which contained a proviso that "nothing herein contained shall give the said company banking privileges," and concluded with a recommendation of a repeal of the charter.

Within a few days after this report was submitted, the secretary of the company — ALEXANDER MITCHELL — presented a communication to the Legislative Assembly dated December 21, protesting against the repeal of the charter, and submitting a bill for its amendment, the principal features of which were that a list of the stockholders should be filed with the Secretary of the Territory, and all changes be from time to time reported, and that the stockholders should be individually liable for all the debts and liabilities of the company; that the debts and liabilities of the company should never exceed the amount of capital actually paid in, and that its failure for ten days to redeem in coin any of its evidences of debt, should be deemed and taken as a forfeiture of its charter. The secretary requested that this draft of a bill might be considered and adopted. It was referred to the committee on corporations with instructions to report on the sixth day of January.

The committee were unable to agree upon any report and made none until the 19th of January when a majority and a minority report were submitted.

In the meantime, on the 8th of January, the secretary addressed another communication to the Legislative Assembly which, among other things, stated that the company

"Positively denies that it has in any way, as complained of, transcended its powers. It "questions both the fact and the law as stated by your committee. It can not conceive "that the Legislature can determine its rights while acting in the threefold capacity of a "party interested, a jury and a court."   *   *   *   *   *   *   *

"The company, as it believes, relies upon its plainest rights, in insisting that the *question* of the violation or forfeiture of a charter can only be determined by a competent "legal tribunal.   *   *   *   To the decree of the proper tribunal the company will "cheerfully submit."

The majority of the committee reported —

"That a court of law is the proper place to determine the question whether or not the company have violated their charter." * * * * * * * *

"They are not satisfied that it would, at this time, be expedient to commence any new Territorial suits."

This report was signed by Messrs. ELMORE, HOPKINS, and PARSONS.

The report of the minority was signed by Messrs. ELLIS and MEEKER, and was largely devoted to an argument to show a violation of its charter by the company, and that the passage of the bill proposed by the company would estop the Legislature in the future from setting up the forfeiture of the charter, and claimed for the Legislature the right of absolute repeal.

The remedy proposed by the committee was the commencement of suit to vacate the charter, and for that purpose reported a joint resolution.

When this resolution came up for consideration, an amendment was offered, that Congress be requested to pass a law approving and confirming the act of incorporation, or restricting it to such business operations as were intended to be conferred by the Legislative Assembly.

Another amendment was offered, that Congress be requested to take similar action with regard to the Fox River Hydraulic Company.

Mr. ELMORE moved that the resolution and proposed amendments do lie on the table until the fourth day of July next, which was decided in the affirmative by a vote of 13 to 11, and thus ended for that session the excitement which was very considerable in relation to the Wisconsin Marine and Fire Insurance Company.

The act authorizing defendants who shall be defeated in actions to recover lands of which they have been in possession, to recover pay for valuable improvements made by them on such lands, generally known as the betterment law was first passed at this session and with some modifications in its details has ever since remained a part of the law of the State.

An act was passed altering and fixing the times of holding the district courts in the second and third judicial districts.

Trespass upon the university and school lands, and upon the even sections of the canal grant, was by a law passed at this session declared to be a misdemeanor and punishable by imprisonment.

Some very material changes were made in the law relating to the redemption of land sold for taxes.

It was provided that the clerk of the board of supervisors should be elected annually for the term of one year. Previously he had been appointed by the board. He was also required to give an official bond.

The time for the redemption of lands sold for taxes was extended from two to three years, and until the recording of a tax deed, and the rate of interest was reduced from thirty per cent. to twenty-five. The provision of law limiting the time within which actions could be commenced for the recovery of lands forfeited for taxes to three years from the recording of the deeds of sale, was first passed at this session.

A bill passed the House of Representatives to divorce WEBSTER PEASE from his wife LUCINDA PEASE, which in the Council, on motion of Mr. WHITON, was laid on the table "till WEBSTER PEASE, the petitioner, furnished satisfactory proof to the Council that he has notified LUCINDA PEASE of the pendency of this bill." No other divorce bill was introduced.

The progress of the settlement of the country created a desire for the organization of several new counties and in some instances opposition was developed. A bill was introduced to organize Portage county in relation to which there were petitions and remonstrances, and the bill was at first indefinitely postponed, and afterwards passed in a novel mode.

A bill had been introduced to incorporate the Southport brass band, which was considered in committee of the whole, and was reported back with an amendment striking out all after the enacting clause. The bill was then laid on the table without any action upon the report of the committee of the whole. Subsequently, on motion of Mr. MARTIN, it was taken up and amended by inserting the entire bill to organize Portage county and in that form was passed, the title amended so as to read "a bill to organize Portage county for judicial purposes," and sent to the House. The next day it passed the House with some amendments which were immediately concurred in by the Council, and the bill to incorporate the Southport brass band became a law to organize Portage county.

At the same session the county of Fond du Lac was organized and the counties of Sheboygan, Calumet and Marquette attached to it for judicial purposes.

Dodge county was also organized and provision made for the location of the county seat by a board of five commissioners, one in each of the four election precincts then existing, and one from the county at large.

Sauk county was also organized and three commissioners appointed by the act to locate and establish the seat of justice. They were NOAH PHELPS of Green county, CHARLES HART of Milwaukee county and JOHN MORRISON of Jefferson county.

The first election of county officers was held on the second Monday of March. JOHN E. ABBOTT was elected Sheriff, PRESCOTT BRIGHAM Judge of Probate and E. M. HART Register of Deeds.

The Registers of Deeds of several counties which had been organized from other counties, were required by law to procure from the records of the several counties of which they had previously formed a part, copies of the records of deeds, mortgages and other instruments recorded in such counties.

The counties in which the Registers of Deeds were at this session required to procure such copies were Grant, Green, Portage and Winnebago.

The legislative authority was exercised in setting off and organizing the towns of Howard, in Brown county; Brighton, in Racine county; Bloomfield, Hudson, Linn and Geneva, in Walworth county; Stockbridge, in Calumet county and Oconomowoc; and in declaring that *Mequanego* should be known and distinguished as *Mukwonago*, and that Nemahbin should be known and called by the name of Delafield.

Special acts to incorporate the villages of Mineral Point and Geneva were passed.

The erection, construction or maintenance of dams was authorized by law on the Peshtigo River, in town 30, range

23, on Rock River, in section 3 in the town of Watertown; on the Milwaukee River, in section 4, in the town of Milwaukee; on the Oconto river, in town 28, range 21 east, and on Sugar River, in the town of Albany, in Green county.

The construction of a float bridge, to rest on water-tight scows or boxes, with a convenient draw, across the Milwaukee River, "from the foot of Water street in the east ward of the town of Milwaukee, to the foot of Ferry street in said town," which when completed should forever remain FREE, was authorized by a special law.

SIDNEY S. SAGE and his associates of the village of Racine were authorized to erect and maintain a free bridge across Root River, one end of which should be in Fourth street in said village.

Territorial roads were authorized to be laid out from house of SEYMOUR WILCOX near Waupun, north of Fox Lake, to section twenty-seven, town thirteen, range eleven east.

From Watertown *via* Waterloo to intersect the Madison road.

From Helena in Iowa county to Cross Plains in Dane county.

From Lake Mills in Jefferson county to "the settlement now known as the Beaver Dam" in Dodge county.

From Boatyard Hollow in Grant county to White Oak Springs in Iowa county.

Acadamies were incorporated in the towns of Burlington, in Racine county and in Madison in Dane connty.

The municipal authorities of the town of Milwaukee and of the villages of Racine and Southport were each authorized by special laws to borrow money to aid in constructing harbors at each of these places and to levy special taxes to repay such loans. The sums thus authorized to be obtained were fifteen thousand dollars for Milwaukee, five thousand dollars for Racine and ten thousand dollars for Southport.

This session was not as prolific in gubernatorial vetoes, as the one which preceded it.

Four of the acts, which had passed both houses of the Legislative Assembly, were returned by the Governor without his approval.

Two of these were passed by a majority of two thirds of each house, notwithstanding the objections of the Governor, the other two passed the Council by the necessary two thirds, but were defeated in the House, the one lacking one and the other two votes of two thirds.

One of these four acts was entitled " an act extending the time for the redemption of certain lands in the Territory on the Canal Grant." It passed the Council by a vote of 13 to 0 and the House by 23 to 2.

Another was entitled " An act to provide for the payment of the expenses of the Legislative Assembly therein named." It originated in the House, where on re-consideration it passed by a vote of 17 to 4, and in the Council by 7 to 0.

Of the two defeated acts, one was entitled "An act to provide for the election of a printer to the Legislative Assembly," which passed the Council by a vote of 8 to 3, the vote in the House being 17 to 9 (not two thirds).

The other was entitled "An act to amend an act to provide for the election of Sheriffs, Judges of Probate, Justices of the Peace, and for other purposes." The vote in the Council upon reconsideration of this act was 11 to 0, and in the House was 16 to 10, being two less than the requisite two thirds.

It must not be supposed that the dignified attention of the members to their ordinary duties, was not occasionally relieved by some displays of wit and exhibitions of mirth. As an illustration the following incident is mentioned: A member from one of the western counties had introduced into the House of Representatives a memorial to the Secretary of the Treasury for the purpose of correcting some abuses which were complained of, in the manner in which the United States Marshal disbursed — or failed to disburse — the public moneys provided for paying expenses of the courts. The language of the memorial was mere fustian and rodomontade; and contained, among other things, the expression, that during a certain period of time the marshal had not paid out "one solitary cent." It was allowed to pass the House as an act of courtesy to the member who introduced it. When it came before the Council, Col. CROCKER moved to amend by inserting between the words "solitary" and "cent," the word "red," so as to read "one solitary red cent." The amendment was adopted, and the memorial returned to the House with the amendment. The House refused to concur, and the Council refused to recede, and the bombastic memorial was lost.

TERRITORY OF WISCONSIN IN 1844. 453

On the 17th of January the Adjutant General sent to the Council, in conformity with a resolution which it had adopted, a report stating that the moneys received by him during the years 1841, 1842 and 1843 were $316.82; expenditures $241.50, and balance on hand $75.32.

Memorials to Congress were adopted, asking for appropriations for the completion of the improvement of the Fox and Wisconsin Rivers;

For a re-appropriation of certain moneys to complete a light house on Grassy Island, near the mouth of Fox River;

For a donation of land to improve the Grant Slough;

For the laying out of a road from Prairie du Chien to La'Pointe on Lake Superior, and

For the indemnification of ELBERT DICKINSON for damages sustained by him, by reason of the forcible possession and occupation by Winnebago Indians of his farm and buildings near the site of the present village of Columbus, and the consumption of his provisions.

A joint committee who were instructed to report

"How long the present session of the Assembly can continue, consistent with keeping the expenses within the appropriation of $17,275, and the cause of the decrease of the appropriation from former years",

reported that with rigid economy the appropriation would defray the expenses of the session of sixty days. That the reason of the deficiency in the appropriation is an error of the Governor in making out his estimates of the expenses of this session.

On the 8th of January, a joint resolution was passed that the session should terminate on the 29th January. On Saturday, the 27th January, a resolution passed the House rescinding that resolution and declaring that the session should terminate on the 1st day of February. On the same day the resolution was amended in the Council by substituting the 31st of January, and late in the evening of that day the House concurred in the amendment of the Council, and on the 31st of January, after a session of fifty-nine days, both houses were adjourned *sine die*, having previously passed an act that hereafter the annual session of the Legislative Assembly should commence on the first Monday of January, in each year.

About the first of April, Mr. ROBERT D. LESTER, sheriff of Crawford county, while descending the Mississippi alone in a canoe, was murdered by an Indian lying in ambush about one hundred miles above Prairie du Chien.

The year 1844, although in "the States" it witnessed a most exciting political contest, resulting in the election of JAMES K. POLK over HENRY CLAY, was comparatively devoid of political interest in Wisconsin. The interest was limited to the election of members of the House of Representatives, and county officers, there being no election for Delegate to Congress.

A convention of the Democratic Whig members of the Legislature and other Whigs of the Territory was held on the 30th of January, when JOHN M. CAPRON, JOHN H. ROUNTREE, GEORGE MESSERSMITH, GEORGE H. SLAUGHTER, M. M. JACKSON, ALONZO PLATT, GLENDOWER M. PRICE, A. W. STOWE, JARED THOMPSON and JAMES TRIPP were appointed delegates to attend the National Convention of the Whigs to be held at Baltimore, in May, for the purpose of nominating a Whig candidate for the presidency.

A committee of six was appointed to report a preamble and resolutions expressive of the sense of the convention, and report the same at the evening session. At the evening session the committee, through its chairman, M. M. JACKSON, reported a series of resolutions, of which he was the putative author, and which were unanimously adopted.

RUFUS PARKS was removed from the office of Receiver of Public Moneys at Milwaukee, and J. A. HELFENSTEIN appointed in his place.

NATHANIEL P. TALLMADGE was appointed Governor of the Territory, in place of JAMES D. DOTY. His appointment was announced as early as July, although his commission was not issued until September, when Governor DOTY's term expired.

CHAPTER XXVI.

TERRITORY OF WISCONSIN — 1845.

The ever ready and almost ever effective argument of the opponents of a change from a Territorial to State government, was the large appropriations annually made by Congress for the maintenance of civil government, and the consequent freedom of the people from taxation for this object.

This argument was deprived of much of its force and effect by the smallness and insufficiency of the appropriation made by the act of March 3, 1845.

The smallest appropriation ever before made for compensation and mileage of the members of the Legislative Assembly, pay of officers, printing, stationery, fuel, postage and other incidental and miscellaneous objects, for any session had been $17,275, while in other years they had ranged from $25,000 to more than $36,000. The appropriation in 1845 for the fiscal year ending June 30, 1846, was only $13,700.

The only appropriation for harbors was $15,000, " for the purpose of aiding in the completion of the harbor already commenced at the town of Southport."

The harbor at the more important port of Milwaukee, which had attained the dignity of being placed among the works of *national* importance, shared the fate of all other works in the same category, which was to fail of being fostered or aided by any appropriations whatever. Nor did the harbor at Racine or any other lake port receive aid at this session of Congress.

The sum of ten thousand dollars was appropriated for the construction and improvement of roads in the Territory, which was distributed as follows :

"From Sheboygan by way of Taychedah and Fond du Lac to the Fox River in the vicinity of Green Lake, $3,000."

"For repairing the United States military road between Fort Howard and Fond du Lac, $2,000."

"From Southport, by way of Geneva to Beloit, $5,000."

Pursuant to the law passed at the last session, changing the time of its annual meeting to the first Monday of January, the fourth Legislative Assembly commenced its third session on the 6th day of January, 1845.

Six of thirteen members of the Council had resigned and new members had been elected to fill the vacancies, while a new election had been had for the entire body of the House of Representatives.

In the Council, RANDALL WILCOX was elected, *vice* MORGAN L. MARTIN, resigned. In Milwaukee county JACOB H. KIMBALL, JAMES KNEELAND and ADAM E. RAY were elected, in place of HANS CROCKER, DAVID NEWLAND and LEMUEL WHITE, resigned. The place of THEOPHALUS LA'CHAPPELLE, of Crawford county, resigned, was filled by WIRAM KNOWLTON, and JOHN CATLIN, of Dane county, was chosen to fill the vacancy created by the resignation of LUCIUS I. BARBER, of Jefferson county, in the same district.

The following members constituted the House of Representatives:

Brown county and the counties attached: ABRAHAM BRAWLEY, MASON C. DARLING and WILLIAM FOWLER.

Crawford and St. Croix: JAMES FISHER.

Dane, Dodge, Green, Jefferson and Sauk: CHARLES S. BRISTOL, NOAH PHELPS and GEORGE H. SLAUGHTER.

Grant: THOMAS P. BURNETT, THOMAS CRUSON and FRANKLIN Z. HICKS.

Iowa: JAMES COLLINS, ROBERT C. HOARD and SOLOMON OLIVER.

Milwaukee and Washington: CHARLES E. BROWN, PITTS ELLIS, BYRON KILBOURN, BENJAMIN H. MOOERS, WILLIAM SHEW and GEORGE H. WALKER.

Racine: ROBERT MCCLELLAN, ALBERT G. NORTHWAY and ORSON SHELDON.

Rock and Walworth: STEPHEN FIELD, JESSE C. MILLS, JESSE MOORE and SALMON THOMAS.

Eight of the twenty-six members had formerly been members of the Territorial Legislature. Messrs. BURNETT and WALKER were elected to the abortive session held at Green Bay in 1836. The former was an unsuccessful applicant for a seat in the Council at Belmont in 1836, and Mr. WALKER was a member at the sessions of 1842-3 and 1843-4. Mr. COLLINS was a member of the House in June, 1837, and of the Council continuously from 1838 to 1842. Messrs. CRUSON and SHEW were both elected to the House in 1838 and served until 1840. Messrs. MILLS and DARLING were members at the sessions of 1840-1 and 1841-2, and Messrs. DARLING and HICKS at those of 1842-3 and 1843-4. The other eighteen members took their seats in the Legislative Assembly for the first time.

The Council was organized temporarily on the first day of the session, and on the second day permanently, by the election of MOSES M. STRONG President, BEN. C. EASTMAN Secretary, and CHARLES H. LARKIN Sergeant-at-Arms.

In the House, GEORGE H. WALKER was appointed Speaker *pro tem.* on the first day and the next day was elected for the session. On the third day LA'FAYETTE KELLOGG was elected Chief Clerk and CHAUNCEY DAVIS, Sergeant-at-Arms.

The counties of Rock and Walworth had continued to form one election district since 1838, and in the fourth Legislative Assembly were entitled to two members of the Council and four members of the House, which by common consent of the people of the two counties were divided equally between them. But in 1845 the proportionate increase of population had been so much greater in Walworth than in Rock county, that it was provided by law that Walworth county should constitute one election district, with one member of the Council and three members of the House, and Rock another district with one member of the Council and only one member of the House. Thirty-five years produced a wonderful change. By the census of 1880 the population of Rock county was nearly fifty per cent. greater than that of Walworth.

No conflicts between the Legislative Assembly and the newly appointed Governor disturbed the harmony of this session.

Governor TALLMADGE with prompt courtesy responded to the formal communication informing him of the organization of the two houses, and on the second day of the session met them in joint convention and delivered in person the customary message.

It exhibited a marked difference with similar papers of his immediate predecessor; chiefly in the absence of all claim of executive prerogative, and of any disposition to assume anything like dictation, and it was with the utmost modesty and deference to the recognized superior knowledge of the representatives that even a positive recommendation found a place in the message.

It opened with the statement that the enactment of the laws devolved upon the Legislative Assembly — not Congress; and upon the Governor that of seeing them faithfully executed. And he added that so far as his

"Co-operation is required in the enactment of laws, you will find in me a disposition to harmonize with your legislative action and to appreciate your patriotic motives."

The Governor did not —

"Deem it out of place to allude to an act passed by the last Legislature in relation to the qualification of voters for State government, and the election of delegates to form a State constitution." He "congratulated" the Legislative Assembly "on the putting to rest in this manner of that important question," and expressed the opinion that "the adoption, by a decided majority of both branches of the Legislature, of the enlightened and constitutional provisions of that act, will contribute to the harmony of our growing population, and facilitate the organization of a sound and wholesome State government whenever that important step shall be deemed necessary."

He said:

"I have no doubt of the right of the Legislature to pass such a law, as well under the ordinance of 1787, as on general principles, when the people, in their primary capacity, undertake the organization of a new government;" and added: "I can not now consent to recommend any material modification or change of the principles secured by that law, without doing violence to my own, and to my long-cherished sentiments of public policy and constitutional right."

The message next speaks of —

"The subject of our naturalization laws," and says: "The movement now in progress in various parts of the Union, to extend the period of naturalization to twenty-one years, is calculated, if successful, materially to abridge the rights which this portion of our population (foreigners) have expected to enjoy."

"A more efficient organization of the militia" is suggested, with the statement that —

"We have no sufficient returns of the numerical force of the militia to enable us to receive from the general Government the quota of arms to which we should otherwise be entitled;" and the remedy is left to the better judgment of the Legislature.

A liberal portion of the message is devoted to remarks upon the subject of internal improvements — particularly the improvement of the navigation of the Fox and Wisconsin rivers — a railroad from Lake Michigan to the Mississippi River, roads generally, and plank roads particularly, and harbors on the lake coast. The importance of all these is forcibly presented, but no practicable mode suggested for their attainment.

The subject of the indebtedness of the Territory, as one of vital importance to its pecuniary interests, as well as to its public character, is given prominence in the message. The adoption of measures to ascertain its nature and extent are recommended and, says the message

"When the amount is thus ascertained, let Congress be asked to do what is just in relation to it, and in any event let means be provided for the payment of interest and the speedy liquidation of the principal. Let it not be said that this young and thriving Territory sanctions, even in name, the doctrine of repudiation."

The subject of education — the education of the great mass of the people — was mentioned, with the remark that

"Whether any and what further measures are necessary to this object, is respectfully submitted to your consideration."

The subject of agriculture was mentioned as well worthy of the profoundest attention of the Legislature. Agricultural schools, pattern farms and agricultural societies were favorably mentioned, and the whole subject submitted to the wisdom of the representatives of the people.

The message concludes with the pious statement that

"Our bosoms should swell with emotions of gratitude to the all-wise Dispenser of human events, that He has here graciously cast our lot; and our action, public and private, should be such as to ensure a continuance of His blessing."

Seven hundred and fifty copies of the message were ordered to be printed in the German language, a precedent set for the first time, which has since been frequently followed.

The emphatic vote of the inhabitants of the Territory at the recent election in September in opposition to the formation of a State government, which question had then for the first time been submitted to them with Legislative sanction, appeared to have set at rest, at least for this session, the further agitation of that question. The Governor, in his message referring to the recommendation of his predecessors that the necessary steps be taken for the formation of a State government, said —

"Desirous of conforming my action to an ascertained public sentiment, it would not become me at this time to renew that recommendation."

A bill, however, passed the Council by a vote of 9 to 3, which provided that at every annual election thereafter, a vote should be taken for or against State government, and the result returned to the Legislative Assembly. This bill was defeated in the House by a vote of 12 to 13.

The only perfected action of the Legislative Assembly upon the subject was the passage of a joint resolution requesting the delegate in Congress —

"To urge upon that body the passage of a law making an appropriation to defray the expenses of taking a census of the inhabitants of the Territory preparatory to the formation of a State government, and also to make an appropriation to provide for the expenses of holding a convention to form a constitution and State Government."

This resolution was not passed until the 24th of February, and Congress adjourned on the 3d of March, without passing any law upon the subject.

Opposition to the act of the last session in relation to the qualifications of voters for State government and for the election of delegates to form a State constitution, was very early developed in the House of Representatives. It was able, determined, well directed and persistent, but futile. It was lead by Mr. BURNETT of Grant county, assisted by Messrs. COLLINS of Iowa, SLAUGHTER of Dane, and seven others.

Immediately upon the organization of the two houses Mr. BURNETT gave notice of the introduction of a bill to repeal the act, and subsequently, for that purpose, introduced the first bill of the session.

The bill came up for consideration on the 27th of January, when Mr. DARLING proposed an amendment by striking out all after the enacting clause, and inserting the following:

"That no person shall hereafter vote upon the subject of State government, or for delegates to form a State Constitution, who shall not have resided three months within the Territory, and who shall not be a citizen of the United States, or shall have declared his intention to become such, as the law requires."

The bill was fully and ably discussed from day to day, until the 3d of February, when the amendment offered by Dr. DARLING was adopted, with a modification extending the period of residence from three to six months, and thus amended, it passed the House by a vote of 16 to 6, and was concurred in by the Council without a division.

The opponents of the measure were not satisfied and renewed the contest, with equal zeal, but no greater success. On the 15th of February a resolution was introduced, which, as modified, instructed the committee on Territorial affairs to report a memorial to Congress for the passage of a law authorizing the people of this Territory to form a constitution and State government *and to define the qualification of voters.*

Dr. DARLING moved to strike out the words "and to define the qualification of voters", which, after a long debate, was adopted and the resolution passed, in pursuance of which the joint resolution of instructions to the Delegate already mentioned was reported and passed both houses — which was all the action had at this session on the subject of State government.

In the last chapter it was stated that the Governor's nomination of ALEXANDER BOTKIN as Auditor, and JAMES MORRISON as Treasurer, had been rejected by the unanimous vote of the Council. No other nominations were sent to the Council at that session, so that at the next session no official information existed showing who were the incumbents of these offices.

On the 10th of January, resolutions were adopted by the Council, on motion of Mr. KNEELAND, requesting the Governor to inform the Council who was the Treasurer and who the Auditor, when they were appointed and when their terms of office would expire.

The next day the Governor answered the request by stating that it appeared from the records of the executive department

"That JAMES MORRISON was Treasurer, and ALEXANDER BOTKIN, Auditor; that they were appointed on the 3rd of February, 1844, and that their term of office would expire at the end of the present session."

On the 4th of February, 1845, Governor TALLMADGE sent to the Council the following nominations:

"JONATHAN LARKIN to be Territorial Treasurer in place of JAMES MORRISON, appointed after the adjournment of the last Legislative Council.

"GEORGE P. DELAPLAINE to be Auditor of public accounts, in place of ALEXANDER BOTKIN, appointed after the adjournment of the last Legislative Council."

These nominations were on the same day confirmed by the Council without reference or a division.

On the 20th of January, the Auditor submitted a report of the claims against the Territory, registered by him as per act of the Legislative Assembly, approved January 31, 1844, which amounted to $6,270.64.

The annual report of the Treasurer, submitted on the 10th of January, showed that the receipts during the year had been $1,285.23; disbursements, $3,259.18, and that there were yet returns to be made of the five per centum for Territorial purposes, from the counties of Racine, Jefferson, Fond du Lac, Crawford, and St. Croix for the year 1843, and from the counties of Dodge, Iowa, Jefferson, Milwaukee, Portage, Racine, Rock, Sheboygan and St. Croix for the year 1844.

The Secretary of the Territory submitted reports of his receipts and disbursements, and so satisfactory was the manner in which his official duties were discharged, that on the last day of the session a resolution was unanimously adopted by the House, tendering the thanks of the House

"For his gentlemanly deportment in his intercourse with the members thereof, and his punctuality and efficiency as a public officer, and in his impartiality and promptness in the disbursement of the public funds."

The protracted absence of Judge IRVIN — especially during the autumn, winter and early spring — was a subject of much complaint; so much that a joint resolution was adopted

"That the Hon. DAVID IRVIN, Judge of the Second Judicial District, be and he is hereby requested either to remain in the Territory in the performance of his duties, so that the public can have the benefit of his services, or that he resign his office, in order that another person may be appointed in his place, who will reside among the people."

An act was passed to abolish the office of Supreme Court Commissioner, and transfer his duties to Judges of Probate.

The Territorial suits experienced another year's delay, without any definite result having been arrived at.

In pursuance of the decision of Judge MILLER refusing to take jurisdiction of the suits against DOTY, O'NEILL and BIRD, the venue of which had been changed from Walworth county to Milwaukee, the records and papers were again remitted to Walworth county, and at the spring term (1845) of the court in that county, Judge IRVIN decided that the venue having been changed from that county, and the case not having been returned by any process known to the law, he could not take jurisdiction.

By direction of the Superintendent of Territorial Property, a writ of mandamus was applied for to the Supreme Court at the July term, 1845, against the District Court of Milwaukee county, requiring said court to try the cause. The Supreme Court, at the same term, directed that a peremptory writ of mandamus do issue, to the District Court of Milwaukee county, commanding that court to —

"Proceed to trial of said cause, in the same manner, and to give judgment and award execution as though the said cause had not been removed."

This decision will be found reported in 1 Pinney R., 569.

At the next term of the court in Milwaukee county, in November, the cause on the part of the Territory was ready for trial, but on the affidavit of AUGUSTUS A. BIRD, one of the defendants, alleging prejudice in the judge, the venue was again changed, and this time to Grant county, in the same district in which it was commenced. The practical effect was to postpone the trial until March, 1846, which was the earliest period at which any term of court was to be held in Grant county.

The suit against JAMES MORRISON and his sureties, pending in Iowa county, was continued on the affidavit of the defendant of the absence of a material witness.

The suit against DOTY and his sureties, still pending in Walworth county, was continued by consent, to await the disposition of the suit against the commissioners.

JOHN Y. SMITH was re-elected Superintendent of Territorial Property by joint ballot of the two houses on the 19th of February, having received 19 votes, to 12 for AUGUSTUS A. BIRD and 6 scattering.

The BAXTER claim, arising out of work done upon the Capitol, was again before the Council, and the committee on Territorial affairs reported in favor of an allowance of $1,008, but the report failed to receive the favorable action of the Council, and went over the session without action.

In a suit which had been commenced by WILLIAM DOUGHTY against the Territory, upon a bond issued to aid in the construction of the Milwaukee and Rock River Canal, it was decided by Judge IRVIN, of the Second District, that the Territory could not be sued.

The decision appears to have been acquiesced in, and the case carried no further.

The friends of the policy of providing a permanent though moderate Territorial revenue for the payment of the debt of the Territory, were more successful at this session than at the preceding one.

The amount of indebtedness registered by the auditor under the act of the last session was only a little over $6,000, yet it was well known that a much larger sum was outstanding which had not been registered.

During the third week of the session a bill was introduced in the Council by Mr. KNEELAND "To provide means to pay the public debt of the Territory." It was referred to the committee on Territorial expenditures which reported it back without amendment. It was subsequently referred to a select committee of one from each election district, consisting of Messrs. ROUNTREE, KNOWLTON, CATLIN, BAKER, KNEELAND, MARSHALL M. STRONG and MOSES M. STRONG, which reported an amendment. Afterwards it was referred to the committee on the judiciary under instructions, in conformity with which a substitute was reported by that committee, which subsequently passed both houses without material alteration, and was substantially the law which was enacted.

The act prescribed the mode of assessment in the several counties. It then provided for the annual levy in each of the counties of a Territorial tax of one and a half mills on the dollar on the assessed value of the property within such county, which was to be collected by the county treasurers and by them paid over to the Territorial Treasurer.

Evidences of Territorial indebtedness issued by authority of law were receivable in payment of the Territorial tax, and it was made the duty of the Auditor to issue warrants on the Territorial Treasurer for such indebtedness, in such sums as the creditor might elect, corresponding in the aggregate with the amount of such indebtedness.

The Territorial indebtedness was further increased by an appropriation of two thousand, six hundred and sixteen dollars to the county of Dane, the amount expended by said county in the completion of the Capitol, payable out of any money in the Territorial treasury, not otherwise appropriated, after all the debts then existing against the Territory should be paid, and not before.

An act to divide the county of Crawford and to organize the county of Chippewa, provided: That the county of Crawford should be limited to that district of country which lies north of the Wisconsin and east of the Mississippi Rivers, and south of a line beginning at the mouth of Buffalo River, thence up the main branch of said river to its source, thence in a direct line to the most southern point on Lake Chetac, thence in a direct line drawn due east, until it intersects the western boundary line of Portage county, as enlarged by an act approved February 18, 1841; and west of the western boundary lines of the said counties of Portage and Richland.

It provided that all that district of country lying west of Portage county, enlarged as aforesaid, north of the northern boundary line of Crawford county aforesaid, east of the Mississippi River, and south of the boundaries of the county of St. Croix, as prescribed in the act approved January 9, 1840, organizing said county, be known under the name of Chippewa county.

The new county of Chippewa was organized for all purposes of county government, and attached to the county of Crawford for judicial purposes. The county seat was located temporarily at or near the residence of Mr. LAMB, at the junction of the Menomonee River with the Chippewa.

Sixteen days later (February 19th) an act was approved

"to divide the county of St. Croix and organize the county of La'Pointe," which enacted—

"That all that district of country within the limits of St. Croix county, as prescribed by an act organizing said county, approved January 9, 1840, be and the same is hereby divided into two counties; beginning at the mouth of Muddy Island River, thence running in a direct line to Yellow Lake, and from thence to Lake Courterille, so as to intersect the eastern boundary line of the county of St. Croix at that place; thence to the nearest point on the west fork of Montreal River, thence down said river to Lake Superior. All that portion of St. Croix county as heretofore bounded, lying south of said lines, be and remain the county of St. Croix, and all the country lying north of said line and within this Territory, shall be known as the county of La'Pointe."

The county of La'Pointe was organized for all purposes of county government, and attached to the county of Crawford for judicial purposes. The "seat of justice" was temporarily located at the town of La'Pointe.

An act was passed that from and after the first day of November, 1845, the county of St. Croix should be organized for judicial purposes, and form a part of the first judicial district, and the district court be held by the judge of that district on the first Monday of June annually: Provided, that at the next general election the qualified voters of the county should vote either "for district court" or "against district court"; and if a majority was *for* it, the act should take effect, otherwise it should be void.

Washington county was organized for judicial purposes from and after the second Tuesday of April, and made a part of the third judicial district, the judge of which was required to hold court on the second Tuesday of September, 1845, at the school-house at the county seat, unless the county commissioners should, sixty days before that time, name some other place in an order to be filed with the clerk of the court, and thereafter the regular terms were required to be held on last Tuesday of March and the second Tuesday of September in each year.

In Dodge county, the county seat was located in this wise at a place afterwards called Juneau, in honor of SOLOMON JUNEAU.

An act was passed which provided that whenever the owner or owners of the land at and about the quarter section stake dividing sections numbers 21 and 22, in township 11 of range 15 east, should lay out into a town plat forty acres of land, of which the said quarter section stake shall be the center, reserving a square of four acres; and whenever the county commissioners should select such square as a site for the public buildings, and the owners should convey the said square and every alternate lot in said plat to the county of Dodge, then the seat of justice of Dodge county should be located upon the site so selected for public buildings. And all former acts conflicting with this were repealed.

The county seat of Winnebago county was located by three commissioners, elected at the annual town meeting in April, 1845, by the white male persons who had resided in the county one month. This was in pursuance of a special law for that purpose.

At the same session a law was passed which provided for an election by the qualified electors of the county, for or against the removal of the seat of justice of Milwaukee county. The vote was to be taken at the spring election, 1846, and if a majority of the votes were in favor of "removal", the seat of justice of said county was to be removed to Prairieville (now Waukesha).

If any election was held in pursuance of this law, the returns of it can not be found, and in view of the action of the Legislative Assembly at the next session, dividing the county of Milwaukee and organizing the county of Waukesha, are of comparatively little importance.

The system of county government was changed by law in Marquette county, from the "Town System," to the "County System," and in Brown county it was submitted by law to a vote of the voters of the county at the annual town meeting held in April, 1845, whether such change should be made.

Petitions for and remonstrances against the formation of a new county from parts of Jefferson and Dodge counties, of which Watertown should be the county seat, were numerously signed and presented to the Legislative Assembly.

Other petitions were presented for the formation of a new county, by taking the west range of towns in Dodge county and the east two ranges of Portage (now Columbia) county and the location of a county seat at Columbus.

Both these propositions were reported upon adversely by a committee of the Council, and never reached a vote in either house.

In the House of Representatives, the committee to which was referred the petition of sundry inhabitants of Sauk county praying for the passage of a law authorizing an election to be held to locate the seat of justice of that county, reported "That in the opinion of the committee, legislative action at the present session is inexpedient."

The report of the committee was accepted and the matter ended.

Several amendments were adopted to the act to provide for the government of the several towns, and for the revision of county government. Some of these related to the mode of electing town officers, and the duty of the chairman and some to matters relating to schools and school taxes but principally to the subject of highways and matters pertaining thereto.

An act of Congress was passed May 23d, 1844, by which it was provided that whenever any portion of the surveyed public land not exceeding 320 acres had been or should be settled upon and occupied as a town site, that it might be entered at the minimum price, in trust for the occupants thereof, the trust to be executed in the manner prescribed by the legislative authority of the State. At this session of the Legislative Assembly an act was passed providing a mode in which such trust might be executed in relation to any lands in this Territory which had been entered in pursuance of the provisions of that act of Congress. It was supposed that the title to a portion of the site of Portage City, in Columbia county could be obtained in pursuance of the provisions of this act, but it was deemed more advisable to proceed under another law subsequently passed in 1852.

For the purpose of enabling the inhabitants residing upon section twenty-five, town one, range two west, in Grant county, to avail themselves of that act of Congress, an act was passed by the Legislative Assembly at this session, constituting them a body corporate by the name of "The trustees of the village of Fairplay." But this act is believed not to have been effective and that the title was subsequently acquired in another mode.

The act to change the corporate limits and powers of the town of Milwaukee, passed March 11, 1839, was amended by extending the corporate boundaries of the town so as to include section 32, town 7, range 22, and so much of section

33 as lies west of the middle of the Milwaukee River, which were made to constitute the South ward of said town, with authority to elect five trustees to act in conjunction with the other trustees of the town.

The powers of the board of trustees were also enlarged.

The village of Beloit was incorporated, and the several acts to incorporate the villages of Racine and Geneva were amended.

A bill to incorporate the village of Madison passed the Council, but in the House it was laid on the table and not again taken up.

The towns of Lake Mills and Sullivan in the county of Jefferson, Beaver Dam and Hustisford in Dodge county, Ceresco in Fond du Lac county, and Lima in Rock county, were created by special acts for that purpose.

The subject of banks and unauthorized banking occupied much of the attention of the Legislative Assembly.

At an early day of the session a bill was introduced in the Council by Mr. KNOWLTON, to repeal an act to incorporate the Mississippi Marine and Fire Insurance Company, passed March 11, 1839, which had ostensibly assumed to do business at Sinipee, in Grant county, and which, under the authority to receive deposits and issue certificates therefor, had issued certificates of deposits in the similitude of bank notes, and was engaged in "banking business" in violation, as it was alleged, of its charter.

The bill passed the Council without opposition.

In the House, a motion was made by Mr. COLLINS, of Iowa, to substitute for the bill a provision that the Attorney General should institute proceedings against the company for the purpose of vacating its charter. This motion was decided in the negative by a vote of 4 to 22, and the bill was then passed by a vote of 22 to 3.

The Attorney General reported to the House of Representatives that in the case of the Attorney General of Wisconsin vs. The Bank of Wisconsin (at Green Bay), which had been pending in the District Court of Brown county, a decree had been entered that the charter of the bank be forfeited, and that ALEXANDER J. IRWIN be appointed the permanent receiver of the institution.

The "Bank of Milwaukee" was incorporated by an act of the Legislative Assembly, passed November 30, 1836, and approved and confirmed by an act of Congress passed March 3, 1837.

By an act of the Territorial Legislature, approved March 11, 1839, the act of incorporation was unconditionally repealed.

In July, 1844, the persons who claimed to be the stockholders of the bank endeavored, through JONATHAN E. ARNOLD, their attorney, to make an arrangement with the Attorney General by which the question of the validity of the repeal of the charter might be presented to the Supreme Court for its decision, upon an agreed case, at a term of the court then in session.

The Attorney General declined any action in the matter on behalf of the Territory at that term of the court and until specially authorized and instructed by the Legislature.

At the next session of the Legislative Assembly, the bank by its officers applied to the Legislature to repeal the repealing act, supported by a petition numerously signed by prominent citizens of Milwaukee.

The memorial and petition were referred to the committee on incorporations in the Council, a majority of which submitted a report in conformity with the wishes of the bank and the petitioners, accompanied by "a bill for the relief of the Bank of Milwaukee," which in terms repealed the repealing act of 1839 and revived the charter.

When the bill came up for consideration, after free discussion in a full Council, it was indefinitely postponed by a vote of 9 to 4, Messrs. KIMBALL, KNEELAND, WHITON and WILCOX voting in the negative.

In relation to the Wisconsin Marine and Fire Insurance Company, a resolution was adopted in the Council instructing the committee on the judiciary to inquire into the legality of passing a law repealing its charter, with liberty to report by bill or otherwise.

The committee, consisting of MARSHALL M. STRONG, JOHN CATLIN and WIRAM KNOWLTON, reported unanimously that "the company have forfeited their charter" but that the Legislature had no power to repeal it.

The committee recommend

"That the Attorney General of this Territory be requested to institute legal proceedings against the company, that the act incorporating them may, as it ought to be, declared void; and that this 'soulless being' be brought to a 'lively sense' of its duties and behold its 'enormous iniquities'."

The report was accompanied by a joint resolution authorizing such proceedings. The resolution was afterwards taken up for consideration by a vote of 7 to 5, and after discussion was laid upon the table. It was again taken up but before any action upon it, the two houses adjourned.

A resolution was adopted in the House, directing the committee on the judiciary to inquire into the expediency of providing by law for the suppression of the circulation of bills, checks, notes, certificates of deposit or other evidences of debt in circulation in the Territory, as money by any company or corporation not expressly authorized thereto by law. And providing also that the circulation of any such issues in the form or similitude of bank bills should be declared to be *prima facie* evidence of the violation of the charter of any such corporation.

A report was submitted by the committee, through Mr. BURNETT, the chairman, in favor of the suppression of the circulation, referred to in the resolution, but adverse to the proposition contained in the latter clause of it. It was accompanied by a bill to amend the existing law to restrain unauthorized banking, and give more effect and stringency to its provisions.

While the bill was under consideration Mr. COLLINS moved to strike out all after the enacting clause and insert —

"That the Attorney General of the Territory be and hereby is directed to institute proceedings against the Milwaukee Marine and Fire Insurance Company and the Mississippi Marine and Fire Insurance Company, with a view to have said charters vacated for violation of the provisions thereof."

This motion was lost by a vote of 7 to 19, and the bill was then ordered to a third reading by a vote of 21 to 5, and passed the next day without a division.

In the Council the bill was indefinitely postponed by a vote of 7 to 6, and thus ended for the session legislative action on the subject of banks and banking.

Governor DOTY had persisted in spelling Wisconsin with a "k" and an "a"—Wis-*k*on-s*a*n,—and some of the newspapers and his admirers imitated his example, so that the Legislative Assembly thought it a matter of sufficient importance to pass a joint resolution, declaring that the orthography should be that adopted in the organic act.

No difference of opinion existed as to the proper orthography, but only as to the wisdom of passing any resolution on the subject. The final vote on the resolution in the House, where it originated, was 16 to 9, and in the Council it was 7 to 6.

The election of a Territorial printer was at this session provided for by law. He was to be elected by joint ballot of the two houses, his term of service to commence at the close of the session at which he was elected, and continue one year and until his successor was elected. He was to give bond in the sum of three thousand dollars and take an oath faithfully to discharge his duties. He was to print the laws and journals and do all the incidental printing, and receive such compensation as should from time to time be established by law.

SIMEON MILLS of Madison was the first Territorial printer elected under this law, having received 24 votes out of 38 cast. JOHN A. BROWN received 13 and McCABE 1.

The revision of the law regulating taverns and groceries attracted the attention of the Legislative Assembly at this session.

It was provided by the Revised Statutes of 1839, that the county commissioners of the several counties might grant licenses to the keepers of inns and taverns, to sell strong and spirituous liquors and wines, and to determine the sum to be paid therefor, which should not be less than five dollars nor more than twenty-five, and that they might grant licenses to as many persons as they might think proper, to keep groceries for the sale of strong or spirituous liquors and wines, and that the sum to be paid for such grocery license should be one hundred dollars.

The sum to be paid for a license to sell in any quantity not less than one quart, was to be not more than seventy-five dollars nor less than twenty dollars, in the discretion of the commissioners.

Penalties were prescribed by the law for each violation of its provisions, but no specific mode for their enforcement was provided.

The law passed at this session provided that these penalties might be prosecuted for and recovered in the name of the United States, and that it should be the duty of the board of supervisors of every town, and the board of commissioners of every county, to prosecute for all violations of the law, and any person might do so.

While the bill was pending in the House, an amendment was proposed, that any person might keep a house of entertainment without obtaining a license therefor, provided that no person should sell any spirituous liquors or other liquors prohibited by law, without obtaining a grocery license.

This amendment was lost by a vote of 10 to 16, and in the Council a like amendment was defeated by a vote of 5 to 8. Another bill, giving to the legal voters of each municipality an option to restrain the granting of licenses therein, was reported by the judiciary committee in the House and was defeated by the close vote of 12 to 13, Mr. THOMAS of Walworth not voting.

An act passed in 1840, prescribing a penalty for the sale of intoxicating liquors to Indians, was amended so as to make the offense indictable, and punishable by fine and imprisonment.

From a communication made by the Governor to the Council, in response to a resolution of that body, the same facts in relation to the amount of selected and unselected University lands were presented as were contained in the report at the previous session of the committee on Territorial affairs.

An act was passed at this session which provided that JOHN T. HAIGHT of Jefferson county be appointed the agent of the Territory to select all the lands authorized to be set apart and reserved from sale by act of Congress, which had not been set apart and reserved from sale by the Secretary of the Treasury.

County treasurers were required by special law to hold their offices at county seats.

The clerk of the board of county commissioners or county supervisors was authorized, in case he had failed to advertise unredeemed lands as required by law, to again advertise them.

He was also authorized to make deeds for lands sold for taxes and unredeemed, where the tax certificates had been lost, upon the certificate of the district judge that he was satisfied of such loss.

Judges of probate were authorized by law to require from executors or administrators new or additional bonds.

They were also authorized to grant letters of administration upon the estates within the Territory of non-residents.

Commissioners were appointed to lay out Territorial roads:

From Milwaukee to Fort Winnebago *via* county seat of Dodge county.

From Milwaukee to Fox Lake, crossing Rock River near the outlet of the Winnebago Marsh (Horicon).

From Spring street in Milwaukee to intersect the road leading from Milwaukee to Mukwanago.

From Third street in Milwaukee until it intersects the United States road from Milwaukee to Green Bay south of Mad Creek.

From Milwaukee to Fond du Lac, passing near the centre of Washington county.

From Prairieville (Waukesha) to Fond du Lac.

From Prairieville, *via* Menomonee Falls, to the county seat of Washington county.

From Potters' Lake to the east line of Walworth county.

From Waupun, *via* Ceresco, to the county seat of Portage county.

From section thirty-five, town six, range seventeen east, in town of Ottawa to Prairieville.

From Monroe to Janesville.

From house of JARED S. WALSWORTH in Portage county to Grand Rapids.

From section twenty-eight, town three, range nine east, to Janesville.

From Exeter in Green county to Beloit.

From section thirty-one, town one, range nine east, to Madison.

From Watertown, by county seat of Dodge county, to Fond du Lac.

From Sheboygan, *via* county seat of Dodge county, to Madison.

From Madison, *via* Fountain Prairie, to Fox Lake.

From Summit to Fond du Lac.

From Fond du Lac, *via* Ceresco, to Fort Winnebago.

From Washington harbor (Ozaukee) to Fond du Lac.

From Columbus to Dekora.

From Columbus, *via* Washara (Fox Lake), to Watertown.

From Isaac Noyes, in Dodge county, to Seymour Wilcox's, in Fond du Lac.

From Janesville, *via* Indianford and Catfish Mills, to Madison.

From northeast corner of section 35, town 1, range 3 east, in Iowa county, *via* Spafford's branch, to Monroe.

From Janesville, *via* Exeter, to Mineral Point.

From the county seat of Washington county, to Hustis' Rapids.

From Eagle, *via* Spring Lake, to Prairieville.

From Watertown to Milwaukee; and

From Watertown to Mineral Point.

The compensation of road supervisors was fixed by law, and provision made for the application of delinquent road taxes to the repair of highways.

The board of supervisors of Milwaukee county were specially authorized to levy and collect three thousand dollars, subject to the approval of the tax-payers at town meeting, to be expended in the construction of roads and bridges.

The supervisors of Brown county were authorized to levy a tax not exceeding one per cent. annually, subject to a vote of the people of the county, for the purpose of constructing a McAdam, plank, or turnpike road from the foot of the Grand Kakalin to Winnebago Lake.

The controversy which had existed for several years in Milwaukee, at one time threatening violence and bloodshed, appears to have found a quietus in the passage of a law at this session, which authorized the trustees of the east, the west, and the south wards, or of either of them, or the people who inhabit them —

"To build, maintain, repair, rebuild and keep in operation at the expense of said wards, or either of them, bridges at the following places: From the foot of Cherry street to Water street, from the foot of Wisconsin street to Spring street, and from the foot of Water street to Walker's Point."

Commissioners were appointed for carrying into effect an act of Congress of June, 1844, appropriating a section of land for the improvement of Grant River, in the town of Potosi.

The commissioners were to cause the section (section 34, town 3, range 3 west) to be surveyed into lots, and to decide upon and award pre-emptions. The lots were to be appraised and sold. A receiver was appointed who was to receive all moneys paid for lots, and give certificates of such payments, which entitled the purchaser to receive from the Governor of the State a patent for the lot.

The commissioners were to cause a survey and estimate to be made of the improvement provided for by the act of Congress, and report to the next Legislative Assembly.

The moneys were to remain in the hands of the receiver, to be applied to the improvement in such manner as the Legislative Assembly should thereafter direct.

A select committee of one from each election district was appointed to inquire into the expediency of erecting a penitentiary or State prison. They submitted a report setting forth the great necessity of such a penal institution, but not recommending any other measure looking to its attainment except a memorial to Congress soliciting an appropriation of a sufficient sum to enable the Territory to erect a portion at least of a suitable building in which the criminals of the Territory may be confined and employed. The memorial was adopted, but no appropriation made by Congress for the purpose.

The Wisconsin River Navigation Company was incorporated, with authority to erect a dam across the Wisconsin River below the Little Bull Falls, of such height as would raise the water on the falls as high as the surface of the water above them, with a slide for the passage of rafts, and to receive tolls for the passage of lumber, shingles and timber.

JOHN HUSTIS, his associates, successors and assigns, were authorized to build and maintain a dam across Rock River upon the east half of section 9, town 10, range 16 east (Hustisford), in Dodge county.

J. CARY HALL, his associates, successors and assigns, were authorized to build and maintain a dam on such part of the Menomonee River as was within the jurisdiction of the Territory, in section 1, town 32, range 22 east.

HORACE R. JEROME, his associates, successors and assigns, were authorized to build and maintain a dam on such part of the Menomonee River as was within the jurisdiction of the Territory, at a place called White's Rapids, on unsurveyed land.

JOACHIM GRENHAGEN, his associates, successors and assigns, were authorized to erect and maintain a dam across the Milwaukee River, on sections 19 or 20, town 8, range 22 east, in Milwaukee county, at what has since been called Good Hope.

Applications for divorce were made in the Council by MARIA WOODFORD MCELWAIN from her husband, and in the House by URIEL B. SMITH, SETH H. MARQUISSE, and MATTHIAS CHILTON, from their wives respectively.

The first passed both houses and became a law. The bill to divorce URIEL B. SMITH from his wife passed the House by a vote of 14 to 10, and was rejected in the Council on its second reading by a vote of 7 to 4.

In the cases of SETH H. MARQUISSE and MATTHIAS CHILTON, the committee on the judiciary in the House made adverse reports, and no further action was had in relation to them.

The name of FRANCES ADELLE CRANDALL was changed to that of FRANCES ADELLE WHITING by a special act, which declared that she should thereafter be known and recognized as the adopted child of JOHN WHITING, of Bloomfield, Walworth county, and as such be capable of inheriting and holding his property.

JOEL T. LANDRUM of Iowa county petitioned the Legislature to pass an act changing the name of his natural son JOSEPHUS MATTHEWS, an infant of about ten years, and to legitimatize his said natural son so as to enable him to inherit the property of his father, which was done so far as an act of the Legislative Assembly could do it.

A co-operative association was incorporated under the name of the "Wisconsin Phalanx." It was located in the township of Ceresco, in Fond du Lac county, to which its business was restricted. WARREN CHASE, LESTER ROUNDS and URIEL FARMIN were authorized to receive subscriptions to stock. Afterwards the officers of the association were to be one president, one vice-president, secretary, treasurer and nine councillors. The act prescribed the duties of the officers and the manner in which the affairs of the corporation should be conducted.

The Janesville Academy was incorporated.

Certain citizens of Milwaukee and their associates and such persons as thereafter might be associated with them were incorporated by the name of the "First Congregational Society in Milwaukee." The act of incorporation contained the *unique* provision that "nothing herein contained shall be so construed as to give to said society banking powers."

Besides the memorial to Congress, soliciting an appropriation for a penitentiary, already mentioned, several others were adopted by the Legislative Assembly.

One in relation to the lands granted by Congress to aid in the construction of the Milwaukee and Rock River canal, asking, among other things, that the proceeds of the sales of the lands might be donated to the Territory to be appropriated to beneficial public uses, of which the payment of the debt incurred in completing the Capitol; $50,000 for building a penitentiary, and $20,000 for a normal school, were suggested.

One, asking for the passage of a bill which had passed the Senate at the previous session making an appropriation for the improvement of the Fox and Wisconsin Rivers.

Two, asking for the establishment of mail routes from Racine, *via* Beloit, to Galena, Ills., and from Milwaukee, *via* Whitewater and Fort Atkinson, to Madison.

Three, asking appropriations for roads, from the Falls of St. Croix to La'Pointe; from Prairie du Chien to La'Pointe, and from Fort Howard, Green Bay to Fort Wilkins, Copper Harbor on Lake Superior.

An itemized fee bill for services rendered by the clerk of the Supreme Court, and also by the Secretary of the Territory, was at this session, for the first time, prescribed by law.

An act was passed " for the protection of sheep "; which provided that if any dog should be found killing, wounding or worrying any sheep, it should be lawful for any person forthwith to kill the dog. It also prohibited rams from running at large between the months of August and December, by imposing a penalty of five dollars on the owner.

The appropriations made by the Legislative Assembly at this session for its incidental expenses, printing, postage, etc., exclusive of pay and mileage of members and pay of officers was $6,600.60.

After the passage of an act that the laws passed at that session should take effect on the first day of June, unless otherwise specially provided in the act itself, the Legislature adjourned on the 24th of February *sine die,* after a session of fifty days.

An act of Congress was passed in 1807, by which it was enacted that the several lead mines in the Indiana Territory shall be reserved for the future disposal of the United States, and the President was authorized to lease any such lead mine for a term not exceeding five years.

The lead mines of Wisconsin and Illinois were then in Indiana Territory.

Pre-emption laws were passed in 1830, 1832, 1834, 1838 and 1840.

Another act was passed June 26, 1834, creating additional land districts in Illinois and Missouri and creating two land districts in Wisconsin (Green Bay and Mineral Point) which authorized the President to cause to be offered for sale all the lands lying in said districts

" Reserving only section sixteen, the tract reserved for the village of Galena, such other tracts as have been granted to individuals, and the State of Illinois, and such reservations as the President shall deem necessary for military posts, any law of Congress heretofore existing to the contrary notwithstanding."

It was claimed by the occupants of lands containing lead mines that they were entitled to pre-emptions under some of these pre-emption laws, and especially that such lands were subject to private entry under the act of June 26, 1834.

This claim was not recognized by the General Land Office nor by the local land offices.

A case was finally decided during the December term, 1844, of the Supreme Court of the United States, of The United States *vs.* H. H. GEAR, reported in 3d Howard's Reports, p. 120, in which the court decided that —

"It was not intended to subject lead mine lands in the districts made by the act of June 26, 1834, to sale as other public lands are sold, or to make them liable to pre-emption by settlers."

In its reasoning the court say that the authority to sell these lands —

"Can only mean all lands not prohibited from being sold, or which have been reserved from sale by force of law." * * * "A power to sell all lands given in a law subsequent to another law expressly reserving lead mine lands from sale, cannot be said to be a power to sell the reserved lands when they are not named, or to repeal the reservation."

This decision was by a divided court, Judges STORY, MCLEAN and MCKINLEY dissenting, and a dissenting opinion prepared by Judge MCLEAN was read, and concurred in by Judges STORY and MCKINLEY.

After this decision was promulgated, the superintendent of the lead mines at Galena, on the 26th May, 1845, issued a circular notice that —

"In consequence of a recent decision, in which the rights of the United States to the lead mines have been clearly defined and established,"—

All persons mining or wishing to mine upon any lands to which a patent had not issued, were required to pay whatever rents may be due and take out a lease for mining, and that he had been instructed in case of necessity, to take legal measures to carry into effect the notice.

Although this decision and the notice of the superintendent caused much uneasiness among the occupants of the lead mine lands, but few of them paid any rents or took any leases, as a very general feeling prevailed that an act of Congress would be passed by which titles to the lands could be obtained. Subsequent events showed that this feeling was well founded.

The President of the United States in his message December 1, 1845, said:

"The present system of managing the mineral lands of the United States is believed to be radically defective. More than a million acres of the public land, supposed to contain lead and other minerals, have been reserved from sale and numerous leases upon them have been granted to individuals upon a stipulated rent. The system of leases has proved to be not only unprofitable but unsatisfactory to the citizens who have gone upon the lands and must, if continued, lay the foundation of much future difficulty between the government and the lessees."

"According to the official records, the amount of rent received by the government for the years 1841 '42, '43 and '44 was $6,344.74, while the expenses of the system during the same period, including salaries of superintendents, agents, clerks and incidental expenses were $26,111.11 — the income being less than one fourth of the expenses. The system has given rise to much litigation between the United States and individual citizens, producing irritation and excitement in the mineral region and involving the government in heavy additional expenditures." * * * * * * * *

"I recommend the repeal of the present system and that these lands be placed under the superintendence and management of the General Land Office as other public lands and brought into market and sold upon such terms as Congress in their wisdom may prescribe."

On the 13th of May, 1845, Hon. HENRY DODGE was appointed Governor of the Territory in place of NATHANIEL P. TALLMADGE removed, being thus restored to the place from which in 1841, he had been removed by President TYLER to give place to JAMES D. DOTY.

On the 6th of May, Gov. DODGE returned from Washington to his residence five miles from Mineral Point, where, after a few days he was waited upon by a committee appointed at a large meeting of the citizens of Mineral Point without distinction of party, by whom he was tendered a public dinner. He accepted the invitation and at the time fixed for the ovation, the 5th of June, a large concourse assembled. The Governor was escorted from his residence to Mineral Point by the Mineral Point Dragoons, under command of Capt. JOHN F. O'NEILL, where he was met by the citizens of the town and others, who formed in procession and marched to the Court House, where the Governor was welcomed on behalf of the people in an appropriate address to which he briefly responded. The procession again formed and marched to the Mansion House and partook of a dinner which was followed with numerous toasts. The festivities of the day were followed by a ball at the Court House.

During the month of May, GEORGE W. JONES was restored to the office of Surveyor General of Wisconsin and Iowa, from which he had been removed by President TYLER in 1841.

Soon after the 4th of March, JOHN S. ROCKWELL was appointed Marshal of the Territory in place of CHARLES M. PREVOST whose commission had expired.

Subsequently WM. P. LYNDE was appointed United States Attorney, in place of THOMAS W. SUTHERLAND removed.

PASCHALL BEQUETTE was appointed Receiver of Public Moneys at the Mineral Point Land Office.

GEORGE H. WALKER was appointed Register of the Land Office at Milwaukee in place of PARACLETE POTTER whose term of service had expired.

The Democratic Territorial convention was held at Madison on the 25th of June, and resulted in the nomination of MORGAN L. MARTIN of Green Bay on the eighteenth ballot, as candidate for delegate.

The following table exhibits the results of the several ballots :

CANDIDATES.	1	2	3	4	5	6	7	8	9	10	11	12	13	14	15	16	17	18
MORGAN L. MARTIN	21	23	23	21	22	24	21	23	18	23	23	23	16	17	7	5	3	49
D. A. J. UPHAM	31	25	24	31	28	27	24	19	22	26	24	24	21	22	23	24	26	20
FRANCIS J. DUNN	30	21	20	20	19	19	20	15	19	20	20	22	21	19	19	19	19	0
MOSES M. STRONG	2	3	3	4	5	4	5	11	3	5	5	2	1	1	1	0	0	0
MASON C. DARLING	1	5	7	2	2	1	2	7	15	2	0	4	12	16	27	29	26	6
MICHAEL FRANK	0	0	0	0	0	0	1	1	0	2	4	1	5	1	1	1	1	0
SCATTERING	2	1	1	0	2	3	5	2	1	1	2	2	2	1	0	0	0	3

Mr. MARTIN being at Madison was waited upon by a committee who informed him of his nomination. He immediately addressed a letter to the committee, in which, after expressing his acknowledgments for the honor conferred, he said:

> " Encouraged by the approbation heretofore expressed in my favor by my fellow-citizens during a long residence among them, I accept the nomination, and trust that the fondest expectations of my friends will be realized in the coming contest."

The Territorial Whig convention was first called to be held at Madison on the 9th day of July, and by order of the Territorial central committee the time was postponed to the 24th of July, at which time the convention met and, without much controversy, nominated Hon. JAMES COLLINS, of Iowa county, as the candidate of that party for delegate in Congress.

Both candidates made a very thorough canvass of the Territory.

EDWARD D. HOLTON, of Milwaukee, was also a candidate, having been nominated by the anti-slavery party, then designated as the "Liberty" party.

The election was held on the fourth Monday (22d) of September, and the result was:

Whole number of votes cast was	13,393
Of which MORGAN L. MARTIN received	6,803
JAMES COLLINS	5,787
EDWARD D. HOLTON	790
Scattering	13

Mr. MARTIN took his seat as delegate on the first Monday of December.

Railroads were much talked of and anticipated as one of the developments of the near future, but as yet no work of construction had been commenced. The demands of the young community, however, for public means of inter-communication had not been overlooked.

By the joint enterprise of Messrs. FRINK, WALKER & Co., of Chicago, L. P. SANGER of Galena, and DAVIS & MOORE of Milwaukee, a daily line of four-horse post coaches ran from Milwaukee to Galena, through in three days. The line, which left Milwaukee on Mondays, Wednesdays, and Fridays, went *via* Troy, Janesville, Monroe, Wiota, Shullsburg and White Oak Springs, lodging at Janesville and Shullsburg.

The line which left Milwaukee on Tuesdays, Thursdays

and Saturdays, went *via* Prairieville, Whitewater, Fort Atkinson, Madison, Blue Mounds, Dodgeville, Mineral Point, Platteville and Hazel Green, lodging at Madison and Mineral Point.

Another line left Whitewater tri-weekly, *via* Milton, Janesville and Beloit for Rockford, where it connected with the Galena and Chicago daily line of stages.

Another tri-weekly line ran from Milwaukee for New Berlin, Vernon, Mukwonago and Troy, returning every alternate day, forming a daily line between Milwaukee and Troy.

Another tri-weekly line ran from Milwaukee *via* Oak Creek, Racine, and Southport to Chicago, returning alternate days.

At Madison, connection was made with a stage line to Fort Winnebago, and at Platteville with another to Prairie du Chien.

There were other less important lines in different parts of the Territory.

On the 6th of April, Milwaukee was visited with the most disastrous conflagration which it had ever experienced. The fire broke out in a small wooden building opposite the Cottage Inn, and spread with frightful rapidity, burning down two entire squares before its progress was arrested. The Cottage Inn, and every other building between Michigan and Huron streets, except a barn and two or three small tenements, were destroyed by the fire.

It was a serious calamity for Milwaukee in its infancy, and many of its citizens sustained very severe losses. Most of the buildings were of wood, and Milwaukee had reached that state of progress and prosperity that the demands of its business required the erection of more imposing and commodious structures.

CHAPTER XXVII.

TERRITORY OF WISCONSIN — 1846.

The last half of the tenth year of the tutelage which commenced with the organization of the Territorial government in 1836, furnished unmistakable evidence that a decided majority of the hundred thousand or more of its inhabitants were now disposed to exchange their dependent relations to a distant paternal government, for the responsibilities and the anticipated advantages of an independent sovereignty as a State in the Union of States.

The existence of this disposition had been officially demonstrated by a direct vote of the electors in April, and the "shadow of the coming event" was so distinctly discernible early in the year that a superficial observer could not fail to see it, so that the important preliminary laws were enacted both by Congress and the Territorial Legislature for the creation of a State government.

The radical and important changes in the political condition of the inhabitants of Wisconsin, which were felt to be so certain to occur during the year 1846, gave to the anticipated events of the year a significant interest.

At the first session of the Twenty-ninth Congress, which commenced in December, 1845, an act commonly called an "enabling act," was passed, which authorized the people of the Territory —

"To form a constitution and State government for the purpose of being admitted into the " Union on an equal footing with the original States in all respects whatsoever, by the " name of the State of Wisconsin, with the following boundaries:"

The entire boundaries are particularly described, and are the same as subsequently adopted in the constitution and as now exist.

The unjust exercise of its power by the National Government, in violation of the rights guaranteed to the "Fifth State" by the ordinance of 1787, while Wisconsin had no voice with which to protest, seconded by the greed of Illinois for an unwarranted extension of her northern boundary, and her adverse occupancy for twenty-eight years of 7,500 square miles of our Territory, closed the door to all controversy over our southern boundary.

The concession by Congress to Michigan of the Northern Peninsula, in consideration of the release by her to Ohio of the territory in dispute between those states, prevented any controversy in relation to our northeastern boundary.

But upon the northwest, the territorial rights of the Fifth State under the Ordinance of 1787, as far as the Mississippi River to its head waters in Itasca Lake, were clear and undisputed, and had been impaired by no previous action of Congress. To have extended its northwestern boundary to the extreme limit to which Wisconsin was entitled, would have given her all that part of Minnesota east of the Mississippi, extending west to about the 95th degree of longitude, and intersecting the boundary line of the British possessions near where it leaves the Lake of the Woods in latitude forty-nine degrees.

It was however the policy of Congress — at least of the non-slaveholding states, which were now in a majority — to provide for a "Sixth State" out of the old Northwest Territory, supplemented by a small part of the "Louisiana Territory."

To accomplish this object it was provided in the enabling act that the boundary after passing through Lake Superior to the mouth of the St. Louis River, should follow

"Up the main channel of said river to the first rapids in the same above the Indian village, according to Nicollett's map; thence due south to the main branch of the St. Croix River; thence down the main channel of said river to the Mississippi."

The enabling act extended the laws of the United States over the State of Wisconsin, provided for a district court, a judge, marshal and attorney, and that the State should be entitled to two representatives in Congress.

It submitted to the convention which should assemble for the purpose of forming a constitution the following propositions, which if accepted by the convention and ratified by an article in the constitution, should be obligatory on the United States, viz.:

First. That section sixteen in every township should be granted to the State for the use of schools.

Second. That the seventy-two sections set apart for a University by the act of June 12, 1838, are granted to the State solely for the use and support of such University.

Third. That ten sections be granted to the State for the purpose of completing the public buildings, or for the erection of others at the seat of government of the State.

Fourth. That all salt springs in the State not exceeding twelve, with six sections of land adjoining or as contiguous as may be to each, be granted to the State.

Fifth. That five per cent. of the net proceeds of sales of all public lands lying within the State, shall be paid to the State for the purpose of making public roads and canals in the same.

These five propositions were on the condition that the constitution or an irrevocable ordinance should provide that the State should never interfere with the primary disposal of the soil within the same by the United States, that no tax should be imposed on lands, the property of the United States, and that in no case should non-resident proprietors be taxed higher than residents.

The parsimoniousness of Congress in the matter of appropriations to promote the welfare and prosperity of the Territory was well calculated to increase the feeling in favor of a change from a Territorial to a State government.

A bill passed both houses of Congress making appropriation for the improvement of rivers and harbors, which included the more important harbors on Lake Michigan but the veto of President POLK prevented it from becoming a law.

A bill was reported in the House appropriating $25,000 to aid in the construction of roads, but it did not become a law. It distributed the appropriations as follows: Milwaukee and Fond du Lac road $4,000; Milwaukee and Madison $4,000; Beloit to Winnebago $4,000; Racine and Madison $3,000; Green Bay and Fond du Lac $2,000; Green Bay and Chicago $4,000; Sheboygan and Fox River $2,000; and Platteville and Potosi $2,000.

The Delegate in Congress was Hon. MORGAN L. MARTIN, who resided at Green Bay, and had always as a member of the Territorial Legislature, and by his unofficial actions, manifested a deep interest in the improvement of the navigation of the Fox and Wisconsin Rivers.

An act was passed at this session, the result, it was believed, in a great measure of the active efforts of the Delegate, which granted to the State on its admission into the Union, for the purpose of improving the navigation of these rivers, and connecting them by a canal; every alternate section of land, for three sections in width, on each side of the said Fox River and the lakes through which it passes, and of the canal.

Complaints were made that this grant was obtained at

the cost of the neglect of other interests by the Delegate. But there is no evidence of any foundation for such complaints.

The appropriation for salaries of United State officers of the Territory were the same as usual, but that for the Legislative expenses was only $13,700.

An act was passed giving to the Surveyor-General of Wisconsin and Iowa the same annual salary as the other Surveyors-General, and the same amount for clerk hire as the Surveyor-General northwest of the Ohio. The effect of this was to increase the amount of salary and clerk hire from $3,100 to $8,300.

The act for the relief of the Stockbridge tribe of Indians, approved March 3, 1843, was repealed, and the tribe or nation was restored to its ancient form of government. The repealing act provided for giving to such of the Indians as chose to become citizens, their proportion of the Indian land in severalty, and that the remainder of the land should be held in common by the remainder of the tribe.

The only other act passed at this session of Congress especially affecting the interests of the people of the Territory was one

"To authorize the President to sell the reserved mineral lands in the States of Illinois and Arkansas and the Territories of Wisconsin and Iowa supposed to contain lead ore."

The fourth annual session of the fourth Legislative Assembly commenced at Madison on the 5th day of January, 1846.

In the Council but one change from the previous year had occurred. Mr. RAY, of Milwaukee county, had resigned, and Mr. CURTIS REED was elected in his place.

In the House more than half the members had resigned and new ones elected to fill the vacancies.

In Brown county ELISHA MORROW succeeded Mr. FOWLER.

In the district composed of Rock and Walworth, all the members, being Messrs. FIELD, MILLS, THOMAS, and MOORE resigned, and Messrs. WARNER EARL, GAYLORD GRAVES, and CALEB CROSWELL, of Walworth county, and Mr. IRA JONES, of Rock county, took their places.

In Racine county Messrs. MCCLELLAN and NORTHWAY gave place to Messrs. ANDREW B. JACKSON and JULIUS WOOSTER.

In Milwaukee county Messrs. BROWN, ELLIS, KILBOURN, SHEW, and WALKER were succeeded by Messrs. SAMUEL H. BARSTOW, JOHN CRAWFORD, JAMES MAGONE, LUTHER PARKER and WILLIAM H. THOMAS.

In Iowa county Messrs. COLLINS and OLIVER had resigned and Messrs. H. M. BILLINGS, and CHARLES POLE were their successors.

In Grant county, in place of Mr. HICKS, ARMSTEAD C. BROWN was the member.

The Council was organized by the election of NELSON DEWEY, President, BEN C. EASTMAN, Secretary, and JOSEPH BRISBOIS, Sergeant-at-Arms. Mr. EASTMAN resigned on the 18th of January, and WILLIAM R. SMITH was elected his successor.

In the House MASON C. DARLING was elected Speaker, LA'FAYETTE KELLOGG, Chief Clerk, and DAVID BONHAM, Sergeant-at-Arms.

The following table exhibits the names, place of nativity, age, residence, and occupation of each of the members of the Legislative Assembly:

MEMBERS OF THE COUNCIL.

NAMES.	NATIVITY.	AGE.	RESIDENCE.	OCCUPATION.
CHARLES M. BAKER	N. York City	41	Geneva, Walworth Co.	Lawyer.
JOHN CATLIN	Vermont	41	Madison, Dane Co.	Lawyer.
NELSON DEWEY	Connecticut	32	Lancaster, Grant Co.	Lawyer.
MICHAEL FRANK	New York	30	Southport, Racine Co.	Printer.
J. H. KIMBALL	Maine	45	Prairieville, Milwaukee Co.	Farmer.
JAMES KNEELAND	New York	28	Milwaukee	Merchant.
WIRAM KNOWLTON	New York	30	Prairie du Chien	Lawyer.
CURTIS REED	Vermont	30	Summit, Milwaukee Co	Farmer.
JOHN H. ROUNTREE	Kentucky	40	Platteville, Grant Co.	Merchant.
MARSHALL M. STRONG	Massachusetts	36	Racine, Racine Co.	Lawyer.
MOSES M. STRONG	Vermont	35	Mineral Point, Iowa Co	Lawyer.
EDWARD V. WHITON	Massachusetts	40	Janesville, Rock Co.	Lawyer.
RANDALL WILCOX	Massachusetts	51	Depere, Brown Co.	Farmer.

MEMBERS OF THE HOUSE OF REPRESENTATIVES.

Names.	Nativity.	Age.	Residence.	Occupation.
Samuel H. Barstow...	Connecticut ..	39	Pewaukee, Milwaukee Co. ...	Farmer.
Henry M. Billings ...	New York....	39	Centreville, Iowa Co.	Miner.
Abraham Brawley...	Pennsylvania.	32	Pinery, Portage Co.	Lumberman.
Armstead C. Brown ..	Missouri......	30	Potosi, Grant Co.	Justice of Peace
Thomas P. Burnett...	Virginia.......	45	Grant Co.	Lawyer and far.
Mark R. Clapp........	Vermont	42	Aztalan, Jefferson Co.......	Farmer.
John Crawford.......	Vermont	53	Wauwatosa, Milwaukee Co.	Farmer.
Caleb Croswell......	New York....	34	Delavan, Walworth Co.	Printer.
Thomas Cruson	Kentucky	43	Platteville, Grant Co........	Farmer.
Mason C. Darling.....	Massachusetts	45	Fond du Lac................	Physician.
William M. Dennis...	Rhode Island.	36	Watertown, Jefferson Co ...	Farmer.
Warner Earl.... ...	New York....	30	Whitewater, Walworth Co..	Lawyer.
James Fisher	Pennsylvania.	30	Prairie du Chien	Carpenter.
Gaylord Graves......	New York....	41	East Troy, Walworth Co. ...	Farmer.
Robert C. Hoard... .	Tennessee	58	Mineral Point, Iowa Co.	Miner.
Andrew B. Jackson ..	Connecticut ..	31	Bristol, Racine Co..........	Farmer.
Ira Jones	Ohio..........	36	Union, Rock Co.............	Farmer.
James Magone	New York....	37	Milwaukee	Shipwright.
Benjamin H. Moores.	New York....	52	Hamburg, Washington Co..	Farmer.
Elisha Morrow.......	New Jersey...	26	Green Bay, Brown Co.......	Lawyer.
Luther Parker.......	N. Hampshire	45	Muskego, Milwaukee Co....	Farmer.
Noah Phelps	New York....	37	Monroe, Green Co..........	Farmer.
Charles Pole.........	Maryland.....	31	Shullsburg, Iowa Co.	Miner.
Orson Sheldon	Vermont	38	Burlington, Racine Co.......	Merchant.
William H. Thomas ..	New York	24	Lisbon, Milwaukee Co.	Farmer.
Julius Wooster	Connecticut ..	32	Caledonia, Racine Co.	Farmer.

The annual message of Governor Dodge was delivered by him in person to both houses assembled in the Representatives Hall on the second day of the session.

The first and most important part of it, recommended the passage of a law submitting to the people, the question of the formation of a State government.

A revision of the laws regulating common schools was recommended.

The Territorial debt it was said should be paid as early as possible.

Some steps, it was said, should be taken to raise funds for

the erection of a penitentiary, and that it would be proper to memorialize Congress, asking for an appropriation for that object.

The message recommended memorializing Congress on the subject of the sale of the lead mines and mineral lands. The importance of completing harbors at Milwaukee, Racine and Southport, and of constructing them at Sheboygan and Manitowoc, of the removal of the obstructions to the navigation of the Mississippi at the upper and lower rapids, of the improvement of the navigation of the Fox and Wisconsin Rivers, and of Rock River, as also the construction of a rail or macadamized road from Lake Michigan to the Mississippi, were each strongly set forth in the message, and the asking of appropriations by Congress recommended, accompanied, however, with the expression that it appeared to be the settled policy of the government to reduce the appropriations as low as possible, believing, as it would seem that the proper time had arrived, when Wisconsin should take the proper steps for the formation of a State government.

The subject of the militia and the public arms was referred to. The Indians were represented as peaceably disposed, except the Winnebagoes, of whose depredations complaint was made.

So much of the Governor's message as related to State government, and all petitions, remonstrances and documents relating to the subject, were referred to a joint select committee consisting of Messrs. MOSES M. STRONG, FRANK, MORROW, MOOERS, SHELDON, and BURNETT.

A very able report from the pen of Mr. FRANK, in favor of the early formation of a State government was submitted by the committee, accompanied by a bill for that purpose.

The report undertook to demonstrate that the change would result in pecuniary advantage. It stated that the average amount of appropriations made to the Territory for all purposes did not exceed about $38,000, while the interest upon the proceeds of 500,000 acres of land, which the State would receive on its admission into the Union at six per cent., and the five per cent. of the net proceeds of the sales of the public lands in the State, it was estimated would amount to about $55,000.

Great importance was attributed by the report to the full

control and disposal of our school lands, and the grant for a university, while it was assumed that the same liberality which had been extended to the other new States, would secure to us still further grants of land.

The advantages of a political character were adverted to as being important, and were presented in a striking and forcible manner.

The bill reported by the committee was amended in some of its details, and then passed the Council without a division.

In the House some slight amendments were made, but the only proposition which elicited much discussion was an amendment offered by Mr. POLE to strike out that part of the bill which authorized the inhabitants who had only *declared their intentions* to become citizens of the United States to vote for delegates to the convention. Upon this amendment the vote was 7 to 18 — those who voted for it being Messrs. BROWN, BURNETT, CRUSON, HOARD, JONES, PHELPS, and POLE.

An amendment was proposed to strike out the word "white" wherever it occurred in the bill, upon which the vote stood 10 to 16. Those voting in the affirmative were Messrs. BARSTOW, BRAWLEY, FISHER, GRAVES, JACKSON, MORROW, PARKER, SHELDON, WOOSTER and DARLING.

The bill was then passed by a vote of 17 to 9. Those who voted in the negative were Messrs. BRAWLEY, BROWN, BURNETT, CRUSON, FISHER, JONES, MORROW, POLE and DARLING.

As soon as the bill was enrolled and presented to the Governor, it received his signature and became a law.

Its principal features were that on the 1st Tuesday of April,

" Every white male inhabitant above the age of of twenty-one years, who shall have resided in the Territory for six months, next previous thereto, and who shall either be a citizen of the United States or shall have filed his declaration of intention to become such according to the laws of the United States on the subject of naturalization ",

should be authorized to vote for or against the formation of a State government.

That the Governor should appoint some person in each county to take the census of the inhabitants on the first day of June.

If a majority of all the votes were "for State government", the Governor was to make an apportionment among the several counties of delegates to form a State constitution. The basis was one delegate for every 1,300 inhabitants, and an additional delegate for a fraction greater than a majority of said number, but there was to be one delegate to each organized county, and no two counties could be united in the same election district. The Governor was to make proclamation of the apportionment.

The election was fixed for the first Monday of September, and the time of the annual election was changed from the fourth to the first Monday of September.

The qualifications of voters for delegates were the same as those for voting on the preliminary question of the formation of a State government.

The delegates were to meet at the Capitol on the first Monday of October, with full power and authority to form a republican constitution, which should be ratified by the people, in such manner and at such time as the convention should prescribe.

It was provided by another act that the Governor should make a new apportionment of the Legislative Assembly among the several counties, based upon the census to be taken in June.

Next to that of providing for the formation of a State Government, no subject engaged the attention of the Legislature more than that of the Wisconsin Marine and Fire Insurance Company.

Incorporated for the ostensible purpose of conducting an insurance business, it was alleged that it had engaged in a general banking business, and thereby violated its charter.

The act of incorporation contained this provision:

"This corporation may likewise receive money on deposit, and loan the same on bottomry, respondentia, *or other satisfactory security*, at such rates of interest as may be done by individuals by the laws of this Territory; may also make insurance upon life or lives and *employ such capital as may belong or accrue to said company* in the purchase of public or other stock, or *in any other monied transactions or operations for the sole benefit of the said company*, and in general the said company may transact all business usually performed by insurance companies, *provided nothing herein contained shall give the said company banking privileges.*"

The company issued what is called certificates of deposit in small sums — $1, $2, and $5. They were in the similitude of bank notes and circulated as money, and to a large extent filled the channels of circulation. It claimed that these issues were authorized by its charter.

No complaint was made that the company did not redeem

in coin all its issues, or that it was not entirely responsible but it was claimed that the issue was an exercise of "banking privileges," and a violation of its charter.

There was a decided majority in each house in favor of taking some course to put a stop to these issues, and to the continued exercise of its corporate powers, and so great was the feeling of hostility to the corporation, that when a respectful communication from ALEXANDER MITCHELL, its secretary, was presented in the House, a motion to return it to him received 12 out of 26 votes, and on a motion to print it only five voted in the affirmative.

Three measures were introduced in the House with a view to deprive the company of its corporate powers.

One was a bill for the unconditional repeal of its act of incorporation.

Another, a joint resolution, instructing the Attorney General to institute the necessary legal proceedings to procure a forfeiture of its franchise, and the other a memorial to Congress asking for the repeal and disapproval of the act of incorporation.

The repealing act passed both houses and became a law. The vote in the House was 18 to 8, and in the Council 9 to 4.

The passage of this law, however, had no practical effect in restraining the company from issuing certificates of deposit as a circulating medium.

The joint resolution failed of adoption in consequence of an irreconcilable disagreement between the two houses upon an amendment adopted by the Council.

The memorial was ordered to a third reading in the House and then laid on the table and was never again taken up.

A joint resolution was passed appointing a committee to examine the affairs of the Bank of Mineral Point. The bank had been practically defunct for more than four years and an examination could serve very little useful purpose, except to gratify curiosity.

The report of the committee stated that the liabilities of the bank at the time of its failure consisted mainly of its circulating notes, which were supposed to have amounted to about $136,000. Of these $101,863 had been taken out of circulation, some having been received on debts due the bank and for property sold; some paid in St. Louis by attachment suits against the debtors of the bank and $9,131 had been redeemed by the receivers; some at fifty cents on the dollar, some at twenty-five and some at ten, leaving a balance of $34,137 in circulation, a portion of which was undoubtedly lost or destroyed.

The nominal assets of the bank were $58,933. These consisted of notes, drafts, and bills of exchange, most of which were worthless, many of the debtors having been discharged under the bankrupt law; and of the amount, $33,491.54 was against SAMUEL B. KNAPP, the defaulting and absconding cashier, and it did not appear probable that the amount which would be realized would pay more than ten per cent. of the liabilities.

The report did not appear to require any legislation, and none was had.

The subject of the indebtedness of the Territory, although not large, continued to occupy the attention of the Legislative Assembly.

The aggregate amount of the assessments in the several counties, made in pursuance of the law of the last session, as returned to the auditor, was $9,324,405.

A bill was reported in the Council by the committee on Territorial affairs to increase the revenue of the Territory by raising the rate of the Territorial tax from 1½ mills to 3 mills on the dollar of assessed valuation, which would have produced a revenue of about $28,000. The bill was ordered to a third reading in the Council, but afterward laid on the table and not again taken up.

The amount of tax due to the Territory under the law passed in 1845, as reported by the Auditor, was $11,691.47, and the amount of tax unpaid prior to 1845 was $1,270.49.

These sums were entirely inadequate to the payment of the debt, but it was impossible to determine the exact amount of the deficiency.

The appropriations by the Legislature in 1846, payable out of the Territorial Treasury, were $3,919.24, and was an addition of that sum to the existing deficiency.

A portion of the scrip which had been received into the Territorial Treasury was issued for legislative expenses, and provision was made for the payment of it by the United States, through the Secretary, who had been provided with funds for that purpose.

The claim of DANIEL BAXTER was again presented and a favorable report made in the House, which adopted a resolution to pay him a certain sum of money in full payment. This resolution was defeated in the Council, where another resolution was passed, which was concurred in by the House and approved by the Governor, which authorized and directed the Territorial Treasurer to pay over to Mr. BAXTER eight of the remaining Territorial bonds (of $100 each) issued for the completion of the Capitol, provided he would receive the same in full satisfaction and relinquishment of all his unsettled claims and demands.

At an early day of the session, a joint resolution was introduced by Mr. CRAWFORD, requiring the Superintendent of Territorial Property to discontinue all suits now pending in which the Territory is plaintiff.

The resolution was referred to the committee on Territorial affairs, which reported that

"Any action on the part of the Legislature, with a view to their discontinuance at this time, would be inexpedient and uncalled for. Nor with the knowledge which they have been able to possess themselves of, would they desire a public disclosure of all the facts relating to the same. They have therefore good and substantial reasons for recommending that no further action be had on this subject."

Mr. CRAWFORD made an earnest argument in support of his resolution, placing it chiefly on the ground of the great expense of prosecuting suits, especially for attorney's fees, and the worthlessness of any judgments that might be obtained. The resolution was then laid on the table by a vote of 18 to 7 — Mr. BURNETT, who was attorney for the defendants not voting. Having been called up at a subsequent day, the House refused to adopt it without a division.

These suits had been commenced and hitherto prosecuted under direction of the Superintendent of Public Property, as authorized by law. For that purpose he had employed attorneys other than the Attorney General.

In an act passed at this session making an appropriation for professional services rendered and expenses incurred by one of these attorneys, a section was inserted that:

"Hereafter there shall be no fees or compensation paid to any attorney except the Attorney-General, for any service to be performed in the management of any suit or suits in behalf of the Territory."

The Superintendent of Territorial Property construed this section as placing the entire control and management of these suits in the Attorney General, and neither the Superintendent nor the former attorneys had any further connection with them.

In compliance with a resolution of the Council, the Attorney General reported that JAMES T. WATSON, then late of the city of New York, died seized of about two thousand four hundred acres of land in the county of Rock, about twelve miles west of Janesville. That he died leaving no relatives surviving him nearer than second cousins, and in the opinion of the Attorney General the lands had accrued to the Territory for want of heirs to inherit.

It does not appear that anything further was done to give effect to the escheat, if the land had escheated.

At this session of the Legislative Assembly, the county of Waukesha was formed out of Milwaukee county, La Fayette out of Iowa and Columbia out of Portage. The act creating Waukesha county was to be effective if approved by a majority of the voters of the proposed new county west of range 21, excluding those of the remaining part of Milwaukee including the city. The requisite majority of votes was cast and Waukesha county was organized.

The creation of the new county of La Fayette was submitted to a vote of all the voters of the whole of Iowa county. The result was 1,115 for division, and 882 against it.

The creation of Columbia county was unconditional and dependent upon no vote whatever.

The inhabitants of Watertown, which is partly in Jefferson and partly in Dodge counties, and other inhabitants of that vicinity had long desired a new county from parts of each. For the purpose of ascertaining the wishes of the people of these counties, a proposition was submitted to them to be voted on, that a new county be established to be composed of towns 9 and 10 of ranges 13, 14, 15, 16 and 17 in Dodge county, and town 8 of ranges 13, 14, 15 and 16 in Jefferson county. The result was to be certified to the Secretary of the Territory and laid before the Legislature.

The vote was adverse to the proposition.

The form of county government was changed in the counties of Dodge, Dane and Washington, and the act of 1841 to provide for "township" government, was declared to be in force in those counties.

In the county of Dodge the following towns were created and their boundaries prescribed, viz.: Portland, Emmett, Lebanon, Ashippun, Elba, Calamus, Lowell, Clyman, Hustisford, Rubicon, Beaver Dam, Fairfield, Hubbard, Burnett, Williamstown, Le'Roy, Chester, Trenton and Fox Lake.

The following in the county of Dane, viz.: Rutland, Rome, Albion, Dunkirk, Sun Prairie, and all the remaining townships in the county constituted the town of Madison.

In the county of Washington, the following, viz.: Erin, Richfield, Germantown, Mequon, Wright, Polk, Jackson, Grafton, Addison, West Bend and Port Washington.

The county of Sheboygan was organized for judicial purposes.

An act was passed providing for a change of the location of the county seat of Sauk county by a popular vote.

The boundary line between the counties of Crawford and Chippewa was established.

The county seat of St. Croix county was established at Stillwater.

The following new towns were organized in other counties:

In Jefferson county Aztalan, Ixonia, Sullivan, Concord, Tunbridge, Palmyra, Bark River and Farmington.

In Rock county, Magnolia and Oak.

In Walworth county, Elk Horn, Sugar Creek, Turtle, Bradford, Spring Valley and Newark.

In Racine county, Blackhawk, Yorkville and Raymond.

In Fond du Lac county, Rosendale, Lime, Metomen and Byron.

The town of Stillwater and the town of Saint Paul — now in Minnesota — were declared to be election precincts at either of which the electors of St. Croix county might vote, and have their votes returned to and canvassed by the officers of Crawford county.

Milwaukee was first incorporated as a city at this session of the Legislature. The territory embraced in the city limits was the south half of town seven, of range twenty-two, except the northwest quarter of section twenty and the north half of section nineteen.

The city was divided into five wards, and the elective officers were a mayor for the city, three aldermen, one justice of the peace and one constable in each ward.

SOLOMON JUNEAU was elected the first mayor.

The villages of Madison, Prairieville, Sheboygan and Potosi were incorporated by special acts, and an act of the previous year vacating an alley in the village of Southport was repealed.

The Governor submitted the report of JOHN T. HAIGHT, who had been appointed an agent on the part of the Territory to select the unlocated lands granted by Congress for a university.

It appearing from the report that the granted lands had not all been yet selected, another act was passed by which NATHANIEL F. HYER was authorized to select all the lands authorized, which had not been set apart and reserved from sale by the Secretary of the Treasury for the purposes of a university by virtue of the act of Congress of June 12, 1838.

Beloit College was incorporated by a special act of incorporation. It was required to be located in the township of Beloit, Rock county, and to —

"Be erected on a plan sufficiently extensive to afford instruction in the liberal arts and sciences."

The first corporators were Reverends A. KENT, D. CLARY, S. PEET, F. BASCUM, C. WATERBURY, J. D. STEVENS, A. L. CHAPIN and R. M. PEARSON, and Messrs. G. W. HICKOX, A. RAYMOND, C. M. GOODSELL, E. W. POTTER, L. G. FISHER, W. TALCOTT, CHARLES S. HEMPSTEAD and SAMUEL HINMAN.

The name of Prairieville Academy was changed to Carroll College, and the trustees incorporated as a collegiate institution.

The "Madison Academy" was authorized to receive from the county commissioners of Dane county the sum of $2,216, which was a special fund appropriated to the county for the purpose of building an academy at Madison.

During the session of the Legislature an educational convention assembled at Madison, which appointed a committee to prepare and submit some plan for the advancement of common school education in Wisconsin.

The committee, which consisted of MORTIMER M. JACKSON, LEWIS H. LOSS, LEVI HUBBELL, M. FRANK, CALEB CROSWELL, C. M. BAKER and H. M. BILLINGS, prepared a report, which was submitted to the Legislature and which recommended the appointment of an agent —

' "To visit the different school districts, ascertain the condition of common schools, collect statistics with regard to the subject of education, and organize educational associations in the several counties and teachers' associations, and report to the Legislative Assembly, with his own suggestions and recommendations."

The committee on schools, in the Assembly, to which the subject had been referred, reported upon it favorably, together with a bill to provide for the appointment of a superintendent of common schools. The bill passed the Assembly without a division, but was defeated in the Council, only three votes—Messrs. BAKER, FRANK, and MOSES M. STRONG—being in favor of it.

Special provision was made by law for the appointment of a board of school commissioners for the city of Milwaukee.

School District No. 1, in the town of Fond du Lac, was created a corporation by the name of the "Trustees of the Franklin School." The election of a board of trustees, and the power to levy taxes, were specially provided for.

Owing to the inadequacy of the general laws, special acts were passed authorizing the levying of taxes, generally for the erection of school-houses, in School Districts Nos. 3, 4, and 16, in Dane county; in Nos. 3 and 7, in the town of "Snake Hollow," and No. 1 in the town of Wisconsin, and No. 1 in the town of Platteville, all in Grant county; No. 5 in the town of Elk Horn, Walworth county; No. 1 in the town of Rochester, Racine county, and District No. 1 in Sheboygan county.

Courts were now held in the counties of Dane, Sauk, Jefferson, Green, Rock, Walworth, and Portage, in the Second Judicial District, and an act was passed re-arranging the times of the sessions, which were semi-annual in all the counties except Portage, where only an annual term was held, on the second Monday in September.

Some important provisions were also enacted in relation to the practice and proceedings in the Circuit and Supreme courts, especially in relation to writs of *mandamus* and *quo warranto*.

An act was also passed to provide for the more convenient contesting of the election of county and other offices before the district courts.

The time had not yet come for beginning the work of constructing a railroad across the Territory from Lake Michigan to the Mississippi River, but the subject had for two or three years occupied the thoughts of the more sanguine and far-seeing.

TERRITORY OF WISCONSIN IN 1846. 499

At this session numerous petitions were presented from almost every section of the Territory asking for charters between each of the most important lake ports and some point on the Mississippi River.

Many members appeared to entertain the idea that the granting of a charter for a railroad upon any particular route would injure the prospects of the construction of one upon any other route. Some were opposed to granting any charters, and others were in favor of granting charters for any and all roads that were asked for in good faith, with an honest intention of making a serious effort to construct the work.

The feeling in the Council was much more liberal than in the House, and after much debate and delay, the Council finally passed four charters:

One from Milwaukee, *via* Janesville, to Potosi.

One from Milwaukee, *via* Madison, to Potosi.

One from Lake Michigan to the Mississippi River, leaving the termini to be defined by the company, and

One from Shebyogan, *via* Fond du Lac, to Fort Winnebago.

None of these were passed until the last day but one of the session, and owing to the shortness of the time, no action was taken upon them in the House, and if there had been, they would probably have been defeated.

A correspondent of the Galena *Gazette*, writing from Madison, and who probably gave expression to the opinions of many at that time, said:

"The only points on Lake Michigan and the Mississippi River to be connected by a railroad for the next fifty years are Chicago and Galena."

Plank roads were then regarded as more practicable and better adapted to the wants of the community, in reaching a market for their agricultural products, of which at that time wheat was the principal.

A charter was passed incorporating a company with authority to construct a road

"Of timber or plank, so that the same form a hard, smooth and even surface" from the place "where the north Madison Territorial road now crosses the range line, dividing range 19 and 20", to "within one mile of the Milwaukee River, in right direction to the west ward of Milwaukee village."

The company was also authorized to extend the road from such range line to the village of Watertown.

The company was organized, the capital subscribed and

paid by citizens of Milwaukee, the road built from Milwaukee to Watertown, and was not only of great advantage to the people of the whole Territory, but a remunerative investment for a time to the stockholders.

Another improvement of a somewhat like character, but to be constructed in a very different manner, was "a McAdam, plank, rail or turnpike road from the foot of Grand Kakalin to Winnebago Lake"—for the purpose of constructing which, the county authorities of the counties of Calumet, Fond du Lac, Winnebago and Marquette, were authorized by a special act to levy a tax not exceeding one per cent. per annum. The levying of the tax was contingent upon a vote in its favor by the legal voters of the several counties, and but little public benefit resulted from the enactment.

The growth of the Territory was by successive, if not rapid steps of progress. None of these steps were of more importance than the locating of Territorial roads which were annually authorized by the Legislative Assembly and it is the province of history to re-present these numerous steps, although they may not possess for the present generation the interest which inspired them.

Territorial roads were authorized by special laws:

From Prairieville, *via* Delafield and Summit, to the point where the United States road from Milwaukee to Madison crosses Battle Creek, in Jefferson county.

From Waupun to Winnebago Rapids in Winnebago county.

From Delafield to Hustis' Rapids.

From Milwaukee to Fond du Lac.

From Whitewater, *via* Indian Ford on Rock River and Cook's mills on section six, town four, range eleven east, and thence to the Territorial road from Milwaukee to Mineral Point, at or near the Peckatonica.

From the range line between ranges ten and eleven, corner of section eighteen and nineteen, to the house of JOHN COOK in town of Janesville.

From Jefferson, *via* Dunkirk and Cooks' Mills, to Campbell's bridge on Sugar River.

From a point on the United States road from Washington harbor to Dekora, in a northwesterly direction, *via* West Bend, to again intersect said United States road.

From Duck Creek Settlement, in Brown county, to the outlet of Winnebago Lake.

From Beloit to White Oak Springs.

From the Combe Settlement in Richland county to the Kickapoo copper mines.

From Jefferson to Madison.

From Watertown, *via* Hustis' Rapids, to Fond du Lac.

From Burlington to Janesville.

From Decora to Beaver Dam.

From section thirteen, town nine, range twelve east, to Lake Puckawa.

From the forks of the Madison and military road in Dane county to Wingville in Grant county.

From Hustis' Ford, *via* May and Foster's Mills, to Fond du Lac.

From Milwaukee, *via* Hustis' Ford, to the Fox Lake and Watertown road, at or near Major PRATT's.

From Columbus to Green Lake.

From Sheboygan, *via* Hustis' Ford, to Madison.

From Calumet to the Sheboygan and Fond du Lac road.

From Fort Winnebago, on the south side of Swan Lake, to the old road between Fort Winnebago and Madison.

From East Troy to Elk Horn.

From Columbus to Waterloo.

From Elkhorn, *via* Palmyra, to Hustis' Ford.

From Milwaukee to Fort Atkinson.

From Exeter, *via* Badger Mills, to Fort Winnebago.

From Madison to the State line between Sugar River and Pearce's Creek.

From Beloit to Madison.

From Green Bay, due west, to the Wisconsin River.

From Manitowoc, westward, to intersect the United States road from Green Bay to Fond du Lac.

From Sinipee, in Grant county, to Oak Creek pier in Milwaukee county.

From Waterloo to Beaver Dam.

From Hustis' Ford to Piperville.

From Rising's Rapids, Dodge county, to Fort Winnebago.

From Waupun to Fort Winnebago.

From Watertown to Madison.

From Watertown, *via* West Bend, to Sheboygan.

From Watertown to Lowell.

From Burlington to Delavan.

Special provision was made by law for the rebuilding and maintaining, by the town of Milwaukee and the several wards in the city of Milwaukee, of three bridges across the Milwaukee River, from the foot of Water street in the Third ward, to the foot of Ferry street in the Fifth ward; from Wisconsin street to Spring street, and from Water street in the First ward to Cherry street.

JEMISON HAMILTON was granted the privilege by special act, of erecting a toll bridge across the Peckatonica River at or near his house "in the town of New Bedford." This point is now in the heart of the city of Darlington, La'Fayette county.

The commissioners appointed at the preceding session of the Legislative Assembly, for carrying into effect an act of Congress of June, 1844, appropriating a section of land for the improvement of Grant River in the town of Potosi, submitted their report together with the report of the receiver, from which it appeared that they had caused the section (section 34, town 3, range 3 west) to be surveyed in town or village lots and "out lots." That they had examined and determined all claims to pre-emption rights presented, the valuation of which had been assessed by persons appointed by the Surveyor General, and that they had in pursuance of the act of the last session, sold all of the lots in said section of land. That the aggregate amount of all the sales was the sum of $4,130.64. That the expenditures under the said act of the Legislative Assembly were $1,405.21, leaving a balance in the hands of the receiver of $2,725.43.

The commissioners also submitted a report of Capt. JOSHUA BARNEY, U. S. civil engineer, superintending the improvement of the Dubuque harbor, who after making an examination and estimates of several different plans of improving the harbor of Potosi, recommended a direct cut from the Mississippi River to Grant River slough, the cost of which he estimated at $20,041.45.

The reports of the commissioners, receiver and engineer were referred to a committee of the House, of which Hon. THOMAS P. BURNETT was chairman which reported that:

"Although the cost of the proposed canal greatly exceeds the fund now available for its construction, and may seem a large sum to apply to such a work, yet the committee are of the opinion that the importance of the improvement to the western part of the Territory, is of such magnitude that the work ought to be undertaken and a commencement made with the funds now applicable to that purpose. This sum will be very nearly or quite sufficient, according to the estimate that has been made, to pay for the clearing and grubbing of the ground and making the first course of excavation. This much of the work can be completed during the present year, and it may reasonably be expected that Congress will appropriate a sufficient sum to finish the improvement after it shall have been commenced."

The Legislative Assembly adopted the views of the committee, and passed an act appointing JAMES F. CHAPMAN a commissioner to expend the fund in the hands of the receiver, upon the plan recommended by Capt. BARNEY. The money was faithfully expended, but the canal was not completed.

A memorial to congress was adopted asking for an additional appropriation of $17,316.02, but no appropriation was obtained.

At the same session the exclusive right and privilege, for ten years, of keeping a ferry across the Grant and Mississippi Rivers, at the place of this improvement, was granted to JAMES F. CHAPMAN, his heirs and assigns.

The construction of a dam across, the Milwaukee River, in the town of Saukville, nearly west of Ozaukee, was authorized by special act.

ABRAHAM BRAWLEY was authorized to build and maintain a dam and boom on the Wisconsin River between sections 31 and 32, town 24, range 8 east.

A boom was erected, which afterward became the property of the Stevens Point Boom Company, and is a valuable adjunct to the lumbering interests at and near the City of Stevens Point.

The "Rochester Cemetery Company," at Rochester, Racine county, was incorporated, with power to hold real and personal estate.

A general law was enacted, authorizing religious societies, by application to, and decree of, the District Court, to sell or mortgage their houses of worship or other real estate. Also of their own volition to sell or lease seats and pews in their respective houses of worship.

An act was passed to incorporate the —

"Carrollton Manufacturing Company, of Ormsbeeville, Wisconsin," with "power to manufacture cotton and woolen goods, iron and wooden wares, and merchandise, construct dams, canals, or waterways and reservoirs, flumes and races."

The business to be confined to section 28, town 15, range 23, in the county of Sheboygan, which was on the Sheboygan River, about midway between its mouth and Sheboygan Falls.

Petitions were presented in the House of Representatives complaining that the act requiring ministers of the gospel to file a copy of their credentials with the clerk of the District Court, and have the same recorded, before they should be authorized to solemnize marriages, was burdensome and expensive. The petitions were referred to the judiciary committee, which, by Mr. BURNETT, the chairman, submitted a report, setting forth the importance that the records of the county should always show the authority of officers to perform the civil rite of matrimony, and concluding

"That the inconvenience and expense complained of are not so great as to be a grievance, and that whatever it may be, it is not expedient to grant the relief prayed for, by altering the law as it now exists."

The causes for which divorces might be granted were increased by adding to the number the sentence to a State's prison or penitentiary for a term of two years or more.

Five special applications for divorce were presented, two in the Council and three in the House, upon all of which adverse reports were made by committees, except that of JOHN J. DRIGGS. In the latter case a bill was passed divorcing him from his wife, the vote in the House being 19 to 5, and in the Council 7 to 6. None of the others were brought to a vote.

The name of ADELBUT H. BISHOP, was by special law changed to ADELBUT H. HUBBARD.

The subject of the sale of intoxicating liquors and the granting of license therefor, was one which, at this time, excited the popular mind to a very great degree, and the feeling of the people was reflected by numerous petitions to the Legislative Assembly.

The prevalent idea of those who sought reform through legislative action was the repeal of all laws authorizing license, while many were in favor of total prohibition.

A bill was introduced, which provided for a novel kind of local option.

It provided that the legal voters of each town should vote for "license" or "no license." If a majority voted for "license", then the sale of liquors was to be unrestrained and *unlicensed*. If a majority voted "no license", then the sale was to be totally prohibited, and of course *unlicensed*.

It was urged in support of the bill that it took away one of the arguments of the rumseller, that he was engaged in business recognized by the law as lawful.

When the bill came up for consideration in the Council it was moved to strike out all after the enacting clause, and substitute for it that —

"Hereafter no license shall be granted for the sale of intoxicating liquors; any law of this Territory conflicting with the provisions of this section is hereby repealed."

This substitute was adopted by a vote of 7 to 6, and the bill so amended was refused a third reading by a vote of 1 to 12.

A bill upon the subject was reported in the House differing from the Council bill, in that it did not provide for local option. The House was nearly evenly divided upon all questions which arose upon it.

The first was to strike out all after the enacting clause. This prevailed by a vote of 14 to 11.

An amendment was then offered —

"That no consideration or sum of money shall be hereafter demanded or received for any tavern or grocery license to be granted within this Territory."

This was adopted by a vote of 14 to 12, and by a like vote the bill was ordered to be engrossed and read a third time.

On the next day, when the question was put on the passage of the bill, Mr. Speaker, who had voted for its third reading, changed his vote, and the bill was defeated by a tie vote, the vote being 13 to 13.

A very elaborate report was submitted by the Adjutant General, which contained a very complete history of the progress of the militia organization during the existence of the Territory — nearly ten years — and concluded with a deprecation of the policy which had substituted *enrollment* for *mustering* and training. But no change in the policy was adopted.

The occupation by the military forces of the United States of the territory upon the left bank of the Rio Grande, which by the annexation of Texas had recently been brought under the protection of the flag of the United States, resulted in a hostile collision between armed troops of Mexico and the United States, which culminated in the declaration by Congress of the existence of a war between the two nations and the providing of men and means for its prosecution.

A call was made for fifty thousand volunteers to take the field, which were apportioned among the several states, but the Territory of Wisconsin was not called upon for any organized force, except for the enrollment of one regiment as a contingent force, and the opportunity was not presented to its patriotic citizens to take an active part in the war, except as they volunteered to form part of the regiments of other states, which many of them did. One company was organized near the Illinois State line, of which JAMES COLLINS was the Captain, and joined an Illinois regiment of which Capt. COLLINS became the Colonel and AMASA COBB his Adjutant.

On the last day of the session of the Legislature, the Governor sent to the House of Representatives the proceedings of a meeting of the citizens of Muscoda, representing that an armed collision had occurred between a band of the Winnebago Indians and the citizens of that locality, which resulted in a fatal conflict, in which four of the Indians were severely, if not not mortally wounded, and that more serious consequences were expected to ensue.

It was further stated that the citizens had organized into a military company, had elected their officers, and were determined not to rest until they had killed or driven to their own ground, west of the Mississippi, every Indian on the Wisconsin.

The Governor recommended the adoption of a memorial to the Secretary of War asking that a corps of the United States dragoons be ordered to this Territory for the protection of our frontier settlements.

Resolutions to that effect were immediately adopted by the House, under a suspension of all rules, and sent to the Council where they were amended by the addition of authority to the Governor to raise a battalion of mounted volunteer riflemen for the protection of the frontier from the depredations of the Winnebago Indians.

There were no more hostile collisions between the Indians and the inhabitants.

On the 24th of February, JOHN CATLIN was appointed Secretary of the Territory in place of GEO. R. C. FLOYD, removed.

During the session of the Legislative Assembly, numerous nominations to office were made by the Governor, every one of which was confirmed by the Council, and with only one exception, without a division.

On the 29th of January, both houses met in joint convention, when SIMEON MILLS was elected Territorial printer and JOSEPH GILLETT KNAPP was elected Superintendent of Public Property.

Memorials to Congress were adopted on various subjects:
The reserved mineral lands;
A road from Prairie du Chien to La'Pointe;
For a collection district west of Lake Michigan and a port of entry at Milwaukee;
For the improvement of the Fox and Wisconsin rivers;
Relative to the "canal land," and to reduce the price of the even sections;
For an appropriation for the Potosi harbor;
For the appropriation of Fort Howard for educational purposes;
For numerous mail routes; and
For an appropriation for a penitentiary.

A very important joint resolution was adopted by the Legislative Assembly, which provided that the receiver of the canal land should pay over to the Treasurer of the Territory all moneys which might arise from any sale of the canal lands — less the expenses of the sale — and that it might be used for the same puposes as any other money in the treasury, and that so much of it as might be necessary be appropriated to the payment of the expenses of holding the convention to form a constitution for the State of Wisconsin.

With whatever justice this appropriation of a trust fund for objects entirely foreign to the trust may be criticised, it certainly provided means for paying the expenses of the convention to form a constitution, for which there did not appear to be any other available resource.

A gloom was cast over the closing days of this session, by the awful news that the dwelling house of one of the members — MARSHALL M. STRONG, of Racine — had been consumed by fire, and that his wife and his two only children had perished in the flames.

Upon the receipt of this heart-rending news on the 28th of January, both houses immediately adjourned, filled with the profoundest grief for the sad calamity which had befallen their associate.

Both houses adjourned on the 3d of February, after a session of only thirty days, which terminated the last session of the fourth Legislative Assembly.

With the close of this political year, the terms of the members of both houses closed also—the members of the Council who had been elected for four years, and of the House for two.

In the early part of this year (January) Mr. FLOYD was removed from the office of Superintendent of Lead Mines, and JAMES MITCHELL, of Galena, was appointed in his place, but he held the office only about a year before his occupation was gone.

In November a proclamation was issued by the President for the sale, in pursuance of a law passed at the previous session, of all the lands reserved on account of having been supposed to contain lead mines. The sale was to be at Mineral Point May 24, 1847.

This proclamation, indeed the passage of the law by which it was authorized, made the duties of the Superintendent of the Lead Mines merely nominal.

Notwithstanding these reservations, the official returns showed that the land sales for the previous years were quite large.

In 1844 the number of acres sold was......... 27,347.35 Amount of sales........ $34,234 19
In 1845 the number of acres sold was......... 44,437.65 Amount of sales........ 55,547 06

In both years the number of acres sold was............................. 71,785.00 Amount of sales........ $89,781 25

At different times during the ten years of Territorial government attempts had been made to organize parties with reference to national politics. Although these attempts had met with a large measure of success, the political divisions were not as perfect in local elections, with reference to national issues, as in the States. Still, those attached to the Democratic party constituted a very decided and acknowledged majority.

For some years previous to 1846, the *"Argus"* had been the only Democratic paper at Madison. It was owned and managed by two or three gentlemen, of whom SIMEON MILLS was one. Mr. MILLS was not a practical printer, although an excellent business man, and had been elected Territorial Printer, supposed to be a lucrative office.

Mr. BERIAH BROWN was a professional printer, an accomplished writer, a popular editor, and had many devoted friends. He had been elected to a responsible county office in Iowa county, and had been led by his party zeal to aid largely in establishing a Democratic paper at Mineral Point, which proved unfortunate, and cost him, as he said, "one half of all he received from the county of Iowa for official services."

Mr. BROWN determined to establish a Democratic paper at Madison, which he did, called the "*Madison Democrat*," the first number being issued on the 10th of January, 1846.

This movement was hailed with satisfaction by many who had become dissatisfied with the managers and management of the "*Argus*," and was regarded with feelings of regret by a large number of loyal and conservative Democrats, who were apprehensive that it would have the effect of splitting into fragments the Democratic party of the embryo State.

Several motives for this movement were assigned by Mr. BROWN in the first number of his paper. That to which he gave the most prominence was thus expressed :

"In common with the practical printers of the Territory, we felt it as an unjust reproach upon mechanics, that the Legislature should elect to the office of Territorial Printer a man who was not a mechanic and was at the same time enjoying another lucrative office, and from having no knowledge of the business, could not perform the duties of the office himself, or even supervise their execution in a proper manner."–

The principal other reasons were :

"Complaints from nearly all parts of the Territory of the manner in which the Territorial paper was conducted," and that its editor "had involved himself in several quarrels, both personal and local, with individuals and portions of the democratic party."

Whatever the motives, or whatever the justification, the effect was seriously to impair the harmony and effectiveness of the Democratic party.

The vote of the people, in April, was about six to one in favor of State government, every county having voted for it except Grant, where the vote was 351 for and 537 against State government.

The census showed a population of 155,277, exclusive of Chippewa, La'Pointe and Richland counties, from which no returns were received.

On the 1st of August, the Governor issued two proclamations; one making an apportionment of the members of the Council and House of Representatives among the twelve election districts into which the Legislative Assembly had divided the Territory.

The other made an apportionment of the delegates to form a constitution, among the several counties, on the basis of one delegate to each 1,300 inhabitants as provided by law.

The following table is arranged so as to show the population of each county, by election districts, as well as the number of members of each branch of the Legislative Assembly, apportioned to each election district and the number of delegates apportioned to each county:

No. of Election District.	Name of County.	Population of the County.	Population of the Election District.	No. of Members of Council.	No. of Members of Ho. of Reps.	No. of Delegates in Convention.
1	Racine	17,983	17,983	2	2	14
2	Walworth	13,439	13,439	1	2	10
3	Rock	12,405	12,405	1	2	10
4	Iowa	14,916	14,916	1	3	11
	Richland	No returns				1
5	Grant	12,034	12,034	1	2	9
6	Green	4,758				4
	Dane	8,289	14,050	1	3	6
	Sauk	1,003				1
7	Crawford	1,444				1
	St. Croix	1,419	2,863	3	1	1
	Chippewa	No returns				1
	La Pointe	No returns				1
8	Dodge	7,787	16,467	1	3	6
	Jefferson	8,680				7
9	Milwaukee	15,925	15,925	1	3	12
10	Washington	7,473	9,110	1	1	6
	Sheboygan	1,637				1
11	Manitowoc	620				1
	Brown	2,662				2
	Calumet	836				1
	Winnebago	732	12,292	1	2	1
	Fond du Lac	3,544				3
	Marquette	989				1
	Portage	931				1
	Columbia	1,969				2
12	Waukesha	13,793	13,793	1	2	11
	Totals	155,277	155,277	13	26	125

The estimate of population assumed by the Legislative Assembly for fixing a basis for the number of delegates was 117,000, which would have given about one hundred members of the convention, but the excess exhibited by the census over this estimate resulted in a much more numerous body than had been anticipated.

As a rule, to which however there were some exceptions, party nominations were made by both parties for delegates to the convention, and the persons elected were generally attached to the party which was in the ascendant in the particular county in which they were elected.

It was a subject of remark that the ablest men of both parties were willing to be, and not unfrequently desirous of being candidates for member of the convention to frame the fundamental law of the State. The result was that both the parties generally nominated their best men, and while men of the highest order of talent in the majority party in any particular county were elected, others of equal, if not superior talents in the minority party were defeated solely upon political issues.

A very large majority of the convention was composed of men elected by the Democratic party, but there was a sufficient number of the members who belonged to the Whig party of that day to constitute a respectable minority. Among these it is not invidious towards others to mention the names of HENRY S. BAIRD, J. ALLEN BARBER, JAMES D. DOTY and JOHN H. TWEEDY, as being the most prominent.

There were others who prided themselves upon being independents, and who attached but little importance to party association and disclaimed party allegiance. The most marked and able of this class were THOMAS P. BURNETT and ANDREW E. ELMORE

It was, however, among those who were devoted to the principles and the policies of the Democratic party, perhaps for the reason stated, that the greatest number of the most brilliant names in the convention were to be found. Of these many have since occupied positions of distinction in the State. Some of them, alphabetically arranged, are mentioned:

CHARLES M. BAKER, HIRAM BARBER, SAMUEL W. BEALL, WARREN CHASE, WM. M. DENNIS, STODDARD JUDD, FREDERICK S. LOVELL, DAVID NOGGLE, THEODORE PRENTISS, ALEXANDER W. RANDALL, GEORGE REED, EDWARD G. RYAN, A.

HYATT SMITH, GEORGE B. SMITH, JOHN Y. SMITH, WILLIAM R. SMITH, ELIJAH STEELE, MARSHALL M. STRONG, D. A. J. UPHAM and NINIAN E. WHITESIDES.

On the day fixed by law, October 5, the delegates elect assembled at the Capitol at noon. In the absence of any mode of organization previously prescribed, the venerable WILLIAM R. SMITH, by the request of many delegates, called the convention to order when *pro tem.* officers were elected on motion and without division.

A committee was appointed to examine the credentials of the delegates.

The following were the delegates who were elected:

BROWN.
DAVID AGRY,
HENRY S. BAIRD.

CALUMET.
LEMUEL GOODELL.

COLUMBIA.
JEREMIAH DRAKE,
LA'FAYETTE HILL.

CRAWFORD.
PETER A. R. BRACE.

DANE.
JOHN M. BABCOCK,
ABEL DUNNING,
BENJAMIN FULLER,
NATHANIEL F. HYER,
GEORGE B. SMITH,
JOHN Y. SMITH.

DODGE.
HIRAM BARBER,
WM. M. DENNIS,
BENJAMIN GRANGER,
STODDARD JUDD,
JOHN H. MANAHAN,
HORACE D. PATCH.

FOND DU LAC.
WARREN CHASE,
MOSES S. GIBSON,
LORENZO HAZEN.

GRANT.
J. ALLEN BARBER,
LORENZO BEVANS,
THOMAS P. BURNETT,
DANIEL R. BURT,
THOMAS CRUSON,
JAMES GILMORE,

GRANT.
NEELY GRAY,
FRANKLIN Z. HICKS,
JAMES R. VINEYARD.

GREEN.
DAVIS BOWEN,
HIRAM BROWN,
WILLIAM C. GREEN,
NOAH PHELPS.

IOWA.
ANDREW BURNSIDE,
ELIHU B. GOODSELL,
THOMAS JAMES,
THOMAS JENKINS,
WILLIAM I. MADDEN,
MOSES MEEKER,
DANIEL M. PARKINSON,
WM. R. SMITH,
MOSES M. STRONG,
JOSHUA S. WHITE,
NINIAN E. WHITESIDES.

JEFFERSON.
ELIHU L. ATWOOD,
SAMUEL T. CLOTHIER,
GEORGE HYER,
THEODORE PRENTISS,
AARON RANKIN,
PATRICK ROGAN,
PETER H. TURNER.

LA'POINTE.
JAMES P. HAYS.

MANITOWOC.
EVANDER M. SOPER.

MARQUETTE.
SAMUEL W. BEALL.

MILWAUKEE.
CHARLES E. BROWNE,
HORACE CHASE,
JOHN COOPER,
JOHN CRAWFORD,
GARRETT M. FITZGERALD,
WALLACE W. GRAHAM,
FRANCIS HUEBSCHMANN,
ASA KINNEY,
JAMES MAGONE,
JOHN H. TWEEDY,
DON A. J. UPHAM,
GARRET VLIET.

PORTAGE.
HENRY C. GOODRICH.

RACINE.
STEPHEN O. BENNETT,
JAMES B. CARTER,
NATHANIEL DICKINSON,
HAYNES FRENCH,
JAMES H. HALL,
DANIEL HARKIN,
CHAUNCEY KELLOGG,
FREDERICK S. LOVELL,
CHATFIELD H. PARSONS,
EDWARD G. RYAN,
ELIJAH STEELE,
MARSHALL M. STRONG,
T. S. STOCKWELL,
VICTOR M. WILLARD,

ROCK.
JAMES CHAMBERLAIN,
JOHN HACKETT,
GEORGE B. HALL,
SANFORD P. HAMMOND,
ISRAEL INMAN, Jr.,
JOSEPH KINNEY, Jr.,
DAVID L. MILLS,
DAVID NOGGLE,
JOSEPH S. PIERCE,
A. HYATT SMITH.

RICHLAND.
EDWARD COMBE.

SAUK.
WILLIAM H. CLARK.

ST. CROIX.
WILLIAM HOLCOMBE.

SHEBOYGAN.
DAVID GIDDINGS.

WALWORTH.
CHARLES M. BAKER,
WILLIAM BELL,
WILLIAM BERRY,
JOSEPH BOWKER,
JOHN W. BOYD,
M. T. HAWES,
LYMAN H. SEAVER,
SEWALL SMITH,
JOSIAH TOPPING,
SOLOMOUS WAKELY,

WASHINGTON.
HOPEWELL COXE,
EDWARD H. JANSSEN,
CHARLES J. KERN,
BOSTWICK O'CONNOR,
PATRICK TOLAND,
JOEL F. WILSON.

WAUKESHA.
BARNES BABCOCK,
CHARLES BURCHARD,
ELISHA W. EDGERTON,
PITTS ELLIS,
ANDREW E. ELMORE,
WILLIAM R. HESK,
BENJAMIN HUNKINS,
JAMES M. MOORE,
RUFUS PARKS,
ALEXANDER W. RANDALL,
GEORGE REED.

WINNEBAGO.
JAMES DUANE DOTY.

No delegate was elected from Chippewa county.

At the assembling of the convention ninety-five delegates were present and twenty-nine absent. Of the absentees, eight took their seats during the first week, eighteen during the second week, one on the 6th of November, and two, Messrs. STOCKWELL of Racine and HAWES of Walworth, did not attend the convention at all. So that of the 125 possible delegates, only 122 were ever in attendance, and there was never a day when less than 13 of these were absent, and some times the absentees numbered forty or more.

The journal shows that the ayes and noes were called 274 times, and that the highest vote recorded was 109, while the lowest was 67, but it generally ranged from 80 to 100 and one fifth part of the votes were from 100 to 109.

The members were not sworn, although at the beginning of the fifth week of the session, Mr. RANDALL introduced a resolution, that each of them take an oath to faithfully and impartially perform his duties as a member and support the constitution of the United States. The resolution was laid on the table and not again called up.

The establishment of a second Democratic paper at Madison has been mentioned. As a consequence there was a divided sentiment among the Democratic members of the convention in reference to the bestowal of the little patronage at their command.

The question of an elective judiciary was one which had been considerably discussed before the meeting of the convention. Some of the Democratic members were well-known to favor it; others to be opposed to it, and others to be undecided. The *Democrat* was in favor of it while the *Argus* had neither advocated it nor opposed it. The opinions of the delegates in reference to the *Democrat* and *Argus,* and in reference to an elective judiciary were used with much effect in the election of the President of the convention. DON A. J. UPHAM, who was elected on the fifth ballot, was ranked with those who called themselves "progressive" Democrats, of whose views the *Democrat* claimed to be an exponent and advocate, as he was also classed with the friends of an elective judiciary.

On the first ballot Mr. UPHAM received thirty-three votes against sixty for other members of the convention, who either had no opinions upon these questions or else such as were opposed to those of Mr. UPHAM. His vote continued to increase, and on the fifth ballot he received fifty-two votes, against forty-one for all others.

There was a little strife over the election of Secretary, for which office LA'FAYETTE KELLOGG and WM. W. TREADWAY were candidates. Mr. KELLOGG was elected, having received 48 votes to 41 for Mr. TREADWAY and 3 scattering.

The other officers were elected *viva voce* on nomination and without much division. The principal ones were HIRAM TAYLOR, Assistant Secretary, and JOHN STARKWEATHER, Sergeant-at-Arms.

A resolution was adopted as soon as the officers were elected,—

"That the Secretary be directed to invite the resident clergymen of Madison to attend alternately and open the convention each morning with prayer."

When the convention met it was of course without any rules regulating its proceedings. It was a rule unto itself.

Mr. A. HYATT SMITH on the first day offered a resolution that the rules of the Council, so far as applicable, be adopted as the rules of the convention until others were adopted.

On motion of Mr. JUDD this resolution was laid on the table and a committee of seven appointed to draft rules for the convention, of which Mr. JUDD was appointed chairman, who on the next day reported a series of seventeen rules, regulating the most important of the proceedings.

The fifth of the rules was an innovation upon the usual proceedings of deliberative bodies. It was, that all propositions should be considered in the convention, and not in committee of the whole. The convention refused to adopt it.

A part of the eighth rule provided that no member should speak longer than —————————— at any one time. After an unsuccessful attempt to fill the blank, that part of the rule was stricken out.

The twelfth rule provided that the ayes and noes might be called at the request of any eight members. This was amended by striking out eight and inserting fifteen.

The thirteenth provided that one fourth of the members present might make a call of the convention and require absent members to be sent for. This was amended by striking out "one fourth" and inserting "fifteen or one fifth," and so amended was adopted.

A new rule was then adopted in lieu of the fifth, providing for the mode of conducting proceedings in committee of the whole, when the rules reported, with these modifications, were adopted.

In about two weeks these rules were revised and an entire new series adopted.

Various propositions were made in reference to the mode of determining the number of standing committees to be appointed, with their appropriate designations, when the matter was referred to a committee of thirteen, which the next day made a report recommending the appointment of twenty-two distinct committees to consist of five members each.

In the afternoon of the next day (the fourth of the convention) the President announced the appointment of the twenty-two committees. There was nothing remarkable about the appointment, except what subsequently occurred in reference to the committee "on the organization and functions of the judiciary."

That committee as appointed by the President consisted of Messrs. BAKER, RYAN, HIRAM BARBER, WM. R. SMITH and O'CONNOR. It was well understood that all the members of this committee were in favor of an elective judiciary, which at that time was an experiment, except Mr. RYAN, whose opinions as subsequently disclosed were in favor of a judiciary appointed by the Governor, with the advice and consent of three fourths of the Senate.

As soon as the committees were announced Mr. HIRAM BARBER moved that the judiciary committee be increased by the appointment of four additional members. The motion was opposed by Mr. MOSES M. STRONG and supported by Mr. WILLIAM R. SMITH, and was adopted.

Mr. RYAN stated that he regarded the action of the convention as a direct censure upon the committee and the chair. The original proposition, he said, referred to the committee of thirteen, was that the committee should consist of seven members, and that committee had recommended a reduction of the number to five. Nothing, he continued, had been said all this time against the number of the judiciary committee, but as soon as it was announced a motion was made to increase the committee and it was sustained. Messrs. JUDD and HIRAM BARBER denied that any censure was implied or intended and the latter disclaimed any such intention in making the motion. Mr. RYAN still persisted and said that the action of the convention would be judged by the act itself and not by the unexpressed intentions of the mover. It would appear on the journal with no proviso. The fact was that the convention had voted five a sufficient number, but when the committee was announced they voted not only that the number was not enough but that those who were appointed were incompetent.

Mr. GEO. B. SMITH did not so construe the action of the convention. He hoped the committee would be increased, and that the gentleman from Racine (RYAN) would still retain his station in the committee.

Mr. MARSHALL M. STRONG said the effect of the motion was as his colleague (RYAN) thought. He was on trial. The convention said they were not satisfied with the committee. The suspicion of incompetency was on the record.

Mr. A. HYAT SMITH said he was satisfied that it might be construed into censure. He would, therefore, move a reconsideration of the vote.

The motion was reconsidered but the question recurring again on the motion to increase the committee, it was carried by a vote of 48 to 42.

Mr. RYAN then asked to be excused from serving on the committee, and he was excused.

The chair then announced the following additions to the committee, Messrs. BAIRD, J. ALLEN BARBER, MOSES M. STRONG, MARSHALL M. STRONG and STEELE.

Mr. MOSES M. STRONG said he could not consent to serve on the committee after what had transpired. The gentleman from Racine (RYAN) thought the motion and the first vote a reflection on him. If so the last was a direct insult. He asked to be excused and his request was granted. Messrs. MARSHALL M. STRONG and STEEL were also by their request excused, and the committee was filled up to the number of nine by the appointment of Messrs. AGRY, GEO. B. SMITH and TWEEDY.

The matter of the disposition of the printing of the convention and its journal, was one which created no inconsiderable feeling among many members of the convention.

On the second day of the session Mr. GRAY proposed by resolution the appointment of a committee to receive proposals.

On the fourth day the resolution offered by Mr. GRAY was taken up, when Mr. BAKER proposed an amendment that BENJAMIN HOLT (he was the representative of the *Argus*) be employed to do the incidental printing of the convention and print the journal of its proceedings.

Mr. ELMORE offered a substitute for this amendment —
"That a printer to the convention be elected forthwith *viva voce*."

The substitute was adopted. The names of the members were then called, who responded with the names of the persons for whom they voted. The result was 50 votes for BERIAH BROWN, 44 for BENJAMIN HOLT and 2 for WM. W. WYMAN.

These preliminary and comparatively unimportant matters having been disposed of, the convention was ready to enter upon the important work of framing a constitution.

There was not much delay. On Friday, the fifth day of the session, the committee on banks and banking, by Mr. RYAN, its chairman, submitted the first report, accompanied by an article designed to prohibit banks of issue, and to inhibit the exercise by corporations of any banking powers whatever.

This article was the real prominent cause which resulted in the rejection of the constitution, and although it was somewhat modified in form, the spirit of it was retained and adopted. It is deemed of sufficient importance to insert the article at length as it was reported, and to state the important modifications, as well as the article, in the form it was finally adopted.

The article, as reported, was as follows :

"1. There shall be no bank of issue within this State.

2. The Legislature shall have no power to create, authorize or incorporate in any manner or form, any bank or other institution or corporation having any banking power or privilege whatever.

3. The Legislature shall have no power to confer in any manner or form, upon any person or persons, corporations or institutions whatever, any banking power or privilege whatever.

4. No person or persons, corporation or institution, whatever, shall under any pretense or authority whatever, in any manner or form whatever, make sign or issue within this State any paper money, or any bank note, promissory note, bill, order, check, certificate of deposit, or other evidence of debt whatever, intended to circulate as money; and any person or persons, or any officer or other agent of any corporation or institution so doing shall, upon conviction thereof, be fined in a sum not less than ten thousand dollars, and imprisoned in the penitentiary not less than five years.

5. No person or persons shall utter, pass or pay or give or receive in payment, any paper money or any bank note, promissory note, bill, order, check, certificate of deposit, or other evidence of debt, whatever, intended to circulate, as money which shall purport to have been issued in this State, before or after the adoption of this constitution, by any person or persons, corporation or institution whatever; and any person or persons so doing shall, upon conviction thereof, be fined in a sum not less than five hundred dollars or imprisoned not less than three months, or both.

6. No corporation within this State shall receive deposits of money, make discounts or buy or sell bills of exchange, and any officer or other agent of any corporation so doing shall, upon conviction thereof, be fined in a sum not less than five thousand dollars, and imprisoned not less than two years.

7. It shall be the duty of the Legislature, from time to time as may be necessary, to pass all acts requisite to enforce any provision of this article.

E. G. RYAN,
Chairman."

This article, with another on the same subject submitted two days later, by Mr. GIBSON, the minority of the committee, were considered in committee of the whole for four days and a most exhaustive discussion of the subject of banks and banking ensued.

At this time the paper money currency of the whole country was in a deplorable condition. Most of the banks of issue had suspended specie payments, and the bank notes in circulation were regarded with great distrust. In the southwestern part of the Territory the circulating medium was exclusively gold and silver, mostly foreign coin. English sovereigns were paid out and were received at $4.90, French five-francs at 95c. In the eastern part a heterogeneous currency existed, made up of the bank notes of the Eastern States — mostly New York and New England — and of the certificates of deposit of the Wisconsin Marine and Fire Insurance Company, usually known as "Mitchell's Bank." These had never been discredited or their redemption at the bank in coin refused, and notwithstanding the general belief and the deliberate declaration of the Legislative Assembly, that their issue was not authorized by the charter, they had the general confidence of the community in the whole valley of the Mississippi.

In this condition of the currency there was an almost universal sentiment throughout Wisconsin of opposition to the conferring by law of banking powers and privileges upon individuals or corporations, especially the power of issuing paper money currency. At the same time there was a very prevalent sentiment that all departments of banking, except the issue of currency, including deposits, discount and exchange, should be left entirely free and untrammelled to individuals.

These sentiments were almost unanimously reflected by the delegates to the convention, while there was a respectable minority who regarded them as transient and temporary, and that the time would come in the growth and progress of the State when the creation of corporations, with all the usual powers of banks, would be demanded by the wants of the people.

The "RYAN report," as it was called, to the extent that it

provided a constitutional prohibition of the creation of banking corporations, or the issue in any way or by any means, of paper money currency, expressed the sentiment of about four fifths of the members of the convention, while there was not a majority who were willing to carry their opinions to what the report presented as the logical result of providing "pains and penalties" for violating the constitutional prohibition.

Hence there was little room and less need for argument upon the important principles contained in the report, and the discussion was limited mainly to the question of detail whether the remedy for the violation of the constitution should be contained in the constitution itself, or left to subsequent legislative action.

Although the question of incorporating "pains and penalties" into the constitution was the only one about which there was much difference of opinion, yet the discussion took a very wide range.

Those who spoke in favor of the article as reported by the committee were Messrs. RYAN, A. H. SMITH, J. Y. SMITH, WHITESIDES, ELMORE, NOGGLE, BEVANS, CLARK, KELLOGG, HARKIN and MOSES M. STRONG.

Those who spoke against it, and in favor of various modifications of it were Messrs. GIBSON, WM. R. SMITH, GEORGE B. SMITH, BAKER, BURNETT, HIRAM BARBER, RANDALL, JUDD, BEALL, STEELE, DENNIS, PARKS, HICKS, HORACE CHASE, HUNKINS, BURCHARD and MOORE.

Numerous amendments were proposed both in committee of the whole and after it was reported back to the convention, several of which were adopted.

When it became apparent that a majority were opposed to the penal features of the article, Mr. RYAN proposed a substitute for those sections containing such features, which was adopted, as was also a new section proposed by him declaring that it should not be lawful to circulate after 1847 bank notes less than ten dollars, nor after 1849 less than twenty dollars.

The following is the article as finally adopted:

"ON BANKS AND BANKING.

SECTION 1. There shall be no bank of issue within this State.

SECTION 2. The legislature shall not have power to authorize or incorporate by any general or special law any bank or other institution having any banking power or privilege or to confer upon any corporation, institution, person or persons any banking power or privilege.

SECTION 3. It shall not be lawful for any corporation, institution, person or persons within this State, under any pretense or authority, to make or issue any paper money, note, bill, certificate or other evidence of debt whatever, intended to circulate as money.

SECTION 4. It shall not be lawful for any corporation within this State, under any pretense or authority to exercise the business of receiving deposits of money, making discounts or buying or selling bills of exchange or to do any other banking business whatever.

SECTION 5. No branch or agency of any banking institution of the United States or of any State or Territory within or without the United States shall be established or maintained within this State.

SECTION 6. It shall not be lawful to circulate within this State after the year 1847, any paper money, note, bill, certificate or other evidence of debt whatever, intended to circulate as money, issued without this State of any denomination less than ten dollars, or after the year 1849 of any denomination less than twenty dollars.

SECTION 7. The legislature shall, at its first session after the adoption of this constitution, and from time to time thereafter, as may be necessary, enact adequate penalties for the punishment of all violations and evasions of the provisions of this article."

An amendment was proposed by Mr. TWEEDY which provided that banking associations might be formed under general laws but that any such law should be submitted to a vote of the electors at a general election and be approved by a majority of the voters at such election before it becomes a law. For this amendment there were but 21 votes and 80 against it.

Another proposition was submitted by Mr. REED for the separate submission of an article, giving to the legislature powers similar to those proposed in the amendment offered by Mr. TWEEDY. But the convention would have no separate submission and the proposition of Mr. REED was indefinitely postponed by a vote of 65 to 30.

The next article considered by the convention was that " ON SUFFRAGE AND THE ELECTIVE FRANCHISE."

In view of the opposition and excited feeling which had been exhibited to the acts of the Legislative Assembly conferring upon unnaturalized foreigners the right of voting for or against State government, and for delegates to the convention, it would seem reasonable to have expected some exhibitions of that feeling in the convention.

The article, in that respect, only required the declaration of intention as a qualification of the right of suffrage. And, although there might have been, in committee of the whole, some attempt to restrict the right to citizens, yet if there was, it was so feebly sustained that it was never renewed in the convention, where the ayes and noes could be had.

The principal controversy in the discussion of this article was upon the subject of negro suffrage.

This arose in the first instance upon a proposition of Mr. BAKER for a separate submission of an article giving the right of suffrage to "colored male citizens." The proposition was discussed at great length, and defeated by a vote of 47 to 51.

The article was then adopted substantially as reported by the committee, except that voting by ballot was substituted for a *viva voce* vote, as recommended by the committee.

Afterward a resolution was introduced by Mr. RANDALL for the separate submission of a separate article, which provided that all colored male citizens should have the right to vote for all elective officers, and after being amended so as to provide that they should also be eligible to all offices, was adopted by a vote of 53 to 46. The delegates who changed votes on this question were Messrs. BURCHARD, GRAHAM, HACKETT, JANSSEN, and WILSON.

THOMAS P. BURNETT, one of the delegates from Grant county, was one of the most distinguished members of the convention.

Detained at his residence by the sickness of his wife and mother, he did not take his seat until the 14th of October, and remained only ten days, when he was called to his home by their more serious illness.

On the first day of November his mother died at the age of seventy-three, and four days later, on the fifth, Mr. BURNETT and his wife both, on the same day, yielded to the same fatal disease, and their mortal remains were buried in one common grave.

It was not until Tuesday, the 10th of November — so slow were the means of communication at that time between the Capital and his secluded home — that Mr. J. ALLEN BARBER made the announcement to the convention of the death of his illustrious colleague.

The usual resolutions of respect and sorrow were adopted and as a further mark of respect the convention adjourned over until the following Thursday.

THOMAS PENDLETON BURNETT was born in Pittsylvania county, Virginia, September 3, 1800. When he was but a child his father migrated to Kentucky. He studied law, was admitted to the bar, and commenced practice at Paris, Kentucky. In October, 1829, he was appointed sub-Indian agent at Prairie du Chien, and removed there in the following month of June.

In December, 1836, he married LUCIA MARIA, second daughter of Rev. ALFRED BRUNSON, then about twenty years of age. In the spring of 1837 he changed his residence to Cassville in Grant county, and soon after removed to a large and valuable farm, which he had made in the town of Patch Grove, where he continued to live until his death.

On the 27th of October, the committee on the organization and functions of the judiciary, in the formation of which there had been so much trouble, by Mr. C. M. BAKER, its chairman, submitted an extended report, accompanied by an article on the subject, which was proposed as part of the constitution.

The report says :

"The leading features of the system proposed for adoption are briefly these:

First, a supreme bench composed of three justices distinct from the circuit judges.

Second, five circuit courts subject to increase or modification as the Legislature shall deem expedient.

Third, the union of law and equity powers in the judges of the supreme and circuit courts, reserving to the Legislature the right to establish a distinct court of chancery whenever it shall be deemed expedient.

Fourth, interchange of circuits by the circuit judges, so that no judge shall preside in the same circuit more than one year in five successive years; and

Fifth, the election of the supreme and circuit court judges by the people, the former by general ticket, the latter by districts."

The largest part of the report was devoted to presenting the arguments in favor of an elective judiciary.

Two members of the committee, Messrs. GEORGE B. SMITH and O'CONNOR, submitted the next day a minority report, which differed from the majority report in only one very important feature.

It proposed a separate supreme court of three judges, elected by the State at large, and five district judges, one to be elected in each of the five districts, and that moreover there should be elected in each county, two or three associate judges, and that the district judge and the associate judges should form the district court of that county, and that the associate judges in each county should have jurisdiction of all probate matters.

It was not until the 19th of November that the articles relative to the judiciary came up for consideration. They were then considered in committee of the whole where they were discussed and amended for four days and some very material changes were made.

The sentiment in favor of an elective judiciary proved to be so strong, that only a small part of the time was spent upon that question. The vote in favor of it was 78 to 20. The twenty were Messrs. ATWOOD, J. M. BABCOCK, BAIRD, BRACE, CLOTHIER, DRAKE, ELMORE, HACKETT, HUNKINS, GEO. HYER, KELLOGG, PRENTISS, RANDALL, ROGAN, RYAN, MARSHALL M. STRONG, MOSES M. STRONG, TWEEDY, VLIET and WILLARD.

The principal controversy was, whether there should be a separate Supreme Court, or whether the circuit judges should constitute the Supreme Court. This was known as the *nisi prius* system.

These differences were adjusted by a proposition which was finally adopted by a vote of 77 to 12, in this form:

"For the term of five years from the first election of the judges of the circuit courts, and thereafter until the Legislature shall otherwise provide, the judges of the several circuit courts shall be judges of the Supreme Court," etc.

Mr. RYAN moved, while this proposition was pending, to strike out the "five year" provision, so as to make the *nisi prius* system permanent and unchangeable.

This amendment was lost by a vote of 30 to 58.

It was proposed to strike out the provision in these words:

"No election for judges, or for any single judge, shall be held within thirty days of any other general election."

The motion to strike out was lost by a vote of 30 to 63.

The article as finally amended was adopted by a vote of 86 to 13. The thirteen were Messrs. BAIRD, J. ALLEN BARBER, CLOTHIER, COXE, CRAWFORD, ELMORE, GEORGE HYER, PRENTISS, RANDALL, RYAN, MOSES M. STRONG, TWEEDY, and WILLARD.

Wisconsin was a pioneer in many reforms. Perhaps the most noteworthy of novelties in its first attempt to adopt a State constitution, was the incorporation into the fundamental law of a provision securing to married women the right to their separate property, and to debtors the exemption of a homestead from the claims of their creditors.

The article upon these subjects met with strenuous opposition. With some, because they were opposed to the ideas which it embodied; with others, who, while they would have consented to the experiment as a legal enactment, liable to repeal, were unwilling to adopt it as a constitutional provision; while still others objected that the two ideas, of married women's rights and homestead exemption, had no necessary connection or association with each other, and that incorporating the two in one article was a species of "log rolling" which ought not to be permitted.

The article as finally adopted was as follows:

"SECTION 1. All property, real and personal, of the wife, owned by her at the time of her marriage, and also that acquired by her after marriage, by gift, devise, descent, or otherwise than from her husband, shall be her separate property. Laws shall be passed providing for the registry of the wife's property, and more clearly defining the rights of the wife thereto, as well as to property held by her with her husband, and for carrying out the provisions of this section. Where the wife has a separate property from that of the husband the same shall be liable for the debts of the wife contracted before marriage.

"SECTION 2. Forty acres of land to be selected by the owner thereof, or the homestead of a family not exceeding forty acres, which said land or homestead shall not be included within any city or village, and shall not exceed in value one thousand dollars or instead thereof (at the option of the owner) any lot or lots in any city or village, being the homestead of a family and not exceeding in value one thousand dollars, owned and occupied by any resident of this State, shall not be subject to forced sale on execution for any debt or debts growing out of or founded upon contract, either express or implied, made after the adoption of this constitution. *Provided*, That such exemption shall not affect in any manner any mechanic's or laborer's lien or any mortgage thereon lawfully obtained, nor shall the owner, if a married man, be at liberty to alienate such real estate unless by consent of the wife."

While the article was under consideration a substitute for the first section was offered by Mr. TWEEDY, providing that the Legislature should enact suitable laws to effect the objects of the section. This was defeated by a vote of 43 to 56.

Much controversy arose as to the phraseology of the second section, and several different forms of expression were proposed and rejected, but to MR. NOGGLE belongs the honor of proposing the form of words in which it was adopted.

No separate vote was taken upon each of the two sections, but the entire article was passed by a vote of 61 to 34.

Mr. MARSHALL M. STRONG had been a strenuous opponent of this article and of each of its component parts, and had proposed several amendments to it which were rejected. After recording his vote against it as one of the 34, he left the hall of the convention to return no more, and on the evening of that day the President presented his resignation as a member of the convention.

The resignation contained no reason, but it was generally understood that the passage of this article was the immediate moving cause. At any rate, from that time forward he opposed the adoption of the constitution, and the adoption of this article was a prominent cause assigned for his opposition.

It was provided in the schedule, which formed a part of the constitution, that it should be submitted to a vote of the electors on the first Tuesday of April, 1847.

The history given of the first convention is limited to the subjects of banks and banking, negro suffrage, judiciary and the article in relation to the rights of married women and homestead exemption. This is not because the interest of the convention was confined to these, but because they constituted the principal points of attack of those who opposed the ratification of the constitution and succeeded in defeating it.

The convention adjourned on the 16th December, and during the remaining two weeks of the year nothing occurred of sufficient importance to be worthy of record.

CHAPTER XXVIII.

TERRITORY OF WISCONSIN — 1847.

There was a very great contrast between the anticipations of a change from a Territorial to a State government that pervaded the people of the Territory in the early part of the year 1846, and those which existed at the beginning of the year 1847.

Then little doubt existed that a change was imminent, and the vote in April of five eighths of the voters in favor of it seemed to insure it. As soon as circumstances would admit a convention to form a constitution was held, the result and many of the details of whose proceedings have been given.

Now, at the advent of what had been generally supposed would be the last year of Territorial government, a great change and with many a great disappointment had fallen upon the spirit of their anticipations.

The resignation a few days before the adjournment of

the convention, of one of its most prominent, able and influential members, and withal one of the recognized leaders of the Democratic party, for the avowed reason of dissatisfaction with the constitution, and the avowed purpose of making that dissatisfaction effective in its defeat if possible, produced a marked effect in promoting the opposition to its adoption, and with the co-operation of other prominent democrats, rendered it impossible to obtain for it the support of the dominant party as a party measure.

The result was the development of a very powerful opposition to the adoption of the constitution, consisting of almost the entire body of voters in the Whig party, and a large number — perhaps a moiety — of those in the Democratic party.

This opposition was exhibited from and before the beginning of the year until the decision of the question on the first Tuesday of April. But a statement of the grounds of it and its modes must be postponed for some account of the congressional and home legislation affecting the Territory which was occurring during this period.

The twenty-ninth Congress which commenced its second session on the seventh day of December, 1846, did not act on the hypothesis that the constitution would not be adopted by the people, but during that session passed "An act for the admission of the State of Wisconsin into the Union."

The preamble recited that

"WHEREAS, the people of the Territory of Wisconsin did on the sixteenth day of December, 1846, by a convention of delegates called and assembled for that purpose, form for themselves a constitution and State government, which said constitution is republican; and said convention having asked the admission of said Territory into the Union as a State on an equal footing with the original states." The act then prescribed "That the State of Wisconsin be, and the same is hereby declared to be, one of the United States of America, and is hereby admitted into the Union on an equal footing with the original states in all respects whatever."

The first constitution declared that the State consented to and accepted the boundaries prescribed in the act of Congress of August 6th, 1846, which adopted the St. Croix River from near its source to its mouth as the western boundary, but proposed to Congress, in the article on boundaries, the following alteration

"As the preference of the State of Wisconsin, and if the same shall be assented and agreed to by the Congress of the United States, then the same shall be and forever remain obligatory on the State of Wisconsin, viz.: Leaving the aforesaid boundary line at the first rapids in the River St. Louis; thence in a direct line southwardly to a point fifteen miles east of the most easterly point in Lake St. Croix; thence due south to the main channel of the Mississippi River or Lake Pepin; thence down the said main channel as prescribed in said act."

This "direct line southwardly," if it had been adopted as the boundary between Wisconsin and Minnesota, would have run near the range line between ranges seventeen and eighteen west, leaving out of Wisconsin the whole of the St. Croix River below where the boundary intersected it, about half of Pierce, St. Croix and Polk counties and a large part of Burnett county.

The act of Congress gave its assent to the change of boundary proposed in the first article of the constitution, and if the constitution had been adopted, the western boundary of the State would have been that expressed as the "preference of the State" in the constitution.

But another section of the act of admission declared it to be a fundamental condition of the admission of said State of Wisconsin into the Union, that the constitution adopted at Madison on the 16th day of December, 1846, shall be assented to by the qualified electors in the manner and at the time prescribed in the ninth section of the twentieth article of said constitution.

The appropriations by Congress for the salaries of the Territorial officers and for legislative expenses, were the same as the preceding year.

No appropriations were made at this session for rivers or harbors. A few were made for light-houses, among which was one for a light-house at Southport of $4,000, and at or near Tail Point, at the Mouth of Fox River, $4,000.

An act was passed creating a new land district, called the Chippewa Land District, which included all the territory between the Mississippi River, and the fourth principal meridian north of town 22, and all between the fourth meridian and the Wisconsin River north of town 29.

The right to enter two hundred acres of land, at $1.25 per acre, was granted to the citizens of Beetown, in Grant county, for the use and benefit of the occupants thereof. It had been reserved from sale as mineral lands, and the village of Beetown had been built upon it.

The right of pre-emption to the northeast quarter and east one half of the northwest quarter of section 26, town 1, range

TERRITORY OF WISCONSIN IN 1847.   529

1 east, was granted to PHILIP F. DERRING and ROBERT H. CHAMPION. This was valuable mineral land, had long been "claimed" by Messrs. DERRING and CHAMPION, though reserved from sale, and the village of New Diggings had grown up upon it.

The first session of the fifth Legislative Assembly was convened at Madison on the 4th day of January, 1847.

The members were elected under a new apportionment made by the Governor, in pursuance of a law passed at the preceding session, and was based upon the population June 1, 1846, as shown by the census taken that year.

The effect of the apportionment was to give to the eastern counties an increased representation, which was taken from the western counties.

The following is a list of the members of each house:

COUNCIL.

Brown, Columbia, Fond du Lac, Manitowoc, Marquette, Portage and Winnebago: MASON C. DARLING.
Milwaukee: HORATIO N. WELLS.
Racine: FREDERICK S. LOVELL and MARSHALL M. STRONG.
Walworth: HENRY CLARK.
Rock: ANDREW PALMER.
Iowa and Richland: WILLIAM SINGER.
Waukesha: JOSEPH TURNER.
Crawford: BENJAMIN F. MANAHAN.
Grant: ORRIS MCCARTNEY.
Dane, Green, and Sauk: ALEXANDER L. COLLINS.
Dodge and Jefferson: JOHN E. HOLMES.
Washington and Sheboygan: CHAUNCEY M. PHELPS.

HOUSE OF REPRESENTATIVES.

Racine: URIAH WOOD and ELISHA RAYMOND.
Walworth: CHARLES A. BRONSON and PALMER GARDINER.
Milwaukee: WILLIAM SHEW, ANDREW SULLIVAN and WILLIAM W. BROWN.
Iowa and Richland: TIMOTHY BURNS, JAMES D. JENKINS and THOMAS CHILTON.
Grant: ARMSTEAD C. BROWN and WILLIAM RICHARDSON.
Dane, Green and Sauk: CHARLES LUM, WILLIAM A. WHEELER and JOHN W. STEWART.
Sheboygan and Washington: HARRISON C. HOBART.

Dodge and Jefferson: GEORGE W. GREEN, JOHN T. HAIGHT and JAMES GIDDINGS.
Rock: JARED G. WINSLOW and JAMES M. BURGESS.
Waukesha: JOSEPH BOND, and CHAUNCEY G. HEATH.
Crawford: JOSEPH W. FURBER.
Brown, Columbia, Fond du Lac, Manitowoc, Marquette, Portage and Winnebago: ELISHA MORROW, and HUGH MCFARLANE:

A very large proportion of the members of both houses were without legislative experience. But three members of the Council and four members of the House had ever been members of the Territorial Legislature.

In the Council, MARSHALL M. STRONG had, previously, often been a member of the Council; MASON C. DARLING had been continuously a member of the House from 1840 to 1846, and HORATIO N. WELLS had been a member of the House in 1839 and 1840.

In the House of Representatives, WILLIAM SHEW had been a member at three different sessions; JOSEPH BOND at two, and ARMSTEAD C. BROWN and ELISHA MORROW were both members at the previous session of 1846.

All the members were in attendance at the opening of the session, except Messrs. STRONG and MANAHAN, in the Council, and Mr. FURBER, in the House.

The two houses were immediately organized, by the appointment of MASON C. DARLING, President *pro tem.* of the the Council, and WILLIAM SHEW, Speaker *pro tem.* of the House, both of whom were subsequently elected by ballot, as the presiding officers of their respective houses.

THOMAS MCHUGH was elected Secretary of the Council and LAFAYETTE KELLOGG, Chief Clerk of the House of Representatives.

The customary messages announcing the organization of both branches of the legislative assembly were interchanged, when the Governor, having been waited upon by a joint committee, met the two houses in joint assembly on the second day of the session and read, in person, his annual message.

The early admission of Wisconsin into the Union was referred to in the message in favorable terms.

The appointment of a joint committee to ascertain if practicable the amount of the indebtedness of the Territory was recommended, one reason for which was that—

"As the present will doubtless be the last meeting of the Legislative Assembly during the Territorial government, it is due to the people as well as the creditors of the Territory that this investigation should take place."

Memorials to Congress for appropriations for harbors at Milwaukee, Racine, and Southport were recommended.

The Governor evinced his interest in the military defense of the Territory against Indian disturbance by a repetition of his recommendation for a reorganization of the militia and its officers. In this connection he also stated that in accordance with a request of the Secretary of War, one company of volunteer infantry composed of citizens of Crawford county, had been mustered into the United States service, to occupy Fort Crawford in the absence of regular troops.

This company was commanded by Captain WYRAM KNOWLTON, afterwards elected judge of the sixth judicial circuit, under the State government, and for about three years one of the judges of the Supreme court.

Our relations with the Menomonee and Chippewa Indians the principal tribes remaining within the Wisconsin superintendency, were represented as "of the most friendly character."

The purchase by the United States of the Menomonee country, at least that portion of it lying between the Wolf River and the portage of the Fox and Wisconsin Rivers, the message represented as "desirable."

E. R. HUGUNIN had been elected Sergeant-at-Arms of the House, and having obtained leave of absence for a few days towards the close of the session, WILLIAM A. BARSTOW, afterwards Secretary of State and then Governor, was elected Sergeant-at-Arms *pro tem.* The fact is worthy of mention as an illustration of the equality of the workings of our republican government.

It was but nineteen days from the time when the convention to form a constitution adjourned, and submitted that fundamental law to the people for their adoption or rejection on the 4th day of April, until the Legislative Assembly met. But within these few days a warm, unmistakable and somewhat vigorous, though unorganized opposition to the adoption of the constitution had been developed.

That opposition had its representation in the Legislative Assembly; much stronger proportionately in the Council than in the house. MARSHALL M. STRONG was by common consent recognized as entitled to the distinction—honorable or otherwise, from the stand-point from which it was viewed—of being the leader of this opposition among the people and in the Council, where he was ably assisted by Messrs. WELLS, LOVELL, COLLINS and others.

A number of petitions, asking for the passage of a law providing for the holding of another convention for the adoption of another constitution in the contingency that the first should not be adopted, were presented, and in the Council referred to the judiciary committee consisting of Messrs. WELLS, STRONG and COLLINS. The committee reported a bill, making all appropriate provisions for such a convention, accompanied by a report, the re-production of which is justified by the interest which then surrounded the question. They say:

"The committee do not feel called upon to express any opinion as to the merits of the constitution already proposed, or to speculate on the probabilities of its rejection.

"It is enough for us to know that the electors of the territory have the power to refuse to it their sanction, and that a respectable portion of them, already looking to such an event, have asked the passage of the law in question.

"The contingency to meet which this provision is asked, has already happened in other territories, and by possibility at least might happen in Wisconsin.

"Provision by law for a second convention subjects the electors to no trouble and the State to no expense, while it leaves the people free to exercise their choice, either to take the constitution now presented to them, or to take prompt measures to secure a better one.

"To withhold such a provision would seem to be assuming on the part of the Legislature to prejudge the question now submitted to the people, or would at least be saying to them 'you must take the constitution now offered to you, or you shall have none with our aid and consent.' Such a position it is presumed this body does not wish to occupy.

"Regarding the rejection of the constitution as barely possible within the sovereign choice of the people, the committee cannot deem it wise or necessary, in case of such contingency to incur the expense of a special session of the Legislative Assembly or to submit to the delay of awaiting the action of a future Legislature.

"Having the power now to make the requisite provisions, and being called upon to do so, the committee deem it the duty of this body to pass the law asked, leaving it to the choice of the people to make use of it or not, as they may deem proper."

The bill reported by the committee provided for a new convention to be held in June and was generally regarded as the most important one of the session. It certainly excited more interest than any other. It was very fully and ably discussed by its supporters and opponents in the Council, where the subject was so thoroughly exhausted that there was little disposition to discuss it in the House.

The leading speech in the Council was that of Mr. STRONG

which not only presented the arguments in favor of the bill itself, but was a very able and exhaustive argument against the adoption of the constitution, and was extensively used as a campaign document in the discussions before the people.

The principal arguments in support of the bill itself were those embodied in the report of the committee.

Some of the arguments against it were that it was an unwarrantable interference by the Legislature with a question then pending before the people, which would be construed into an expression of an opinion by the Legislature in opposition to the constitution, and would tend to impair the free and fair expression of the opinions of the people on the subject.

Another objection was the expense of another convention.

Another, the uncertainty of obtaining any better constitution.

Another, the constitution could be easily amended.

Another — of a party character — that another convention would injuriously affect the Democratic party — then dominant.

The ultimate argument against the bill was that if the pending constitution should not be adopted the Governor could call a special session of the Legislature.

A vote on the bill was had in the Council, on the 6th of February, when it passed by a vote of 7 to 6.

Those who voted in the affirmative were Messrs. COLLINS, HOLMES, LOVELL, McCARTNEY, STRONG, TURNER and WELLS.

The negative votes were those of Messrs. CLARK, MANAHAN, PALMER, PHELPS, SINGER, and DARLING.

The bill came up for consideration in the House of Representatives on the 9th of February, when it was indefinitely postponed by a vote of 18 to 8, all the members being present, and all thus voting to defeat the bill except Messrs. BRONSON, A. C. BROWN, W. W. BROWN, FURBER, GARDNER, HAIGHT, HEATH, and RICHARDSON.

The exciting questions connected with the bill were thus transferred from the Legislative Halls to the forum of the people.

The subject of railroads, and especially the passage of laws granting the franchise of constructing them occupied much of the attention of the Legislature, and excited more interest than any other matter except the questions connected with State government and the constitution.

The first bill upon this subject was the second to be introduced in the House on any subject, and was presented by Mr. HOBART, and incorporated the Sheboygan and Fond du Lac Railroad Company with the franchise of constructing a railroad " beginning at Sheboygan and terminating at Fond du Lac."

The bill was introduced on the 11th of January, referred to one of the standing committees, then considered in committee of the whole, and passed the House on the 18th of January without opposition or even a division. It passed the Council on the 22d of January without serious opposition. The ayes and noes were called on ordering it to a third reading, when twelve voted in the affirmative and only one — Mr. CLARK — in the negative.

This unanimity was remarkable, in view of the differences of opinion which were soon after developed in relation to granting similar franchises in the more southern part of the Territory, and was probably in consequence of a prevalent opinion that a railroad from Sheboygan to Fond du Lac was a visionary chimera, and that if ever built it could not come in competition with a road extending west from Milwaukee, Racine, or Southport.

Simultaneously with the introduction of the Sheboygan Bill by Mr. HOBART, a bill was introduced by Mr. A. C. BROWN, to incorporate the Milwaukee, Madison and Mississippi Railroad Company—Potosi being the contemplated western terminus. This encountered some local hostility, and before it ever came to a vote was laid on the table and the House refused to again take it up.

No one appeared to suppose that more than one railroad could be built or supported across the Territory between the Lake and the Mississippi River, and a proposition to authorize one to be built from either Milwaukee, Racine or Southport westward, was by many of the citizens of the points not named, regarded as a direct blow at their prosperity.

Bills were pending in both houses granting charters to construct railroads, some from one point and some from another; when on the 25th of January Mr. WELLS offered in the council a joint resolution

"That all bills for the construction of railroads from Lake Michigan to the Mississippi

"River, now before either house, be referred to a joint committee of three from each house, "with instructions to report one bill for a railroad, either with or without points."

A motion was made to strike out the words "either with or," so as to leave it "without points." This was defeated by a vote of 6 to 6. The resolution was then adopted in the Council by a vote of 7 to 5. On the next day it was adopted by the House by a vote of 13 to 12.

The committee consisted of Messrs. WELLS, STRONG, and PALMER, of the Council, and HAIGHT, RICHARDSON and RAYMOND, of the House.

The next day after their appointment the joint committee reported a bill to incorporate "the Lake Michigan and Mississippi Railroad Company." The bill created twenty-six commissioners, who were named, to receive subscriptions to the capital stock; of whom four resided in Milwaukee county, four in Racine and two in each of the counties of Walworth, Rock, Green, Grant, Iowa, Dane, Jefferson, Dodge, and Waukesha. The capital was to be $1,500,000, in shares of $100 each, and whenever 10,000 shares were subscribed, and $5 on each share paid, the company was to be organized by the election of nine directors.

The company was authorized to locate and construct a railroad —

"From such eligible point south of township number 8, on Lake Michigan, to such "eligible point on the Mississippi River, in the county of Grant, as shall be determined "upon by a vote of the stockholders."

The bill passed the House on the 30th of January by a vote of 13 to 11, and on the 2d of February it passed the Council by a vote of 12 to 1, Mr. SINGER alone voting in the negative.

The passage of this resolution did not, nor did the passage of the bill reported by the committee, have the effect of suppressing attempts to introduce other bills.

On the same day that the bill "without points" was reported in the House, two bills were introduced by Mr. LOVELL, one (No. 28) to incorporate the "Southern Railroad Company of Wisconsin," the other (No. 29) to incorporate the "Racine and Mississippi Railroad Company," and one (No. 31) by Mr. TURNER, to incorporate the "Milwaukee and Waukesha Railroad Company."

The two bills introduced by Mr. LOVELL were both laid on the table on the 4th of February and not again taken up.

The bill introduced by Mr. TURNER passed the Council without serious opposition. One incident however occurred, which in view of later judicial decisions, is worthy of being reproduced. It was an amendment offered to the bill by Mr. LOVELL and subsequently withdrawn by him.

In the celebrated (so called) "Granger" cases (The Attorney General *vs.* Railroad Companies, 35 Wis. R., 425) Chief Justice RYAN in delivering the opinion of the court says (p. 587) —

"On the argument we called on the Attorney General for information on this point (the power of the Legislature to repeal the charter), we were only informed that the Territorial charter contained a reserved power to alter or repeal. On examination we find this to be a mistake. The only power reserved is in section 20 of the act. And that only provides that in case of violation of the charter by the company, the Territorial or State Legislature might resume the rights and privileges granted by it. The right reserved in this section is dependent on violation of the charter. That must first be established. That is clearly a judicial function."

The court is here speaking of the charter of the "Milwaukee and Waukesha Railroad Company," approved February 11, 1847, under which the Chicago, Milwaukee & St. Paul Railway Company claimed its franchises; and in reference to that the court says (p. 588):

"We hold the territorial charter of 1847, enlarged by the territorial act of 1848 to be the existing charter of the road built under it from Milwaukee to Prairie du Chien." The court further says (p. 592): "We feel bound to hold the territorial charter of 1847, enlarged by the territorial act of 1848, to be a contract within the prohibition of the Federal constitution, the obligation of which the State can pass no law to impair; and that the provisions of chapter 273 of 1874 ('Potter' law), limiting the tolls of the railroads operated by the Chicago, Milwaukee & St. Paul Company, if applied to the road from Milwaukee to Prairie du Chien, built under that charter, would impair the obligation of the contract of that charter, and that, therefore, those provisions of chapter 273 do not apply to that road."

It is evident that if the charter of 1847, had reserved the power to alter, amend or repeal it, an opposite decision of the court would have been made.

It is therefore of some interest to present the fact, that while this bill was pending, Mr. LOVELL offered the following amendment:

"Sec.—This act may be altered, amended or repealed at any time by the Legislature of Wisconsin."

Mr. H. N. WELLS said that the amendment was offered from motives of hostility to the bill, which he attributed to local jealousy of Milwaukee, felt by the members from Racine and Southport. That he was ready to support any bill in favor of Racine or Southport. All he complained of was the hostility which was manifested to any bill which proposed Milwaukee as a point for a terminus.

Mr. LOVELL disclaimed any feeling of hostility toward Milwaukee, and then withdrew his amendment, when the bill was passed without the reservation of these powers to the Legislature.

When the bill came into the House, it met with serious opposition and repeated delays; it was finally ordered to a third reading by a vote of 14 to 11, but when the vote was taken on its passage it was defeated by a vote of 12 to 14. Its friends, however, obtained a re-consideration and it finally passed by a vote of 13 to 12.

It is under this charter, procured under these difficulties, and which so narrowly escaped the insertion of a clause reserving the right of repeal, that the first road was built which constitutes a part of the immense system of railroads operated by the Chicago, Milwaukee and Saint Paul Railroad Company.

A bill was subsequently introduced on the 3rd of February, to incorporate the Fond du Lac and Beaver Dam Railroad Company, which passed both houses without opposition and without division.

JAMES F. CHAPMAN, who by an act approved January 31st, 1846, was appointed commissioner to superintend the work of cutting a canal from the main channel of the Mississippi River to the Grant River at Potosi, made his report, which was presented in the House of Representatives January 15, 1847.

The net proceeds of the sales of a section of land, including the village of Potosi, had been appropiated for that purpose, which, according to the report of the Receiver, amounted to $2,725.

The commissioner reported that the first work performed was the clearing and grubbing of the line of the canal, which was done under contract let to the lowest bidder, for the sum of $688.20. That the estimate of the engineer of the amount of excavation to dig the canal to the depth of six feet below the average surface and fifty feet wide at a slope of $1\frac{1}{2}$ feet to one foot perpendicular, was 31,027 cubic yards, and to have made it one hundred feet wide, the excavation would be double that amount. To dig the canal four feet deep and fifty feet wide at the same slope the excavation would be 17,315 yards.

The citizens of Potosi at a public meeting requested the commissioner to limit the excavation to fifty feet in width and to make it as deep as the funds would admit of. In accordance with that request and in pursuance of his own views he determined to adopt that width, which was rendered necessary by the small amount of funds, which it was not probable after paying contingent expenses, would exceed $1,500 or $1,600. He accordingly let a contract to the lowest bidder for the excavation of 14,000 cubic yards at twelve cents per yard, which he estimated would complete the work to a depth of four feet below the average surface, except the four sections of fifty-five yards each (horizontal) nearest the Grant River. He reported that the contractor had completed and been paid for about 11,000 yards, and that the other 3,000 yards would be completed by the first of April.

The Legislative Assembly adopted a joint resolution ratifying and approving the acts and proceedings of the commissioner as detailed in his report, and authorizing him to proceed in the expenditure of the funds which were or might be applicable to the work upon the plan adopted by him.

A memorial to Congress was also adopted asking for an additional appropriation of lands to complete the work, and the town of Potosi was authorized to borrow $5,000 for the same purpose.

An act was passed authorizing ELIPHALET S. MINER and HENRY CLINTON to improve the navigation of the Grand Rapids in the Wisconsin River, by the erection of four dams at different points specified in the act, with sufficient "slides" in the same, and to collect toll for the passage of rafts of lumber or timber, flat-boats, scows or any other water craft over and through said dams and slides.

A memorial was passed asking Congress to make appropriation for the improvement of the obstruction to the navigation of the Mississippi River, known as the Des Moines Rapids, near the southern boundary of Iowa, and the Rock River Rapids, about one hundred and fifty miles above.

A number of laws were passed authorizing the erection and maintenance of dams across navigable rivers.

One by LYMAN E. BOOMER, JOHN RICHARDS and DANIEL W. KELLOGG, across Rock River, on sections 8 and 9, in town 8, of range 15 east.

Another by WILLIAM JONES, across Sugar River, on section 15, town 2, range 9 east.

Four on the Milwaukee River; one by MICHAEL BRATT, on section 34, town 12, range 21; one by PHINEAS M. JOHNSON, on northeast quarter of section 24, town 10, range 21 east; one on the southeast quarter of the same section by the rightful owners of it, and one by BENJAMIN H. MOOERS, on section 25, town 10, range 21 east.

HARVEY JONES, LOYAL H. JONES, HARRISON REED, CHARLES DOTY and CURTIS REED were authorized to erect a dam on section 22, and specified parts of section 27, in town 20, range 17 east.

Another by SAMUEL H. FARNSWORTH, with a boom, on Wolf River, on or between sections 24 and 25, in town 27 north, range 15 east.

And SAMUEL B. ORMSBEE, across Sheboygan River, on section 28, town 15, range 23.

CHESTER FORD, LUCAS M. MILLER, EDWARD EASTMAN and five other citizens of the embryo city of Oshkosh, were incorporated by the name of "The Fox River Bridge Company," with an authorized capital of $3,000 and power to construct a bridge across Fox River at Miller's Ferry, and to take so much land on the southern bank of said river as might be necessary to rest the said bridge on and also to collect tolls for passing the same.

The trustees of the village of Racine were given power by a special law to levy a special tax of $5,000, each year during the two years of 1847 and 1848, for the purpose of continuing the construction of a harbor at that place.

A corporation was created consisting of fifteen of the leading citizens of Green Bay and the valley of the Fox and Wisconsin Rivers, with a capital of $100,000 and authority to increase it to $200,000, called the "Mississippi and Lake Erie Navigation Company." The object of the company appears to have been the —

"Transporting freight and passengers to and from the Mississippi River and Buffalo by " way of the Wisconsin Rivers and the lakes, and to and from the intermediate points on " said rivers and lakes,"—

Although this object or the power to affect it is nowhere given in the act, except negatively in a proviso, designed to prevent the exercise of banking powers or privileges.

Legislation in relation to the creation of new counties, the organization of those already created, and the establishment or change of county seats, is always a matter of interest to those affected by it. There was no lack of such interest at this session.

In pursuance of an act passed at the last session, so much of Milwaukee county, as lies west of range twenty-one, had, by a large majority of the votes of those authorized to vote on the question, been erected, established and organized into a new county called Waukesha.

To meet the necessities of this change, an act was passed providing for the removal of suits from the district court of Milwaukee county to that of Waukesha county, with the proper details. It also contained a ratification of the acts of the register of deeds.

In relation to the Washington county seat, an act was passed that for the term of five years it should be established at the village of Washington, on section 28, town 11, range 22 east. It was introduced by Mr. HOBART, went through all the stages of legislation in the House, where it passed without opposition or division. But in the Council it was opposed by Mr. PHELPS, of whose district the county was a part, and finally passed by a vote of 6 to 4, three members being absent.

The result of the vote in Iowa county, upon the law for a division of the county, being a majority of 233 in favor of the law, imposed upon the Legislative Assembly the duty of providing for the full organization of both the counties. An act was passed for this purpose. It declared what towns should constitute the county of La Fayette, and that from and after the 1st day of May next, said county should be fully organized for all judicial and county purposes. It also provided for the removal of suits and causes from Iowa to La Fayette county, and for the transfer of records from the office of the register of deeds. It provided that the persons holding county offices should continue to hold the same offices for the counties in which they respectively resided, and that the vacancies thereby created in the other county should be filled at a special election to be held on the first Tuesday of April, whose terms were to commence May 1st.

That the county commissioners should provide rooms for holding courts at such place as they might deem most convenient, which should be the court house of said county for the time being. Courts were to be held on the first Monday of September and the third Monday of April.

The debts and liabilities of the old county, as they existed on the 1st day of May, as well as the proceeds of the property and effects, were to be divided in the proportions of the population of each county, to be ascertained by a special census, provided for in the law.

Iowa, La Fayette and Richland counties were to continue to constitute one election district, entitled to one member of the Council and three members of the House.

Another act provided that on the first Tuesday of April the voters of Iowa county should vote by ballot for some place for the county seat of that county, and that such place as should be designated by a majority of the votes so given, should be and remain the county seat until otherwise provided by the people of the county, and that the county seat should be located at Mineral Point until otherwise provided for.

Acts were passed for the organization of Winnebago county, which had been attached to Fond du Lac county, and of St. Croix county, which had been attached to Crawford county.

The law of the previous session, creating Columbia county from the southern part of Portage, contemplated that the voters of the new county should select, by their votes, some place for its county seat. The votes were divided between Columbus, Wyocena, Dekorra and Winnebago Portage and some scattering points; so that no place received a majority.

Numerous petitions were sent to the Legislature, at this session, in relation to the matter. The result was the passage of a law which purported to legalize the elections held in the months of April and September 1846, in that county and the acts of all officers elected at such elections. It located the county seat, temporarily, at Wyocena, on the northeast ¼ of section 21, town 12, range 10 east, and provided that an election for the site of the county seat should be held at every general annual election, until some place received a majority of the votes, and that in the meantime, the county seat should remain at Wyocena. Provision was also made for the transfer of suits and records, and for other details requisite for the organization of the county, its courts and officers.

Many towns were divided and new towns organized. The names given to the new towns were as follows: In Brown county, Lawrence. In Rock county, Porter and Avon. In Fond du Lac county, Alto, Auburn, Forest, Taychedah and Seven Mile Creek. In Dane county, Christiana, Cottage Grove, Oregon, Montrose, Greenfield, Rome, Springfield, Verona, Windsor, Clarkson and Cross Plains. In Washington county, North Bend, Fredonia and Clarence. In Jefferson county, Hebron and Waterloo. In Winnebago county, Butte des Morts, Neenah, Winnebago, Brighton and Rushford. In Racine county, Norway. The name of Bark River, in Jefferson county, was changed to Cold Spring. Lime, in Fond du Lac county, was changed to Oakfield. Wright, in Washington county, was changed to Hartford. Richmond, in Iowa county, to Linden; and Prairieville, in Waukesha county, to Waukesha.

The villages of Southport and Fond du Lac were incorporated. The name of the incorporated village of Prairieville was changed to Waukesha. The act of 1845 to incorporate the village of Beloit was repealed. The city of Milwaukee was authorized to borrow $15,000 for the purchase of suitable sites for school-houses and for their construction. And the city charter was amended by taking from the common council the power of appointment of treasurer, attorney, marshal, constables, assessors and street inspectors and making those officers elective.

Commissioners were appointed to lay out the following territorial roads:

From Lake Mills, in Jefferson county, to Lowell, in Dodge county.

From Indian Ford in town of Fulton, Rock county, to Madison, Dane county.

From the northwest corner of Jefferson county, south on or near the county line.

From the point where the territorial road crosses the range line between range 17 and 18, *via* Oconomowoc and the bridge across Rock river to a point in the road from Watertown to Waupun.

From Watertown, in Jefferson county, *via* Palmyra, to Delavan, in Walworth county.

From Columbus, in Columbia county, to Sauk village, in Sauk county.

From Lake Puckaway, *via* Wyocena, to Madison, in Dane county.

From Waterford, in Racine county, *via* Hall & Pratt's tavern, in town of Paris, to Southport, in Racine county.

From Janesville in Rock county, *via* Indian Ford, to Fort Winnebago in Columbia county.

From "Tibbitts" in Walworth county on the territorial road from Milwaukee to Janesville, *via* Indian Ford, to the Territorial road from Milwaukee to Mineral Point.

From Dodgeville, *via* Hickox's Mill and WILLIAM RUGGLES', to the Territorial road from Madison to Helena.

From the outlet of Lake Winnebago to the foot of Grand Kaukalin on the east side of the Fox River.

From the section line between sections twenty-one and twenty-eight, town ten, range fifteen in Dodge county; thence east on section lines as near as possible to the road leading from Hustisford to Milwaukee.

From the house of ERASTUS G. SNELL in Jefferson county to Clinton in Dane county.

From Halls' saw-mill on Koshkonong Creek, Jefferson county, to Clinton, Dane county.

From Janesville, *via* Stone's Bridge, Catfish Mills and Dunkirk, to Madison, Dane county.

From Grafton, Washington county, to Fond du Lac.

From Grafton, *via* Cedarburg, to Prairieville.

From Sauk Washington, Washington county, *via* Salisbury's Mills, to Beaver Dam in Dodge county.

From Beaver Dam, Dodge county, to Dekorra, Columbia county.

From Columbus in Columbia county to Green Lake in Marquette county.

From Manitowoc to Winnebago Rapids in Winnebago county.

From Neenah in Winnebago county to the Rapid Decroche in Brown county.

From Hacey's Mills in Dodge county to Columbus in Columbia county.

A memorial to Congress was adopted, asking for a United States road from Prairie du Chien to La'Point or some other place on Lake Superior, in which it was stated that

"Said road will probably run on a ridge of beautiful and fertile prairie, with numerous tracts of valuable timber interspersed."

An act was passed incorporating twenty of the most prominent business men of the city of Milwaukee into "a body politic and corporate," by the name of the "Merchants' Mutual Insurance Company."

A special act was passed by which the male members of full age belonging to any Protestant Episcopal Church were authorized to become an incorporated body, and elect wardens and vestrymen, and take and hold, by purchase, gift or devise, real estate or other property, and to sell and dispose of or lease the same; but the annual income of the real estate, excepting the site of the church, parsonage and school house, should not exceed five thousand dollars.

By another portion of the same act, it was made lawful for the male members of full age of any other church, congregation or religious society to elect trustees, who and their successors should be a body corporate and politic, with all the powers, immunities and privileges conferred by the same act upon Protestant Episcopal Churches.

Five trustees named in another act, and their associates, were created a corporation by the name of "The First Baptist Society in the Town of Prairieville," with the usual powers of such corporations, including that of taking, holding, selling or disposing of real and personal estate, the income of which should not exceed one thousand dollars.

By another act, four persons named therein and their associates and successors were created a corporation by the name of the "Lutheran Evangelical Trinity Church and Society of the Town of Mequon" (Washington county).

By another act, five persons named therein and their associates were created a corporation by the name of the "United Lutheran and Reformed Church of Milwaukee." Similar corporate powers were conferred upon these Lutheran churches, as upon the other churches which were incorporated.

The late Bishop KEMPER and six other persons named in an act for that purpose, trustees and their associates, with such persons as might thereafter be associated with them, were

"Created a body politic and corporate with perpetual succession by the name of 'NASHOTAH HOUSE,' of the Nashotah Lakes, in the town of Summit, Waukesha County, for the purpose of erecting, maintaining and conducting a college of learning and piety."

All the usual and necessary corporate powers were conferred by the act.

The first act of the session was one to incorporate "The Board of Trustees of Lawrence Institute of Wisconsin;" the object of which was declared to be

"Establishing, maintaining and conducting the institution of learning for the education of youth generally."

All the ordinary and necessary corporate powers were given, with the proviso that the annual income of their estate should not exceed ten thousand dollars.

The act provided that the institute should —

"Be located on Fox River, between Little Kaukalau and the foot of Winnebago Lake, at "such place as the trustees should select."

The board of trustees were given —

"Authority to appoint all officers, teachers and agents of the institution, except the "President, who shall be elected by ballot by the annual conference of the Methodist Epis- "'copal Church in Wisconsin."

The bill for this act was introduced in the Council and passed both houses without opposition or division, but an attendant and auxiliary measure, being a "Memorial to Congress asking a grant of land to the Lawrence Institute," introduced into the Council at the same time, although it passed the Council without objection, met with opposition in the House which finally proved fatal. It was ordered to a third reading in the first instance without a division, but such opposition to it was afterwards developed that it was recommitted to the committee of the whole, and after being amended by inserting a provision that any lands granted should not be sold for a sum exceeding $1.25 per acre, it was again ordered to a third reading by a close vote of 13 to 11. But when the question came upon its passage, those opposed to it succeeded in having it postponed from time to time until the last day of the session, when it was laid on the table without a division.

Separate acts were passed to incorporate —

"The Stockholders of the Green County Seminary," at Monroe;

"The Watertown Seminary," at the village of Watertown;

"The Trustees of the Sheboygan Academy," at the village of Sheboygan;

"The Trustees of the Beaver Dam Academy," at the village of Beaver Dam; and

"The Trustees of the Prairie du Sac Academy," at the village of Prairie du Sac, in Sauk county.

Another act was passed to incorporate the "Beloit Mechanics' Library Association."

The question of the passage of what are called *sumptuary* laws occupied the attention of this Legislature, and the result was the passage of a "local option" law, by which the electors of the several municipalities were annually to vote "for license" or "against license," and if a majority of the votes cast in any municipality were "against license," then no license could be granted therein for the year next ensuing.

The report of NATHANIEL F. HYER, who was appointed at the previous session of the Legislative Assembly to select the unselected portion of the University lands, was presented. It appeared that of the seventy-two sections, amounting to 46,080 acres, granted by Congress, there remained 18,580 acres to be selected, all of which, amounting to twenty-nine sections, were selected by Mr. HYER, who made a tabular statement in his report of the particular sections selected by him.

Five acts were passed purporting to dissolve the marriage contract between JOHN MARTIN and his wife, DORCAS B. MARTIN; between JESSE A. CLARK and JEMIMA M. CLARK; between PHOEBA PHILLIPS of Dane county and JOAB PHILLIPS; between CALEB CROSWELL and his wife, E. JANE CROSWELL, of Walworth county, and between SAMUEL HALL and his wife, SARAH HALL.

The name of HARRIET WELLS of Spring Prairie, Walworth county, was changed to HARRIET ARMS; and WILLIAM DICK of Manchester, Calumet county, was to be thereafter known and recognized by the name of WILLIAM HAMLIN DICK.

Provision was made by law for the setting off and admeasurement of the dower of widows in the estates of their deceased husbands, under the jurisdiction of the probate courts, with appeal to the district courts.

In a convention of both houses, held on the 9th of February, an election was held by joint ballot for Territorial printer and for Superintendent of Territorial Property.

For printer, HORACE A. TENNEY received 26 votes, W. W. WYMAN, 8, and BERIAH BROWN, 4. Mr. TENNEY was declared elected.

For Superintendent of Territorial Property, J. GILLET KNAPP received 35 votes and JOHN NELSON, 3, and Mr. KNAPP was declared elected.

The claim of DANIEL BAXTER was again presented and referred to the committee on Territorial expenditures, which reported that they found " that in April, 1843, a committee appointed to settle with Mr. BAXTER reported a balance of $1,372.14 due him, and that under a joint resolution of the last Legislature he had received $800." The committee were of the opinion that the balance, with interest amounting to $732.24 was justly his due, and reported a bill by which that sum was appropriated to him.

This bill, with the report of the committee, was referred to a select committee of five. This committee reported that the joint resolution of 1846 " goes to show a final settlement of all claims between the said BAXTER and the Territory," and " that his accepting the provisions of that resolution would preclude him from any further demand against the Territory."

The report of the select committee was, on motion, " adopted as the opinion of the House," by a vote of 20 to 4, and the bill was indefinitely postponed by a vote of 24 to 1.

The select committee appointed to inquire into the expediency of taking measures for building a penitentiary, made a report near the close of the session, which gives in detail many reasons why—

"They deem it essential to the interests of the State that ample provision should be made for the establishment of a secure and adequate State's prison at an early day."

The report, however, only invited —

"The attention of the Legislature and the people to the matter, in order that due preparation may be made at the next ensuing session, to adopt suitable measures for carrying the project into immediate effect."

A facetious report was made by the chairman of the committee on agriculture of the House, upon a petition referred to that committee, for the passage of a law to prohibit quackery in the science and practice of medicine, from which the following extract is made :

" Of late years the regular practice of medicine, consisting of the general features of bleeding, purging, vomiting, and injections, cataplasms, blisters, poultices and leeching —

handed down to us by our grandsires and respected grandmothers; rendered illustrious by the names of HYPOCRATES and GALEN, and, in modern days, of SANGRADO and GLYSTER, venerable from long usage — has been invaded by a tribe of interlopers, who, without license and without lancets, under the various names of homœopathists, hydropathists, animal magnetizers, phreno-magnetizers, urine doctors, and poudrette doctors, undertake to cure our diseases without any regular system, purging us chiefly of our substance, and bleeding our pockets more than our veins.

"The committee would represent that in their opinion, the enactment of a law subjecting such offenders to be operated on by their own systems, and to swallow their own medicines, would materially, if not effectually, remedy the evil."

This report drew out a minority report, the author of which, while regarding quackery as an evil of great and increasing magnitude, expressed the opinion that any law aimed at its suppression should include all species of quackery,— the quack doctor, the quack lawyer, the quack politician, the quack mechanic, the quack dentist and the quack linguist.

No further action upon the petition seemed to be thought necessary.

In pursuance of an act of Congress passed July 11, 1846, and of the proclamation of the President the 20th of November, 1846, all the lands in the Wisconsin land district which had been theretofore reserved from sale as containing valuable lead mines, were offered at public sale at the land office at Mineral Point, on the 24th day of May, 1847.

The proclamation stated that —

"All of such lands as contain a mine or mines of lead ore actually discovered and being worked, will be sold in such legal subdivisions as will include such mine or mines, at not less than two dollars and fifty cents per acre."

The act of Congress authorizing the sale of these lands required the President, in giving notice of the time and place of sale, to give with it —

"A brief description of the mineral regions, showing the number and localities of the different mines now known, the probability of discovering others, etc."

In pursuance of this requirement the following "description" was appended to and formed part of the proclamation —

"The lands embraced by the above proclamation of the President of the United States, contain many of the most valuable lead mines actually opened and worked, which have yet been discovered; and from indication on the surface and from experiments made in digging it is believed that many others equally valuable exist, and may be explored at a trifling expense.

From the great number of these mines it would be impracticable to give an adequate idea of their character and location, without extending this notice beyond proper bounds. It is sufficient to state that they are situated in the section of country bounded on the south by the Illinois State line, on the west by the Mississippi River, on the north by a line drawn nearly parallel to the south side of the Wisconsin River, at the average distance of ten or twelve miles therefrom, and on the east by a meridian line passing through the source of Sugar Creek, the whole district covering a surface equal to about sixty full townships. All necessary facilities for transporting the products to a market are afforded by the Mississippi and Wisconsin Rivers, and their tributaries, the Blue, Grant, Platte, Pekatonica and other rivers with which the district is intersected.

The above district was explored by Dr. OWEN, the geologist of the State of Indiana, under instructions from the Treasury Department, and in compliance with a resolution of the House of Representatives, passed the 6th of February, 1839. The able report of this gentleman, published in 1844, with the charts and illustrations (Senate Document, 407, 1st session, 28th Congress), contains precise information as to the location of each mine and shows that in 1839 the lead mines in Illinois, Iowa and Wisconsin, though only partially worked, produced upwards of thirty millions pounds of lead, of which those in Wisconsin, it appears, yielded the largest proportion; and farther, that the whole district, if properly mined, would yield one hundred and fifty millions pounds per annum.

Particular lists of sections and parts of sections to be offered at said sale, have been furnished to the register and receiver at Mineral Point, together with maps on which the location of each tract is designated, all of which will be subject to the examination of those wishing to purchase."

Many of the mining "claims" had been held by the miners nearly twenty years, and in numerous instances were in small tracts, often not exceeding ten acres, and frequently less, and in many cases bounded by irregular lines, and without regard to their conformity with the lines of the legal subdivisions of the sections. So that the purchaser of the smallest legal subdivision (40 acres) would almost invariably purchase the "claim" of some one else.

In this condition of things the claimants of lots in each of the different mining communities, organized themselves into mining claim associations, with a president, secretary, treasurer, surveyor and board of arbitrators. All claims within the jurisdiction of the association were required to be filed with the secretary and to be surveyed by the surveyor, when necessary for their proper and definite designation. In the case of conflict of claims the dispute was settled by the board of arbitrators, from whose determination there was no appeal.

Whenever there was more than one "claim" upon any legal subdivision, the different claimants paid to the treasurer such proportion of $100 (the cost of forty acres at $2.50 per acre) as the number of acres in his claim bore to forty acres, and some person was then selected to buy the entire legal subdivision at the sale and to hold it in trust for the different claimants, to whom he made deeds conforming to the claims awarded to them respectively.

At the time appointed for the sale, an army of claimants of mineral lots were in attendance, but the utmost order prevailed and no disposition was manifested by any one to bid against the person selected by the claimants to purchase the land for their use and his bid of the minimum price of $2.50 per acre was in every case accepted, although many of the lands were well known to be worth forty times that sum. Such was the disposition to respect the well earned rights of miners to their mineral lots, that the most greedy speculator was unwilling to incur the detestation with which he would have been visited by the whole community, if he had attempted to bid upon a tract containing any miner's lot, in opposition to the appointed bidder.

The effect of the sale of these "mineral lands," was that every man in the "mineral regions" obtained a secure title to his mineral lot. There was no more "jumping" of claims and no further conflicts in relation to them, and every one was greatly benefited by this condition of affairs except the lawyers, of whom it had become a proverb that whenever a new lead was struck half of it belonged to the lawyers, as there was generally more or less dispute among conflicting claimants. But now, since the land sales had quieted titles, their occupation was gone.

The most important event of the year 1847, and the one that excited the greatest interest among the people and engendered the greatest amount of contention, attended by no small degree of acrimonious feeling, was the submission to a vote, on the first Tuesday of April, of the constitution adopted on the 16th of December, 1846, for ratification or rejection, by all persons who should then have the qualifications of electors to the convention which framed the constitution.

Opposition to the adoption of the constitution by the electors was exhibited before its adoption by the convention. The resignation of one of its leading and ablest members more than a week before the adjournment of the convention, and the reasons for it, was generally and properly regarded as a declaration of war upon the ratification of the instrument, in the framing of which he had so largely participated.

The article " on Banks and Banking" was acknowledged by the committee which reported the original article on that subject, and especially by its eminent chairman, the late Chief Justice RYAN, to be a new departure in constitutional law, and that it was so, was urged as an argument in its favor.

At this time (1846-7) the country was overrun with a depreciated currency, and the channels of circulation were flooded with "wild-cat" bank notes, and the article on banks and banking was intended as a remedy for the evil and a security against its recurrence. It was given at length in the last chapter.

It strictly prohibited banking of every description, whether of issues, deposits, discounts or exchange *by corporations.* And although the Legislature could *confer* no banking power or privilege whatever, upon any person or persons, and although it was declared not to be lawful for any person or persons to *issue* any evidence of debt whatever, intended to circulate as money; yet all the other branches of banking — discounts, deposits and exchange — were left entirely free and open to private enterprise.

It was this prohibition of the power to *issue*, in other words to manufacture currency, that excited the opposition to the constitution of a certain class, especially in Milwaukee, that could not tolerate a constitutional law which would deprive them of the power of making paper money by which they alone would reap all the benefit, while the mass of the people would be subjected to all the hazard of loss in the event of the inability or unwillingness of those who issued it to redeem it.

This class were earnest, determined, and to some extent systematic and organized in their opposition. The great mass of the Whig party, by the teachings of their party, became the ready and willing supporters of the ideas upon which this opposition was founded, and allies of those most interested in their promulgation. This reason for opposing the adoption of the constitution was readily supplemented by other objections to it which were presented; the most prominent of which were the elective judiciary, the rights of married women, exemptions, too numerous a Legislature and that it legislated too much.

A number of able and influential leading Democrats were found ready and willing to aid these opponents of the constitution, so many that a sufficient number of the rank and file, following their lead, united with the nearly solid body of the Whig voters, were able to effect its rejection by a large majority.

Prominent among these leading Democrats were Messrs. STRONG, LOVELL, WELLS and HOLMES — members of the Council — and others whose personal influence was not augmented by official position. Historical justice, also, requires the statement that among the leading opponents in the Whig party, the late Chief Justice WHITON, Messrs. JOHN H. TWEEDY, JONATHAN E. ARNOLD, WM. S. HAMILTON and ALEXANDER L. COLLINS were the most prominent, active and influential, while their successful efforts were seconded by many others, who were either less prominent or whose names are not now remembered.

It would swell these pages beyond all justification to reproduce the arguments and reasons presented for and against the adoption of the constitution. It is, however, worthy of remark that the Democrats who opposed it, made their attacks chiefly upon the article upon the rights of married women and exemption, passing lightly over the bank article, while with the Whig leaders the chief point of attack was the restrictions upon banking and bank circulation.

Mr. STRONG, in his very able speech in the Council, dealt heavy blows at other parts of the constitution, but in speaking of the 6th section of the bank article, said:

"I voted for that section because I thought it abstractly right then and think so still, all the while, however, doubting the expediency of placing it in the constitution."

He said nothing against the prohibitions of banking.

On the other hand, Mr. COLLINS, the recognized Whig leader in the Council, in commenting upon the speech of Mr. STRONG, said:

"I must differ with him in his comments upon that article of the constitution, providing for the exemption of forty acres of land, and in some cases its equivalent. He opposes the article and so do I. He opposes the *principles* of the article, but I do not. The article is defective in form and effect, and not only that, it is not wide enough, broad enough or long enough. Every man should be protected in his homestead, be the same more or less."

The article in the constitution "on the rights of married women and on exemption from forced sale," which was the subject of the vigorous attacks of the opponents of the constitution was the 14th, and was in the words given in the last chapter.

The objection to the numerousness of the Legislature was founded upon the provision that the number of the House of Representatives should never be less than 60 nor greater than 120, and that of the Senate not greater than one third nor less than one fourth of the number of the members of the House, while the number fixed until there was a new apportionment, was 79 members of the House and 21 members of the Senate.

As showing the character of the objections to the constitution, but one other will be mentioned, which is that the bill of rights contained this provision —

"No person shall be rendered incompetent to give evidence in any court of law or equity in consequence of his opinions on the subject of religion."

One objection which was strenuously and with some effect urged, is not especially alluded to, nor the arguments in support of it, viz.: an elective judiciary, for the reason that it was adopted as a part of the second constitution, and almost universally acquiesced in.

The objections to the constitution which were so earnestly and successfully urged in numerous public speeches by its able opponents, and by a vigorous and sometimes unscrupulous press, were met and answered by a large array of able advocates, with powerful and well presented arguments.

Among the leading advocates of the adoption of the constitution, whose names are now recalled, were GEORGE B. SMITH, DAVID NOGGLE, A. HYATT SMITH, CHARLES M. BAKER, HIRAM BARBER, SAML. W. BEALL, JAMES DUANE DOTY, JOHN Y. SMITH, WM. H. CLARK, WARREN CHASE, LORENZO BEVANS, WILLIAM R. SMITH, NINIAN E. WHITESIDES, and towering above all others in the magnetism of his zeal and the power of his eloquence, EDWARD G. RYAN.

It was not denied that the articles (10) "on Banks and Banking," and (14) "on the rights of married women and on exemptions from forced sale," were experimental. But it was claimed that they were experiments in the direction of progress, designed and well calculated by all the security which constitutional law could afford, to protect the masses of the people against the grinding avarice of the few, who are ever ready to avail themselves of the advantages to be derived from fluctuating legislation.

It was argued by them that while it was true beyond successful contradiction that a large majority of the people were opposed to all banks of issue, and to conferring the power of making paper money upon any persons or corporations; they ought, while they could, to render themselves secure by a constitutional provision, against the danger that this power might, in the future by undue influence, which those who desired the privilege of exercising it, understood so well how to use; be conferred upon soulless corporations, who by its exercise would flood the country with worthless and irredeemable bank notes.

In support of the sixth section, which was designed gradually to prevent the circulation of small bank bills and to substitute for them a currency of coin; the experience of the inhabitants of the lead-mine region for the three or four years preceding, where gold and silver coin had formed the exclusively currency in circulation among the people, was referred to as an unanswerable argument in support of this section.

It was argued that any commodity, for which there was a demand — wheat for instance, which was then the principal commodity in the eastern part of the State — would command the best kind of currency in existence, if the sellers chose to demand it, and that the adoption of the sixth section would be the means of inducing the farmers to demand coin in exchange for their wheat, and that a result would be witnessed corresponding with that in the lead mines, by which the buyers of lead had for several years been compelled to comply with the demand for coin which had been so imperatively made by the miners. But so long as wheat growers were content to accept an inferior currency, they would not be able to obtain a currency of coin.

It was denied that there was any force in the objection that the number of members in the Legislature was too large. That the objection involved a mere difference of opinion and the subject admitted of as many different opinions as there were different numbers between a very high and a very low number. That the convention had adopted a medium number. That the first Legislature would consist of only seventy-nine members of the House and twenty-one in the Senate, and could never be increased except by the Legislature itself.

The objection to that section of the tenth article which secured to a married woman as her "separate property," whatever was "owned by her at the time of her marriage," as well as "that acquired by her after marriage, by gift, devise, descent or otherwise than from her husband," was claimed to have been met by the reading of the article itself. It was said that the objections to the section were founded on a perversion of its meaning. That it in truth conferred upon a woman no rights, so far as related to *real* property, which were not already recognized by existing laws — indeed by the common law of England — and that there was no good reason why her rights to *personal* property, derived in a similar manner, should not have the same recognition.

It was further answered that the section contained only a general declaration which would be entirely without practical effect, until legislation should intervene "for carrying out the provisions of this section," and that it was to be supposed that when the Legislature should "define the rights of the wife," it would not leave the rights of the husband undefined.

The objection to that section of the fourteenth article, which provided that "forty acres of land," or its equivalent, as expressed in the section already quoted, should "not be subject to forced sale on execution for any debt or debts growing out of or founded upon contract express or implied, made after the adoption of this constitution," was forcibly met with the statement that it was addressed to the cupidity of the heartless creditor, and that it ignored the humane appeals of the honest debtor whose only crime was his misfortune and his poverty, in which his unfortunate family were sufferers in common with himself.

Besides answering the objections to the constitution made by its opponents, its advocates pointed out what they regarded as its excellencies.

It was said by one:

"The executive powers conferred are extremely limited. The Governor has no power of appointment whatever. Every officer is to be elected. And with the exception of the limited veto power, when we say that the Governor may submit an annual message to the Legislature and issue a proclamation for fast and thanksgiving, we have nearly completed the enumeration of his powers."

Some new provisions in the judiciary article were:
Tribunals of conciliation.
Taxes in civil suits applicable to the salaries of the judges.
Testimony in equity cases to be taken as in cases at law.
Any suitor might be his own attorney.

Some new provisions in the legislative article were :
That the ayes and noes should be taken on the final passage of all bills;
A *viva voce* vote in all elections by the Legislature;
No private or local bill to embrace more than one subject;
Prohibiting extra compensation to officers and others;
Never authorize any lottery;
Provision for suits against the State, to be made by law.

The provisions of the constitution in relation to internal improvements, taxation, and the public debt, were regarded by its advocates as presenting strong reasons for its adoption, and it was asked :

"With our State disencumbered of all banks, and all danger of their blighting influence entirely removed, with no possibility that her energies can be crippled with the incubus of a State debt, the construction of works of internal improvement left entirely free to private enterprise, may we not soon hope to see Wisconsin occupy an eminence that may be justly envied by all her western sisters?"

Many other reasons for the adoption of the constitution were urged by its advocates.

The contest was the most able, the most energetic, and the most exciting that ever occupied the attention of the people and in many respects its like has not been seen in any subsequent controversy in the State, and the feelings of personal antagonism between members of the dominant Democratic party, who were arrayed against each other, were such that their effects were not easily nor for a long time eradicated.

The advocates of the constitution predicted that if those of its features which were most antagonized should be then defeated, they would ultimately be adopted either in a new constitution or by legislative enactment, and their anticipations have been completely verified in every particular except the sixth section of the bank article, which provided for the suppression of the circulation of small bank notes.

The following is the official result of the vote by counties:

COUNTIES.	FOR.	AGAINST.
Brown...	235	120
Calumet — no returns received	......	......
Crawford...	49	150
Columbia	66	354
Dane	592	962

Counties.	For.	Against.
Dodge	803	975
Fond du Lac	624	627
Grant	532	1,898
Green	341	607
Iowa, La'Fayette and Richland	1,414	1,417
Jefferson	780	1,233
La'Pointe — no returns received		
Manitowoc	96	45
Marquette	184	189
Milwaukee	1,678	1,996
Portage	164	209
Racine	1,363	2,474
Rock	987	1,977
Sauk	111	157
Sheboygan	160	374
St. Croix	65	61
Walworth	934	2,027
Washington	1,478	353
Waukesha	1,246	1,823
Winnebago	137	203
Totals	14,119	20,231
Majority against the constitution		6,112

The convention of the Democratic party to nominate a candidate for delegate to Congress was held at Madison on the 21st of July. It was very fully attended, there being 78 delegates in attendance, representing every portion of the Territory.

The candidates were MORGAN L. MARTIN, HIRAM BARBER and MOSES M. STRONG. The preferences of the delegates were nearly equally divided between the three. There were twelve ballots on the first day, upon the last of which the votes were equally divided between the three candidates, each having received twenty-six. The next day there were six ballots, on the last of which Mr. STRONG was nominated, having received 45 of the 78 votes, the accession to his vote coming from those who had voted for Mr. BARBER.

This nomination was immediately denounced as being the work of the supporters of the defeated constitution, and it became at once apparent that the effort would be made to carry the war over the defeated constitution into the election of delegate in Congress.

A leading paper in Racine County which had opposed the constitution, in its first issue after the nomination was known, contained a highly sensational, and not very candid article, from which the following extracts are taken:

"It is probably a fact that Mr. STRONG has commended himself to the favorable notice of many of the leaders of his party by his reckless and unscrupulous course as a partisan. * * * It is well known that of all the advocates of the late constitution there was no one so open-mouthed and violent in its support as he. This service undoubtedly had great weight with the convention in his favor, for, as far as we have been able to ascertain, that convention was composed exclusively of the friends of the constitution; those who opposed the adoption of that instrument having been carefully excluded from all participation in the deliberations of that body. And it is an undeniable fact, that no opponent of the constitution received a single vote in that convention, although in that section or branch of the Democratic party are to be found many possessing superior talent and undoubted integrity. * * * They (the members of the convention) asked themselves, who proclaimed himself the most violent and uncompromising in support of our constitution? This question would be answered at once — MOSES M. STRONG!"

One week after the Democratic convention — on the 28th of July — the Territorial convention of the delegates of the Whig party was held. It was almost as numerously attended as the Democratic convention. After agreeing to the report of the committee on credentials and permanent organization, an informal ballot was had for a candidate for delegate to Congress, which resulted as follows:

JOHN H. TWEEDY	38
E. V. WHITON	10
A. L. COLLINS	10
M. M. JACKSON	10
JOHN H. ROUNTREE	1

Mr. JACKSON, who had been elected president of the convention, withdrew his name as a candidate, when a formal ballot was taken, which resulted in 62 votes for JOHN H. TWEEDY and 7 for A. L. COLLINS, when the nomination was made unanimous.

The Abolition party, in rather an informal manner, had nominated Mr. CHARLES DURKEE as their candidate for delegate.

The election was on the 6th day of September, and the following is an official statement of the votes, by counties, as canvassed:

COUNTIES.	STRONG.	TWEEDY.	DURKEE.	Scattering
Brown	157	151		
Calumet	39	7		
Columbia	198	306	3	
Crawford	152	59		
Dane	400	470	7	
Dodge	442	418	50	
Fond du Lac	274	360	73	1
Grant	897	1,162	3	2
Green	354	398	54	1
Iowa and Richland	557	478		
La'Fayette	647	574		10
La'Pointe	57	4		
Jefferson	503	578	56	2
Manitowoc	67	64		
Marquette	190	154	5	
Milwaukee	797	799	60	1
Portage	123	116		
Racine	743	971	175	6
Rock	683	1,060	80	2
Sauk	117	134		3
St. Croix	92	51		5
Sheboygan	195	294	6	1
Walworth	841	1,008	159	3
Washington	396	198	8	3
Waukesha	583	659	198	
Winnebago	144	197	27	
Totals	9,648	10,670	973	40

TWEEDY's plurality over STRONG ...1,022
TWEEDY's majority of the whole vote, 9

On the 27th day of September, the Governor issued his proclamation, appointing a special session of the Legislative Assembly of the Territory, to be held at the Capitol in Madison on Monday, the eighteenth day of October, to take such action in relation to the admission of the State into the Union and adopt such other measures as in their wisdom the public good may require.

The special session of the Legislative Assembly was commenced at Madison on the 18th of October in pursuance of the Governor's proclamation.

There had been but two changes in the membership of the Council since the preceding session. In Racine county, MARSHALL M. STRONG had resigned and PHILO WHITE had been elected to fill the vacancy. In the district composed of Iowa, La Fayette and Richland counties, NINIAN E. WHITESIDES was elected in the place of WILLIAM SINGER, resigned.

The members of the House at the previous session had all been elected for only one year, and elections were held in September for members of a new House of Representatives. Only two of the old members were re-elected, viz.: TIMOTHY BURNS, of Iowa county, and JOHN M. STEWART, of Green county.

The following were the members of the House at this special session—the second of the fifth Legislative Assembly:

Racine: G. F. NEWELL and DUDLEY CASS.

Walworth: ELEAZER WAKELY and GEORGE WALWORTH.

Milwaukee: ISAAC P. WALKER, JAMES HOLLIDAY and ASA KINNEY.

Iowa, La Fayette and Richland: TIMOTHY BURNS, M. M. COTHREN and CHARLES POLE.

Grant: NOAH H. VIRGIN and DANIEL R. BURT.

Dane, Green and Sauk: E. T. GARDNER, ALEXANDER BOTKIN and JOHN W. STEWART.

Sheboygan and Washington: BENJAMIN H. MOOERS.

Dodge and Jefferson: LEVI P. DRAKE, HORACE D. PATCH and JAMES HANRAHAN.

Rock: DANIEL C. BABCOCK and GEORGE H. WILLISTON.

Waukesha: GEORGE REED and L. MARTIN.

Crawford: HENRY JACKSON.

Brown, Columbia, Fond du Lac, Manitowoc, Marquette, Portage and Winnebago: MOSES S. GIBSON and GEO. W. FEATHERSTONHAUGH.

Of these, besides Messrs. BURNS and STEWART, none had before been members of the Territorial Legislature, except Messrs. POLE, BURT and MOOERS.

The Council was organized by the election of H. N. WELLS, President, THOMAS MCHUGH, Secretary, and EDWARD P. LOCKHART, Sergeant-at-Arms.

In the House ISAAC P. WALKER was elected Speaker, and the other officers were the same as at the previous session.

TERRITORY OF WISCONSIN IN 1847.

The Governor's message was brief and was limited to a recommendation of such action by the Legislature in the early organization of a State government, as would meet the wants and wishes of their constituents. He expressed himself in favor of the admission of the State into the Union in time to be entitled to give its electoral vote at the presidential election of 1848, and again presented many of the advantages which would result from an early formation of a State government.

The Legislative Assembly having determined to confine its action to this one subject, and the incidental one of the expenses of the session, referred the message to a joint committee, which on the fourth day of the session reported a bill in relation to the formation of a State government, to the Council. On Saturday, the sixth day of the session, the bill passed the Council substantially as it came from the committee, and was sent to the House.

On Tuesday, the 26th of October, the second day after the bill passed the Council, the House concurred in it with several amendments, some of which were agreed to, and others which were disagreed to were referred to a committee of conference, where the disagreements were harmonized, and on the same day both houses concurred in the passage of the bill, and on the 27th October it was signed by the presiding officers of both houses, approved by the Governor, and both houses adjourned *sine die* after a brief session of ten days.

The new law provided for an election on the fifth Monday (twenty-ninth day) of November of delegates to form a constitution. The qualification of voters at the election was a residence of six months in the Territory, preceding the day of election, and in every other respect the same as that of voters for delegates to the former convention. Every person authorized to vote was declared eligible to be elected a delegate.

It provided for the election of sixty-nine delegates, who were apportioned among the several counties, as follows: Racine, eight; Milwaukee, seven; Walworth, Waukesha and Rock, each six; Grant, five; Jefferson, four; La'Fayette, three; Iowa and Richland, three; Dane, Dodge and Washington, each three; Green and Fond du Lac, each two; Brown, Calumet and Columbia, each one; Sheboygan and

Manitowoc, one; Winnebago and Marquette, one; Portage and Sauk, one; Crawford and Chippewa, one, and St. Croix and La'Pointe, one.

The delegates were to assemble on the third Wednesday (fifteenth) of December, and have full power and authority to form a republican constitution for the State of Wisconsin.

Each delegate was to receive two dollars and fifty cents per day for his service and ten cents per mile for travel, going and returning; and the officers such compensation as the convention should allow, all to be paid by the Territorial treasurer.

The constitution adopted by the convention was to be published in all the newspapers in the State, at a sum not exceeding twenty dollars per paper. The convention was required to submit it to a vote of the people for their approval (not rejection) and to provide how the votes cast on that subject should be taken, canvassed and returned, and to submit it to the Congress of the United States, and to apply in such manner as they may deem proper for the admission of the State of Wisconsin into the Union.

The act further provided that a census should be taken between the 1st and 15th day of December, of all persons residing in the territory on the 1st day of December. It was to be taken by suitable persons appointed by the Governor—one in each county.

It was further provided, that if the constitution should not be adopted, the Governor should forthwith issue a proclamation for an election of delegates to form another constitution at such time as he might designate, the delegates to meet on the fourth Monday after such election.

The annual session of the Legislature was by the same act postponed from the first Monday of January to the first Monday of February.

The election for delegates to the convention to form the second constitution took place at the time prescribed by law — November 29. The candidates in most of the counties had been nominated by the political parties to which they were respectively attached, and although party lines were not in all cases strictly adhered to, much the larger number represented in their political opinions the party majorities in the counties which they respectively represented. There were about 25 Whigs and about 44 Democrats.

As the convention assembled so near the close of the year, and its session was continued until the 1st of February in the next year, any further notice of its members or their proceedings will be reserved for the next chapter.

The following table exhibits the population of the Territory on the 1st of December, 1847, as shown by the census:

COUNTIES.	POPULATION	COUNTIES.	POPULATION
Brown.....................	2,914	Marquette...................	2,261
Calumet.....................	1,063	Milwaukee.................	22,791
Columbia...................	3,791	Portage.....................	1,504
Chippewa—no returns...		Racine.......................	19,539
Crawford...................	1,409	Richland....................	235
Dane.......................	10,935	Rock........................	14,729
Dodge......................	14,906	Sauk........................	2,178
Fond du Lac.	7,409	Sheboygan	5,580
Grant.......................	11,720	St. Croix	1,674
Green.	6,487	Walworth	15,039
Iowa........................	7,728	Washington.................	15,547
Jefferson...................	11,464	Waukesha..................	15,866
La Fayette.................	9,335	Winnebago..................	2,787
La Pointe...................	367	Total	210,546
Manitowoc.................	1,285		

CHAPTER XXIX.

TERRITORY OF WISCONSIN — 1848.

The second convention to form a constitution for the State, in pursuance of the act of the Territorial Legislature of October 27, 1847, met at Madison on the 15th day of December, at noon.

A large majority of the members-elect were in attendance, and were called to order by STODDARD JUDD, and on motion of F. S. LOVELL, Hon. CHARLES DUNN of La'Fayette county, was appointed president *pro tem.*, and on like motion THOMAS MCHUGH was appointed secretary *pro tem.* Other temporary officers were appointed, when a committee of three was appointed to examine the credentials of members, and report thereon at the next meeting of the convention.

On motion of Mr. WHITON, the rules of the last convention were adopted, until others should be adopted.

The convention then adjourned until 10 o'clock the next day.

On the second day of the session, the committee on credentials reported the names of sixty-three delegates as elected, with regular credentials; that EZRA A. MULFORD was entitled to a seat as a member from Walworth county, although by an error made by one of the clerks of election, fifty votes were returned for *Cyrus* A. MULFORD instead of EZRA A. The result of this error was to give the certificate to TIMOTHY MOWER, Jr., who, the committee reported, was not elected.

CHARLES H. LARRABEE, of Dodge county, ORSAMUS COLE, of Grant county, and WILLIAM MCDONNELL, of Green county, were admitted to seats in the convention, on motion.

Two others of the sixty-nine delegates — WILLIAM H. KENNEDY of Portage, and GEORGE W. BROWNELL of Saint Croix — were absent at the organization of the convention. They appeared on the following Monday, the 20th of December, and were, on motion, admitted to seats.

The following is a complete list of the members of the convention, with their residences, etc. :

TERRITORY OF WISCONSIN IN 1848. 565

NAMES OF THE MEMBERS OF THE SECOND CONVENTION, WITH THEIR RESIDENCES, PLACE OF NATIVITY, AGES AND OCCUPATION.

NAMES.	POST OFFICE.	COUNTY.	NATIVITY.	AGE.	OCCUPATION.
BEALL, SAMUEL W.	Taychedah	Fond du Lac	Maryland	48	Lawyer.
BISHOP, CHARLES	Dodgeville	Iowa	New York	28	Lawyer.
BIGGS, JAMES	Farmer's Grove	Green	N.W. Territ'y	48	Farmer.
BROWNELL, GEO. W.	Falls of St. Croix	St. Croix	Connecticut	37	Geologist,
CARTER, ALMERIN M.	Johnstown	Rock	New York	33	Farmer.
CASE, SQUIRE S.	Waukesha	Waukesha	New York	46	Farmer.
CASTLEMAN, ALFRED L.	Delafield	Waukesha	Kentucky	39	Physician.
COLE, ALBERT G.	Burlington	Racine	New York	28	Lawyer.
COLE, ORSAMUS	Potosi	Grant	MadisonCoNY	27	Lawyer.
COLLEY, JOSEPH	Beloit	Rock	N. Hampshire	65	Farmer.
COTTON, E. P.	Oconomowoc	Waukesha	New York	25	Miller.
CRANDALL, PAUL	Lima	Rock	Connecticut	45	Farmer.
CHASE, WARREN	Ceresco	Fond du Lac	N. Hampshire	35	Farmer.
DAVENPORT, S. A.	Brighton	Racine	New York	40	Farmer.
DORAN, JOHN L.	Milwaukee	Milwaukee	Ireland	32	Lawyer.
DUNN, CHARLES	Belmont	La'Fayette	Kentucky	47	Lawyer.
ESTABROOK, EXPERIENCE	Geneva	Walworth	N. Hampshire	34	Lawyer.
FAGAN, JAMES	Grafton	Washington	Ireland	35	Farmer.
FEATHERSTONHAUGH, G. W.	Pequot	Calumet	Albany, N. Y.	33	Miller.
FENTON, DANIEL G.	Prairie du Chien	Crawford	New Jersey	37	Lawyer.
FITZGERALD, GARRET M.	Milwaukee	Milwaukee	Ireland	38	Farmer.
FOLTZ, JONAS	Jefferson	Jefferson	New York	39	Farmer.
FOOT, EZRA A.	Bachelors Grove	Rock	Connecticut	38	Farmer.
FOWLER, ALBERT	Wauwatosa	Milwaukee	Massachusetts	45	Farmer.
FOX, WILLIAM H.	Fitchburg	Dane	Ireland	34	Physician.
GALE, GEORGE	Elk Horn	Walworth	Vermont	31	Lawyer.
GIFFORD, PETER D	Waterville	Waukesha	New York	34	Merchant.
HARRINGTON, JAMES	Elk Horn	Walworth	New York	37	Carpenter.
HARVEY, LOUIS P.	Clinton	Rock	Connecticut	27	Merchant.
HOLLENBECK, STEPHEN B.	Highland	Iowa	Vermont	47	Farmer.
JACKSON, ANDREW B.	Bristol	Racine	Connecticut	33	Farmer.
JONES, MILO	Fort Atkinson	Jefferson	Vermont	39	Farmer.
JUDD, STODDARD	Waushara	Dodge	Connecticut	50	Physician.
KENNEDY, WILLIAM H.	Plover Portage	Portage	Pennsylvania	28	Lumberman.
KILBOURN, BYRON	Milwaukee	Milwaukee	Connecticut	46	Civil Engineer.
KING, RUFUS	Milwaukee	Milwaukee	New York	31	Editor.
KINNE, AUGUSTUS C.	Sugar Creek	Walworth	New York	37	Farmer.

NAMES OF THE MEMBERS OF THE SECOND CONVENTION WITH THEIR RESIDENCES, PLACE OF NATIVITY, AGE AND OCCUPATION — Continued.

Name.	Post Office.	County.	Nativity.	Age	Occupation.
Lakin, George W.	Platteville	Grant	Maine	30	Lawyer.
Larkin, Charles H.	Milwaukee	Milwaukee	Connecticut	37	Farmer.
Larrabee, Charles H.	Horicon	Dodge	New York	28	Lawyer.
Latham, Hollis	Elk Horn	Walworth	Vermont	35	Farmer.
Lewis, James T.	Columbus	Columbia	New York	28	Lawyer.
Lovell, Frederick S.	Southport	Racine	Vermont	33	Lawyer.
Lyman, Samuel W.	Hustis' Ford	Dodge	Massachusetts	50	Farmer.
Martin, Morgan L.	Green Bay	Brown	New York	42	Lawyer.
McClellan, Samuel R.	Lakeville	Racine	Massachusetts	41	Physician.
McDowell, William	Monroe	Green	Virginia	42	Farmer.
Mulford, Ezra A.	Walworth	Walworth	New York	43	Physician.
Nichols, Charles M.	Cottage Grove	Dane	New York	47	Farmer.
O'Connor, John	Shullsburg	La'Fayette	Pennsylvania	33	Merchant.
Pentony, Patrick	Mequon	Washington	Ireland	35	Farmer.
Prentiss, Theodore	Watertown	Jefferson	Vermont	28	Lawyer.
Ramsay, Alexander D.	Cassville	Grant	Kentucky	44	Farmer.
Reymert, James D.	Norway	Racine	Norway	26	Editor.
Reed, Harrison	Neenah	Winnebago	Massachusetts	34	Farmer.
Richardson, William	Jamestown	Grant	Ohio	40	Farmer.
Root, Eleazer	Waukesha	Waukesha	New York	45	Lawyer.
Rountree, John H.	Platteville	Grant	Kentucky	42	Farmer.
Sanders, H. T.	Racine	Racine	New York	27	Lawyer.
Scagel, George	New Berlin	Waukesha	Vermont	49	Farmer.
Schoeffler, Morritz	Milwaukee	Milwaukee	Bavaria	34	Printer.
Secor, Theodore	Mount Pleasant	Racine	New York	32	Farmer.
Steadman, Silas	Sheboygan Falls	Sheboygan	Massachusetts	63	Farmer.
Turner, Harvey G.	Grafton	Washington	New York	25	Lawyer.
Vanderpool, Abraham	Waterloo	Jefferson	New York	41	Farmer.
Ward, Joseph	Dodgeville	Iowa	New York	43	Merchant.
Wheeler, William A.	Verona	Dane	Connecticut	33	Farmer.
Whiton, Edward V.	Janesville	Rock	Massachusetts	42	Lawyer.
Worden, Allen	Wiota	La'Fayette	New York	26	Merchant.

But six members of the second convention were members of the first; these were Messrs. BEALL, CHASE, FITZGERALD, JUDD, LOVELL, and PRENTISS. All the others were new members.

The convention was permanently organized on the second day of the session, the officers having been elected by ballot.

The number of votes was 66. For president, MORGAN L. MARTIN received 41, JOHN H. ROUNTREE 20, and there were 5 scattering votes. Mr. MARTIN was elected, and at once assumed the duties of the office.

THOMAS MCHUGH was elected secretary, having received 44 votes to 22 for W. W. BROWN.

The other officers were elected by a corresponding division of the votes, which represented the relative strength of the political parties among the delegates in attendance.

On the same day Mr. FENTON presented, by the particular request, as he said, of Col. WILLIAM S. HAMILTON, and as an act of courtesy to him, his petition contesting the seat of JOHN O'CONNOR, to whom a certificate of election had been given as a delegate from La'Fayette county.

On motion of Mr. WHITON the petition was referred to a committee of five, with power to appoint commissioners to take depositions in Iowa and La'Fayette counties, and to receive such proof and allegations as the parties should judge proper to offer.

The committee appointed by the President consisted of Messrs. WHITON, FENTON, ROUNTREE, LOVELL, and KILBOURN, by whom two commissioners were appointed to take depositions, which were returned to the convention and considered by the committee.

Subsequently, on the 13th of January, Mr. WHITON submitted a report of the committee, to the effect that the committee were —

"Unanimously of the opinion that the contestant had not made out such a case as entitles him to the seat in the convention now occupied by Hon. JOHN O'CONNOR, and a majority of the committee are of the opinion that the Hon. JOHN O'CONNOR is entitled to the seat now occupied by him."

The committee reported the following resolution:

"*Resolved*, That WILLIAM S. HAMILTON is not entitled to the seat in this convention now occupied by the Hon. JOHN O'CONNOR."

The resolution was made the special order for the seventeenth of January, when after an able and exhaustive argument by Col. HAMILTON, in favor of his right to the seat, and by Hon. SAMUEL CRAWFORD, in favor of the right of the sitting member, the resolution was adopted by a vote of sixty-three to two. Messrs. CASE and LAKIN alone voting in the negative.

On motion of Mr. SANDERS a committee of seven was appointed by the President to report rules. The committee consisted of Messrs. SANDERS, DUNN, PRENTISS, BISHOP, ESTABROOK, LEWIS and KING, and reported the same day a series of rules, which with some amendments were adopted.

The resident clergymen of Madison were by resolution invited to open the convention each morning with prayer.

Each member of the convention was furnished with sixty-five weekly newspapers, printed in the Territory, during the session.

Considerable difference of opinion was early developed as to the best mode of bringing before the convention the propositions upon which the members were to act, which was disposed of by the adoption of a resolution

"That a committee of nine be appointed to prepare and submit a plan for the progress of the convention, the number of committees to be appointed and such other suggestions as they shall deem proper and expedient."

The next day (Saturday, December 18th) the committee made the following report:

"The committee to whom was referred the resolution to provide for the appointment of standing committees, submit the following:

1st. A committee of fifteen on general provisions, comprising preamble, boundaries and admission of the State, suffrage and elective franchise, internal improvements, taxation, finance and public debt, militia, eminent domain and property of the State, bill of rights and such other provisions as may be referred to them.

2d. A committee of seven on the executive, legislative and administrative provisions.

3d. A committee of five on the judiciary.

4th. A committee of nine on education and school funds.

5th. A committee of five on banks, banking, and incorporations.

6th. A committee of seven on the schedule and other miscellaneous provisions."

The report of the committee was adopted.

At the next session the President announced the appointment of the following standing committees:

1st. Messrs. KILBOURN, ROUNTREE, SANDERS, MULFORD, REED, LARRABEE, FOX, BEALL, CARTER, JONES, SCHOEFFLER, MCDOWELL, SCAGEL, REYMERT and BROWNELL.

2d. Messrs. LOVELL, KING, FENTON, LATHAM, JUDD, O. COLE and TURNER.

3d. Messrs. DUNN, WHITON, A. G. COLE, GALE and MCCLELLAN.

4th. Messrs. ESTABROOK, ROOT, JACKSON, WORDEN, HARVEY, VANDERPOOL, FITZGERALD, STEADMAN and FAGAN.

5th. Messrs. CHASE, LAKIN, BISHOP, CASTLEMAN and WHEELER.

6th. Messrs. PRENTISS, LEWIS, COLLEY, DORAN, FEATHERSTONHAUGH, WARD and COTTON.

Subsequently two other committees were appointed by resolution, viz.:

On Incidental Expenses — Messrs. FOWLER, CASE, SECOR, NICHOLS and HOLLENBECK.

On Engrossment — Messrs. RICHARDSON, KINNE, LARKIN, FOOTE and PENTONY.

The questions as to how to provide for, and in what manner, and what amount to pay for the printing, elicited much discussion. Some members advocated the employment of specified persons, others the election of a printer, and still others the letting of the printing to the lowest bidders, while various modifications of these three principal modes were suggested.

The result was the adoption of a resolution that the Secretary should receive sealed proposals for the incidental printing of the convention, and report the same to the convention.

A motion to amend the resolution by striking out the word "incidental," so that the resolution would apply to all printing, of course including the journal, which was more than all the rest, was lost.

Under this resolution proposals were made by W. W. WYMAN, by BERIAH BROWN and by WELCH and BIRD, to do the incidental printing at specified rates, which, although somewhat variant, contemplated a reasonable compensation. But Messrs. TENNEY, SMITH and HOLT, proprietors of the *Wisconsin Argus* printing establishment, made a proposal to do the incidental printing for *one cent*.

A resolution was then adopted that Messrs. TENNEY, SMITH and HOLT

"Having offered the lowest bid for the same, be and are hereby appointed to do the incidenta printing of this convention; *Provided*, they shall file security for the performance of the same to the satisfaction of the President."

This ended the controversy for the time, and Messrs. TENNEY, SMITH and HOLT having filed the security, performed the work in a satisfactory manner. But the end was not yet. Ten days later Mr. FENTON introduced a resolution:

"That the printers of the convention be directed to print five hundred copies of the daily slips, in Journal form, with a sketch of the debates daily, and to prepare an index therefor, and to have the journal of the convention printed, stiched and bound and ready, so that each member can have a complete copy furnished him at the time of the adjournment, or as soon thereafter as circumstances will permit."

The resolution was considered the next day, when a motion by Mr. GALE to fix a specified and reasonable price for the work was defeated by a vote of 17 to 47.

A motion was made by Mr. BEAL, modified by the suggestion of Mr. HARVEY, that proposals be received by a committee and reported to the convention, for printing as indicated in the resolution, as also for printing the journal alone. This motion was lost by a tie vote of 33 to 33; when the resolution of Mr. FENTON was adopted by a vote of 34 to 31, with a general belief that the profits in printing the journal and debates would compensate the printers for the losses in doing the incidental printing.

The first article reported for the consideration of the convention was that relative to the "Executive," which in the subsequent order of arrangement become Article V.

The discussion of the article elicited quite a number of propositions for amendment.

The first one was offered by Mr. WHITON, to change the term of office of the Governor from two years to one year. This was defeated in committee of the whole by a vote of 27 to 39, and afterward in the convention by a vote of 29 to 34.

The fifth section, as reported by the committee, provided that —

"The Governor shall *reside at the seat of government during his continuance in office, and* receive as a compensation for his services, annually, the sum of one thousand five hundred dollars."

The words in *italics,* requiring a residence at the seat of government, had been stricken out, when, on motion of Mr. BEALL, the section was further amended by reducing the salary from fifteen hundred to twelve hundred and fifty dollars.

The two questions pertaining to this article which principally occupied the attention of the convention, were the Governor's veto and creating the office of Lieutenant Governor.

In reference to the veto power, it was proposed to substitute a majority of the members elected to each house, for two thirds of the members present, as the requisite number to pass a bill notwithstanding the objections of the Governor.

The action of the convention upon this question was very fluctuating. When the vote was first taken it was lost by 27 to 36, and the article was ordered to be engrossed without the proposed change. Three days later, upon a motion to recommit the article, Mr. WHITON moved that the committee be instructed to report the proposed amendment, and his motion was adopted by a vote of 31 to 27. When the committee, on the next day, reported the article, with the amendment proposed by Mr. WHITON, the convention refused, by a vote of 30 to 35, to adopt it, and the article was passed without the alteration proposed.

In reference to the office of Lieutenant Governor, it was proposed to dispense with it entirely, and to provide that in case of the death, etc., of the Governor, the duties of his office should devolve upon the President of the Senate.

The action of the convention upon this proposition was also quite fluctuating. The principal advocates of the proposed amendment were Messrs. ESTABROOK, HARVEY, KILBOURN, LARKIN, and WHITON. Those who spoke against it were Messrs. A. G. COLE, GALE, JUDD, and LOVELL, while Messrs. BEALL and KING were at first in favor of the amendment and finally opposed it.

The remarks of Mr. HARVEY, in the light of his premature death in 1862, are worthy of preservation. He

"Thought the contingency against which it was proposed to guard in general very remote. In the history of the States, very few cases had arisen where the office of Governor had been vacated by death or disability."

He little thought then that within a few years his own untimely death, while holding the office of Governor, would furnish the first illustration of the utility of providing for the contingency.

Mr. BEALL said he

"Thought it was a small matter either way, whether such an office was or was not created. He thought it quite probable, however, that in case it was created there were plenty of persons who would be willing to fill it."

In two years from that time, he demonstrated that one person at least was willing to fill it, by accepting the office to which he was himself elected.

In the early stage of the consideration of the article, the several sections containing the words "Lieutenant Governor" were amended by eliminating those words, without division, and without much opposition or discussion.

But when it came to the question of the engrossment of the article, it was evident that a large number, if not a majority of the members, had concluded that the office ought not to be dispensed with, and a motion was made by Mr. A. G. COLE to recommit the article with instructions to provide for it. This brought out considerable discussion, and the motion at that time was lost by a vote of 30 to 32, and the emasculated article was ordered to be engrossed and read a third time without a division.

When the question came up on its passage, Mr. LOVELL renewed the motion to recommit with instructions, made three days before by his colleague, Mr. COLE, and after much discussion the motion was adopted.

On the next day, the article was reported back with amendments which provided for the office of Lieutenant Governor, when they were adopted upon a call for the ayes and noes by a vote of 40 to 25, and the article in this respect was restored to the condition in which it was originally reported, and was then passed by the convention.

The article as finally passed was a re-adoption of the same article in the first constitution, with only two material amendments. One was that the salary of the Governor was increased from one thousand to twelve hundred and fifty dollars. The other was the omission of a section of the first constitution, which provided that

"The Governor and Lieutenant Governor, or eitner of them, shall not, during the term for which he or they are elected, hold any other office of trust, profit or emolument under this State or the United States, or any other State of the Union, or any foreign state or government."

While the article entitled "executive" was under consideration, articles entitled "administrative," "declaration of rights," "banks and banking," "boundaries," "suffrage," "judiciary," and "militia" were reported to the convention, followed closely with the various other articles which it was proposed should constitute the constitution, so that the convention was at no time without an abundance of work on its hands.

The subjects which developed great diversity of opinion or excited much discussion were comparatively few, and were "boundaries," "judiciary," "legislative," "suffrage"— alien and negro—"exemptions" and "banks and banking."

TERRITORY OF WISCONSIN IN 1848.

Such parts of the constitution as related to other matters, were agreed upon without much difficulty or discussion, and were for the most part a re-adoption of the same or similar provisions in the first constitution.

The article "on the organization and functions of the judiciary," as reported by the committee, differed from a similar article in the first constitution, chiefly in these provisions:

The first constitution provided that

"For the term of five years from the first election of judges of the circuit courts, and thereafter until the legislature shall otherwise provide, the judges of the several circuit courts shall be judges of the supreme court."

While the second provided that

"Until the legislature shall otherwise provide the judges of the several circuit courts shall be judges of the supreme court."

And it provided that the judges should continue in office for such term as the legislature might determine by law, and that the legislature should provide by law for the election and classifying the circuit judges so that one should go out every two years, and thereafter the judge elected to fill the office should hold the same for ten years. The first provided that the judges should hold their offices for the term of five years. It also provided that the circuit judges should interchange circuits, and hold courts in such manner that no judge of either of said circuits should hold court in any one circuit for more than one year in five successive years. This provision for interchange of circuits was omitted from the article of the new constitution as reported and adopted. The judiciary article in the new constitution as reported and as adopted, conferred upon the legislature express power to provide by law for the organization of a separate supreme court to consist of one chief justice and two associate justices, while the first contained no such express power.

Both of the constitutions contained a provision that —

"All votes for either of them (the judges) for any office, except that of judge of the Supreme or Circuit court, given by the Legislature or the people, shall be void."

The object of that provision was to prevent the election of judges to the office of Senator or Representative in Congress, but it has practically proved entirely ineffective and been regarded as in conflict with the provisions of the constitution of the United States prescribing the qualifications of members of Congress.

The judiciary article, as reported by the committee, was amended in the convention, by inserting the provision of the first constitution, that the judges of the Circuit court shall be judges of the Supreme court "for the term of five years and thereafter," until the Legislature shall otherwise provide.

The principal controversy in the convention in relation to the judiciary article was upon the relative merits of the "separate Supreme court system" and what was called the *"nisi prius* system," in which the judges of the Circuit courts constituted the Supreme court. This question was very clearly and fairly presented by an amendment offered by Mr. LOVELL to strike out all the sections relating to the *nisi prius* system, and inserting others establishing the separate Supreme court system. The amendment was lost by a vote of only 15 in its favor to 51 against it.

The question of the location of the northwestern boundary of the State was one which developed some difference of opinion. There were two causes for this difference, one local, the other, while it concerned the whole State was in some sense national.

The article on "Boundaries" reported by the committee to the convention was as follows :

"SECTION 1. It is hereby ordained and declared that the State of Wisconsin 'doth consent and accept of the boundaries' prescribed in the act of Congress, entitled 'An act to enable the people of Wisconsin Territory to form a constitution and State government, and for the admission of such State into the Union,' approved August 6, 1846; *Provided however*, That the following alteration of the aforesaid boundary be and hereby is proposed to the Congress of the United States as the preference of the State of Wisconsin; and if the same shall be assented and agreed to by the Congress of the United States, then the same shall be and forever remain obligatory on the State of Wisconsin; viz.: Leaving the aforesaid boundary line at the foot of the rapids of the St. Louis River, thence in a direct line bearing southwesterly to the mouth of Rum River, where the same empties into the Mississippi River, thence down the main channel of the said Mississippi River, as prescribed in the aforesaid boundary.

SECTION 2. This ordinance is hereby declared to be irrevocable without the consent of the United States."

This "preference of the State of Wisconsin," if it had been assented to by Congress, would have carried the boundary about fifty miles further west than that prescribed by the act of August 6, 1846, and would have included within the limits the entire valley of the St. Croix, and all of the left bank of the Mississippi below the mouth of the Rum River, including St. Anthony and St. Paul.

Mr. BROWNELL, the delegate from St. Croix county, proposed an amendment to the *proviso,* by substituting the following after, "viz.:"

"Leaving the aforesaid boundary line at the head waters of the Montreal River, where the State line of Michigan first intersects the same, from thence in a straight line southwesterly to a point a half degree due north of the highest peak of Mountain Island on the Mississippi River; thence due south over said Mountain Island to the center of the channel of the Mississippi River; thence down the center of the channel of said river as prescribed in the aforesaid boundary."

The boundary proposed by this amendment would have been an average distance of sixty miles southeasterly of that prescribed by the act of Congress, and the territory between it and the "preference" line reported by the committee, would have been sufficient for a State of respectable size.

The "Brownell" line excluded from the State the entire valley of the Chippewa River, except some of its tributaries from the east and northeast. It would have run about ten miles east of the city of Eau Claire, and about the same distance east of Chippewa Falls.

The argument in favor of this line, as far as it was based on local considerations, was that it left the valley of the St. Croix and its inhabitants an entirety instead of segregating them as was done by the adoption of the St. Croix River as a boundary.

That it was so far removed from the Chippewa River, that the larger portion of the population which should in the future inhabit the valley of that river would be under one government, when a new State should be formed northwest of Wisconsin, which, from its proximity to that valley, would better supply the governmental wants of its inhabitants.

It was urged that the extension of the State to the "Rum River" line would make it too large, and that comparatively small states were more conducive to the welfare of the people than large ones.

In a national point of view the consideration of providing for a larger number of free states in the north to offset the possibility of the creation of more slave-holding states, was not lost sight of although not strenuously urged.

On taking the vote there were but five members in favor of the amendment proposed by Mr. BROWNELL. These were Messrs. BROWNELL, CHASE, JACKSON, LARRABEE and REED, while of the other delegates fifty-two voted in the negative.

Mr. BROWNELL then proposed another amendment to the *proviso*, viz.:

"Leaving the boundary line in the middle of Lake Superior, opposite the mouth of Burnt Wood (*Bois Brule*) River, from thence through the said mouth of Burnt Wood River in a direct line southwardly to the head of the most northwesterly bend of Lake Pepin, to the channel of the Mississippi River, thence down the center of the channel of said Lake Pepin and the Mississippi River."

This boundary if adopted would have preserved the integrity of the St. Croix valley and left it outside of Wisconsin. But only two votes—Messrs. BROWNELL and CHASE—were recorded in favor of it, and there were fifty-three against it.

Mr. KING then moved the following substitute for the *proviso* in the article reported by the committee, viz.:

"*Provided however*, That the admission of this State into the Union, according to the boundaries described in the act of Congress, shall not in any manner affect or prejudice the right of this State to the boundaries which were 'fixed and established' for the fifth division or State of the northwestern territory, in and by the fifth article of compact in the ordinance of Congress for the government of the territory northwest of the River Ohio, passed July 13, 1787."

The most effective reasons urged against the amendment proposed by Mr. KING were that its adoption would prevent the admission of the State into the Union.

Mr. KILBOURN said

"The proposed acceptance of the boundaries prescribed by Congress would, with the *proviso* of Mr. KING, be no acceptance at all. It would be enacted in the first section of the article that we do accept the boundaries prescribed by Congress, provided that we do not. * * * Our highest policy was to accept the boundaries of Congress unconditionally. Should the convention adopt the proposition of Mr. KING, we would sacrifice all the provisions offered by Congress, even if we had a right to the boundaries proposed under the ordinance of 1787."

The amendment was defeated by a vote of seventeen to thirty-eight. Those who voted in favor of it were Messrs. BEALL, BIGGS, BROWNELL, CASTLEMAN, O. COLE, COLLEY, ESTABROOK, FAGAN, FITZGERALD, KING, LAKIN, MCDOWELL, REED, RICHARDSON, ROOT, ROUNTREE and WORDEN.

The article entitled "Legislative," as reported by the committee, provided that "the number of the members of the Assembly shall never be less than forty-five, nor more than eighty."

This was amended in committee of the whole by striking out forty-five and inserting fifty-four, and by striking out eighty and inserting one hundred.

In the convention both amendments were adopted on a call for the ayes and noes. That in relation to the minimum number by a vote of 37 to 30, the other — the maximum number — by 36 to 31.

The article entitled "suffrage" elicited much debate, both in relation to granting the elective franchise to unnaturalized foreigners, as well as to negroes.

Section one of the article, as reported by the committee, provided that "all free *white* male persons of the age of twenty-one years or upwards," belonging to certain specified classes, should be qualified electors. Among these classess were "persons not citizens of the United States, who had declared their intention to become such."

Mr. DUNN moved to amend the article by striking out section one and inserting the following :

"SECTION 1. In all elections, every white male citizen, above the age of twenty-one years, having resided in the State one year next preceding any election, shall be entitled to vote at any such election. And every white male inhabitant of the age aforesaid, who may be a resident of the State at the time of the adoption of this constitution, shall have the right of voting as aforesaid."

The amendment offered by Judge DUNN presented fairly and distinctly the proposition that the elective franchise should be limited to citizens of the United States, with the exception of those who were residents of the State at the time of the adoption of the constitution. It was supported by him at length in an able and exhaustive argument in which he was sustained in speeches by Messrs. ROUNTREE, MCDOWELL, O. COLE, RICHARDSON, CASTLEMAN, LAKIN and ROOT.

On the other hand, the amendment was opposed and the policy of granting in the constitution the elective franchise to all persons of foreign birth, who have declared their intention to become citizens, in conformity with the laws of the United States upon the subject of naturalization, was advocated in speeches by Messrs, GIFFORD, BROWNELL, BEALL, SANDERS, FOX, DORAN, GALE, and JACKSON.

On taking the vote by ayes and noes, in a full convention, there were 16 for the amendment and 53 against it.

Upon the subject of negro suffrage, the action of the convention was somewhat unsteady and vacillating.

The first movement was in committee of the whole, when Mr. SCAGEL moved to strike out the word "white," which was disagreed to.

The motion was renewed in the convention by Mr. CHASE, when, upon a call for the ayes and noes, it was decided in the negative by a vote of 22 to 45.

Subsequently Mr. ESTABROOK, who had voted against striking out "white," offered an amendment to add this *proviso:* "*Provided, however,* that the Legislature shall, at any time, have the power to admit colored persons to the right of suffrage on such terms and under such restrictions as may be determined by law."

This amendment was adopted by the close vote of 35 to 34, but on motion of Mr. DORAN, who said he had voted in the affirmative under a misapprehension of the question, the vote was reconsidered, and the question being again put upon the amendment of Mr. ESTABROOK, it was decided in the negative by a vote of 34 to 35.

On the next day Mr. GALE offered an amendment providing for a quadrennial submission to the people, by the Legislature, of the question of equal suffrage to colored persons, which, upon the suggestion of Mr. KILBOURN, he modified so as to provide that the submission might be at any time, when Mr. HARVEY offered the following substitute, viz.:

"The Legislature shall at any time have the power to admit colored persons to the right of suffrage, but that no such act of the Legislature shall become a law until the same shall have been submitted to the electors at the next general election succeeding the passage of the same, and shall have received in its favor a majority of the votes cast at such election."

The substitute for Mr. GALE'S amendment was adopted by a vote of 37 to 29, and then the amendment as thus amended by 45 to 21, when the article was ordered to be engrossed for its third reading without a division.

When the article came up on its passage Mr. KILBOURN moved to recommit it to the committee of the whole, with instructions to substitute the following *proviso* for the one adopted the day before, viz.:

"*Provided,* That the Legislature may at any time extend by law the right of suffrage to persons not herein mentioned, but no such law shall be in force until the same shall have been submitted to a vote of the people at a general election, to be held subsequent to the passage thereof and approved by a majority of all the votes cast at such election."

Mr. KILBOURN said it would be observed that the amendment did not contain the words "colored suffrage" and he believed it would be more acceptable to the people.

The article was recommitted with these instructions by a vote of 45 to 15, and the amendment concurred in without a division, and the entire article on suffrage passed as it now stands in the constitution by a vote of 52 to 13.

The article in the rejected constitution "on exemptions from forced sale" was made a prominent and efficient objection to its adoption. Many members of the second convention were in favor of incorporating in the constitution the principle of exemption, omitting all details. Of this number was Mr. MARTIN, the President of the convention.

While the "declaration of rights," which contained no declaration on the subject of exemption, was under consideration in committee of the whole, Mr. MARTIN moved to amend it by inserting a new section, to stand as section 16, as follows, viz.:

"The right of the debtor to enjoy the necessary comforts of life shall be recognized by wholesome laws, exempting a reasonable amount of property from seizure or sale for the payment of any debt hereafter contracted. Estates held by the courtesy or in dower shall never be subject to execution against the tenant, nor shall the enjoyment thereof be altered or abridged by law."

While the article was in committee of the whole, Mr. MARTIN modified his amendment by striking out the last sentence of it in relation to "estates held by the courtesy or in dower." It was then adopted in committee and reported to the convention, when several amendments were proposed.

One by Mr. FOOT to limit the value of exempted property to $500.

One by Mr. DORAN to insert after the word "necessary" the words "means to procure the."

One by Mr. FOLTS to add to the section the words "which exemption shall in all cases be uniform in amount."

One by Mr. FOX to substitute "common necessaries" for "necessary comforts."

And Mr. CHASE moved as a substitute for the whole section to provide that

"Every person has a right to a place to live, and it shall be the duty of the Legislature to provide by law for such exemptions from forced sale as are necessary to define and secure such rights."

All the amendments were disagreed to, and the amendment proposed by Mr. MARTIN as modified by him, was adopted as section 17 of the declaration of rights by a vote of 43 to 21.

At an early day of the session a select committee of five was appointed to consider and report upon the expediency of incorporating an exemption clause in the constitution.

About two weeks after the adoption of the 17th section of the declaration of rights, a majority of the committee reported a separate article "on exemptions," as follows:

"SECTION 1. The homestead of a family, not exceeding in value five hundred dollars, or at the option of the head of such family the tools and machinery of any mechanic, or other real or personal property of any person, being a resident of this State, not exceeding in value five hundred dollars, shall be exempt from forced sale on execution for any debt or debts growing out of or founded upon contract made after the adoption of this constitution; *Provided*, That such exemption shall not affect in any manner any mechanic's or laborer's lien, or any mortgage lawfully obtained.

"SECTION 2. That the Legislature shall make such other and further exemptions as to them shall seem proper.

"SECTION 3. The Legislature shall, at its first session, pass suitable laws for the purpose of carrying into effect the foregoing provisions."

On motion of Mr. LARRABEE, an amendment was adopted to insert before the article a resolution providing for a separate submission of it to the people, at the same time the constitution was submitted to a vote of the electors, and if a majority were in favor of the article it should form a part of the constitution; otherwise it should be rejected.

Several other amendments were offered, none of which were adopted, and the article preceded by the resolution for a separate submission was ordered to be engrossed and read a third time, by a vote of 34 to 32.

The next day, on motion of Mr. CASE, this vote was reconsidered by a vote of 35 to 31, and the article was of course open to amendment.

Other amendments were offered only to share in a common defeat, when the question was again put on ordering the article to be engrossed and read a third time, and the action of the convention was reversed by a vote of 30 in the affirmative and 36 in the negative; Messrs. BIGGS, CASE, NICHOLS and ROOT having changed from the affirmative to the negative.

For the purpose of "clinching" the defeat of the article, Mr. LOVELL moved a reconsideration of the vote, which was disagreed to without a division, and the question of "exemption" in the convention was ended.

The only remaining question which occupied much of the time of the convention, or developed great diversity of opinions among its members, was that of banks and banking.

The committee on Banks, Banking and Incorporations submitted to the convention a majority and minority report, each accompanied by an article, which it was proposed should be adopted as a part of the constitution. The two articles agreed in their negations, and differed only in their assertions.

They both agreed that the Legislature should not have power to authorize the exercise of banking franchises, except upon the condition that the law conferring the franchise should, after its passage, be submitted to a vote of the electors of the State, and be approved by a majority of such votes.

The article submitted by the majority, authorized the Legislature upon such condition to grant special bank charters, while the article submitted by the minority authorized the formation of banking associations under general laws, subject to the same condition of ratification by a popular vote.

After these reports had been about two weeks before the convention they were taken up for consideration and elicited the most elaborate discussion during a period of four days, in which a very large number of amendments were proposed, none of which of any general importance were adopted.

The discussion and the amendments all demonstrated that the temper of the convention was to limit the exercise by the Legislature of all power over the subject, so that it should not be effective until ratified by a popular vote. But the practical difficulty was in agreeing as to what powers the Legislature might exercise, even upon this restricted condtion.

But the difficulty was at last solved by a substitute proposed by Mr. LARKIN for the second section of the article reported by the majority.

The first section was permitted to remain as follows:

"SECTION 1. The Legislature shall not have power to create, authorize or incorporate by any general or special law, any bank or banking power or privilege, or any institution or corporation, having any banking power or privilege whatever, except as provided in this article."

Mr. LARKIN'S substitute for the remainder of the article was as follows:

"SECTION 2. The Legislature of the State shall have power to submit to the voters at any general election, the question of 'bank or no bank,' and if at such election a number of votes, equal to a majority of all the votes cast at such election, shall be in favor of banks, then the Legislature shall have power to grant bank charters, or to pass a general banking law with such restrictions and under such regulations as they may deem expedient and proper. *Provided*, That said law shall have no force or effect until the same shall have been submitted to a vote of the electors of the State at some general election, and been approved by a majority of all the votes cast at such election."

This substitute was adopted by a vote of 46 to 15, and the article then ordered to be engrossed and read a third time without division.

But the end of the bank article was not yet. The next day Mr. JACKSON moved to recommit it with instructions to report an amendment to the effect that the "majority of all the votes cast," not only on the question of "bank or no bank," but on the adoption of any law passed by the Legislature, should not be the majority "cast at such election," but the majority cast "on that subject."

The motion of Mr. JACKSON was adopted by a vote of 33 to 28.

The two amendments were reported by the committee when the first was adopted by a vote of 34 to 30, and the second by 33 to 31, and as thus amended the article was passed by a vote of 51 to 13.

The schedule provided that the constitution should be submitted to the electors of the State for their ratification or rejection on the second Monday in March, the election of State officers and members of Congress on the second Monday in May, and that the first session of the State Legislature should commence on the first Monday in June.

The convention, having completed its work, adjourned on the first day of February.

On the 13th of March the proposed constitution was ratified by a majority of the electors, and became the constitution of the State of Wisconsin.

The form of the ballot was monosyllabic "Yes" or "No."

The following gives the result of the vote by counties:

COUNTIES.	YES.	No.	COUNTIES.	YES.	No.
Brown	218	6	Marquette	283	133
Calumet	55	5	Milwaukee	2,008	203
Columbia	513	31	Portage	208	58
Crawford	120	16	Racine	1,073	1,231
Dane	871	237	Rock	1,243	511
Dodge	872	282	Sauk	245	12
Fond du Lac	747	183	Sheboygan	431	110
Grant	1,137	428	St. Croix	15	224
Green	510	299	Walworth	1,323	574
Iowa	651	161	Washington	1,090	191
Jefferson	969	422	Waukesha	1,108	798
La'Fayette	659	193	Winnebago	328	71
Manitowoc	122	5	Totals	16,797	6,383

Congress by an act approved May 29, 1848, enacted—

"That the State of Wisconsin be, and is hereby, admitted to be one of the United States of America, and is hereby admitted into the Union on an equal footing with the original States in all respects whatever, with the boundaries, prescribed by the act of Congress approved August 6th, 1846, entitled 'An act to enable the people of Wisconsin Territory to form a constitution and State government, and for the admission of such State into the Union.'"

No consideration appears to have been given to the "preference" expressed for the Rum River boundary, as no reference is made to it.

The last session of the Territorial Legislature, which was the second session of the fifth Legislative Assembly, met at Madison in pursuance of an act of the preceding session on the 7th day of February.

The members of both houses were the same as at the previous October session.

The Council was organized by the election of Horatio N. Wells, President, and Thomas McHugh, Secretary.

The House by the election of Timothy Burns, Speaker, and La Fayette Kellogg, Chief Clerk.

On the second day of the session Governor Dodge met the two houses in joint assembly, and delivered his annual message.

He said—

" The preparatory steps having been taken for the early organization of the State Government, I have not deemed it proper to submit to the Legislative Assembly any subjects of general legislation."

A large portion of the message was devoted to the subject of harbors on the western shore of Lake Michigan, showing the national character of such works, their value and importance to commerce generally, to the government as auxiliaries to war measures, and the benefits resulting from them to the people more immediately interested in them, and recommended—

"That the Legislative Assembly take such action on the subject of memorializing Congress, in relation to harbor appropriations, as the good of their constituents may seem to require."

The message also recommended—

" That a memorial from the Legislative Assembly be forwarded to Congress, asking for an appropriation to complete the improvement of Grant River, at the town of Potosi."

The death of Silas Wright was referred to in the message, which said that—

" When a member of the United States Senate he was an able supporter of the rights of the people of Wisconsin," and it recommended " that a joint resolution of the Council and House be passed, expressive of the high estimation in which the memory of Mr. WRIGHT is held by the people of Wisconsin."

The message contained no other specific recommendation, and in conclusion said :

"From the steps taken by the late convention for the organization of a State government, it would seem that the least legislation done at the present session would best accord with the wishes of the people."

At an early day of the session a committee, to which the subject had been referred, submitted a report, that of the sum of $13,700 appropriated by Congress March 3, 1847, to defray the expenses of the Legislative Assembly for the year, the sum of $5,045.21 had already been paid for the October session, leaving a balance unexpended of $8,654.79, applicable to the expenses of the present session. The committee reported that upon a ratio of expenditures to compare with the October session, this sum would defray the expenses of a session of about twenty-four days.

Very few laws of a general nature were passed. These were the following:

"To make the official certificate of any register or receiver of any land office of the United States, in this Territory, evidence in certain cases."

"To provide for the publication of legal and other notices in the several counties in this Territory."

The act provided that where no newspaper was published in the county to which any legal notice related, it might be published in a newspaper published in the nearest adjoining county, or at the seat of government.

"Concerning conveyances of real estate."

This act related to the mode of executing conveyances out of the Territory.

It also authorized any clerk of any court of record, or clerk of the board of supervisors or county commissioners in the Territory to take the acknowledgment of deeds and administer oaths.

" Concerning commitments."

The object of this act was to authorize officers in making commitments of offenders, to direct their confinement in jails in other counties than those where the commitments were made, when the jails in the latter counties were not safe.

"To provide for the incorporation of cemetery associations."

"Authorizing the construction of electric telegraph lines in Wisconsin."

The act authorized the construction of telegraph lines upon public roads and highways, and upon private property with the consent of the owner, and required an annual tax of twenty-five cents per mile to be paid to the Territory or State in lieu of all other taxes. It also contained some provisions regulating the order of the transmission of messages, and imposed penalties for willful injury to such lines or their appurtenances.

Appropriate joint resolutions by the Council and House were adopted in relation to the death of SILAS WRIGHT, as recommended by the Governor, and of JOHN QUINCY ADAMS, which occurred during the session of the Legislative Assembly.

The message of the Governor referred in a feeling manner to the death of Captain AUGUSTUS QUARLES, of Southport, who it stated —

"Fell nobly, with a large portion of his command, on the battle field before the City of Mexico, with their country's flag waving triumphantly over them, in the face of the enemy. The memory of Captain QUARLES and the men who fell in battle under his command in the defense of the rights of our common country, will long be cherished by the grateful people of Wisconsin."

In harmony with these sympathetic expressions of the Governor, the Legislative Assembly —

"Appropriated three hundred dollars to be paid to his mother, to defray the expenses of conveying for interment the body of Captain QUARLES from New Orleans to this Territory, in a manner befitting the character and dignity of the Territory in noticing the death of one of her distinguished citizens."

The subject of the Territorial suits was one of general interest. Judgment had been rendered in Grant county against DOTY and others, and all the suits were now under the exclusive management of the Attorney General — A. HYAT SMITH.

On the 15th of February he submitted to the Legislative Assembly through the Speaker of the House, the proposition of the defendants for an adjustment of all matters in controversy between them and the Territory.

The proposition was made in May, 1847, and was in substance that all matters in controversy be submitted to the arbitration of five indifferent persons—three to be named by the Legislature and two by the defendants — whose determination should be final.

A bill in conformity with the proposition had passed both houses, but before it had been sent to the Governor for his approval, a reconsideration was had, and a substitute adopted, the substance of which was that if the defendants should pay or secure to be paid within one year the whole amount of costs sustained by the Territory in the prosecution of the suits, the Attorney General should direct the discharge of the said suits and judgment, and the payment of said sum should be received in full payment, satisfaction and discharge of all claims of either party, arising or growing out of the subject matter of said suits and judgment.

The substitute was concurred in by the House, and as thus amended, the bill became a law.

The old claim of DANIEL BAXTER was again presented in the Council, and referred to a committee, which submitted an adverse report.

Memorials to Congress were adopted as follows:

For an appropriation of $17,315, to complete the improvement of the Grant River and the steam-boat landing at Potosi.

For a suitable appropriation for a light house at Port Washington, and for a survey of the harbor at that place.

That the military reservation on the east side of the Mississippi River opposite Fort Snelling may be raised and the right of pre-emption granted to the former settlers thereon.

Also that Fort Howard may be vacated and the reservation of lands thereto attached for military purposes be sold.

A memorial to the Senate of the United States was also adopted in relation to a treaty with the Menomonee tribe of Indians for the lands north of the Fox River.

A joint resolution was adopted repealing and rescinding so much of the resolutions of the Legislative Assembly passed February 18, 1842, as were generally known as the repudiating resolutions.

Of this resolution, Mr. Speaker BURNS in his farewell address, upon the adjournment of the House, said it

"Will in my opinion cause the members of this body to be remembered by the people of Wisconsin with feelings of pride and satisfaction. By this act of the Legislature the foul blot of repudiation has been wiped from our public record."

This, it is believed, comprises a summary of nearly, if not quite all the measures of a general nature, which were adopted at this session of the Legislative Assembly.

Very much of the attention of the Legislative Assembly was directed to the subject of granting divorces.

The constitution of the State, which was then before the people for their consideration, and the adoption of which appeared to be a foregone conclusion, contained a provision that the Legislature should never grant any divorce.

Either this constitutional provision, or something else, brought an avalanche of petitions for divorce upon the Legislature, many of which were for causes that did not come strictly within any of the classes recognized by the law conferring upon the courts power to grant divorces.

The Legislature appeared to assume the functions of the English Ecclesiastical Court, and to have considered the numerous petitions which were presented.

These amounted in the aggregate to forty-two, of which nine were presented in the Council and thirty-three in the House.

Of the nine presented in the Council, seven were acted upon favorably by that body and bills passed for the relief of the petitioners; the other two did not pass the Council.

Of the thirty-three presented in the House, ten failed to receive the favorable action of that body, and bills for the relief of the other twenty-three petitioners passed the House and were sent to the Council, seventeen of which were concurred in and six were not, while all of the seven which passed the Council were concurred in by the House.

Of the whole number, twenty-four became laws, of which seven originated in the Council and seventeen in the House.

One of these acts dissolved the marriage contract between MARY SMITH and her husband JOHN SMITH, without any identification by residence or otherwise, to which of the possible MARY and JOHN SMITHS the act had reference.

Eight acts were passed changing the names of persons. The name of MARY ANN CONNER was changed to that of SARAH BRIGGS, HENRY HEAP to HENRY HEAP KENDALL, WILLIAM WILLIAMS to ARTHUR WILLIAM WILLIAMS, LEONARD HUMPHREY to LEONARD RAVELLA HUMPHREY, CHRISTIAN W. SCHWARTZ to CHRISTIAN W. SCHWARTZBURG. WILLIAM HENRY HILL to WILLIAM HENRY GARDNER, EMILY, JANE RING to EMILY JANE HYER and MARY SMITH, who was divorced from JOHN SMITH, to MARY MOORE.

The sum of seven hundred and fifty dollars was appropriated for the heirs of the late THOMAS P. BURNETT, deceased, to be drawn by their guardian, as a compensation for his services as reporter of the Supreme Court of the Territory for the years 1844, 1845 and 1846.

The legal voters of La'Fayette county were authorized to vote for the permanent location of the county seat of that county, by designating on their ballots the place for which they voted, and the place receiving a majority of all the votes cast thereon was to be located and made the county seat by the next or any future Legislature of the Territory or State. If no place received such majority, a like election was to be held at any annual election until a county seat should be so selected and located.

Until a county seat should be selected and suitable county buildings thereon provided, the county seat was to remain at the village of Shullsburg.

In the county of Grant three propositions were submitted to the legal voters in relation to the division of that county, viz.:

    1st. To divide the county by an east and west line.
    2d. To divide the county by a north and south line.
    3d. For or against any division.

An "east and west line," was defined by the act to mean the town line dividing towns four and five.

A "north and south line" was defined to mean the range line between ranges two and three west, north of Platte River.

An abstract of the votes cast was to be returned to the Governor and by him communicated to the Legislature for its further action.

In the county of Fond du Lac, township thirteen of range eighteen east, townships thirteen, fourteen, fifteen and sixteen of range nineteen east, and townships fourteen, fifteen and sixteen of range fourteen east were declared to be a part of that county.

All that part of Lake Winnebago lying south of a line extended west from the south line of the late Brothertown reservation to the range line between ranges 17 and 18, and all west of such range line and south of the town line between townships 16 and 17, was declared to be a part of Fond du Lac county; and all of the lake north of such east and west line, and west of such range line, was declared to be a part of Winnebago county, and the remainder of the lake a part of Calumet county.

The county of Adams was organized and attached to Sauk county, embracing the territory between Sauk county and the Lemonweir and Wisconsin Rivers.

The next term of the District Court for Sauk county was required to "be held at the new court house in the town of Adams," but the clerk of the court was authorized to hold his office at Prairie du Sac until the commencement of the next term of said court.

The seat of justice of the county of Columbia was established at the village of Columbus for the term of five years.

The county of Manitowoc was organized for judicial purposes.

The board of supervisors of Waukesha county were authorized to appoint suitable persons to procure from the office of the register of deeds, and of the district surveyor, copies of the records and surveys in Milwaukee county, affecting lands in Waukesha county, which copies were to be admitted in evidence in the same manner as the original records.

The second bill introduced in the House was by Mr. MOOERS, of Washington county, entitled: "A bill to enable the inhabitants of Washington county to permanently locate the county seat of said county by a vote."

The county-seat question was one which excited an unusual degree of interest and feeling in the county, the result of which was that numerous delegations were sent to Madison to represent the conflicting interests, and the local feeling, to a considerable extent, was participated in by many of the members.

The bill was first referred to the judiciary committee, a majority of which recommended that it do not pa' ..

It was then recommitted to a select committee, a majority of whom made a report in favor of its passage, with some amendment, and the minority an argumentative adverse report.

When the vote was taken upon the engrossment and third reading of the bill, it was defeated by 11 to 13.

A motion was made to reconsider the vote, and it was lost by a more decisive vote of 9 to 14.

On motion of Mr. MOOERS, the petitioners for the law had leave by their representative to withdraw their petitions.

The Speaker then immediately laid before the House a communication from Mr. MOOERS, by which he resigned his seat as a member of the House, assigning as a reason the rejection of the bill, which he considered, he said in his communication, "a direct reflection upon the integrity, capacity and discretion of the citizens of Washington county."

Quite a number of towns were laid off and created, viz.: In Dane county, Bristol, Pleasant Spring, Middletown, York, Medina, Dunn, Springfield and Blue Mounds, and the name of Clarkson was changed to Dane.

In Dodge county, Harman, Shields and Theresa.

In Rock county, the towns of Harmony and Plymouth.

In Waukesha county, the name of Warren was changed to Merton.

In Washington county, the towns of Taylor, Belgium, Trenton, Sackville and Wayne were created, and the name of Clarence changed to Farmington.

In Fond du Lac county, Eden, Springvale, Eldorado and Forest.

In Winnebago county, Utica and Winneconnah.

The several acts passed at previous sessions, incorporating the villages of Racine, Southport, Madison and Mineral Point, were each amended.

The act of 1846, to incorporate the village of Prairieville, and the act of 1847, amendatory thereof, were repealed.

Two hundred acres of land in section 30, town 4, range 4, in Grant county, having in pursuance of an act of Congress, been entered by the judge of the district court in that county in trust for the use of the inhabitants of Beetown, NELSON DEWEY, M. K. YOUNG and CLOVIS LAGRAVE were appointed commissioners to execute the trust, by causing the land to be surveyed into lots and streets, and to hear and decide upon claims to such lots.

A seminary of learning by the name and style of the "Du Lac Academy" was established and located in the village of Milton, Rock county.

"The President and Trustees of the Sinsinawa Mound College" were created a body corporate and politic for educational purposes, and the college was located at Sinsinawa Mound, in Grant county,

"On a plan sufficiently extensive to afford instruction in the liberal arts and sciences."

"The Wisconsin Medical College" was incorporated and located in or near the city of Milwaukee, the objects of which were declared to be —

"To promote the general interests of medical education and to qualify young men to engage usefully and honorably in the practice of medicine and surgery."

An act was passed to incorporate "the trustees of the funds and property of the Protestant Episcopal Church in Wisconsin."

An act "supplementary to an act to incorporate the Milwaukee and Waukesha Railroad Company approved February 11, 1847," was passed by which the Milwaukee and Waukesha Railroad Company was authorized to extend its railroad from the village of Waukesha to the village of Madison and thence west to such point on the Mississippi River in Grant county, as the company might determine.

The great want and pressing need of the inhabitants of the Territory was that of increased facilities of intercommunication, and especially of reaching the markets which the towns upon the lake shore furnished for the products of the farm.

The time had not yet arrived, although it was rapidly approaching, for the construction of railroads. Home capital was not adequate for that purpose, and it needed the stimulus of a through rail connection to the seaboard to induce eastern capital to enter upon the building of railroads west of Lake Michigan.

Plank roads in this emergency became the favorite mode of meeting the popular need, and numerous applications were made to the Legislature for charters authorizing the construction of these and other turnpike roads.

Sixteen acts of incorporation were passed at this session, giving to the companies authority to construct plank or turnpike roads and collect tolls. In most cases they were to be constructed of plank, but in some cases of other material.

The routes of these sixteen roads were as follows:
1. From Racine to Janesville, with branches to Waterford, Rochester and Burlington.

2. From Southport to Beloit, with branches to Burlington and Elkhorn.

3. From Milwaukee, *via* Big Bend on Fox River, and East Troy to Janesville.

4. From the outlet on Winnebago Lake to Manitowoc, with a branch to the foot of the Grand Kakalin.

5. From Milwaukee, *via* the iron mines and Horicon, to Beaver Dam.

6. From Milwaukee, *via* Hustisford, to Beaver Dam.

7. From Fond du Lac to Beaver Dam.

8. From Madison, *via* Lake Mills, Aztalan and Farmington, to Oconomowoc.

9. From Sheboygan to Fond du Lac, with a branch to Taychedah.

10. From Horicon to Marquette.

11. From Port Washington to Beaver Dam.

12. From Milwaukee, *via* Waukesha, Delafied and Summit, to Watertown, and also from Waukesha to Rock River, *via* Gennessee, Palmyra and Whitewater, with a connecting track to Jefferson and Fort Atkinson.

13. From Port Ulloa in Washington county, *via* Grafton, and thence on to Rock River.

14. From Winnebago Lake to the foot of the rapids of the Grand Kakalin of Fox River.

15. From Milwaukee to the town of Muskego, thence to Fox River, thence to Waterford and to Wilmot.

16. From Hustisford to Columbus.

The following Territorial roads were authorized to be laid out:

From Beloit to White Oak Springs.

From Janesville, *via* the Indian Ford, to Columbus.

From northeast corner of section 6, town 9, range 12, in Dane county (town of York), *via* Bradley's Grove, to Dekora.

From Monroe, *via* Green's Prairie and Blue Mounds, to Arena.

From Green Bay, *via* Oshkosh and Waukau, to Fort Winnebago.

From Hustisford to Milwaukee.

From Fond du Lac, *via* Ceresco and Strong's Landing, to Plover Portage.

From Fond du Lac, *via* Humesville on Fox River, to Plover Portage.

TERRITORY OF WISCONSIN IN 1848. 593

From Sheboygan, *via* Mayville, to Harrison, in Dodge county.
From Fond du Lac, *via* Mayville, Neosha and Oconomowoc, to Summit.
From Fond du Lac to Ceresco.
From Manchester to Sheboygan.
From Southport, *via* Walker's bridge, Noxon's corners, Liberty and Welmot, to Beloit.
From East Waupun, *via* Waukau, to Plover Portage.
From Waukesha to West Bend.
From Clinton to Waterloo.
From Fond du Lac to Oshkosh.
From Hustisford to the Watertown and Fox Lake road.
From Dunkirk Falls, *via* Cambridge and Lake Mills, to Milford.
From Janesville, *via* Clinton, to Columbus.
From Plover Portage to Lake Puckaway.
From the military road in Calumet county to Manitowoc.
From Port Washington, *via* Greenbush, to Calumet.
From Madison to Fort Winnebago.
From Delafield to Fond du Lac.
From Sheboygan to Horicon.
From Whitewater, *via* the Indian Ford and Cook's Mills, to the Territorial road from Milwaukee to Mineral Point.
From Jefferson, *via* Dunkirk and Cook's Mills, to Campbell's bridge, in Green county.
From Madison, *via* Palmer's Mills (Lodi), to Adams, county seat of Sauk county (now Baraboo).
From Beaver Dam to Dekorra.
From Fountain Prairie to Beaver Dam.
From Columbus to the Waterloo and Columbus road near Stephen Linderman's.
Commissioners were appointed to lay out *and improve* a territorial road from Sheboygan and Fond du Lac, and for that purpose a special highway tax of two and a half cents was levied upon the taxable property of certain towns through which the road ran.

The franchises of keeping and maintaining ferries across navigable streams were granted as follows:
To THOMAS NOYES and NATHAN H. STRONG, across the Fox River at Strong's landing (now Berlin), in Marquette county.

To A. L. GREGOIRE and GEORGE W. JONES, across the Mississippi River on section 32, town 1, range 2 west, commonly known as Boat Yard Hollow (opposite Dubuque).

To JOHN MORGAN, across Lake Saint Croix, at Stillwater.

To WILLIAM NOBLE, acoss Lake Saint Croix at the mouth of Willow River (near Hudson).

To CHESTER MATSON, across the Wisconsin River on section two, town ten, range seven east (now Merrimac).

Laws were passed giving authority to construct and maintain dams as follows :

To F. WILLIAM ALLERDING, across the Milwaukee River on section four, town seven, range twenty-two.

To JOSEPH CARLEY and BENJAMIN BROWN, across the Milwaukee River on section six, town eleven, range twenty-one.

To BARTON SALISBURY, across the Milwaukee River on section twelve, of township eleven, range twenty.

To CICERO COMSTOCK and CHARLES H. WILLIAMS, across the Milwaukee River on sections four and five, town seven, range twenty-two.

To A. HYATT SMITH and IRA MILTIMORE, across Rock River on sections one and two in town two, range twelve.

To ELISHA MORROW, across the Oconto River on sections twenty-six and thirty-five in town twenty-eight, range twenty.

To CADWALLADER C. WASHBURN and CYRUS WOODMAN, across the Peckatonica River on sections twenty and twenty-one in township one, range six.

To EDWARD S. HANCHETT, CHARES POWELL and CYRUS WOODMAN, across the Peckatonica River on sections thirty-one and thirty-two in town one, range six.

To WILLIAM A. BARSTOW, across Fox River on section seventeen in town fifteen, range ten.

To J. SPRAGUE PARDEE, across Fox River on section three in town twelve, range ten.

To CURTIS REED, across the north channel or outlet of Winnebago Lake on section twenty-two in town twenty, range seventeen.

Each of the laws authorizing the construction of the three last dams across Fox River passed the House of Representatives without any opposition or division on the vote. And yet with that inconsistency which sometimes characterizes the action of legislative bodies, the committee on corporations in the House unanimously reported upon the petition of HENRY HUSKEY and others, to build and maintain a dam across Fox River, that the navigation of the river was,

<blockquote>"In their opinion, of such paramount importance to the great interests of the section of the country through which it flows, that they cannot, under the views which have been presented to them, discover any good reason why it should be obstructed."</blockquote>

They therefore reported that the prayer of the petitioner ought not to be granted. And it was not granted.

JOHN H. ORR and JAMES WHITE, of Dodge county, and their associates were constituted a corporation by the name of the "Wisconsin Iron Company," "for the purpose of manufacturing iron."

An act was passed that the county of St. Croix should at each annual election, elect a suitable person to be surveyor or measurer of boards, plank or other sawed lumber, and also of saw logs and cord wood.

The Council and House met in joint convention on the, 9th of March and elected by ballot a territorial printer and Superintendent of Territorial Property.

H. A. TENNEY was elected printer, having received 23 votes out of 35, of which WILLIAM W. WYMAN had 9, BERIAH BROWN 2, Blank 1.

For Superintendent, J. GILLETT KNAPP received 23 votes E. M. WILLIAMSON 10, and Blank 2. Mr. KNAPP was elected.

After providing by law that the Superintendent of Territorial Property should put the Capitol and its furniture in suitable condition and order for the use of the first session of the State Legislature, and provide the necessary stationery for the use of its members and officers, the last session of the Legislative Assembly of the Territory, on the 13th of March, 1848, adjourned *sine die.*

On the same day of the final adjournment of the Legislature the constitution of the new State was ratified by the popular vote, and the TERRITORY OF WISCONSIN became only a memory.

CHAPTER XXX.

MILWAUKEE AND ROCK RIVER CANAL.

The reader of the foregoing pages, with but even a slight knowledge of the legislation of the Territory during the twelve years ending with 1848, cannot have failed to notice that no mention has been made of the legislation of that period in relation to the Milwaukee and Rock River canal.

There was no subject that occasioned a greater public interest, and none which appeared to demand or which received a larger part of the time or attention of the Legislative Assembly of the Territory of Wisconsin during its entire existence; and it is for this reason that it has been thought best to devote a chapter exclusively to a connected account of that work, in relation to which such high hopes and expectations of usefulness were entertained only to be disappointed; and of the legislation affecting it.

Such a consecutive account must be more satisfactory than the fragmentary one which would have been presented by the mode adopted in relation to other subjects.

The use of Rock River for downward navigation by flat boats had been made practically available before the Black Hawk war. On the 24th June, 1830, JOHN DIXON, the founder of the town of Dixon, Ill., wrote to the editor of the *Miner's Journal* at Galena —

"The first flat boat built on the Pickatolica passed here this day, bound to St. Louis, with one thousand pigs of lead (70,000 lbs.) for Col. WILLIAM. S. HAMILTON "

Its navigability upward for steam-boats was demonstrated a few years later.

The *Galena Gazette* of May 17, 1838, says:

"The steam-boat 'Gipsy,' Gray master, lately ascended Rock River as far as the mouth of the Pekatoneca."

During the summer of 1836 public attention was directed to the importance of uniting the waters of Lake Michigan with those of Rock River by means of a canal; and, although the country was then but little known, some general examinations were made by Hon. BYRON KILBOURN, who had not only devoted much time to the surveys of the public lands in Wisconsin, but had been in charge as civil engineer of the canal in Ohio, connecting Lake Erie with the Ohio River. Reconnoisances had also been made by other competent persons, all of which resulted in the conviction that such a canal could be constructed, and at a moderate expense.

At the first session of the Legislative Assembly, held at Belmont, in 1836, a petition was presented, signed by numerous citizens, which set forth some of the advantages of such a canal and its feasibility, and asking for the passage of "an act incorporating a company for the purpose of constructing a *navigable canal*, from navigable water in the Milwaukee River, to navigable water in the Rock River."

The petition was referred to a standing committee, which reported a bill " to incorporate the Milwaukee and Rock River Canal Company." The bill was laid on the table, and no further action was had on the subject during that session.

During the year 1837, a preliminary survey was made by Mr. KILBOURN and Hon. INCREASE A. LAPHAM LL. D., a distinguished civil engineer —afterwards Chief Geologist of the state of Wisconsin — by which the entire feasibility of the work was ascertained, and an approximate estimate made of its cost.

During the same year public attention was further directed to the subject by a series of five articles, published in the *Milwaukee Advertiser*, which gave a description of the proposed route, the connection of other water courses with the canal and with Rock River, especially the Pishtika (Fox), Pickatoneca, and the River of the Four Lakes, and contained a most complete view of the bearing which the construction of the work would have upon that part of the Territory through which the canal would pass, and upon other portions of the Territory.

At the next annual session of the Legislative Assembly, held at Burlington, in November, 1837, petitions were presented similar to those presented at the previous session, and asking for a similar act of incorporation.

A bill was reported in the House of Representatives, in conformity with the prayer of the petitions, which, after being amended in both houses, finally passed both, entitled, "An Act to Incorporate the Milwaukee and Rock River Canal Company," and on the 5th January, 1838, received the approval of the Governor.

It provided that such persons as should become stockholders, agreeably to the provisions of the act, should constitute the corporation.

That the capital stock of the corporation should be $100,000, which might he increased to a sum not exceeding $1,000,000 to be divided into shares of $100 each.

That JOHN S. ROCKWELL, ALVIN FOSTER, AUGUSTUS A. BIRD, MADISON W. CORNWALL, SOLOMON JUNEAU, JAMES SANDERSON and BYRON KILBOURN should be commissioners for receiving subscriptions to the capital stock, to whom one dollar on each share subscribed was to be paid by the subscriber at the time of subscribing, and they were to continue receiving subscriptions until $50,000 should have been subscribed, when the books might be closed, and together with the money received on subscription, transferred to the directors provided for by the act.

That the affairs of the company should be managed by a board of seven directors to be annually chosen by the stockholders. The first directors were to be chosen on notice given by the commissioners.

That the corporation should

"Have the right to construct, maintain and continue a navigable canal or slackwater navigation from the town of Milwaukee to Rock River, on such routes and of such dimensions and to terminate at such point as shall be determined on by said corporation, and to construct such navigable feeders of said canal as shall be found actually necessary, and also a branch canal to connect with the Fox or Pishtaka Rivers, at or near Prairie Village, in Milwaukee county."

The right to take private property was given, and a mode provided for making compensation to the owner.

The tolls were to be prescribed by the Legislature of the Territory or future State.

The corporation was authorized to borrow money.

The corporation was required to commence the construction of the works authorized by the act within three years, and in default thereof, the privileges were to be forfeited and the act null and of no effect. The right to complete so much as should not be completed within ten years should be forfeited.

Section twenty-three of the act was as follows:

"That the future State of Wisconsin, at any time after its admission into the Union, shall have the right to purchase and hold for the use of the State, the canal, herein authorized to be constructed, together with all its branches and other improvements by paying to the said corporation, the amount actually expended in the construction and repairs of the same, together with such reasonable interest, not more than seven per centum per annum, as may be agreed upon by and between said State and the corporation;

Provided, however, That in case the Congress of the United States shall make any appropriation or donation, either in land or money, in aid of the construction of the work by this act authorized. the right to the same shall vest in said State whenever the said transfer of the canal shall be made; and the net proceeds of all sales of land and the amount of all money so appropriated or donated, shall be deducted from the amount to be paid to the said corporation for the transfer of said works to the State. And the said corporation are hereby authorized to apply to Congress for such an appropriation, in money or lands, to aid in the construction of the works authorized by this act, as Congress in its wisdom shall see proper to grant."

In case of a donation of lands by Congress to aid in the construction of the canal, if any such lands should at the time be actually improved and settled upon by any person, the corporation was required to sell to such settler the land so settled upon — a quarter section or 160 acres — at $1.25 per acre.

These are the most material provisions of the act.

Books of subscription were opened at Milwaukee under the direction of the commissioners on the second day of February, 1838, and a sufficient amount of stock immediately subscribed, and a meeting of the stockholders notified to be held on the next day.

At the stockholders meeting held February 3, 1838, the following board of directors was elected: BYRON KILBOURN, SOLOMON JUNEAU, JOHN S. ROCKWELL, JAMES H. ROGERS, SAMUEL BROWN, SYLVESTER D. COWLES and WM. R. LONGSTREET.

BYRON KILBOURN was elected president, F. A. WINGFIELD, secretary, C. H. PEAK, treasurer, and I. A. LAPHAM, engineer.

On the 12th of February the directors adopted a memorial of the Company to the Senate and House of Representatives of the United States. It stated the incorporation of the company, its purposes and its authority to apply to Congress in behalf of the Territory or future State, for aid in the construction of a canal to connect Lake Michigan at Milwaukee with the navigable waters of Rock River.

It set forth the importance of the canal to the Territory and to the general government, and the facilities of the navigation and hydraulic power of Rock River and its tributaries.

It represented that the organization of the company had been so shaped as to constitute it an agency for the future

State, which might be erected in the limits of the Territory rather than a company with permanent rights and privileges, and referred to the reserved right of the future State to purchase the canal and its privileges, thus securing to the State whatever the liberality of Congress might grant.

The memorial asked a grant of land similar to the several grants to the states of Ohio, Indiana and Illinois, in aid of similar works, each of which granted to the respective works —

"A quantity of land equal to one half of five sections in width on each side of said canal, and reserving each alternate section to the United States, from one end of said canal to the other."

And expressed -

"The rational hope that just and liberal views and sentiments towards this young and flourishing portion of the United States. will impel your honorable body to appropriate in aid of this work, an amount of land equal to that granted for similar objects elsewhere, as before cited."

On the 14th of February, the Chief Engineer, Mr. LAPHAM, submitted to the directors an estimate of the probable cost of constructing the canal. In making the estimate the work was divided into eight sections, varying in distance from one mile to twenty-two. Separate estimates were submitted upon each section for grubbing and clearing, for excavation and embankment, for masonry in locks, for dams and for a feeder half a mile in length, and showed an aggregate estimated cost of $730,515. The estimated lockage from Milwaukee to the summit was 316 feet, and from the summit to Rock River, 80. The estimated cost of the Pishtaka branch, length five miles, lockage 40 feet, was $68,200. Total estimated cost of canal and Pishtaka branch, $798,715. Total lockage both ways, 436 feet.

A resolution was adopted by the directors, that it was expedient to send some person to Washington to further the interests of the canal and of the company, and that Mr. KILBOURN be requested to act as such agent. In compliance with this resolution Mr. KILBOURN went to Washington with the foregoing memorial and estimate, which, on the 6th of March, were introduced into the Senate by Hon. C. C. CLAY of Alabama and referred to the committee on public lands and ordered to be printed.

The committee on public lands reported on the 9th of April favorably to the application of the company accompanied by a bill making a grant in conformity with it.

The report was quite lengthy, and presented an elaborate argument in favor of making the grant.

It spoke favorably of the feasibility of the work, and the facility with which it could be executed; its importance to the government in case of the invasion of the northwestern frontier and of Indian incursions; its value "as opening a new and important connection with the lead mine district of which it (the Government) is the principal proprietor;" the increased sale of the public lands, and concluded as follows:

"In relation to the canal under consideration, it appears to possess some valuable features. The country through which it passes is represented as being very fertile, and capable of sustaining a dense population. Its agricultural productions are such as are usually found in the northern and middle states; and being intersected in various directions, by streams furnishing valuable hydraulic power, and possessing a moderate climate and wholesome air, it will probably in a few years, become an important section of the Union. The exports of this Territory will always possess much value, especially those of the mineral kind; and where an export trade of large amount is carried on, a large import may be expected also. Resting on the Mississippi, upon the one hand, and on the lakes upon the other, this country is favorably situated for commercial transactions; and by means of the proposed canal, a connecting link is formed by which to effect exchanges between those great thoroughfares: and a communication is opened from the interior to the distant markets of New York and the manufacturing districts of the east, as also of New Orleans and the plantations of the lower Mississippi.

"Being satisfied that the present as well as future interests of the Government both in a local and general respect, will be advanced by the construction of this canal, your committee report herewith a bill to grant the amount of land desired."

The fourth (and last) section of the bill as reported, was as follows:

"SECTION 4. That the alternate sections which shall be reserved to the United States, agreeably to the first section of this act, shall not be sold for a less sum than two dollars and fifty cents per acre."

The bill came up for consideration on the 1st of June. On motion of Mr. BUCHANAN of Pennsylvania, it was amended by adding to the end of the fourth section, these words:

"And not subject to pre-emption,"

and without other amendment it passed the Senate.

But this little amendment was of great importance to the "settlers" and had the effect to remove from the operation of the pre-emption laws subsequently passed, the alternate sections reserved to the government.

The bill in this shape went to the House of Representatives, where it was referred to the committee on public lands, and in the hands of that committee was materially changed by amendments.

The principal amendments reported by the committee and adopted by the House of Representatives, were two recommended by the Commissioner of the General Land Office.

One was designed to fix more definitely the western terminus of the canal. The Senate bill fixed no point of termination on Rock River, and the canal might have been constructed from Milwaukee to the mouth of that river, with a grant of land five miles in width for the whole distance. To obviate this defect, the bill as reported by the House committee, fixed the western terminus

"Between the point of intersection with said river of the line dividing townships seven and eight, and the Lake Koshkonong."

This limitation gave a range of nearly twenty miles of the river.

The other amendment was designed to obviate some ambiguities and indefiniteness in the Senate bill, which made it the duty of the commissioner to select the alternate sections. The amended House bill granted

"All the land in those sections which are numbered with *odd* numbers within the breadth of five full sections taken in north and south, or east and west tiers on each side of the main route of said canal from one end thereof to the other."

The 6th and 7th of June having been set apart for the consideration of Territorial business, this bill was taken up in the House, and some amendments were adopted. One was to increase the minimum price at which the lands granted might be sold, from one dollar and twenty-five cents to two dollars and fifty cents per acre. Another defined the relations of the future State of Wisconsin to the canal, and its rights and liabilities in reference to the stock of the company, and the proceeds of the sales of lands, and required the assent of the future State to the act. Another authorized the Territory to borrow on the pledge of the lands such sum as they might think expedient. And the assent of Congress was given to the act incorporating the canal company.

The amendments of the House were concurred in by the Senate, and on the 18th of June the bill became a law by receiving the approval of the President.

On the 6th of August the Board of Directors adopted a resolution that it would at all times lend its most hearty efforts and co-operation in securing to the settlers the granted lands which have been occupied and improved by them.

On the 27th of September, Mr. KILBOURN was appointed Acting Commissioner, to employ hands, provide the necessary outfit, and direct and superintend the operations of the engineer department, in running and locating the line of canal, and in the field operations generally, subject to the orders of the Board of Directors.

An engineer party was organized, and was engaged in making further preliminary surveys and examinations of the country along the route of the proposed canal during the remainder of the year 1838, preparatory to making a final location of the line, which, however, was not completed until the following month of May.

At the session of the Legislative Assembly which convened on the 26th of November, 1838, the Governor in his annual message referred to the act of Congress making the grant of land, and recommended the propriety of memorializing Congress asking the extension of the right of preemption to all actual settlers on the line of the canal.

A memorial was adopted, but no action was taken upon it in Congress.

At this session a bill drawn by the president of the canal company was presented for the consideration of the members, which contained the plans of the company for utilizing the lands granted by Congress, and effecting the construction of the canal.

The prominent ideas of the bill were, a sale of the lands on a long credit, and what at that time was moderate interest, and obtaining funds for the construction of the work by borrowing money on the credit of the territory, supplemented by the proceeds of the sales of the lands.

It authorized the Governor to borrow on the credit of the Territory not exceeding $500,000, in installments as follows: On the 1st of September, 1839, $50,000; 1840, $100,000; 1841, $150,000; and 1842, $200,000; payable in not less than ten nor more than twenty years from the time when each installment should be received, bearing interest at six per cent. per annum, payable semi-annually.

The proceeds of the land sales, the canal revenues, the canal itself and the faith of the Territory, were inviolably pledged for the payment of the interest and redemption of the principal of the loan.

The Governor was authorized to appoint such agents as he might think necessary and proper for the purpose of obtaining the loan.

The proposed bill provided for the appointment of three persons by the Governor and Council, to be known as *Commissioners of Appraisal.* These commissioners were to make a registry of the lands that had been settled upon and occupied within the grant, to which the occupants would be entitled, for which purpose they were empowered to administer oaths and take testimony.

They were also to make out a schedule and valuation of all the granted lands, in legal subdivisions, annexing to each tract such price as they might consider such tract to be worth, taking into consideration the enhanced value which the canal would give to the lands, and a rule of minimum valuation was prescribed by the bill varying from $2.50 to $10.00 per acre, in proportion to the distance of the tract from the canal, and depending upon other circumstances affecting its value, such as the intrinsic value of the land, the improvements of the surrounding country, the vicinity to towns, town sites, mill improvements, lockage and water power created by the construction of the canal.

The commissioners of appraisal were also to determine upon the right of occupants to purchase at the minimum price, lands claimed by them to have been occupied by them, and were to determine all conflicting claims, and were to issue certificates of such right, and all occupants having such certificate were authorized by the bill to bid off the land described in such certificate, at $2.50 per acre, when the same should be offered for sale, and officers having charge of the sale were prohibited from receiving any bid in opposition to said occupant.

The bill provided for a public sale of the canal lands at stated periods in the following manner, viz.: on the fourth Monday in June, 1839, all the northeast quarters, and all the "occupied" lands; at the same time in 1840 all the southwest quarters; at the same time in 1841 all the northwest quarters; and at the same time in 1842 all the southeast quarters, and such lands as had been previously offered and not disposed of; at the same time in 1843 all the residuary lands were to be offered to the highest bidder, at not less than their appraised value, and at the same time, in 1844, all remaining unsold were to be offered to the highest bidder at not less than $2.50 per acre, and if there still remained any poor and unsalable lands they were to be offered for sale on the fourth Monday of June, 1845, to the highest bidder without reservation.

The bill provided that a register and receiver should be appointed by the Governor and Council, whose duty it should be to superintend the sales of the canal lands and make returns of each sale thereof to the Governor, in the same manner that returns were made from the land offices of the United States to the General Land Office. The compensation of each was to be one per centum on the amount of all sales made by them.

It provided that the canal lands should be put up to sale in tracts of eighty acres or fractions under one hundred acres, according to legal subdivisions, and for each tract sold ten dollars should be paid on the day of sale, and for the balance a bond and mortgage should be taken, conditioned for the payment of one fourth part within five years, one fourth in six years, one fourth in seven years and the remaining one fourth in eight years with interest payable semi-annually from the date of sale, at the rate of seven per cent. per annum, with some exception as to interest in case of occupants—provided full payment might be made at any time.

The bill provided for the appointment by the Governor and Council of a chief engineer on behalf of the Territory, who was to keep a general supervision over the canal and supervise its progress, make or revise and certify for payment estimates for work done and report annually to the Legislature the condition of the work and receive a salary not exceeding ——— dollars.

The bill contained provisions for the application of the proceeds of the sales of the lands to the payment of the interest and redemption of the principal of moneys obtained by the Governor on loan.

It contained other matters of detail, and was supposed to present a complete plan of the modes of operation, desired by the company to enable it to proceed effectively and speedily with the work so far as Legislation was desirable in aid of such modes.

On the 15th December, Hon. DANIEL WELLS, Jr. introduced a bill which conformed substantially to the foregoing bill prepared by Mr. KILBOURN, which was twice read, laid on the table and extra copies ordered printed. No action was had on it at that session, which adjourned on the 22d December, until the 21st January. In the mean time a feeling had been for some time growing in Milwaukee and Jefferson counties, in the supposed interests of the settlers upon the ten mile strip embracing the canal grant, and in favor of promoting settlements on that strip, on the one hand, and of consequent hostility to the construction of the canal on the other. These feelings were founded upon the opinion that the construction of the canal, and the plans of the company for the disposition of the lands, would greatly enhance the cost of the lands and retard the settlement of the country.

Whether these popular feelings influenced the action of the Legislative Assembly or not, it is certain that its action was very different from and far short of what the canal company deemed desirable to promote the effectual and speedy construction of their proposed work.

While the Legislature adopted the idea of long credits and low interest in making sales of canal lands, thus closing the door to any immediate revenue from that source, they declined to authorize the making of a loan on the credit of the Territory of any such sum as was adequate to the construction of the work, or even of its commencement in such a manner as to give promise of its completion.

The bill introduced by Mr. WELLS in December, probably died with the adjourument, but whether it did or not, it was not afterwards considered.

On the 25th of January, a new bill on the subject was introduced by Hon. WM. A. PRENTISS, which was copied largely in its details from the one prepared by the president of the canal company, but differed from that very materially in some of its most essential features.

It was amended in both houses, and on the 26th February received the approval of the Governor, and thereby became a law under the title of

"An act to provide for aiding in the construction of the Milwaukee and Rock River canal."

The first section enacted

"That to aid in the construction of the Milwaukee and Rock River canal, the Governor of the Territory be and he is hereby authorized to borrow *on the pledges hereinafter provided*, any sum or sums of money not exceeding *fifty* thousand dollars." * * *

The "pledges" were :

"The proceeds of the sales of lands granted by Congress to aid in the construction of said canal, together with the interest money accruing thereon, the revenues derived from the use of the canal and accruing to the Territory or State of Wisconsin, the whole or so much of the canal as shall belong to, or by law vest in the said Territory or State."

The words "pledges hereinafter provided" were inserted in lieu of the words "credit of the Territory of Wisconsin," which were in the bill as introduced.

The words "and the faith of the Territory" in the bill as introduced following the other "pledges" above quoted, were stricken out in the Council on motion.

These amendments, reducing the amount to be borrowed from $500,000 to $50,000, and withholding the credit and faith of the Territory, were the most important.

Instead of three "commissioners of appraisal" in addition to the register and receiver, as proposed by Mr. KILBOURN'S bill, the act provided that—

"There shall be appointed by the Governor, by and with the advice and consent of the Council, three commissioners to be styled the Board of Canal Commissioners, one of whom shall be designated as the acting commissioner, one as register and one as receiver."

* * * "The register and receiver shall each receive for their services an annual salary of one thousand dollars, and the acting commissioner an annual salary of twelve hundred dollars."

The board of canal commissioners were to make a registry of the occupied lands, and an appraisal of the other lands, as the "commissioners of appraisal" were by the KILBOURN bill required to do, but the act as passed extended the time to which the making of improvements should relate from the 1st day of December, 1838, as provided in the KILBOURN bill, to the 1st day of February, 1839. It also included among the tracts which might be registered as "occupied,"—

"Any quarter or fractional quarter section, claimed agreeably to the rules of the country adjoining a quarter or fractional quarter of an even numbered section, on both or either of which improvements by cultivation have been made to the amount of three acres, or on which a mill had been built prior to the 1st day of February, 1839."

The rule of minimum valuations, varying from $2.50 to $10 per acre, according to the distance of the tract from the canal and other circumstances, contained in the KILBOURN bill, was not retained in the act as passed.

The plan proposed by the canal company in the Kilbourn bill, of extending the time for the sale of the lands, except the "occupied" lands, through a series of years from 1839 to 1845, was not adopted.

The twenty-second section of this act contained a provision which the canal company regarded as injurious to the progress of the work, which was as follows :

"No canal commissioner, director or stockholder of the canal company, or engineer employed on said canal shall purchase or be interested in the purchase of any of the lands authorized to be sold by virtue of any of the provisions of this act, nor shall be interested in any contract for the construction of any portion of the canal, or furnishing materials therefor."

Another act was passed, approved February 20, 1839, by which the directors were authorized to sell at public sale any shares of stock in the company, upon which assessments were not paid, and the purchaser of any share at any public sale should be liable to pay any assessment that might thereafter become due. Stockholders were by the act authorized to vote by proxy, and the directors were authorized to fill vacancies in the board. This act was accepted by a vote of the directors May 1, 1839.

On the 4th of March, the Governor, by and with the advice and consent of the Council, made the following appointments:

Register — HANS CROCKER.
Receiver — JOHN H. TWEEDY.
Acting Commissioner — LEMUEL W. WEEKS.
Chief Engineer — ALEXANDER M. MITCHELL.

In the month of March an engineer party was again organized by the canal company and a final location of the line was completed, and a report submitted to the directors on the 6th day of May.

It is impossible to give an accurate description of the line of this location, except by a delineation on a map, and only an approximate one will be attempted.

The canal was to unite with the Milwaukee River on its right bank, a very short distance above where Chestnut street came to the river. From thence a canal was to be constructed along the right bank of the river for a distance of about one mile, to where a dam and lock were to be constructed, and the water in the river raised thereby about ten feet. This dam was designed to create slackwater navigation in the river for several miles above, and furnish an adequate supply of water below, not only for the uses of canal navigation, but for the numerous water powers between the canal and the river. The location contemplated the use of the slack water of the river in lieu of the canal

MILWAUKEE AND ROCK RIVER CANAL

to a point in section 5, town 7, range 22, a distance of about four miles, where it was proposed to leave the river and construct a canal running a little north of west, through the town of Granville, to the Menomonee River, at a point in section 36, town 8, range 20, near the southeast corner of the town of Germantown, thence southwesterly in the town of Menomonee to the Pishtaka (Fox) River, in section 29, town 8, range 20; thence to Weaver's Run, in the town of Lisbon, at section 35, town 8, range 19. From Weaver's Run the location passed westerly through the town of Lisbon, in which town the summit was reached.

The Territorial Engineer (Mr. A. M. MITCHELL) in his report to the Governor in October, 1839, says —

"Within two miles of the summit is the beginning of a chain of lakes, presenting almost a connection of waters, easily made navigable to the eastern bend of Rock River, a distance of twelve or fifteen miles." * * * "From La'Belle Lake to Rock River is a valley which appears to have been designed to unite the two."

The location of the canal from the summit to the outlet of La'Belle Lake passed through parts of the towns of Lisbon, Merton, Delafield and Oconomowoc. After leaving the valley of La'Belle Lake it passed through the towns of Summit and Concord, through which last town the location took a southwesterly course to Johnson's Creek, in section 27, township 7, range 15, in the town of Farmington, and thence pursuing a westerly course bearing south for a distance of about six miles it intersected Rock River at a point which was designated Cinniscippi, between Jefferson and Bellville.

This location was adopted by the board of directors on the 6th of May, and plats of the line were immediately forwarded to the Governor and to the Commissioner of the General Land Office, and the lands granted to the Territory were designated and set off by the commissioner agreeably to the act of Congress, being the alternate sections, numbered with odd numbers, ten miles wide, and extending from Lake Michigan to Rock River

The whole number of acres thus designated and set off by the commissioner was 139,190.91.

The next session of the Legislative Assembly convened at Madison December 2, 1839.

On the 9th day of December the report of the board of canal commissioners was presented to the Council, through the President.

The report states that the occupied and improved lands registered as contemplated by the law of the previous session were 43,677.10 acres.

The sale of these registered lands was commenced on the fourth Monday of June, and one tract was sold, when, as no returns had been received of the designation of the canal lands, the sale was adjourned until the 2d day of July.

On the 2d July, the complete returns having been received by the commissioners, they proceeded with the sale, and within three days all registered land was sold, except 240 acres, at the minimum price of $2.50 per acre.

The report states:

The number of acres sold amounted to	$43,447 10
Total value at $2.50 per acre	108,617 75
Ten per cent. required to be paid at the time of sale was	10,861 77
Total amount of receipts	12,337 27

In some instances more than ten per cent. was paid, which increased the total amount of receipts by $1,475.50 over the ten per cent. required to be paid at the time of sale.

The amount of lands granted, after deducting the number of acres sold was 95,743.81, subject to the subsequent action of the Legislature.

In relation to the "settlers" and the registered land, the report says:

"It is with great satisfaction that the undersigned have it in their power to inform you, that the first and immediate object of the canal law, to-wit: the protection of the settlers upon the canal lands, has been happily accomplished, beyond even the most sanguine hopes of the settlers themselves."

"We believe," the report continues, "that in no instance has a meritorious settler been shut out of the equity of any provisions of the act or suffered by the competition of others at the sale."

The Governor in his annual message, delivered December 3d, says that by the act approved February 26, 1839

"The Governor was authorized to borrow the sum of $50,000. Accordingly bonds were issued to that amount on the 5th of August last, executed by me in the name of the Territory, and under authority of an act of Congress, for one thousand dollars each, bearing an interest of six per cent. per annum, payable twenty years thereafter.

"John H. Tweedy, Esq., was appointed the agent of the Territory to make sale of the bonds." * * * * * * * * * * * *

"Mr. Tweedy, in his report to me on this subject, states that stocks of every nature were depressed to a lower point than they had at any time been for many years, not excepting the panic of 1837. The seven per cent. stocks of the city of New York were selling at 95; New York State Bonds — four per cent.— at 7½ and the bonds of most of the other States, least encumbered with debt, were totally unsalable. Money was commanding three times the ordinary interest in all the larger cities and in the smaller places of business."

MILWAUKEE AND ROCK RIVER CANAL.

The Governor in his message further says:

"In the report of the chief engineer, made in obedience to the fifteenth section of the act of February 26, 1839, the estimated cost of the construction of the canal is given at less than twelve hundred thousand dollars."

The board of commissioners in their report say:

"At the time of the passage of the law no difficulty was anticipated in negotiating the loan authorized by the Legislature.

"It is a source of regret that unfortunate circumstances in the matter of the location of the canal prevented an effort being made to sell the bonds of the Territory before the attempt became hopeless. Had the effort been made in April, May or June, we have reason to believe that it would have been attended with success.

"The bonds executed by the Governor and Secretary are now in the custody of the Receiver and can be used again should another attempt be authorized or deemed expedient."

The report further says:

"The establishment at present superintending the interests of the Territory in the construction of the canal, is in many respects liable to serious objections and ought to be reorganized if continued at all, on a reduced and more economical scale. The salaries of the several officers should be reduced to a fair compensation for actual services rendered and required. The provision which would best meet every exigency would be to fix the compensation of the Register and Receiver, or any officer that may be substituted in their places, a percentage on the receipts and disbursements, and fees for recording and other services, and that of the acting commissioner by a per diem allowance for actual services."

The attention of the Legislature was called by the report —

"To the defect of the canal law, in not making any provisions for the payment of the salaries of the officers under that law." * * *

"The Receiver therefore has not felt himself authorized to part with any of the funds in his hands for that purpose, without special instruction from the Legislature, however obvious it may be that it was the intention of that body that such funds should and must be so applied in the absence of any loan."

The Governor, in his annual message before referred to, says:

"I would recommend to the Legislative Assembly the propriety of so amending the act as to authorize the payment of the salaries of the chief engineer and commissioners of the canal out of the proceeds of the sales of the canal lands."

The message of the Governor suggests —

"The propriety of memorializing Congress to place the occupants of the alternate sections (the even numbered sections) in the same situation as other settlers, on the public domain, by allowing them the right of pre-emption, and permitting them to enter their lands at the minimum price of the public lands."

A memorial was adopted by the Legislature praying Congress:

"To grant a pre-emption right at $1.25 per acre, to all those who had settled on the alternate sections previously to the passage of the law by which those lands were reserved to the United States."

On the 9th of December, a memorial adopted by the canal company on the 25th of November, was presented in the House of Representatives. The memorial represented that the 22d section of the act of the last session, which has been quoted, was in violation of the rights of the company, injurious to the progress of the work and to the bests interests of the country. That it presented a bar to subscriptions to the stock of the company by depriving stockholders of the ordinary rights of citizens in the purchase of land and in furnishing material and supplies for the canal.

The memorial said:

"Some of our most enterprising citizens have been restrained from taking the stock of the company who were anxious to do so, for the reason that if the work should be commenced, they wished to take and be interested in contracts. Many of our citizens would be willing to take a few shares each, and pay the amount of such shares by constructing portions of the canal, and in this way give impetus to a work in which they are all alike interested, but they dare not do this lest they should be cut off from the privilege of taking other contracts in the further progress of the work, from the circumstance of their holding stock in the company."

The memorialists stated that they were clearly of the opinion that the effect of this provision would be to give a death-blow to the canal, and if the design had been (which they did not believe) to defeat it entirely, a more effectual method could not have been adopted.

They stated that many of the settlers on the canal lands, on which they had extensive improvements, had before the act containing this restrictive clause was passed, subscribed for stock in the company, who, in order to be entitled to purchase their lands, had been compelled to sell their stock.

They further stated that by the act of congress making the grant, the land was required to be sold to the "highest bidder," and ask if a stockholder should be the "highest bidder," would it be competent for the legislature or any officer to say that such "highest bidder" should not have the land? Would the sale be a legal one if the Register and Receiver were to strike it off to a lower bidder?

The memorialists therefore prayed the Legislature to repeal so much of the 22d section of the act as is contained in the foregoing extract.

A considerable portion of the memorial was devoted to showing that a spirit of hostility existed in certain quarters to the canal which assumed the form of attacks upon the canal company. The memorial sets forth the nature of these attacks, and undertakes to meet them and to demonstrate that they have no foundation in fact, or in any but unworthy motives, and as an evidence of the good faith of the company says:

"Our great and paramount object is to see the canal in successful operation, and we would willingly forego all the direct advantages to result to us growing out of the charter, if by so doing we could have the assurance of its speedy and certain completion by any other means. Let us but have the full assurance that the canal can and will be completed by any other means, and we will gladly lay down our charter at the feet of the Legislature. We ask no rights or privileges which are not open to the people of the whole Territory, and we invite the co-operation of the people of every section to come forward and invest their money and share equally in the benefits to be derived from the work, and we extend this invitation to those who have assailed us most violently and bitterly."

The memorial represented that the salaries of the board of canal commissioners (register, receiver and acting commissioner) and of the chief engineer were extravagantly high, and proposed that the compensation of the register and receiver be one per centum to each on all moneys by them received, and one per centum on all moneys paid out, and fees for other special duties. That the compensation of the acting commissioner should be three dollars per day for such time as was devoted to the discharge of his duties.

"If these prices were this year paid (the memorial states) instead of the salaries allowed by law, the amount chargable to the canal fund for commissioners' salaries would be about $260 instead of $3,200, making a saving of $2,940, without any detriment to the public service."

The salary of the chief engineer was fixed by the law at $3,000 annually, which the memorialists think was $1,000 too much. Upon that subject they say:

"A still further reduction might have been secured, and may in the future be made, by merging the Territorial engineer and the Company engineer in one." * * *

"If that system were adopted here, it is believed that the commissioners on the part of the Territory, and the directors on the part of the company, would be able to agree in the appointment of an engineer, and it will be apparent to every one that one engineer is sufficient to conduct the affairs of a canal sixty miles in length as well as a greater number."

* * * * * * * * * *

" In case of the commissioners and directors so agreeing the salary could be paid, one moiety by the Territory and the other by the Canal Company; consequently if a competent engineer can be employed for $2,000 per annum only $1,000 could be chargeable to the canal fund instead of $3,000 as in the present arrangement. * * * * *

" The present year's expense for commissioners and engineer, amounts to $6,200, without there having been expended one dollar of public funds for the promotion of the canal. The only official duties which have been performed by the commissioners, being to dispose of the occupied lands, the receipts from which are understood to be about $13,000 ($12,337.27 by their report), and the only professional duties discharged being to express his opinion in regard to the location of the canal line and its cost of construction."

In reference to the work on the canal the memorial states:

"In June a letting of jobs took place under the direction of the company, at which several sections of the canal were put under contract. One of the contractors, Mr. PETTIBONE, has commenced operations and has notified the board of directors that he is willing to continue his operations through the winter on a portion of the work which can be done with much better effect at that season than any other, and he will advance his own means for that purpose to be remunerated whenever the Company shall obtain funds to meet it, or whenever a loan shall be obtained by the Territory applicable to that purpose. These jobs have been let on favorable terms and we feel a confidence in their completion within a year or eighteen months; so far as to make the water power at this place available, even if the times remain unfavorable for a loan." * . * * * * * *

" Your memorialists would further respectfully represent that the present amount of population and the increased productions of the country afford facilities for the performance of labor, which would justify the expenditure within the next year of at least $100,000. This sum could be economically and beneficially expended, and should the condition of the money affairs of the country be such as to enable the Territory to effect a loan to that amount, we feel justified in expressing the opinion that good policy would dictate the measure. This would require an additional appropriation of $50,000, which could be negotiated with the present bonds for $50,000."

Immediately after this memorial was introduced, it was, on motion of Mr. WELLS of Milwaukee, laid on the table, and he offered the following resolutions, which were immediately adopted:

"*Resolved*, That the officers of the Milwaukee and Rock River Canal Company be requested to report to this House as soon as may be, upon the following points:

"First. That the President state under oath, the quantity of land given by individuals, in consideration of the location and termination of said canal, at different points upon the route, to whom and to whose benefit said lands were donated.

"Second. That the secretary of said company state on oath the amount of capital stock taken, the amount actually paid in, by whom it was taken, the names of the present holders, and the amounts held by each; also state on oath the number of offices created by said company, by whom held, and the compensation allowed to each of said officers and to each member of said company during the past year.

"Third. That the treasurer of said company state on oath the amount and kind of money actually paid and now in his hands.

"*Resolved*, That the chief clerk transmit a copy of these resolutions to each of said officers.

On the 28th of December the Speaker laid before the House a communication from Mr. KILBOURN, the president of the company, in answer to these resolutions.

He stated that he was on the eve of his departure for Madison when he received the resolutions; that the time required to make a detailed statement upon all the points requested would be such as probably to defeat the beneficial results designed; that the resolutions were, however, laid before the directors, who by resolution authorized the president to give such information generally, touching the affairs of the company, as might be desired by the Legislature, or by any committee of either house, and to state definitely the views of the board on the following points:

1st. That if desired the company would report annually to the Legislature all the facts connected with their operations relative to the canal, embracing the points covered by the aforesaid resolutions, and such other matters as they might deem useful to the public or of interest to the Legislature. That the company are not required by their charter to make such report, and were not requested to do so until it was too late for the present session, and had the Legislature expressed at an earlier day its desire to receive such a report, the company would promptly and voluntarily have complied. They had nothing to conceal, and would freely at all times, when desired, exhibit their books and transactions to the Legislature, to the canal commissioners, or to the public.

2d. That so long as the company exists in their corporate capacity, and bear a part in the prosecution of the canal, they conceive themselves entitled to exercise all the rights and privileges conferred by the act of incorporation.

3d. That the company will at any time surrender into the hands of the Territory all the privileges conferred by the charter, and all property purchased by or donated to the company, or to any person on behalf of the company, on condition that they can be assured of the vigorous prosecution and early completion of the canal by the Territory.

4th. That during the two years since the formation of the company their expenditures have been but about $8,000. This includes all the expenses of the company, in running the first experimental levels, the subsequent random levels, and the final survey of location and the obtaining the grant of land.

"It was not the province of the President (he said) to institute a comparison between this expenditure of the company for *two* years past, and the amount of business transacted by them, with the territorial expenditures of the last year, and the necessarily small amount of busines transacted by its officers in furtherance of its work. Such a comparison will readily be made by the Legislature, who are in possession of all the material facts, and might be considered invidious in me."

On motion of Mr. BILLINGS, of Iowa county, a resolution was adopted by the House of Representatives on the 26th December:

"That the President of the Milwaukee and Rock River Canal Company be requested to inform the House upon what terms said company will surrender to the Territory the privileges conferred upon them by the act of incorporation."

In response to this resolution the President of the company, on the 28th December, submitted the following propositions:

"First. Satisfactory assurance to be given that the work will be commenced by the Territory as soon as the money affairs of the country will enable a loan to be effected, or if such loan cannot be obtained before September next, that the funds then on hand and thereafter accruing will be currently applied to the work, from. that time until a loan can be effected, said funds to be applied to the performance of work on the jobs now under contract, and for which the company are held liable to the contractors.

"Second. The company will transfer to the Territory all lands and contracts for lands held by the company, or by others on behalf of the company, subject to the conditions of the original contracts between the grantors and the company, the Territory to exonerate the company from all liabilities under or growing out of such contracts.

"Third. That no material alteration be made in the line of the canal, as now located, without the concurrence of the company."

"Fourth. That an amount of work be performed on the canal from and after the first loan can be obtained equal to $50,000 or upwards each year, and the canal be completed in ten years from the passage of the act of grant by congress.

"Fifth. That the Territory pay to the company in the manner prescribed in the charter, the amount which they have expended prior to the time of transfer."

Appended to each of the propositions was a statement of its object and the reasons for it, and the response contained a statement of the estimated cost of the work, and concluded as follows:

"In estimating this work, the prices affixed to each item are believed to be from twenty to twenty-five per cent. above what they will actually cost, in order to render the estimates entirely safe, and yet the aggregate estimate falls a little short of a million of dollars, after adding ten per cent. for incidental expenses. The estimates of the company in detail are subject to the inspection of the Legislature whenever desired.

"I am clearly satisfied that these estimates will be found to cover the entire cost, and would not hesitate to enter into contract at any time to perform the work at the prices estimated. Should the Legislature take the work off the hands of the company, I will as an individual, if desired, enter into a contract to that effect, and perform the work in advance of the payments monthly."

On motion of Mr. MARTIN, of Brown county, it was resolved by the Council on the 30th December

"That the President of the Milwaukee and Rock River Canal Company be requested to lay before the Council the plans and estimates of the cost of construction of the said canal and such other information as he may deem proper to submit."

In compliance with this resolution, the President on the same day submitted the detailed estimates of the cost of constructing the canal, which he stated had been revised by the Territorial Engineer, and approved by him.

In making the estimates, the whole work was divided into sixty-one sections of various lengths from a half mile to two miles or more, but usually about one mile long, and the estimated cost of each section given under the different heads of grubbing, excavation, embankment, cost of locks, dams and culverts, to which was added an estimate for three feeders. The total estimates were $901,043.31, to which was added ten per cent. for contingencies, making a total of $991,148.73.

In the House a committee of one from each election district was on the 20th of December appointed to consider the several matters before the House relating to the canal and the canal company.

On the 28th of December, the committee submitted the following report:

"That after having the matter under consideration, your committee deem it inexpedient to attempt to prosecute the work on the canal at present for the following reasons:

"First. The embarrassed state of the currency of the United States your committee believe would render it difficult, if not impossible for the Territory to effect a loan on its bonds without selling them at a discount.

"Second. Your committee are of the opinion that to go on and expend the proceeds of the lands granted by Congress to aid in the construction of said canal, would be placing the Territory in a situation either to be liable to the general government for the repayment of the money or to incur a much heavier debt for the completion of said work, which would be useless without being finished.

"Third. Your committee did not deem satisfactory the answers of the president of the canal company to the resolution of this House, calling on the officers of said company for an exposition of their affairs, that the Territory might judge as to the propriety of prosecuting said work in connection with said company.

"Fourth. That in the location of said canal your committee believe that great injustice was done to some of the settlers living on the government lands, by locating said canal and having the lands selected and sold without the acceptance of the Territorial engineer, and after this having been done, a new location made by the said company, by which a number of occupants on said lands were thrown from six to eight miles from the line of said canal, and still compelled to pay $2.50 per acre for their lands and not entitled to the right of pre-emption.

"Fifth. Your committee find a proposition in the communication from the president of the canal company to this House, that they (the company) would surrender their charter to the Territory, on conditions that they can be assured that the Territory will prosecute and complete the work.

"Your committee believe that it would be a very improper course for the Legislature to take to bind the Territory to perform certain things with her own means.

"Your committee deem it unnecessary to give any further reasons, believing that the above are sufficient, and beg leave to report the accompanying bill for the consideration of the House."

This bill, entitled "A bill to amend an act entitled 'An act to provide for aiding in the construction of the Milwaukee and Rock River canal,' approved February 26, 1839, and for other purposes," provided for the unqualified repeal of the act of February 26, 1839, except sections 10, 11, 12 and 13, which provided for the issuing of patents and giving of mortgages for lands sold. It contemplated the abandonment of the construction of the canal, and the withdrawal and cancellation of the bonds authorized by the act of 1839 to be issued.

When the bill came up for consideration in the House, amendments were proposed contemplating an opposite policy, by applying to the construction of the canal the proceeds of the sales of the lands, in case a loan should not be effected. The amendments were adopted by a vote of 15 to 11, the eight members of the committee which reported the bill being equally divided.

The bill as it was amended in the House finally passed the Council, and on the 11th of January, 1840, became a law.

The main features of this law were:

In section 1. That the compensation of the register and receiver should be a percentage on the amount of money received by them, and the acting commissioner and engineer should receive a per diem compensation, instead of the salaries which those officers had previously received, and the maximum pay of the register and receiver was to be reduced to $300 per annum.

Section 2 authorized the Governor to pay out of the canal fund the back salary of these officers.

Section 3 provided that the canal commissioners should be elected by joint ballot of the two houses, instead of being appointed by the Governor and Council.

Section 4 enacted that in case a loan should not be effected by the first day of September, the money of the canal fund should be applied to the construction of the canal, in the same manner that money obtained by loan was authorized by law to be applied. but when a loan should be effected, all moneys in the canal fund should be applied to the payment of interest and the liquidation of the loan, as prescribed by the act of 1839.

Section 5 regulated the details of payments.

Section 6 related to reports of the canal company to the Legislature. Under this law the Legislature made the following elections:

GEORGE H. WALKER, *Acting Commissioner.*

MILWAUKEE AND ROCK RIVER CANAL.

JOHN HUSTIS, *Register.*
JOHN H. TWEEDY, *Receiver.*
The Governor appointed
I. A. LAPHAM, *Chief Engineer.*

On the 14th of March Gov. DODGE appointed BYRON KILBOURN agent in behalf of the Territory to negotiate the canal loan of $50,000 authorized by the act of February 26, 1839, and delivered the bonds to him and appointed the Bank of America, in the city of New York, as the depository of the loan.

On the 21st of April Mr. KILBOURN communicated to the Governor a proposition from S. HIGGINBOTHAM to take $25,000 of the loan at par on condition that four years interest was paid in advance, and at the same time he communicated a resolution adopted by the canal company on the 20th of April, that the company would pay to the Territory as a gratuity, if the loan should be effected on these terms:

"An amount equal to six per cent. interest on all installments of interest which shall be so paid prior to the time when the same would become due in semi-annual payments on said loan, whereby the said loan will be secured to the Territory at '*the par or nominal value or amount thereof,*' in accordance with the *terms* of the act without subjecting the Territory to any loss or deduction for interest so paid in advance."

In his letter to the Governor, Mr. KILBOURN advised the acceptance of the proposition of Mr. HIGGINBOTHAM for the reasons that the Territory had the money on hand to pay the interest in advance and it was lying entirely useless to the Territory, and by making this diposition of it a fund might be obtained for active use, which would confer a very essential benefit on the Territory.

"But," he said, "as it might leave room for those who are disposed to cavil at anything to endeavor to make it appear that the loan was obtained as much below the 'par or nominal value or amount thereof' as the use of the interest money would be worth so paid in advance," * * * the Canal Company "propose to pay to the Territory *six* per cent. on the amount so advanced, which will in fact amount to a *premium* on the bonds to that amount more than the Territory would receive if the canal fund should be permitted to lie dormant as at present."

The Governor, in his reply to the letter of the loan agent, said:

" I do not think I have any discretionary powers that would authorize me in drawing a draft on the receiver of the canal fund, for the interest of $25,000 for the term of four years in advance. He might refuse the payment of any amount not authorized by the existing laws. And any proposition of the board of directors, which they may deem advantageous for the prosecution of the work of the canal, it appears to me belongs entirely to the Legislative Assembly of the Territory, who, I have no doubt would readily agree to the passage of such a loan as would meet the provisions contained in the resolutions of the board of directors of the 20th ultimo. It would certainly have my concurrence."

The correspondence was laid before the Legislative Assembly, at an extra session held on the first Monday of August, but no action was taken upon the subject, nor was anything done at that session relative to the canal, or the loan in aid of its completion.

No part of the authorized loan of $50,000 was negotiated during the year 1840.

A loan not having been effected by the first day of September, the money belonging to the canal fund, became, by the act of January 11, 1840, applicable to the construction of the canal.

Mr. KILBOURN, agent to negotiate the loan, wrote to the Governor on November 19th, from Ohio, that he had

"Opened negotiations with several capitalists, with a view of obtaining said loan. Owing, however, to the peculiar state of the money market, and the depressed condition of the business affairs of the country, I have not thus far (he said) been able to accomplish that object."

The agent also suggested an amendment of the act authorizing the loan, by increasing the interest to seven per cent., and permitting the money to be received at any specie paying bank wherever it would best suit the convenience of the parties taking up the loan. He thought a speedy negotiation of the loan could be made with these two modifications of the law.

The next annual session of the Legislative Assembly was held on the first Monday (7th day) of December, 1840.

On the 10th the Speaker laid before the House the annual report of the canal company, and on the 15th Mr. BARBER presented the report of the canal commissioners.

An extra number of both reports was ordered to be printed, and both referred to a select committee—Messrs. BARBER, RAY and GRAY.

Both reports recommended the adoption of the two modifications of the law authorizing the loan suggested by the loan agent.

Both concurred also in recommending the substitution of wooden locks in place of stone, with some exceptions.

The report of the canal company presented a view of its operations during the year, and that of the canal commissioners exhibited a full account of their official actions for the same time. They both showed harmonious co-operation, and that of the commissioners presented a roseate view of the condition and prospects of the canal.

It showed that the amount of work under contract was	$25,158
The amount of work done	3,430
The amount paid for work	3,141
The amount to be paid	22,017

It states

"That the contract prices of that portion of the work now in progress are forty per cent. below the original estimates of the same work, and upon which the estimates of the entire cost of the canal were based."

It contained an estimate of the reduced price of the whole work on the hypothesis that a corresponding difference should be found between the estimates and contracts. It adopted 25 per cent. as a safer calculation than 40, of the actual difference.

The original estimates of the total cost were	$991,148 73
A difference of 25 per cent. would be	247,787 18
The actual estimated cost	$743,361 55

It estimated that the saving by substituting wooden locks for stone would be $120,000, and that the estimate of $23,760 for the construction of a tow path along the Milwaukee River from the point where the canal connects with the river to its mouth, and of $1,295 for a pier at the harbor, might be entirely dispensed with or materially diminished. These reductions of cost amount to $145,055 and would reduce the total cost of the canal to a sum below $600,000.

In concluding the report the commissioners say:

"To the Territory, the path of duty and policy is clearly pointed out. Every consideration of her own interest, or her duties to the people, or justice to the settlers, should prompt her to embrace the cause of the canal with her whole soul and energy. What liability she can incur, she has already incurred. Recede she cannot. To advance easy and safe. Delay and vacillation alone are difficult and dangerous. Doing as she will do, her whole duty, she will in a few short years, without a dollar of debt contracted, or a, dollar of liability assumed, or if so, only when amply secured, have achieved an enterprise which will enrich her with constant, copious streams of wealth, and shed an imperishable glory on the rising State of Wisconsin."

On the 14th of January, Mr. BARBER, from the select committee to which the various reports had been referred, submitted a report, which coincided with the views expressed in the report of the canal commissioners, and embodied them in a bill, which passed the House without a division, and the Council by a vote of 11 to 2, and having been approved by the Governor on the 12th of February, became a law on that day.

The material provisions of this law were:

That in the construction of the locks on the canal it should be lawful to substitute wood instead of stone, whenever, in the opinion of the chief engineer, approved by the canal commissioners, such substitution shall be deemed expedient.

That the Governor of the Territory be authorized to execute and issue bonds in the name of the Territory, for any sum not exceeding $100,000, bearing an interest of *seven* per cent. per annum, payable semi-annually; provided, that the moneys might be deposited in any sound specie-paying banks, which shall be selected by the canal commissioners and the Governor of the Territory, subject to the draft of the receiver of the canal funds, whenever the same may be required for expenditures on the canal.

The act further provided that the bonds previously issued for $50,000, which should not have been negotiated should be recalled, and if any of them had been sold, then the new bonds should be issued to such an amount only as should with the loan thus effected be equal to the sum of $100,000.

This act also contained provisions for the sale of such of the unsold canal lands as were wanted for immediate occupation and improvement, and all the details requisite to give effect to such provisions.

It made it the duty of the acting commissioner to protect from trespass and waste all timber on any of the canal lands.

Another act approved December 24, 1840, postponed the collection of the semi-annual interest until the Legislature should provide by law for its collection, and a later act approved February 19, 1841, made it the duty of the canal commissioners, whenever any loan should be negotiated, so to fix the time when payment of interest should be made as to meet the interest semi-annually, accruing on such loan and to give three months' notice thereof by newspaper publication.

On the 9th of February the canal commissioners were elected by joint ballot of the two houses.

Messrs. WALKER, HUSTIS and TWEEDY were re-elected to the offices of *acting commissioner, register* and *receiver* respectively.

The act of February 26, 1839, by the twentieth section of which the Governor was authorized to appoint agents for obtaining loans, was specially recognized as being in force, and consequently the authority of the Governor to appoint agents to negotiate the bonds for $100,000, authorized to be issued by the act of February 12, 1841, remained in force.

Governor DODGE, acting upon this construction of his authority, on the 13th of May, 1841, renewed the appointment of Mr. KILBOURN as loan agent and authorized him

"Upon receiving from any person or persons a certificate of the cashier of either of the safety fund banks in the State of New York, or any specie paying bank or banks that he or they have deposited with the said cashier any specified amount of money, subject to the order of the receiver of the canal funds as mentioned in the last aforesaid act (of February 12, 1841), to deliver over to such person or persons so many of the said certificates (bonds), aforesaid, as shall not exceed in amount the sum so deposited."

During the summer of 1841 Gov. DODGE was removed from the office of Governor by President TYLER, and JAMES D. DOTY appointed his successor.

On the 1st day of September, 1841, Governor DOTY addressed a communication to Mr. KILBOURN at Milwaukee, he then being in the state of New York or Ohio, notifying him that all authority as loan agent conferred upon him by Governor DODGE was "revoked and annulled."

On the next day (September 2d) notice was —

"Given to the public that BYRON KILBOURN, Esq., of Milwaukee, is not authorized to sell or otherwise dispose of any bonds or certificates of stock made by the late executive of the Territory of Wisconsin, in virtue of the provisions of the act entitled 'an act supplementary to the several acts relating to the Milwaukee and Rock River canal,' for the sum of one thousand dollars each, and bearing date the 15th day of March, A. D. 1841, as no authority was given by said act or any other act, to said KILBOURN to negotiate a loan upon the said bonds or certificates of stock.

MADISON, September 2, 1841.   J. D. DOTY, Governor."

Under date of December 27, 1841, Mr. KILBOURN made a report of his proceeding under his appointment as the accredited agent of the executive.

The following extract from this report gives, he said, "a simple detail of the transactions:"

"On the 22d of June last I closed negotiations at Cincinnati for loans amounting to thirty-one thousand dollars, one thousand of which was then deposited, and certificates of deposit forwarded to JOHN H. TWEEDY, Esq., receiver of canal funds. The remainder of $30,000 was to be deposited in monthly installments of $3,000 per month, for the purpose of meeting current payments on the canal, as the same fell due at the close of each month, beginning on the last day of July, and thereafter on the last day of each month, until the whole amount shall be paid.

"For this purpose bonds were deposited in the Bank of the Ohio Life Insurance and Trust Company in Cincinnati to the same amount, with instructions to deliver said bonds whenever the funds were deposited as above stated. This arrangement was broken in upon by the receiver, in the manner set forth at length in my report to the Legislature, and the fund has in consequence thus far remained unproductive to the Territory. The person however with whom this negotiation was made (GEO. REED, Esq.,) has evinced his readiness to perform his part of the agreement, and has been subjected to some inconvenience by the preparation to perform, and the delay which has occurred on the part of the Territory by the interposition of the receiver.

"This loan can still be commanded by the Territory by a compliance on their part in the delivery of the bonds, which bonds still remain in suspense, they not having been delivered to Mr. REED, nor subject to be withdrawn by the Territory without a mutual agreement to that effect.

"On the 4th of August I closed an arrangement for a loan of $5,000 in the city of New York, the funds being deposited in the Bank of America. The certificates for this amount I have not delivered to the receiver for the reasons set forth in my report to the Legislature. But I am ready to pass those funds over to that officer whenever one shall be appointed who regards the law rather than his own will as his rule of action.

"On the 14th of August I closed an arrangement at Oneida for a loan of $15,000, to be deposited in the bank of Vernon at any time prior to the 1st of August, 1842, on which the first interest falls due on the 20th December, 1842, and bonds to the same amount were deposited in the bank of Vernon, subject to this arrangement. The object of this loan was to furnish a fund for the commencement of business at the opening of the next season, up to which time it was thought other loans had been or would be made, sufficient to keep the work in progress."

"On the 26th of August I closed an arrangement at Albany for a loan of $5,000, the funds to be deposited in the Albany City bank and State bank. The certificates for this amount I have not delivered to the receiver for the same reasons I withheld those obtained in the city of New York, but am in like manner ready to account for them to any successor to the late receiver.

"These several loans in the aggregate amount to $56,000, and are all the loans which have been made. The bonds sold are numbered from 1 to 56 inclusive, and the remainder of the bonds (44 in number) numbered from 57 to 100 inclusive, are subject to the disposal of the Governor and Legislature."

The manner in which the arrangements made by the loan agent "were broken in upon by the receiver" are stated in the following extracts from the report of the loan agent to the Legislature.

"Having completed my arrangements at Cincinnati for the $31,000, I wrote Mr. TWEEDY June 23, notifying him officially of the loan, and stated as clearly as I could find language to convey, the nature of the loan, in the following words: 'This loan I have been obliged to make in funds bankable at the Life and Trust Company, and consider even that very favorable under present circumstances, as that institution, being itself a specie paying bank, is very circumspect in the kind of funds it receives. I conceive that this is a discretion devolving solely on myself, but hope, as I trust, it will be satisfactory to you and the other commissioners. I shall leave to-morrow morning for New York, and shall spare no pains in my exertions to negotiate the remaining $69,000, wherever it can be found, and hope to find it at some of the eastern banks in their own funds.'"

* * * * * * * * * * *

"Mr. LAPHAM was at Cincinnati at the date of my letter, and by him I sent to Mr. TWEEDY two certificates of deposit amounting to $1,000, a part of the loan of $31,000, which, as has been before stated, were received by him and paid out for work on the canal."

* * * * * * * * * * *

"In reply to my letter of June 23d, I received, while in New York, a letter from Mr. TWEEDY, dated July 17th, in which he informs me that he 'wrote by the last mail to the

MILWAUKEE AND ROCK RIVER CANAL. 625

President of the Ohio Life Insurance and Trust Company, stating our views at large, and desiring him to suspend the transfer of the bonds until these objections were removed by you, at the same time expressing the belief that you would be able to make a satisfactory arrangement after your return from New York.' And soon after the receipt of this letter, I received one from Mr. WILLIAMS, the president of the bank, stating that he had 'received an official letter from JOHN H. TWEEDY, Esq., receiver of the canal fund, *objecting distinctly* to your sale of the bonds for *current bank notes*, or any other than legal currency, meaning, of course, coin. He objects to the Trust Company certificates because it is not payable in legal currency, and he says that you are not authorized to sell the bonds for any thing but legal currency,' etc."

"Whatever may be Mr. TWEEDY's professions in regard to the canal, I consider his *acts* more strongly indicative of his feelings than his *professions*." * * * *

"Such feelings, coupled with secret feelings of hostility toward me individually, for which I can assign no adequate cause, have in my opinion actuated him in the infliction of a public wrong." * * * * * * * * * *

"The difficulties thus interposed have arisen from an assumption of power on the part of said commissioners to interfere with and dictate *unconditionally* as to the loan and the kind of funds which might or might not be received, and to present clearly and under standingly the unjustifiable nature of this assumption, I will premise that by the law, the duty of making the loan devolves *entirely* and *exclusively* on the Governor alone; either by his own act or through means of agents to be by *him* appointed. (See act of February, 1839, sections one and twenty, and the act of February, 1841, section 2, quoted in the preceding part of this report.) Neither of said acts nor any other act, confers any power whatever on the commissioners to negotiate any loan, nor are they in any manner authorized to direct the Governor as to the manner in which he shall discharge the official duties devolving on him by law, or sit in judgment on his acts, whether they be right or wrong. Certain duties were to be discharged *by the Governor*, and if in the discharge of those duties, he violates the law he is responsible *to the law* and *to the country* for such violation and *not to the board of canal commissioners*, nor are they in any manner responsible for his acts. The law has not even *named* the commissioners in connection with the negotiation of the loan; neither as associating with them the Governor or otherwise; much less has it conferred on them a dictatorial supervisory control and absolute veto over his acts. Yet these same commissioners have by their acts assumed that the law has, or *ought* to have conferred on them this power." * * * * * * * *

"The law does not require the loan to be made in specie, and it is a fair presumption that it did not intend any such thing; but that if nothing better could be done, the territory would receive and disburse such funds as are used for the purposes of business throughout the western states, internal improvements of every kind included."

* * * * * * * * * * * *

"Notwithstanding all the difficulties which have had to be thus encountered to effect any loan; notwithstanding my loan at Cincinnati was a better one than has been made by any western state for years; notwithstanding the emergency of the case, and the importance of the present vigorous prosecution of the work; notwithstanding the total absence of any legal right to interfere with the loan, Mr. TWEEDY, backed up by Mr. HUSTIS, reckless of all consequences to the canal, to the rights of the people and the interests of the Territory, issues his imperial ukase, that the loan *shall not be paid out*, and that consequently the work *must stop!*"

* * * * * * * * * * *

"Out of the amount which has been placed in my hands ($11,000), I remitted to the receiver $1,000, leaving $10,000 in my hands to be accounted for. This fund I have declined

40

placing in the hands of Mr. TWEEDY, being well satisfied that if placed in his possession, he would, under some technical plea, refuse to disburse it at all, and thus consummate what had been well begun, a total overthrow of the whole work. It has not, therefore, been placed at his disposal, but in lieu thereof I have individually provided funds and paid on certificates of the engineer, a sum which, added to the contingent expenses of negotiating the loan and the remittance to discharge interest on the bonds, amounts to $10,041.87, being $41.87 more than I have received on the loan. These certificates are the proper vouchers on which the law makes it the duty of the register to draw his check on the receiver for payment, but on demand for such checks Mr. HUSTIS, the register, refused to issue them, without assigning any satisfactory reason. His acts, however, have made the reason so palpable that I am at no loss to comprehend it. It is simply, as I fully believe, a pre-determination on the part of Mr. HUSTIS, to aid in sustaining the untenable position of Mr. TWEEDY. though it should involve him in an open violation of his *duty* under the law."

* * * * * * * * * * * * *

"Considering the tone of feeling which has been but too clearly exhibited, and which I had no doubt would actuate Mr. TWEEDY in the disposal of the funds obtained on the loan, I would sooner have rescinded the loan or assumed it myself on behalf of the canal company, than permitted it to go into his hands to be locked up as a fund for him and other politicians to quarrel about. Even now, if the Territory prefers to stand indebted to the canal company for the same amount, bearing the same rate of interest (as it must do under our charter for all company expenditures) instead of these bonds, I have but little doubt but that the company would freely assume the debt. It would, however, be a useless transfer of securities, for sooner or later the Territory or State will have the whole cost of the work to pay either to the canal company or to those from whom the loans may be made to construct it."

A communication of JOHN H. TWEEDY to a select committee of the Council, to which was referred the report of the loan agent from which the foregoing extracts are taken, was called out by that report, and some extracts from the communication are submitted, which it is thought present the vindication of the conduct of Mr. TWEEDY and his associates, so far as that conduct is assailed in the foregoing extracts from the report of the loan agent.

"The personal and political relations between the loan agent and myself, which have been brought into view in the report, its many imputations, its lofty defiance and its vituperation and abuse I shall pass unnoticed.

* * * * * * * * * *

"The report charges in substance that the receiver has been guilty of an arbitrary and unwarranted interference with the duties of the loan agent, from motives of secret hostility to the canal, and has by such interference arrested and defeated a loan of $30,000.

* * * * * * *

"The truth of these charges and the justice of the credit or odium imputed to myself and others, will clearly appear from a true presentment of the facts.

* * * * * * * * *

"In the certificates or bonds delivered to the agent, the time and place, when and where the principal of the loan should be reimbursable, and also the names of the persons to whom the same should be due and payable were left in blank, which the said agent was (by said letter of authority) authorized to fill in such manner as should correspond with the loan which should be made.

MILWAUKEE AND ROCK RIVER CANAL. 627

"The canal commissioners by letter under their hands and seals in May or June, 1841, selected and designated any of the specie paying safety fund banks of New York, the Ohio Life Insurance and Trust Company of Cincinnati and two specie paying institutions of Columbus, as proper banks for the deposit of any moneys borrowed by the loan officer.

"These are the powers and the only powers given to the loan agent.

"Under this law and these powers the steps to be taken and the conditions to be observed in the sale of the bonds cannot be mistaken.

"1st. The money in equal amount to the bonds to be sold must be deposited.

"2nd. It must be deposited in a *sound specie paying bank*.

"That bank must be one selected or designated by the Governor and Commissioners.

"Certificates of the deposit of such money in such bank, signed by the cashier thereof, must be delivered by the agent.

"The certificates must be payable to the order of the Receiver of the canal fund.

"Then, and not till then, the agent is authorized to fill the blanks with the times, places and names corresponding with the loan and to deliver the certificates to the person entitled thereto.

"Here then was a special agent or attorney entrusted with a few simple and limited powers so plainly prescribed that they could not be misunderstood.

"There was no discretion to exercise, no responsibility to assume. He was authorized to do a particular act in a particular manner. He could not lawfully transfer, sell or contract for the sale of any of the bonds in his hands unless in the manner pointed out by the law and his instructions.   *   *   *   *   *   *   *   *

"I wish the attention of the committee to be here directed to two requisitions of the law, made part of the instructions of the loan agent, to which reference will be made hereafter.

"First. That the funds deposited or certificates, should be subject or payable to the order of the receiver of the canal fund.

"By the first provision not a dollar of the loan to be negotiated could be touched, controlled or come into the hands of the agent, who was not required to give any bonds to faithfully account for money received.

"That officer had no more authority by law and the instructions under which he acted, to take, keep and expend any of the funds for which the bonds might be negotiated, than he had to take, keep and expend any other funds of the Territory, without law or license.

"Second. To the kind of funds to be received on the loan.

"The law declares that the deposit should be made in *money*. The term *money*, unless qualified, can mean nothing but specie, or legal currency or its equivalent.
      *   *   *   *   *   *   *   *   *   *   *   *   *

"The law, in designating the character of the *bank*, intended to designate the character of the *funds*, and not only intended to secure the receipt of the loan in funds of the same character with the bank, to wit: the bills of sound specie paying banks, but also in the bills of such specie paying banks as the Governor and commissioners should select, as furnishing the best circulating medium.
      *   *   *   *   *   *   *   *   *   *   *   *   *

"The objections of the commissioners to the loan proposed by the agent were clearly drawn from their views of the law, and of the authority directing the agent, and may be distinctly stated as follows:

"The funds to be received were not the bills of the specie paying bank selected by the commissioners, where the deposit was to be made.

"They were not payable in the bills of any specie paying bank.

"They were not convertible into money at the place of deposit without a serious loss.

"They were liable to another objection.

"They were not for practical purposes equivalent, even to depreciated but current paper of suspended western banks, whose paper was designed to be excluded by law.

* * * * * * * * * * * *

"These are some of the objections to the proposed loan, honestly entertained by myself and the commissioners, and which fixed me in the resolution not to use the funds receivable on such loan.

"This resolution being formed, it became plainly my duty to give notice thereof to the parties whose arrangements might be affected thereby, that is to the loan agent, the depository of the bonds and to the contractors.

"That duty was performed by my letters to Mr. WILLIAMS and to Mr. KILBOURN.

"The loan agent not being at Cincinnati, I thought it prudent to desire Mr. WILLIAMS to cause the arrangements for the loan to be, for the time being, suspended, before the delivery of the bonds, until the objections to the loan could be avoided by converting the funds to be deposited into legal currency or its equivalent.

"I feared that unless the transfer of the bonds was suspended, the bonds might pass beyond the control of the agent.

"But the letter did 'distinctly object' to the kind of funds proposed to be received; did 'pronounce' such loan to be illegal; did give notice of the determination of the receiver not to sanction such loan by acceptance of the funds; did propose by a timely intervention to prevent any mischief or embarrassment likely to result from a transfer of the bonds."

Governor DOTY, in his annual message to the Legislative Assembly, on the 10th of December, 1841, said:

"I am bound to express to you my belief that it is quite impracticable to make a canal, upon the route surveyed from Milwaukee to Rock River, which will be of any utility to the public; and I am equally positive that under the system as it is now managed the work ought not to be continued."

This portion of the Governor's message was referred in the Council to a select committee of five, consisting of Messrs. TWEEDY, UPHAM, MARTIN, MAXWELL and STRONG, and subsequently the report of the loan agent was referred to the same committee, and the communication of Mr. TWEEDY, addressed to that committee, was also considered by it.

On the 3d of February, this select committee submitted a report, which, after giving the history of the conduct of the Governor, loan agent and canal commissioners in relation to the negotiation of a loan, concluded as follows:

We feel bound to express the opinion, that the 55 bonds of one thousand dollars each, said to have been negotiated by Mr. KILBOURN, have been illegally and fraudulently disposed of, and that the Territory is not liable for their redemption. A similar objection would be valid to the bond for one thousand dollars, issued by Mr. KILBOURN to himself, but inasmuch as a part at least of its par value has been received by the proper officer of the Territory, we consider his acts in negotiating it to have been thus virtually ratified, and that its redemption ought to be provided for.

"The committee therefore deeming legislative action on this subject to be necessary to assert the rights of the Territory, and to take proper measures to protect them, beg leave to submit the accompanying resolutions.

M. L. MARTIN, Chairman.

The resolutions were afterwards known as the repudiating resolutions.

The report of the committee was not concurred in by Mr. STRONG, although be did not submit a minority report.

The preamble was somewhat amended and enlarged, but the resolutions were adopted substantially as reported, and the following is a copy of them, as approved by the Governor on the 18th of February:

"*Resolved*, That in the opinion of the Legislative Assembly, the said bonds or certificates of stock numbered from 1 to 30 inclusive, and from 32 to 56 inclusive for $1,000 each, and being on interest of seven per cent. per annum are null and void; and that there is not, nor can be any obligation, either legal or equitable, resting upon the territorial government, to reimburse the amount of said bonds or certificates, or any part thereof.

"*Resolved*, That the bonds numbered from 57 to 100, both inclusive, are hereby declared to be null and void.

"*Resolved further*, That the Governor of the Territory be requested to take such measures as may be deemed expedient to recover possession of the bonds for $100,000, dated March 15, 1841, and entrusted to BYRON KILBOURN, Esq., by the late Governor of the Territory, except bond numbered thirty-one for $1,000, which is hereby declared to be valid."

Upon the passage of these resolutions in the Council, those who voted in the affirmative were Messrs. BULLEN, BRIGHAM, JANES, LEARNED, MARTIN, MAXWELL, ROUNTREE, TWEEDY, UPHAM and COLLINS (President).

Mr. STRONG voted in the negative.

In the House the vote was 14 in the affirmative and 11 in the negative.

These resolutions and some other measures adopted at the same session, which will presently be noticed, practically and effectually put a stop to all further work on the canal except such as was necessary to make the water power created by the dam and that part of the canal in the city of Milwaukee available.

The repudiating resolutions remained unrescinded for a period of more than six years. During that time one of the bonds had been paid, and the others surrendered and canceled, except ten for $1,000 each, which remained unpaid and were held as a subsisting debt against the Territory.

During the session of 1848, Governor DODGE sent a communication to the House of Representatives under date of February 15th in which he called the attention of the Legislative Assembly to the repudiating resolutions in which he said:

"Holding as I do the opinion that a great injustice is done by these resolutions, not only to the creditors, but to the good reputation for honor and integrity of the Territory, I feel impelled by a sense of justice to the former and a desire that the latter in changing her condition from a Territory to a State government, may enter the Union with her character untarnished by the stain of repudiation, to urge upon you the propriety of rescinding these resolutions and providing for the payment of the outstanding bonds of the Territory, amounting in the whole to the sum of ten thousand dollars, exclusive of interest.

* * * "It remains for you to say as the representatives of the people of this Territory, whether the State of Wisconsin shall enter the Union with the blot of repudiation on her escutcheon or whether she shall take a high and noble position by the side of the highest and proudest states of the Union."

The following joint resolution was adopted by both houses:

"That so much of the resolutions of the Legislative Assembly of the Territory of Wisconsin, passed February the eighteenth, A. D. 1842, as declares that certain bonds of which the ten now outstanding against the Territory are a part, are null and void, and that there is not nor can be any obligation either legal or equitable resting upon the Territorial government to reimburse the amount of said bonds or certificates or any part thereof, be and the same are hereby rescinded."

The vote upon the passage of this resolution in the Council was 11 to 2, and in the House it passed unanimously and was approved by the Governor March 11, 1848.

The other measures before referred to, adopted at this session, were:

Joint resolutions declaring:

First. "That all connection of the Territory with the Milwaukee and Rock River Canal Company ought to be henceforth dissolved; that all prosecution of the work of the canal by the Territory ought to be henceforth abandoned; that the Territory ought not further to proceed to execute the office of trustee imposed upon her by the act of Congress, approved June 5, 1838.

Second. "That the Congress of the United States be and is hereby requested to repeal so much of the said act of June 5, 1838, as directs the application of the fund and prescribes the conditions of the grant, and that the cession of the same land be made to the Territory upon the terms following, viz.:

"That the minimum price of the even numbered sections reserved by Congress be reduced to $1.25 per acre.

"That the odd numbered sections be made subject to the disposal of the Territory or future State of Wisconsin, for purposes of internal improvement, to be designated by the Territory, subject to the approval of Congress.

"That no other conditions or restrictions be annexed to such grant, excepting that the Territory may be prohibited from selling any portion of said land at a price less than $1.25 per acre.

Third. "That if Congress shall decline to alter the act of cession so as to conform to the terms herein set forth, or to terms equally satisfactory, that Congress be and is hereby requested to repeal the act of June 5, 1838, unconditionally, and to sell and dispose of so much of the lands as shall by such repeal revert or be retroceded to Congress, in the same manner and upon the same terms as other public lands are sold by the government."

Another of the measures was an act by which all interest on purchases of the canal lands was remitted and discharged, except such small sum as might become necessary to pay interest on loans, and expenses of the same.

The other measure referred to was an act by which the 1st, 16th and 17th sections of the act of February 26, 1839, the 4th section of the act of January 11, 1840, and the 2d and 3d sections of the act of February 12, 1841, were repealed.

These were the sections which authorized the issue of bonds and making loans, and contained all the authority of law for those purposes, and also authorized the application of the proceeds of the sales of canal lands, and of loans to the construction of the canal.

In response to a resolution of the House of Representatives, Mr. KILBOURN in behalf of the canal company said:

"The canal company are willing to surrender their right to construct the canal beyond the point where the line leaves the Milwaukee River, provided that the Legislature adopt such measures as will secure the construction of a railroad through the same tract of country."

The communication containing this response presented the full details of a plan for effecting a change of object from a canal to a railroad. Nothing, however, was done in reference to it, except the adoption of the resolutions previously quoted.

At a meeting of both houses in joint convention on the 18th of February, the following officers of the canal board were elected:

ALLEN W. HATCH, *Register;* JOSHUA HATHAWAY, *Receiver;* ALVIN FOSTER, *Acting Commissioner.*

The second section of an act passed February 19, 1841, provided that if any purchaser of any tract of canal lands should not have filed a bond and mortgage within six months from the passage of that act, as required by the act of February 26, 1839, and should not make payment of the interest and principal moneys becoming due on such land, at the time when the same should become due, such purchaser should forfeit his right to such lands.

At the session of 1843, an act was passed which repealed

said second section of the act of 1841. It also repealed so much of any law as authorized any person to make application for the sale of any portion of the unsold canal lands, and such parts thereof as authorized the sale of any portion of said lands, by proclamation of the Governor or otherwise.

In 1844, by an act passed January 25th, the payment of all principal and interest due or to become due from purchasers of the canal lands was indefinitely postponed, and it was provided that no suit should be instituted for the same until such time as the Legislature should thereafter determine.

And that all persons, whose lands on said canal grant had been sold for taxes and redeemed by the Territory, might pay to the receiver the amount which may have been paid for such redemption, with seven per cent. interest, and that such payment should defeat any title or claim of the Territory to such lands.

At the next session of the Legislative Assembly, by an act approved February 24, 1845, it was provided that so much of the canal lands as remained unsold at the passage of the act should be offered at public sale to the highest bidder on the second Tuesday of April, 1846, at the minimum price of $1.25 per acre, to be paid on the day of sale in gold or silver coin, unless such sale should be thereafter prohibited by act of Congress.

The public sales were to be continued from day to day, until all the lands had been offered for sale, and all such as should remain unsold at the close of the public sale should be subject to entry on the same terms as the public lands of the United States.

The 6th section of the act provided that purchasers of lands theretofore sold might, if Congress should approve the act, avail themselves of it by paying on or before the first Monday of July, 1845, ten per cent. of the balance due on such lands, estimating the original purchase at $1.25 per acre, without interest, and by paying the remainder in the legal currency of the United States between the first Monday and the second Tuesday of April, 1846.

The receiver was authorized and required to pay out of the moneys derived from the installments of ten per cent. to be paid by the first Monday of July, 1845, to sundry persons named in the act certain specified sums amounting to

$1,644.25, and to the holder of canal bond "No. 31" the sum of $1,000, with interest to the day of such payment.

All other moneys, paid into the hands of the receiver, were to be deposited by him in the bank of America in the city of New York, to the credit of the Territory, and to be drawn out only in such manner as the Legislative Assembly should thereafter direct.

The 17th section contained this provision:

"If Congress shall approve this act, then the foregoing provisions shall be in full force, and the land shall be sold at the minimum price of $1.25 per acre. But if Congress does not disapprove, or shall fail to approve of this act, then the said lands shall be sold at the minimum price of $2.50 per acre, one half of such bid to be paid in cash on the day of sale."

It also contained a provision for the security for payment of the balance by mortgage.

Simultaneously with the passage of this act a memorial to Congress was adopted, requesting —

"Congress to pass a law authorizing the Territory to effect a final settlement with the canal company, and to purchase the canal with all its privileges, to be paid for out of the proceeds of the sale of the canal lands, and that the same may be granted to the Territory. That the canal lands, or the balance of the proceeds thereof, may be donated to the Territory, to be appropriated to beneficial public uses."

No action was taken by Congress on the subject.

JOHN WHITE was elected *Register*, and DAVID MERRILL, *Receiver* of the canal lands.

On the 12th of January, 1846, the register and receiver presented their report to the Legislative Assembly, showing that 158 of the 277 original purchasers of the canal lands had paid ten per cent. of the balance due on such lands by the 1st of July, 1845, amounting to $2,230.75, and that $50.83 had been paid for the redemption of lands sold for taxes; total receipts, $2,281.58. That the receiver had paid to the several persons named in the act of February 24, 1845, the sum of $1,644.25, and the further sum of $155.62, for office rent, commissions and other claims; total payments, $1,799.87, leaving balance on hand of $481.71.

JOHN WHITE was re-elected *Register*, and DAVID MERRILL, *Receiver*.

On the 3d of March, 1846, the Legislative Assembly, by joint resolution, directed that the receiver of the canal lands should pay over to the Treasurer of the Territory all moneys which might arise from any sale of the canal lands, except the sum which should be required to defray the expenses of the sale. That such moneys should be liable for all debts due from the Territory.

That the money so received be appropriated to the payment of the expenses of holding the convention to form a constitution for the state of Wisconsin, and be paid out in such manner as the convention should provide.

That the faith of the Territory and future State be pledged to repay to the canal fund the sum diverted, whenever the same shall be required to be repaid for the purpose of executing the trust created by Congress in making the canal grant.

A memorial to Congress was adopted at the same session calling the attention of Congress to the act of February 24, 1845, authorizing a sale of the canal lands at $1.25 per acre, provided the same should be approved by Congress, and to the condition of the settlers on the lands. This memorial however was no more effective in inducing congressional action on the subject than that of the previous year.

The annual report of the Register and Receiver to the Legislative Assembly was presented in the Council on the 11th of January, 1847. It stated that the public sales of the canal lands were opened on the first Tuesday in April, 1846, and continued for three days, when adjournments were had from time to time until the tenth day of November, when the last and final sale was had, continuing two days.

That the quantity of land sold was 24,193 71-100 acres, all of which was sold at $2.50 per acre, of which $1.25 per acre was paid at the time of sale, except 83½ acres of which the entire amount was paid and the unpaid portion was secured by mortgages.

That the total amount of moneys paid to the Receiver on these sales, and on mortgages given to the Territory upon sales made prior to the act of 1845, was. $39,074 04
Amount paid for commissions, rents, printing and other expenses.... .... 1,291 06

Leaving a balance belonging to the Territory of..... .... $37,782 98
Amount paid to the Treasurer of the Territory..... .... 35,257 86

Balance in the hands of the Receiver... $2,525 12

JOHN WHITE and DAVID MERRILL were re-elected *register* and *receiver*.

An act was passed February 8, 1847, which provided that the register and receiver should cancel and release all mortgages executed in pursuance of the act of February 24,

1845, and that no mortgage should be required to be given by any purchaser under said act upon lands sold or to be sold.

That upon the payment of $1.25 per acre, including payments heretofore made, the register and receiver should deliver all patents issued on sales previously made, and that all mortgages executed under acts prior to the year 1845 should be canceled and released.

That the register and receiver should proceed to sell all the unsold canal lands agreeably to the act of 1845, and that section seventeen of that act and so much of the act as relates to the prohibition of a sale by act of Congress be repealed.

Another act was passed at the same session appropriating to JOHN ANDERSON for work done under his contract in the construction of a dam across Milwaukee River, which supplied water for the canal in Milwaukee and created the water power, the sum of ten thousand dollars and interest thereon at the rate of seven per cent. per annum from the date of the respective estimates of the engineers of the Territory in charge of the work.

The last session of the Legislative Assembly of the Territory convened on the 7th of February, 1848. On the twenty-fourth day of that month the annual report of the register and receiver was presented in the Council.

It stated that a public sale of the unsold canal lands was commenced on the seventh day of June, 1847, and was continued from day to day until all the lands were offered for sale, and that since the 15th of October the unsold lands have been subject to private entry.

That since the commencement of the public sales, there had been sold in all 53,330.33 acres, and there remained unsold 15,680 acres.

That the balance in the hands of the receiver at last report was...		$2,525 12
Amount paid on sales and on mortgages		82,286 20
		$84,811 32
Paid for commissions, expenses, etc.	$2,634 52	
Paid to JOHN ANDERSON	14,489 35	
Paid in full for Territorial Bond No. 31	1,408 75	
Deposited with Treasurer of the Territory	57,500 00	
		76,032 62
Balance in the hands of the receiver		$8,778 70
That there remained due and unpaid on mortgages about		$12,000 00

On the 9th of March, in joint convention, JOHN WHITE and DAVID MERRILL were re-elected *register* and *receiver*.

A joint resolution was adopted requiring the receiver to pay the interest due on the ten canal bonds, which had been repudiated by the resolutions of February 18, 1842, and which were rescinded at this session, and providing for the payment of future interest.

Another resolution was also adopted, directing the register to ascertain the number and names of all persons who had purchased canal lands prior to January, 1847, and paid for the same a sum exceeding $1.25 per acre, which sum was to be refunded by the receiver.

By an act approved March 11, 1848, the duties of the register were to be transferred to the *Secretary of State,* and those of the receiver to the *State Treasurer* of the STATE OF WISCONSIN, within ten days after the first Monday of January, 1849, in case such officers should be elected and qualified.

Appended to the State constitution, adopted February 1, 1848, were resolutions to the effect that Congress so alter the provisions of the act of June 18, 1838, making the canal grant, that the odd numbered sections unsold might be held and disposed of as part of the 500,000 acres grant, and that the even numbered sections reserved by Congress be offered for sale by the United States for the same minimum price as other public lands of the United States.

That Congress be requested to pass an act whereby the excess price over $1.25 per acre, which may have been paid by the purchasers of any of the even numbered sections which have been sold by the United States, be refunded to the owners thereof, or that they be allowed to enter any of the public lands to an amount equal in value to the excess so paid.

By the act of Congress for the admission of the State of Wisconsin into the Union, approved May 29, 1848, the assent of Congress was given to these resolutions, and the acts of Congress referred to therein were amended so that the lands granted by the provisions of said acts, and the proceeds of said lands shall be held and disposed of by the State in the manner and for the purposes mentioned in said resolutions; *provided,* that the liabilities incurred by the Territorial government of Wisconsin under the land grant act of June 18, 1838, shall be paid and discharged by the State of Wisconsin.

No settlement between the canal company and the Territory having been arrived at, although several attempts were made, those matters of difference, and the various other cognate subjects resulting from the canal grant and the attempt to utilize it, were left as a legacy to the STATE OF WISCONSIN, whose sovereign attributes as one of the States of the Union were now recognized by the Congress of the Nation.

INDEX

ABBOTT, John E 450
ABERCROMBIE, Gen 44 Lt 102
ACCAU, 29
ADAMS, Capt 134-135 John Quincy 585 President 131
AGRY, David 388 512 Mr 388 410 517
AIRD, James 88
ALDRIDGE, Owen 232
ALEXANDER, 138 146 Gen 145-146 Lt 103
ALLERDING, F William 594
ALLOUEZ, 27 Father 77 Pere Claude 26
AMHERST, Gen 46 48
ANDERSON, Capt 91-92 John 635 Maj 117 Thomas 90 William S 388
ANDREWS, Constant A 75
ANDRICK, Jacob 248 Mr 248
ANGE, Augustin 87
ANSLEY, John D 181
ANSON, Admiral 153
ANTUA, Pierre 87
APPLE, 142
ARGEMAIT, De 36
ARMS, Harriet 546
ARMSTRONG, 76 John 156-157
ARNDT, 383 Charles C P 83 263 302-303 381 John P 82 84 181 222-223 350 Judge 84 Mr 83 223 229 381-383
ARNOLD, J E 250 Jonathan E 350 356 469 552 Mr 338
ASHBURTON, Lord 415 434
ATCHINSON, John 226
ATKINSON, Gen 126-127 130 134-136 138-142 144-149
ATWOOD, Elihu L 512 Mr 524
AUBREY, James 141
AUBRY, 45

BABCOCK, Barnes 513 Daniel C 560 J M 524 John M 512
BAILEY, Maj 134
BAIRD, Henry S 82 222-224 233 250 252 285 511-512 Mr 83 223 229 517 524
BAKER, C M 497 523 Charles M 439-440 487 511 513 553 E S 382 Enos S 347 381 Mr 387 418 427 429 431 463 498 516-517 520 522
BALDWIN, Russell 269 303
BANCROFT, 34 44-45
BANKS, William H 339 Wm H 293
BARBER, A L 242 Dr 422 427 Hiram 511-512 516 520 553 557 J Allen 511-512 517 522 524 Lucius I 245 269 280 302 325 374 456 Mr 330 364 387 395-396 427 429 431 620-621
BARCELLOW, Lallotte 46 Mr 46
BARCHELDER, George 357
BARCLAY, Mr 434
BARNEY, Capt 503 Joshua 502
BARSTOW, Mr 490 Samuel H 487-488 William A 531 594
BARTH, 100-101 Laurent 100
BARTLETT, Mr 388 426 William A 388
BARTON, William 156
BASCUM, F 497
BATCHELDER, George 325 356 Mr 330
BATES, David G 75
BAUPREZ, 80
BAXTER, 377 406 408 444 463 Daniel 334 376 409 443 493 547 586 Mr 494
BEAL, Mr 570
BEALE, Samuel W 82 176

BEALL, Capt Brevet Maj 101 Lt 102 Mr 520 566 568 570-571 576-577 Saml W 553 Samuel W 511-512 565
BEARDSLEY, Mr 312 Othni 269 304
BEATTY, George 253 263 268 325 358
BEAUBIEN, John B 105
BEAUCHAMP, 124
BEAUHARNOIS, Marquis De 153 Mr 35-36
BEAUJEU, De 43-44 M De 44
BELDEN, Philo 357
BELFOUR, Capt 78 104
BELL, William 513
BELLERIVE, Saint Ange De 59
BELT, Mr 94
BENNETT, Jesse L 423 Mr 94 Stephen O 513
BEQUETTE, Pascal 142 346 Paschall 480
BERRY, William 513
BERTRAND, Joseph 74
BEVANS, John 222 Lorenzo 512 553 Mr 520
BIDDLE, John 158 181
BIENVILLE, 32 De 31
BIGGS, James 565 Mr 576 580
BILLINGS, H M 487 497 Henry M 269 303 488 Mr 615
BIRCHARD, Ezra 422
BIRD, 441 462 569 A A 244-245 263 292 347 350 377 409 Augustus A 231 250 263 308 310 407 462-463 598 Mr 282 310
BISHOP, Adelbut H 504 Charles 565 Mr 568-569
BLACK, 143 154 Samuel 143
BLACKSTONE, John W 222 269 273 280 303 Mr 283 314
BLAIR, Mr 229 Thomas 224
BOILVIN, Nicholas 88 94-95 97
BOISBRIANT, Monseur 32
BOND, Joseph 325 530 Mr 208 330 357 Shadrack 157
BONHAM, David 487

BONNETERRE, 80
BOOMER, Lyman E 538
BORIEGUILLOT, Mr De 86
BOTKIN, Alexander 441 460-461 560
BOUCHARD, Ed 143
BOUCHER, 80
BOURASSA, Charlotte 42 Rene 42
BOUTHILLIER, Frances 98 Francis 94 97
BOWEN, Davis 512
BOWKER, Joseph 513
BOWYER, John 80 97
BOX, John 224 Mr 229
BOXLEY, James 144
BOYD, Col 140-141 John W 513 Thomas A B 194
BOYLES, Mr 229 William 222 224
BRACE, Mr 524 Peter A R 512 Porter 339
BRACKEN, Charles 142 150 269 303
BRADDOCK, 43-44 62 Gen 56
BRADSTREET, Gen 64
BRADY, Gen 140 Hugh 81 140
BRATT, Michael 539
BRAWLEY, Abraham 456 488 503 Mr 490
BRAZELTON, Jacob 325 Mr 330
BREBEUF, 25
BREED, A O T 241 244
BREVOORT, Henry B 98
BRIGGS, Sarah 587
BRIGHAM, David 263 350 Ebenezer 222 224 269 384 Mr 229 312 361 365 367 369 383-384 629 Prescott 450
BRISBOIS, Antoine 91 94 Joseph 125 302-303 316 487 M 96 Michael 87-88 91-92 94 97 120 Mr 88
BRISQUN, 80
BRISTOL, Charles S 456
BROCK, E E 247
BRODHEAD, 298 Mr 272
BRONSON, Alfred 368 Charles A 529 Ira B 252 Mr 533

INDEX

BROWN, A C 533-534 Armstead C 487 529-530 Benjamin 594 Beriah 508 518 547 569 Charles E 388 456 Henry Saunders 416 Hiram 512 John A 471 Joseph R 320 325 330 357 Margaret 320 Mr 330 487 490 509 Samuel 106 206 244 599 W W 533 567 William Jr 106 William W 529
BROWNE, Charles E 513
BROWNELL, Geo W 565 George W 564 Mr 568 575-577
BRUCE, Mr 328-329 W H 194-195 William H 325 327-328 330 Wm H 319
BRUNET, Baptist 79 Jean 98 125
BRUNETT, 67 Jean 98 252
BRUNSON, A 348 Alfred 86 325 330 357 523 Dr 86 88 Ira B 269 303 J H 279 Lucia Maria 523 Mr 312 329-330 335 357
BRUSH, Charles R 263
BUCHANAN, Mr 209 276 601
BULL, John 141
BULLEN, John Jr 182 Mr 370 629 William 232 270 273 280 302-303
BURBANK, Lt 102
BURCHARD, Charles 513 Mr 520 522
BURDICK, Paul 245
BURDINE, Lt 117
BURGESS, James M 530
BURNETT, 297 Baptist 67 Ellsworth 249-250 Jacob 156 Lucia Maria 523 Mr 140 194-195 197 199 201-202 223 456 460 470 489-490 494 504 520 Thomas P 97-98 193 223 233 270-271 297 357 456 488 502 511-512 522 588 Thomas Pendleton 522 Thos P 140
BURNS, Mr 560 586 Timothy 529 560 583
BURNSIDE, Andrew 512
BURT, Daniel R 325 512 560 Mr 330 334 560
BUTLER, Symmes 182

BYRD, Charles Willing 157
CADILLAC, De La Motte 31 153
CADLE, Mr 82 Rev Mr 82 Richard F 82 423
CALHOUN, John C 109 113
CAMERON, Mr 298 Murdoch 89 Simon 272
CAMP, Col 252 Hosea T 224 252 Mr 229
CAMPBELL, 88 101 Gen 46 Maj 74 Mr 52 67 100 William 232
CAPRON, John M 388 403 454 Mr 395-396 409 411
CARBONNO, Amable 249-250
CARBOUNSAU, 80
CARDINELLE, 86
CARDRONE, 80
CARLEY, Joseph 594
CARNS, Wm 143
CARON, Mons 78
CARR, Christopher 374
CARTER, Almerin M 565 James B 513 Mr 568
CARVER, 40 48-50 52 Capt 48-49 51-53 65 87 Jonathan 47 262 Ralph 269 302
CARY, Bushnell B 263 Mr 276
CASE, Mr 567 569 580 Squire S 565
CASEY, Mr 209
CASS, 139 Dudley 560 Gen 109 Gov 72 79 97 110-111 119 125-126 173 Lewis 171 175
CASTLEMAN, Alfred L 565 Mr 569 576-577
CATLIN, John 233 249 253 263 268 312 325 347 351 358 388 423 456 469 487 506 Mr 463
CAVAGNAC, Marquis De Vaudreuil De 153
CENTRE, W A 102
CHADANAU, John B 74
CHALIFOUX, 80
CHAMBERLAIN, James 513
CHAMBERS, Col 81 92 Talbot 92
CHAMPION, Robert H 529
CHAMPLAIN, 24 152
CHANCE, David R 224 Mr 229 232

CHAPIN, A L 497
CHAPMAN, James F 503 537 W W 220 William W 233
CHAPPUE, 105
CHARDON, Rev Father 35
CHARLES V, King Of 151
CHARLEVOIX, 50 59 Father 57
CHASE, Dr 106 Enoch 106 241 244 Horace 106 249 513 520 Mr 566 569 575-576 578-579 Warren 476 511-512 553 565
CHATEAUMORAND, Marquis 31
CHEVALIER, 80
CHILDS, Capt 128 Col 84 E 274 348 Ebenezer 83 127 141 223-224 269 302-303 330 Mr 106 223 229 330
CHILTON, Matthias 476 Thomas 529
CHOUTEAU, Auguste 71
CHURCHILL, Ezekiel 269 302
CILLEY, 271 276 Jonathan 255 Mr 256-260
CLAPP, Mark R 488
CLARK, 60 411 Asa 374 Col 65-66 Gen 119 George Rogers 65 Gov 89 Henry 529 Jemima M 546 Jesse A 546 Julius T 410 Mr 410 520 533-534 Sat 292 William 182 William H 513 Wm 71 Wm H 553
CLARKE, Capt 149 Dr 106 James 233 245 251
CLARY, D 497
CLATYON, Senator 251
CLAY, C C 600 Henry 454
CLAYTON, John M 231
CLIGANCOURT, 35
CLINTON, Henry 538
CLOTHIER, Mr 524 Samuel T 512
CLYMAN, James 106 206 Lt 106
COBB, Amasa 506
COLBERT, 152
COLE, A G 568 571-572 Albert G 565 Mr 572 O 568 576-577 Orsamus 565
COLLEY, Joseph 565 Mr 569 576
COLLIER, 281

COLLINS, 290 A L 558 Alexander L 529 552 Capt 506 James 222 267 269 280 302-303 348 350 358 382 456 481 506 Mr 333 338 456 460 468 470 487 532-533 629
COLTER, Hugh R 232
COLUMBUS, 23
COMBE, Edward 513
COMSTOCK, Cicero 594
CONKEY, Theodore 445
CONNER, Mary Ann 587
CONROE, Jacob W 269 303 Mr 310
COOPER, John 513
CORIELL, William W 263
CORNWALL, Madison W 223-224 598 Mr 229
COTHREN, M M 560
COTTON, E P 565 Lester H 284 Mr 569
COURCELLES, 152
COWLES, S D 245 Sylvester D 599
COX, James P 135 222 224 Mr 229
COXE, Hopewell 513 Mr 524
CRAIG, Jonathan 302-303 Mr 276
CRAM, Capt 336-337 T J 336 Thos J 314
CRANDALL, Frances Adelle 476 Paul 565
CRAWFORD, 88 101 John 487-488 513 Mr 494 524 Samuel 567
CRESPEL, Father 35
CROCKER, Col 389 452 H 403 Hans 233 250 312 456 608 Mr 387 389 400-401 413 419 425 427-429 438 444
CROGHAN, George 73
CROSSMAN, Lyman 388 Mr 426 443
CROSWELL, Caleb 486 488 497 546
CROWSWELL, E Jane 546
CRUSON, Mr 307-308 456 490 Thomas 222 269 303 456 488 512
CUSHING, Mr 276
D'AMARITON, 35

D'ARTAGUETTE, Dirau 32
D'ARTAQUETTE, Diron 153
D'IBERVILLE, M 31
DABLON, 27 Claude 26
DALLAM, James B 223-224 233 252 Mr 229
DANIEL, 25
DANIELS, Lyman I 233
DARLING, Dr 330 389 391 401 411 426 429 446 460 Enoch 106 Enoch G 374 Mason C 325 330 388 456 480 487-488 529-530 Mr 330 388-389 410 426 430 456 460 490 533
DAVENPORT, S A 565
DAVIESS, Col 72
DAVIS, Chauncey 457 Jeff 102 Jefferson 150 Mr 136 481
DE'SEELHORST, Justus 232
DEAVILES, Pedro Melendez 151
DEBAUHARNOIS, Marquis 38
DECALLIERS, 153
DELANGLADE, 41
DELAPLAINE, George P 461
DEMENT, John 144 Maj 144
DEMING, Mr 330 Reuben H 325 356
DEMUYS, 153
DENNIS, Mr 520 William M 249 488 Wm M 511-512
DERRING, Philip F 529
DESOTO, Ferdinand 24 151
DEVA, 143
DEWEY, Mr 325 330 364 387 410 427 429 Nelson 269 303 316 325 349 487 590
DICK, William Hamlin 546
DICKINSON, Elbert 453 Joseph 127 223 252 Nathaniel 513 William 81-82 181
DICKSON, Capt 150 Col 73 Robert 73 90
DINWIDDIE, Gov 55 154
DIXON, Capt 147 John 596
DODGE, 127 146 Augustus C 135 192 Col 127 130 132-133 135-142 145-150 Gen 142 261 355-356 419 Gov 236 262 298 325

DODGE (cont.) 351 356 397 488 619 623 629 Henry 126 138 142 178 187 219 235 237 346 351-352 479 Henry L 263
DORAN, John L 565 Mr 569 577-579
DOTY, 297 306 333 440-441 462 585 Charles 356 398 539 Gov 347 356 361-363 375 381 389 398-399 408 411 454 470 623 628 J D 323 372 376-377 381 390 404 407 442 623 James D 82 102 162-163 179 182 203 231 270-271 275 308 310 346 396-397 409 443 454 479 511 623 James Duane 84 192-193 228 233 276 282 292-293 513 553 Judge 85 94 130 192 203 228 271 279 284 294-295 305 312 324 Mr 84 271 276 291 308 311 332 443
DOUGHERTY, John 278
DOUGHTY, William 463
DOUGLASS, B 106
DOUSMAN, 80 G D 245 George D 106 246 H L 90 Hercules L 96 98 Mr 99 T C 206 Talbot C 106
DRAKE, Jeremiah 512 Levi P 560 Mr 524
DRAPER, Mr 47
DRIGGS, John H 504
DROCOUX, Jean Charles 26
DUBUISSON, Monsieur 38
DUCHANO, 80
DUCHARME, 80
DUGAY, 29
DULHUT, 78 Daniel Greysolon 30 Lt 77
DULUTH, 100
DUMAIS, Chevalier 44
DUMOND, 80
DUNCAN, Asa 143 Joseph 132
DUNMORE, Gov 61
DUNN, Charles 145 219 233 263 289 564-565 Chief Justice 312 384 F J 311 354 Francis J 325

DUNN (cont.)
　346 356 480 Judge 577 Mr 330
　354 568 577
DUNNING, Abel 512
DUQUESNE, 44 Marquis 153
DURKEE, Charler 223 Charles 224
　558
DURKINS, Mr 229
DURLEY, 138
DUTCHER, Joseph 249
EARL, Warner 486 488
EASTMAN, Ben C 423 457 487
　Edward 539 Jonathan 356-357
　Mr 487
EATON, Gen 112
EDGERTON, B H 349 Benjamin H
　193 E W 106 Elisha W 513 Mr
　194-195 202
EDWARDS, James E 273 Ninian 71
ELLIS, A G 194 361 Albert G 82 84
　223-224 252 263 325 327-328
　330 388 Gen 79 84 Mr 83 194
　223 229 335 358 364 388 425
　429-430 448 487 Pitts 456 513
ELMORE, Andrew E 70 388 511
　513 Mr 401 426-427 430 448
　517 520 524
ENGLE, Mr 229 Peter Hill 224 231
　233 251
ESTABROOK, Experience 565 Mr
　568 571 576 578
ETHERINGTON, Capt 63 79 Maj
　63-64
EVERETT, Charles 241
EWING, William L D 147
FAGAN, James 565 Mr 568 576
FARMIN, Uriel 476
FARNSWORTH, Samuel H 345
　539
FARRIBAULT, Jean Baptiste 94
FEARING, Paul 157
FEATHERSONHAUGH, George W
　272
FEATHERSTONHAUGH, G W
　565 Geo W 560 Mr 569
FENTON, Daniel G 565 David G
　233 Mr 567-570

FIELD, A P 354 384 Alex P 357
　Alexander P 346 Col 391 Mr
　354 486 Secretary 354-355
　Stephen 456
FIELDS, Abner 126 Capt 126
FILY, Laurent 101 105
FINCH, B W 106 206 245 Benjamin
　182 Benoni 182 Benoni W 106
FINDLAY, James 156
FINDLEY, John L 94 97
FISHER, James 456 488 L G 497
　Mr 490
FITCH, Matthew G 143
FITZGERALD, Garret M 565
　Garrett M 513 Mr 566 568 576
FLANIGAN, John 379
FLEMING, Judge 299
FLOYD, Mr 508 R C 506
FOLEY, John 224 Mr 229
FOLTS, Mr 579
FOLTZE, Jonas 565
FOOT, Ezra A 565 Mr 579
FOOTE, Mr 569
FORCE, 141
FORD, Chester 539
FORSYTH, Maj 95 Thomas 95
FORTIER, 80
FOSTER, Alvin 598 631 Dwight
　241
FOWLER, 140 Albert 106 182 244
　565 John 138 Mr 486 569
　William 456
FOX, Mr 568 577 579 William H
　565
FRANK, Jacob 80 M 497 Michael
　422 480 487 Mr 427-429 431
　489 498
FRANKS, 80 Jacob 105
FRAZER, Judge 227 233 250 Maj
　60 William C 249 Wm C 219
　263
FRENCH, Haynes 513
FRINK, Mr 481
FRONTENAC, Count 152
FULLER, Benjamin 512
FURBER, Joseph W 530 Mr 530
　533
GAGE, Gen 60 65

GAGNIER, 123 128 130 Mrs 121-122 Rijeste 121
GAINES, Gen 132
GALE, George 565 Mr 568 570-571 577-578
GALISSONERE, Count 153 De La 153
GANIER, 86
GARDINER, Palmer 529
GARDNER, E T 560 Mr 533 W N 250 William Henry 587 William N 263 Wm N 233 263
GARRIEPY, 80
GATES, John P 94 97
GEAR, H H 478
GEHON, Francis 220
GENTRY, Capt 141 149 James H 132 142 222 Judge 135
GIBAULT, M 66
GIBSON, Moses S 512 560 Mr 519-520
GIDDINGS, David 325 513 James 530 Mr 329-330
GIFFORD, Mr 577 Peter D 565
GILLETT, Benoni R 222
GILMAN, Joseph 156 W W 106
GILMORE, James 222 247 512
GIRGNON, Augustin 104
GIST, 55
GLADWYN, Maj 64
GODDARD, 78 104
GOODELL, Lemuel 512 Nathan 181
GOODRICH, Henry C 513
GOODSELL, C M 497 Elihu B 512
GORRELL, James 78 104 Lt 64-65 78-79
GRAHAM, Duncan 88 121 Lt 92 Mr 121 522 Wallace W 513
GRANGER, Benjamin 512
GRANT, Levi 422 Maj 45 Mr 425
GRATIOT, Charles 81 Col 133 137 Maj 81 Mr 133
GRAVEL, 80
GRAVES, 271 276 Gaylord 486 488 Mr 256-260 490 Wm J 255
GRAVIER, Father 31

GRAY, Mr 330 517 620 Neeley 325 Neely 512
GREEN, 141 Charles 195 George W 530 William C 512
GREENVILLE, 68
GREGOIRE, A L 594
GRENHAGEN, Joachim 473
GRIFFIN, James 182
GRIGNON, Augustin 40 47 67 90-91 101 Charles L 141 Domitelle 46 Hypolite 105 Lewis 176 Mr 67 79 Peirre Sr 79 Pierre 46 Pierre Sr 47 Robert 318
GUIRD, Bazil 87
HACKETT, John 325 513 Mr 330 334 522 524
HAIGHT, John T 444-445 472 497 530 Mr 533 535
HALE, 140 William 138
HALL, 136 138 146 George B 513 J Cary 473 James H 513 Samuel 546 Sarah 546
HAMILTON, Alexander 186 Col 141 143 179 186 198-199 201-202 419 422 567 Gov 46 66 Henry 66 Jemison 502 Mr 194 197-198 201 388 396 410 William S 126 186 194 350 388 419 567 596 Wm S 140 179 193 552
HAMMOND, Sanford P 513
HANCHETT, Edward S 594
HANKS, Lt 73
HANRAHAN, James 560
HARDIN, Mr 209
HARKIN, Daniel 513 Mr 520
HARMAR, Gen 68
HARMON, C 106
HARNEY, Capt 101-103
HARRINGTON, Alva 241 James 565
HARRIS, Carey A 262
HARRISON, Gen 72 79 157 321 Jesse M 224 William H 157 William Henry 70 131 321 Williamhenry 346
HART, Charles 450 E M 450

HARVEY, Louis P 565 Mr 568 570-571 578
HATCH, Allen W 631
HATHAWAY, J Jr 106 Joshua 438 631
HAWES, M T 513 Mr 513
HAWLEY, 140 Aaron 138
HAYS, James P 512
HAZEN, Lorenzo 512
HEALD, Capt 74
HEAP, Henry 587
HEATH, Chauncey G 530 Mr 387-388 422 533
HEDRICK, Solomon U 107
HELFENSTEIN, J A 454
HELM, Capt 66
HEMPSTEAD, Charles S 497
HENNEPIN, 28-30 78 86 100
HENRY, 138 146 148 Col 147 Gen 145-146 Patrick 65 William 224
HERBIN, M 42
HESK, William R 513
HICKCOX, Gen 419 George W 419
HICKOX, G W 497
HICKS, Franklin Z 388 456 512 Mr 422 427 430 456 487 520
HIGGENBOTHEM, Alexander 143
HIGGINBOTHAM, Mr 619 S 619
HILL, Allen 142 193 Lafayette 512 Mr 194 William Henry 587
HINMAN, Samuel 106 241 244-246 497
HOARD, Mr 194 490 Robert C 193 341 456 488
HOBART, Bishop 108 Harrison C 529 Mr 534 540
HOCQUART, 38
HODGES, Henry W 247
HOLCOMBE, William 513
HOLLENBECK, Mr 569 Stephen B 565
HOLLIDAY, James 560
HOLLISTER, David S 246
HOLMES, John E 529 Mr 533 552
HOLT, Benjamin 517-518 Mr 569
HOLTON, Edward D 481
HOOD, John 143
HOOE, Alexander S 89

HOPKINS, John 388 Mr 389 396 426 448
HORNER, Acting Gov 198 207 Gov 197 207 J S 197 John S 191 193 195 197 219 233 248-249 Secretary 194 207
HOULL, 80
HOULRICH, 80
HOWARD, John 241 Peter 341 Sarah 341
HOWEL, Mr 209
HOWELL, Mr 209
HOYT, Mr 312 Tristram C 270 304
HUBBARD, Adelbut H 504 H M 244 Henry M 246 Oliver C 374 Otis 106 206
HUBBELL, Levi 497
HUEBSCHMANN, Francis 426 513
HUGHLETT, Mr 246
HUGUNIN, Daniel 346 E R 531 Edgar R 232 Mr 387-388 419 422
HULL, Gen 73-74
HUMPHREY, Leonard 587 Leonard Ravella 587
HUNKINS, Benjamin 388 513 Mr 410 426 430 520 524
HUSKEY, Henry 595
HUSTIS, John 473 619 Mr 622 625-626
HYER, Emily Jane 587 Geo 524 George 512 524 N F 241 244-245 Nathaniel F 497 512 546
HYOTTE, 80
INDIAN, Ash-e-co-bo-ma 250 Ash-o-wa 250 Black Bird 39 74 Black Hawk 70-71 73 131-136 141 143-144 146-150 Black Sparrow Hawk 71 131 148 Cari-mau-nee 128 Cha-e-tar 149 Chic-hon-sic 121-123 130 176 Chien 94 De-kau-ray 130 143 Dog 94 La Fourche 41 Little Priest 137-138 140 Little Thunder 137 Ma-kau-ta-pe-na-se 39 Muck-e-ta-me-che-ka-ka 71 Nis-so-wa-quet 41 One-eyed De-cor-ra 149 Pauquette 146

INDEX 647

INDIAN (cont.)
> Pontiac 59 62 64 Prophet 149-150 Red Bird 101 121 123 127-130 176 Red Wing 95 Souligny 73 Spotted Arm 137-138 140 Tecumthe 72 The Fork 41 The Leaf 95 The White Elk 73 To-pen-e-bee 74 Tomah 73 Wa-man-doos-ga-ra-ka 120 Wabashaw 76 95 We-kau 121-123 130 176 Whirling Thunder 138 140 White Crow 137 145

INGERSOLL, John V 321 346 388 405
INGHRAM, Arthur B 223 253 Mr 229
INGRAM, Arthur B 268
INMAN, Israel Jr 513
IRVIN, David 163 192 219 233 290 384 462 Judge 227 442 462-463
IRWIN, Alexander J 82 223-224 252 269 302 468 Matthew 80 97 Mr 176 223 229 Robert Jr 81-82 97 173 176
JACKSON, 139 Andrew 163 210 218 Andrew B 486 488 565 Gen 112 192 197 218 248 321 Henry 560 M M 347 384 454 558 Mortimer M 497 Mr 490 558 568 575 577 582 President 150
JACOBS, 80
JAMES, Edward 266 346 Thomas 512
JAMES I, King Of England 170
JANES, Lorenzo 302-303 Mr 332 358 367 629
JANSSEN, Edward H 513 Mr 522
JAY, 67 96 170
JEFFERSON, Mr 359 364-365
JENKINS, 143 James D 529 Mr 229 307 312 314 366 Thomas 143 269 303 356 512 Warren S 224
JENNINGS, Jonathan 157
JEROME, Horace R 473
JEWETTE, Lt 63
JOGUES, 25
JOHNSON, Cave 208-209 Col 117 George 141 James 117

JOHNSON (cont.)
> John W 94 96-98 Phineas M 539 Richard M 72 117

JOHNSTON, George 97
JOLIET, 27 78 86 100 Sieur 27
JONES, Capt 150 Col 221 270 Delegate 251 Gen 192 207 235 257 Geo W 192 George W 158 193 195 207 221 231 255 257 270-271 275-276 293 346 480 594 George Wallace 192-193 234 Harvey 539 Ira 486 488 Loyal H 539 Milo 106 565 Mr 207-208 257-260 270 276 291 490 568 William 539
JONQUIERE, Admiral 153 De La 153
JOURDIN, 80
JUDD, Mr 515-516 520 566 568 571 Stoddard 346 511-512 565
JUDSON, Mr 388 422 Philander 388
JUMONVILLE, 55
JUNEAU, Mr 105 Solomon 105 186 241 244-246 426 465 496 598-599
KAURY, De 48
KELLOGG, Chauncey 513 Daniel W 538 John C 249 La'fayette 457 Lafayette 487 514 530 583 Mr 520 524
KEMPER, Bishop 544
KENDALL, Amos 249 D G 374 Gilmore 374 Henry Heap 587
KENNEDY, William H 564-565
KENNESLEY, Aid-de-camp 90
KENNON, Mr 209
KENT, A 497
KERCHEVAL, Mr 178
KERN, Charles J 513
KILBOURN, Byron 105 241-242 244-246 263 293 456 565 596 598-599 619 623 629 Mr 293 295 297 487 567-568 571 576 578 597 600 603 605 607 614 619-620 623 628 631
KILLBOURN, 297

KIMBALL, J H 487 Jacob H 456 Mr 469
KING, Mr 568 571 576 Rufus 565
KINNE, Augustus C 565 Mr 569
KINNEY, Asa 513 560 Joseph Jr 513
KINZIE, James 105 John H 102
KIRKER, 138
KIRKPATRICK, Francis C 289 R H 143
KNAPP, Gilbert 182 193 223-224 289 292 348 J Gillet 547 J Gillett 595 Joseph Gillett 507 Mr 194-195 200 202 229 595 R C 339 S B 339 Samuel B 493
KNEELAND, James 456 487 Mr 461 463 469
KNIGHT, Thomas 224
KNOWLTON, Mr 463 468 Wiram 456 469 487 Wyram 531
L'ECUYER, 101 Duncan 100 Jean 100 John 100 Mrs 101
LACHAPELLE, Mr 400
LACHAPPEL, Mr 387
LACHAPPELLE, Mr 389 423 427-429 441 Theophalus 330 357 456
LAFRAMBOISE, Alexander 104
LAGRAVE, Clovis 590
LAKIN, George W 445 Mr 567 569 576-577
LALLEMAND, 25
LAMB, Mr 464
LAMMIOT, 78
LAMOTTE, Lt 102
LANDER, Henry 246
LANDRUM, Joel T 476
LANGEVIN, 80
LANGLADE, 47 81 Agate De 41 Augustin 42 Augustin De 41-42 78 Charles 42 Charles De 40-43 46 67 79 Charles Dr 64 Charlotte 42 De 43 45-46 54 79 Domitelle 46 Dr 44 Lallotte 46 Sieur 44
LANGWORTHY, Lucius H 267
LAPHAM, I A 241 244-246 599 619 Increase A 597 Mr 600 624

LAQRAL, 79
LARKIN, Charles H 457 566 George W 566 Jonathan 461 Mr 569 571 581
LAROCK, 80
LARRABEE, Charles H 564 566 Mr 568 575 580
LASALLE, 29-30 57 78 152 Robert Cavelier De 26 Sieur 28
LATHAM, Hollis 566 Mr 568
LAVIGNE, 80
LAW, John 32
LAWE, George W 195 John 80 82 98 193 293 Judge 80 Mr 194 199
LAWHEAD, Benjamin 143
LEACH, Levin 143
LEARNED, C J 350 Charles J 316 350 Mr 334 338 365 629
LEAVENWORTH, Col 95-97
LEBOEUF, 80
LECARON, 24
LEE, Mr 96
LEFFLER, Isaac 224 253 Mr 229
LEFRANC, M L 42
LEJEUNI, Pere 25
LEROY, Francis 102
LESLIE, Lt 63
LESTER, Robert D 453
LESUEUR, 100 M 31
LEWIS, James T 566 Mr 568-569 Warner 224
LIGNERY, De 36 39 42 78 Marchand De 35
LINDSAY, Allen 122 Capt 122 124
LINN, L F 423 Lewis F 231 235 423 Senator 251
LIPCAP, 122 130 Solomon 121
LIVINGSTON, Robert R 69
LOCKHART, Edward P 560
LOCKWOOD, James H 76 93 96-98 121 223-224 232-233 252 Judge 93-94 125 Mr 76 94 229 Mrs 121
LONG, Hugh 325 356 Mr 330 423 Robert M 388 403 William B 194

INDEX

LONGSTREET, Mr 312 W R 245-246 William R 244 302 304 Wm R 599
LOOMIS, Mr 106
LOSS, Lewis H 497
LOUIS XVIII, King Of France 24
LOUVIGNY, De 33-35 78
LOVELL, F S 564 Frederick S 511 513 529 566 Mr 532-533 535-537 552 566-568 571-572 574 580
LOW, Capt 103
LULL, Almon 347 Mr 409
LUM, Charles 529
LURWICK, George 374
LYMAN, Samuel W 566
LYNDE, Wm P 480
LYON, Lucius 158 177 Mr 178 279
MADDEN, William I 512
MAGONE, James 487-488 513
MAITLAND, W 106
MANAHAN, Benjamin F 529 John H 388 403 512 Mr 410 430 530 533
MANDERVILLE, John 241 246
MANDEVILLE, Jack 124 Saucy Jack 124
MARCHAND, 79
MARIN, 37 39 Perriere 36 Sieur 38-39
MARITN, Morgan L 316
MARQUETTE, 27-29 77-78 86 100 Father 77 James 26
MARQUISSE, Seth H 476
MARSH, John 140 Mr 141
MARTIN, Dorcas B 546 John 546 L 560 M L 358 629 Morgan L 85 178-179 192 222 269-270 292-293 303 312 318 349 404 456 480-481 485 557 566-567 Morgan Lewis 193 Morganl 319 Mr 179 333-334 338 361 387-389 403 425 427 429 431 449 481 579 616 628-629
MASON, Acting Gov 179 207 Ex-gov 347 Gov 190 193 196 207 294 305 John T 111 Mr 276

MASON (cont.)
   Stevens T 182 190-191 228 282 419
MASTERS, Mr 443 Robert 241 388
MASTON, Stevens T 305
MATSON, Chester 594
MATTHEWS, Josephus 476
MAXWELL, James 269 303 325 Mr 308-309 628-629
MAYNARD, J B 98
MCCABE, 471
MCCALL, James 111
MCCARTNEY, Dennis 247 Francis 247 Mr 533 Orris 529
MCCLELLAN, Mr 486 568 Robert 456 Samuel R 566
MCCONNELL, 143
MCCRANEY, Mr 229 Thomas 223
MCDONNELL, William 564
MCDOWELL, Mr 568 576-577 William 566
MCFARLANE, Hugh 530
MCGRAW, Dominick 143
MCGREGGOR, A W 252 Alexander 303
MCGREGOR, Alexander 267 269
MCHUGH, Thomas 530 560 564 567 583
MCILWAIN, 141
MCKAY, 78 Col 74 90-92 William 90
MCKINLEY, Judge 478
MCKINNEY, Thomas L 111
MCKNIGHT, Mr 229 Thomas 222 224
MCLEAN, Judge 478
MCMILLAN, Wm 157
MCNAIR, 121 126 Alexander 94 Capt 125-126 Gov 75 Thomas 94 96-97 125
MCNEILL, John 81
MCSHERRY, Edward 224
MCWILLIAMS, George 223 Mr 223
MEEKER, Moses 221 235 388 512 Mr 389 430 448
MELENDEZ, 151
MENARD, Charles 92

MENNEVILLE, Marquis Du
  Quesne De 153
MERRILL, David 633-634 636
  Henry 103 181
MESNARD, Father 77 Pere Rene 26
MESSERSERSMITH, Jr 143
MESSERSMITH, George 347 422
  454 Mr 445
METHODE, 120 122 Madame 120
MICHOLS, Charles M 566
MILLER, Andrew G 290 Col 81
  Gaines 102 John 81 Judge 373
  442 462 Lucas M 539
MILLION, 141
MILLS, David L 513 Jesse C 325
  456 Mr 330 456 486 508
  Simeon 471 507
MILTIMORE, Ira 594
MINER, Eliphalet S 538
MIREANDEU, Jean Baptist 104
MIRUELO, Diego 23
MITCHELL, A M 609 Alex 373
  Alexander 447 492 Alexander
  M 608 James 508
MONROE, James 69 Mr 109
MONTCALM, 41 44-45
MOOERS, Benjamin H 456 539 560
  Mr 489 560 589-590
MOORE, Col 135 James M 513
  Jesse 456 Josiah 341 Levisee
  341 Mary 587 Mr 481 486 520
MOORES, Benjamin H 488
MORGAN, Alfred 241 Col 117
  John 594
MORRIS, 143
MORRISON, 332-333 378 441
  James 261 283 307-308 350
  376-377 409 441 443 460-462
  John 450 Mr 334 407
MORROW, Elisha 486 488 530 594
  Mr 489-490
MORSE, Dr 109 Jedediah 107 S F B
  107
MORTON, A B 346
MOWER, Timothy Jr 564
MUHLENBERG, Maj 96
MULFORD, Cyrus A 564 Ezra A
  564 566 Mr 568

MURRAY, James 153 272 Mr 298
  William 53
NAGLE, James 233
NARVAEZ, Pamphilo De 23
NEGRO, Peter 123
NELSON, John 547
NEWELL, G F 560
NEWLAND, David 325 456 Mr 330
  358 387 395 415 427 429 432
NEWMAN, Zadoc 270 304
NICHOLS, Mr 569 580
NICOLET, 100
NICOLLET, 27 77 152 M 25
NOBLE, William 594
NOGGLE, David 511 513 553 Mr
  520 525
NOONAN, J A 312
NORMAN, 80
NORTHWAY, Albert G 456 Mr
  486
NOWLIN, Hardin 224 Mr 229
NOYELLE, Sieur De 38
NOYES, Thomas 593
O'CONNOR, Bostwick 513 John
  566-567 Mr 516 523
O'DONNELL, John 249
O'NEIL, John F 231
O'NEILL, 441 462 J F 308 377 John
  F 407 409 480 Mr 282
OGDEN, David A 107 Ephraim F
  325 John 246 Mr 330 357
OLIN, Mr 426 431 Thomas H 242
  388
OLIVER, Edward E 271 Mr 487
  Robert 156 Solomon 456
ORENDORFF, Alfred 241
ORMSBEE, Samuel B 539
ORR, John H 595
OWEN, Col 72 Dr 549 William P
  345
OWENS, Wilfred 76 97
PALEN, Mr 94
PALMER, Andrew 529 Isaac H 388
  Mr 396 410-411 430 443 533
  535
PALMERSTON, Mr 52
PARDEE, J Sprague 594
PARISH, Thomas J 222

PARKE, Benjamin 157
PARKER, John 193 Luther 241 487-488 Mr 194 490
PARKINSON, Capt 150 D M 126 136 143 Daniel M 222 224 325 512 Mr 229 330 357 364 N T 347 Peter Jr 143
PARKMAN, 25
PARKS, Mr 520 Rufus 454 513
PARMELEE, Mr 330 357-358 Thomas E 356
PARMELER, Thomas E 325
PARSON, Judge 156
PARSONS, Chatfield H 513 Jonathan 388 Mr 426 448 Samuel Holden 156
PATCH, Horace D 512 560
PATRICK, Samuel 143
PATTERSON, J B 143
PATTON, Mr 208-209
PAUQUETTE, 146 Pierre 101-102 249
PAYNE, Joseph 248 Mr 248
PEAK, C H 599
PEAKE, C H 244
PEARSON, R M 497
PEASE, L S 346 Lucinda 449 Webster 449
PEET, S 497
PENDLETON, Thomas 192
PENTONY, Mr 569 Patrick 566
PERKINS, 76 Hardin 76 Lt 89 91
PERRIN, F 250
PERROT, Nicholas 26 50 86
PERRY, Joseph 249 Nathaniel 318
PETTIBONE, Mr 614 Sylvester 241 246
PETTIS, 281
PEYSTER, Capt De 46
PHELPS, Chauncey M 529 Mr 490 533 540 Noah 450 456 488 512
PHILIP II, King Of 151
PHILLIPS, Joab 546 Phoeba 546
PIATT, Benjamin M 157
PIERCE, Joseph S 513
PIERNAS, 59
PIKE, Gen 95 Zebulon 71
PINKNEY, Col 81 Ninian 81

PIZARRO, 24
PLATT, Alonzo 388 454 Mr 416
POHLMAN, Capt 90 92
POINSETT, Joel R 261 298-299
POLE, Charles 487-488 560 Mr 490 560
POLK, James K 454 President 485
PONCE*DE*LEON, Juan 23
PONCEDELEON, 151 214
POPE, John 310 Mr 311 Nathaniel 158
PORLIER, Jacques 79 98 100-101 James 79
PORTER, 142 George B 113 Peter B 434
POSEY, 138 Gen 144-146
POTTER, E W 497 Mr 356 Paraclete 346 356 480
POWELL, Chares 594
PRENTICE, Nathaniel C 284
PRENTISS, Mr 377 524 566 568-569 N C 306 334 376 Nathaniel C 310 Theodore 511-512 566 William A 245-246 269 303 316 324 348 350 Wm A 246 350 606
PREVOST, Charles M 480
PRICE, G M 247 Glendower M 222 388 454 Mr 222 247 425 430 445 Thomas H 143
PRIERE, Father 95
PRITCHETTE, Kintzing 282
PROUDFIT, W P 245
PUTNAM, Judge 156 Rufus 156
PUTNEY, Jeremiah 242
QUARLES, Augustus 585 Capt 585
QUERRE, Jean De 25
QUIGLEY, Mr 229 267 Patrick 224
RAMSAY, Alexander D 566
RANDALL, Alexander W 511 513 Mr 514 520 522 524
RANDOLPH, Mr 276
RANKIN, 143 Aaron 512
RAY, Adam E 302-303 325 456 Mr 325 330 486 620 Richard 249
RAYMBAULT, 25
RAYMOND, A 497 Elisha 529 Mr 535
REAM, Mr 376 Robert L 375

REAUME, Charles 79 97 100
REED, Curtis 486-487 539 594 Geo 624 George 106 511 513 560 Harrison 539 566 Mr 521 568 575-576 624
REID, Col 60
RENAULT, Philippe Francis 32
RESZILLY, 152
REYMERT, James D 566 Mr 568
REYNOLDS, Eli 224 Gov 132-133 135 Mr 229
RICHARD, Father 83 Gabriel 83 158
RICHARDS, D H 244 Daniel H 106 233 John 538
RICHARDSON, Mr 533 535 569 576-577 William 529 566
RICHELIEU, 152
RICHLIEU, Duke De 24
RING, Emily Jane 587
ROBERTSON, George 87
ROBINSON, Mr 246
ROCHEBLAVE, 66
ROCKWELL, John S 241 325 480 598-599 Mr 330
ROGAN, Mr 524 Patrick 512
ROGERS, Gov 48 53 James H 106 246 374 599
ROLETTE, 94 Capt 90-92 Joseph 76 89-90 93-94 96 98 101 Mr 76
ROOT, Eleazer 566 Erastus 111 Mr 568 576-577 580
ROUNDS, Lester 476
ROUNTREE, 387 John H 132 232 269 303 348 383 454 487 558 566-567 Mr 333 358 380 396 427 429 463 567-568 576-577 629
ROY, Agate 41 Amable 41 79 Francis 101 Joseph 79
RUGGLES, George D 181 William 543
RUSSELL, John 271 John B 233
RYAN, 517 Chief Justice 536 551 E G 519 Edward G 511 513 553 Mr 516-518 520 524
SAGE, Joel 182 Sidney S 451
SAINT, Ange M 60

SAINTCLAIR, Arthur 156 Gen 68 Gov 156 170
SAINTCYR, Hyacinth 97
SAINTJEAN, Jean B 94
SAINTPERRE, Gardeur De 55
SAINTPIERRE, Capt 50
SAINTVRAIN, 138 140
SALISBURY, Barton 594
SALTONSTALL, Col 48
SANBURN, Samuel 241
SANDERS, H T 566 Mr 568 577
SANDERSON, Henry 182 James 106 206 242 244 598
SANGER, L P 481
SANVOLE, 31
SARGEANT, John Jr 110 Winthrop 156-157
SAUNDERS, Henry Brown 416
SCAGEL, George 566 Mr 568 577
SCHERMERHORN, John F 263
SCHOEFFLER, Morritz 566 Mr 568
SCHOOLCRAFT, 50 Henry R 175 Mr 176
SCHWARTZ, Christian W 587
SCHWARTZBURG, Christian W 587
SCOTT, Gen 149 Martin 103
SEARGEANT, John 107
SEAVER, Lyman H 513
SECOR, Mr 569 Theodore 566
SEE, William 182
SEYMOUR, Wm N 293
SHACKELFORD, B 410 Barlow 269 316 347 409 Mr 290 312 316
SHACKLEFORD, Barlow 232-233 303
SHANLEY, Mr 229 Thomas 224
SHANLY, Thomas 222
SHARRIER, Oliver 97
SHAW, Capt 75 John 75 93 116 Mr 75 94
SHELDON, John P 293 321 405 Maj 321 Mr 229 489-490 Orson 456 488 William B 223-224 268 293 Wm B 345
SHEPARD, Mr 330

INDEX 653

SHEPHARD, William F 325
SHEPLEY, Mr 209
SHEW, Henry 241 Mr 307 314 456 487 William 269 303 456 529-530
SHOLES, C Latham 351 Charles C 83 245 252 269 303 316 Henry O 83 Mr 314 316
SIBLEY, Solomon 158
SILL, Elisha S 357
SINCLAIR, Patrick 87
SINGER, Mr 533 535 William 529 560
SKINNER, Henry C 269 302
SLAUGHTER, Col 199 George H 263 454 456 Mr 194 197 199-200 202-203 460 William B 248 Wm B 193
SMITH, A H 520 A Hyat 517 585 A Hyatt 511-513 515 553 594 Col 81 109 Gen 115 261 Geo B 517 George B 512 520 523 553 George F 222 224 267 J Y 520 Jeremiah 193 Jeremiah Jr 223 John 587 John Y 377 406 443 512 553 Johny 463 Joseph L 81 Mary 587 Mr 194 229 377 569 Sewall 513 Uriel B 476 William 233 William R 23 261 487 512 516 553 Winfield 81 Wm R 512 516 520
SMYTHE, Brevet Gen 92 Col 92
SNELL, Erastus G 543
SNELLING, Col 122 124-127 Mr 125 William J 124
SOPER, Evander M 512
SOULIGNY, 41 Agate 41 M 78
SPAFFORD, 141
SPENCER, 141 Capt 101
STAMBAUBH, Samuel C 112
STAMBAUGH, Col 112 141 S C 141
STANGE, Sieur De 38
STANLEY, Webster 374
STARKWEATHER, John 515
STARR, W Henry 267
STEADMAN, Mr 568 Silas 566
STEEL, Mr 517

STEELE, Elijah 512-513 Mr 517 520
STEPHENSON, Benjamin 157 Capt 138 140 143-144
STERLING, Levi 194 269 303 346 356 Mr 194 William T 347
STEVENS, J D 497 Orrin R 270 304
STEVENSON, William 83
STEWART, 123 John M 560 John W 529 560 Mr 560
STILLMAN, 135 Maj 134-135
STIRLING, Capt 60 65
STOCKWELL, Mr 513 T S 513
STORER, Mr 207
STORY, Augustus 269 303 Judge 478 Mr 290
STOWE, A W 454
STPHENSON, Capt 149
STREET, Gen 97 140 149 Joseph H D 232 269 303 Joseph M 96 98 176 Mr 312 314
STRINGHAM, H 285 Henry 263
STRONG, 387 559 M M 311 Marshall M 263 270 290 302 419 422-423 427 429 463 469 487 507 512-513 517 524-525 529-530 532 560 Moses M 266 274 281 312 328 346 356 384 388 427-429 432 457 463 480 487 489 498 512 516-517 520 524 557 Mr 358 365 369 380 382-384 395 400 415 530 532-533 535 552 558 628-629 Nathan H 593
SULLIVAN, Andrew 529 Capt 90
SUTHERLAND, Daniel S 269 303 James 325 Mr 312 Thomas W 346 480
SUYDAM, J V 82 John V 84 289 Mr 82
SWEET, Alanson 106 223-224 Mr 229
SYMMES, John Cleves 156
TALCOTT, W 497
TALIAFERRO, Maj 76
TALLMADGE, Gov 457 461 N P 85 Nathaniel P 454 479

TALON, 152
TANNER, Edward 40
TAYLOR, Hiram 515
TEAS, George W 224 Joseph 233 Joseph B 193-194 223 Mr 194-195 229
TENNEY, H A 595 Horace A 547 Mr 569
TERRY, John B 222 224 Mr 229
THAYER, J L 306 James L 284
THEBEAU, 80
THIBEAU, Augustin 80
THOMAS, Martin 117 126 Mr 276 472 486 Salmon 456 William H 487-488
THOMPSON, Jared 388 454 John 144 Mr 426-427 445
TIERCOURT, Mr 94
TIFFANY, George O 106
TILLOU, 282
TODD, John 155
TOLAND, Patrick 513
TONTI, 28-30
TOPPING, Josiah 513
TOWNSEND, 143
TRACY, 152
TREADWAY, Wm W 514
TRIPP, James 356 388 454 Mr 389 427
TROWBRIDGE, C C 110 John T 388 John W 423 Mr 110 388 441
TULLAR, Charles 181
TURNER, George 156 Harvey G 566 Joseph 529 Mr 533 535 568 Peter H 512
TWEEBY, John H 513
TWEEDY, J H 382 John H 356 511 552 558 608 610 619 623 625-626 Mr 367 369 517 521 524-525 622 624-626 628-629
TWIGGS, David E 101
TYLER, John 321 346 396 President 479-480 623
UNDERWOOD, Mr 208
UPHAM, A J 325 D A J 480 512 Don A J 513-514 Mr 361 381-382 514 628-629

VAIL, Aaron 52 C S 423
VANBUREN, Mr 321 323 President 84
VANCE, David 156
VANDENBERG, Henry 156
VANDERPOOL, Abraham 566 Mr 568
VANDYKE, Mr 52
VANVLEIT, Peter 388
VANVLIET, Mr 388 422
VANWAGNER, 143
VARNUM, James Mitchell 156
VAUDREUIL, 44 Gov 34 45 M La Marquis De 34 Marquis 43 Marquis De 153
VAUN, 80
VELIE, Capt De 39 78
VERVILLE, Gautier De 41 Mr De 41
VIEAU, 80 Jacques 105
VILLIERS, Neyon De 58 Sieur De 38
VINEYARD, 383-384 James R 193 222 224 269 303 381 383 512 Mr 194 198 202-203 222 229 252 308 312 333 380-383
VINTON, Mr 208
VIRGIN, Noah H 560
VLIET, Garret 513 Mr 524
WAKELY, Eleazer 560 Solomous 513
WALKER, George H 105 193 197 206 388 423 456-457 480 618 Isaac P 426 560 Mr 194 389 396 456 481 487 622
WALSWORTH, Jared S 473
WALWORTH, George 560
WARD, J 409 Joseph 566 L 409 Mr 409 569
WARREN, Rear Admiral 153
WASHBURN, Cadwallader C 594
WASHINGTON, 45 55 154
WATERBURY, C 497
WATSON, James T 495
WAYNE, Anthony 68 Gen 68
WEBB, Col 256-259 J W 256 James Watson 255
WEBSTER, Daniel 415 Mr 209 434

WEDGE, Hugh 246
WEEKS, Lemuel W 608
WELCH, 569
WELL, Daniel Jr 303
WELLS, 143 Capt 74 Daniel Jr 106 244 269 324 605 H N 250 293 312 347 536 560 H W 285 Harriet 546 Horatio N 285 302 304 328 351 529-530 583 Mr 312 532-535 552 606 614
WEST, Henry 106
WESTON, Josiah D 346
WHALEN, Nicholas 242
WHEELER, Loring 224 Mr 229 569 William A 529 566
WHISTLER, Maj 127-130
WHITE, 427 Col 72 James 595 John 426 633-634 636 Joshua S 512 Lemuel 456 Mr 387 429 Philo 560
WHITESIDE, Gen 134-135 Samuel 134
WHITESIDES, Mr 520 Ninian 560 Ninian E 512 553
WHITING, Frances Adelle 476 John 476
WHITNEY, Daniel 81-82
WHITON, 429 Chief Justice 552 E V 337 558 Edward V 269 290 302 304 312 316 325 348 350 403 487 566 Judge 312 Mr 290 325 330 333 338 340 357 364 367 387-388 395-396 400 427 429 431-432 449 469 564 567-568 570-571

WILCOX, Mr 469 Randall 456 487 Seymour 343 451
WILKINS, Col 60-61
WILLARD, Mr 524 Victor M 513
WILLIAMS, 114 Arthur William 587 Charles H 594 Eleazer 107 113 Mr 109-110 625 628 William 587
WILLIAMSON, E M 595
WILLISTON, George H 560
WILSON, George 269 302 James 346 Joel F 513 John 267 Mr 522 William 232
WING, Austin E 158 187
WINGFIELD, F A 599
WINSLOW, Jared G 530
WISE, Henry A 257 Mr 257-260
WOLFE, 45 Gen 48 56
WOLFINGER, Leslie 13
WOOD, Uriah 529
WOODBRIDGE, 143 Mr 207 William 193 195 Wm W 158
WOODBURY, Levi 218
WOODMAN, Cyrus 594
WOODWARD, Augustus B 171
WOOSTER, Julius 486 488 Mr 490
WORDEN, Allen 566 Mr 568 576
WRIGHT, Hoel S 319 Silas 583 585 Thomas 350
WYMAN, W W 547 569 William W 595 Wm W 518
YEISER, Capt 91
YEIZER, Capt 90
YOUNG, M K 590 Mr 380
ZANDER, Jeremiah B 289

www.ingramcontent.com/pod-product-compliance
Lightning Source LLC
Chambersburg PA
CBHW070905300426
44113CB00008B/935